IGCSE

English as a Second Language Third edition

Teacher's book

Peter Lucantoni

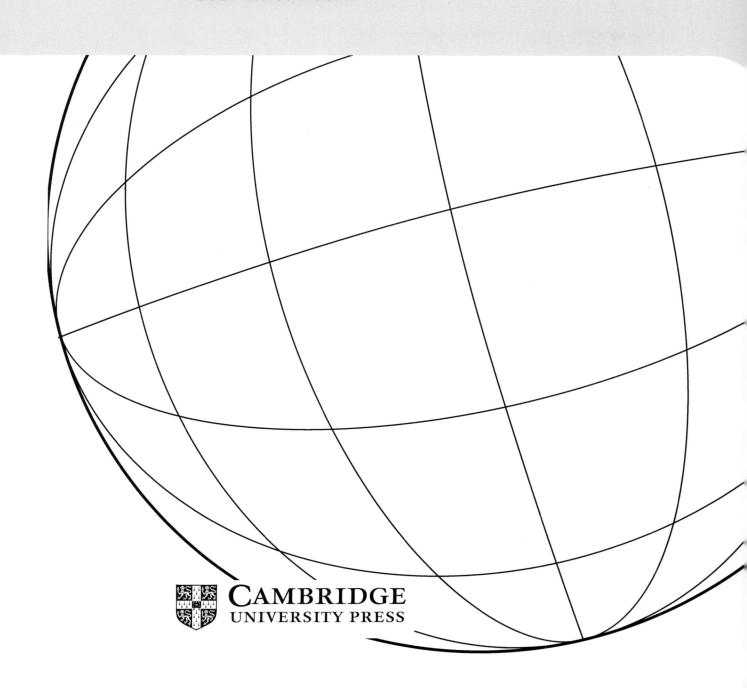

CAMBRIDGE
UNIVERSITY PRESS

CAMBRIDGE UNIVERSITY PRESS
Cambridge, New York, Melbourne, Madrid, Cape Town,
Singapore, São Paulo, Delhi, Tokyo, Mexico City

Cambridge University Press
The Edinburgh Building, Cambridge CB2 8RU, UK

www.cambridge.org
Information on this title: www.cambridge.org/9780521736015

First published 2009
4th printing 2011

Printed in the United Kingdom at the University Press, Cambridge

A catalogue record for this publication is available from the British Library

ISBN 978-0-521-73601-5 Paperback

ACKNOWLEDGEMENTS

Cover image: © ImageState/Alamy

As always, thanks and all my love go to Lydia, Sara and Emily, who
continue to support my efforts – I couldn't do it without you.

Contents

Level 1

Introductory unit:

Part 1: The world around us

Part 2: Human endeavour

Concluding unit:

This Teacher's book supports the core components of the *Cambridge IGCSE English as a Second Language* series, Third edition, which are Coursebook 1 and Workbook 1 (Level 1) and Coursebook 2 and Workbook 2 (Level 2). (There is also an additional component for Level 2 – the *Exam Preparation Guide: Reading and Writing*.) The Level 1 and Level 2 books together form a complete and comprehensive study programme for students who plan to take the IGCSE English as a Second Language (E2L) examination. Level 1 is a one-year, theme-based intermediate English course for students who are not yet ready to start an exam course and need to focus on developing language skills and grammar awareness. Level 2 is a two-year, exam-focused course for the IGCSE which will properly prepare students for the E2L examination.

The combined Teacher's book for the two Levels provides the following:

*   an overview of the IGCSE English as a Second Language syllabus 0510 or 0511
*   menus for the two coursebooks and the two workbooks
*   a grid for marking and grading Core and Extended writing
*   answers to the exercises in the two coursebooks and the two workbooks
*   answers to sample exam-practice questions
*   suggestions for alternative approaches to tasks.

It is assumed that students following the Level 2 course will be in a position to focus on the exam itself, while the new Level 1 course is more appropriate for consolidating language and language skills. The two Levels therefore provide more than adequate preparation in terms of exam skills and language skills, and the content-based approach of the new Level 1 coursebook exposes students to a wide variety of lexis and knowledge.

Level 1

The completely new Level 1 course is designed to provide students with a broad content-based coursebook (Coursebook 1), exposing them to a wide variety of topics and themes, while at the same time consolidating essential language and vocabulary. Each themed unit is divided into sections, covering speaking and thinking skills, reading and vocabulary, listening, writing, language focus, study skills and research, and a unit review quiz.

Coursebook 1 is divided into two parts: Part 1, The world around us, and Part 2, Human endeavour. Each part is subdivided into units covering topics such as Space, Living creatures, The senses, Explorers, Sport, and Wonders of the world. In addition, there are two further units which focus on aspects of the English language.

Throughout Coursebook 1 and Workbook 1, students are encouraged to learn inductively, by applying thinking and learning strategies. While the book is content-based, it does not assume or require any previous knowledge of a particular subject. However, students are continually encouraged to work things out for themselves and to use alternative sources of information to find solutions to tasks and problems. There is hardly any mention of the IGCSE E2L exam in the Level 1 course (only an optional prepatory activity on pages 141-2), although it is clearly an introduction to the exam-based content found in the Level 2 course.

Level 2

Coursebook 2 is divided into units, each focusing on particular aspects of the IGCSE E2L exam. Speaking skills are integrated throughout the book and are practised through discussion work, role play and specific tasks. Although candidates in the exam are not assessed in role-play situations, these provide invaluable practice for the techniques required and, of course, help to build confidence. While it is probably best to follow the units in Coursebook 2 consecutively, there is no reason why teachers should not choose to focus on a particular language skill or exam question.

The material in Coursebook 2 and Workbook 2 becomes progressively more demanding, with longer and more advanced reading and listening texts in the second half of the book. The exercises in the Further practice section of each unit are particularly useful for homework, for early finishers, or for practice outside the classroom. Note that the word limit for writing activities is 100–150 words for the Core curriculum and 150–200 for the Extended curriculum. The first three exam-practice units (Units 5, 10 and 15) contain a selection of exercises related to material covered in the preceding units, whereas exam-practice Unit 20 is a complete sample exam paper. The author is wholly responsible for the answers to the sample exam questions.

The progressive step-by-step approach of Level 2, including exam tips, will help to build students' confidence in all the main skill areas, while also developing the techniques and additional skills necessary for success in all the papers of the IGCSE E2L exam. Workbook 2 provides an additional source of extra material for home or classroom practice.

Additional materials

Throughout both Levels it is suggested that students refer to a dictionary to help them with problem vocabulary and to check the meanings of unknown words. At IGCSE level, students should feel comfortable using a learner's monolingual dictionary, of which there are many available. Bilingual dictionaries may be used as a last resort, but they will not help students to understand vocabulary 'in English'. If students are not familiar with using a dictionary, teachers should spend time getting them used to how a dictionary is laid out, what the various symbols mean, and, more importantly, how a dictionary can help them to improve their English.

Using the Internet for research

In both Level 1 and Level 2, students are actively encouraged to use the Internet as a research tool and the following guidelines about how to use the Internet effectively and safely may be of use to teachers.

Remind students that when they search the Internet for information, they need to identify **key words** for their search – just as they do when scanning a text for the answer to a question! To find out more about a famous person (e.g. Coursebook 1, Unit 9, Exercise 20), students should first write down the person's name and a few facts that they already know about them. They could also think about other things that they might want to include – for example, where the famous person went to school. Students can then pick out the key words to use in their search(es). The following tips may help:

- Try to use more than just one or two key words – the best number is between six and eight.
- The best key words are nouns.
- Most search engines allow you to enter phrases in quotation marks. For example, entering the key words **Will Smith** tells the search engine to look for web pages containing the words 'Will' and 'Smith' – but not necessarily together. A search for **"Will Smith"**, however, will return only pages that include the two words together and in that order.
- Some search engines use Boolean commands:
  - Use **AND** if you want documents that include both/all your key words/phrases. For example, a search for **"Will Smith" AND film AND music** will return pages that contain all three key words/phrases.
  - Use **OR** if you want documents that include any of your key words/phrases. For example, a search for **"Will Smith" OR film OR music** will return pages that contain any one of the key words/phrases.
  - Use **AND NOT** if you want documents that contain one or more key words/phrases, but not those that also contain another word/phrase. For example, a search for **"Will Smith" AND film AND NOT music** will return pages that include the key words/phrases 'Will Smith' and 'film', but not those that also contain the word 'music'.

Students also need to be aware that not all websites are reliable. For example, it is generally safe to assume that large organisations such as the BBC have verified their information, but the same cannot be said of all websites. It is also important to consider the purpose of a website, as this may affect what information is presented, as well as how it is presented. You should advise students that they may want to verify the information they find on sites they are not sure about by using a trusted site or an encyclopaedia.

Overview of syllabus

The revised IGCSE English as a Second Language syllabus 0510 is based on practical communication and on students' ability to express themselves effectively in both written and spoken English. It aims to:

- develop the ability to use English effectively for the purpose of communication
- form a sound base for the skills required for further study or employment using English as the medium
- develop an awareness of the nature of language and language-learning skills, along with skills of a more general application
- promote students' personal development.

Reading and listening comprehension are assessed through a wide range of material and language registers. An IGCSE English as a Second Language qualification at Grade C or above is usually accepted by most United Kingdom universities and by many colleges in the United States, as well as in other places throughout the world, as an indication of English language proficiency. However, students are advised to confirm requirements with the university of their choice.

The syllabus is normally assessed through three separate papers: Reading and Writing, Listening, and Speaking. Speaking is assessed independently of the other two papers and candidates receive a separate grade for their oral skills. (See the University of Cambridge International Examinations current syllabus for details of component percentage weightings, length of papers, etc.)

Thirteen examples of Speaking test cards (taken from various recent examination sessions) are given in Appendix 1 of Coursebook 2. You should stress to students that the test is one of speaking skills and not of detailed topic knowledge.

Guidance on conducting Speaking tests, exam requirements, and information on the Core and Extended options of the syllabus can be found in the syllabus booklet for the relevant year of examination, and this is available from the University of Cambridge International Examinations.

Mark band	CONTENT: relevance and development of ideas (AO: W1, W2, W6)	Mark band	LANGUAGE: style and accuracy (AO: W1, W3, W4, W5)
8–9 Extended	**Highly effective:** • *Relevance:* Fulfils the task, with consistently appropriate register and excellent sense of purpose and audience. • *Development of ideas:* Shows independence of thought. Ideas are well developed, at appropriate length and persuasive. Quality is sustained throughout. Enjoyable to read. The interest of the reader is aroused and sustained.	8–9 Extended	*Fluent:* • *Style:* Almost first language competence. Ease of style. Confident and wide-ranging use of language, idiom and tenses. • *Accuracy:* None or very few errors. Well-constructed and linked paragraphs.
6–7 Extended	**Effective:** • *Relevance:* Fulfils the task, with appropriate register and good sense of purpose and audience. • *Development of ideas:* Ideas are well developed and at appropriate length. Engages reader's interest.	6–7 Extended	**Precise:** • *Style:* Sentences show variety of structure and length. Some style and turn of phrase. Uses some idioms and is precise in use of vocabulary. However, there may be some awkwardness in style making reading less enjoyable. • *Accuracy:* Generally accurate, apart from occasional frustrating minor errors. There are paragraphs showing some unity, although links may be absent or inappropriate.
4–5 Core & Extended	**Satisfactory:** • *Relevance:* Fulfils the task, with reasonable attempt at appropriate register, and some sense of purpose and audience. A satisfactory attempt has been made to address the topic, but there may be digressions. • *Development of ideas:* Material is satisfactorily developed at appropriate length.	4–5 Core & Extended	**Safe:** • *Style:* Mainly simple structures and vocabulary, sometimes attempting more sophisticated language. • *Accuracy:* Meaning is clear, and work is of a safe, literate standard. Simple structures are generally sound, apart from infrequent spelling errors, which do not interfere with communication. Grammatical errors occur when more sophistication is attempted. Paragraphs are used but without coherence or unity.
2–3 Core & Extended	**Partly relevant:** • *Relevance:* Partly relevant and some engagement with the task. Does not quite fulfil the task, although there are some positive qualities. Inappropriate register, showing insufficient awareness of purpose and/or audience. • *Development of ideas:* Supplies some detail and explanation, but the effect is incomplete. Some repetition.	2–3 Core & Extended	**Errors intrude:** • *Style:* Simple structures and vocabulary. • *Accuracy:* Meaning is sometimes in doubt. Frequent, distracting errors hamper precision and slow down reading. However, these do not seriously impair communication. Paragraphs absent or haphazard.
0–1 Core & Extended	**Little relevance:** • Limited engagement with task, but this is mostly hidden by density of error. **Award 1 mark.** • No engagement with the task, or any engagement with task is completely hidden by density of error. **Award 0 marks.** If essay is completely irrelevant, no mark can be given for language.	0–1 Core & Extended	**Hard to understand:** • Multiple types of error in grammar/spelling/word usage/punctuation throughout, which mostly make it difficult to understand. Occasionally, sense can be deciphered. Paragraphs absent or haphazard. **Award 1 mark.** • Density of error completely obscures meaning. Whole sections impossible to recognise as pieces of English writing. Paragraphs absent or haphazard. **Award 0 marks.**

The grid applies to Exam Exercises 6 and 7 of the Reading and Writing component of the IGCSE E2L syllabus.

The English language 1

This is an introductory unit designed to give your students the chance to get to know each other better. There is no corresponding Workbook unit.

Coursebook exercises

A Speaking

1 Make sure everyone understands how to approach this speaking activity. If you think your students may have problems forming the questions, you could do this with them orally first, and then allow them to 'find someone who …'. Also, help them with some prompts for the follow-up questions.

2 Students report back on their survey. For example, *Manuel supports Manchester United because his father was a keen fan.*

3 & 4 As students decide what they can say in English, get them to give each other examples. This activity will make your students more aware of what they can already say in English – self-assessment is not always easy for learners.

5 & 6 This is similar to the previous exercises, although more challenging as your students need to now express themselves more fully in English.

7 Learners often want to be able to do or say something in another language but can't. This exercise encourages them to think about this and to make a list. Get them to compare their lists with each other's – they will probably find that they have a lot in common.

8 This exercise encourages learners to think about problems they may have with speaking skills, and to focus on why they are not always confident about speaking. Again, get your students to discuss their 'fears' and see whether they share any with their classmates.

9 This is a fun activity to end Section A. Make sure you demonstrate the activity first, and then put students in groups to try it out.

B Reading and speaking

10 & 11 If your students are not familiar with the idea of first and second language speakers, you could combine these exercises and simply get them to make a list of countries where they think English is spoken. They will find out the answers later in the section.

12 The paragraph in Exercise 13 gives students some facts and figures about English as a world language. These two pre-reading questions check students' knowledge of long numbers (this issue is revisited later in the book).

> **Answers**
> **a** six (1,000,000)   **b** nine (1,000,000,000)

13 & 14 Students read the text and complete the gaps with the numbers from the box. They can then check their answers to the previous exercises by looking at the completed map and text. Are they surprised by anything?

> **Answers**
> **a** 6,000
> **b** 75 per cent
> **c** 60 per cent
> **d** 5,300
> **e** 350
> **f** 400

15 Students now answer the questions by looking at the map in more detail.

Answers

a North America
b India
c South Africa
d Canada
e the Bahamas or Guyana (both have a population of less than a million)
f no
g Africa

C Reading and vocabulary

16 Learners tend to think of a dictionary as the only method of finding the meaning of an unknown word. Here they should be encouraged to think of alternative sources, and to make a list.

17 Check with your students that they understand the three words given – if they are not sure, they should use a method from the previous exercise to check.

18

Answers

a Auditory
b Visual
c Kinaesthetic

19

Answers

a visual – it mentions pictures
b kinaesthetic – it mentions making something, which involves physically handling items
c auditory – it mentions reading aloud, listening

20 Get your students to read the text quickly and check their answers to the previous exercises. They do not need to understand everything in the text in order to check their answers.

21 Ask your students which of the three learning styles they think applies to them. Point out that we tend to favour one style, but we often show signs of the others as well.

D Language focus: questions and short answers with *do/does*

22 Students need to re-read the text and find and underline all the *do … ?* questions. There are three in each of the paragraphs about the different learner types.

23 Some learners need a 'rule' to help them understand an aspect of language.

Answers

Do + subject (not *he* or *she*) + infinitive verb (no *to*)?
Does + third person single subject, *he* or *she* + infinitive verb (no *to*)?

24 Point out the position of time adverbs in imperatives, and how this contrasts with their position in *do/does* questions.

Answers

Do + subject (not *he* or *she*) (+ adverb) + infinitive verb (no *to*)?
Does + third person single subject, *he* or *she* (+ adverb) + infinitive verb (no *to*)?

25 If students are unfamiliar with the term 'short answer', give some examples of both long and short answers.

Answers

Yes, I do / No, I don't.
(Long answers would be: Yes, I always make written notes … / No, I don't always make written notes … .)

26 *Does … ?* questions have different short answers.

Answers

Yes, she does / No, she doesn't.

27 This exercise gives students some practice in word order for *do/does* questions.

Answers

a Does your teacher always use the whiteboard?
b Do you sometimes forget to switch off your mobile?
c Do you often listen to cassettes in class?
d Do you usually draw pictures in your mind to remember things?
e Does your teacher ever ask you to make things in class?

28 If possible, get your students to stand up and move around the class asking each other the questions, rather than always asking the student sitting near them.

E Listening and speaking

CD 1,
Track 1

29 Make sure your students understand the focus of the interview, as this will help them to think of questions that Yousef might have asked Mr Peter. However, this is a pre-listening and prediction exercise and as such it does not matter what questions your students think of.

30 Students listen and check whether any of their questions appear in the interview.

31 In the table, students write down Yousef's actual questions (from the transcript on pages **148–9**). They then listen to the interview again and make notes about Mr Peter's answers.

32 Let students check with each other. They can also look at the transcript for further clarification if necessary.

F Reading and writing

33 Make sure your students are comfortable with the language in this exercise, and then let them match Yousef's questions to Mr Peter's answers.

Answers

a C
b A
c B

34 Refer students back to Yousef's questions on pages **148–9**. Then get them to skim the text to find how he wrote out Mr Peter's answers.

Answers

a Everybody has their own individual learning style …
b There is no 'right' way to learn …
c There are three distinct learning styles …
d To find out what your particular learning style is …
e If we 'see' the number …

35 & 36 Using the information given, students write the rest of the article. Guide them and point out how Yousef wrote the first part of the article. Encourage students to assist each other and to read each other's writing.

Unit 1: Space

Coursebook exercises

A Speaking and thinking

1   If you think that students will not know many of the planets, you could prompt them by bringing in visuals. Give them time to think and discuss their ideas with each other. Perhaps they know all the planets in their own language. They will see the English words in the next exercise.

2 & 3

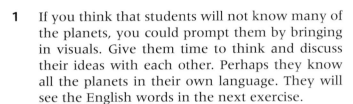

Answers
horizontal: Neptune, Jupiter, Mercury, Pluto
vertical: Saturn, Venus
diagonal: Mars, Earth, Uranus

Position	Name	God/Goddess
1	Mercury	Winged messenger of the gods
2	Venus	Goddess of love and beauty
3	Earth	
4	Mars	God of war
5	Jupiter	God of the sky and heavens, and son of Saturn
6	Saturn	God of farming and agriculture, and father of Jupiter
7	Uranus	King of the gods
8	Neptune	God of the sea
9	Pluto	God of the underworld

B Listening and vocabulary

CD 1,
Track 2

4   Give students time to think about the information in the table and to guess how the planets got their names. It does not matter what they think as they will find out the information in the next exercise. This is simply a pre-listening activity.

5   Play the recording. Students listen and check whether their ideas from Exercise 4 are correct. Let students listen a second time if they want to.

6   You could have a class competition and see which student can think of the best new name for Earth. Perhaps get them to design a logo as well.

C Reading and vocabulary

7   If you can show your students a real telescope (or a picture), this might help to generate some ideas if none are forthcoming. You could tell students the various parts (e.g. eyepiece, lens, etc.) and get them to show you where they are on the telescope.

8   Ask students if anything else in the classroom contains a lens (mobile phone with camera, for example).

Answers
a   camera
b   projector
c   microscope
d   contact lens
e   glasses

9   Throughout the Coursebook students will be encouraged to use a dictionary to check meanings, so make sure dictionaries are available, either class sets, individual copies, or perhaps online versions. If students are new to using dictionaries independently, spend some time training them in how to do so efficiently. Try to get them to give reasons for their choices in this exercise.

10   Encourage students to read the text quickly, and not to spend time worrying about unknown words.

11 You will need to guide your students when they write the definitions. You could do one as an example: *Optical is an adjective, and it refers to something visual, or something which uses the human eye.*

D Language focus: passive forms

12 The verbs are all in the passive form (voice).

13

Answers
a all of the planets; Jupiter, Saturn, Mars, Venus and Mercury
b this colour
c Pluto
d The lenses in glasses and contact lenses
We do not know who the doer is.

14

Answer
The passive is formed with the verb *to be*, followed by the past participle of a main verb.

15

Answers
a is seen   d is seen
b are made   e is perceived
c is held

E Study skills and research

16 Each unit contains a small research project. Depending on time and resources available, students could do this at home, in school, on their own, or with other students – you will need to decide. Encourage students **not** to simply copy information from books and the Internet, but to put things into their own words. Also try to get them to use visuals to support what they are trying to say in their projects.

F Reading and writing

17 This is a pre-reading exercise, so it does not matter what your students think. The idea is to get them thinking about the topic, and to make some predictions.

18

Answers
chimpanzees
dogs
insects (fruit flies)
monkeys
mice
rabbits
rats

19 This is a vocabulary exercise where students need to discuss their ideas with each other and use a dictionary for further help. Remind students to use the context of the text first, rather than rushing immediately to a dictionary.

20

Answers
a gives reasons for sending animals into space
b paragraph 3 – *was launched*, *was killed*, *were sent*
c find out about space conditions, effects of weightlessness, and effects of stress
d rocket hit the Earth on its return
e a passenger in a rocket which does not return
f *problems*
g 253 km, 9,426 km/h
h next step was human flight

21 Some students respond well to seeing information on a timeline. If you have time and if your students would enjoy it, you could get them to draw a simple visual for each event.

Answers

The timeline should show the following events:
August 1948 – first mouse in space
early 1950s – Russians put mice, rats, rabbits into space as one-way passengers
January 1961 – first chimp in space (Ham)
May 1961 – first human in space (American Alan Shepard)

22 This is a short piece of writing. Make sure your students use the five pieces of information from the timeline. They can exchange their writing and check each other's work.

 Review quiz

23 Each unit in the Coursebook ends with a 'Review quiz' section. The purpose of this section is to give a quick and not too demanding review of some of the key lexis and grammar from the unit, and its themes. Students can work on the questions on their own or with a classmate, but it is important that they do not look back at the information in the unit itself, in order to ensure that the quiz is both competitive and fun. Once students have worked through the questions, they can look back at the unit and self-check their answers, which is in itself a useful skill to develop. When more full and structured practice of the Coursebook content is required, teachers can direct their students to the Workbook.

Workbook exercises

 Vocabulary

1 **a** Neptune
   b Jupiter
   c Mercury
   d Mars
   e Pluto
   f Venus
   g Earth
   h Saturn
   i Uranus

2

Mercury, Venus, Earth, Mars, Jupiter, Saturn, Uranus, Neptune, Pluto

3 **a** Optical
   b images
   c refraction
   d rays
   e transparent
   f glass
   g air

4 horizontal: rabbit, chimpanzee, turtle, insect
vertical: snake, fish, monkey
diagonal: rat, mouse, dog, cat, frog

Language focus: passive forms

5 are produced
were given
have been sent
had been trained
will be required

6 **a** are produced
   b is hit
   c are bent
   d is formed
   e is changed

Reading

9

Basic qualifications and requirements	*Special skills and special training, degree in science or maths …*
Classification of astronaut	commander/pilot, mission specialist, payload specialist
Length of basic training	two years
Training subjects	basic science (maths, astronomy, physics, geology, meteorology, oceanography), technology (navigation, mechanics, materials processing), space shuttle systems
Flight training	pilots – 15 hours per month in T-38 jets mission specialists – 4 hours
Other information	also taught parachute jumping, land and sea survival, scuba diving, ways to overcome different pressure conditions

10 a fulfil
   b vision
   c vehicle
   d geology
   e micro
   f contingency

Listening

CD 1,
Track 1

12

Word from listening text	Meaning
miniature	smaller version
into thin air	completely
dishevelled	untidy
paradisiacal	like paradise
humanoid	like a human
frail	physically weak
pedestal	base for something to stand on
courage	bravery or strength to do something
ultimately	finally
whizzes	moves very quickly
exhausted	very tired

13 a False   **f** False
   b False   **g** False
   c True   **h** False
   d True   **i** True
   e True   **j** True

14 a he produces a miniature machine
   b he tells the story after dinner
   f he tries to find it
   g the Time Traveller finds fire is a good defence
   h he starts the fire accidentally

Unit 2: Living creatures

Coursebook exercises

A Speaking and thinking

1   UFO = unidentified flying object. Ask your students what they know about UFOs – it does not matter if they know nothing!

2   Similarly, it does not matter if your students don't know what an alien is. However, get them to discuss their ideas, and perhaps show them a visual to encourage discussion.

3   You may need to deal with some of the vocabulary in the 'no' and 'yes' answers before you get students to read. Make sure they understand what the question is (*Are UFOs alien spacecraft?*). There are no right or wrong answers – this section is designed to get your students thinking and speaking about the unit theme. Check the vocabulary before you ask students to vote.

B Listening and vocabulary

CD 1,
Track 3

4   Students may not realise that everyday objects have been mistaken for UFOs. Go through the list of objects and ask them which, if any, they think could have been mistaken for alien spacecraft.

> **Answers**
> All of them have been mistaken for UFOs, apart from *camcorder*.

5   Throughout the book there are many opportunities for students to work on vocabulary together, and using a dictionary. This repeated activity will make your students more confident about using a dictionary, and will also encourage them to think more about words they are unsure about.

6   Get your students to think about the information and decide whether it is true or false – it does not matter what they think.

7   Refer back to the objects in Exercise 4. Tell students to listen for them, and to number them as they hear the objects.

> **Answers**
> 1   aeroplane   5   bird
> 2   glider   6   tennis ball
> 3   helicopter   7   frisbee
> 4   balloon
> Note: *camcorder* is mentioned at the end, but not as an object mistaken for a UFO.

8   Students listen again and check whether the information in Exercise 6 is true or false – in fact everything is true.

C Reading and vocabulary

9   Students find out what the words mean and look for pictures on the Internet or in books.

10

> **Answers**
> *uniform + constant*
> *various + diverse*

11 The language in the list here is quite difficult so make sure you are ready to help your students. If they do not understand the terms, they will not be able to do the following activity.

12 The matching exercise should not be challenging, as there are plenty of key words to help students.

D Language focus 1: word building

13 There are several word building exercises in the book. An awareness of how words 'build' on themselves to form other words is an extremely useful skill in developing proficiency in a language. Adding a translation is also useful, and can be used in quizzes and self-checking.

Verb	Noun	Adjective	Adverb	Translation
vary	variety	various, varied	variously	
diversify	diversity	diverse	diversely	
–	uniformity, uniform	uniform	uniformly	
specialise	specialisation, specialist, speciality	specialised	–	

E Language focus 2: signpost words

14 There are various terms used to describe what I call 'signpost' words. A signpost tells you in which direction to go, and signpost words (or sequence/discourse markers) do exactly this. Ask your students to complete the blank 'branches' on the signpost with their own words.

15 & 16 Depending on your situation, you could allocate one column to different groups of students and give them a time limit in which to think of, for example, five more words.

When	Contrast	In addition
firstly	although	also
secondly	however	and
next	even though	furthermore
finally	on the other hand	so
subsequently	or	either ... or
	but	for example
	though	

F Study skills and research

17 It can be difficult to define or find synonyms for some words, particularly scientific and technical language. Using translation is an effective method for checking understanding.

18 & 19 Try not to assist your students too much with projects. The whole point is for them to become more independent and autonomous in their learning. Encourage them to discuss their ideas with you, however, and check progress regularly to make sure they are on target.

G Reading and writing

20 Look at the pictures and discuss what is happening in each one. If appropriate, introduce some of the new vocabulary (see Exercise 21 and the article on page 24), such as *conceal, incubate*.

21 Students match the words to the pictures in Exercise 20.

22 Students read the text and compare the content with their ideas from the previous exercises.

23

24 This writing exercise encourages the use of signpost words from earlier in the unit. You could do the activity orally first, encouraging students to think about the order of events and what exactly happens at each stage.

H Review quiz

24 Students can self-check their answers in the unit.

Workbook exercises

 Vocabulary

1 umbrella, frisbee, aeroplane, hoverscraft, bird, balloon, glider, ball, kite, camcorder

2 a organ
   b molecule
   c atom
   d tissue
   e cell
   f organism

3 a atoms
   b molecules
   c cells
   d organism
   e tissues
   f organs

4 a embryo
   b foetus
   c toddler
   d adolescent

5 Various answers are possible, depending on your students' first language.

Language focus: word building and signpost words

6

When	Contrast	In addition
finally	although	also
firstly	but	and
lastly	even though	furthermore
secondly	however	so
	on the other hand	
	or	

7 a However
   b although
   c but
   d On the other hand
   e Even though
   f but

8 a launched
   b visitors
   c extremely
   d expensive
   e companies
   f leaders

Reading

11

Verb	Noun	Adjective	Adverb
–	–	*unique*	*uniquely*
thrill	*thrill/thriller*	*thrilling/thrilled*	*thrillingly*
–	landmark	landmark	–
strike	strike/striker	striking	strikingly
–	roughness	rough	roughly
ripple	ripple	rippling	–
–	cone	conical	–
–	dusk	–	–
dawn	dawn	–	–
witness	witness	–	–
appear	appearance	apparent	apparently
gravitate	gravity	gravitational	gravitationally
weigh	weight	weightless	weightlessly
intrigue	intrigue	intriguing/intrigued	intriguingly
survey	survey/surveyor	surveyed	–

Listening

CD 1,
Track 2

13 1 gone forever
    2 natural extinction
    3 declines in numbers
    4 adapt to changes in climate
    5 dinosaurs
    6 human population
    7 polluted some habitats
    8 indirect destruction
    9 hunted and killed wildlife
    10 tourist souvenirs

14 a True
    b True
    c False – about 100 million years ago
    d True
    e True
    f True
    g False – but numbers getting smaller
    h True

Unit 3: Natural disasters

Coursebook exercises

A Speaking and thinking

1   Point out to students the difference between weather events and natural events, then get them to look for pictures of the events listed on the Internet and in books.

2   Students copy and complete the table. They could add other events, if they can think of any, and of course some events may go in both columns.

Violent weather	Violent Earth
hailstorm	volcano
flood	avalanche
tsunami	tsunami
drought	earthquake
hurricane	
tornado	

3   It may be that you and your students live in a hurricane zone, in which case you will be able to answer this question easily! If not, help students describe the five stages.

> **Answers**
> Stage 1: Warm ocean water causes more evaporation than usual, creating humid air and clouds.
> Stage 2: Winds meet and force air upward.
> Stage 3: Above the storm, winds flow outward; the air below rises.
> Stage 4: Humid air rising causes clouds to form.
> Stage 5: Winds cause the hurricane to move and grow.

4   Give your students time to talk about the five pieces of information and decide whether each is true or false. Everything is true.

B Listening and vocabulary

CD 1,
Track 4

5–7   These exercises all focus on vocabulary, and are all for pre-listening. Students will hear all the phrases when they listen to the news item, so it is important for them to spend time on the matching activities first. If time is short, you could allocate different groups of students just one of the exercises and then allow them to exchange answers. In some cases more than one matching is possible. They can listen for the correct matchings during the news item.

5

A	B
ripping away	storefronts
peeling back	roofs
forcing	tourists
sideswiping	Cuba
carrying out	bags
terrifying	residents

6

Nouns	Verbs
Hurricane Wilma	punished
waves	slammed
winds	tore
people	looted
others	dragged
buildings	shook

7

Adjective phrases	Nouns
luxury	hotels
alligator-infested	lagoon
knee-deep	water
eerily electric	air
hiding	spots
debris-filled	streets
destroyed furniture	store
sweltering, dark	shelters
popular beach	resort

8 From the matchings, students should begin to get an idea of what happened. Get them to tell each other what happened when Hurricane Wilma hit Mexico's Caribbean coastline, and to make notes. In this sort of exercise, one student does most of the speaking and the other mostly listens, so make sure that as you progress through the book all students are given an opportunity to take on the roles of both speaker and listener.

9 Play the news item. During this first listening, get students to check whether they matched the words correctly in Exercises 5–7.

10 Students listen again and this time focus on the order of events, and compare them with their own ideas from Exercise 8. If necessary, you can let your students read the transcript on page 151–2 of their Coursebook.

C Reading and vocabulary

11 In some parts of the world, snow and avalanches are unknown, while in others, they are a very common occurrence. You could have a quick competition, asking students to think of five countries where snow falls, and five more countries where it doesn't. Afterwards, get them to tell you what they think snow actually is.

12 Using their dictionaries, students discuss and decide on the meanings of the six words. Then they try to find a picture of each on the Internet or in books.

13 Here there are seven more words for students to check.

14

> **Answers**
>
> | | | | |
> |---|---|---|---|
> | a | rain | f | identical |
> | b | crystals | g | moist |
> | c | clouds | h | hillside |
> | d | melt | i | cylindrical |
> | e | hexagonal | | |

15 This is a pre-reading exercise to help students deal with the text which follows.

> **Answers**
>
> a single file
> b a long stick
> c a small spade
> d a personal tracking device
> e an anchor

D Language focus: the 0 conditional for advice and suggestions

16 The text contains five *if* clauses, including the example given:

> **Answers**
>
> If you are in an avalanche area, <u>take notice of warning signs</u>.
> If you are in an avalanche area, <u>always carry safety equipment</u> …
> If you are caught in the path of an avalanche, <u>try to get to the side of it</u>.
> If you can't do this, <u>hold on to an anchor, such as a tree</u>.
> If you are hit by an avalanche, <u>'swim' with the snow</u> …

17 The verbs in the *if* clauses are present tense, and those in the main clauses are all present tense without a subject = imperative forms. Point out to students that, where further advice is given in a second sentence, the imperative is used again (e.g. *Stay alert in the countryside …*).

> **Answers**
>
> If you are in an avalanche area, take notice of warning signs.
> If you are in an avalanche area, always carry safety equipment …
> If you are caught in the path of an avalanche, try to get to the side of it.
> If you can't do this, hold on to an anchor, such as a tree.
> If you are hit by an avalanche, 'swim' with the snow …

18 This conditional form is used to do both b and c, although in the examples so far the meaning is for instructions, warnings, advice, suggestions.

19 Make sure your students understand what the pictures are showing, and do the example with them first. Then do the questions orally before getting students to write their answers. There are various possible answers.

Possible answers

a *If you have an emergency radio,* keep it turned on.

b *If you don't have a basement,* stay in the bathroom.

c *If you know a hurricane is coming,* keep the windows shuttered.

d *If you live in a hurricane area,* buy a power generator.

e *If you live in a mobile home,* move out when a hurricane approaches.

f *If you live on a boat,* don't stay on it.

g *If you see broken power cables,* don't go near them.

---

20 Using the examples in the previous exercise, students now write their own pieces of advice.

E Study skills and research

21 This exercise requires students to think about their own country and the weather events that occur there. They should find out how to say the events in their own language.

22 & 23 This project is based on the weather, and students can use information from the unit as well as their own research. As already mentioned, do not assist students too much, but talk to them about their progress and guide them where necessary.

F Reading and writing

24 The pictures should prompt students to discuss volcanoes and Vesuvius in particular. Find out if they know the story of Pompeii. If not, do not tell them too much as they will be reading about the disaster in the following exercises.

25 This is a vocabulary exercise, and the words are quite demanding, so give students plenty of time to discuss the words and check what they mean. They should also select eleven which they think they will find in the text.

26

Answers

monstrous	collapse	remains
debris	phenomenon	annihilation
dust	eruption	pyroclastic
ashes	molten	

27

			p	h	e	n	o	m	e	n	o	n	
	a	s	h	e	s								
			p	y	r	o	c	l	a	s	t	i	c
					c	o	l	l	a	p	s	e	
			d	u	s	t							
a	n	n	i	h	i	l	a	t	i	o	n		
		r	e	m	a	i	n	s					
		m	o	n	s	t	r	o	u	s			
		d	e	b	r	i	s						
	e	r	u	p	t	i	o	n					
		m	o	l	t	e	n						

28 Check students' understanding of Pliny's letter, and then get them to start imagining what happened next. Their thoughts can then be developed into a piece of creative narrative writing.

G Review quiz

29 Students can self-check their answers.

Workbook exercises

Vocabulary

1   horizontal: avalanche, drought
    vertical: hailstorm, flood
    diagonal: tornado, earthquake, tsunami, hurricane, volcano

2   a   earthquake
    b   tsunami
    c   drought
    d   avalanche
    e   hurricane

4   Possible answers:
    volcano – ashes, eruption, lava, molten, pyroclastic
    hurricane – Category 2, drowning, hide in basement, knee-deep water, pick up speed, wind
    flood – drowning, knee-deep water

Language focus: the 0 conditional for advice and suggestions

5   a   If you are in an avalanche area, take notice of warning signs.
    b   If you are caught in the path of an avalanche, try to get to the side of it.
    c   If you are hit by an avalanche, try to swim with it.
    d   If a hurricane approaches, hide in the basement.
    e   If you live on a boat, be careful of broken power cables.

6   a   If you **see** an eruption, **warn** others.
    b   If you **see** buildings shaking, **move** to an open area.
    c   If you **walk** in an avalanche area, never **travel** alone.
    d   If you can't **avoid** an avalanche, **try** to hold on to something solid.
    e   If you **live** in a mobile home, **move out** if danger is approaching.

Reading

12 a   … the long drought is over
    b   … in flooding tragedies
    c   … cars off the roadway
    d   … death by drowning
    e   … hunger and disease

Listening

CD 1, Track 3

15 a   Arabic word meaning 'season'
    b   tropical regions, e.g. northern Australia, Africa, South America, the USA
    c   cold and warm air over land and sea
    d   countries in south-east Asia, particularly India
    e   both flooding and droughts

16 1   winds
    2   rainfall
    3   South America
    4   India
    5   land and sea
    6   over 35 °C
    7   drop in temperature
    8   flood hazards

Unit 4: Water

Coursebook exercises

A Speaking and thinking

1   If your students find the answers and write them correctly in the puzzle, the word *ocean* is made.

a	s	h	a	l	l	o	w		
b	s	u	r	f	a	c	e		
c				d	e	p	t	h	
d				s	e	a	w	e	e	d
e	f	r	o	z	e	n			

2   Allow students enough time to think about the information and decide whether it is true or false – in fact everything is true.

3   The pictures and names all represent records of some type. See if students can match the names and pictures, but do not give them too much assistance yet.

> **Answers**
> a   Mount Everest, Nepal–China border
> b   the world's tallest tree (a redwood), California
> c   the world's deepest cave (Voronya Cave), Georgia
> d   the Arabian Sea
> e   the Antarctic Plateau
> f   the world's highest volcano (Ojos del Salado), Argentina–Chile border
> g   the Eiffel Tower, France
> h   the tallest living man (Bao Xishun)
> i   the Pacific Ocean
> j   the Burj Tower, Dubai

4   Using the information given, students now decide how high or deep everything is.

> **Answers**
> a   8,850 m   f   6,887 m
> b   115 m   g   300 m
> c   2,191 m   h   2.57 m
> d   2,734 m   i   10,924 m
> e   4,572 m   j   2,313 m

5   Show students how they can illustrate graphically all the information from the previous exercises. This could be a simple graph showing heights and depths, or something more adventurous using pictures. Once students understand what is required of them, they will probably think of their own ways of representing the information.

B Reading and vocabulary

6   Zeros can cause students to misunderstand large numbers, so this exercise gives them the chance to think about zeros and how many are needed with various numbers.

> **Answers**
> ten = one zero
> hundred = two zeros
> thousand = three zeros
> million = six zeros
> billion = nine/twelve zeros
> trillion = twelve/eighteen zeros

7   Unfortunately, the USA and the scientific world use numbers differently from some other countries, although the US system is now more and more accepted as the norm. Get students to complete the table with the information given. They should be able to see how the two systems work.

Number of zeros	US and scientific community	Other countries
1	0	*ten*	ten
2	00	*hundred*	hundred
3	000	*thousand*	thousand
6	000 000	million	*million*
9	000 000 000	billion	1,000 million
12	000 000 000 000	*trillion*	billion
15	000 000 000 000 000	quadrillion	1,000 billion
18	000 000 000 000 000 000	*quintillion*	trillion

8 This is a pre-reading exercise. Encourage students to discuss the vocabulary before using their dictionaries.

9 Set a time limit for your students to skim the text and think of headings for each paragraph. It does not matter what they think of – the important thing is that the headings they choose have some connection with the content of each paragraph. They can compare their choices and decide which ones they think are the best.

10 Students read again and complete the eight gaps with the words from Exercise **8**.

Answers

a saline
b continuous
c gigantic
d descending
e equator
f portions
g evaporation
h evolved

11 This exercise gives practice in writing long numbers as figures. Make sure they remember to include a unit of measurement after each number, if necessary.

Answers

70 per cent / 70%
361,000,000 km²
3,000 m
35 parts per 1,000 (3.5 per cent / 3.5%)
30 to 38 parts per 1,000
70 per cent / 70%
3,000,000,000 (US) years

C Listening and speaking

CD 1, Track 5

12 Encourage students to discuss the idea of going down deep into the ocean, and to think about what they might find. Prompt them if necessary (submarines, bathyscopes, etc.). Use pictures of sea monsters if you think this might help.

13 Give students sufficient time to look at the words and to think about what they mean. Make sure they use a dictionary to help them.

14

Answers

1 reptiles
2 mammals
3 extinct
4 continents
5 fertile
6 herbivorous
7 thrived
8 carnivorous
9 insects
10 reefs
11 mass
12 asteroid

15 Allow students to digest the information in the table and to predict what is missing – they may even remember some information from the first listening. Let them listen again and complete the gaps. They should check their answers with a classmate, and use the transcript if they disagree.

Triassic period	Jurassic period	Early Cretaceous period	*Late Cretaceous period*
250–200 million years ago (MYA)	*200–145 MYA*	145–83 *MYA*	83–65 MYA
Large reptiles and tiny mammals ruled the Earth; dinosaurs lived on land and in sea	*Sea monsters extinct ; dinosaurs dominated; continents merged, split apart again; fertile and green; herbivorous dinosaurs, meat-eating animals; first birds, flowers, insects*	*Continents continued to move and separate; took on modern form*	*Many animals died out; mass extinction at end; possible impact from asteroid; age of mammals began; mountain ranges formed*

D Language focus: superlatives

16 Go through the rules, which your students should already be aware of. However, mistakes are often made, particularly with spelling.

old	oldest
fat	*fattest*
thin	thinnest
far	furthest
tiny	tiniest
simple	*simplest*
amazing	most amazing
fertile	most fertile
shallow	*shallowest*
modern	most modern

17 Various answers are possible.

> **Possible answers**
> a This is the most uncomfortable bed in the whole hotel.
> b I think she's the worst singer in the group.
> c Maria is the most intelligent of all the students.
> d Marco is the naughtiest and cleverest in his class.
> e I am the happiest person in the world.
> f Ahmed cannot answer the most difficult questions.
> g That song is the most beautiful music I have ever heard.
> h Bao Xishun is the world's tallest man.
> i Voronya Cave is the deepest cave in the world.

E Study skills and research

18 More words for students to translate. Get them to check with a classmate and make sure they agree.

19 & 20 As mentioned in previous units, do not assist students too much, but talk to them about their progress and guide them where necessary.

F Reading and speaking

21 Many words in English have multiple meanings, and the word *hot* is a good example. Get students to think of some different meanings, although they may not be able to come up with many.

22 In the table there are ten different uses of the word *hot* and students need to match the example sentences to the correct meaning. Some variations may be possible.

A	B
His shirt was hot pink with blue spots.	bright, vivid colour
I think that topic is too hot to discuss.	something which causes an argument
Listen to this news hot off the press!	recent or topical
Martha has a very hot temper.	quickly angered
Petros is really hot on jazz.	keen, eager
That curry was too hot for me.	very spicy
The competition was too hot for our team.	knowledgeable
It's the hottest day of the year.	very warm
The protest got too hot and he left quickly.	dangerous
This car is the hottest in our range.	successful

23 See if your students can think of different meanings for the word *cold*. Let them discuss their ideas and use a dictionary to help them.

24 & 25 Students are going to read about the hottest and coldest places on Earth. Get them to predict where they think these places are. Give them some prompts if they cannot think of anywhere.

26 This is an information-transfer exercise. Students should look at the table first and decide what information is being asked for. Then they read the text and complete the table.

	Hottest place/s	Coldest place/s
Name	1 Dallol Depression 2 Death Valley	Antarctica
Location	1 Ethiopia 2 California, USA	Antarctica
Temperature	1 63 °C in the sun 2 49 °C in the sun	−89 °C
Geographical features	1 desert, some places 100 m below sea level, one of lowest places on Earth not covered by water 2 miles of sand dunes, salt lake, mountains, volcanic rock	one of driest places on Earth, sun rises and sets only once a year – six months of darkness and six months of daylight
Other information	1 Earth tremors frequent, several active volcanoes 2 Big tourist attraction	penguins live along the coast, but none inland, very little food, nothing to build shelter from

Review quiz

27 As before, get students to check their answers by looking back through the unit.

Workbook exercises

 Vocabulary

1 a asteroid
  b carnivores
  c continent
  d fertile
  e herbivorous
  f insect
  g mammal
  h dinosaur
  i reptile
  j extinct

3 a Dinosaurs
  b carnivores
  c continents
  d climate
  e extinction

 Language focus: superlatives

5 a largest
  b smallest
  c lowest
  d hottest, coldest
  e loneliest
  f most treacherous

Reading

8

Word or phrase from text	Meaning
precipitation	rain, snow or hail
vegetation	plants in general
attuned to survive	adapted to live and not disappear
harsh conditions	difficult environment
endowed	given, provided
roots	underground part of plant
dunes	hills of sand
vast tract	enormous area
barrenness	being without vegetation
uninhabited	with nobody living there

9 All true

10 a Saudi Arabia
   b Yemen
   c Oman
   d UAE
   e Qatar
   f Jordan

 Listening

CD 1,
Track 4

13

Planet name	Earth weight	Planet weight	Information about temperature	Other information
1 *Mercury*	60 kg	*25 kg*	Very cold at night	*Spins very slowly, very close to sun*, smaller than Earth, less gravity
2 Venus	*30 kg*	slightly less	*Hottest average temperature*	Similar size to Earth, very hostile planet, thick cloud cover, impossible to see surface, active volcanoes, venusquakes
3 Mars	30 kg	12 kg	Mild temperature, similar to Earth's	Once had rivers and lakes, today water is frozen or underground
4 Jupiter	30 kg	85 kg	–	*The sky becomes the ocean*, has super hurricane winds, no solid surface

Unit 5: Plants

Coursebook exercises

A Speaking and thinking

1 Give students some time to think about the question and to suggest what the three groups might be.

> **Answers**
> grasses, fruit-bearing plants, grains

2 Now students need to think about the things that animals eat.

	Grasses	Fruit-bearing plants	Grains
What can eat it?	cat cow frog rabbit sheep	bear fly human mouse spider wolf	chicken human mouse

3 Get your students to think about what animals eat – use animals they will be familiar with. See if they can understand the meaning of the words *carnivore* (meat-eating), *omnivore* (meat- and non-meat-eating) and *herbivore* (non-meat-eating).

4

Herbivores	Carnivores	Omnivores
sheep cow rabbit mouse chicken	cat spider wolf	human bear fly frog

B Reading and vocabulary

5 This section deals with ecosystems. Allow your students to read the text and to check the meaning of the words printed in green, and then to compare their meanings with a classmate's.

6 This is an information-transfer exercise. Students should read the text again and, while they read, label the diagram.

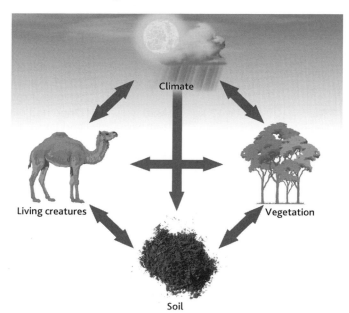

C Listening and reading

CD 1, Track 6

7 Make sure your students understand what they have to do in this exercise. They need to listen and draw a diagram of the ecosystem the speaker describes, and they can also take notes if they wish. You may like to pause after each section, to give your students time to draw and write.

8 Using their diagrams and notes to help them, students read the jumbled instructions and put them into the correct order. They can then check with each other.

> **Answer**
> 1, C, E, F, A, B, D, 8

9 If students need to, let them listen again and check the order of the instructions.

D Language focus: imperatives

10 The language focus here should not prove too demanding as it was covered in the previous unit when students looked at the 0 conditional.

> **Answer**
> The verbs give you instructions.

11

> **Answers**
> imagine   choose   write   underline
> make   choose   write   underline
> choose   draw   remember   add
> write

12 Review the signpost words from Unit 2, and then do this exercise orally with your students before they write out the instructions. Various answers are possible.

E Study skills and research

13–16 As mentioned in previous units, do not assist students too much, but talk to them about their progress and guide them where necessary.

F Reading and writing

17 Focus on the picture and make sure students understand what is being shown, and what has happened to the insect.

18 Check that students remember what *carnivorous* means – it is the adjective from *carnivore*, which they saw earlier in this unit. Look at the verbs in the text extract and check students understand what they mean – they should use a dictionary to help them.

19

> **Answer**
> *A carnivorous plant must be able to do the following things:*
> * *attract its victim into its trap, usually using colour and smell*
> * *capture its victim*
> * *kill its victim*
> * *eat its victim*
> * *absorb nutrients from its victim*

20 Students look at the section headed 'A beautiful plant' and then match the words printed in green with the words given. Do not allow them to use a dictionary here; they should use the context to get the meanings.

> **Answers**
> a dissolves
> b grooved
> c prey
> d cavity

21 Now students focus on the third part of the text and find words or phrases with a similar meaning to those given. Again, try to get them to do this without dictionaries if possible.

22 This writing exercise exploits students' understanding of what the pitcher plant does when it kills an insect. Get students to go through the process orally first, and then to write their story. They should be as descriptive and as imaginative as possible! Perhaps they could illustrate their story with a picture.

G Review quiz

23 The answers to these questions can be found by looking back through the unit.

Workbook exercises

 Vocabulary

1 herbivores, grasses, omnivores, grains, nutrients, ecosystem, carnivores, biotic

2 a herbivores, carnivores, omnivores (any order)
  b grasses, grains (any order)
  c ecosystem
  d biotic
  e nutrients

3 a bear
  b cat
  c chicken
  d fly
  e mouse
  f rabbit
  g sheep

4 a digest
  b victim
  c kill
  d smell
  e colours
  f cavity
  g liquid
  h odour
  i dissolves

Language focus: imperatives

5 a instruction
  b suggestion
  c infinitive
  d subject

Reading

7 man of the jungle

8 a desperately
  b stall
  c limp
  d dumped
  e trader

9   a   contribute
    b   running out
    c   on a large scale
    d   mission
    e   forester
    f   droplets
    g   rapidly

10 a   because they are closely related to humans
    b   they hold butterflies and flowers, enjoy the beauty around them
    c   1,000
    d   donations from local schools

Listening

CD 1,
Track 5

11 & 12
    a   feathers
    b   shrimp
    c   chick
    d   bill
    e   nest
    f   pieces of egg shell
    g   cracked egg
    h   mud
    i   feet

13 a   False – found all over the world
    b   False – does not face any danger from mankind
    c   True
    d   True
    e   False – both male and female look after the egg
    f   False – parents help
    g   False – remain with parents for a further month (after ten weeks)

Writing

14

Paragraph	Information
1	countries they live in, eating habits, feathers, captivity, colours
2	nest-building materials and method, laying eggs, hatching, baby birds, flying

Unit 6: Animals

Coursebook exercises

A Speaking and thinking

1   Brainstorm with your students to make a list of animals, focusing on very large and very small creatures. Then get students working in pairs to complete the six sentences, using the information given.

Answers

a	African Elephant	d	giant tortoise
b	30 metres	e	1.5 grams
c	Australian tiger beetle	f	bee

2   Make sure students understand the idea that everything can be classified in some way. Use music as an example (see page **50** of the Coursebook), and then get students to think about how to classify animals.

3 & 4   Various answers are possible here, depending on how your students decided to classify animals. As an example, use the number of legs, and then show them how the creatures listed could be classified.

Answers

two legs: chicken, human
four legs: bear, cat, cow, frog, mouse, rabbit, sheep,
    wolf
six legs: fly
eight legs: spider

B Reading and vocabulary

5   Get students to think about fear, and what might frighten different animals. Give the example of

mice frightening elephants, and ask them why this is the case. Get students to think also about other things that frighten animals, apart from other animals, such as fire.

6   The newspaper reports that elephants are being frightened away by the noise of angry bees.

7   Students will need to use a dictionary for the words and phrases. Get them to discuss the words as well and to come up with final ideas about meanings.

8   Get students to look at the information and decide whether it is true or false – they will find out when they read the text, so do not tell them anything at this point.

9   Give students a few minutes to skim the text to find the words and phrases from Exercise **7** and to check whether the meanings they agreed on with each other make sense.

10   Students read the text in more detail and check the information from Exercise **8**.

Answers

a   True
b   True
c   True
d   True
e   False – a bee cannot sting an elephant
f   True
g   False – elephants are intelligent animals

C Listening and speaking

CD 1,
Track 7

11   Students will probably not know the word in English (*invertebrates*), so let them tell you in their first language, if they can. Ask students for any examples they can think of.

12   All the creatures listed are invertebrates.

13   Give students plenty of time to go through the list of information and decide together whether it is true or false. Dictionaries should not be necessary as all the vocabulary has been seen before.

14   Students listen and number the creatures in the order the scientist mentions them.

> ### Answers
>
> | 1 | jellyfish | 7 | grasshopper |
> |---|-----------|---|-------------|
> | 2 | worm | 8 | ant |
> | 3 | octopus | 9 | spider |
> | 4 | crab | 10 | scorpion |
> | 5 | butterfly | 11 | squid |
> | 6 | beetle | 12 | mosquito |

15   Students listen again and check whether the information in Exercise **13** is true or false.

> ### Answers
>
> **a** False – jellyfish have no eyes
> **b** True
> **c** False – 1 million species of insect are known
> **d** False – there are some similarities between humans and insects
> **e** True
> **f** True
> **g** True
> **h** True
> **i** False – very few people have seen a living giant squid
> **j** False – the most dangerous invertebrate is the mosquito

D Language focus: question tags

16   Question tags can be rather bewildering for students, as in many languages there is only one possible form for a tag, whereas in English the form of the tag is determined by the verb in the preceding sentence. In the transcript students need to find and copy eight examples.

> ### Answers
>
> | aren't they? | isn't it? |
> |--------------|-----------|
> | don't they? | weren't they? |
> | isn't it? | doesn't it? |
> | don't they? | won't you? |

17   Before students listen again to the interview, make sure they are clear about how the meaning changes depending on a rising or falling intonation.

> ### Answers
>
> aren't they? – down
> don't they? – up
> isn't it? – down
> don't they? – down
> isn't it? – up
> weren't they? – up
> doesn't it? – up
> won't you? – down

18   There are some rules for forming question tags. Refer your students to examples in the transcript and then get them to complete the four rules.

> ### Answers
>
> • negative
> • negative
> • tag
> • *do*

19

> ### Answers
>
> **b** aren't they?
> **c** aren't there?
> **d** aren't they?
> **e** hasn't it?
> **f** doesn't it/she?
> **g** are they?
> **h** isn't it?
> **i** have they?
> **j** doesn't it?

E Study skills and research

20 & 21 As mentioned in previous units, do not assist students too much, but talk to them about their progress and guide them where necessary.

F Reading and writing

22 The best way to introduce the topic of *Twenty Thousand Leagues Under the Sea* would be to show the cover of the book, or perhaps a DVD picture. Get students to tell you what they know about the story, and find out if anyone has read the book or seen the film.

23 Students read the summary of the story, or, if you prefer, you could read it aloud to them first for extra listening practice.

24 When students read the summary the second time, ask them to focus on the words and phrases printed in green, and to work out what they mean with a classmate. They should use their dictionaries for this exercise. Then get students to summarise the summary, orally, to check they have understood.

25 & 26 Students are going to read a translation of the end of the story. There is some difficult vocabulary, so you will need to deal with this before they read. However, the purpose is to prepare students for some creative writing, in which they take on the role of one of the main characters and describe what happened *during that night*. If possible, get your students to focus on the questions the narrator asks in the final two paragraphs of the story.

G Review quiz

27 Students should check their answers by looking back through the unit.

Workbook exercises

 Vocabulary

1 horizontal: frog, sheep, cat
vertical: mouse, cow
diagonal: fly, bear, spider, rabbit, wolf, chicken, human

2 a beetle
   b crab
   c jellyfish
   d mosquito
   e spider

Language focus: question tags

4 a aren't they?
   b are you?
   c have they?
   d are they?
   e have they?

5 a wasn't it?
   b isn't it?
   c doesn't it?
   d aren't they?
   e had he?
   f do they?

Reading

8

English	Arabic	Greek	German	Latin
duck bull	giraffe	hippopotamus rhinoceros shark elephant python crocodile	poodle	leopard shark salmon trout elephant

9

Behaviour	Appearance	Neither
duck	giraffe	elephant
hippopotamus	hippopotamus	python
poodle	rhinoceros	
bull	leopard	
salmon	shark	
trout	crocodile	

 **Listening**

CD 1,
Track 6

13 1 volcano

   2 coral

   3 isolated

   4 different atmospheres

   5 natural beauty

   6 desert

   7 Honolulu

   8 rainforests

   9 hospitable population

14 Various answers are possible, but students will probably include phrases such as: *ring of coral*, *barren rock*, *live volcanoes*, *breathtaking beaches*, etc.

Level 1, Part 1

Unit 7: The senses

Coursebook exercises

A Speaking and thinking

1   Before they open their Coursebooks, ask students what their five senses are. If they are unable to do this, let them look in their books and decide in pairs what the five human senses are.

2   Now students match the pictures to the five senses.

> **Answers**
>
> sight – eyes
> touch – fingers
> taste – tongue
> smell – nose
> hearing – ears

3   Obviously there are no right or wrong answers here. Get your students talking about their senses, and thinking about which they use the most and the least. Prompt them if necessary. Ask them if they use any of their senses more or less depending on where they are.

4   Animals use their senses in different ways from humans. Give students some time to read through the statements (they are all true) and to discuss them in pairs.

B Listening and vocabulary

CD 1,
Track 8

5

> **Answers**
>
> Various answers are possible. This is one suggestion:
>
> | 1 Sight | 2 Touch/feel | 3 Taste | 4 Hearing |
> |---------|--------------|---------|-----------|
> | air | feel | buds | frequencies |
> | eyeball | pressure | sense | hearing |
> | eyes | sense | taste | Hz |
> | lens | touch | tongue | sense |
> | movement | | | sound |
> | sense | | | |
> | vision | | | |

6   Allow students to add any words they think are appropriate.

7   Students listen to the talk to confirm their predictions from Exercise **4**. All the information is true.

C Reading and vocabulary

8   The words, which all mean 'chess', are from the following languages:
     shakki   Finnish
     échecs   French
     ajedrez   Spanish
     xadrez   Portuguese
     schaken   Dutch
     catur   Malay and Indonesian
     shah   Albanian

9 Give students 2–3 minutes to read and answer the questions, but do not prolong it. Also, at this stage, it does not matter what answers they give to the questions. They will find out whether they were right during the next exercise.

10 Give your students a couple of minutes to check their answers to the questions in Exercise **9**.

Answers
a a way of life that no longer exists
b thousands of years (it is the oldest skill game in the world)
c Noor uses his memory instead of sight

11 You can get your students working in pairs for this exercise. They can also use dictionaries if you have any available.

Answers
a set up   e blind
b represent   f cerebral
c no longer exists g fix
d medieval   h assistance

12

Answers
There are various possibilities, but the following words could be listed:
think   teach   touch
learn   remember

D Language focus: comparative and superlative adjectives

13 It is important for students to be able to recognise grammatical patterns as this can lead to a better understanding of meaning. Students match the sentences with the questions.

Answers
a i & iv
b ii & iii
c bigger than, better than
d the oldest, the best

14

Possible answers
a A dragonfly has better sight than a human. / A dragonfly's sight is better than a human's.
b A catfish has the most taste buds.
c My eyeball's length is smaller than that of an eagle.
d The box jellyfish has more eyes than a scorpion.
e Chess is trickier than other games.
f My hearing is worse than a rat's.
g A bat has the best hearing.

15 This exercise gives students the chance to personalise the use of comparative and superlative adjectives. You can do this as an oral activity, followed by writing.

E Study skills and research

16 In English, the pieces are king, queen, rook/castle, bishop, knight and pawn.

17–19 As mentioned in previous units, do not assist students too much, but talk to them about their progress and guide them where necessary.

F Reading and writing

20 & 21 This e-mail provides your students with a model for the writing they are going to do later in this section. Before they read it, ask them what they know about Indonesia: where it is, its population, its climate, and so on.

Answers

20 *is made up of*	comprises
have people living on them	inhabited
stretch	are strung out
people	inhabitants
edge	outskirts
grow	cultivate

21 The capital of Indonesia is Jakarta.

22

Answers

a	seven	**d**	paragraph 5
b	paragraph 2	**e**	paragraph 6
c	paragraph 3	**f**	paragraph 7

23 Make sure students understand how the model e-mail can be used as a guide to help them write their own e-mail in reply. They should try to include information about the points given.

Review quiz

24 As usual, students can check their answers by looking back through the unit.

Workbook exercises

Vocabulary

1 horizontal: jellyfish, penguin
vertical: butterfly, chameleon
diagonal: fly, eagle, ant, dragonfly, mouse

2

Singular	Plural
dragonfly	dragonflies
penguin	penguins
eagle	eagles
chameleon	chameleons
jellyfish	jellyfish
ant	ants
fly	flies
butterfly	butterflies
mouse	mice

3 smell – nose
hearing – ear
taste – mouth/tongue
sight – eye
touch – fingers/toes

4 **a** independently
b frequencies
c multiple
d skill
e medieval
f blind
g cerebral
h comprises
i inhabitants
j cultivates

Language focus: comparative and superlative adjectives

5 **a** Dragonflies have better sight than humans.
b Catfish have the most taste buds.
c My eyeball's length is smaller than that of an eagle.
d A box jellyfish has more eyes than a scorpion.
e Chess is trickier than other games.
f My hearing is worse than a bat's.
g A bat has the best hearing.

6
  a Sumatra, Java, Sulawesi, Kalimantan and Papua are the **biggest** islands.
  b The population of Indonesia is **more** than 240 million.
  c There are many animals in Indonesia. The **most** beautiful for me is the Sumatran tiger.
  d My two sisters are **older** than me.
  e Is your country **bigger** or **smaller** than Indonesia?

 # Reading

9

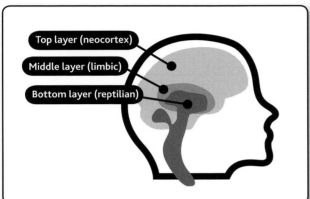

	Name	Function
Top layer	neocortex	deals with creativity and logic
Middle layer	limbic	controls emotions; deals with sense of identity, beliefs and long-term memory
Bottom layer	reptilian	controls body's functions and instincts

10 *features*   characteristics
    part or side   hemisphere
    sensible   logical
    involving original or
    imaginative ideas   creative
    producing a positive result   effective

 # Listening

CD 1,
Track 7

12 1 brain
   2 senses
   3 emotions
   4 beliefs
   5 memory
   6 birthday party
   7 historical date
   8 temperature
   9 danger
  10 learning

13
  a True
  b False – humans have no problem remembering happy occasions
  c True
  d False – your blood pressure and body temperature are controlled by the bottom layer of the brain
  e True

Unit 8: Edible plants

Coursebook exercises

A Speaking and thinking

1 This unit focuses on food and in particular how food affects the human body. Get students to think first of all about spicy food, and to give examples of different foods or dishes they would describe as spicy.

2 Students now think about the natural (and beneficial) ingredients that we add to food to improve the flavour (e.g. salt) and make a list with a classmate.

3 Students need to unjumble the letters and match the words to the pictures.

> **Answers**
>
> | | | | |
> |---|---|---|---|
> | a | onion | d | chilli |
> | b | garlic | e | pepper |
> | c | salt | f | sugar |

4 Ask students which of the ingredients in Exercise 3 are healthy, and then which of the ingredients make food spicy hot.

B Reading and vocabulary

5 Depending on where you are in the world, chilli peppers may be more or less common in cooking. However, most students should know that chillies can make food very spicy, depending on how much is used. Students should read the information about chilli peppers and decide whether it is true or false.

6 The text students are going to read about chillies is in four sections. Before they read, tell them to predict where the information from Exercise 5 will appear in the text.

7 Students skim the text to check whether they predicted correctly, and to check their answers to Exercise 5.

> **Answers**
>
> | | | | |
> |---|---|---|---|
> | a | True, D | e | True, D |
> | b | True, C | f | True, A |
> | c | True, D | g | True, B |
> | d | True, B | | |

8 If you do not have enough time for students to deal with all the vocabulary, you could allocate different words to different groups of students, and then share the answers at the end.

> **Answers**
>
> | | | | | | |
> |---|---|---|---|---|---|
> | a | mild | h | minimal | o | gradually |
> | b | indigenous | i | indoors | p | thermal |
> | c | cultivated | j | edible | q | calories |
> | d | rate | k | loaded | r | sweat |
> | e | potent | l | boosts | s | evaporates |
> | f | triggers | m | immune | t | sore |
> | g | relieve | n | mature | | |

C Listening and writing

CD 1,
Track 9

9 In pairs, students think about rainforests, and in particular the types of plants that grow there. Do not worry if students do not know very much at this point.

10 Students listen to someone talking about rainforest plants. As they listen, they should check whether anything they thought of in Exercise 9 is mentioned. Also, they should listen for the name of one animal (armadillo).

11 Several numbers are mentioned. During the second listening, tell students to listen out for the numbers, and make a note of the order in which they hear them.

> **Answers**
> **1** 1 per cent   **5** 2,000
> **2** 3 million   **6** 300
> **3** 25 per cent   **7** 1,300
> **4** 80 per cent

12 Students now complete the sentences using the numbers from Exercise 11. They can check their answers by reading the transcript on pages **156–7**.

> **Answers**
> **a** 1 per cent   **e** 2,000
> **b** 3 million   **f** 300
> **c** 25 per cent   **g** 1,300
> **d** 80 per cent

13 Students now use the completed sentences from Exercise 12 to help them write a paragraph about how rainforest plants are used in medicine and for food.

D Language focus: referring words

14 & 15 English uses a lot of referring words to avoid repeating nouns, and these words can be the key to whether something is understood. Students now look back at the text on page **65** and decide which word or phrase each of the words in green refers back to (the first three are used in the example).

> **Answers**
> *this* refers back to *measuring the strength of capsicums*
> *which* refers back to *computers*
> *it* refers back to *capsaicin*
> *they* refers back to *Chillies*
> *they* refers back to *Chillies*
> *these* refers back to *Many varieties … indoors*
> *their* refers back to *capsaicin levels*
> *these* refers back to *capsaicin levels … at their highest*

E Study skills and research

16–19 As mentioned in previous units, do not assist students too much, but talk to them about their progress and guide them where necessary.

F Reading and writing

20 & 21 The text students are going to read is about fish and how it can affect our health. They are given the first half of the opening sentences from each of the five paragraphs and need to decide in what order they think the sentences appear in the text. They are then given the second halves of the sentences and are asked to match them up to make complete sentences.

> **Answers**
> *Three recent scientific studies suggest that your mother might have been right.*
> *The smallest study looked at 404 Dutch people aged between 50 and 70.*
> *Norwegian scientists studied more than 2,000 (e) …… people.*
> *The largest study looked at more than 2,400 people in New Zealand.*
> *These studies show that there could well be a link.*

22 Students look at the words with a classmate and check the meaning.

23 Students skim the text and check their answers to Exercises **20** and **21**.

24 The words from Exercise **22** now need to be put back into the text as students read it in more detail.

Answers

a	cognitive	**f**	compelling
b	consumption	**g**	consistent
c	markedly	**h**	trials
d	decline	**i**	establish
e	elderly	**j**	prevalence

---

25 Using information from the unit, as well their own ideas, students write an article for their school newspaper or magazine on the topic of healthy food. They can illustrate their article if they wish.

 Review quiz

26 Students can check their answers by looking back through the unit.

Workbook exercises

 **Vocabulary**

1 chilli, garlic, onion, pepper, salt and sugar

2 **a** Indigenous
 b cultivated
 c developed
 d mild
 e cultivate
 f edible
 g potent
 h immune
 i mature

3 fatty acids
 higher levels
 elderly people
 similar conclusion
 physical health
 brain function
 compelling link
 cognitive decline
 clinical trials

 Reading

6 All the statements are referred to in the text. They are all true.

7 **a** vary
 b essential
 c habits
 d cope with
 e ashamed
 f relieve
 g bottle things up
 h cause
 i low self-esteem
 j regardless of
 k racial

8 **a** paragraph 4
 b 8
 c 1
 d 7
 e 3, 5
 f 4

Listening

CD 1,
Track 8

10 b, j, a, h, d, c, g, e, f, i

11

Character	Who they are
Andie Bradley	gymnast
David Blair	coach
Leslie	other team member
Josh	boyfriend
Holly	best friend

Language focus: referring words

12 *This* refers back to *the chance to train*
she refers back to *Andie*
her refers back to *Andie*
He refers back to *David Blair, the coach*
she refers back to *Andie*
her refers back to *Andie*
her refers back to *Andie*
her refers back to *Andie*
herself refers back to *Andie*
they refers back to Andie's *parents*
where refers back to *the gym*
she refers back to *Andie*
She refers back to *Andie*
her refers back to *Andie*

13 *both* refers back to *Food and eating* (paragraph 1)
our refers back to *we* (1)
it refers back to *food* (3)
it (final) refers back to using food *to help you with painful situations ... stress* (3)
it refers back to *how you deal with emotions and feelings* (4)
it refers back to *bottl[ing] things up* (4)
It (second) refers back to *eating disorder* (5)
These refers back to *factors, events, feelings or pressures* (5)
they refers back to *people with eating disorders* (6)
their refers back to *people with eating disorders* (6)
these refers back to *high academic expectations, family issues or social pressures* (8)
you/your refers to the reader throughout

Unit 9: Explorers

Coursebook exercises

A Speaking and thinking

1 You might need to prompt students with pictures or events to help them if they cannot think of any explorers. The visuals in the Coursebook should also help. Students may be able to think of modern-day explorers.

2 & 3 It does not matter if your students cannot match the pictures to the names and the dates – these are awareness-raising exercises designed to get students thinking about the topic.

Answers
a Abel Tasman, 1642, Australia's western coast mapped
b James Cook, 1770, Australia's eastern coast claimed for Britain
c Edmund Hillary and Norgay Tenzing, 1953, first men to climb Mount Everest
d Roald Amundsen, 1911, first journey to South Pole
e Vasco da Gama, 1497, Portuguese sailor sailed around Cape of Good Hope to India
f Juan Sebastian del Cano, 1519–1522, first voyage around the world
g Robert Peary, 1909, first man to reach North Pole
h Amerigo Vespucci, 1499–1501, coast of South America explored
i Christopher Columbus, 1492, Caribbean reached from Europe
j Leif Ericsson, 1000, first settlement on North America continent, named Vinland
Check students' timelines.

4 Encourage your students to give reasons for their choices. Help them with any difficult vocabulary.

B Reading and vocabulary

5 Once students have completed the timeline, they should skim the text and check whether they have got everything in the right place. If they haven't, they can correct things now.

6 Some of the countries and nationalities mentioned may be unfamiliar to students, but the best way to help them to find everything is to remind them to look for words with capital letters (although some are of course names of people and areas). Note that, although *Holland* and *the Netherlands* are often used interchangeably, Holland is actually a region in the Netherlands; however, do not penalise students who give the answer as *Holland*.

Answers
a Australia
b China
c Portugal
d Spain
e Holland / the Netherlands
f New Zealand
g England
h Turkey
i Iran
j Afghanistan
k India
l Mongolia
m North America
n Italy
o the Caribbean
p Cuba
q Haiti
r Norway

7

Country	Adjective	Country	Adjective
Australia	Australian	Italy	Italian
China	Chinese	Caribbean	Caribbean
Portugal	Portuguese	Cuba	Cuban
Spain	Spanish	Haiti	Haitian
Holland / the Netherlands	Dutch	Norway	Norwegian
New Zealand	(New Zealander)	South America	South American
England	English		
Turkey	Turkish		
Iran	Iranian		
Afghanistan	Afghan		
India	Indian		
Mongolia	Mongolian/ Mongol		
North America	North American		

8

Verb	Noun (person)	Noun (thing)	Adjective	Adverb
–	*adventurer*	adventure	adventurous	adventurously
–	–	*fame*	famous	famously
–	–	*fortune*	fortunate	fortunately
reward	–	*reward*	rewarding	rewardingly
explore	*explorer*	exploration	explored, explorative	exploratively
navigate	*navigator*	navigation	navigated	–
travel	*traveller*	travel	travelled, travelling	–

C Reading and speaking

9 Give students some time to think about the equipment past explorers might have had with them, to guide them and to help them survive. They should work in pairs and produce a list which they can compare with others in the class.

10 We tend not to think of modern explorers, but there are still parts of our world which are unexplored, in particular space and the oceans. Encourage students to compare past explorers with their modern-day equivalents, and to think about the equipment they use, the clothes they wear, the food they eat, and so on.

11 An oceanographer is a scientist who studies the oceans and seas. Ask your students to answer the questions in the Coursebook and to think about the technology oceanographers have at their disposal in the 21st century.

12 Students work in pairs and use a dictionary to help them match the words and definitions.

A	B
interactions	ways of communicating
unique	special, different from others
remote	far away
crew	staff on ship
consistent	reliable
a mixed blessing	having advantages and disadvantages
respondents	those who answer questions
primary appeals	important attractions
onshore	on land
fulfil	achieve or satisfy
substitute	replace

13 Give students a time limit to skim the text for the means of communication listed in Exercise 11. Everything listed is mentioned in the text.

14 This is an exercise for checking the meaning of the words and phrases previously studied by the students in Exercise 12. This gives them a chance to see the vocabulary in its context, and to check the meaning.

15

Advantages	Disadvantages
People can be alone, but have chance to tell others	You can never get away from modern life
Ship can operate better	Communications interrupt personal life
Researchers and crew can maintain relationships with family and friends	Crew worry about home
	Communications often inconsistent

16 Get students to compare the lifestyle of a past explorer, such as Marco Polo, with Cassandra's from the text. What are the similarities and differences? Which lifestyle do students prefer, and why?

D Language focus: the past perfect

17 If anything, once students learn about the past perfect, they tend to overuse it, making it sound very unnatural, so point out the reasons it is used in English.

> **Answers**
> a *After they <u>had crossed</u> Turkey, ... the Polos <u>spent</u> 17 years ...*
> b *Before <u>this</u> ... Roald Amundsen <u>had made</u> the first journey ...*

18 Various answers are possible. Students need to look at the text to check the order of events.

> **Possible answers**
> a Captain James Cook charted Australia's eastern coast after Abel Tasman had mapped Australia's western coast.
> b Traders had brought back travellers' tales before Marco Polo set off on an epic expedition.
> c Columbus reached the Caribbean in October 1492, two months after he had left Italy.
> d Roald Amundsen made the first journey to the South Pole in 1911, after Robert Peary had reached the North Pole.
> e Amerigo Vespucci explored the coast of South America after Vasco da Gama had sailed from Portugal to India.

E Study skills and research

19–21 As mentioned in previous units, do not assist students too much, but talk to them about their progress and guide them where necessary.

F Listening and writing

CD 1,
Track 10

22 Get students to think about the skills and training that an explorer or an adventurer needs to have.

What might an advertisement for an explorer or adventurer include?

23 & 24 Students are going to listen to a radio programme about NASA, which most students will probably have heard of. Before they listen, get them to think in pairs about the phrases given; they should use a dictionary to check anything they are unsure of. They should also decide which of the phrases they think they will hear on the radio programme.

25 All of the phrases appear in the programme.

> **Answers**
> 1 lunar rover
> 2 real-world environment
> 3 external fuel
> 4 lunar-like obstacles
> 5 lunar crater
> 6 life-size replica
> 7 design criteria
> 8 Apollo missions
> 9 lunar landing
> 10 simulated lunar course

26 Allow students to read the incomplete notes and to predict (or perhaps remember) what goes in each gap. Then play the radio programme again so that students can write their answers.

> **Answers**
> a design
> b Friday
> c 14
> d engineering
> e maths
> f vehicles
> g LEM
> h lunar crater area
> i answer depends on current year first race was held in 1994
> j 1 February
> k www.sciencetomorrow.eur

27 Let students check their answers with each other, and look at the transcript if necessary.

G Review quiz

28 Students can check their answers by looking back through the unit.

Workbook exercises

 Vocabulary

2 Various answers are possible (depends on countries chosen for Exercise 1).

3
a fulfil
b remote
c a mixed blessing
d onshore
e interactions
f crew
g consistent
h substitute

4
Apollo missions
design criteria
external fuel
life-size
lunar-like
lunar rover
lunar crater
real-world

Reading

6
1 Wind power
2 Even faster
3 Spaceships with sails
4 Inter-planet transport
5 Warp speed
6 Today's technology

Listening

CD 1,
Track 9

9

A	B
expedition	organised trip, journey
summit	highest point
peak	highest point
previous	which went before
victorious	winning, successful
rapid	very fast
repercussions	consequences
gruelling	exhausting, hard work
terrain	land or countryside

10

Name of film	How long (mins)	Countries and places	People	Film category
Conquest of Everest	90	*Mount Everest*	*Sherpa guides, Sir Edmund Hillary, Tensing Norgay*	Best documentary
Return to Penguin City	48	*Antarctica*	*Viola Toniolo, Grant Ballard*	Best science exploration film
Dog Gone Addiction	67	Alaska, Yukon	*Canadian mother, Polish adventurer, Alaskan dog sled leader*	Best adventure film
Ice Challenger	48	Alaska, Russia	*Steve Brooks*	*Best film*

Language focus: the past perfect

11 15th and 16th centuries

12
a was renamed
b had worked
c was
d had helped
e was described
f became
g began
h had flown
i made
j (had) worked
k joined
l learned
m entered
n had completed
o married
p became
q was
r were killed
s crashed

Writing

13

Date	Event
9 March 1934	Gagarin born, Klushino, Russia
1955	entered military flight training at Orenburg Pilot's School, before this completed technical schooling
1957	married Valentina Goryacheva
1959	became Senior Lieutenant in Soviet Air Force
12 April 1961	first human to travel into space in *Vostok 1* and return
27 March 1968	killed in crash during training flight
1968	town of Gzhatzk renamed Gagarin in his honour

14 Various answers are possible.

Unit 10: Jobs

Coursebook exercises

A Speaking and thinking

1 & 2 The jobs discussed in previous units have been quite exciting. Ask students now to think about jobs that they think are boring, and to make a list which they can later discuss with each other. Prompt them if they find it difficult to think of any boring jobs; the illustrations on page **78** of the Coursebook may help.

3 Briefly discuss with students why they think the jobs they have chosen are boring, then ask them to add their reasons to their list. For example: *It's very repetitive* or *It doesn't need any special skills*.

4 Get students to compare their lists. Combine all the information into a table or graph about the most boring jobs.

B Reading and writing

5 Here are five different jobs which might be considered boring. Students look at the pictures and decide what each one shows.

Answers
a cornflakes checker
b chalk counter
c bottle watcher
d toll collector
e sandwich filler

6 & 7 Students decide which of the five jobs is the most boring and say why. They should also try to predict what each job involves, as this is something they will check when they read about the jobs.

8

Answers
horizontal: watch
vertical: poke
diagonal: flick, sit, put

9 Get students to choose three jobs from their initial list and to write a short description of each one, including why they think the jobs are boring. They should use the descriptions on page **79** of the Coursebook as a guide for their writing.

C Reading and vocabulary

10 A boring job may not necessarily be a bad or dangerous job. Now students need to think about the worst jobs imaginable, and to make a list with a classmate. They should give reasons for their choices.

11 Get the students to tell you what they think each job is. Explain that these are jobs from 170 years ago, when conditions were very different from today.

12 Get students to skim the texts and give each one a job title from Exercise 11.

Answers
Job 1 navvy
Job 2 rural child labourer
Job 3 child chimney sweep
Job 4 scavenger
Job 5 match girl

13 There is quite a lot of vocabulary to deal with here; if time is short, you could allocate a different job to five different groups of students.

<table>
<tr><td colspan="2">Answers</td></tr>
<tr><td>a</td><td>wheelbarrow</td><td>k</td><td>domestic</td></tr>
<tr><td>b</td><td>soil</td><td>l</td><td>discarded</td></tr>
<tr><td>c</td><td>shovelling</td><td>m</td><td>sewers</td></tr>
<tr><td>d</td><td>dawn</td><td>n</td><td>filth</td></tr>
<tr><td>e</td><td>sowing</td><td>o</td><td>bench</td></tr>
<tr><td>f</td><td>poverty</td><td>p</td><td>permitted</td></tr>
<tr><td>g</td><td>soot</td><td>q</td><td>poison</td></tr>
<tr><td>h</td><td>narrow</td><td>r</td><td>vapour</td></tr>
<tr><td>i</td><td>reluctant</td><td>s</td><td>rot</td></tr>
<tr><td>j</td><td>wriggle</td><td></td><td></td></tr>
</table>

14 Get students to vote for the job they think is the worst, and to say why.

D Language focus: word building

15 Once again, if time is short, you could allocate the vocabulary to different students, and then get them to share their answers to provide the complete table.

Verb	Noun (person)	Noun (thing)	Adjective	Adverb
produce	producer	produce, production, product	productive/ producing	produc- tively
manufacture (ing)	manufac- turer	manufac- ture	manufac- tured	–
convey	conveyor	*conveyor/ ance*	conveyed	–
bore	bore	boredom	*boring/*ed	boringly
collect(ing)	collector	collection	collectable	–
commune	–	commune	*communal*	commu- nally
frighten	–	fright	*frightening/* ed	frighten- ingly
–	pauper, the poor	*poverty*	poor	poorly
encourage	–	*encourage- ment*	encouraging/ ed	encour- agingly
discover	discoverer	discovery	discovered	–
permit	–	permit/ permission	*permitted*	–

16 Various answers are possible for this short writing exercise.

E Study skills and research

17–19 As mentioned in previous units, do not assist students too much, but talk to them about their progress and guide them where necessary.

F Listening and writing

CD 2,
Track 1

20 & 21 This is a lateral thinking exercise. Make sure students understand the context and situation, and then see what answers they come up. The surgeon is, of course, the boy's mother. The activity often confuses students as we tend to stereotype people in various professions.

22 Get students to think of jobs which are traditionally for men, women or both, and to complete the table. Give them some examples to get them started (for example, nurse, sailor, doctor).

23 Explain that a counsellor gives people advice about something. Students are going to listen to a careers counsellor talking about different jobs. During the first listening, students should listen for any jobs they listed in the previous exercise.

24

> **Answers**
> **Advantages**
> Follow your dreams
> May lead to positive attention from opposite gender
> All jobs should be accessible to all people in 21st century
> **Disadvantages**
> Lack of guidance
> Opposite gender may not accept you
> May be physically demanding for women
> May attract unwanted attention

25 Get students to read the transcript to check their answers to Exercise **24**. They should then write two short paragraphs describing the advantages and disadvantages, using their notes for guidance.

G Review quiz

26 Students should check their own or each other's answers by looking back through the unit.

Workbook exercises

 ## Vocabulary

1 a cornflakes checker
  b chalk counter
  c bottle watcher
  d toll collector
  e sandwich filler
  f chimney sweep
  g navvy
  h match girl
  i glass blower

3 a traditional
  b career
  c gender
  d conversely
  e gender
  f categories
  g labour-intensive
  h cons
  i pros

 ## Reading

6

A	B
consistently	time and again
occupations	jobs
aspects	parts
catwalk	platform, stage
epitome	the best example of
glamour	elegance and excitement
tedious	boring
adoring	loving
hauling	moving something with effort
dingy	dark, not clean
brush up	revise

8 a actor
  b pilot
  c model, actor
  d rock star
  e model

 ## Listening

CD 1,
Track 10

11

Word or phrase from text	Meaning
opportunity	chance
employment	job
experience	practical knowledge
environment	surroundings, setting
openings	jobs
funding	financial support
wage	salary
hired	given a job
orientation	familiarisation
resident	someone who lives in

 ## Language focus: word building

14

Verb	Noun (person)	Noun (thing)	Adjective	Adverb
consist (of)	–	consis-tency	consistent	*consistently*
occupy	occupant	*occupation*	occupied	–
–	–	*glamour*	glamorous	glamorously
–	–	tedium	*tedious*	tediously
adore	–	adoration	*adoring*/ed	adoringly
–	–	–	*dingy*	–
apply	*applicant*	application	applying/ied	–
employ	employer/ee	*employ-ment*	employing/ed	–
supervise	supervisor	*supervision*	supervising/ed	–
interview	interviewer/ee	interview	*interview*ed	–

Unit 11: Running

Coursebook exercises

A Speaking and thinking

1   Ask students what they know about the word *marathon* and what the race involves. See if they know anything about the history of marathon running.

2   Students read the information and discuss it in pairs, deciding whether each statement is true or false.

3   Sports shoes have become fashion items over the years, and there is an amazing choice of shoes available for different sports and ages, and, of course, just for fashion. Get students to think about their own sports shoes, and to consider why they bought a particular pair.

4   Women and men have different shaped feet (men tend to have longer and broader feet than women of similar stature), and therefore running shoes need to be made differently for men and women. Get students to think about how these shoes might be different.

B Reading and vocabulary

5   Everyone's feet are different, but in what ways? Get students to think about this, and to think about factors they need to consider when they buy sports shoes.

6   An arch has a very specific shape, and the underside of a human foot mimics this shape, although the shape of everyone's arches is unique to them. The sole is the whole of the underside of the foot, the heel is at the back of the foot, and the ball is at the front, before the toes.

7   Explain that water is used for the wet test, and see if students can guess what the test is.

8   Get students to look at the four diagrams and the four instructions for the wet test, and to match them. If possible, you could get some of your students to actually do the test in class.

> **Answers**
> 1 Pour a thin layer of water into a shallow pan.
> 2 Wet the sole of your foot.
> 3 Step onto a blank piece of paper.
> 4 Step off and look down.

9   *Pronation* is a technical term used to describe the movements of the foot when in contact with the ground. It is not important for students to remember it or to use it after the lesson, but it is used in the text on page **86** of the Coursebook.

> **Answers**
> top – Nektarios
> middle – Marios
> bottom – Stelios

10 Get students to read the texts in more detail and do the vocabulary exercise.

> **Answers**
> a contrary to popular belief
> b collapses
> c absorbs
> d stability
> e entire
> f resulting in
> g excessive
> h motion
> i firmer
> j vital

C Listening and writing

CD 2,
Track 2

11 & 12 Make sure students know where Kenya is. Discuss the climate there, and the problems the Maasai might face, and then check they understand why the warriors ran in the London marathon. They wore pieces of car tyres on their feet and carried shields and sticks. They also wore traditional dress.

13 & 14 Read the information with the students, then ask them to decide whether it is true or false. They will find out when they listen to the interview that it's all true.

15 Using all the information from this section, students now write a short paragraph about the Maasai warriors' visit to London to take part in the marathon, and in particular their reasons for doing so.

D Language focus: *-ing* forms

16 While it does not matter too much if students do not understand the terminology here, it is important for them to know that *-ing* does not always indicate a continuous verb form.

> **Answers**
> a continuous verb form
> b noun (gerund)
> c adverb (describes how she left the room)
> d adjective (describes the tap)

17 In the transcript there are seven examples of *-ing* words. Firstly, get your students to read the transcript and underline the seven words; then they should decide with a classmate how the *-ing* words are used.

> **Answers**
> *stopping*   noun – gerund
> *taking*   noun (*taking part in* = noun phrase)
> *running*   adverb (part of adverbial phrase)
> *showing*   adjective (part of adjective phrase)
> *eating*   adverb (part of adverbial phrase)
> *killing*   continuous verb form
> *threatening*   continuous verb form
> *extracting*   noun – gerund

18 In this exercise students practise using *-ing* forms in complete sentences. Check they spell the forms correctly. You can also get students to tell you how the forms are being used.

> **Answers**
> a Smoking – noun
> b are eating – continuous verb form
> c Talking – noun
> d crying – adverb describing how she went to bed
> e winding – adjective describing the path
> f singing – adjective describing the birds
> g dressing – noun
> h knowing – adverb
> i sitting – adjective describing the man
> j is working – continuous verb form

E Study skills and research

19 & 20 As mentioned in previous units, do not assist students too much, but talk to them about their progress and guide them where necessary.

F Reading and writing

21 Get students to think about the idea of unusual sports. Give them an example if they cannot think of anything. Then ask them to match the pictures with the four sports.

Answers

a	man versus horse	**c**	cheese-chasing
b	tuna-throwing	**d**	underwater rugby

22 Once students understand what the four sports are, they can predict in which text the words and phrases given will appear. They will find out whether they are correct in the next exercise.

23 Students skim the texts and check whether their predictions were correct.

24 This is a vocabulary exercise. Students need to read the text again and find words or phrases which are similar to those given.

Answers

a	marathon	**g**	steep
b	cross-country	**h**	contestants
c	obstacles	**i**	ban
d	endurance	**j**	attempt
e	every year	**k**	manoeuvres
f	in excess of	**l**	strategies

25 Students now find which sports match the information given.

Answers

a	man versus horse, tuna-throwing
b	tuna-throwing
c	underwater rugby
d	man versus horse, cheese-chasing
e	underwater rugby

26 Using the four previous sports as models, students choose one of the new sports given here and write a descriptive paragraph. They can include anything they want, as the sports do not (to my knowledge!) actually exist.

 G Review quiz

27 Students can check their answers by looking back through the unit, or with each other.

Workbook exercises

 Vocabulary

1 horizontal: ball, olympics, basketball
vertical: arch, running
diagonal: sole, marathon, shoes, heel, athletics, size

2 **a** stability shoes
b performance training shoes
c motion-control shoes
d neutral cushioned shoes

3 4 metre deep
cheese-chasing
cross-country
grown adult
normal rules
Olympic Gold medallist
steep hill
swimming pool
tuna thrower
underwater rugby
village council

 Reading

7 **a** BASE jumping
b Free diving
c Cave diving
d Speed skiing
e Rock fishing
f Bull riding
g Supercross
h Solo yacht racing
i Street luging
j Bike riding

 Listening

CD 2,
Track 1

10

Word or phrase	Meaning
get into	become interested in
stage fright	fear of performing in front of people
overcome	solve a problem
have a go	take part in something

11 a mom (mother)
   b get up and learn dance
   c sleeps
   d dreams
   e brother
   f 5
   g 11
   h beat
   i ability
   j power
   k female
   l nervous
   m brother
   n younger

Language focus: *-ing* forms

12 *-ing* forms can be used as verbs, adjectives, adverbs and nouns. Check students' sentences.

13

including	adjective
diving	noun
getting	adjective
racing	adjective
fishing	noun
casting	noun
riding	noun
raging	adjective
doing	adverb
taking	adverb
death-defying	adjective
hitting	continuous verb
riding	noun

14
a listening, was, took, watch, happened, learning
b dancing, trained, enjoyed, decided, dancing
c was, danced, told, didn't have

Unit 12: Sport

Coursebook exercises

A Speaking and thinking

1   Make sure students distinguish between sports they like participating in and those they prefer to watch. Also, get them to think about sports on TV, and going to see an event in a stadium.

2   Lead the discussion into talking about sports equipment, and get students to think about what they need in order to play a particular sport. Does having better and more expensive equipment really make a difference to performance?

3   Students think about the equipment needed for the three sports. If time is limited, you could give a different sport to different groups of students and then let them share their answers.

4 & 5   In the wordsearch there are eight items of equipment for the three sports. Students need to find the words and then match them to the sports. They should then discuss in what way they think the equipment is important for each sport.

> **Answers**
> horizontal: goggles, computer
> vertical: trisuit, monitor
> diagonal: shoes, wetsuit, helmet, socks

B Reading and vocabulary

6   See if students can come up with term *triathlete*.

7 & 8   Allow students to use a dictionary for this exercise, and get them to give reasons for their choices.

> **Answers**
> a   *thick material, better body fit*
> b   *some of the face, use contact lenses*
> c   *a good fit, better ventilation*
> d   *under your wetsuit, two-piece for women*
> e   *current speed, distance travelled*
> f   *properly measured, ultra-lightweight*
> g   *feet are soft, absorb moisture*
> h   *within your limits, tell the time*

9   Students read the texts in more detail and answer the questions.

> **Answers**
> a   not flexible, body movement difficult (because made of thick material)
> b   mask-type
> c   it will not give good protection
> d   can be worn under wetsuit, so immediately ready for next event
> e   price
> f   ultra-lightweight trainers
> g   protect soft feet
> h   an HRM

C Listening and vocabulary

CD 2,
Track 3

10   Check that students know where Malawi is, and then explain what they are going to listen to in this section. Students need to look at the words and phrases given and decide in pairs which ones they think they are going to hear.

11   Now get students to focus on the four questions and think about what the triathlete's answers might be.

12 All of the words and phrases are used in the interview.

> **Answers**
> 1 *time*
> 2 *transition*
> 3 *as smooth and as fast as possible*
> 4 *safe technique*
> 5 *baby oil*
> 6 *the wetsuit can get stuck*
> 7 *bike pedals*
> 8 *you won't need to wear socks*
> 9 *elastic laces*
> 10 *wet, slippery fingers*

13

> **Answers**
> a yes, but only if you have a safe technique
> b you need baby oil, talcum powder and Vaseline®
> c inside your cycling shoes
> d around five minutes

D Language focus: signpost words

14 Get students to review the signposts words studied in Unit **2**. Give them the three headings – *When, Contrast, In addition* – and see how many they can remember. They should make lists in pairs.

15 The five sentences from the triathlon text all contain examples of signpost words. Students read the sentences and identify the signpost words in each one.

> **Answers**
> a but, and
> b and
> c Furthermore
> d In addition, and
> e However

16 In this exercise students rewrite each sentence, replacing the signpost words with suitable alternatives

> **Answers**
> Various answers are possible, but as an example:
> d *Furthermore, they are more aerodynamic as well as offering better ventilation.*

E Study skills and research

17–20 As mentioned in previous units, do not assist students too much, but talk to them about their progress and guide them where necessary.

F Reading and writing

21 This exercise gives students practice in forming questions which they will later ask and answer in pairs. Explain the theme here – choosing holidays – and give your students some background information (if they need it) on the Maldives and Mauritius.

> **Possible answers**
> a Where is the holiday?
> b How much is the lowest holiday price?
> c How many nights is the holiday?
> d What is included in the price?
> e What is not included in the price?
> f When does the holiday depart in October?
> g How much is a departure in December?
> h What meals are included?
> i Are there any additional costs?
> j Where can I get more information?

22 Divide students into pairs: one student in each pair should read the text on the Maldives (Coursebook page **144**) and the other should read the text on Mauritius (Coursebook page **145**). They should not look at each other's text. Students should then take it in turns to ask the questions they prepared in Exercise **21**, and note down the answers.

23 Once students have collected the information, they write a short comparison of the two holidays, focusing on the details collected from their questions. Give your students time to read each other's writing and to compare it with their own.

G Review quiz

24 Students can check their answers by looking back through the unit in the Coursebook.

Workbook exercises

 Vocabulary

1 swimming, shoes, socks, cycling, wetsuit, running, goggles, monitor, trisuit, computer

2
cheap wetsuits	loose helmet
thick material	good protection
different thicknesses	expensive models
greater flexibility	better ventilation
small goggles	average speed

3
a	Scattered	d	spectacular
b	amazing	e	wonderful
c	surrounded		

Reading

6

A	B
lodge	small building, often in a forest or jungle
canals	waterways
trails	paths or tracks
daring	brave

8 The following appear in the text: bird watching, hanging bridges, mountains, palm trees, scenic boat trip, tropical nature, volcano, waterfalls.

9
a	interactive exhibits	e	hot springs
b	narrow waterways	f	fireworks display
c	banana plantations	g	bird's eye view
d	rafting trip		

Listening
CD 2, Track 2

13 a vibrant city, growing rapidly
b magnificent sand dunes; warm, white sands
c Arabic-style, Arabic music
d swimming, desert sand-boarding, jet ski, water ski, banana ride
e sun shining brilliantly, twinkling stars, spectacular desert sunrise

Language focus: signpost words

14 well, firstly, then, (what) next, the next thing, then, as soon as, then, even though, after, what next, after, then, also
Note that *and* appears throughout.

Unit 13: Science

Coursebook exercises

A Speaking and thinking

1   The focus for this unit is science. Introduce the topic and ask your students whether they like studying science at school. Get them to give their reasons for liking or disliking it, and what they find easy or difficult about it.

2   Give students a time limit to find the twelve words in the wordsearch. If your students find this demanding, or if you think it will be difficult for them, you could give them some or all of the words, or even just the first letter of the words. Another way to help your students might be to tell them how many words are written horizontally, how many vertically and how many diagonally.

> **Answers**
> horizontal: elements, chemistry, electricity, magnetism
> vertical: gravity, science
> diagonal: atoms, force, physics, biology, reaction, compounds

3   There are no wrong answers here. Tell students that they must be prepared to give reasons for their choices.

For example:

Physics	Chemistry	Other
forces	reaction	biology
atoms	elements	science
gravity	compounds	
magnetism		
electricity		

4

> **Answers**
> a   Chemistry
> b   Physics

5   Use the definitions of chemistry and physics as models to help students prepare to write a definition of biology. The words and phrases given can be used to help.

> **Possible answer**
> Biology is the science of life and living organisms, which can be one cell or several cells, as well as the study of plants and animals.

B Reading and vocabulary

6 & 7   This section gives students more definitions from science. You might prefer to focus on the picture-matching exercise first, and then get students to complete the gaps in the text.

> **Answers**
> a   elements, picture vii
> b   compounds, picture ii
> c   reactions, picture iv
> d   force, picture v
> e   gravity, picture i
> f   magnetism, picture iii
> g   electricity, picture vi
> h   atoms, picture viii

8 & 9 Give students time to look at these verbs and nouns in context, and to discuss meanings in pairs, before allowing them to use dictionaries to check.

10 Make sure students understand how to complete the word puzzle.

a		e						
t		x		f	t			
t		e	d	o	i	i	m	
r		r	r	c	e	d	a	
p	**a**	**r**	**t**	**i**	**c**	**l**	**e**	**s**
o	c	e	s	v	u	d	s	s
l	t	p		e	r			
e	i	e						
s	o	l						
n								

C Listening and speaking

CD 2,
Track 4

11 This is a pre-listening exercise. There are eight questions here to be answered, so if time is limited, you could allocate different questions to different groups of students to answer, and then they could give feedback to the whole class.

12 This is another pre-listening prediction exercise. Give students time to think about the words and phrases, and to use their dictionaries if they need to.

13 & 14 As they listen, students should make notes about the answers given to the eight questions. Make sure they understand that they need to write notes only. They should then compare these answers with their own predictions from Exercise 11.

Answers

a   water is the liquid form of H_2O
b   yes, water is all around us
c   all living creatures need water to survive
d   between one and seven litres per day
e   dehydration
f   routine / have a glass of water every morning / carry bottle of water / eat more fruit and vegetables
g   the world has a water crisis
h   very simply – shower instead of bath, brush teeth using glass of water, use water butt to collect rain, fish tank water for garden

15 All of the words and phrases from Exercise 12 are spoken.

Answers

1   H_2O
2   freeze
3   water vapour
4   Polar ice caps
5   sweat
6   weight
7   temperature
8   health problems
9   fruit and vegetables
10 sinks and toilets
11 poor hygiene
12 400 litres
13 brushing your teeth
14 fish tank

D Language focus: word building

16

Verb	Noun	Adjective	Adverb
limit	limitation	*limited*	–
discover/ed	discovery	discovered	–
differ	difference	*different*	differently
include	inclusion	*including*/ed	–
combine	combination	combining/ed	–
react	*reaction*	reacting/ed	–
exert	exertion	exerting/ed	–
attract	*attraction*	attracting/ed/ive	attractively
power	power	*powerful*/ed	powerfully
contain	container	containing/ed	–
depend	dependence	dependant/ent	–
replace/d	replacement	replaced/ing	–
shorten	*shortage*	short	shortly
remove	removal	removed/remote	remotely

E Study skills and research

17–20 As mentioned in previous units, do not assist students too much, but talk to them about their progress and guide them where necessary.

F Reading and writing

21 Give students a time limit to come up with a list of everything they can think of which uses water. You could prompt them with pictures of water being used in various situations. Get them also to think about how much water they waste (or save).

22 Before students read the article, ask them to think about washing machines and how much water they use. Give them some figures and ask them to guess how much water a washing machine uses.

23 & 24 All five statements are taken from the text and are therefore true, but do not tell students this yet. Ask them to read the information and decide in pairs whether it is true or false. They should then skim the text and find out whether they were right.

25 This is a vocabulary exercise. Before students try to find the words and phrases in the text, get them to think of possible synonyms, sharing their ideas with each other. They should then look at the text in more detail.

Answers
a conventional
b drawback
c granules
d stains
e virtually
f get rid of
g astonishing
h fraction
i recyclable

26 You will probably need to give students quite a lot of planning support here. They will need to think carefully about the household item they have chosen, and then make careful notes about how they are going to make it more environmentally friendly. Once they are ready, they can write their e-mail, telling their friend what the item would look like, and how it would work. Encourage them to include a diagram.

G Review quiz

27 Students can check their answers by looking back through the unit.

Workbook exercises

Vocabulary

1
  a elements
  b chemistry
  c biology
  d force
  e gravity
  f magnetism

  g atoms
  h compounds
  i fraction
  j physics
  k science

2

e	l	e	m	e	n	t	s		
	b	i	o	l	o	g	y		
	s	c	i	e	n	c	e		
	f	r	a	c	t	i	o	n	
		a	t	o	m	s			
		f	o	r	c	e			
g	r	a	v	i	t	y			
		c	o	m	p	o	u	n	d	s
c	h	e	m	i	s	t	r	y	
m	a	g	n	e	t	i	s	m	
	p	h	y	s	i	c	s		

Reading

4

Word from the text	Definition
consequently	therefore
likelihood	possibility
monitor (verb)	check
devices	instruments, equipment
ratings	number of people watching
images	pictures
likeness	similar image

5
  a because it uses a radio signal
  b a mobile phone has a very limited range
  c electromagnetic waves are sent through the air
  d devices can sometimes stop working
  e lets parents block TV programmes
  f V-chip electronically reads ratings embedded in programmes
  g sending documents to any phone number with fax machine

6
  a fax machine (converts the image on a page into a series of light and dark dots)
  b regular phone line (for sending sound tones)
  c receiving fax machine (interprets tones and prints a likeness of the original page)

Listening

CD 2, Track 3

10
  1 atmosphere
  2 air molecules
  3 animals
  4 gases
  5 photosynthesis

  6 ozone layer
  7 South Pole
  8 global warming
  9 forest fires
  10 coal, oil and gas

11
  a air is made up of different gases, mostly nitrogen and oxygen
  b air is essential for almost all forms of life on Earth
  c not really, changes as you move up through the atmosphere
  d in the stratosphere layer
  e it is in some places
  f most caused by humans, but some is natural
  g yes

Language focus: word building

12

Verb	Noun (thing)	Noun (person)	Adjective	Adverb
connect	connection, connector	–	connecting/ed	–
convert	*converting*, converter	–	converted	–
endanger	danger	–	*dangerous*	dangerously
–	invisibility	–	*invisible*	invisibly
receive	receipt, receiver	receiver	receiving/ed	–
–	–	–	recent	*recently*
regulate	regulation	regulator	regular, regulated	regularly
scan	*scanning*, scan/ner	scanner	scanned	–
surround	surrounds	–	*surrounding/ed*	–
translate	*translating*, translation	translator	translated	–

Unit 14: Technology

Coursebook exercises

A Speaking and thinking

1 & 2 This unit focuses on oil as a natural resource, and what it is used for. Get students to think about the importance of oil, and where it comes from. If oil is extracted close to home, it may be something students know a lot about; other students may know very little about oil and plastic. Students should discuss their ideas in pairs and make a list of products made from oil – the pictures in the Coursebook will give them lots of ideas, so you may prefer to introduce the unit with books closed.

3 Get students to focus on the pictures and to decide in pairs which of the products are made from oil. First, check that students know what all the items are in English.

Answers

a	mobile phone	j	pens
b	deodorant	k	perfume
c	pillows	l	credit cards
d	hair colour	m	fishing rod
e	toilet seat	n	shoes
f	blister pack	o	curtains
g	golf balls	p	glasses
h	shampoo	q	laptop
i	tennis rackets	r	headphones

---

4 Students now will realise that many things around us are made of plastic. See if they can guess when plastic was invented, and then lead them into a discussion about the impact of plastic on the environment, and why it is such a problem.

B Reading and vocabulary

5 Students are going to read two versions of a gapped text 'Grow your own plastic'. In order to complete the gaps, students need to ask each other questions – this is therefore an information-transfer activity. First, students read their text (Student A's text is on Coursebook page **146**, Student B's is on page **147**) and then prepare five questions using the five question words given.

6 & 7 In their pairs, students now take it in turns to ask and answer questions, and complete their texts. They should then read each other's text in order to check their answers.

8 Students can remain in their pairs for this vocabulary exercise.

Answers

a	extent	g	rocketed
b	emigrated	h	decades
c	oven	i	ivory
d	synthetic	j	versatility
e	moulded	k	widespread
f	variant		

C Reading

9 Students will probably be very familiar with mobile (cell) phones. Get them to answer the six multiple choice questions on their own, and then to compare their answers with a classmate. You do not need at this stage to tell them whether they are right or wrong.

10 Give students a time limit for skimming the text and checking their answers to the multiple choice questions in Exercise 9.

Answers

a	1940s	**d**	a briefcase
b	all of these	**e**	all of these
c	1983	**f**	4

11 Students now need to look through the text in more detail and answer the questions.

Answers

a yes, (*in one form or another ... 2G*)
b less reliable, more static, more noise interference
c no (very large, not mobile, expensive)
d faster, quieter, smaller, more energy-efficient
e no (*created very soon after ...*)
f can transfer e-mail, information and instant messages as well as voice data
g faster, more affordable
h no (*industry continues to grow*, *keep ... users coming back for more*)

D Language focus: question forms

12 & 13 Get students to look back to the questions they wrote earlier in the unit, all of which began with a question word. Remind students that question words 'force' information in the answer. Point out the position of the auxiliary verb after the question word.

Answers

a How <u>do</u> you know?
b –
c How <u>do</u> you know?
d Why <u>were</u> 2G phones more popular than 1G phones?
e How <u>do</u> you know?
f How <u>is</u> 3G an improvement over 2G?
g What <u>does</u> 4G do that 3G cannot do?
h How <u>do</u> you know?

14 Go through the grammar with your students, making sure they understand how the questions are formed. Do the exercise orally first, and then allow students to write their answers. Other answers are possible, including the tense in the questions.

Possible answers

a What is the car called? / What will the car be called?
b How much does/will it cost?
c How/Where is it made?
d When will it be available?
e Who invented it? Where was it invented?
f What does it look like?
g Why is it so economical?
h Who will use the new car?
i Where will the car be produced?
j How will the car be powered?

E Study skills and research

15–17 As mentioned in previous units, do not assist students too much, but talk to them about their progress and guide them where necessary.

F Listening and writing

CD 2,
Track 5

18 & 19 Make sure students understand the difference between an invention and a discovery, and then get them to discuss when they think each item was invented. If they find this difficult, give them some clues about the dates. Once they have decided when the various things were invented, they can complete the timeline. Do not check their answers yet as they can do this themselves in the next exercise.

20 Let students listen once and check their answers.

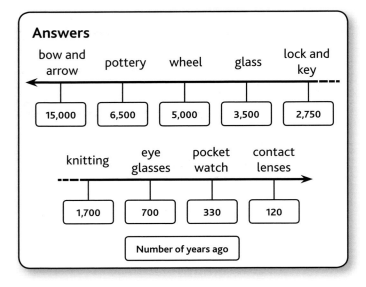

Answers

bow and arrow — 15,000
pottery — 6,500
wheel — 5,000
glass — 3,500
lock and key — 2,750

knitting — 1,700
eye glasses — 700
pocket watch — 330
contact lenses — 120

Number of years ago

21 Give students time to think about this before they start writing. Make sure they know enough about the invention in order to write about it. Then help them through the planning and drafting stages.

G Review quiz

22 Students can check their answers by looking back through the unit.

Workbook exercises

Vocabulary

1
a pillow
b pen
c MP3 player
d shoes
e perfume
f deodorant
g shampoo
h aspirin
i laptop
j credit card

2 mobile phone
hair colour
toilet seat
golf balls
tennis racket
fishing rod
eye glasses
bow and arrow
contact lenses
lock and key
pocket watch

3 The verbs are *discover* and *invent*.

Reading

6
a jams
b idea
c colleagues
d geniuses
e knowledge
f out of place
g projections
h fail
i viable option

7
a 1983
b vertical take-off and landing
c 1989
d slow speed
e eight small 120 hp engines
f 500 km/h
g range
h pollution
i 'vertiports'/parking
j large distances between Skycars

Listening

CD 2, Track 4

11 1 zoo
2 dolphins
3 engineers
4 whale
5 feathers
6 futuristic boats
7 high-tech ships

12 a more than 15 km/h
b propellers
c withstand stormy conditions, change direction quickly, sense currents or waves and respond in a split second
d any three from: like hard, stiff paddle, has small feathers, shaped like aeroplane wing, can move up and down, can move forward and backward, can twist around
e as many as 50

Language focus: question forms

14 a When was Moller International founded?
b Where was Paul Moller born?
c What did Moller's colleagues say about his dream?
d When was the M200x produced?
e What did the M200x look like?
f How many engines does the M400 have?
g How fast can the M400 fly?
h What does Moller predict will be on the top of buildings?
i How far will Skycars be from each other in the sky?

15 a 1983
b Canada
c that it couldn't be done
d 1989
e flying saucer
f eight
g 500 km/h
h 'vertiports'/parking
i nearly 2 km

Level 1, Part 2

Unit 14: Technology **57**

Unit 15: Buildings

Coursebook exercises

A Speaking and thinking

1 & 2 The topic for this unit is bridges and other structures. Get students to think about the word *bridge* in their own language and to compare it with the English word, and any other languages they know. Then see if students can match the translations to the languages.

Translation of *bridge*	Language
ブリッジ	Japanese
мост	Russian
الجسر.	Arabic
most	Polish
köprü	Turkish
架橋	Chinese
다리	Korean
Γέφυρα	Greek

3 Now see how much students know about bridges in their own country, and around the world. You could prompt them with some pictures, if necessary.

4–6 Students look at the pictures and try to match them with the names and locations. They then think about how long the bridges might be, and when each could have been opened.

Answers
a Rio Antirio Bridge (Greece), 2,880 m, 2004
b Golden Gate Bridge (USA), 2,700 m, 1937
c Tsing Ma Bridge (Hong Kong), 1,377 m, 1997
d Tower Bridge (England), 244 m, 1894
e Mahatma Gandhi Setu Bridge (India), 5,850 m, 1982
f Akashi-Kaikyo Bridge (Japan), 3,911 m, 1998

B Reading

7 When students read the text they will be able to check their answers to Exercises 4–6. First, get students to skim the text and decide which paragraph describes each of the six bridges.

Answers
1 Akashi-Kaikyo Bridge (Japan)
2 Rio Antirio Bridge (Greece)
3 Mahatma Gandhi Setu Bridge (India)
4 Tsing Ma Bridge (Hong Kong)
5 Golden Gate Bridge (USA)
6 Tower Bridge (England)

8 Now students look at the text in more detail and answer the questions.

Answers
a Tsing Ma Bridge and Golden Gate Bridge
b Akashi-Kaikyo Bridge, Tsing Ma Bridge and Golden Gate Bridge
c Tower Bridge
d Tsing Ma Bridge
e Tower Bridge
f Golden Gate Bridge
g Akashi-Kaikyo Bridge

C Reading

9 Ask students if they have ever heard of the Icehotel, and to predict where it is, what it is, and what they think it looks like. The picture shows the outside – what do students think the inside looks like?

10 & 11 Make sure students understand what each of the pieces of information means, and then get them to form questions, as in the example.

> **Possible answers**
> a   How old is the hotel?
> b   What facilities does the hotel have?
> c   Where is the hotel (located)?
> d   How big is the hotel?
> e   Where does the ice come from?

12 Students look quickly at the text and decide where they will find the answers to the questions they have just made.

> **Answers**
> a   paragraph 1
> b   3 and 4
> c   1 and 4
> d   4
> e   3

13 Students look at the text again and answer the questions they wrote in Exercise 11.

> **Answers**
> a   now in its fifteenth year
> b   bar, reception, art gallery, cinema, chapel/church
> c   Jukkasjärvi, in the heart of Swedish Lapland
> d   the world's largest igloo
> e   the Torne river

D Language focus: nouns, verbs and adjectives

14 There is a small group of English verbs which end in *-en*, and which are to do with measurement. The *-en* suffix means 'make'.

> **Answers**
> depth – deep – deepen
> length – long – lengthen
> height – high – heighten

15 Students could start to build up a table for these *-en* verbs.

> **Answers**
> a   widen – wide – width
> b   broaden – broad – breadth
> c   strengthen – strong – strength
> d   weaken – weak – weakness
> e   thicken – thick – thickness

16

> **Answers**
> a   strengthened
> b   height
> c   depth
> d   weaknesses, length
> e   thickness/strength
> f   widened

E Study skills and research

17–19 As mentioned in previous units, do not assist students too much, but talk to them about their progress and guide them where necessary.

F Reading and writing

20 Use the picture in the Coursebook if your students are unsure what Atlantis is. However, do not be too concerned as this exercise is designed simply to find out how much (if anything) they know.

21 Tell your students that it does not matter if they are unsure about the information, but they should make a guess. They will find out the answers later in the section.

22 Students now need to ask each other the questions in order to get the information required. This will involve them in moving around the room; if this is not feasible, pair students with different texts so that they can question each other.

Answers

a 9,000 years ago
b nobody
c any four from: Gibraltar, the south-west of England, Bolivia, the Caribbean, the Azores, the Canary Islands, Iceland, Sweden, Western Africa, the Sahara Desert
d they did not believe it and made fun of him
e a devastating earthquake
f an island sank
g nobody knows
h parts of Europe and Africa

23 If it is easier, students could use the Internet to answer these questions.

Answers

a south – Bolivia
   north – Iceland and Sweden
   east – the Caribbean
   west – Sweden
b approximately 11,000 km
c approximately 8,500 km
d Iceland – approximately 4,000 km
   Gibraltar – approximately 2,500 km
   the Canary Islands – approximately 3,500 km

G Review quiz

24 Students can check their answers by looking back through the unit, or with each other.

Workbook exercises

 Vocabulary

1

Adjective	Noun	Verb
wide	width	widen
broad	breadth	broaden
strong	strength	strengthen
weak	weakness	weaken
thick	thickness	thicken
high	height	heighten
long	length	lengthen
short	shortness	shorten

2 professional, toughest, troublesome, dangerous, miserable, funny, famous, bad, deadly, moody

 Reading

4 Pictures a, c, d and e are real.

5

Word or phrase from text	Definition
array	collection
curved	rounded
goals	aims
harbour	port, marina
high-rise buildings	very tall structures, skyscrapers
lagoon	small lake
mimics	copies
sloping	higher on one side
smog	pollution
sustainable	does not destroy the environment
tracks	path of a railway

6 Picture a shows the Urban Cactus
Picture c shows the Anti-smog Building
Picture d shows the Treescraper Tower of Tomorrow
Picture e shows the Ascent at Roebling Bridge

7 a high-rise buildings
b curved
c array
d tracks
e lagoon
f smog
g goals
h sloping
i harbour
j sustainable
k mimics

8 a The Urban Cactus
b The Anti-smog Building, the Urban Cactus, the Treescraper Tower of Tomorrow
c The Anti-smog Building, the Ascent at Roebling Bridge
d The Anti-smog Building

 Listening

CD 2, Track 5

12 1 maiden voyage
2 double-bottomed hull
3 watertight compartments
4 buoyancy
5 unsinkable
6 perished
7 on board
8 wreck
9 upright
10 tear

13 All the information is true.

Language focus: nouns, verbs and adjectives

14

Verb	Adjective	Noun
calculate	calculated/ing/able	calculator/ion
consider	considerate/ed	consideration
design	designing/ed	design/er
divide	dividing/ed	divider/ision
estimate	estimated	estimate/ation
explore	exploring/ed/atory	exploration/er
mention	mentionable	mention
sink	sinking/able/sunken	sinking
sustain	sustainable/ed	–
wonder	wonderful/ing	wonder

15 a unsinkable
b designs, calculations
c sustainable
d wonderful
e mentioned
f estimated
g considered
h divided
i exploration

Unit 16: Wonders of the world

Coursebook exercises

A Speaking and thinking

1 Give students some prompts to get them thinking about the Seven Wonders of the Ancient World, if they need help. Get them to think about the countries where the Wonders were located.

2 Students now match the pictures to the names – if they don't know all the names, these can be given.

> **Answers**
> 1 the Temple of Artemis
> 2 the Statue of Zeus
> 3 the Great Pyramid of Giza
> 4 the Colossus of Rhodes
> 5 the Lighthouse of Alexandria
> 6 the Mausoleum of Maussollos
> 7 the Hanging Gardens of Babylon

3 Students now decide in which countries the Wonders were located, and write the numbers on a copy of the world map in the Coursebook.

> **Answers**
>
>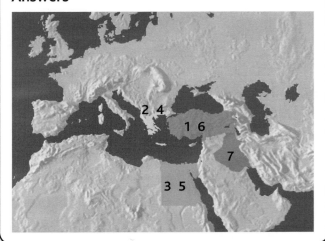

4 Students will realise that all the Wonders are in the same geographical region, that is, the eastern Mediterranean and the Near East.

5 The Seven Wonders of the Ancient World were built between about 2585 and 280 BC; it should be fairly clear by now that all but one (the Great Pyramid) of the original Seven Wonders of the Ancient World no longer exist.

B Reading and vocabulary

6 Students work in pairs and use a dictionary to check the meaning of the words, which will, of course, appear in the text they are going to read.

7 Give students a time limit to skim the text and decide which Wonder is being described in each of the seven paragraphs.

> **Answers**
> 1 The Great Pyramid of Giza
> 2 The Hanging Gardens of Babylon
> 3 The Temple of Artemis
> 4 The Statue of Zeus
> 5 The Mausoleum of Maussollos
> 6 The Colossus of Rhodes
> 7 The Lighthouse of Alexandria

8 The words from Exercise 6 now need to be put back into the text, so students need to read it in more detail. Let them compare their answers in pairs.

During the second listening, students complete the notes and then check their answers in pairs.

Answers

a	2001	e	structures
b	history	f	Mexico
c	public awareness	g	Brazil
d	online poll/vote	h	damage

Answers

a	tomb	g	fame
b	Constructed	h	erected
c	borders	i	throne
d	lush	j	disassembled
e	irrigation	k	entire
f	controversy		

9 Students will need to refer to the text in order to answer these comprehension questions.

Answers

a four (the Hanging Gardens of Babylon, the Mausoleum of Maussollos, the Colossus of Rhodes and the Lighthouse of Alexandria)
b one (the Great Pyramid of Giza)
c the Hanging Gardens of Babylon
d the Colossus of Rhodes
e the Statue of Zeus and the Colossus of Rhodes
f Herostratus (the Temple of Artemis)
g the Great Pyramid of Giza and the Mausoleum of Maussollos

C Listening and writing

CD 2,
Track 6

10 There have been several attempts to name wonders of the modern world. New7Wonders is an organisation which is concerned with the preservation and protection of our heritage and history, and it has organised an online poll to establish seven new wonders.

11 Students will need to work in pairs and use dictionaries to check the meaning of the words and phrases given, and to decide which, if any, they think they will hear in the interview.

12

Answers

horizontal: Peru, Italy, Mexico
vertical: England, India
diagonal: China, Brazil, Jordan, Switzerland

13 Now let students listen to the interview and check their answers to the previous exercises.

15 Students can discuss the seven wonders and make suggestions for additions or deletions. There may be buildings in their own country which they think should be added to the list.

D Language focus: *is thought/said/believed*, etc.

16 This is quite a tricky structure for students to deal with, and it is unlikely that they will be able to produce it accurately. However, they should be able to recognise and understand it in context.

Answers

a was thought to have been
b is said to have destroyed

17 Do a couple of the questions orally with your students as examples, making sure that they use the structure explained here.

Answers

a The Colosseum is believed to have been built in the years 70–82.
b The Great Wall of China is thought to have been constructed about 2,200 years ago.
c The Great Wall of China is said to have been guarded by more than one million soldiers.
d Machu Picchu is thought to have been deserted by the Incas because of disease.
e 'El Castilla' in the middle of Chich'en Itza is considered to have been a temple.

Level 1, Part 2

E Study skills and research

18–21 As mentioned in previous units, do not assist students too much, but talk to them about their progress and guide them where necessary.

F Reading and writing

22 Mumbai (formerly Bombay) is a vibrant place. Students are going to read a quite demanding text which describes various aspects of the city. Before they read, find out what knowledge they already have of Mumbai.

23 & 24 For this exercise students should work in pairs, with Student A in each pair working on the words in paragraphs 1–3, and Student B looking at paragraphs 4–8. Let students use their dictionaries. Once they have finished, they should share their answers with each other.

A	B
graced (paragraph 1)	made something look pleasant
staggering (1)	amazing
amidst (2)	within
mayhem (2)	chaos
characterises (2)	is a perfect example of
ceded (2)	gave up
trousseau (2)	items collected by a bride
leased (2)	gave on loan
swept aside (3)	replaced
metropolis (3)	large city
grease the city's wheels (4)	make the city work well
upmarket (4)	luxurious
neglected (5)	forgotten
slain (5)	killed
prominent (5)	well-known, important
overdose (6)	too much of something
enhance (6)	improve
snarl-ups (8)	jams
notwithstanding (8)	despite
'give and take' (8)	cooperation

25 Now students can skim the text and find the words they worked on in Exercises **23** and **24**. They should look at the words in context and check their meanings.

26 Students look at the text again, this time in more detail, and answer the questions.

> ### Answers
> **a** two (twin structure)
> **b** ten o'clock
> **c** from about 1668
> **d** Apollo Bunder
> **e** Indian and multinational companies, banks and financial houses
> **f** the arts
> **g** in memory of those slain (killed) in the First Afghan War
> **h** clothes, jewellery, leather, ornaments, brass, antiques, furniture, bric-a-brac
> **i** often chaotic
> **j** the locals' spirit of 'give and take'

G Review quiz

27 Students can check their answers to these questions by looking back through the unit.

Workbook exercises

 Vocabulary

1 **a** construct   **b** erect

2 **a** construction   **b** erection

3 Switzerland, Egypt, Italy, China, Turkey, India, Jordan, Iraq, Peru, Brazil, England, Greece, Mexico

4 **a** staggering
   b mayhem
   c prominent
   d swept aside
   e upmarket

Reading

9 **1** History
   2 Carriages
   3 Life on board
   4 Dining

10 afternoon tea (section 4)
    cosy confines (2)
    French silverware (4)
    panoramic views (3)
    personal steward (3)
    romance, adventure and pleasure (1)
    Sleeping Car 3309 (2)
    snowdrifts (1)

11 **a** any two from: *each has a history of its own*, *in 1929*, *Second World War, long years of service*
   b Turkish, German, French, Italian; Romania, USA; Europe
   c 1929, sleeping car stuck in snowdrift for ten days
   d lunch, dinner, brunch, breakfast, afternoon tea
   e any four from: bombed and shot at, stuck in a snowdrift for ten days, part of the Orient-Express service used by King Carol of Romania, taken over by the German Army during World War II, used by the US Transportation Corps during World War II
   f wood, brass, linen
   g three Restaurant Cars – Lalique, Etoile du Nord or Chinoise; passengers' compartments

Listening

CD 2, Track 6

13 **1** London
    2 Paris
    3 Innsbruck
    4 Verona
    5 Venice

14 **a** 3
   b 4
   c ticket
   d current
   e 1,475
   f 2,140
   g 325
   h 11.15
   i Paris
   j Innsbruck
   k Verona
   l 18.12
   m Friday
   n next/following

Language focus: passive forms

15 **a** ran
   b was
   c were ferried
   d boarded
   e was completed
   f was started
   g became
   h were taken
   i began
   j remained
   k were carried

Level 1, Part 2

Unit 17: Leisure

Coursebook exercises

A Speaking and thinking

1 This unit focuses on entertainment and leisure time, as well as fashion. To start, get your students to think about what they do in their free time, and to make a list which they can compare with a classmate's (for example, *go shopping*, …).

2 Find out whether students like to be on their own or with others in their free time, and make sure they give reasons.

3 You might need to give students some help with ideas about how their grandparents entertained themselves. Use pictures or words on the board to prompt them. They should write a list of activities and then compare this with a classmate's (for example, *listened to the radio*, …).

4 Now get your students to think about the future, and how they think their free time will change.

B Reading and vocabulary

5 The word *digit* comes from the Latin *digitus*, meaning finger or toe, and it was originally used in its numerical sense because numbers under ten were counted on the fingers. Go through the words and phrases in the list and then get students to complete the text.

Answers
a	digits	f	black or white
b	computer	g	dots
c	information	h	continuous
d	movies	i	transmit
e	digitised		

6 Go through the statements with your students, checking they understand the vocabulary. Then get them to decide whether they think the statements will appear in the following text about digital entertainment.

7 There is quite a lot of difficult vocabulary in this text, but at this point students do not need to have a deep understanding of the content. Give them some time to match the headings given with the seven paragraphs.

Answers
1 A new study
2 Where will our money go?
3 What will we be downloading?
4 What will the mobile TV market be worth?
5 And cinema?
6 Home TV
7 Mobility

8 All the statements appear in the text.

9 Students will need to refer to the text in far more detail in order to answer the questions. Let them use a dictionary to check any unknown words.

Answers
a $422 billion = the amount that will be spent on entertainment purchases around the world in 2011
$260 billion = the figure in 2005
b mobile 30 per cent, online 41 per cent
c between $5 and $10 per month
d $22 billion
e cinema
f the market will decline
g the pay TV market

C Reading and speaking

10–12 Find out what your students think about fashion, and whether or not it affects their lives in any way. They should try to talk about their favourite clothes and fashions, and whether they have special clothes for different occasions. Also, get them thinking about the future, and how fashions may or may not change. They can discuss their ideas in small groups.

13 Let students use a dictionary to check the meaning of the words in English, and then allow them to translate them into their own language.

14 & 15 Once students understand the concept of a biometric bodysuit, they should be able to make a good guess about what it could do. All the things listed are mentioned as possibilities in the article.

16 Students need to look closely at the text to find words or phrases which have a similar meaning to those listed.

Answers

a detect
b version
c lightweight
d monitor
e wearable
f incorporated
g aesthetic
h civilian
i embedded
j promote
k diagnose
l blending
m fabric
n generate

---

17 Students should now have a good idea of the potential a biometric bodysuit has, so they should be able to think of more uses for their own personal clothes of the future!

D Language focus: modal verbs

18 You could do this activity as a game or race. In pairs or small groups, students write down as many different modals as they can think of, and then compare as a class.

19 Make sure students understand the form of modal verb + main verb, and then tell them to find **nine** more examples in the text they have just read. For the moment, avoid any examples using *will*.

Answers

can monitor
should reach
could give
might be incorporated
could be embedded
could diagnose
could all be made
could produce
would help

---

20 This exercise requires students to think about the function of the various modals they have identified in the text.

Possibility	Ability
should reach	can monitor
could give	
might be incorporated	
could be embedded	
could diagnose	
could all be made	
could produce	
would help	

Other modals for possibility include *may*.

21 If you think students may find this demanding, it might be an idea to give them some example sentences, similar to the one in the Coursebook, to help them.

E Study skills and research

22–24 As mentioned in previous units, do not assist students too much, but talk to them about their progress and guide them where necessary.

F Listening and vocabulary

CD 2,
Track 7

25 Give students some time to check the meaning of any unknown words or phrases in the list, and to decide which they think they will hear in the talk about clothes people wore in the past.

26

Answers

1 engine-powered machines
2 naked
3 leather
4 wool
5 rich people
6 a girl or a boy
7 linen tunics
8 west Asia
9 Islamic period
10 sari
Not in text: hat, shopping mall

27 Students listen again and complete a copy of the notes. There are many variations possible. Let students listen again if they need to.

For example:

	Information about clothes
Stone Age	*made of leather or fur, or woven grasses*
Bronze Age	many clothes, especially coats, still made of leather or fur, most clothes made of wool, linen or cotton; rich people wore silk
Middle Ages	clothes less expensive, but people still only had one or two outfits
Mediterranean region	people wore wool or linen tunics – women long, men short; wool cloaks
West Asia	tunics and pants common, made of linen
China	tunics, and many people wore trousers; hemp, ramie, silk, cotton
India and Africa	clothes without sewing, one big piece of cloth wrapped around the body, e.g. sari in India, kanga in central Africa; made of cotton or silk

G Review quiz

28 Students can check their answers by looking back through the unit.

Workbook exercises

Vocabulary

1   horizontal: continuous, information
     vertical: digitised, transmit
     diagonal: movies, digits, computer, dots

3

A	B
detect	notice
lightweight	not heavy
aesthetic	concerned with looking good
non-military	civilian
embedded	placed inside
improve	promote
identify an illness	diagnose
cloth or material	fabric
produce	generate

Reading

5

Word or phrase from the text	Definition
dodgy	risky
illegal	against the law
not the case	not true
generated	created
grainy	not visually clear
muffled	quieter and unclear
receipt	proof of payment
spot	recognise
cast list	names of actors and actresses
over the counter	in shops

8 1   What is piracy?
    2   Film and music piracy
    3   How do I know it's a pirate copy?
    4   Cheap
    5   Illegal music downloads
    6   Copying CDs

9   All the statements are true.

10 a   because nobody gets hurt
     b   any five from: sound quality bad, picture quality grainy, no receipt, no plastic case, foreign languages on case, problems with cast list, no recognisable film certificate

c   markets, car boot sales, online
d   because it is cheaper than shops
e   share photos, self-produced music or video files
f   you could be fined thousands of pounds
g   lend to friends

Listening

CD 2,
Track 7

12 a   *theft* – a crime of stealing (by a thief)
     robbery – stealing from a bank or shop
     burglary – stealing from someone's home/house
     piracy – stealing from ships at sea; copying without permission
    b   thieve, rob, burgle, pirate (but we commonly use *steal* for all four)
    c   thief, robber, burglar, pirate

13 a   at sea   g   American
    b   on land   h   bad skin
    c $13 billion   i   stomach problems
    d $16 billion   j   1689
    e   Caribbean   k   1719
    f   European   l   pistols

Language focus: modal verbs

14   modal verb = *may*, main verb = *be*, function = possibility

15

Modal verb	Main verb	Function
may	*be*	*possibility*
can	be used	possibility
could	be (grainy)	possibility
will	(often) be	possibility
won't	be given	prediction
might	not be able	ability
should	look out for	advice
will	(definitely) be	prediction
might	have been produced	possibility
may	be (a pirate copy)	possibility
may	come across	possibility
will	be (cheaper)	prediction
(wi)ll	(probably) have been	prediction
can	choose	ability
can	be used (legally)	possibility
should	not use	prohibition
(wi)ll	be copyrighted	prediction
may	be faced	possibility
can	lend	permission

Unit 18: Films

Coursebook exercises

A Speaking and thinking

1   This unit focuses on the cinema and entertainment in general. Introduce the topic by asking students how often they go to the cinema, and what type of films they enjoy watching. Do they watch films at home?

2   Get students to talk about their favourite film stars, and to give reasons for their choices.

3   Read through the seven facts, and make sure students understand them. Then focus on the list of figures and discuss with students what the figures might refer to. Let them work in pairs to complete the gaps.

Answers

a   1895
b   258
c   300
d   800, 948
e   85
f   300,000
g   75, 211

4 & 5 Give students a time limit to quickly match the questions and answers. Then find out if anything surprises them about the information they have read.

Answers

a   B
b   A
c   D
d   C

B Reading and vocabulary

6   Make sure students understand what the five headings mean (i.e. check they know what a *blockbuster* is, and the meaning of *era* and *animation*) Then get them to discuss what information they think each paragraph might contain.

7   Now students need to decide in which paragraphs they think the words and phrases given will appear. Try to get them to give reasons for their choices.

8   This is a prediction-checking exercise. Give students a time limit to skim the text and check whether their ideas from Exercise 6 appear anywhere.

9   This is another prediction-checking exercise. Again, give students a time limit, this time to find the words and phrases from Exercise 7.

Answers

a   Directors paragraph
b   Silent era
c   Blockbusters
d   Blockbusters
e   Film animation
f   Hollywood
g   Directors
h   Film animation
i   Silent era
j   Hollywood

10 Students look at the text again and make a list of all the films mentioned, along with the type (or genre) of each.

Answers

The Great Train Robbery (1903), western
Cutthroat Island (1995), action
Indiana Jones (series), adventure
Star Wars (series), science fiction
Batman (series), action
Lord of the Rings (series), epic adventure
Harry Potter (series), adventure
Citizen Kane (1941), suspense
Reservoir Dogs (1992), crime drama
Pulp Fiction (1994), crime drama
Madagascar (2005), animation
Happy Feet (2006), animation
Ratatouille (2007), animation
Kung Fu Panda (2008), animation

C Listening and vocabulary

CD 2,
Track 8

11 Give students as much help as they need to complete the wordsearch activity. If they have problems, you could give them the genres and tell them to find the words in the puzzle.

Answers

horizontal: science fiction, historical, adventure
vertical: crime, musical
diagonal: war, drama, action, western, comedy, horror

12 Focus on the two symbols for comedy and western. Get students to suggest icons for the other nine film genres. If time and space permit, you could hold a competition for the best visual for each film genre.

13 In pairs, students should go through the list of words and phrases checking they understand what they mean, using a dictionary if necessary. Then they should decide which film genre or genres each word or phrase might be connected to; for example, aliens would probably appear in a science fiction film.

14 & 15 When students listen for the first time, they complete the 'words and phrases' column; during the second listening, they add the film examples.

Film genres	Words and phrases	Film example
action	high energy, martial arts	–
adventure	exciting stories, disaster films	*Pirates of the Caribbean, Titanic*
comedy	*jokes, slapstick*	*Mr Bean*
crime	criminals, gangsters	The three *Godfather* films
drama	character development, biographical films	–
historical	heroic figures, lavish costumes	films about Alexander the Great, gladiators, Braveheart
horror	shocking finales, serial killers	*Frankenstein*
musical	song and dance, choreography	*The Sound of Music*
science fiction	aliens, mad scientists	*Star Wars* series
war	combat fighting, military operations	*Saving Private Ryan*
western	*horses, cowboys and indians*	*The Magnificent Seven*

16 Once students have noted as much information as they can, ask them which if any films they like/dislike, and to give their reasons. You could also ask them to add more film names to the table.

D Language focus: word building

17 & 18 This is another word-building exercise – if time is limited you could share the words among students and get them to share answers.

Verb	Adjective	Adverb	Person/Thing
silence	*silent*	silently	silencer/silence
–	*earliest*	early	–
produce	producing/ed	–	*producers/ production*
locate	located, locational, locatable	–	*locations*
direct	directing/ed	–	director/direction
differs	different	differently	difference
categorise	categorised	–	*categories*
include	including/ed, inclusive	inclusively	inclusion
–	comical	comically	comic/*comedy*
involves	involving/ed	–	involvement

develop	developing/ed	–	developer, *development*
interact	interacting/ed	–	*interaction*
terrify	*terrifying*/ied	terrifyingly	terror
sadden	sad	sadly	*sadness*
operate	operational	operationally	operator, *operations*

E Study skills and research

18–20 As mentioned in previous units, do not assist students too much, but talk to them about their progress and guide them where necessary.

F Reading and writing

21 Get students to discuss the information they think a film review should contain. Give them prompts if necessary; for example, actors, length of film, and so on.

22 Film reviews may contain different types of information, and the answer given here is just an example. Use it for students to compare with their own ideas.

23 Get students to skim the text and check whether it contains all the information they would expect from a film review. They do not need to read it in detail.

24 Students should now have enough ideas and information to write their own film review.

G Review quiz

25 Students can check their answers by looking back through the unit.

Workbook exercises

 Vocabulary

1
a crime
b western
c comedy
d musical
e sci-fi
f historical
g adventure
h drama

2
a The first film-makers
b multi-million-dollar business
c exotic locations
d art form
e stop-frame cinematography

3
a B
b A
c D
d E
e C

Reading

6
a marvelled
b quest
c devouring
d labour-intensive
e interacting
f animation
g scenery
h merged
i jerky
j passed away
k isolate

7
a six
b they are no longer convincing
c because it experimented with early special effects
d models are moved, filmed and moved again 24 times for one second of film
e filming things separately and then putting them together
f blue screen
g Tom Hanks shaking hands with JFK

Listening

CD 2,
Track 8

10 1 brain power
2 steam engines
3 competition for power
4 stellar distances
5 liquid water
6 semiconductors
7 people get old and die
8 colonise the other planets
Not in the text: chocolate bars, football fans

11 a they will grow more intelligent
b many thousands of years in the future
c any four from: process information quickly, can be switched off and on again for years, can be made very small, work together in networks, electronics do not need water, semiconductors can turn sunlight into energy, computers do not fight, quick to load with information, information can be passed easily from one computer to another
d plants
e the information on an old computer can be passed onto a new one, but when an old person dies their knowledge dies with them
f computers

 # Language focus: word building

12

Verb	Noun	Adjective	Adverb
marvelled	marvel	marvellous	marvellously
convince	–	*convincing*/ed	convincingly
experiment	experiment	experimental	experimentally
animate	animation/or	*animated*/ing	animatedly
express	*expressions*	expressive/ing/ed	expressively
separate	separation	separate	*separately*
projected	projection/or/ile	projected/ing	–
remember/memorise	memory	*memorable*	memorably
compete	*competition*/or	competitive	competitively
know	*knowledge*	knowledgeable/known	knowledgeably

Level 1, Part 2

Unit 18: Films   **73**

The English language 2

This final unit has a different format from the others in the Coursebook and focuses on vocabulary. There is no corresponding Workbook unit.

Coursebook exercises

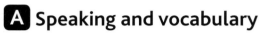 A Speaking and vocabulary

1 Check that students understand the two words: *metaphorical* and *literal*.

2 & 3 You could do these exercises as competitions, with pairs or small groups of students making lists of all the prefixes and suffixes they can think of, and then compound words.

B Reading and vocabulary

4 & 5 The idea here is for students to start thinking about how they can work out the meaning of words and phrases without using a dictionary.

6 Students make notes about how they deal with unknown words and phrases. Hopefully they will list strategies such as using context, thinking about similar words, and so on.

7 Let students read the text and focus on the words that they have already looked at in Exercise 4, and check their meaning.

8 If you think students will find this too difficult, give them the words to find in the wordsearch.

Answers

horizontal: reverse, humorous, monolingual, related to
vertical: limit, definition
diagonal: envisage, illustrate, distribute, compile

9 Give students a few minutes to skim the text and find the words from Exercise 8.

C Speaking and vocabulary

10 Students need to think about the hints and strategies in the previous text, and talk about which ones they already knew about or follow and which they don't. Do they have any suggestions of their own?

11 Recording words in groups or sets is an effective strategy for learning vocabulary. See if students can work out the patterns.

Answers

a same root (derivatives)
b same topic/theme (methods of transport)
c similar meanings (synonyms)
d opposites (antonyms)
e same sound, different spelling and meaning (homophones)

12 Now get students to match the descriptions to the word sets.

Answers

a iv
b i
c v
d ii
e iii

13 & 14 Find out if students use word groups as a strategy for remembering them or understanding them, and get them to categorise words they already know.

D Reading and vocabulary

15 Students should be able to work out the answers even if they do not know what the words in the list mean!

> **Answers**
> **a** *okay*
> **b** *the capital*
> **c** *lethologica*
> **d** *four*
> **e** *typewriter*
> **f** *checkmate*
> **g** *uncopyrightable*
> **h** *Canada*
> **i** *stewardess*
> **j** *karaoke*
> **k** *dreamt*

16 Ask students which words from the previous exercise they think are useful and which they might need to use; also, find out where they are going to record the useful words.

17 Students can now apply some of the strategies they have looked at in the unit to work out the meaning of the words printed in red. All the information is true.

E Introduction to IGCSE

18 You need to give students access to a past examination paper (Paper 2) so that they can answer the questions. They also need to refer to the text in the Coursebook.

> **Answers**
> **a** International General Certificate of Secondary Education
> **b** E2L
> **c** students who are studying English
> **d** education or employment
> **e** 2 hours (Extended) / 1.5 hours (Core)
> **f** no
> **g** centre number, candidate number, name
> **h** on the question paper
> **i** both reading, both short answers; Exercise 2 has more questions, longer text, graphics included
> **j** Exercise 3 is a form-filling exercise; Exercises 1 and 2 are comprehension questions
> **k** note-taking
> **l** word count, using own words
> **m** up to 9 (5 Core) marks for content, up to 9 (5 Core) marks for language

F Review quiz

19 Students can check their answers by looking back through the Coursebook.

Unit 1: Focus on reading skills

Exam Exercise 1

In Exercise 1 of the IGCSE E2L Reading and Writing papers, candidates are tested on their ability to read and understand short texts presented in a variety of forms, such as advertisements, brochures, leaflets, guides, reports, manuals, instructions or notices, and answer questions on factual details using skimming and gist-reading skills. In order to improve their chances of success in this part of the examination, it is important that candidates skim and scan texts, and avoid the type of intensive reading which they may be used to doing in other situations. Intensive reading can be laborious, and in an examination situation there is not always time to read in this way. Thus students must be trained to find the **key words** in questions, and to get into the habit of 'reading against the clock'. This unit focuses on these skills, and allows students to practise skimming and scanning and giving short answers.

Coursebook exercises

A Speaking and vocabulary

1 With these types of questions, there are no right or wrong answers. Encourage your students to speculate and to discuss their ideas, and to give reasons for their choices. Use the question to promote discussion in English. You may wish to focus on pronunciation problems here, and to encourage students to consider derivatives of the words they suggest – for example, *entertainment – entertain – entertaining – entertainer*.

2 As above. Encourage students to use the gerunds, for example *watching cartoons on TV*.

Exam tip

These occur throughout the book. They are designed to make students aware of what the examiners are looking for, or to advise them of a certain approach which can help them to be successful in the examination.

B Reading

3 Discuss with your students **how** they read. What reading strategies do they use? Ask them if they always read in the same way, or if they use different techniques for different types of text, such as magazines, dictionaries, novels, and so on. Ask them how they approach reading in their **own** language. Try to establish that we use different reading strategies depending on **what** we are reading, and **why** we are reading. If we want to find something quickly in a text, skimming and scanning are the best techniques. Make sure that your students actually understand what these techniques involve.

4 This exercise practises skimming for gist. Set students a time limit, say 20 seconds. They will realise that there is no need to read everything in the text, nor is it necessary to understand every word in order to answer the two questions.

Answers

a seven
b SONIKS millennium game

5

Answers

skimming for gist
no
quickly

6

Answer

SONIKS baseball cap

7 While all the answers would no doubt receive a mark, the **best** answer here is **d** (*SONIKS baseball cap*) because it is short and concise. No time is wasted in writing a long answer, which is not required in this part of the examination. Make sure your students understand that the key to a good answer in this part of the examination is to include all the necessary information, which may only be one or two words. Complete sentences will not normally be necessary.

8 Students do not need to write anything yet. Encourage them to ask and answer, and to discuss their answers.

9 Students should check that the other pair have written short, concise answers which include all the necessary information. They should remember that complete sentences will not normally be required.

> **Answers**
> a three
> b by joining the SONIKS loyalty scheme
> c SONIKS watch
> d a million
> e a 21-day money-back guarantee, a quarterly newsletter and a membership card
> f SONIKS share cards
> g SONIKS baseball cap

> **Exam tip**
>
> This exam tip introduces the idea of **key words**. It is important for students to identify the word or words in the question which will lead them to the answer in the text. The key word/s will help students to skim and scan more efficiently.

10 Encourage students to speculate. This type of advertisement would probably appear in a magazine or newspaper.

11 Students need to have an effective strategy for answering questions. Reading the question first saves a lot of time.

> **Answers**
> b, d, c, a

12 When students do this for the first time, there may be some disagreement over their choice of key words. Encourage them to discuss their choices and to give reasons. In some cases it may not be possible to agree, or there may not even be a particular word or words which help to find the answer. Tell them they do not need to write anything yet.

> **Possible answers**
> a view   f postage
> b pay to order   g alternative method
> c receive for free   h payment
> d SONIKART software   i wait
> e rolls of film   j other products

13 Students should understand that the whole text is about photographs and pictures, and therefore choosing one of these words is not necessarily going to lead them to the place in the text where the answer is. It is therefore essential to look quickly at the text in order to understand what the general topic is, and then to read the questions. Students should write short answers, then exchange them with a classmate and check each other's. Remind students that answers do not usually need to be complete sentences.

> **Answers**
> a on your home computer or laptop
> b £1.00
> c interactive guide
> d any six from: edit, create special effects, crop, enlarge, stretch, change colours, add hair, remove spots, print, e-mail
> e one
> f 60p
> g take advertisement and film to local SONIKS retailer
> h cheque, credit card
> i up to 14 days
> j tick the box

C Language focus: word building

This section deals with adjectives, which are prominent in both the texts.

14

> **Possible answers**
> Adjectives are used to provide **information about nouns**.

15

Adjective	Noun	Adverb	Verb
exciting	*excitement*	*excitingly*	*excite*
amazing	amazement	amazingly	amaze
digital	digit	digitally	digitise
removable	removal	–	remove
delightful	delight	delightfully	delight
creative	creation	creatively	create
interactive	interaction	interactively	interact
incredible	–	incredibly	–

16 English uses a variety of adjectival endings. If students can learn to recognise these endings, comprehension and spelling can be improved. They should be able to find several more endings in the texts, for example *fantastic, coloured, local*.

17 This exercise (like the previous one) encourages students to build up their vocabulary range, and to think about word formation. If they have access to their own or a class dictionary, encourage them to check words.

D Speaking: showing preference and making suggestions

18 Let students think of different ways of making suggestions and showing preference. Accept colloquial language (e.g. *How about doing ... ?* and *No way!*) as well as more formal language (e.g. *Would you like to ... ?*), but point out that in the Speaking assessment, students should not lapse into slang. Also, remind students that it is usual to give a reason for not wanting to do something.

19 Students need to use their phrases from Exercise **18** to carry out the dialogues. Make sure they give reasons for their preferences. Students may want to add more examples to the list given. After oral practice, students could write down their mini-dialogues as a way of consolidating the correct forms.

20 In the Speaking assessment, students are given a task or a topic to think about, and are then required to talk about it and to answer the examiner's questions. This exercise is good practice in helping students to plan their ideas before speaking. Encourage students to brainstorm their ideas, and to make lists or draw spidergrams (simple diagrams linking elements from a central idea – as shown in the Coursebook). Students may find this approach strange, and may want to write full sentences, but this should be discouraged. There are no right or wrong answers. Note that in the IGCSE E2L Speaking assessment, students are not allowed to make any written notes.

E Further practice

The exercises in the Further practice sections at the end of each unit provide students with the opportunity to practise their general language skills. The exercises do not always focus on the main skill area of the unit, in this case reading.

21–23

> **Answers**
> Various answers are possible.

24

> **Answers**
> a £1,355
> b camping under the stars / African music and dance / golf / tennis / squash / badminton / swimming / bowls / relaxing in the gardens / shopping / cinema
> c six nights
> d 30 km
> e breathtaking waters / Victoria Falls
> f under the stars / campsite / in a tent / in the African rainforest
> g Zimbabwe National and Plaza
> h Victoria Falls
> i day 5
> j day 6
> k breakfast
> l Air Zimbabwe

25

> **Answers**
> a all countries (*global*)
> b on the reverse/back (usually)
> c game may be frightening (for young children)
> d consultations with parents, consumers and religious groups
> e because of different cultures and attitudes
> f supersede

Workbook exercises

Vocabulary

1 & 2 These first two questions review work from the Coursebook. Answers can be checked there.

Reading 1

3 a number
    b noun
    c list of nouns
    d noun
    e number
    f action
    g name (proper noun)
    h name (proper noun)

5 Answer **b** would be best because it provides all the information that is necessary.

6 a two
    b a boat
    c any four from: exotic plants, wild flowers, ancient cairns, crumbling castles, sparkling white sands, an azure sea
    d the Tropics
    e 2,000
    f check times and tides for availability
    g St Mary's
    h St Agnes

Reading 2

10 For example:
    ramps on pavements
    wide doors
    special toilets

12 a Special drop-off/pick-up spaces
    b Parking
    c Special check-in counters and waiting areas
    d Toilets
    e First Aid
    f Free telephones and information desks

13 For example:
    Passport control: Easy access to and through passport control for customers in wheelchairs.
    Shopping: Wide aisles in our shops for customers in wheelchairs and special low-level tills/counters.

 **Writing 2**

14 Outside the airport building
- *dedicated drop-off spaces*
- *pavements have* wheelchair ramps
- adequate parking in convenient locations
- shuttle buses equipped with ramps
- further assistance available on request

Inside the airport building
- dedicated check-in counters
- disabled toilets
- *signs and notices in Braille*
- *four First Aid rooms*
- telephones with free connection
- text phones for people with hearing problems

 Language

15 For example:
- Whether you go or not, I want to go to the party.
- Whether he had worked harder or not, he would not have passed the exams.
- Shall we go whether it rains or not?

16

Adjective	Adjective opposite	Noun	Verb	Adverb
beautiful	*ugly*	*beauty*	beautify	beautifully
exotic	familiar	exoticism	–	exotically
inhabited	uninhabited	habitation	inhabit	–
available	unavailable	availability	avail	–
commercial	–	commerce	commercialise	commercially
accessible	inaccessible	*access*	access	–
additional	–	addition	add	*additionally*
assisted	unassisted	*assistance*	assist	–
medical	–	medication	medicate	medically
special	normal	specialist	specialise	specially

17 For example:
- That is the person who won the prize.
- These are the reasons why they left school.
- This is the team that won the championship.

18 a Regarded as one of the best on the African continent, this hotel has been voted the best in Zimbabwe.
b Starting with a meal cooked by our head chef, your evening continues with a programme of African music and dance.
c Offering a full range of 5* facilities, the hotel has its own cinema, as well as a pool complex with diving boards.

19 For example:
Regarded as one of the best films ever made, it continues to attract viewers.
Beginning with the lowest level, the students work themselves up to the top.
Considered to be the best restaurant in town, it is always busy.

Unit 2: Focus on reading skills

Exam Exercise 2

In Exercise 2 of the IGCSE E2L Reading and Writing papers, candidates are tested on their ability to understand and respond to information presented in a variety of forms (e.g. a report or newspaper/magazine article), and to select and organise material relevant to specific purposes. Candidates answer a series of questions testing more detailed understanding of the text. The text may incorporate a graphical element such as a picture, map or graph/chart.

Coursebook exercises

 **A Speaking and vocabulary**

1

> **Possible answers**
> drama, comedy, documentary, film, cartoon

2 Do this as a timed activity, encouraging students to work quickly to find the ten words. Make sure you remind students that the words are written either horizontally and vertically, but not diagonally or backwards.

> **Answers**
> horizontal: music, cartoon, documentary, weather, horror
> vertical: comedy, news, sport, drama, western

3 Students think about the programmes discussed so far, and then add them to their tables. Get them to compare their lists with each other's.

4 Students complete the table. It is important that they use minutes and not hours, as the information they will see on the graph is in minutes. You may need to give students some examples to get them started. The theme should be leisure activities, but you may decide to accept 'doing my homework' as well. This is another excellent opportunity for extended discussion in English. As always, encourage students to give reasons for their opinions.

5 Students use the list of activities and decide which one each column (A–G) on the graph represents. Remind them that the times given are averages, in minutes, per week, and that they should give reasons for their choices. Discuss with students whether anything surprises them. Ask them how this compares with young people's activities in their own country.

6 Much of the information students will come across in their daily lives is in the form of graphs and charts. They may also have to interpret graphical information in the IGCSE examination. This exercise is the first of several in the Coursebook which asks students to produce a graph based on information they have read or researched. Help them to decide how best to display graphically the information they have collected.

B Reading

7 This exercise is a reminder of the work done on approaches to reading in Unit **1**. Students should understand that they will probably need to look at the texts in more detail for Exercise 2 of the examination.

> **Answers**
> **a** ... get the general idea / the gist.
> **b** ... find specific facts/details.

8 General discussion. As with all these exercises, the aim is to generate spoken language which is as realistic as possible. Students need to be monitored, but feedback should be saved for later when the activity is completed. Do not interfere while students are discussing. Give a time limit of 2–3 minutes.

9 Throughout the book, you will notice that students are advised to use their dictionaries to help them with vocabulary. If your students do not have their own dictionaries, you may like to make a habit of taking a set to each lesson, or at least enough so that students can share. However, note that in the IGCSE E2L examination, candidates are not allowed to use dictionaries.

10 Once students feel confident about the meanings they have agreed on in pairs in the previous exercise, give them 5–6 minutes to scan the text in order to decide where the words and phrases fit. Tell them to think about **grammar** (i.e. what part of speech fits the gap) as well as **meaning**.

> **Answers**
> a inequalities
> b theatre-goers
> c academics
> d handy
> e positive light
> f overwhelmingly
> g a strong showing
> h elders
> i contrary to popular belief
> j flaunt
> k hang-ups

11 Students may not agree, so encourage them to discuss and give reasons for their choices of key word/s. Various answers are possible.

12 The purpose of this exercise is to demonstrate to students that the words they identify in the question may not always be exactly the same in the text itself. Thus, in the first question, one of the key words is *percentage*, but in the text itself the phrase *one in four* is used.

13 Answer **a** would not be acceptable because it does not adequately answer the question: a student who gives this answer may have realised that the popularity of soaps and reality TV shows is connected to social interaction, but not fully understood that connection. Answer **b** would probably receive a mark, but it doesn't explain why the fact that people talk about these programmes makes them popular. The best answer is **c**, because it contains all the necessary information. Stress to students that examiners are looking for evidence of understanding of the text and the question.

14

> **Answers**
> a 25 per cent (one in four)
> b because young people visit museums less, and spend more time chatting on the Internet, watching TV etc.
> c any four from chat on the Internet / read / watch American soaps / watch reality TV shows / listen to music / play computer games / cinema / clubbing / sport / listening to radio
> d music
> e people talk about them and this encourages social interaction
> f 81 per cent say that computers will never replace books
> g i greater variety of media
>   ii admit to liking things previous generations would have been ashamed of

C Writing: adverbs

15 There are many possibilities here. Do three or four examples orally to show students the diversity of possible responses, and to ensure that they understand that a phrase is required, not just a word or two. If students simply complete question a with *it was expensive*, they have avoided using an adverb or an adverb phrase.

D Speaking: *would do / wouldn't do*

16 Encourage students to talk about the information given, and to compare it with their own situation. You might like to remind students of the types of language structures which would be useful in this discussion – for example, comparatives and conditionals. Ask students to find out what their classmates spend their pocket money on.

17 The purpose here is for students to consider specific functional language: requesting in informal and formal situations. You could give a time limit and ask students to think of as many different phrases as possible.

18 Students continue to discuss their ideas, using speculative language, and add phrases to the lists.

E Reading

19 This exercise is designed to generate interest in the topic and to provide students with an opportunity to talk about the subject from a personal point of view. The theme of leisure activities continues, although it is no longer specifically related to young people.

20 Make sure students have access to a monolingual dictionary for this exercise. In some cases, students can only speculate at this stage about which dictionary meaning might be the right one, but this will be clarified once they read the text. The important thing is that students are getting further practice in using a monolingual dictionary, and in discussing alternatives with a classmate.

21 Here, students need to find the words from the previous exercise, and decide with a classmate which of the dictionary meanings fits the text.

22 Make sure students identify the key word/s in each question before they attempt to answer.

Answers

a   20 million
b   they risk banging into their neighbours
c   because of the congestion
d   with electronic games
e   to maintain order
f   too many people selling products on the beach / prices of products sold are very high
g

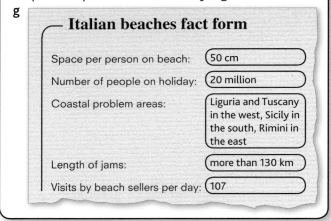

Italian beaches fact form

Space per person on beach:	50 cm
Number of people on holiday:	20 million
Coastal problem areas:	Liguria and Tuscany in the west, Sicily in the south, Rimini in the east
Length of jams:	more than 130 km
Visits by beach sellers per day:	107

F Further practice

23

Nouns	Adjectives	Adverbs
strength	strong	*strongly*
part	partial	*partially*
clarity	clear	clearly
regularity	regular	regularly
–	*particular*	particularly
relation/relative	*relative*	relatively
–	*incredible*	incredibly
total	total	*totally*
completeness	*complete*	completely

24–26

Answers

Various answers are possible.

Workbook exercises

 ## Vocabulary

1
a elder
b academic
c flaunt
d handy
e overwhelmingly

2
a academics
b overwhelmingly
c flaunt
d elders
e handy

Order: a, e, b, d, c

 ## Reading 1

3 the spread of the plague through Europe during the 14th century, showing where the plague was at different times

4 & 5
a infection
b made sense of
c greatly damaged
d deadly
e germ
f causes
g unaffected by
h rats
i different types
j killed
Not used: expectations, security

6 & 7
a deciphered
b threat
c first affect Europe
d Where, survive today, transferred to humans
e four other diseases
f Black Death, 14th century
g travel across Europe, 14th century
h How, vet, infected
i What form, 1,500
j two varieties
k 'Pasteuralla pestis'
l 855 people killed

8
a Yersinia pestis
b as a chemical weapon in a war
c in the 6th and 8th centuries
d survives in rodents, transferred by an infected insect bite
e cholera, malaria, leprosy and meningitis
f wiped out one third of Europe's population
g westwards
h an infected cat sneezed on him
i stomach infection
j the lethal pneumonic variety and the bubonic variety
k named after Louis Pasteur
l India in 1992

Reading 2

12 & 13
a activities
b routine
c digging out
d complex
e legends
f careful
g community
h expedition
i discovered
j strength
k puzzled

The word in the shaded area is *Argonauts*.

14
a myths
b excavating
c settlement
d perplexed
e stumbled across
f determination
g exploits
h mundane
i painstaking
j composite
k quest

15
a What, archaeologists
b shape, 'tholos'
c When, community first discovered
d Vasso Adrimi feel
e Who encouraged
f What put together the evidence
g legend of Jason
h three items, moulds

16
a the remains of what they believe is ancient Iolcus
b a beehive shape
c nearly 25 years ago
d perplexed
e her professor
f modern technology
g the exploits of a seafaring people who sailed on the Black Sea
h jewellery, weapons and tools

 **Language**

18 a deciphered, made sense of
 b greatly damaged, devastated
 c deadly, lethal
 d microbe
 e poses
 f resistant to
 g rats, rodents
 h strains
 i removed

19 For example:
- The insects were resistant to the chemical and could not be killed.
- The town was devastated after the bombing.
- A mouse is another example of a rodent.

20 For example:
- We buy two types of chocolate: dark and milk. I prefer the former; my wife prefers the latter.
- Lewis Milestone's film *Ocean's Eleven* was remade in 2001 by Steven Soderbergh. I think the former version was better than the latter.
- My favourite flowers are daffodils and bluebells. I have vases of the former around the house, but the latter look best left growing outside.

21 a The Solar System was formed by gases about 4,600 million years ago.
 b The planet Earth was dominated by dinosaurs about 235 million years ago.
 c Copper and gold were used by man during the Bronze Age.
 d Bubonic plague was brought to Europe by rats around 1346.
 e English was spoken by only five million people worldwide in the 16th century.
 f Rubber was brought to Europe from Latin America in the 18th century.
 g The radio was invented by Marconi in 1894.
 h The first man, Yuri Gagarin, was launched into space in 1961.
 i The Olympic Games were held in Athens, Greece, in 2004.

22 a World Health Organization
 b British Broadcasting Corporation
 c digital versatile disc
 d video cassette recorder
 e United Nations Children's Fund (formerly United Nations International Children's Emergency Fund)
 f North Atlantic Treaty Organization
 g Short Message Service
 h unidentified flying object

Unit 3: Focus on writing skills

Exam Exercises 6 and 7

In Exercises 6 and 7, candidates are required to demonstrate that they can communicate clearly, accurately and appropriately, and convey and express their opinions effectively. They should use a variety of grammatical structures as well as a range of appropriate vocabulary, and demonstrate that they are aware of the conventions of paragraphing, punctuation, spelling and styles of writing.

Candidates are required to write 100–150 words (Core curriculum) or 150–200 words (Extended curriculum) of continuous prose, in response to a short stimulus. A purpose, format and audience will always be supplied. The type of writing required in Exercise 7 will always differ from that required in Exercise 6.

Coursebook exercises

A Speaking

1   Encourage students to discuss their reasons. It does not matter what criteria they use to classify the various foods.

2   The discussion continues on the theme of food: students' likes and dislikes, and their favourite foods.

3   Predicting what a text will be about from its title can help to take away some of the fear that students may feel when faced with a new text. This is a 'top-down' reading activity, which is an effective strategy when used alongside other pre-reading activities. There are no right or wrong answers. Do not worry if students fail to grasp the play on words with *pasta* and *present*.

4   It does not really matter what students predict: the point of the exercise is to generate discussion in English about the topic.

B Writing and vocabulary

5 & 6   Put students into pairs, or with smaller classes this could be done in groups. Working on unknown or difficult vocabulary is an important skill which needs to be developed, so these exercises give students further practice. Allow them to discuss their ideas and to use a dictionary, and encourage them to look carefully at the context.

7   This exercise gives students writing practice using the vocabulary they have been working on in the previous exercises. Make sure students demonstrate the meaning of the key words in their sentences.

8   This is a scanning activity so make sure students do not spend too long on checking their predictions from Exercise 4. Set a time limit and observe your students as they scan the text – are they really scanning, or reading slowly?

> **Answers**
> a   False – together with Burger King, McDonald's has only 5 per cent of the market
> b   True   c   True   d   True

C Reading

9   The aim of this exercise is for students to focus on the information rather than on the wording of their answers. They should think about key words in the questions and use these to identify their answers in the text. Try to make your students understand that key words will lead them to the part of the text where the answer is. They do **not** need to write anything yet.

10 Encourage some discussion about the answers. Check whether the key words helped – it is important for students to feel confident about the strategies we want them to use.

> **Answers**
> **a** by 20 per cent
> **b** central and southern Italy
> **c** because these areas are the heartland of the Mediterranean diet
> **d** traditional restaurants
> **e** it has been a hit
> **f** a pizza chain
> **g** 11 minutes 30 seconds
> **h** chips like cardboard, bread poor

D Writing: informal letter

11 Making notes is a vital writing skill which students often find difficult, so this exercise provides help in this area. Students make notes about different types of restaurants, and their relative advantages and disadvantages. The table will help them to organise their ideas.

12 Ask students to think about the key words taken from the exam-type question: *explain*, *describe*, *write*, *say*, and to discuss with you what each one means.

13 Now students complete the exam-type question with the words from the previous exercise.

> **Answers**
> **a** Write   **c** describe
> **b** explain   **d** say

14 An address and date are not normally required for an Exercise 6 or 7 letter task. Students should make a list of possible beginnings and endings for an informal letter. There are many possibilities, but encourage them to use something like *Dear Mum and Dad* or *Dear Maria*. Remind students that, in English, openings such as *Dear friend* and *My dear parents* may seem inappropriate for the context. There are many possibilities for the ending too, but again it may be wise to encourage

students to 'play safe' with a set phrase such as *Best wishes from … .*

15 Identifying errors is an excellent way of encouraging students to analyse writing and it should motivate them to look at their own writing in the same critical way. Make sure students do not attempt to write anything yet, but simply identify language errors, and discuss any problems with the content.

16 This is a simple idea for improving writing. Encourage your students not simply to look for errors when they check their writing, but also to think about how to improve the overall quality. Using a wider vocabulary range can make a real difference to a piece of writing, even if there are errors in language accuracy.

17 Students write their own answer. Make sure they focus carefully on the question and exclude any irrelevant information. If the writing is done in class, you will be able to provide students with support and guidance. Students should exchange their letters with a classmate and provide feedback.

E Speaking: expressing opinions

18 Students need to use a range of functional language, and this exercise encourages them to think of appropriate phrases for giving opinions. There are many possible answers. They will get the chance to use the language in the next exercise.

19 Students often fail to perform well in discussions. This may be because they have not had enough time to think about what they want to say or because they have not been given the appropriate language. This exercise should help students with both these problems.

Further practice

20

> **Answers**
> a eight glasses
> b no
> c it is said to break up kidney stones and aid digestion
> d eight
> e Evian
> f to prevent bacterial contamination

21 & 22 See assessment criteria for Extended writing on page **xii**.

23

> **Answers**
> a because research into marine life is growing stronger
> b because of the pearls they contain
> c the shores of Dhofar
> d it has only one shell
> e young ones live in small groups underneath medium-sized rocks; adults live in groups of up to twelve in cracks in rocks
> f cold, nutritious water
> g face mask and knife (not fins)
> h fins

Workbook exercises

Vocabulary

1 Remember that students may not agree about what constitutes fast food and traditional food.

Fast food	Traditional food
burger	goulash
sandwich	rice
	moussaka
	falafel
	samosa

2 a Decades
b outlets
c turnover
d launched
e palate
f gourmets
g ambience

Reading 1

3

absorption	process where something takes in something else
adequate	enough, sufficient
chronic	continuing for a long time
conform to	obey a rule
dairy foods	milk, cheese, butter, etc.
derived from	developed or coming from something else
free of	not containing
humane	not treating animals and people in a cruel way
poultry	meat from birds such as chicken and ducks
sparingly	only a little
strict	obeying all the rules

4 a poultry
b dairy foods
c derived from
d humane
e adequate
f Strict
g free of
h conform to, chronic
i sparingly
j absorption

6 a What is a vegan?
   b Why veganism?
   c Caring
   d Vegan nutrition
   e Protein
   f Fat
   g Vitamin D
   h Calcium
   i Zinc
   j Iron
   k For more information

   Additional questions
   a green beans, peas and red beans
   b soya

 ## Research

8 a 1 cup = 240 ml
   b 2 tablespoons = 30 ml
   c 5 ounces = 140 g

 ## Reading 2

13 a Health dangers of obesity
    b Shoppers' habits
    c Statistics on the sales of fattening foods
    d Sales of healthier products
    e Not just what you eat
    f Class and trends

 ## Language

15 For example:

Advantages	Disadvantages
One thing in its favour is …	A bad thing about it is …
A good thing about it is …	A point against it is …

16 For example:
   • Once people used to walk everywhere; today they travel by car.
   • Once only some children went to school; today they all go to school.

17 a A healthy and varied vegan diet includes fruits, vegetables and plenty of leafy greens in addition to wholegrain products, nuts, seeds and legumes.
    b In addition to being free of cholesterol, vegan diets are also generally low in fat.
    c Calcium is found in dark green vegetables in addition to many other foods commonly eaten by vegans.
    d In addition to 160 quick and easy recipes, *Simply Vegan* contains a complete discussion of vegan nutrition.

Unit 4: Focus on listening skills

Exam Questions 1–6

In the IGCSE Listening papers, candidates need to be able to understand and respond to information presented in a variety of forms, and to select information which is relevant. Candidates will need to answer a series of questions based on individual statements or dialogues.

Students benefit enormously from hearing English inside as well as outside the classroom, so the use of English is to be encouraged at all times. Throughout the book, teachers and students will find questions and activities which supply integrated speaking and listening practice.

Coursebook exercises

A Listening and speaking

CD 1,
Track 1

1 This activity can be done against the clock.

2

> **Answers**
> horizontal: plane
> vertical: bus, train, cab, balloon, camper, motorbike
> diagonal: bicycle, coach, car

3 Encourage students to talk about each of the ten methods of transport, and to give reasons for their opinions. Prompt them with different types of holiday if they find it difficult to think of any (e.g. *skiing, sightseeing*).

4 Students complete a copy of the table with their own ideas. There are no right or wrong answers. They should try to think of two or three ideas for each method of transport.

5 Students decide which transport method is the most expensive. Allow them to discuss this in pairs. Students should be prepared to give reasons for the order they choose.

6 **a** Students discuss which of the methods given they think they will hear about, and give reasons for their choices.
   b Make sure that students know exactly what is required, and that they are ready to listen before you start the CD. The questions are designed to give students a reason for listening, and to test gist comprehension.

> **Answers**
> i   train, balloon, coach, ferry
> ii speakers 2 and 4
> iii speaker 2

7 This exercise encourages students to think about **how** and **why** they identified the methods of transport the speakers are describing. Which words were clues?

8

> **Answers**
> *Speaker 1*
> a platform 13E
> b four (wife and three children)
> c (quite) excited
> d the platform was empty
> e went to the booking office to make enquiries
> f had misread the time on the tickets
> *Speaker 2*
> a birthday present
> b 23
> c because she had never enjoyed flying
> d 30 minutes
> e exhilarated, delighted (not actually given in text, students need to infer)

Speaker 3
a cheaper, able to see countryside
b four – slow, uncomfortable, difficult to sleep, no toilets or washing facilities
c every 4–5 hours
d nearly 48 hours

Speaker 4
a evening
b the petrol and diesel from the cars
c the breeze blew away the fumes
d extremely cold
e hum of the engines, spray falling

9 Encourage students to compare and discuss their answers. Allow them to listen again if they need to.

10 Students complete as much as they can. Not all the gaps can be filled.

	Speaker 1	Speaker 2	Speaker 3	Speaker 4
Departure time	8.30 a.m.	9 a.m.	–	evening
Length of journey	–	30 minutes	48 hours	–
Arrival time	–	–	–	–
Weather / time of year	beautiful summer day	sunny, May	–	extremely cold, mid-winter
Speaker's feelings	excited, then anxious	worried, then happy	not worried, then tired and uncomfortable	relaxed, totally alone
Speaker with who?	wife and three children	–	–	–
Cost	–	free (a gift)	$275	–

11 Students read the transcript and check their answers to Exercises 8 and 10. Allowing students to take control of checking their own answers is excellent for building confidence, and makes the lesson less teacher-centred.

B Reading

12 You might like to lead in to this by bringing in some photos of car accidents. Many countries have campaigns that use shock tactics, showing photographs of accident victims or wrecked cars, or horrifying statistics.

13 Ask your students to describe what might happen in an accident which is not too serious. They will probably not know the word *whiplash*, but they might come up with the idea. Do not tell them what *whiplash* means – they will find out when they read the article on page **29** of the Coursebook.

14 Students speculate about the content of the article. There are no right or wrong answers.

15 Encourage students to discuss their ideas and to use their dictionaries.

16 This exercise is also designed to get students to think and to speculate about the missing information. There are many possible answers – students will find out what is actually written when they read the text.

17 Students can now check their answers to the previous exercises by scanning the article.

C Language focus: tenses

18 Students need to look at the sentences given and think about what time is being referred to. As an additional task, you could ask them also to tell you what tense each of the verbs printed in red is.

> **Answers**
> a the past few years up to the present; present perfect simple
> b between 2000 and 2005; past simple
> c the present / now; present continuous (and the second example is passive)
> d 2020; future

Answers

a *have/has* + past participle
   Function: to indicate recent past events with present effects
b past tense
   Function: for past events
c *am/is/are* + present participle (*-ing*)
   Function: to indicate a present ongoing activity or trend
d *will* + infinitive without 'to'
   Function: to state a future fact or opinion

20 There may be more than one possible answer, but the most obvious and natural-sounding are given here.

Answers

a will get
b have seen
c are thinking
d told, caught / had caught
e is trying
f will be
g has had

D Speaking

21 & 22 Encourage students to discuss the information they have read, and to make comparisons with their own country.

23 *Garda* is the Irish word for *police*. There is a lot of information in the tables, so give your students enough time to read it and understand what is being shown. You may need to guide them. Ask your students to display the information graphically – you should decide together whether to have a table, chart or graph. Make sure they think about how much information they want to show, as well as how.

24 Get your students to focus on the traffic situation in their town, and to discuss the various transport problems. They can imagine that they are responsible for traffic and suggest ways to improve the situation.

Answers

a 216
b the number of pedestrians killed
c in 2006
d October 2005
e 2005

E Listening

CD 1,
Track 2

25 Allow students time to read through the questions. Make sure they understand that these questions are similar to the type they will see in Part 1 of the IGCSE Listening papers. Students need to think about what information each question is asking for. Encourage them to condense their ideas into single words or short phrases – for example, a date, a study subject, a number.

Answers

1 subject to study
2 reference number
3 period of time
4 weather details
5 price
6 place which sells tickets

26 Students should discuss and speculate, and give reasons for their answers.

27

Answers

1 Italian
2 CD39–2BK
3 19th–21st
4 any two from: sunny spells in the morning, possibly heavy showers in the afternoon, temperature will reach maximum 18 °C, strong breeze all day
5 £5.80 per hour
6 booking office at venue

28 Students compare their answers and then read the transcript to check them.

F Further practice

CD 1,
Track 3

29

> ### Answers
> a Out of Asia
> b Beach Camp
> c Children's Festival, Inflatable Day
> d Firework Fantasia
> e Children's Festival
> f Hello There!
> g Out of Asia

30

> ### Answers
> a £3.50
> b eight
> c value for money
> d Buckingham Palace
> e all good bookshops

31

> ### Answers
> Various answers are possible.

32 Students give a short talk.

Workbook exercises

Vocabulary

1

Air	Land	Sea
plane	car	yacht
balloon	bicycle	hovercraft
helicopter	coach	ferry

Reading

3 a i, iv – children understand the concept of advertising
   b iii, vii – children need to be exposed to advertising
   c viii, ix – children's programming would suffer from restricted advertising
   d v – advertising can influence requests
   e ii, vi – about food

4 a impact
   b intent
   c persuasive
   d purchasers
   e insulate
   f correlation
   g revenue
   h expenditure
   i banned
   j substantial
   k pestering
   l influence
   m explicit

5 a False
   b True
   c True
   d False
   e True
   f False
   g True
   h False

Listening

Track 1

8 & 9
a iv   c iii   e ii
b vi   d v   f i

10 **a** choose things
   b seven- to nine-year-olds
   c 86 per cent of parents
   d TV advertising to children is banned
   e one of the major influences
   f three or four
   g negatively
   h critical comparisons

 # Language

12 *contra*   against
   con   together, with

13 *in-*   shows a negative, an opposite; in, on
   ex-   former and still living; out, from
   en-   to cause to become; make
   pro-   in favour of
   per-   thoroughly, very; through
   ad-   in the direction of; towards, to
   sub-   under

15 For example:
   a A good thing is that they have the opportunity to
      be well educated; a bad thing is that many find that
      they would rather be out at work.
   b On the plus side they are not taken advantage of; a
      drawback is that many families need the money.
   c It is lovely to experience the change in the seasons,
      but people don't always like all the seasons.
   d People need to be computer literate in our society.
      Not everybody can afford one, so this leads to
      unfairness.
   e Children need to exercise their bodies to stay
      healthy even though some children are not good
      at sports.

16

Adjective	Noun	Adverb	Verb
childlike, childish	*children*	childishly	–
encouraging/ encouraged	encouragement	encouragingly	*encourage*
developing/ developed	development	–	*develop*
comprehensive	*comprehension*	comprehensively	comprehend
advertised/ing	*advertisement*	–	advertise
producing, productive	*product*	productively	produce
decisive	decision	decisively	*decide*
aware	awareness	–	–

17 positive   negative
   partially   fully
   minor   major
   oldest   youngest
   useless   useful
   dissuasive   persuasive
   narrower   wider
   misinformed   informed
   indirect   direct
   small   substantial
   specific   general
   broaden   restrict

Unit 5: Exam practice

This is the first of four examination-practice units. This unit focuses on examination Exercises 1 and 2 (reading), 6 and 7 (writing), and Questions 1–6 (listening).

Coursebook exercises

Reading: Exam Exercise 1

1

Answers
a nothing
b beating the traffic, having fun
c (children) under 10 years
d under the floor
e 15 km
f 4–5 hours
g foot safety cut-off switch, handlebar brakes
h still use the scooter

2

Answers
a because of Aste Nagusia celebrations/festivities
b eight days and nights
c stone lifting, log chopping, hay-bale tossing
d bus stops and street crossings painted, bright scarves draped on statues
e on the Nervion river
f two (Calle Rodrigo Arias and the airport)
g very important

Reading: Exam Exercise 2 (Extended)

3

Answers
a a library card
b by getting a list from the school office or personnel department
c it is placed inside the reader ticket, filed alphabetically
d if it has been requested by another user
e any four from: get students to design them, include school logo, include school name, tickets could be colour copied, write users' names on tickets, tickets could be laminated or put into plastic pockets
f more durable and reduce librarian time, but can be more costly
g can cause damage
h any four from: lack of use, damaged beyond repair, information out of date, information has become culturally insensitive

Writing: Exam Exercise 6 or 7

See assessment criteria for Extended writing on page xii.

Listening: Questions 1–6

CD 1,
Track 4

Answers
1 upstairs on the left
2 seven rupees
3 tickets are $9.50, open at 3 p.m. every day
4 sunny
5 a week, to phone other branch
6 supermarket, across the road (close by)

Workbook exercises

 Reading: Exam Exercise 2 (Core)

a they are exposing themselves to a range of potential hazards
b as many as 20 per cent
c because of lack of sleep / because they spend so much time in front of video screens
d over 1,100
e six to eleven
f repetitive movements and sleep deprivation
g overuse of games
h mouse elbow, video eyes, joystick digit, vibration finger, nerve trap

 Reading: Exam Exercise 1 (Extended)

a 20.00 hours
b £255
c two
d restaurant
e have an initial consultation
f regular reviews
g state-of-the-art machines and user-friendly equipment

 Listening

Track 2

a life skill
b on the stairs
c Falls
d stored properly
e the condition of your electrical equipment
f Fires
g matches, lighters
h ovens, hot drinks
i scald

Unit 6: Focus on reading skills

Exam Exercise 2

Coursebook exercises

 **Reading**

1   Encourage students to focus on the facilities and services that a language school might offer.

2   Students could rank their facilities and services in order of importance. They should be prepared to give reasons.

3   Allow students to use their dictionaries if necessary.

4

> **Answers**
> a   Two computer centres
> b   Library and bookshop
> c   University counselling service
> d   Cafeteria
> e   Social and leisure programme
> f   Accommodation
> Unused: Banking facilities, Sports centre

5   The school's facilities are the paragraph headings. Ask students to check whether they are the same as the ones they thought of in Exercises **1** and **2**, and to add any that they think should be included.

6   This exercise helps students to check the vocabulary work they did earlier.

7   While this writing skill is not assessed in the IGCSE examination, it is useful practice in language manipulation. Various answers are possible.

 Language focus: prefixes

> **Language box** Prefixes change the meaning or function of a word.

8   For example:

Prefix	Definition	Word/s
self-	referring to oneself or to personality	self-conscious
multi-	more than one	multiracial
inter-	from one to another, between	international
con-	together, with	concurrent
micro-	*very small, on a small scale*	*microchip*
audio-	to do with hearing or sound	audio-visual
dis-	not, the opposite of	disadvantage
pro-	in favour of, supporting	pro-education

9

> **Answers**
> The new words are:
> automatic   biannual
> hypermarket   monolingual
> submarine   antidote
> transcontinental   ex-president
> equidistant   contradiction

 Speaking: telephone skills

Each pair of students will need one copy of the leaflet on page **43** of the Coursebook, one copy of the leaflet on page **44**, and one copy of the form on page **45**.

10 First, you need to allocate the two roles, A and B, to your students. Then get all the As in one group and all the Bs in another. Give them plenty of time to read their instructions, and check that they understand exactly what they have to do. Their first task is to make lists of phrases which might be useful when they eventually perform the role play.

11 When they are ready, each student A joins with a student B, and acts out the conversation. As this role play is a telephone conversation, students should not be able to see each other's faces, so have them sit back to back during the activity. As an extension to this activity, you could ask your students to write a letter or an e-mail to a language school asking for a copy of their latest brochure and price list. By actually sending students' letters, the writing becomes an authentic writing activity which will receive a response. Names and addresses of language schools can be obtained from the Internet.

D Speaking: giving advice

12 Students will eventually read an article about children changing schools. This exercise helps to build up their confidence by getting them to think about the topic before they read the article. There are no right or wrong answers. Encourage students to use this activity to practise and develop their speaking skills in English.

13 Students discuss their ideas in pairs and then make a list of 'advice phrases'.

14 Students change pairs and give each other advice about preparing for a change of schools. Encourage students to use the advice phrases from the previous exercise, and their ideas from Exercise **12**. Make sure they look at the example.

E Reading

15 Students discuss the vocabulary and use their dictionaries to help them.

16 This exercise not only asks students to predict what they think they are going to read in the text, but also helps them to focus more deeply on the text content by finding references to the topics.

17 Students read the text in more detail and use the words from Exercise **15** to complete the gaps.

Answers
a significant transition
b plunged into
c bullying
d involvement
e potential problems
f stability
g traumatic
h 'rights' and 'wrongs'
i responsibility

18

Answers
a because it marks a transition between childhood and being a teenager
b bullying
c because teenagers make their own way to and from school
d staying with friends from primary school
e because teenagers need to 'fit in' and not feel left out
f because it is simply a continuation of secondary or high school in the same building
g encouraging teenagers to talk about their own views
h when they want independence

F Further practice

19 See assessment criteria for Extended writing on page xii.

20

> **Answers**
> a all levels
> b word-for-word transcript, mini-glossary,
>   information about the listening materials
> c a few hours each month
> d visit the website www.LanguageLearning.eur
> e Bonjour!
> f a gondola-maker
> g £103.50
> h four (order form, telephone, fax, online)

21 & 22

> **Answers**
> Various answers are possible.

Workbook exercises

 ## Vocabulary

2

Noun	Verb	Adjective	Adverb
discovery	*discover*	discovered	–
environment	–	environmental	environmen-tally
problem	–	problematic	
education	educate	educated/ional	educationally
communica-tion	communicate	communi-cated	–
preparation	prepare	*prepared*/atory	–
continuation	continue	continued/al/ous	continually/ously
independence	–	independent	independently

 ## Reading 1

4 a True
   b False
   c False
   d True
   e True
   f True
   g False
   h True

6 a children themselves
   b because they take away the natural ability to learn things
   c when they see a change for the worse in their children
   d unhappy, angry people who can't communicate
   e it makes children socially and academically ahead of schooled peers
   f children are not in charge and may be exposed to bullying, peer pressure and bad language

Reading 2

10 a academic
   b salary
   c short
   d expenses
   e initially
   f contribute
   g reputation
   h graduate
   i depend

12 c left out = not included in a group

14 a when she got her IGCSE results
 b she was worried that she would not be accepted by the other students **or** she believed that other students would be better than her
 c everyone
 d contribute money to the home
 e and saved nearly everything
 f a good academic reputation
 g of being left out
 h that there are many advantages in going to university

Language

17 Possible answers:

teaching	learning
hard	easy
wonderful	awful
often	rarely
recent	old
worse	better
artificial	natural
strong	weak
confident	shy
wide	narrow

18 a university
 b pressure
 c interrupt
 d playground
 e structured
 f siblings
 g concept
 h absolutely
 i encouragement
 j assisting

19 a siblings
 b absolutely
 c university
 d assisting
 e concept
 f playground
 g encouragement
 h structured
 i interrupt
 j pressure

20

Phrasal verb	Meaning
get off	get little punishment
go in for	take part in something
go for	try to get something
point out	call attention to
try out	test
put out	extinguish

Unit 7: Focus on reading and writing skills

Exam Exercise 4

Coursebook exercises

A Reading: looking for details

1   Students often have fairly fixed ideas about their future careers; many have already planned their education in line with their career goals. This exercise gives students the chance to talk about their futures, and to consider any negative aspects of their chosen careers.

2   Students look at the wordsearch and find the seven jobs.

> **Answers**
> horizontal: accountant
> vertical: pilot
> diagonal: doctor, carpenter, gardener, teacher, astronaut

3   Students write definitions of the seven jobs.

4   This pre-reading activity will help build students' confidence. They may need some prompting, so be prepared to give help. You could provide some of the information from the text itself.

5   Students look quickly through the text to see if they can find any of their answers from Exercise 4.

6 & 7   These exercises guide students in the skills required for note-taking and summary-writing.

B Writing: making notes and writing a paragraph

8 & 9   Again, these exercises guide students in the skills required for note-taking and summary-writing.

10   In this exercise, students write notes based on the text. They can use their ideas and notes from Exercises 6–9 to help them.

> **Answers**
> a   agile hands   g   19
> b   concentration   h   husband
> c   lifting   i   backgammon boards
> d   carrying   j   drinks trays
> e   60   k   nerves in hands
> f   Nicosia   l   lungs/breathing

11   This exercise gives students useful practice in writing a paragraph from notes. Encourage students to use their own words as far as possible.

12   Students should check for style, number of words, relevant information, use of own words, etc.

C Speaking: giving advice

13   In this exercise, students identify phrases which give advice.

> **Answers**
> You ought to … .   What about … ?
> Why don't you … ?   You should … .

14

> **Answers**
>
> *You ought* + verb.
> *Why don't you* + verb without 'to'?
> *What about* + *-ing* verb?
> *You should* + verb without 'to'.

15 Students think of some other ways of giving advice.

16 This exercise gives students the chance to practise using some of the advice phrases along with their ideas from Exercise 1.

17 Students think about the advantages and disadvantages of the five jobs listed. Make sure they give valid reasons for their decisions.

D Reading

18–20 These are all pre-reading exercises to encourage students to think and speculate about the text.

21 Make sure your students have access to a dictionary for this exercise.

22 Allow students to speculate here – they have a lot of freedom, but obviously their answers need to match the questions.

23

> **Answers**
>
> **c** What has it been like spending so much time in a relatively small space?
> **d** How have you kept your relationship with your family strong over this long absence?
> **h** What is the best part of walking in space?
> **a** You have been shown playing a music keyboard up there. What have you been playing and singing?
> **f** Did you have the problems with nausea that many first-time astronauts experience?
> **b** What are some of the things that surprised you about orbital life?
> **g** What have you missed the most?
> **e** How does it feel being unable to take a shower for so long?

24

> **Answers**
>
> **a** container   **f** spectacular
> **b** claustrophobia   **g** fortunate
> **c** crew   **h** orbit
> **d** ample   **i** gravity
> **e** massive   **j** anchor

25 Students compare their predictions from Exercise 22 with Clayton's actual answers.

E Writing

26

> **Answers**
>
> **a** three
> **b** electronic files
> **c** have liquid soaps and shampoos
> **d** views of space and other planets
> **e** EVA
> **f** claustrophobic or SAS
> **g** in zero gravity

27 Make sure students include the information from the previous exercise in their summary.

F Further practice

28 Students should include some or all of the following information in their paragraph:

- one of the best universities in Britain
- choice of 168 courses
- can study in your own time
- personal tutor support
- chance to meet fellow students
- various levels of course
- wide range of subjects
- no previous qualifications needed
- value for money
- monthly instalments
- high-quality materials
- variety of forms

29

> **Answers**
> Various answers are possible.

30 This is a form-filling exercise: see below.

> **Answers**
>
>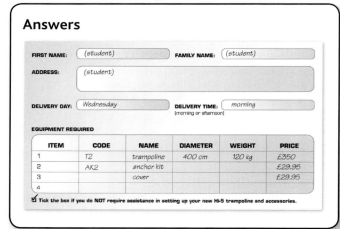

31

> **Answers**
> a by e-mail
> b no, there was plenty of space
> c today they have e-mail, video conferences, can receive electronic files, make phone calls
> d going out into space from the space station
> e not enough time
> f how difficult simple tasks become in zero gravity
> g outdoor smells, the breeze, changes in temperature

Workbook exercises

 Vocabulary

1 astronaut, gardener, teacher, carpenter, pilot, doctor, accountant

2 a claustrophobia
   b ample
   c massive
   d spectacular
   e orbit, gravity

Reading 1

3 a paragraph 4
   b 6
   c 1
   d 3
   e 5
   f 2

5 For example:

Paragraph 1
- Periodontal disease is the most common of all diseases.
- Most people are aware of the basics of dental and oral health.

Paragraph 2
- Xylitol is seen as the latest effective anti-plaque weapon.
- It is seen as the most promising development since the introduction of fluoride.

Paragraph 3
- Hyaluronic acid, which is found naturally in the gum and the eye, has been used to treat eyes after surgery and now is being used for gum health.

Paragraph 4
- Halitosis plagues many people and is not caused by oral bacteria and does not come from the stomach.
- Basic oral cleanliness can avoid halitosis.

Paragraph 5
- Another hazard for oral health is smoking.

Paragraph 6
- Some nutrients, like vitamin C and calcium, are important for oral health.

6 a any two from: twice daily toothbrushing, regular flossing, dental checks, visits to the hygienist, low sugar intake

b any two from: anti-plaque and anti-caries (tooth decay) agent, related to sugar and extracted from birch wood, can't be converted to acid in the mouth, suppresses unfavourable mouth bacteria, inhibits plaque formation

c misconceptions that bad breath comes from the stomach or from sulphurous gases, brush and floss teeth and remove bacteria from mouth before breakfast, bacteria react with food to create acid

d citrus fruit, kiwi, strawberries, broccoli and cabbage provide vitamin C; yoghurt, cheese, green leafy vegetable, nuts, seeds, tinned sardines or salmon, and bread provide calcium

Research

8 Students could visit the following sites to find out about becoming a dentist:
- www.bda.org
- www.ada.org

Reading 2

10 It does not matter if your students are unfamiliar with the programme – they should be able to predict its content from the title!

11 a host
b occupational duties
c alongside
d pilot
e juxtaposition
f wit
g hazards
h spin-off from
i graphic
j inundated with
k commissioned
l concept
m promos

12 a *Dirty Jobs*
b Discovery
c November 2003
d 20
e the US
f Australia
g the situations
h the personalities of the people he encounters
i dangerous
j disgusting
k *Somebody's Gotta Do It*

Writing 2

13 Make sure students use the information from the previous exercise to write their summary.

Language

14 a There is a film on at the cinema (which/that) I would like to see.
b A fireman is a person who loves his job.
c Is this the article in the newspaper that talks about the best hotels?
d Do you know the reason (why) they went on strike?
e Do you think they would forget the day (that) they got married?
f A cathedral is a place that/which is usually quiet and peaceful.
g That was the girl who passed all her exams.
h The carpenter is from a place that/which is a small island.
i Their craft is from a time when it was valued more than it is now.
j Wimbledon is a club where people play tennis.

15 a assume/assertion
b assertion/assume
c bassoon
d passport/passive
e cassette
f message
g massive
h tissue
i successful
j passive/passport

16 a tissue
b massive
c passive
d assertion
e passport
f assume
g successful
h cassette
i message
j bassoon

17 a i watchful
ii menacing
iii total
iv accidental
v delicate or dust filled

b dangerous – more dangerous – most dangerous
different – more different – most different
aware – more aware – most aware
professional – more professional – most professional

c milli + metre
crafts + man/men
work + shop
dress + making
any + thing
foot + steps

d i highly, extremely
ii delicate
iii timber
iv sterotypical, unique
v current

Unit 8: Focus on writing skills

Exam Exercises 6 and 7

Coursebook exercises

A Spelling

1 & 2 In an extended writing exercise, students will not be penalised for individual spelling mistakes. However, general poor spelling does not give a good impression and it is therefore important that students are aware of the importance of correct spelling. You may like to give your students some spelling rules (e.g. the use of -*ize* (rather than -*ise*) in American English (AmE), and the spelling of words such as *licence* in AmE, which is the same for both the noun and the verb). This exercise could lead into a more general discussion of how some vocabulary is different in AmE, for example *sidewalk* (AmE) and *pavement* (BrE). Stress that both AmE and BrE are acceptable in the examination as long as they are used consistently.

3 Students will see these words later on in the unit and so will be able to check the spelling.

4 Students may have their own 'favourites' which they consistently misspell. Ask students which of the methods in the list they think is the best. Encourage them to think of other ways of recording new vocabulary items, and what information they should include (e.g. part of speech, antonyms, collocation, phonology).

B Reading

5

Words	Definitions
logic	reasons
nuisance	something which annoys or causes problems
bid farewell	say goodbye
mayhem	confused situation
grappling with	trying to deal with a difficult problem
upsurge	sudden increase
ratify	sign an agreement

Unused: speak the language of a country or area, reduce the size of something

6

Order	Paragraph
1	A
2	F
3	D
4	B
5	C
6	E
7	G

7 Make sure students give reasons for their choice.

8 Encourage students to think about parts of speech, and to look at the context as well as the word/s immediately before and after the gap.

> **Answers**
> Paragraph B: bid farewell
> Paragraph C: mayhem
> Paragraph D: nuisance
> Paragraph E: grappling with, upsurge
> Paragraph F: logic
> Paragraph G: ratify

9 Students check their spelling from Exercise **3** by finding the words in the text.

10

> **Answers**
> a variants   d spilled over
> b widespread   e smuggle through
> c canvassed   f endorsed

C Speaking

11 Students need to have a clear understanding of what each man says and thinks. Encourage them to look closely at the text again and then discuss their own feelings with a classmate.

> **Answers**
> a Phil Coogan   b Frank Haden

12 & 13 It is actually quite difficult for learners to correctly identify the type of mistakes which they make in English, so you may have to give them some help here. There are examples in the Coursebook. Encourage students to discuss their ideas with a classmate. Get them to ask each other what sort of mistakes they make and then present their information in the form of a table or graph.

14 It is interesting to discover whether students make similar mistakes in spoken and written language; often this is not the case. Students are rarely proficient in all language skills, and tend to be stronger in some and less able in others.

D Writing: formal letter

15 Students need to think carefully about formal letter-writing, as the style requires a more specific layout than an informal letter. However, students are likely to have had plenty of letter-writing practice over the years and so this activity should not take too long. Draw students' attention to the Exam tips.

16 Students should think about the beginning and ending of a formal letter. They should begin with *Dear Madam/Sir* or *Dear Sir/Madam* when they do not know the name of the person to whom they are writing, and end with *Yours faithfully*. When the name of the receiver is known, the letter should begin with, for example, *Dear Mrs Peterson* and end with *Yours sincerely* (see Exam tip on page **64**). Encourage students to stick to one format, and not to use other greetings and salutations.

17 As more complex language (such as conditionals, modals and compound tenses) tends to be used in formal letters, phrases **a**, **d** and **f** would be appropriate. Phrases **e** and **g** might also be appropriate, depending on the context, but **b**, **c** and **h** could sound rude. Ask students to think of more phrases that they could use.

18 A common problem in the IGCSE E2L examination is that students fail to read the question properly and thus do not include everything that is required. Tell students to read the stimulus material and the question itself very carefully, and then discuss with a classmate what they have to do. They do **not** need to write anything yet.

19 Students read the sample response and try to identify its weaknesses, focusing on grammar and spelling. They do **not** need to rewrite the letter.

20 Students now focus on content and layout, and discuss how the letter can be improved. They do **not** need to rewrite the letter.

21 Students compare this 'model' answer with the one in Exercise **19**, and identify in what ways it is an improvement. There is no need for them to write their own answer to the question.

22 Students write a letter in response to the advertisement. As this is their first attempt at this type of letter, allow them plenty of time for planning and checking. Make sure students read the 'rules' for writing formal letters. You could ask them to exchange their letters with a classmate.

Level 2, Part 2

E Speaking: job interview

23 This exercise is preparation for the speaking task which follows. Allocate roles to your students so that they can think about the type of language they need for the role play. Give them plenty of time to do this.

24 If you have the space and the resources, it would be a good idea to video or at least record some or all of the interviews; alternatively ask some students to carry out their interviews in front of the class. If you have an uneven number of students, there is no reason why you could not have two interviewers with each interviewee.

F Further practice

25

> **Answers**
> **a** business and social functions, casual conversation
> **b** in the book *Adventures in Speaking and Writing*
> **c** by what you say and how you say it
> **d** it has certain fundamental rules and principles
> **e** to acquaint readers with easy-to-follow rules for developing speaking and writing skills
> **f** telephone, return the coupon, write

26

> **Answers**
> Various answers are possible.

27 & 28 See assessment criteria for Extended writing on page **xii**.

Workbook exercises

Vocabulary

1 advertisement, association, available, believe, decreased, dictionary, government, increasingly, literacy, materials, secondary, studying

2 horizontal: dictionary, believe, literacy, advertisement
vertical: available, studying, government, decreased
diagonal: association, increasingly, materials, secondary

Reading 1

6 **a** paralysed   **g** raise
b trains   **h** primates
c quadriplegics   **i** manipulate
d lap   **j** furnished
e companion   **k** donations
f foster parents

7 **a** fetch the phone, remove food from freezer, put food in microwave
b bringing items, turning on a light, follow laser pointer, change a CD, turn pages of book, pour water bottle, scratch an itch
c because it no longer met his needs
d from a friend
e eight
f it's like an apartment with furniture
g practise what they have learned

Research

8 For general information about guide dogs for the blind and hearing dogs for the deaf, students could visit www.guidedogs.org.uk and www. hearingdogs.org.uk.

Writing 1

11 **a** I'm writing to let you know
b I've never done
c I like the idea of
d I'd like to play
e My idea is to
f we could have
g we never have much chance to
h I think having
i I hope that you will

Reading 2

14 a Be positive at all times
   b Know what to do
   c Good preparation is a pre-requisite
   d Practise, practise, practise
   e Use various materials and aids
   f Be open to criticism

16

Noun	Verb	Adjective	Adverb
topic	–	topical	topically
effect	affect	effective	*effectively*
hesitation	*hesitate*	hesitant	hesitatingly
–	–	*considerable*	considerably
confidence	–	confident	confidently
illustration	*illustrate*	illustrated/ illustrative	illustratively
attraction	*attract*	attractive/ed	attractively
science	–	scientific	*scientifically*
disappointment	disappoint	*disappointed*	disappointedly
suggestion	suggest	suggested/ ive	suggestively

 Language

18

BrE	AmE
colour	*color*
analyse	analyze
travelled	traveled
programme	program
cheque	check
labour	*labor*
theatre	*theater*
doughnut	*donut*
centre	center
metre	meter
gaol	jail
humour	*humor*
pyjamas	*pajamas*
honour	honor
catalogue	*catalog*
manoeuvre	*maneuver*
tyre	*tire*
practise (v)	practice
practice (n)	
aeroplane	airplane

19 horizontal: signature, address, dear, informal, sincerely
   vertical: faithfully, formal, date, reply, yours

20

buzzy	lively and exciting
click	press the button on a computer mouse
tweenager	a child between the ages of ten and fourteen
retail therapy	the practice of shopping to make you feel happy
attachment	a computer file appended to an e-mail
digital divide	division between those who have and those who don't have computers
mobe	mobile phone
adultescent	a middle-aged person associated with youth culture
format	determine the size, shape and form of a written document
cargo pants	loose-fitting cotton trousers with large pockets

21 a digital divide
   b tweenager
   c retail therapy
   d adultescent
   e attachment
   f buzzy
   g mobe
   h click
   i format
   j cargo pants

Unit 9: Focus on listening skills

Exam Questions 9 and 10

Coursebook exercises

A Speaking

1 Each of the clippings contains the letters 'CV'.

2 Encourage students to check the meaning of CV (curriculum vitae) in their dictionary. (Note: The word *résumé* is used in AmE.)

3 Depending on students' knowledge of CVs, this may be either a short or a long activity. Prompt students with information if they are stuck for ideas (e.g. date of birth, education). They will, in fact, get more ideas in the next exercise.

4 The content of a CV often depends on the job being applied for. However, there is certain basic information which should always be included. The best order is probably: personal information, education, qualifications, work experience, hobbies, languages, referees; but allow students a different order if they give reasons for their choice.

B Listening: radio interview-

CD 1,
Track 5

5 Students first listen simply for gist. Tell students they only need to check the order of the items in a CV which they chose in Exercise 4. In fact the order is exactly as listed above.

6 Identifying key words in listening questions is just as important as in reading questions.

7 Students listen again and decide whether the seven statements are true or false. They can check their answers with a classmate.

> **Answers**
> | a | False | c | False | e | True | g | True |
> |---|-------|---|-------|---|------|---|------|
> | b | False | d | True | f | False | | |

8 Allow students to read the transcript to make a final check on their answers.

C Writing: CV

9 This is the planning stage before the writing. Students will probably not have written a CV before, so it is important for them to think about what needs to be included, as well as what can be left out. They may find this quite challenging. Consider giving them a real CV – you could use your own or prepare a model.

10 Although writing a CV is not a skill which is assessed in the IGCSE examination, it is a useful skill to acquire, not least because it gives students practice in organising information. Furthermore, because CVs usually appear in note form, it also enables students to practise their note-writing skills. Students should be encouraged to look at and comment on each other's CVs.

D Listening: job interview

CD 1,
Track 6

11 & 12 These pre-listening exercises will help to build up students' confidence before they listen. There are no right or wrong answers. Students will need to refer back to Exercise 22 in Unit 8. In pairs, they decide what kind of questions the interviewer might ask, and make notes. They then discuss what responses the interviewee should give, and again make notes.

13 Students listen and make notes about the interviewee's mistakes. There are many – for example, the use of informal language or slang (*Thanks, Nope, 'cos I checked it out, Yeah, What else do you want to know?* etc.), as well as failing to supply the required information. Your students should appreciate that the interviewee does not perform very well!

14 For the second listening, the interviewee's responses are missing. Students should make notes about what they would say if they were asked the questions. You could then play the CD again and ask students to respond orally.

E Speaking: job interview

15 As with all role plays, you will need to ensure that your students know exactly what they have to do before they begin. Give them time to think about their questions and answers. If possible, video or record their questions and answers. Alternatively, ask some students to act out their interview in front of the class.

F Reading

16 & 17 Give students a time limit for this exercise. They will need to supply some of the countries or nationalities themselves. There is quite a lot of information for students to find, so make sure they have enough time to complete the table. Ask them to work in pairs and check their answers with other students. (Not all the spaces can be filled.)

Country/ continent	Nationality	Include	Exclude
Germany	German	references from previous employers, copies of education certificates, details about parents	cover letter, personal interests
France	French	handwritten cover letter, personal interests, languages spoken, photo	
America/ USA	American		age, sex, marital status, photo
Italy	Italian		
Britain	British	language skills, foreign travel, cultural experiences	
Spain	Spanish		
Scandinavia	Scandinavian		self-centredness
Norway	Norwegian		overplaying achievements, self-centredness

18

> **Answers**
> a global   e contacts
> b skills   f overplay
> c voluntary   g prospective
> d binder   h discriminate

G Further practice

19

> **Answers**
> Various answers are possible.

20 See assessment criteria for Extended writing on page **xii**.

21 & 22

> **Answers**
> Various answers are possible.

23

Student	1	2	3	4
Name	Ahmed Yousuf	Mani Saleki	Weerahennadige Ishanka Nirmali Fernando	Alia Al Naggar
Nationality	Nigerian	Iranian	Sri Lankan	Swedish
Similarities between home and Dubai				Education just as hard
Differences between home and Dubai	Home town cooler than Dubai; approach to education different		Dubai more developed, better education	More reading to do, more assignments
Advantages of living in Dubai	Most people speak English	Upcoming city; plenty to do	Good schools, experienced staff	Education easier
Disadvantages of living in Dubai	Heat takes some getting used to; expensive to rent accommodation	Getting more expensive and crowded; traffic problems; lack of support for students; part-time jobs not allowed		
Any other information	Various answers are possible for this row.			

Workbook exercises

 Vocabulary

1 & 2
Personal information
Education
Qualifications
Work experience
Hobbies
Languages
Referees

Reading

3 A famous traditional dancer who is now too old to dance

4 a line 10 – age new dancers are trained from
   b line 12 – year Moiseyev was born
   c line 13 – year Moiseyev was enrolled in a dance school
   d line 16 – year Moiseyev formed a small company
   e line 16 – year the dance group travelled abroad
   f line 17 – year the dance group toured France and Britain
   g line 27 – school founded
   h line 28 – number of pupils who graduate
   i line 28 – how often pupils graduate

5 a False
   b False
   c True
   d False
   e True
   f True
   g False
   h True
   i False
   j False

6 a Igor Moiseyev continues to go to work every day.
   b He first became a classical dancer at the Bolshoi Theatre.
   d The best dancers are guaranteed a place in his dance group.
   g He travelled abroad in 1945.
   i He thinks that folk dance is overshadowed by pop culture.
   j Every four years, pupils graduate from the school.

Listening

Track 3

9

Words from text	Similar words
classical	traditional
crucial	vital
debutante	newcomer
critics	reporters
judgement	decision
raved	enthused
prestigious	important
choreography	compose a dance
irrespective of	with no regard to
impoverished	poor
connoisseurs	experts
promote	support

11 a The Arangetram performance is crucial for a dancer
  b A special offering by the debutante
  c The judgement of the critics is crucial
  d Has the unique distinction of making over 1,600 live performances
  e To dance at the prestigious residence of the President
  f Leading dance gurus of India
  g Different dance forms such as Indian folk dancing
  h Enjoys teaching children and the poor
  i She has her own group of 60 performers

12 a a special offering by the dancer to her teacher, family, friends and critics
  b extremely complimentary
  c she was one of the youngest dancers
  d four from: history, theory, dance music, development and dance technique
  e children and the poor
  f poverty
  g three hours
  h five from: United Kingdom, France, Germany, the former Soviet Union, Canada, Singapore, Malaysia, Japan, USA

✏️ Writing 2

13 a What can you tell us?
  b You were born in a theatre?
  c How did you become interested in dancing?
  d Why is this dance, the Arangetram, so important?
  e What happened after that?
  f What else do you do in your busy schedule?
  g Do you teach a particular age or ability?
  h Could you tell us something about your dance performances?

 Language

14 *has refused, has kept*   present perfect
   helped   past
   continues, takes   present

15

Present	Present perfect	Past
continues	has refused	helped
takes part	has kept	said
think	has overshadowed	got
works		worked
says		enrolled
don't want		moved
is		was
spends		formed
enjoys		became
trains		toured
needs		recalled
receives		was
see		admitted
are		cultivated
receive		
says		
keeps		
graduate		

17 For example:
  a We must win the race irrespective of how tired we feel.
  b I am determined to complete the puzzle irrespective of how difficult it is.
  c I want to go for a walk irrespective of the weather.
  d We should go swimming irrespective of how warm the water will be.
  e I think we should visit China irrespective of any problems with the language.

18

Unit 10: Exam practice

This is the second of four examination-practice units. In this unit, the exercises focus on examination Exercises 2 (reading), 3 and 4 (reading and writing), 6 and 7 (writing), and listening (Questions 9 and 10).

> **i** any four from: transported to factory, lifted by magnet, placed in oven, heated (to 1,600 °C), melted, poured into over-sized pan, rolled into sheets

Coursebook exercises

Reading: Exam Exercise 2 (Extended)

1

> **Answers**
> **a** within two decades / 20 years
> **b** personal privacy
> **c** provide expiry dates for products / identify damaged or expired products / check prices and inventory
> **d** Uniform Product Code symbol and barcodes
> **e** a message is sent to a computer in the store or factory
> **f** unlocking doors, sending information to a security guard
> **g** alert us when we run out of something, expiry of medicine, automatic delivery of products, supply details to marketers about eating and hygiene habits
> **h** Various answers are possible.

2

> **Answers**
> **a** cans for fruit or vegetables, caps for bottles, screw caps for jars, sides and bases of drink cans
> **b** rolled into thin sheets, coated with 2 grams of tin
> **c** to prevent corrosion, to rule out changes in taste
> **d** can easily be melted down
> **e** about 6 million tonnes
> **f** because magnets are used to remove/sort tin cans from other metals on a conveyor belt
> **g** 23 tonnes
> **h** 318,086 tonnes

Reading and writing: Exam Exercise 3

> APPLICATION FORM
> THE GULF DAILY TIMES, DUBAI
>
> SECTION A
> JOB APPLIED FOR: Trainee journalist
>
> **PERSONAL DETAILS**
> NAME (BLOCK CAPITALS PLEASE): AHMED HASSAN
> ADDRESS: 23 Al Falaj Street, Dubai United Arab Emirates
> MOBILE: 73-918247
> E-MAIL: ahmed@dubainet.com
> DATE OF BIRTH: 19 October 1985
>
> **EDUCATION**
> NAME OF SCHOOL: Dubai High School
> QUALIFICATIONS: IGCSEs C grade: Arabic (First Language), English as a Second Language; D grade: Maths, History, Physics, French (Foreign Language)
>
> POSITIONS OF RESPONSIBILITY AT SCHOOL: President of Debating Society, organised 'Let's Recycle' group
>
> HOBBIES AND INTERESTS: Football, using the Internet, Arabic language
>
> IF YOU ARE OFFERED THE JOB, CAN YOU START WORK IMMEDIATELY?
> (PLEASE TICK)
>
> YES ✓   NO ☐
>
> SECTION B
>
> IN THE SPACE BELOW, WRITE ONE SENTENCE OF BETWEEN 12 AND 20 WORDS EXPLAINING WHY YOU THINK YOU ARE A SUITABLE APPLICANT FOR THE JOB.
>
> [Various answers are possible.]

Writing: Exam Exercises 6 and 7

1 & 2 See assessment criteria for Extended writing on page **xii**.

Listening: Questions 9 and 10

CD 1,
Track 7

Answers

Core questions

a	True	e	True	i	True
b	True	f	True	j	False
c	True	g	False	k	False
d	True	h	False	l	True

Extended questions

a 3,000
b for their fur
c from marble and other stones
d within ten years
e to blast open the ground
f tigers don't have enough food and water
g the big cosmetics manufacturers are not convinced of the damage they are doing

Workbook exercises

📖 Reading: Exam Exercise 2 (Core)

a it increases
b about 40 kg
c Benedictine monks
d it is placed in a net-like bag and then into a mould
e each wheel of Parmesan has its own personal air-conditioning system
f used as security for loans by banks, they increase in value as they mature, offer short-term financing for local people, for banks the cheese offers a very low security risk

📖✏️ Reading and writing: Exam Exercise 3 (Extended)

COURSE APPLICATION FORM

Name of your organisation: _Instituto Acapulco_

Address: _6 San Miguel de Allende, 1022 Mexico City, Mexico_

Course required: _Humanities_

Total number of people: _28 students and 3 teachers_

Duration of stay:
From: _Saturday 18th June_   To: _Saturday 25th June_

Student accommodation:
Male rooms: _6_   Female rooms: _8_

Activities for group (please tick):
☑ Swimming ☐ Basketball ☑ Sightseeing ☐ Indoor games

Suggestions for other activities:

tennis/shopping

Meal times:
Please delete times NOT required
Breakfast   ~~07.00~~ 08.00
Lunch   ~~12.00~~ 13.00
Dinner   19.00 ~~20.00~~

Special requests:
a _Three people are vegetarians_
b _One student is partially sighted and needs the course material in large print_
c _We are studying IGCSE South American Geography_

In the space below, write one sentence of between 12 and 20 words in which you say why your class wants to attend the Humanities course in Belize.

[Various answers are possible.]

📖 ✏️ Reading and writing: Exam Exercise 4

a   birth and death of August Ferdinand Möbius
b   Möbius published his discoveries
c   Gary Anderson designed recycling symbol
d   one side
e   one edge
f   black arrows + white circle
g   outline arrows + no circle
h   car fan belt

💿 Listening
Track 4

a   they help in the study of codes
b   over 4 million
c   because by the time the prime has been written out another one will have been found
d   discovery of the first million-digit prime number
e   45 days
f   he had use of a computer that was to be left on all day
g   we have no idea

Unit 11: Focus on reading skills

Exam Exercises 1 and 2

Coursebook exercises

A Speaking

1   The *Guinness Book of World Records* is known globally. The first edition was published in the UK in 1955. Today, the English language version is distributed in 70 different countries, and it is translated into 22 foreign languages. Worldwide, sales of the book have reached 100 million.

2   Encourage students to think about the type of records which people try to break. Are they all to do with sport? Do students think that some are rather pointless? Students should try to decide which record they would like to break.

3   Quiz! You may like to give students some more examples. Up-to-date records can be obtained from www.guinnessworldrecords.com or you can e-mail info@guinnessrecords.com.

4   Students read the texts quickly to check their answers to the quiz in Exercise **3**.

> **Answers**
> a   45   c   90 cm   e   21.64
> b   309.9 m   d   205 days

B Reading

5

> **Answers**
> a   From left to right: 100 m (running), 400 m (running), long jump, high jump, shot put
> b   The five pentathlon events, plus hurdles, 1,500 metres (running), discus, javelin, pole vault

6

> **Answers**
> a   Various answers are possible.
> b   horizontal: now (*current*), successful (*glittering*), opportunity (*springboard*)
> vertical: collected (*amassed*)
> diagonal: increase (*boost*), excellent (*outstanding*), destroyed (*shattered*), started (*initiated*)

7

> **Answers**
> Various answers are possible.

8

> **Answers**
> a   outstanding   e   glittering
> b   current   f   springboard
> c   shattered   g   boost
> d   amassed   h   initiated

9

> **Answers**
> a one year / 12 months
> b it is better than the under-17s record
> c 400 m
> d three (75 m hurdles, shot put, 800 m)
> e Daley Thompson
> f she should be delighted
> g they are about learning how to compete and how to win
> h training and travel expenses
> i 2005

C Reading and vocabulary

10 Once again, make sure students discuss the vocabulary and use their dictionaries if necessary.

Words	Definitions
stumbled	walked unsteadily and almost fell
blizzard	severe snow storm
dissuade	try to stop someone from doing something
amputation	the action of cutting off a person's arm or leg
rations	a fixed amount of food or water
depot	a place where food and other things are stored
legible	written clearly enough to be read

Not needed: full of liquid or gas, a situation where something cannot continue

11 It is important for students to understand that they do not have to know the meaning of every word in a passage. However, it may be that certain vocabulary items hinder a student's understanding of particular parts of the text. Allow students to focus on five words, and to ask a classmate for help. They should continue to use their dictionaries as well.

12 These are gist questions.

> **Answers**
> a four (Wilson, Scott, Bowers, Oates)
> b Scott

13 Students take notes about the events in the text. There is a lot of detail for each date, but students need only select key points.

Date	What happened?
16 or 17 March	Oates wanted to stay in his sleeping bag, but struggled on when others insisted
day after	Oates left tent and disappeared
20 March	raging blizzard, Scott's right foot a problem, blizzard stopped them continuing
29 March	Scott made last diary entry
12 November	search party found tent

14 Make sure students write answers which include all the necessary information.

> **Answers**
> a because Wilson was too weak to help them
> b the explorers lost track of the date
> c there was a blizzard blowing
> d there was a problem with it and he was afraid the trouble would spread
> e the blizzard
> f he wanted to die naturally, not by any other means
> g he wanted his notes to be sent to his widow
> h it was almost buried in snow
> i about eight months
> j because he had been starving and almost frozen to death

D Speaking

15–18 Use the question prompts to encourage students to discuss the idea of heroes and heroines. This topic is typical of the type set in the Speaking examination.

19 The two paragraphs can be used as models for writing in the next exercise. Point out to students how the writers have given reasons for their opinions.

E Writing

20 Students think of a famous person whom they consider to be a hero or a heroine. They should give clear reasons for their opinion.

21 This is quite a demanding exercise which requires students to imagine themselves as Katarina Thompson. Make sure students understand that the diary entry should be written in note form, and not in continuous prose. You could discuss possible details before students write. A further possibility is for students to rewrite their notes in continuous prose form.

F Further practice

22–24

> **Answers**
> Various answers are possible.

25

> **Answers**
> | | | | | | |
> |---|---|---|---|---|---|
> | a | False | d | True | g | True |
> | b | False | e | False | h | False |
> | c | True | f | True | i | False |

Workbook exercises

 Vocabulary

1 a wireless Internet provider, 45
    b cartoon strip, 309.9
    c fingernail, 90
    d tightrope, 205
    e 21.64, influenza

2

Throw	Jump	Run
shot put	long jump	100 metres
discus	high jump	400 metres
javelin	pole vault	1,500 metres
		hurdles

Reading 1

3 A deep-sea diver
    B goldminer
    C steeplejack
    D forest firefighter

4 a perils, hazards
    b reduced
    c tremors
    d falling
    e soak/wet

5 the North or South Poles / the Arctic or Antarctic

7
auroral	at the start of the day
motives	reasons to do something
devoted	dedicated
reigns	exists
insomnia	sleeplessness
swell	increase
maintain	look after
tang	flavour

8 a maintain
    b reigns
    c auroral
    d swell
    e insomnia
    f tang
    g devoted
    h motives

9 a cold and windy
   b 27 °C (winter lowest is −55 °C and summer lowest
      is −28 °C)
   c they can't sleep
   d they were crushed by ice
   e atmospheric pollution, sea-level rise, climate
      change and geology
   f take warm clothes, be prepared to get little sleep,
      need to be sociable, be prepared to have a diet with
      little fresh fruit

Reading 2

13 Help students to put the events in the text on a
    timeline. Various answers are possible.

Language

15 For example:
   a *determine* → determined, determination,
      determiner
   b *achieve* → achievement, achieved, achiever
   c *succeed* → success, successful, successfully,
      successor
   d *perish* → perished, perishable, perishing
   e *dissuade* → dissuasive, dissuaded, dissuasively
   f *explore* → exploration, explorer, explored
   g *isolate* → isolation, isolated
   h *climb* → climber, climbed, climbing

16 For example:
   a successor
   b climbed
   c achieved
   d isolated
   e perishable
   f dissuaded
   g explorer, climber
   h determined, successful

17

Adjective	Comparative	Superlative
tall	*taller*	*tallest*
thin	thinner	thinnest
cheap	cheaper	cheapest
good	better	best
bad	worse	worst
unhappy	unhappier	unhappiest
untidy	untidier	untidiest
clever	cleverer	cleverest
lonely	lonelier	loneliest
far	farther	farthest
much	more	most
shy	shyer	shyest

18 a longest
    b heaviest
    c longest
    d greediest
    e deepest
    f most destructive
    g oldest

Unit 12: Focus on reading and writing skills

Exam Exercises 4 and 5

Coursebook exercises

A Reading

1   With musicians and film stars being so much a part of young people's lives today, students should not have any problems in deciding what qualities or characteristics they believe are important.

2   More vocabulary work. Allow students enough time to think about the words and phrases and to check the meanings in their dictionaries.

3

Words	Definitions
assist	help by a team player
debut	first appearance
role	work position
runner-up	in second place
sign for	have a contract with
tenure	job
versus	against

4

> **Answers**
>
> All the phrases from Exercise **2** can be found in the text about David Beckham.

5

> **Answers**
>
> a   runner-up   e   sign for
> b   tenure   f   versus
> c   role   g   assist
> d   debut

6   Students do not need to discuss the meaning of the words and phrases here, but should try to predict who or what the text is going to be about. It does not matter if their predictions are wrong. If students have difficulty with any of the words or phrases, they can check in their dictionaries. Some of the words and phrases have been removed from the text.

7   Students scan the text and put the six paragraphs into a logical order. They do **not** need to worry about the gaps yet. Encourage them to check their order with a classmate, and to give reasons for their choice. There are several possibilities, but the following is the order of the original article:

> **Possible answer**
>
> B, E, F, C, A, D

8   Students should read the text again, this time more intently, and use some of the words and phrases from Exercise **6** to complete the gaps.

> **Answers**
>
> Paragraph A: repertoire
> Paragraph B: child prodigy
> Paragraph C: exceptional achievement
> Paragraph E: classical, pop and jazz, mesmerised audiences, dressed unconventionally

9

> **Answers**
>
> a   music album
> b   released three classical CDs, toured with orchestras, made many TV appearances
> c   first classical musician to be nominated for the award
> d   because it was popular music packaged/sold as classical music
> e   Various answers are possible.

B Writing: making notes

10 Students read the question and discuss what they are being asked to do.

11 The point here is for students to understand that notes need to be short but precise; in other words, notes should provide all the necessary information in brief.

> **Answer**
>
> c provides all the information required, as does e, although this also includes Vanessa-Mae's name, which is not really necessary

12 Students make notes about the various events in Vanessa-Mae's life, linking them with the dates in the text.

Year/age	Event
1978	born in Singapore
age 3	moved to London from Singapore
by age 13	already released three classical CDs
age 14	started working on *The Violin Player*
age 16 (1995)	dramatic entry into music scene with release of first popular music album *The Violin Player*
1996	nominated for Best Female Artist in BRIT Awards
2001	*Subject to Change* album

13 Students compare their notes in pairs.

C Speaking and vocabulary

14 The next text is about twins. The words *double*, *duo* and *identical* are leading students towards this theme.

15

> **Answers**
>
> twins are two children born at the same time to the same mother
> three = triplets
> four = quadruplets (quads)
> five = quintuplets (quins)

16 Encourage students to discuss and share their experiences.

17 There is some quite demanding vocabulary here, so make sure students have enough time to discuss the words and phrases, and to use their dictionaries if necessary.

18

Words	Definitions
encounter	meeting
compassion	kindness
intrusive	interfering
impulse	desire
disenchanted	let down
inappropriate	unsuitable

D Reading

19 Students now look at the text and decide whether their earlier decisions about the vocabulary items were correct or not. You should not need to interfere too much in any of these vocabulary-based activities.

20 This is an excellent exercise for encouraging students to think about how words are formed from roots. Initially, they should do the exercise without using their dictionaries, and look up only words they are unsure about. Most of the new words are nouns, so you could extend the exercise by asking students to give other parts of speech as well.

Verb	New word	Part of speech
enthuse	*enthusiasm*	*noun*
situate	situations	plural noun
familiarise	familiar	adjective
care	care	noun
think	thoughtful	adjective
differ	different	adjective
emphasise	emphasis	noun
multiply	multiples	plural noun
able	abilities	plural noun
feel	feelings	plural noun
disapprove	disapproval	noun
behave	behaviour	noun
defend	defence	noun

21

> **Answers**
> a 20 years ago in her local supermarket
> b when someone asked her which twin was good and which one was bad
> c as a 'matched set', they are compared and contrasted
> d the twins were more caring and compassionate
> e they compare their twins' characters and abilities
> f they keep their feelings to themselves
> g bad behaviour should be disapproved of, and not the individual child
> h outside the family circle
> i to demonstrate a positive attitude towards twins and the differences which may exist

E Writing

22 Another type of note-taking exercise is one which does not focus on biographical events, but on pieces of advice, as in the text students have just read.

23 Students look again at the text and pick out the advice given.

> **Possible answers**
> • give twins completely different names
> • never dress them alike
> • avoid emphasis on twinship
> • allow them to grow up fulfilling their individual potential and developing their own strengths
> • resist impulse to favour one or other
> • emphasise positive points
> • disapprove of bad behaviour
> • control behaviour of relatives

24 Students use their notes from the previous exercise to write their summary. Make sure they respect the word limit of 100 words.

F Speaking

25–27 Encourage discussion of the twin myth, and on the treatment of twins in general.

G Further practice

30

> **Answer**
> Twins reunited after 35 years apart

31

> **Answers**
> a 35
> b given for adoption as part of experiment
> c 2003
> d they had been dropped from the survey
> e asked lots of questions, continued his study
> f records of study are sealed until 2066
> g because twins are very close

32

> Important dates and times
> * separated for 35 years
> * 2003 contacted agency
> * records of study sealed until 2066
>
> How the twins met
> * Elyse contacted agency
> * arranged to meet in café
> * looked similar, but each unique
>
> The twins' feelings now
> * still want answers
> * don't regret their lives
> * have to get to know a stranger
> * challenging but joyful experience

Workbook exercises

 Vocabulary

1

against	versus
first appearance	debut
have a contract with	sign for
help by a team player	assist
in second place	runner-up
job	tenure
work position	role

2 horizontal: individual, triplets, personality
vertical: opposites, pair
diagonal: myth, parents, multiples, twins, polar

3
a myth
b twins
c pair
d polar
e opposites
f Parents
g multiples
h individual

Reading 1

4
a innate
b pioneering
c profoundly
d distinct
e random

5
a the result of a baby just moving its jaw;
it is an inborn rhythm vital for learning a language
b normal, hearing babies of profoundly deaf parents;
random hand movements made by all babies;
'silent babbling' using simple signs
c with their hands;
different from other hand movements
d a lower, more rhythmic activity
e could be used to help handicapped children to
speak earlier

 Writing 1

8 For example:
Babies are born with a natural rhythm which helps
them to develop their speaking patterns as they get
older. It is believed that the results of this research will
help children who have speaking problems themselves

or are the children of parents who are deaf. It was
thought that the sounds that babies make and their
hand movements were merely random but it has now
been proven that this is in fact a natural process in
their development and one which guides and helps
them to speak.

Reading 2

9 Bahrain's nearest neighbours are Iran, Kuwait, Saudi
Arabia, Qatar, United Arab Emirates

10 All the statements are true.

13 a because of rising global sea levels
b if the sea rose by two metres
c ice shelves are melting
d 0.1 per cent of global total
e any three from: reports have been commissioned,
ratified Kyoto agreement, royal initiative planting
9,000 saplings, wind turbines in WTC building

Writing 2

14

What is sea-level rise?

• humans putting more CO_2 into atmosphere

• as a result **global temperatures are rising**

• and so **ice shelves melting**, which means more
water in oceans and so **sea levels rise**

Where does Bahrain come into this?

• world's **third-largest polluter**

• annual CO_2 output per person = **30.6 metric
tonnes per annum**

What is Bahrain doing to prevent this?

• Kyoto protocol ratified, although **as a developing
country Bahrain is not obliged to take part**

• trying to raise **public awareness**

• three wind turbines at World Trade Centre
**provide up to 15 per cent of the building's energy
needs**

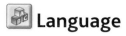
Language

15 **a** *chameleon* – French
    b *husky* – Inuit
    c *quartz* – German
    d *kindergarten* – German
    e *thugs* – Hindi
    f *sari* – Hindi
    g *waltz* – German
    h *chauffeur* – French
    i *lieutenant* – French
    j *rendezvous* – French
    k *pretzels* – German
    l *igloo* – Inuit

16 For example:

Word	Guessed meaning	Dictionary definition
chameleon	lizard	small lizard that can change its colour to match its surroundings
husky	dog	large working dog with thick hair that lives and works in cold climates
quartz	stone	hard mineral used for making watches and clocks
kindergarten	nursery	school for young children
thugs	violent men	violent men, especially criminals
sari	Indian dress	a graceful dress especially worn by Hindu women
waltz	a dance	slow, formal dance performed in a ballroom
lieutenant	military rank	an officer of low rank
rendezvous	to meet	meet a at a certain time and place
pretzels	biscuits	hard, salty biscuits
igloo	ice house	house made of hard blocks of snow

17 For example:
    a The tycoon was a millionaire by the time she was 22.
    b The chimpanzee learned how to count.
    c This part of town is full of sleazy bars.
    d She was wearing a long sable coat.
    e Cocoa is used to make chocolate.
    f The cosmonaut stepped out of her spaceship to loud applause.

Unit 13: Focus on writing skills

Exam Exercises 6 and 7

Coursebook exercises

A Speaking

1 & 2 Encourage students to speculate about the organisation, and its aims.

B Writing: paragraphs

3 & 4 This is a fairly free writing exercise in which students put together the notes from Exercises 1 and 2. They should use linking words and expressions, and avoid producing a 'shopping list' of information. Make sure students exchange their work and check each other's writing. It would be a good idea to set a time limit.

C Reading

5 Students could practise saying each number if you feel that there may be problems. Set a time limit for this scanning exercise.

Answers
a the area of the Asia–Pacific Scouting Region
b the population of the region
c the number of Scouts in the region
d the percentage of worldwide Scouts in the region
e the amount of money raised in eight years in the region
f the year by which the committee hopes to raise a further US$1 million

6

Answers
a recruitment   e potential
b branches   f undertakings
c worthy   g oversees
d donations   h trustee

7 There are various possibilities here, but the following are the most likely choices:

Answers
a aim to attract money
b objectives
c potential for raising funds
d 2005
e financial support to projects
f member
g more information

8

Answers
a by recruiting new members and obtaining donations
b to help fund Scout projects in the region, and to support research projects
c because of its large area and population
d it hopes to have raised an additional US$1 million
e Bangladesh and the Philippines
f individuals, national Scout organisations and their branches, and corporations
g by mail, phone, fax, or e-mail

D Vocabulary

9 This vocabulary list is quite demanding, so give students plenty of time to think about the words and to make decisions about what they might mean. Do **not** allow students to use their dictionaries yet. You may choose to divide the words into two groups and have students work on different sets of words.

10 Once students have had time to discuss the words, they can check them in their dictionaries. Later, when they read the text, they will be able to use context to confirm meaning.

E Reading and writing

11 These are gist questions to help students get a preliminary understanding of the text. They will also have gained some ideas from the previous vocabulary exercise.

> **Answers**
> **a** an adolescent is neither a child nor an adult
> **b** 25

12 Students read the text again, this time more closely, and complete each gap with a word from Exercise **9**.

> **Answers**
>
> | | | | |
> |---|---|---|---|
> | **a** | vulnerable | **h** | neglects |
> | **b** | transition | **i** | nutritional |
> | **c** | compromised | **j** | prevalent |
> | **d** | adequate | **k** | sanitary |
> | **e** | counterparts | **l** | self-esteem |
> | **f** | preferential | **m** | curricula |
> | **g** | discriminate | **n** | peer |

13 This question-writing skill is not assessed in the IGCSE E2L examination, but it is useful practice for students, who invariably have difficulties in forming correct questions. Students should exchange their questions with a classmate and write answers.

F Writing

14 Encourage your students to discuss the difference in meaning between the key words.

15 This type of writing, based on an idea or information from a text, is common in the IGCSE examination. Here, students need to refer back to the passage they have just read in order to get a picture of what the HARP girls do. Their writing will be based on this picture. Make sure students study the question carefully and discuss its content in pairs.

> **Answers**
> **a** Write
> **b** describe
> **c** explain
> **d** suggest

16 There is no specific task here, but allow students time to read the article so that they get an idea of what is required. Point out to students that it is not a model answer in terms of accuracy, although the content is quite good.

17 Students now focus on errors, although there is no need for them to rewrite the article. Encourage them to think about content, style and layout as well as language errors. It is important for students to decide whether or not the writer has answered the question. In fact, the writer has not written anything about 'ways in which your school and your friends could help HARP', and there is little in the way of a description of the girl and where she comes from.

18 Students now write their own answer to the question in Exercise **15**, using the notes supplied.

19 Students exchange their work and check each other's writing. Make sure they have a list of important items to check: content, style, question answered, spelling, number of words, grammar, vocabulary range and appropriateness, layout, repetition.

G Speaking

20 & 21 Students discuss their opinions of HARP and ways of helping people less fortunate than themselves.

 H Further practice

22 See assessment criteria for Extended writing on page **xii**.

24 The site www.wagggsworld.org might be a good place to start researching Guides and Scouts.

25

> **Answers**
> **a** to offer knowledge and new ideas to the youth of Cyprus, to reinforce the ideals of good citizenship, to raise awareness of environmental issues
> **b** an elected council
> **c** into five groups / by age
> **d** experience of working with children of all ages, graduates, people with high ideals, desire to offer something back to society
> **e** maps and compasses
> **f** European Union, United Nations
> **g** regular visits to archaeological sites, traditional villages and museums

 # Workbook exercises

Vocabulary

1	a	fun	f	skip
	b	memories	g	illegal
	c	lifetime	h	peers
	d	volunteer	i	impact
	e	impact	j	donate

 **Reading 1**

4	a	fragrant
	b	dye
	c	revive
	d	ground
	e	soaking
	f	ornamental

Research

5 Students can find out more about henna at www.hennapage.com.

Writing 1

6

Student A		Student B	
Weak	**Strong**	**Weak**	**Strong**
no paragraphs	length of sentences	*spelling*	correct number of words
spelling	answers the question		good introduction and conclusion to article
grammar			written in an interesting way
punctuation			punctuation
the article is too short			good grammatical structures
incorrect vocabulary use			

7 Various answers are possible, but encourage students to give reasons.
For example:

a Yes, in the second piece, as it is directed at the reader and written in an interesting style.

b Yes, in both pieces, but in the second there is a clear introductory paragraph as well as a concluding one.

c Yes, in both pieces there are mistakes in grammar, punctuation and spelling, but the first is worse than the second. Spelling is a problem for both pieces, but grammar and punctuation are more a problem for the first.

d Yes, in both the pieces, but in the second they are more clearly laid out.

e Yes, very much so.

 # Reading 2

9 Various answers are possible. Again, ask your students to give reasons for their choices.

10 a What is it?
b History
c Goal
d Purpose
e Target group

 # Writing 2

12 Some of the spelling and grammar problems are listed below; the correct spelling or phrasing is given for each word/phrase.

Student A

spaceship	the spaceship
offeres	offers
quick transporting	fast transport
peoples	people
by animals	on animals
nowdays	nowadays
it benefits to me	It would be a benefit to me
mars	Mars
in a very quick time	very quickly
people use to die	sometimes die
be able ever to pay a ticket	ever be able to buy a ticket
until I die	before I die

Student B

concidered	considered
comfortible	comfortable
mobil	mobile
youre	your
wich	which
becouse	because
messiges	messages
completly	completely
writting	writing

 # Language

14 a Meeting often is a good solution.
b Eating late is not good for the digestion.
c Going to sleep early is a healthy option.
d Assisting the old is beneficial to society.
e Saving money is a good investment.

17

Verb	Noun	Adjective
establish	*establishment*	*established*
–	environment	*environmental*
activate	*activity*	active
direct	direction	direct, directed
–	*objective*	objective
campaign	*campaign*	campaigning
participate	participant	*participatory*
train	trainer	trained
consume	*consumer*	consuming/ed
investigate	investigation	investigative

18 a consume
b objective
c trainer
d direct
e investigate
f participatory
g campaign
h activity
i environment

19 a establishment
b environment
c activity
d direction
e objective
f campaign
g participant
h trainer
i consumer
j investigation

Level 2, Part 3

Unit 14: Focus on listening skills

Exam Questions 7 and 8

Coursebook exercises

A Writing and speaking

1   This is a demanding exercise, so do not allow it to go on for too long if students are having problems in thinking of vocabulary items. However, remember that there are no right or wrong answers, and that the most important thing is for students to focus on the topic, and to be prepared to give reasons for their word choices. You may like to ask some students to think of adjectives, and others to think of nouns.

2   Make sure you do not give too much away yet. Let your students look at the words and phrases and try to get a feel for what they mean, but do not explain anything.

3   This exercise practises skimming skills, something your students should be quite competent at by now. However, further practice is always useful.

4   Now students can use a dictionary to check understanding.

5   Give students a time limit for this short piece of writing. Read out as many paragraphs as you can to the whole class and ask students to decide on the best.

6   Florence Nightingale should be a well-known figure to many students. If not, they will find out about her in the first listening exercise.

B Listening 1

CD 1,
Track 8

7 & 8 Students need to listen intently to find the information required. This type of note-taking listening exercise is often used in the IGCSE examination. Students should check their answers in pairs. Make sure students understand that their answers need only be in note form – complete sentences are not required.

Answers		
a	1820	born 12 May in Italy
b	1850	returned to England after travelling in Italy, Greece, Egypt and Germany
c	1853	started work at a clinic in London
d	March 1854	Britain at war with Russia
e	autumn 1854	Russians defeated
f	November 1854	arrived in Scutari with 38 female nurses
g	1907	received a medal
h	1910	died on 13 August

9   This note-completion exercise is also very typical of what students will find in the IGCSE Listening exam. Ensure that students read the notes carefully before they listen. You could ask them first to predict the type of answers required – for example, a number, a place, a noun.

Answers	
a academic	f Germany
b hospitals and nursing	g 1853
	h 38 nurses
c considered suitable for a well-educated woman	i large number of casualties
	j medal
d Greece	k blind
e Egypt	

10 Students compare their answers in pairs, then check them against the transcript.

C Reading

11 Students are asked to speculate on what the Florence Nightingale Foundation does. You may have to give some help with the word *foundation*.

12 Some of these words are quite demanding, so allow students time to discuss them, and to make use of their dictionaries.

13 Students scan the text and complete each gap with a word or phrase from Exercise **12**.

> **Answers**
> | | | | |
> |---|---|---|---|
> | a | universally | e | envisaged |
> | b | founder | f | footsteps |
> | c | pay tribute | g | broaden |
> | d | memorial | h | observe trends |

14 Students check their answers with a classmate.

15 Make sure students identify the key words before they write anything.

> **Answers**
> a 1820
> b because she led the way in modern nursing
> c they decided to set up an educational foundation
> d to help nurses follow the example set by Florence Nightingale
> e because of the 1914–18 war
> f London
> g gives them the opportunity to develop professionally through travel
> h by writing to the Foundation or visiting one of the websites listed

16 Students check their answers with a classmate.

D Speaking and vocabulary

17 & 18 The letters ICRC stand for the International Committee of the Red Cross. However, like other organisations which make up the Red Cross and Red Crescent Movement, the ICRC often use their initials rather than their full name, since the final C could stand for either *cross* or *crescent* (in some countries, the use of *cross* rather than *crescent* could cause offence, and vice versa). Students should be able to come up with plenty of ideas about what the ICRC does.

19 There is some quite demanding vocabulary here, so give students the time they need to check the meanings.

20 This is purely a prediction exercise, and there are no right or wrong answers. However, it should be interesting to establish what students think. They will, of course, be able to check their predictions when they hear the interview in Exercise **21**.

E Listening 2

CD 2,
Track 1

21 Students listen to the interview and check the predictions they made in Exercise **20**.

22 Students listen a second time and complete the notes.

> **Answers**
> | | | | |
> |---|---|---|---|
> | a | famine | l | medical care |
> | b | drought | m | before |
> | c | economic crisis | n | after |
> | d | political instability | o | seeds |
> | e | ethnic | p | tools |
> | f | political | q | cholera |
> | g | economic | r | typhoid |
> | h | food | s | construction |
> | i | water | t | engineering |
> | j | essential goods | u | humanitarian work |
> | k | hygiene | v | stress/pressure |

23 Students check their answers in pairs. You may also wish to let them read the transcript.

F Speaking

24 Students should now be able to provide a lot more information about the ICRC. As an extension to this exercise, students could prepare a talk which you could video or record.

25 & 26 These types of topic-based questions are typical of what students may be asked in the IGCSE Speaking examination.

G Further practice

27 See assessment criteria for Extended writing on page **xii**.

28 You will need to give your students time to prepare for this, either in class or as a homework exercise.

29 You may need to advise your students on a suitable radio channel to listen to, or a suitable website for on-line listening. The BBC site offers a reliable service: www.bbc.co.uk/worldservice.

30 Students should complete the application form with their own personal details, and write a short paragraph explaining why they want to do the course.

 Workbook exercises

Vocabulary

1 provide care
restore health
alleviate suffering
diagnose and treat common illnesses
prescribe and dispense medicines
perform minor surgery
promote people's health
prevent illness

2 a alleviate suffering
  b provide care
  c diagnose and treat common illnesses
  d perform minor surgery
  e promote people's health

Reading

5 a marsupial
  b mammal
  c immature
  d pouch
  e rear
  f obstacles
  g bulky
  h survive

6 a Paragraph 5
  b Paragraph 2
  c Paragraph 6
  d Paragraph 1
  e Paragraph 4
  f Paragraph 3

7 a it represents progress
  b wallabies
  c 2 cm long
  d in its mother's pouch
  e by using its tail
  f walking or moving backwards easily
  g it rests in the shade

Listening

10 a D
b G
c A
d E
e B
f F
g H
h C

11 A small
B snakes
C Predators
D smallest
E No
F 10 per cent, extinct
G three, sites
H conservation

 Language

13

	s	p	e	c	i	e	s	
			a	n	i	m	a	l
c	o	n	s	e	r	v	a	t	i	o	n
				l	i	z	a	r	d
	b	i	r	d				
	f	r	o	g				
		i	n	s	e	c	t	
			m	a	m	m	a	l
	r	e	p	t	i	l	e	
	s	n	a	k	e			
		t	a	i	l			

The word which means 'our surroundings' is *environment*.

14 a an offer
b an obligation
c past habit
d 'if' structure

15 For example:
a We should get up earlier.
b Every morning he would catch a bus to town.
c I should/would like to visit you next week.
d If I had the money I would buy a yacht.
e Would you like a lift?

Unit 15: Exam practice

This is the third of four examination-practice units. This unit focuses on examination Exercises 1 and 2 (reading), 4 and 5 (reading and writing), 6 and 7 (writing) and listening.

Coursebook exercises

Reading: Exam Exercises 1 and 2

1

Answers

a very limited
b shower
c wastes more water than one person needs to drink in a week
d vegetables are washed with the plug in the sink
e if they have leaks
f because they undergo regular training in environmental issues

2

Answers

a airways close, making it difficult to breathe
b any two from: exercise, environmental factors, emotional situations
c partly inherited, partly environmental factors
d their asthma may disappear or cease to be a problem, but may return in later life
e increases or differences in environmental pollutants may be responsible
f relievers and preventers
g any two from: relievers used during an attack, preventers taken regularly over a period of time; reliever medication inhaled, preventer medication may be inhaled or taken as tablets; relievers re-open blocked airways, preventers reduce over-sensitivity
h any two from: support organisations, patient groups, doctor, specialist nurse, pharmacist

Reading and writing: Exam Exercises 4 and 5

1

Possible answers

Two notes under each heading.
  For example:
a Maldives: development of tourism
   • attempted to avoid tourism's negative effects on local economy and environment
   • strict controls on development of resorts
   • only certain islands can be developed
b Maldives: scuba-diving
   • plenty of dive sites
   • one of best diving regions in world
   • warm water
   • excellent visibility up to 50 m
   • abundance of sea life
c Mauritius and Réunion: geography
   • volcanic islands
   • beautiful beaches
   • lunar-like landscapes
   • central plateau of Mauritius surrounded by mountains
d Seychelles: the islands
   • more than 90 islands
   • abundant in coral reefs
   • 40 are mountainous
   • over 50 are coral islands
   • only largest islands inhabited
   • tropical climate (heavy rainfall but plentiful vegetation)

2 Students should include some/all of the following details in their paragraph summary.

> **Possible answers**
>
> The development of pizza up to and including 1858
> - Romans baked bread called *picea*
> - by end of first millennium, word *pizza* in use
> - pizza at this time very different from what we eat today
> - 1858 recipe describes pizza similar to today's food
> - also mentions folded pizza, known today as *calzone*
>
> The popularity of pizza today
> - pizza in *Guinness Book of World Records*
> - society of pizza-makers organises competitions
> - pizza eaten all over the world
> - delivery services available in many towns and cities
> - supermarkets sell frozen pizza as well as ingredients for making pizza at home

Listening

CD 2,
Track 2

> **Answers**
>
> | | |
> |---|---|
> | **a** 2.5 million | **g** budgets |
> | **b** killed | **h** research |
> | **c** injured | **i** cyclists |
> | **d** air pollution | **j** bus users |
> | **e** World Health | **k** cars banned |
> | Organization | **l** derelict |
> | **f** economic | |

Workbook exercises

Reading: Exam Exercise 1

a the ancient cities of Petra in Jordan and the oases in Saudi Arabia
b any time of the year
c in the National Museum
d $92
e Egypt
f Kenya and Gabon
g Hammamet, Tunisia
h telephone or visit the website

Reading: Exam Exercise 2

a outside front doors, on balconies and inside the home
b the right soil mix, a fertiliser and plenty of irrigation
c books and the local garden centre
d the temperature
e because of local climate conditions and local demand
f by its height
g because they are not yet established
h roots are loosened from the soil and leaves and branches may get knocked and broken
i they provide a tropical atmosphere, they are tolerant of a wide range of interior conditions, they are practically maintenance-free, they need only a little sunlight and a little water
j they grow too much
k advantage: easy to control / no leaves to clear up disadvantage: can grow very tall in a small area of land

Reading and writing: Exam Exercise 4

Two notes under each heading. For example:
a Three billion years ago
- did not exist as a separate continent
- connected to South America and Australia
b Between 150 million and 70 million years ago
- separation of continents
- Antarctica became isolated
- land mammals began to populate all the continents of the world
- trees suited to cooler temperatures flourished

Level 2, Part 3

c Between four and one million years ago
- trees died out
- Antarctica became glaciated

d 1977–today
- covered by polar ice
- fossils show plant and animal life
- susceptible to earthquakes

 **Listening**

Track 6

a if one side got scratched you could still use the other side

b video cassettes

c in the early 1990s

d 'layer' them, remove moving pictures

e a DVD will play only in a DVD player, DVD recorders are expensive

Unit 16: Focus on reading skills

Exam Exercises 1 and 2

Coursebook exercises

A Speaking and vocabulary

1   Most students should be able to add more to the list, even if they do not have access to e-mail or a mobile phone.

Answers

tomorrow	just for today
parent watching	bad hair day
away from computer	really unhappy
'bye for now	

2 & 3   Allow students to discuss these points for as long as they wish. There are no right or wrong answers.

4   Students predict what they are going to read about.

5   This is a matching exercise which students should complete on their own, without their dictionaries.

Answers

a	abbreviations	d	sloppy	g	concise
b	evolved	e	lexicon	h	jargon
c	missives	f	signify	i	threat

6   Students check their answers and refer to their dictionaries if necessary.

B Reading

7   Students scan the text, identify the words from Exercise **5** needed to complete the gaps, then check their answers in pairs.

Answers

a	lexicon	f	evolved
b	jargon	g	concise
c	sloppy	h	missives
d	threat	i	abbreviations
e	signify		

8   Students refer back to the predictions they made in Exercise **4**.

9

Answers

a   the jargon and symbols
b   sloppy pronunciation
c   to keep down costs, speed up response times and inject emotion into messages
d   the new shorthand style
e   because letters will be replaced by messages
f   because intonation is important in very brief messages
g   it shows that you are joking and not being nasty
h   46 per cent
i   dropping grammar and replacing sentences with abbreviations
j   the ability to separate themselves even more from adults

C Writing

10 Many ideas will come from the text, but encourage students to think of their own points as well.

Advantages	Disadvantages
adults find them difficult to understand	poses threat to language
reduce message costs	difficult to improve literacy skills
speed up response times	writing skills not improving
inject emotion	language is being damaged
new ways of expressing emotions	letter-writing skills becoming obsolete

11 Students use their notes from the previous exercise to write a short paragraph.

D Speaking and vocabulary

12 Encourage students to work quickly to make a list of the different functions on a mobile phone. You could make this into a team competition.

13 Give your students time to think about the various possibilities in this matching exercise.

A	B
store	contact information
make	tasks or to-do lists
keep	track of appointments
set	reminders
use	the built-in calculator
send or receive	e-mails
get	information from the Internet
play	games
watch	TV
send	text messages
integrate	other devices

14 Students look at the first part of the text and check their answers to the matching exercise above. Get them to think about the functions on their own phones, and how many they actually use.

15 The words in the wordsearch are taken from the text the students will read, but all of them should be familiar. Once students have found the ten words, do a quick check to make sure they understand what they mean – perhaps use your own or a student's mobile phone to indicate the various components.

> **Answers**
> horizontal: keyboard, microphone, wireless
> vertical: memory, antenna, speaker
> diagonal: digital, radio, battery, display

E Reading

16 Students read the text and complete the gaps using the words they found in the wordsearch.

> **Answers**
> a radio   f microphone
> b wireless   g speaker
> c digital   h battery
> d antenna   i memory
> e keyboard   j display

17 Get students to find and underline the key words in each question, and then write their answers.

> **Answers**
> a 11 (counting sending and receiving as two functions)
> b it's actually a radio
> c telephone and wireless
> d processes millions of calculations or compresses and decompresses the voice stream
> e handles everything for the keyboard and display, deals with command and control signalling, co-ordinates the rest of the phone's functions
> f by the radio frequency and power section
> g because of the number of features in the phone

F Speaking

18 & 19 These exercises should lead into a general discussion about mobile phone technology, and the advantages and disadvantages of using mobile phones.

G Further practice

20

> **Answers**
> mind your language
> unfortunately
> anyone
> teachers are watching
> way cool
> pet dog
> staring at a screen for 15 hours

21 See assessment criteria for Extended writing on page xii.

22

> **Answers**
> a within five years
> b it is no bigger than a car radio or cassette player
> c share prices, traffic updates, details of nearest petrol stations, restaurants, hotels, shops, football results
> d next year
> e they will be able to download audio books
> f system will indicate nearest hospital
> g about £2,000 to buy it and £20 per month to link to the Internet

23 Make sure your students are confident in using language to give directions, i.e. using imperatives (*do this, don't do that*), and prepositions of place/location (*on the left, at the bottom*), before they do this pairwork exercise.

Workbook exercises

 Vocabulary

1 horizontal: jargon
vertical: missives, concise, signify
diagonal: lexicon, threat, evolved, sloppy

2 a evolved
b missives
c sloppy
d lexicon
e signify
f concise
g jargon
h threat

Reading 1

5

Public transport	Places of interest	Leisure activities	Food
fare	Reichstag	clubs	cuisine
trams	Palace of Princesses	entertainment	eaterie
U-Bahn	Olympic Stadium	shopping	tasty
S-Bahn			restaurants

7 a U-Bahn, S-Bahn, trams
b single-fare ticket
c at midnight
d for the Olympic Games in 1936
e in Bonn
f at 10.00 p.m.

Reading 2

10 architectural plans have been shown

11

A	B
variable	different
dome	hemisphere
piloted	tested
suburban	out of the town centre
constructed	built
hexagonal	six-sided
adjusted	changed
enhance	strengthen
morale	feelings
impact	effect

 Writing 2

12 a are variable-sized classrooms and glass domes
   b 180
   c will be built to save space
   d have outdoor classrooms
   e it can be adjusted according to the number in the group being taught
   f light and airy effect, using materials which enhance sunlight
   g believed they will have a positive impact
   h are expected to have a working life of 30–60 years

Language

13 For example:
   a may not, should not
   b could, may
   c must, should
   d must not, can't
   e would, might
   f might, would
   g Should
   h can't, won't

Unit 17: Focus on reading and writing skills

Exam Exercises 4 and 5

Coursebook exercises

A Speaking and vocabulary

1   There is an environmental theme to this unit. This quiz is designed to encourage students to think – it does not matter if they are not sure about the answers. They will find out if they are right or wrong later in the unit.

2   The newspaper headlines are all genuine. Spend some time with students thinking about what the content of the articles might be; this should initiate general discussion which can be continued with the question prompts (a–c).

3

Words	Definitions
shrinking	becoming smaller
severe	serious, worrying
rapid	very fast
pollution	dirtying, contamination
meltdown	process in which something turns from solid to a liquid
latitudes	areas of the globe
fossil	something preserved in rock
flourish	to grow well and be healthy
consistent	is the same as or follows the same pattern as

4

Answers

c	o	n	s	i	s	t	e	n	t	
f	l	o	u	r	i	s	h			
		r	a	p	i	d				
m	e	l	t	d	o	w	n			
		s	h	r	i	n	k	i	n	g
		p	o	l	l	u	t	i	o	n
	f	o	s	s	i	l				
		l	a	t	i	t	u	d	e	s
	s	e	v	e	r	e				

The area of the globe revealed by the shaded area is *North Pole*.

B Reading

5   Students skim the text and choose an appropriate headline from Exercise **2**. They should say why they have chosen it. The original headline was *North Pole icecap melts as global warming increases*.

6

Answers

a	True	e	False	i	False
b	True	f	True	j	False
c	True	g	True	k	True
d	True	h	True		

7   Students look back at the list they made in Exercise **2** and check whether anything they wrote appears in the text. They then add new information to their list.

Level 2, Part 4

8 Students are again encouraged to identify the key words in questions before attempting to answer them.

9

> **Answers**
> a 55 million years ago
> b gases are released by burning fossil fuels, which then trap heat in the atmosphere and warm the Earth
> c there was no ice at the North Pole
> d the Gulf Stream
> e because of evidence from fossils
> f it will eventually disappear completely
> g human activities
> h there is no agreement after 2012
> i greenhouse emissions must be reduced
> j it will disappear completely

10 Students combine their ideas to produce a model answer for each question.

C Writing

11 Students should look at the question carefully and identify exactly what information needs to be summarised.

12 The text is quite challenging and there is a lot of detail in it, but only a limited amount of information is required to answer the question satisfactorily. Encourage students to remember that they need only find information about two aspects of the text: the melting of the polar icecap, and the 1997 Kyoto climate-change agreement. Has the sample answer done this? Ask students to give reasons for their opinions.

13 This is a note-taking exercise. Students should look at the notes carefully before reading the text again.

> **Answers**
> a James McCarthy
> b oceanographer
> c 3 metres
> d 2–3 degrees
> e Greenland icecap
> f reduce greenhouse emissions
> g no agreement
> h reduce greenhouse emissions to 60 per cent of 1990 levels by 2050

D Speaking and vocabulary

14 This is a prediction exercise. The phrases should lead students to the conclusion that the text is going to be about a hot country with a water problem.

15 Once the topic has been established in Exercise 14, students should be able to think of other related vocabulary and phrases.

16 This vocabulary is demanding, so students will probably need to refer frequently to their dictionaries.

E Reading

17 & 18 Students skim and then scan the text and check if their predictions in Exercises 14 and 15 were correct.

19

> **Answers**
> a barren   e dislocation
> b outskirts   f swathes
> c Drought   g sporadic
> d play down   h conserve

20

> **Answers**
> a because he has no crops and no cattle
> b the soil crumbles to dust and then disappears in the wind
> c it is dirty
> d it has given a 9.5-billion-rupee relief package and has asked for public donations
> e because it has not rained for three years
> f from a government tanker that distributes water two or three times a week
> g some use tin pots on their heads and other tie bags to their bicycles
> h there are areas of green in the baked brown landscape
> i the towns are full of traffic and the fruit and vegetable markets are full of goods
> j they hope that it will collect more water when the rains return

F Writing

21 Students focus on the question and think about what is required.

22 Students look at the text again and identify the key points. They then make notes, using their own words as far as possible, about these key points. They should compare their notes in pairs. The information students need is in paragraphs 5 and 6. Their notes should be similar to the following:

> **Possible answer**
> • water distributed from government tanker
> • comes two/three times each week
> • tanker empties water into trough
> • at end of day villagers walk towards town to meet the tanker
> • some carry tin pots on their head
> • others use bags on bicycles
> • farmers walk all day to find water for their cattle
> • sometimes takes one or two hours to find
> • others go to the city

23 Students write their summary.

> **Possible answer**
> Two or three times a week, the villagers of Jamnagar walk towards the town at the end of the day to meet the government tanker that delivers water. The water is put into a trough, from where the local villagers fill their tin pots, which they carry home on their heads. Some of them use bags tied to their bicycles. The farmers walk all day to find water for their cattle. Others go to the city to find water. (79 words)

G Speaking

24 & 25 It is often said that water, not oil or anything else, will cause the next global conflict. Do your students know this? Are your students aware of the global shortage of water? Encourage them to discuss and speculate, and to be prepared to give reasons for their opinions.

H Further practice

26 & 27

> **Answers**
> Various answers are possible.

28 The main point of this exercise is to develop writing skills, but your students need also to include some graphics or visuals to support their writing and create their leaflet. You could bring some information leaflets to class to give your students an idea of what is required.

Answers

Results of hyponatraemia
- apathy and lethargy
- dizziness and mental confusion
- nausea

People at risk
- very young and very old
- people who exercise for a long time
- people in nightclubs

Advice about drinking water
- everyone should drink water, especially during hot and humid weather
- we should drink liquids with carbohydrates in them
- drink sports drinks when exercising

Workbook exercises

📖 Reading 1

5 a significant
   b low self-esteem
   c peer pressure
   d factors
   e reluctant
   f diagnosing
   g body image
   h self-conscious
   i acknowledge
   j genuine

6 a They are becoming much more aware of the warning signs. (paragraph 4)
   b They also have to have a genuine desire to get better. (paragraph 6)
   c ... it is hard for a doctor to diagnose an eating disorder. (paragraph 3)
   d Males face similar peer pressure ... (paragraph 2)
   e If a male has a well-muscled body ... (paragraph 3)
   f ... significant increases (paragraph 1)

7 a no government department or agency has collected any statistics
   b low self-esteem
   c their problems / their feelings
   d diagnose the diseases in males
   e increased public information and awareness
   f they could cause boys to be more self-conscious
   g acknowledge and recognise the problems

✏️ Writing 1

8 a Fruit can reduce the risk of certain illnesses.
   b Controlled consumption of starch is fine as it reduces fat and increases fibre.
   c Snacks and sweets, if limited, shouldn't affect a balanced diet.
   d Meat, fish and pulses are important sources of protein.
   e Drinking enough water is a vital part of a healthy diet.
   f Dairy products are essential for strong bones and healthy teeth.

Reading 2

9 Students may be surprised at all the things that coconuts are used for! Give them a limited amount of time to brainstorm.

10 a setting sail
  b reluctance
  c solitude
  d luring
  e verdant
  f entices
  g seek refuge
  h double
  i debris
  j husks

 Writing 2

13 a Arabian Sea
  b in the east
  c wooded hills, coastal beaches
  d tourism
  e fishing
  f coconut farming
  g drinks
  h flavouring sweets or curries
  i oil
  j 45 days
  k Thiruvananthapuram
  l Cochin
  m Thrissur
  n 30

14 Various answers are possible, but students should include most of the information from the notes they made in Exercise 13.

 Language

15 For example:
  a Temperatures are higher this year, but in spite of this they are still below average for this time of year.
  b He studied very hard. Nevertheless, he failed to obtain the grade he needed.

  c She worked very hard until late last night. However, she did not manage to finish off the project.
  d In spite of filling the tank before they left, they ran out of petrol.
  e People on the island are extremely friendly in spite of being quite cut off from the rest of the world.
  f She speaks at least four languages. However, she is not fluent in any of them.
  g His doctor told him to go on a strict diet. Nevertheless, he chose to ignore the advice.
  h The team played very well all year. However, they didn't do so in their last match.

16 For example:

Fruit	Dairy products	Liquids	Meat/fish	Cereals
bananas	*cheese*	*cola*	beef	wheat
apples	milk	milk	lamb	corn
apricots	butter	water	cod	rice
pears	yoghurt	juice	shark	barley
mangoes	cream	squash	mutton	millet
papayas		tea		
pineapples		coffee		

18 a bananas are not round
  b chicken is poultry
  c elephants don't live in cold climates
  d cats are pets
  e China is not part of the same land mass
  f drought has no water

19 a chicken
  b cat
  c beef
  d India
  e bananas
  f donkey
  g droughts
  h penguin

Unit 18: Focus on writing skills

Exam Exercises 6 and 7

Coursebook exercises

A Speaking

1 Initiate a discussion about chewing gum, covering the points raised.

2 & 3 Encourage students to speculate. It does not matter if they are not sure. In fact, all the statements are true. Students should think about the statements and consider which ones (if any) surprise them.

B Writing

4 This writing exercise will encourage students to write to a strict word limit. The eleven statements contain about 100 words. Ask your students to paraphrase and to use their own words as far as possible, and to remember to use linking words rather than simply writing a list.

5 Students check each other's work. By now, they should be very clear about what to look for.

C Speaking and vocabulary

6 Students speculate.

> **Answers**
> The correct answer is **b**.

7 This vocabulary list is demanding, so allow students plenty of time to check meanings.

8 Students will confirm the order of these sentences in Exercise 11.

9 Encourage students to speculate and to think carefully about what they are going to read.

D Reading

10 Students scan the text and check whether their prediction in Exercise 6 was correct.

11 Students look at the text again and complete the gaps (**a–j**) with a word from Exercise 7. They then decide which sentence from Exercise 8 goes first in each paragraph. This will confirm (or otherwise!) the order they chose earlier.

> **Answers**
> Sentences:
> **1 c** (*Our cities are …*)
> **2 a** (*City councils …*)
> **3 b** (*In Birmingham …*)
> **4 d** (*The Tidy Britain Group …*)
> Words:
> **a** hideous
> **b** discarded
> **c** dislodging
> **d** defacers
> **e** blight
> **f** lingers
> **g** draconian
> **h** culprits
> **i** envisage
> **j** urging

12

> **Answers**
> a because the pavements are covered with black spots of chewing gum
> b this is where young people tend to socialise
> c gumbuster machines which spray hot or cold pressurised water, and a trigger spray which shoots out a citrus-based oil
> d because the machines spray out water everywhere and people would get wet
> e when the black spots are removed, white patches are left
> f it is difficult to see and catch people dropping gum on the pavements
> g the gum would need to be wrapped in paper first, otherwise it would stick to the bins, and young people are unlikely to use them

13 Students compare their answers and produce a model response.

E Writing

14–19 Students should read the question carefully and decide what they have to do. They then go through the various stages of writing: planning and making notes, drafting, and so on. Students should work in pairs, exchanging ideas and checking each other's work at every stage. Advise students that they are not required to lay out their answer to look like a newspaper/magazine article.

F Reading

20 & 21 This text is quite long and demanding, and there will no doubt be quite a few words with which students need help. Encourage them to use the context as far as possible, and to ask each other for help. They should also make use of their dictionaries.

G Speaking

22 & 23 The content of the article should provide students with plenty of material for discussion and speculation.

H Writing

24–26 See notes on Exercises **14–19** above.

I Further practice

27 See assessment criteria for Extended writing on page **xii**.

28

> **Answers**
> a he works on Saturdays as a DJ
> b because of the construction boom
> c because of the number of homeless people on the streets
> d early in the morning of the day before the pick-up
> e in case of a shortage, or someone getting married who might need something in their new home
> f the taps and metal piping
> g ordinary household refuse and debris from building sites
> h they will be cannibalised
> i because the professionals always take anything worth having early on

29

> **Answers**
> Various answers are possible.

30 See assessment criteria for Extended writing on page **xii**.

Workbook exercises

 Reading 1

3 Girls play a more participatory role than passive one.

4 For example:
   a Girls can't leave some tasks to boys.
   b Girls are not distracted by boys.
   c Girls do better academically.

6 **a** lines 21–22 (*They plan careers in Maths, Science and Technology four times more often*)
   b lines 22–23 (*They score 30 per cent higher in tests*)
   c lines 4–5 (*Girls' self-esteem and confidence ... fall during the middle-school years*)
   d line 9 (*lowered teacher expectations*)
   e line 15 (*Girls experience the freedom to speak out*)
   f lines 23–25 (*almost 100 per cent of school-leavers from girls' schools go on to university and they are twice as likely to earn doctorates*)
   g lines 2–3 (*many girls attending co-educational ... schools do not receive equal opportunities*)
   h line 8 (*fewer opportunities to participate*)

✎ Writing 1

7 • Read the question carefully.
   • Make sure you follow the instructions.
   • Look for the main points and key words of the question.
   • Plan what you are going to write first.
   • Make sure your answer is relevant to the question.
   • Check the number of words you have written.

8 The second one, because it first introduces the topic and prepares the reader for the contents of the article.

10 The first one, because it considers both sides of the issue before coming to a conclusion.

📖 Reading 2

13 **a** *In so-called advanced countries,*
   b *Not so in the developing world.*
   c *As recycling has become the craze across the world,*
   d *But even Egypt*
   e *Al Attar Street in downtown Cairo*

14 **a** any four from: cell phone, VCR, DVD player, PS, radio, watch, camera
   b circuits, keyboards, compact-disc lenses
   c because recycling is a necessity – when something fails, they can't afford just to buy a new one
   d cheap electronics are arriving from China
   e they buy a whole product and disassemble it

🧊 Language

17 For example:
   a I'd rather not lend you the money.
   b I'd rather watch TV than go for a walk.
   c I'd rather not eat anything now, sorry.
   d I'd rather go to the cinema than the theatre.
   e I'd rather go on Monday as I am not so busy that day.
   f I'd rather not speak, actually.

18–20

A	B	C	D
huge shop	hypermarket	basement	basement
come out	emerge	battered	battered
unusual	exotic	emerge	emerge
doctor	surgeon	exotic	exotic
lucky	fortunate	flats	flats
lacking a job	unemployment	fortunate	fortunate
apartments	flats	hopeless	hopeless
cellar	basement	hypermarket	hypermarket
rules	regulations	regulations	regulations
broken	battered	stacked	stacked
piled	stacked	surgeon	surgeon
impossible	hopeless	unemployment	unemployment

Unit 19: Focus on listening skills

Listening exercises

Coursebook exercises

A Speaking

1–3 These exercises are for discussion and speculation.

4 Students read the statements and decide whether they are true. They should be prepared to give their reasons.

5 & 6 More prompts for discussion and speculation.

B Listening

CD 2,
Track 3

7 The vocabulary items are all connected – the theme is 'clothing'. Allow students to use their dictionaries to check meanings.

8 Finding key words should have become automatic by now!

9–11 Students listen twice and answer the questions. They then check with a classmate.

Answers
a the fibres
b four (spin, weave, cut, sew)
c GHK: mobile phone and MP3 technology
  Conte: designed clothes
  Jeane Company: made clothes
d in the hood or collar
e the MP3 player will stop
f using a keyboard hidden beneath a pocket flap
g from clothes from all over the world
h military uniforms
i a face-recognition camera

j would provide information about a person when you meet them again, and parents could keep an eye on their children
k because of all the built-in technology, which could make them look ugly

C Writing

12–15 The planning, note-making and drafting processes should be clear for all students by now. Let students read all the entries and decide which one should win first prize.

D Listening

CD 2,
Track 4

16–18

Answers
a shoes made to fit your feet only
b a Ferrari car, a Gucci handbag
c none
d any three from: small, dark, cramped, full of antique-looking tools and rolls of leather, 'old-fashioned' smell
e the technology is completely unchanged
f at least three times
g shoemaker draws round your foot and takes four measurements
h a wooden model of the foot
i clients do not want new fashions

Level 2, Part 4

E Reading

19 Students predict the text content from the list of words.

20 Students complete the gaps in the text using suitable words from the list in Exercise **19**.

> **Answers**
> a photo shoot   e make-up artist
> b fashion-dominated   f commercials
> c supermodel   g exotic location
> d auditions

21 Students identify the key words, and then answer the questions.

> **Answers**
> a in the Seychelles
> b people in more than 25 million homes twice a week
> c actress and supermodel
> d a series of auditions
> e four (stylist/designer, make-up artist, fashion photographer, Malaika Arora)
> f India and Sri Lanka

F Speaking

22 Students think back to their earlier predictions about changes in fashion and decide whether they still feel the same way.

G Further practice

23 See assessment criteria for Extended writing on page xii.

24–26

> **Answers**
> Various answers are possible.

Workbook exercises

Thinking and vocabulary

3 From top to bottom: c, g, h, f, a, e, b, d

Listening
Track 7

7

A	B
PA	personal assistant
relevant	connected
vital	very important
deadline	time something must be completed by
invaluable	necessary
fickle	changeable
options	choices
on the pulse	up to date

9 a on a website
 b Marketing Assistant
 c a lot of relevant work experience, and a large contacts list
 d communication skills, computer skills and meeting deadlines
 e so you can see which part of the industry you want to go into
 f jobs and opportunities
 g limit your options
 h it will help you to keep in touch

Writing 1

11 a Why do you think you were so suitable for the job?
 b How important was it that you went to university?
 c Such as?
 d What steps would you recommend to someone who wanted to go into the world of fashion?
 e What else?
 f What do you mean, exactly?
 g what other advice can you give our listeners?

Reading and vocabulary

14

Reasons for school uniforms	Reasons against school uniforms
create atmosphere of pride, loyalty, equality	erases individuality
image of professionalism	
businesslike approach to learning	
no fashion dilemma	
involve students more	
make them feel part of a team	
cost	
children avoid being laughed at because of clothes	

19

a	c	o	n	f	i	d	e	n	t	
b		c	a	r	e	e	r			
c			s	h	y					
d			p	h	o	t	o	g	r	a	p	h
e		b	u	y	i	n	g			
f	f	a	c	t	o	r	y			
g			n	e	r	v	o	u	s	

 # Writing 2

16 There are many reasons given, so students should make sure they keep to the word limit.

Language

18

a *retailing*   sale to a consumer
   buying   purchasing something with money
b *marketing*   promoting or advertising something before it is sold
   selling   offering something for money
c *styling*   giving something its own characteristics
   designing   creating the initial product
d *career*   a job you are trained for and plan to follow for the rest of your life
   job   something you do where earning a salary is the priority
e *picture*   could be printed, painted, drawn, etc.
   photograph   taken by a camera
f *industry*   general word used for an area of business in which a product is made or sold
   factory   where a product is made
g *shy*   uncomfortable with other people
   nervous   frightened of a situation or certain people, etc.
h *confident*   calm and unworried about people or situations
   brave   feeling strong about confronting a particular situation

Unit 20: Exam practice

This final exam-practice unit takes the form of a complete examination paper.

Coursebook exercises

Reading: Exam Exercise 1

> **Answers**
> 1 nutritional information on the food label/labels
> 2 medium
> 3 choose these foods
> 4 on the front of (some) packs
> 5 they show levels of salt, sugar, fat and saturated fat
> 6 to eat small amounts / eat occasionally
> 7 canned soups and TV dinners
> 8 MSG / monosodium glutamate

Reading: Exam Exercise 2

> **Answers**
> 1 30,000 hectares
> 2 any three from: large rivers, clear streams, waterfalls, red soil, bright green jungle
> 3 100 different species of trees, more than 2,000 identified plant species, more than 400 species of birds, mammals and reptiles
> 4 all sorts, from couples and honeymooners, to larger groups of family and friends, young and old
> 5 come with a private group of friends
> 6 contact local travel agent or direct
> 7 plane and four-wheel drive vehicle
> 8 distance is further

> 9 any six from: observing wildlife, walking photo safari, discovering forest waterfalls, driving through the jungle, exploring local villages, relaxing, strolling through gardens, eating, drinking
> 10 wood stoves provide heating
> 11 electric generator, kerosene lamps
> 12 13 (4 × 2 = 8, plus 5)

Reading and writing: Exam Exercise 3

Summer ...
Volunteer helper application...

Use BLOCK CAPITALS in Section A – Part 1

Section A – Part 1

Surname:	ANDREOU
Initials:	N
Address:	32 KALYMNOU STREET, NICOSIA, CYPRUS
e-mail:	NEK@CYPRUS.MED
Age:	17

Section A – Part 2

Number of camps attended: 2

Total time spent at camp (please circle one):
- less than four weeks
- four to eight weeks
- more than eight weeks

Camp location (please underline):
   Nicosia   Troodos   Rome

Most children from: Rome / Italy

Ages taught   6–8 ☐   8–12 ✓   12–16 ☐
(please tick one):

Activities taught: Football
Other duties: Teaching English / English conversation

Did you...
please s...

What v...
the can...

Sectio...
In the s...
saying ...

helper application form

Did you experience any problems at the camp? If YES, please specify what they were:

> YES Very hot, no swimming pool
> No mobile signal, could not contact family

What was the best thing about your previous work at the camp?

> Free time speaking Italian to students

Section B

In the space below, write one sentence of 12–20 words, saying why you want to work at the camp again.

> [Various answers are possible.]

Reading and writing: Exam Exercise 4

Answers

Two notes under each heading. For example:

a Cost and aim
  • £200 million
  • to find evidence of life on another planet
b Research equipment on *Beagle 2*
  • cameras
  • drill
  • 'mole'
  • instruments for analysing soil samples
c Landing on Mars
  • lander protected by heat shield
  • parachutes will slow lander's descent
  • gas-filled bags to cushion landing
d Water on Mars
  • water once flowed on Mars
  • pictures show evidence
  • huge quantities of water may be trapped under the surface
  • *Mars Express* will search using radar
  • if there is water, there may be life

Reading and writing: Exam Exercise 5

Answers

What the system will do
  • aerial system to protect Brazilian rainforest
  • monitor meteorological data and aerial activity
  • project 95 per cent ready
  • jobs for 1,000 experts
  • system will catalogue and map Amazonian land
  • detect forest fires and deforestation
  • locate illegal airstrips

Writing: Exam Exercises 6 and 7

See assessment criteria for Extended writing on page xii.

Listening

CD 2,
Tracks 5–9

Note: The exercise and question numbers follow those given on the CD.

Answers

Questions 1–6
1 a sales
  b Tuesday 10 a.m.
2 so Mary can watch her favourite wildlife programmes
3 half-price tickets only sold on day of performance
4 very heavy traffic is expected
5 a 2–3 weeks
  b go to other branch
6 problems with fridges

Question 7

7
a 9 a.m.
b 6 p.m.
c checking systems
d feeding fish
e sharks are used to eating fish, not humans
f having to be in the freezing water
g teacher / something in educational side of marine biology
h its international aspect / opportunities for travel

Question 8

8
a reception desk
b welcome party in the dining room
c noticeboard list
d map-reading skills
e camera
f wildlife park
g football match
h farewell party and barbecue

Question 9

9
a any two from: he knows when they are ill, when they're well, when people die, when babies are due
b nobody else has wanted his job
c smallest in region, with twelve children
d because of talking/chatting with people
e when the letter looks important
f they do not know their postman as well as people in the country do

Question 10

10
a it generates its own power, similar to a car
b 224 kw
c any five from: kitchen or galley, electronic systems, hydraulic systems, technical systems, air conditioning, lighting, in-flight entertainment, de-icing systems, water pipes
d to ensure vital systems are powered
e any two from: auxiliary power unit (APU), external power unit (EPU), parking places have own power supply

Workbook exercises

📖 Reading: Exam Exercise 1 (Extended)

a in the Eco class
b in the Eco organic gardens
c the amazing view of Carlstown and the river
d pay a small extra charge
e special meals at reduced prices, children under eight are supervised in the Eco organic gardens, Eco class for children
f any three from: great choice of snacks and drinks, wide range of vegetarian dishes, access for wheelchair users, large-print food menus
g at 7 p.m.

📖 Reading: Exam Exercise 2 (Extended)

a because it is a refreshing change from the beach
b opportunity to breathe in some clean air and enjoy the stunning views
c hikers, bikers, nature lovers and skiers
d any two from: the slopes are not too demanding, the slopes are not long, excellent facilities
e on the western side of Cyprus
f information on the trees, flowers and shrubs
g about 1,700–1,750 m
h churches, monasteries and rustic mountain villages
i Archbishop Makarios III, the first President of Cyprus, was born there
j cherries, plums, apples, grapes and pears
k Agros and Kakopetria
l because of its tragic past, when it was hunted almost to extinction

📖 ✏️ Reading and writing: Exam Exercise 3 (Extended)

Application Form

SECTION A – please complete in block capitals

Surname: ADALLAN   Initial: K   Age: 16

Male/~~Female~~ (please delete as appropriate)

Home address: 46 Ruwi Street, Muscat, Oman

Telephone: 246993   E-mail: kadilrunner@hotmail.glo

SECTION B

Running experience & competitions entered: 100 and 200 metres
Won Oman under-15s 200 metre race two years ago
Won inter-school 100 metre race for students

Name & address of proposed sponsor: Mrs Fatima Indiri,
                              719 Salalah Road, Muscat

Telephone: 246114   E-mail: Doesn't have one

SECTION C

Arrival date and time: 26 June at 6 a.m.

Departure date and time: 28 June at 7 a.m.

Do you require transport?   (YES)   NO

Type of transport: (bus)   plane

Type of ticket (return/single): return

Ticket price enclosed: $ 15

Entry fee enclosed: $28   ($45)

Do you require accommodation?   (YES)   NO

Number of nights: 2

Special food requirements (please list): none

Entertainment (please tick first and second choices):

27 June   ☐ basketball   ☑ film night   ☐ beach walk   ☑ exhibition

28 June   ☐ volleyball   ☐ exhibition   ☐ shopping   ☐ film night

SECTION D

Write one sentence of 12–20 words telling us why you think your application to join our sports day should be accepted.

[For example:]

It would inspire me to become a better athlete as I hope to represent my country abroad in international championships.

📖 ✏️ Reading and writing: Exam Exercise 4 (Extended)

Answers

Two notes under each heading. For example:

a 15th–17th centuries
- whales hunted by Europeans as well as by Eskimos and American Indians
- large fleets of whaling ships built when enormous value of whale products was realised

b 18th century
- over-whaling reduced numbers of whales rapidly

- blubber or fat could be dealt with at sea to prevent ships stopping frequently to offload supplies

c 19th century
- Pacific and Arctic Oceans became the new hunting grounds
- USA dominated the world industry

d present day
- helicopters, sonar and high-powered harpoon guns are used for hunting
- on-board equipment and laboratories process whales in less than an hour

Vauxhall/Opel Vectra
Owners Workshop Manual

John S. Mead

Models covered

Hatchback, Saloon & Estate

Petrol: 1.8 litre (1796cc) & 2.2 litre (2198cc)
Turbo-Diesel: 1.9 litre (1910cc)

Does NOT cover 1.6 litre or 2.0 litre turbo 4-cyl petrol, 2.8 litre V6 petrol, or 3.0 litre V6 diesel engines
Does NOT cover CVTronic transmission or dual fuel models

(4887 - 384)

© **Haynes Publishing 2010**

ABCDE
FGHIJ
KLMNO
PQRST

A book in the **Haynes Owners Workshop Manual Series**

ISBN **978 1 84425 887 1**

British Library Cataloguing in Publication Data
A catalogue record for this book is available from the British Library.

Printed in the USA

Haynes Publishing
Sparkford, Yeovil, Somerset BA22 7JJ, England

Haynes North America, Inc
861 Lawrence Drive, Newbury Park, California 91320, USA

Haynes Publishing Nordiska AB
Box 1504, 751 45 UPPSALA, Sverige

Contents

Contents

REPAIRS AND OVERHAUL

The Vauxhall/Opel Vectra was introduced in the UK in October 1995 as a replacement for the Cavalier. It was originally available in Saloon and Hatchback versions with 1.6, 1.8, 2.0 and 2.5 litre petrol engines and 1.7 litre normally-aspirated diesel engines. The Estate range was launched in October 1996. Since its introduction, the Vectra has had various mechanical revisions and facelifts during the course of the production run. This manual covers versions from October 2005, which were the subject of the third facelift, together with further mechanical revisions. Earlier models are covered in previous editions of the Haynes Vauxhall/Opel Vectra Owners Workshop Manual.

A variety of engines are available in the Vectra range, comprising 1.8 and 2.2 litre petrol engines and 1.9 litre diesel engines. All engines are of the four-cylinder, in-line type, featuring single, or double overhead camshafts. The engines all have fuel injection, and are fitted with a range of emission control systems. 1.6, 2.0 and 2.8 litre petrol, and 3.0 litre diesel engines are also available, but are not covered in this manual.

The Vectra is available in Saloon, Hatchback and Estate body styles, with a wide range of fittings and interior trim depending on the model specification.

Fully-independent front and rear suspension is fitted; the front being of the MacPherson-strut type and the rear being of multi-link design.

According to engine type, the manual gearbox is of the five- or six-speed all synchromesh type, with five- and six-speed electronically-controlled automatic transmissions, and an 'Easytronic' manual/automatic transmission, optionally available on certain models.

A wide range of standard and optional equipment is available within the Vectra range to suit most tastes, including power steering, air conditioning, remote central locking, electric windows, electric sunroof, anti-lock braking system, electronic alarm system and supplemental restraint systems.

For the home mechanic, the Vectra is a relatively straightforward vehicle to maintain, and most of the items requiring frequent attention are easily accessible.

Your Vauxhall/Opel Vectra manual

The aim of this manual is to help you get the best value from your vehicle. It can do so in several ways. It can help you decide what work must be done (even should you choose to get it done by a garage), provide information on routine maintenance and servicing, and give a logical course of action and diagnosis when random faults occur. However, it is hoped that you will use the manual by tackling the work yourself. On simpler jobs, it may even be quicker than booking the car into a garage and going there twice, to leave and collect it. Perhaps most important, a lot of money can be saved by avoiding the costs a garage must charge to cover its labour and overheads.

The manual has drawings and descriptions to show the function of the various components, so that their layout can be understood. Then the tasks are described and photographed in a clear step-by-step sequence.

References to the 'left' or 'right' are in the sense of a person in the driver's seat, facing forward.

Project vehicles

The main vehicle used in the preparation of this manual, and which appears in many of the photographic sequences, was a Vauxhall Vectra Hatchback with a 1.9 litre DOHC diesel engine. Other vehicles included a Vectra Estate with a 1.9 litre SOHC diesel engine and a Vectra Hatchback with a 2.2 litre petrol engine.

Acknowledgements

Certain illustrations are the copyright of Vauxhall Motors Limited, and are used with their permission. Thanks are also due to Draper Tools Limited, who provided some of the workshop tools, and to all those people at Sparkford who helped in the production of this manual.

We take great pride in the accuracy of information given in this manual, but vehicle manufacturers make alterations and design changes during the production run of a particular vehicle of which they do not inform us. No liability can be accepted by the authors or publishers for loss, damage or injury caused by any errors in, or omissions from, the information given.

Working on your car can be dangerous. This page shows just some of the potential risks and hazards, with the aim of creating a safety-conscious attitude.

General hazards

Scalding

• Don't remove the radiator or expansion tank cap while the engine is hot.
• Engine oil, transmission fluid or power steering fluid may also be dangerously hot if the engine has recently been running.

Burning

• Beware of burns from the exhaust system and from any part of the engine. Brake discs and drums can also be extremely hot immediately after use.

Crushing

• When working under or near a raised vehicle, always supplement the jack with axle stands, or use drive-on ramps.
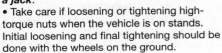
Never venture under a car which is only supported by a jack.
• Take care if loosening or tightening high-torque nuts when the vehicle is on stands. Initial loosening and final tightening should be done with the wheels on the ground.

Fire

• Fuel is highly flammable; fuel vapour is explosive.
• Don't let fuel spill onto a hot engine.
• Do not smoke or allow naked lights (including pilot lights) anywhere near a vehicle being worked on. Also beware of creating sparks (electrically or by use of tools).
• Fuel vapour is heavier than air, so don't work on the fuel system with the vehicle over an inspection pit.
• Another cause of fire is an electrical overload or short-circuit. Take care when repairing or modifying the vehicle wiring.
• Keep a fire extinguisher handy, of a type suitable for use on fuel and electrical fires.

Electric shock

• Ignition HT and Xenon headlight voltages can be dangerous, especially to people with heart problems or a pacemaker. Don't work on or near these systems with the engine running or the ignition switched on.

• Mains voltage is also dangerous. Make sure that any mains-operated equipment is correctly earthed. Mains power points should be protected by a residual current device (RCD) circuit breaker.

Fume or gas intoxication

• Exhaust fumes are poisonous; they can contain carbon monoxide, which is rapidly fatal if inhaled. Never run the engine in a confined space such as a garage with the doors shut.

• Fuel vapour is also poisonous, as are the vapours from some cleaning solvents and paint thinners.

Poisonous or irritant substances

• Avoid skin contact with battery acid and with any fuel, fluid or lubricant, especially antifreeze, brake hydraulic fluid and Diesel fuel. Don't syphon them by mouth. If such a substance is swallowed or gets into the eyes, seek medical advice.
• Prolonged contact with used engine oil can cause skin cancer. Wear gloves or use a barrier cream if necessary. Change out of oil-soaked clothes and do not keep oily rags in your pocket.
• Air conditioning refrigerant forms a poisonous gas if exposed to a naked flame (including a cigarette). It can also cause skin burns on contact.

Asbestos

• Asbestos dust can cause cancer if inhaled or swallowed. Asbestos may be found in gaskets and in brake and clutch linings. When dealing with such components it is safest to assume that they contain asbestos.

Special hazards

Hydrofluoric acid

• This extremely corrosive acid is formed when certain types of synthetic rubber, found in some O-rings, oil seals, fuel hoses etc, are exposed to temperatures above 4000C. The rubber changes into a charred or sticky substance containing the acid. *Once formed, the acid remains dangerous for years. If it gets onto the skin, it may be necessary to amputate the limb concerned.*
• When dealing with a vehicle which has suffered a fire, or with components salvaged from such a vehicle, wear protective gloves and discard them after use.

The battery

• Batteries contain sulphuric acid, which attacks clothing, eyes and skin. Take care when topping-up or carrying the battery.
• The hydrogen gas given off by the battery is highly explosive. Never cause a spark or allow a naked light nearby. Be careful when connecting and disconnecting battery chargers or jump leads.

Air bags

• Air bags can cause injury if they go off accidentally. Take care when removing the steering wheel and trim panels. Special storage instructions may apply.

Diesel injection equipment

• Diesel injection pumps supply fuel at very high pressure. Take care when working on the fuel injectors and fuel pipes.

 Warning: Never expose the hands, face or any other part of the body to injector spray; the fuel can penetrate the skin with potentially fatal results.

Remember...

DO

• Do use eye protection when using power tools, and when working under the vehicle.

• Do wear gloves or use barrier cream to protect your hands when necessary.

• Do get someone to check periodically that all is well when working alone on the vehicle.

• Do keep loose clothing and long hair well out of the way of moving mechanical parts.

• Do remove rings, wristwatch etc, before working on the vehicle – especially the electrical system.

• Do ensure that any lifting or jacking equipment has a safe working load rating adequate for the job.

DON'T

• Don't attempt to lift a heavy component which may be beyond your capability – get assistance.

• Don't rush to finish a job, or take unverified short cuts.

• Don't use ill-fitting tools which may slip and cause injury.

• Don't leave tools or parts lying around where someone can trip over them. Mop up oil and fuel spills at once.

• Don't allow children or pets to play in or near a vehicle being worked on.

The following pages are intended to help in dealing with common roadside emergencies and breakdowns. You will find more detailed fault finding information at the back of the manual, and repair information in the main chapters.

If your car won't start and the starter motor doesn't turn

☐ If it's a model with automatic transmission, make sure the selector is in P or N.
☐ Open the bonnet and make sure that the battery terminals are clean and tight.
☐ Switch on the headlights and try to start the engine. If the headlights go very dim when you're trying to start, the battery is probably flat. Get out of trouble by jump starting (see next page) using a friend's car.

If your car won't start even though the starter motor turns as normal

☐ Is there fuel in the tank?
☐ Is there moisture on electrical components under the bonnet? Switch off the ignition, then wipe off any obvious dampness with a dry cloth. Spray a water-repellent aerosol product (WD-40 or equivalent) on ignition and fuel system electrical connectors like those shown in the photos.

1 On petrol engines, remove the engine cover and check that the wiring to the ignition module is connected firmly.

2 Check that the air mass meter wiring is connected securely.

3 Check the security and condition of the battery connections.

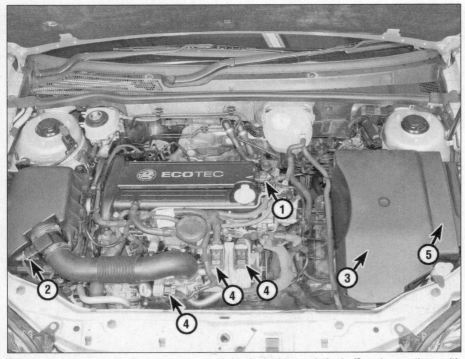

Check that electrical connections are secure (with the ignition switched off) and spray them with a water-dispersant spray like WD-40 if you suspect a problem due to damp.

4 Check all multiplugs and wiring connectors for security.

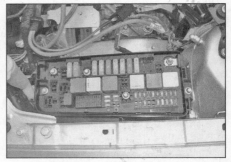

5 Check that all fuses are still in good condition and none have blown.

Jump starting

When jump-starting a car using a booster battery, observe the following precautions:

✔ Before connecting the booster battery, make sure that the ignition is switched off.

Caution: Remove the key in case the central locking engages when the jump leads are connected

✔ Ensure that all electrical equipment (lights, heater, wipers, etc) is switched off.

✔ Take note of any special precautions printed on the battery case.

✔ Make sure that the booster battery is the same voltage as the discharged one in the vehicle.

✔ If the battery is being jump-started from the battery in another vehicle, the two vehicles MUST NOT TOUCH each other.

✔ Make sure that the transmission is in neutral (or PARK, in the case of automatic transmission).

Jump starting will get you out of trouble, but you must correct whatever made the battery go flat in the first place. There are three possibilities:

1 *The battery has been drained by repeated attempts to start, or by leaving the lights on.*

2 *The charging system is not working properly (alternator drivebelt slack or broken, alternator wiring fault or alternator itself faulty).*

3 *The battery itself is at fault (electrolyte low, or battery worn out).*

1 Connect one end of the red jump lead to the positive (+) terminal of the flat battery

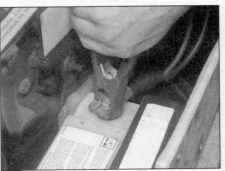

2 Connect the other end of the red lead to the positive (+) terminal of the booster battery.

3 Connect one end of the black jump lead to the negative (-) terminal of the booster battery

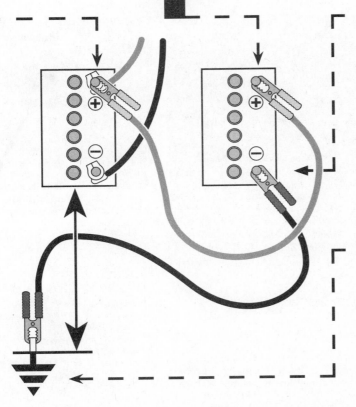

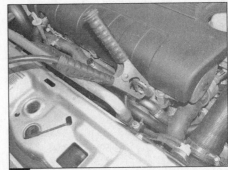

4 Connect the other end of the black jump lead to a bolt or bracket on the engine block, well away from the battery, on the vehicle to be started.

5 Make sure that the jump leads will not come into contact with the fan, drive-belts or other moving parts of the engine.

6 Start the engine using the booster battery and run it at idle speed. Switch on the lights, rear window demister and heater blower motor, then disconnect the jump leads in the reverse order of connection. Turn off the lights etc.

Wheel changing

⚠️ *Warning: Do not change a wheel in a situation where you risk being hit by other traffic. On busy roads, try to stop in a lay-by or a gateway. Be wary of passing traffic while changing the wheel – it is easy to become distracted by the job in hand.*

Preparation

- [ ] When a puncture occurs, stop as soon as it is safe to do so.
- [ ] Park on firm level ground, if possible, and well out of the way of other traffic.
- [ ] Use hazard warning lights if necessary.

- [ ] If you have one, use a warning triangle to alert other drivers of your presence.
- [ ] Apply the handbrake and engage first or reverse gear (or Park on models with automatic transmission).

- [ ] Chock the wheel diagonally opposite the one being removed – a couple of large stones will do for this.
- [ ] If the ground is soft, use a flat piece of wood to spread the load under the jack.

Changing the wheel

1 Lift the floor covering and unscrew the spare wheel clamp nut. Lift out the spare wheel and position it under the sill in case the jack fails.

2 Remove the tools from the carrier stored beneath the spare wheel.

3 On models with steel wheels, use the special tool to pull the wheel trim from the wheel. Note that if the wheel bolts are visible, the wheel trim is removed with the wheel bolts. On models with alloy wheels, use the screwdriver provided inserted at the wheel bolt holes to prise off the trim.

4 Slacken each wheel bolt by half a turn. Locate the jack head below the jacking point nearest the wheel to be changed.

5 The jacking point is indicated by an arrow in the sill. Turn the handle until the base of the jack touches the ground ensuring that the jack is vertical. Raise the vehicle until the wheel is clear of the ground. If the tyre is flat make sure that the vehicle is raised sufficiently to allow the spare wheel to be fitted.

6 Remove the bolts and lift the wheel from the vehicle. Place it beneath the sill in place of the spare. Fit the spare wheel and tighten the bolts moderately with the wheelbrace.

7 Lower the vehicle to the ground, then finally tighten the wheel bolts in a diagonal sequence. Refit the wheel trim. Note that the wheel bolts should be tightened to the specified torque at the earliest opportunity.

Finally . . .

- [ ] Remove the wheel chocks.
- [ ] Stow the jack and tools in the correct locations in the car.
- [ ] Check the tyre pressure on the wheel just fitted. If it is low, or if you don't have a pressure gauge with you, drive slowly to the next garage and inflate the tyre to the correct pressure.
- [ ] Have the damaged tyre or wheel repaired as soon as possible, or another puncture will leave you stranded.

Identifying leaks

Puddles on the garage floor or drive, or obvious wetness under the bonnet or underneath the car, suggest a leak that needs investigating. It can sometimes be difficult to decide where the leak is coming from, especially if an engine undershield is fitted. Leaking oil or fluid can also be blown rearwards by the passage of air under the car, giving a false impression of where the problem lies.

 Warning: Most automotive oils and fluids are poisonous. Wash them off skin, and change out of contaminated clothing, without delay.

 The smell of a fluid leaking from the car may provide a clue to what's leaking. Some fluids are distinctively coloured. It may help to remove the engine undershield, clean the car carefully and to park it over some clean paper overnight as an aid to locating the source of the leak. Remember that some leaks may only occur while the engine is running.

Sump oil

Engine oil may leak from the drain plug...

Oil from filter

...or from the base of the oil filter.

Gearbox oil

Gearbox oil can leak from the seals at the inboard ends of the driveshafts.

Antifreeze

Leaking antifreeze often leaves a crystalline deposit like this.

Brake fluid

A leak occurring at a wheel is almost certainly brake fluid.

Power steering fluid

Power steering fluid may leak from the pipe connectors on the steering rack.

Towing

When all else fails, you may find yourself having to get a tow home – or of course you may be helping somebody else. Long-distance recovery should only be done by a garage or breakdown service. For shorter distances, DIY towing using another car is easy enough, but observe the following points:

☐ Only attach the tow-rope to the towing eyes provided. A towing eye is provided with the tool kit in the luggage compartment. To fit the towing eye, remove the circular cover from the front or rear bumper, as required, then screw in the towing eye anti-clockwise as far as it will go using the handle of the wheel brace to turn the eye. **Note that the towing eye has a left-hand thread.**

☐ Use a proper tow-rope – they are not expensive. The vehicle being towed must display an ON TOW sign in its rear window.

☐ Always turn the ignition key to the 'on' position when the vehicle is being towed, so that the steering lock is released, and the direction indicator and brake lights work.

☐ Before being towed, release the handbrake and select neutral on the transmission. On models with automatic transmission, special precautions apply. If in doubt, do not tow, or transmission damage may result.

☐ Note that greater-than-usual pedal pressure will be required to operate the brakes, since the vacuum servo unit is only operational with the engine running.

☐ Greater-than-usual steering effort will also be required.

☐ The driver of the car being towed must keep the tow-rope taut at all times to avoid snatching.

☐ Make sure that both drivers know the route before setting off.

☐ Only drive at moderate speeds and keep the distance towed to a minimum. Drive smoothly and allow plenty of time for slowing down at junctions.

Introduction

There are some very simple checks which need only take a few minutes to carry out, but which could save you a lot of inconvenience and expense.

These *Weekly checks* require no great skill or special tools, and the small amount of time they take to perform could prove to be very well spent, for example:

☐ Keeping an eye on tyre condition and pressures, will not only help to stop them wearing out prematurely, but could also save your life.

☐ Many breakdowns are caused by electrical problems. Battery-related faults are particularly common, and a quick check on a regular basis will often prevent the majority of these.

☐ If your car develops a brake fluid leak, the first time you might know about it is when your brakes don't work properly. Checking the level regularly will give advance warning of this kind of problem.

☐ If the oil or coolant levels run low, the cost of repairing any engine damage will be far greater than fixing the leak, for example.

Underbonnet check points

◀ **1.8 litre Z18XE petrol engine**

1 *Engine oil level dipstick*

2 *Engine oil filler cap*

3 *Coolant reservoir (expansion tank)*

4 *Brake and clutch fluid reservoir*

5 *Washer fluid reservoir*

6 *Battery*

◀ **1.8 litre Z18XER petrol engine**

1 *Engine oil level dipstick*

2 *Engine oil filler cap*

3 *Coolant reservoir (expansion tank)*

4 *Brake and clutch fluid reservoir*

5 *Washer fluid reservoir*

6 *Battery*

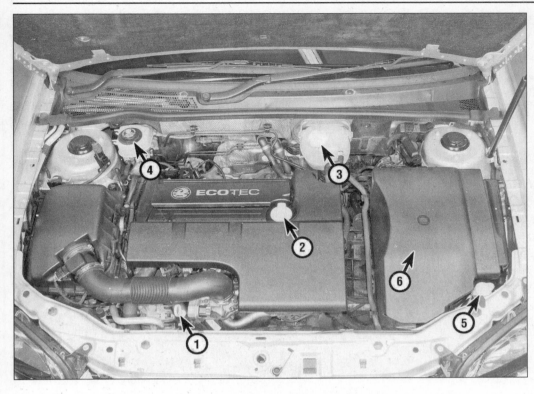

1 *Engine oil level dipstick*
2 *Engine oil filler cap*
3 *Coolant reservoir (expansion tank)*
4 *Brake and clutch fluid reservoir*
5 *Washer fluid reservoir*
6 *Battery*

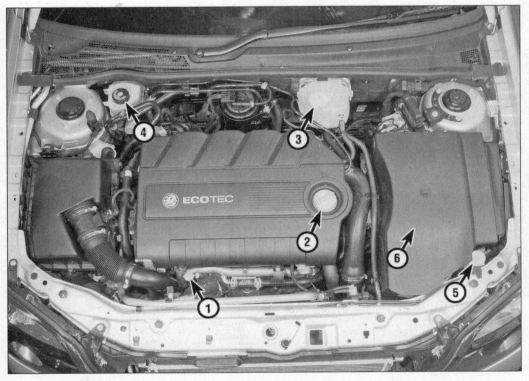

◀ 1.9 litre DOHC diesel engine

1 *Engine oil level dipstick*
2 *Engine oil filler cap*
3 *Coolant reservoir (expansion tank)*
4 *Brake and clutch fluid reservoir*
5 *Washer fluid reservoir*
6 *Battery*

Engine oil level

Before you start

✔ Make sure that the car is on level ground.
✔ The oil level must be checked with the engine at normal operating temperature, however, wait at least 5 minutes after the engine has been switched off.

HAYNES HiNT *If the oil is checked immediately after driving the vehicle, some of the oil will remain in the upper engine components, resulting in an inaccurate reading on the dipstick.*

The correct oil

Modern engines place great demands on their oil. It is very important that the correct oil for your car is used (see *Lubricants and fluids*).

Car care

● If you have to add oil frequently, you should check whether you have any oil leaks. Place some clean paper under the car overnight, and check for stains in the morning. If there are no leaks, then the engine may be burning oil, or the oil may only be leaking when the engine is running.
● Always maintain the level between the upper and lower dipstick marks (see photo 3). If the level is too low, severe engine damage may occur. Oil seal failure may result if the engine is overfilled by adding too much oil.

1 The dipstick is brightly coloured for easy identification (see *Underbonnet check points* for exact location). Withdraw the dipstick.

2 Using a clean rag or paper towel remove all oil from the dipstick. Insert the clean dipstick into the tube as far as it will go, then withdraw it again.

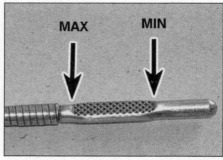

3 Note the level on the end of the dipstick, which should be between the upper (MAX) mark and lower (MIN) mark. Approximately 1.0 litre of oil will raise the level from the lower mark to the upper mark.

4 Oil is added through the filler cap. Unscrew the cap and top-up the level. A funnel may help to reduce spillage. Add the oil slowly, checking the level on the dipstick frequently. Avoid overfilling (see *Car care*).

Coolant level

Warning: Do not attempt to remove the expansion tank pressure cap when the engine is hot, as there is a very great risk of scalding. Do not leave open containers of coolant about, as it is poisonous.

Car care

● With a sealed-type cooling system, adding coolant should not be necessary on a regular basis. If frequent topping-up is required, it is likely there is a leak. Check the radiator, all hoses and joint faces for signs of staining or wetness, and rectify as necessary.

● It is important that antifreeze is used in the cooling system all year round, not just during the winter months. Don't top-up with water alone, as the antifreeze will become diluted.

1 The coolant level varies with the temperature of the engine. When the engine is cold, the coolant level should be slightly above the KALT/COLD mark on the side of the tank. When the engine is hot, the level will rise.

2 If topping-up is necessary, **wait until the engine is cold**. Slowly unscrew the expansion tank cap, to release any pressure present in the cooling system, and remove it.

3 Add a mixture of water and antifreeze to the expansion tank until the coolant is up to the KALT/COLD level mark. Refit the cap and tighten it securely.

Brake (and clutch) fluid level

Before you start
✔ Make sure that the car is on level ground.
✔ Cleanliness is of great importance when dealing with the braking system, so take care to clean around the reservoir cap before topping-up. Use only clean brake fluid.

Safety first!
● If the reservoir requires repeated topping-up, this is an indication of a fluid leak somewhere in the system, which should be investigated immediately.

● If a leak is suspected, the car should not be driven until the braking system has been checked. Never take any risks where brakes are concerned.

 The fluid level in the reservoir will drop slightly as the brake pads wear down, but the fluid level must never be allowed to drop below the MIN mark.

 Warning: Hydraulic fluid can harm your eyes and damage painted surfaces, so use extreme caution when handling and pouring it. Do not use fluid which has been standing open for some time, as it absorbs moisture from the air, which can cause a dangerous loss of braking effectiveness.

1 The MAX and MIN marks are indicated on the front of the reservoir. The fluid level must be kept between the marks at all times.

2 If topping-up is necessary, first wipe clean the area around the filler cap to prevent dirt entering the hydraulic system. Unscrew the reservoir cap.

3 Carefully add fluid, taking care not to spill it onto the surrounding components. Use only the specified fluid; mixing different types can cause damage to the system. After topping-up to the correct level, securely refit the cap and wipe off any spilt fluid.

Washer fluid level

● Screenwash additives not only keep the windscreen clean during bad weather, they also prevent the washer system freezing in cold weather – which is when you are likely to need it most. Don't top-up using plain water, as the screenwash will become diluted, and will freeze in cold weather.

 Warning: On no account use engine coolant antifreeze in the screen washer system – this may damage the paintwork.

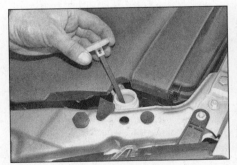

1 The reservoir for the windscreen, rear window and headlight (where applicable) washer systems is located on the front left-hand side of the engine compartment. If topping-up is necessary, prise open the cap and lift out the dipstick attached to it.

2 When topping-up the reservoir a screen-wash additive should be added in the quantities recommended on the bottle.

Tyre condition and pressure

It is very important that tyres are in good condition, and at the correct pressure - having a tyre failure at any speed is highly dangerous. Tyre wear is influenced by driving style - harsh braking and acceleration, or fast cornering, will all produce more rapid tyre wear. As a general rule, the front tyres wear out faster than the rears. Interchanging the tyres from front to rear ("rotating" the tyres) may result in more even wear. However, if this is completely effective, you may have the expense of replacing all four tyres at once! Remove any nails or stones embedded in the tread before they penetrate the tyre to cause deflation. If removal of a nail does reveal that the tyre has been punctured, refit the nail so that its point of penetration is marked. Then immediately change the wheel, and have the tyre repaired by a tyre dealer.

Regularly check the tyres for damage in the form of cuts or bulges, especially in the sidewalls. Periodically remove the wheels, and clean any dirt or mud from the inside and outside surfaces. Examine the wheel rims for signs of rusting, corrosion or other damage. Light alloy wheels are easily damaged by "kerbing" whilst parking; steel wheels may also become dented or buckled. A new wheel is very often the only way to overcome severe damage.

New tyres should be balanced when they are fitted, but it may become necessary to re-balance them as they wear, or if the balance weights fitted to the wheel rim should fall off. Unbalanced tyres will wear more quickly, as will the steering and suspension components. Wheel imbalance is normally signified by vibration, particularly at a certain speed (typically around 50 mph). If this vibration is felt only through the steering, then it is likely that just the front wheels need balancing. If, however, the vibration is felt through the whole car, the rear wheels could be out of balance. Wheel balancing should be carried out by a tyre dealer or garage.

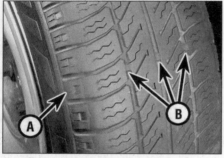

1 *Tread Depth - visual check*
The original tyres have tread wear safety bands (B), which will appear when the tread depth reaches approximately 1.6 mm. The band positions are indicated by a triangular mark on the tyre sidewall (A).

2 *Tread Depth - manual check*
Alternatively, tread wear can be monitored with a simple, inexpensive device known as a tread depth indicator gauge.

3 *Tyre Pressure Check*
Check the tyre pressures regularly with the tyres cold. Do not adjust the tyre pressures immediately after the vehicle has been used, or an inaccurate setting will result.

Tyre tread wear patterns

Shoulder Wear

Underinflation (wear on both sides)
Under-inflation will cause overheating of the tyre, because the tyre will flex too much, and the tread will not sit correctly on the road surface. This will cause a loss of grip and excessive wear, not to mention the danger of sudden tyre failure due to heat build-up.
Check and adjust pressures
Incorrect wheel camber (wear on one side)
Repair or renew suspension parts
Hard cornering
Reduce speed!

Centre Wear

Overinflation
Over-inflation will cause rapid wear of the centre part of the tyre tread, coupled with reduced grip, harsher ride, and the danger of shock damage occurring in the tyre casing.
Check and adjust pressures

If you sometimes have to inflate your car's tyres to the higher pressures specified for maximum load or sustained high speed, don't forget to reduce the pressures to normal afterwards.

Uneven Wear

Front tyres may wear unevenly as a result of wheel misalignment. Most tyre dealers and garages can check and adjust the wheel alignment (or "tracking") for a modest charge.
Incorrect camber or castor
Repair or renew suspension parts
Malfunctioning suspension
Repair or renew suspension parts
Unbalanced wheel
Balance tyres
Incorrect toe setting
Adjust front wheel alignment
Note: *The feathered edge of the tread which typifies toe wear is best checked by feel.*

Wiper blades

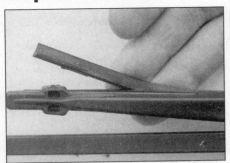

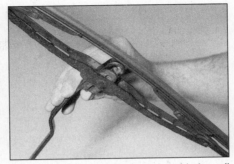

1 Check the condition of the wiper blades; if they are cracked or show any signs of deterioration, or if the glass swept area is smeared, renew them. Wiper blades should be renewed annually.

2 To remove a windscreen wiper blade, pull the arm fully away from the screen until it locks. Swivel the blade through 90°, press the locking tab with your fingers and slide the blade out of the arm's hooked end.

3 Don't forget to check the tailgate wiper blade as well. To remove the blade, depress the retaining tab and slide the blade out of the hooked end of the arm.

Battery

Caution: Before carrying out any work on the vehicle battery, read the precautions given in 'Safety first!' at the start of this manual. If the battery is to be disconnected, refer to 'Disconnecting the battery' in the Reference Chapter, before proceeding.

✔ Make sure that the battery tray is in good condition, and that the clamp is tight. Corrosion on the tray, retaining clamp and the battery itself can be removed with a solution of water and baking soda. Thoroughly rinse all cleaned areas with water. Any metal parts damaged by corrosion should be covered with a zinc-based primer, then painted.

✔ Periodically (approximately every three months), check the charge condition of the battery as described in Chapter 5A.

✔ If the battery is flat, and you need to jump start your vehicle, see *Roadside Repairs*.

1 The battery is located at the front, left-hand side of the engine compartment, housed in a protective plastic box. Open the battery box, for access to the terminals, by releasing the lid at the front and pivoting it upwards. Where fitted, unclip the insulation jacket and lift open the jacket cover.

2 Check the tightness of battery clamps to ensure good electrical connections. You should not be able to move them. Also check each cable for cracks and frayed conductors.

Battery corrosion can be kept to a minimum by applying a layer of petroleum jelly to the clamps and terminals after they are reconnected.

3 If corrosion (white, fluffy deposits) is evident, remove the cables from the battery terminals, clean them with a small wire brush, then refit them. Automotive stores sell a tool for cleaning the battery post . . .

4 . . . as well as the battery cable clamps

Electrical systems

✔ Check all external lights and the horn. Refer to the appropriate Sections of Chapter 12 for details if any of the circuits are found to be inoperative.

✔ Visually check all accessible wiring connectors, harnesses and retaining clips for security, and for signs of chafing or damage.

> **HAYNES HiNT** *If you need to check your brake lights and indicators unaided, back up to a wall or garage door and operate the lights. The reflected light should show if they are working properly.*

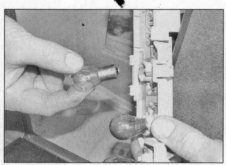

1 If a single indicator light, stop-light or headlight has failed, it is likely that a bulb has blown and will need to be renewed. Refer to Chapter 12 for details. If both stop-lights have failed, it is possible that the switch has failed (see Chapter 9).

2 If more than one indicator light or headlight has failed, it is likely that either a fuse has blown or that there is a fault in the circuit (see Chapter 12). The main fuses are located behind a cover on the left-hand edge of the facia. Pull open and remove the cover for access to the fuses.

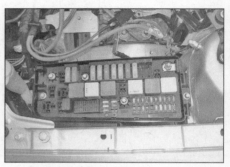

3 Additional fuses and relays are located in the fuse/relay box on the left-hand side of the engine compartment . . .

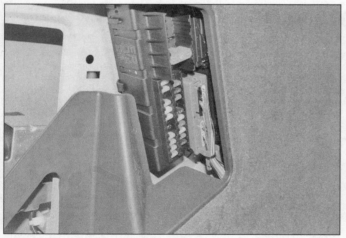

4 . . . and in the left-hand side of the luggage compartment. Refer to the wiring diagrams at the end of Chapter 12 for details of the fuse locations and circuits protected.

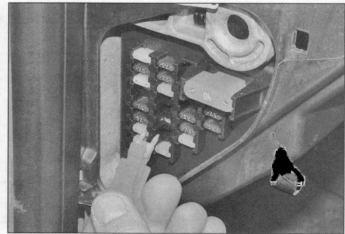

5 To renew a blown fuse, remove it, where applicable, using the plastic tool provided. Fit a new fuse of the same rating, available from car accessory shops. It is important that you find the reason that the fuse blew (see *Electrical fault finding* in Chapter 12).

Lubricants and fluids

Engine

Petrol . . . .   Multigrade engine oil, viscosity SAE 0W/30, 0W/40, 5W/30 or 5W/40 to Vauxhall/Opel specification GM-LL-A-025

Diesel . . . .   Multigrade engine oil, viscosity SAE 0W/30, 0W/40, 5W/30 or 5W/40 to Vauxhall/Opel specification GM-LL-B-025

Manual and Easytronic transmissions . . . .   Vauxhall/Opel gear oil (09 120 541)

Automatic transmission:

AF23 . . . .   Vauxhall/Opel automatic transmission fluid (93 160 393)

AF40 . . . .   Vauxhall/Opel automatic transmission fluid (93 165 147)

Power steering reservoir . . . .   Vauxhall/Opel steering fluid (93 160 548)

Cooling system . . . .   Vauxhall/Opel silicate-free coolant (09 194 431)

Brake/clutch fluid reservoir . . . .   Hydraulic fluid to DOT 4

Tyre pressures (cold)

Note: *Pressures apply to original-equipment tyres, and may vary if any other make or type of tyre is fitted; check with the tyre manufacturer or supplier for correct pressures if necessary.*

Normal load (up to 3 passengers)	Front	Rear
1.8 litre petrol models		
All tyre sizes	2.0 bar (29 psi)	2.2 bar (32 psi)
2.2 litre petrol models		
195/65 R 15 and 205/55 R 16 tyres	2.3 bar (33 psi)	2.3 bar (33 psi)
215/55 R 16, 215/50 R 17, 225/45 R 17 and 225/45 R 18 tyres	2.2 bar (32 psi)	2.2 bar (32 psi)
1.9 litre Z19DTH diesel models		
195/65 R 15 and 205/55 R 16 tyres	2.4 bar (35 psi)	2.4 bar (35 psi)
215/55 R 16, 215/50 R 17, 225/45 R 17 and 225/45 R 18 tyres	2.3 bar (33 psi)	2.3 bar (33 psi)
1.9 litre Z19DT diesel models		
195/65 R 15 and 205/55 R 16 tyres	2.3 bar (33 psi)	2.3 bar (33 psi)
215/55 R 16, 215/50 R 17, 225/45 R 17 and 225/45 R 18 tyres	2.2 bar (32 psi)	2.2 bar (32 psi)
Fully laden		
1.8 litre petrol models		
All tyre sizes	2.2 bar (32 psi)	2.7 bar (39 psi)
2.2 litre petrol models		
195/65 R 15 and 205/55 R 16 tyres	2.5 bar (36 psi)	3.0 bar (44 psi)
215/55 R 16, 215/50 R 17, 225/45 R 17 and 225/45 R 18 tyres	2.3 bar (33 psi)	2.8 bar (41 psi)
1.9 litre Z19DTH diesel models		
195/65 R 15 and 205/55 R 16 tyres	2.5 bar (36 psi)	3.0 bar (44 psi)
215/55 R 16, 215/50 R 17, 225/45 R 17 and 225/45 R 18 tyres	2.4 bar (35 psi)	2.9 bar (42 psi)
1.9 litre Z19DT diesel models		
195/65 R 15 and 205/55 R 16 tyres	2.5 bar (36 psi)	3.0 bar (44 psi)
215/55 R 16, 215/50 R 17, 225/45 R 17 and 225/45 R 18 tyres	2.3 bar (33 psi)	2.8 bar (41 psi)
Space-saver temporary spare tyre		
All models	4.2 bar (61 psi)	4.2 bar (61 psi)

Chapter 1 Part A:
Routine maintenance and servicing – petrol models

Contents

Degrees of difficulty

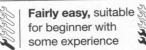 **Easy,** suitable for novice with little experience

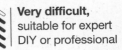 **Fairly easy,** suitable for beginner with some experience

Fairly difficult, suitable for competent DIY mechanic

Difficult, suitable for experienced DIY mechanic

 Very difficult, suitable for expert DIY or professional

Lubricants and fluids............................... Refer to *Weekly checks* on page 0•17

Capacities

Engine oil (including oil filter)
1.8 litre engines:
    Z18XE engines .... 4.25 litres
    Z18XER engines .... 4.5 litres
2.2 litre engines .... 5.0 litres
Difference between MIN and MAX dipstick marks .... 1.0 litre

Cooling system
1.8 litre engines .... 5.5 litres
2.2 litre engines:
    Manual transmission without air conditioning .... 6.9 litres
    Manual transmission with air conditioning .... 7.2 litres
    Automatic transmission with or without air conditioning .... 7.4 litres

Transmission
Manual transmission:
    F17+ transmission .... 1.6 litres
    F23 transmission .... 1.55 litres
    M32 transmission .... 2.2 litres
Automatic transmission (at fluid change) .... 3.0 to 3.5 litres (approximately)
Easytronic transmission .... 1.6 litres

Washer fluid reservoir
Without headlight washers................................. 2.9 litres
With headlight washers .... 5.6 litres

Fuel tank
Saloon and Hatchback models .... 60 litres
Estate models... 61 litres

Cooling system
Antifreeze mixture:
    40% antifreeze .... Protection down to -28°C
    50% antifreeze .... Protection down to -40°C

Ignition system

Spark plugs:

	Type	Gap
1.8 litre engines	Bosch FQR 8 LEU2	0.9 mm
2.2 litre engines	Beru 14 FGR-8DQU7	0.8 mm

Brakes
Friction material minimum thickness (including backing plate):
    Front brake pads .... 9.0 mm
    Rear brake pads.. 8.0 mm

Torque wrench settings

	Nm	lbf ft
Oil filter housing cap to filter housing (paper element filter)	25	18
Roadwheel bolts	110	81
Spark plugs	25	18
Sump drain plug:		
1.8 litre engines	14	10
2.2 litre engines	25	18

The maintenance intervals in this manual are provided with the assumption that you, not the dealer, will be carrying out the work. These are the minimum maintenance intervals based on the standard service schedule recommended by the manufacturer for vehicles driven daily. If you wish to keep your vehicle in peak condition at all times, you may wish to perform some of these procedures more often. We encourage frequent maintenance, because it enhances the efficiency, performance and resale value of your vehicle.

If the vehicle is driven in dusty areas, used to tow a trailer, or driven frequently at slow speeds (idling in traffic) or on short journeys, more frequent maintenance intervals are recommended.

When the vehicle is new, it should be serviced by a dealer service department (or other workshop recognised by the vehicle manufacturer as providing the same standard of service) in order to preserve the warranty. The vehicle manufacturer may reject warranty claims if you are unable to prove that servicing has been carried out as and when specified, using only original equipment parts or parts certified to be of equivalent quality.

Every 250 miles or weekly

- [ ] Refer to *Weekly checks*

Every 10 000 miles or 6 months – whichever comes first

- [ ] Renew the engine oil and filter (Section 3)

Note: *Vauxhall/Opel recommend that the engine oil and filter are changed every 20 000 miles or 12 months if the vehicle is being operated under the standard service schedule. However, oil and filter changes are good for the engine and we recommend that the oil and filter are renewed more frequently, especially if the vehicle is used on a lot of short journeys.*

Every 20 000 miles or 12 months – whichever comes first

- [ ] Check all underbonnet and underbody components, pipes and hoses for leaks (Section 4)
- [ ] Check the power steering fluid level (Section 5)
- [ ] Check the Easytronic clutch hydraulic fluid level (Section 6)
- [ ] Check the condition of the brake pads (renew if necessary), the calipers and discs (Section 7)
- [ ] Check the condition of all brake fluid pipes and hoses (Section 8)
- [ ] Check the condition of the front suspension and steering components, particularly the rubber gaiters and seals (Section 9)
- [ ] Check the condition of the driveshaft joint gaiters, and the driveshaft joints (Section 10)
- [ ] Check the condition of the exhaust system components (Section 11)
- [ ] Check the condition of the rear suspension components (Section 12)
- [ ] Check the bodywork and underbody for damage and corrosion, and check the condition of the underbody corrosion protection (Section 13)
- [ ] Check the tightness of the roadwheel bolts (Section 14)
- [ ] Lubricate all door, bonnet, boot lid and tailgate hinges and locks (Section 15)
- [ ] Check the operation of the horn, all lights, and the wipers and washers (Section 16)
- [ ] Check the headlight beam alignment (Section 17)
- [ ] Carry out a road test (Section 18)
- [ ] Reset the service interval indicator (Section 19)

Every 40 000 miles or 2 years – whichever comes first

- [ ] Renew the pollen filter (Section 20)
- [ ] Check the auxiliary drivebelt and tensioner (Section 21)

Every 2 years, regardless of mileage

- [ ] Renew the battery for the remote control handset (Section 22)
- [ ] Renew the brake and clutch fluid (Section 23)
- [ ] Renew the coolant (Section 24)*
- [ ] Exhaust emission test (Section 25)

* Note: *Vehicles using Vauxhall/Opel silicate-free coolant do not need the coolant renewed on a regular basis.*

Every 40 000 miles or 4 years – whichever comes first

- [ ] Renew the air cleaner filter element (Section 26)
- [ ] Renew the spark plugs (Section 27)
- [ ] Renew the timing belt, tensioner and idler pulleys – 1.8 litre engines (Section 28)*
- [ ] Renew the fuel filter (Section 29)

* Note: *The normal interval for timing belt renewal is 60 000 miles or 6 years, for the 1.8 litre Z18XE engines, and 100 000 miles or 10 years for the 1.8 litre Z18XER engines. However, it is strongly recommended that the interval used is 40 000 miles on vehicles which are subjected to intensive use, ie, mainly short journeys or a lot of stop-start driving. The actual belt renewal interval is therefore very much up to the individual owner, but bear in mind that severe engine damage will result if the belt breaks.*

Every 100 000 miles or 10 years – whichever comes first

- [ ] Check, and if necessary adjust, the valve clearances – 1.8 litre Z18XER engines (Section 30)

Underbonnet view of a 1.8 litre Z18XE engine model

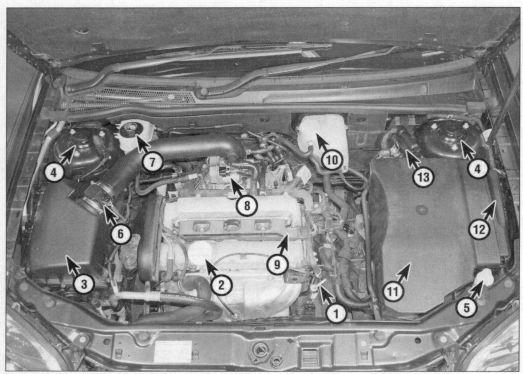

1   Engine oil level dipstick
2   Engine oil filler cap
3   Air cleaner assembly
4   Front suspension strut
    upper mounting
5   Screen washer fluid
    reservoir
6   Airflow meter
7   Brake (and clutch) fluid
    reservoir
8   Throttle housing
9   Ignition module
10 Coolant expansion tank
11 Battery
12 Fuse/relay box
13 ABS hydraulic modulator

Underbonnet view of a 1.8 litre Z18XER engine model

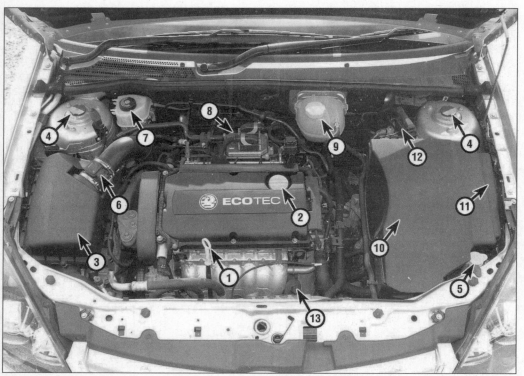

1   Engine oil level dipstick
2   Engine oil filler cap
3   Air cleaner assembly
4   Front suspension strut
    upper mounting
5   Screen washer fluid
    reservoir
6   Airflow meter
7   Brake (and clutch) fluid
    reservoir
8   Engine management ECU
9   Coolant expansion tank
10 Battery
11 Fuse/relay box
12 ABS hydraulic modulator
13 Oil filter

Underbonnet view of a 2.2 litre engine model

1   Engine oil level dipstick
2   Engine oil filler cap
3   Air cleaner assembly
4   Front suspension strut
    upper mounting
5   Screen washer fluid
    reservoir
6   Airflow meter
7   Brake (and clutch) fluid
    reservoir
8   Throttle housing
9   Ignition module
10 Coolant expansion tank
11 Battery
12 Fuse/relay box
13 ABS hydraulic modulator
14 Oil filter
15 Engine management ECU

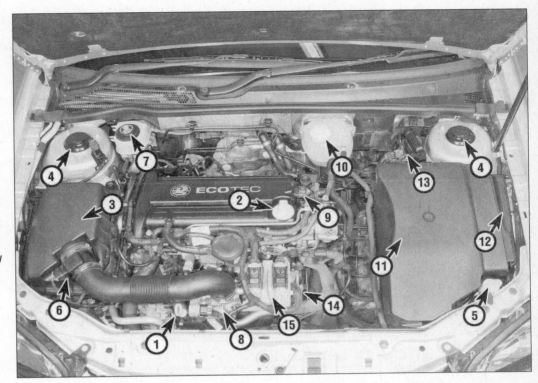

Front underbody view of a 1.8 litre model

1   Exhaust front pipe
2   Steering track rods
3   Front suspension lower
    arms
4   Front brake calipers
5   Engine mounting front
    torque link
6   Engine mounting rear
    torque link
7   Right-hand driveshaft
8   Final drive cover plate
9   Manual transmission
10 Engine oil drain plug
11 Engine oil filter
12 Air conditioning
    compressor
13 Electric cooling fan
14 Front subframe

Rear underbody view of a 1.8 litre model

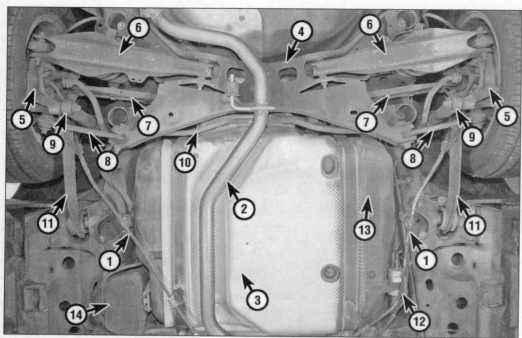

1   Handbrake cable
2   Exhaust tailpipe and silencer
3   Exhaust heat shield
4   Rear axle body
5   Rear hub carrier
6   Lower control arm
7   Upper control arm
8   Auxiliary control arm
9   Shock absorber
10 Rear anti-roll bar
11 Rear suspension trailing arm
12 Fuel filter
13 Fuel tank
14 Charcoal canister

Maintenance procedures

1   General information

1 This Chapter is designed to help the home mechanic maintain his/her vehicle for safety, economy, long life and peak performance.
2 The Chapter contains a master maintenance schedule, followed by Sections dealing specifically with each task in the schedule. Visual checks, adjustments, component renewal and other helpful items are included. Refer to the accompanying illustrations of the engine compartment and the underside of the vehicle for the locations of the various components.
3 Servicing your vehicle in accordance with the mileage/time maintenance schedule and the following Sections will provide a planned maintenance programme, which should result in a long and reliable service life. This is a comprehensive plan, so maintaining some items but not others at the specified service intervals, will not produce the same results.
4 As you service your vehicle, you will discover that many of the procedures can – and should – be grouped together, because of the particular procedure being performed, or because of the proximity of two otherwise-unrelated components to one another. For example, if the vehicle is raised for any reason, the exhaust can be inspected at the same time as the suspension and steering components.
5 The first step in this maintenance programme is to prepare yourself before the

actual work begins. Read through all the Sections relevant to the work to be carried out, then make a list and gather all the parts and tools required. If a problem is encountered, seek advice from a parts specialist, or a dealer service department.

2   Regular maintenance

1 If, from the time the vehicle is new, the routine maintenance schedule is followed closely, and frequent checks are made of fluid levels and high-wear items, as suggested throughout this manual, the engine will be kept in relatively good running condition, and the need for additional work will be minimised.
2 It is possible that there will be times when the engine is running poorly due to the lack of regular maintenance. This is even more likely if a used vehicle, which has not received regular and frequent maintenance checks, is purchased. In such cases, additional work may need to be carried out, outside of the regular maintenance intervals.
3 If engine wear is suspected, a compression test (refer to the appropriate part of Chapter 2) will provide valuable information regarding the overall performance of the main internal components. Such a test can be used as a basis to decide on the extent of the work to be carried out. If, for example, a compression test indicates serious internal engine wear, conventional maintenance as described in this

Chapter will not greatly improve the performance of the engine, and may prove a waste of time and money, unless extensive overhaul work is carried out first.
4 The following series of operations are those most often required to improve the performance of a generally poor-running engine:

Primary operations

a) Clean, inspect and test the battery (refer to Weekly checks).
b) Check all the engine-related fluids (refer to Weekly checks).
c) Check the condition and tension of the auxiliary drivebelt (Section 21).
d) Renew the spark plugs (Section 27).
e) Check the condition of the air cleaner element, and renew if necessary (Section 26).
f) Renew the fuel filter (Section 29).
g) Check the condition of all hoses, and check for fluid leaks (Section 4).
5 If the above operations do not prove fully effective, carry out the following secondary operations:

Secondary operations

All items listed under *Primary operations*, plus the following:
a) Check the charging system (refer to Chapter 5A).
b) Check the ignition system (refer to Chapter 5B).
c) Check the fuel, exhaust and emission control systems (refer to the appropriate Parts of Chapter 4).

Every 10 000 miles or 6 months

3 Engine oil and filter renewal

> **HAYNES HiNT** *Frequent oil and filter changes are the most important preventative maintenance procedures which can be undertaken by the DIY owner. As engine oil ages, it becomes diluted and contaminated, which leads to premature engine wear.*

1 Before starting this procedure, gather together all the necessary tools and materials. Also make sure that you have plenty of clean rags and newspapers handy, to mop-up any spills. Ideally, the engine oil should be warm, as it will drain more easily, and more built-up sludge will be removed with it. Take care not to touch the exhaust or any other hot parts of the engine when working under the vehicle. To avoid any possibility of scalding, and to protect yourself from possible skin irritants and other harmful contaminants in used engine oils, it is advisable to wear gloves when carrying out this work.

2 Access to the underside of the vehicle will be greatly improved if it can be raised on a lift, driven onto ramps, or jacked up and supported on axle stands (see *Jacking and vehicle support*). Whichever method is chosen, make sure that the vehicle remains level, or if it is at an angle, that the drain plug is at the lowest point. The drain plug is located at the rear of the sump.

3 Remove the oil filler cap from the camshaft cover (twist it through a quarter-turn anti-clockwise and withdraw it) **(see illustration)**.

4 Using a spanner, or preferably a suitable socket and bar, slacken the drain plug about half a turn. Position the draining container under the drain plug, then remove the plug completely **(see Haynes Hint)**.

5 Allow some time for the oil to drain, noting that it may be necessary to reposition the container as the oil flow slows to a trickle.

6 The oil filter is located on the front left-hand side of the cylinder block, and two different types may be encountered. On all 2.2 litre engines, the oil filter is of the paper element type. On 1.8 litre engines the oil filter may be either a paper element type or a metal canister type. Proceed as described under the following sub-Sections, according to engine.

1.8 litre engines

7 Position another container under the oil filter.

8 Where a canister-type oil filter is fitted, use an oil filter removal tool to slacken the filter initially, then unscrew it by hand the rest of the way **(see illustration)**. Empty the oil from the old filter into the container. In order to ensure that all the old oil is removed, puncture the 'dome' of the filter in two places and allow the oil to drain from the filter completely.

9 Where a paper element-type oil filter is fitted, unscrew the filter cap and withdraw it, together with the element, then separate the element, and remove the O-ring seal from the cap **(see illustrations)**.

10 Use a clean rag to remove all oil, dirt and sludge from the oil filter housing, or the oil filter sealing area on the cylinder block.

11 On the canister-type filter, apply a light coating of clean engine oil to the sealing ring on the new filter, then screw the filter into position on the engine. Tighten the filter firmly by hand only – **do not** use any tools.

12 On the paper element-type filter, locate a new O-ring seal in the groove on the retaining cap, then locate the new element in the cap and insert them both in the filter housing. Screw on the cap and tighten to the specified torque.

2.2 litre engines

13 Position another container under the oil filter.

14 Unscrew the filter cap and withdraw it, together with the element, then separate the element, and remove the O-ring seal from the cap **(see illustrations)**.

15 Use a clean rag to remove all oil, dirt and sludge from the oil filter housing and cap.

16 Locate a new O-ring seal in the groove on the retaining cap, then locate the new element in the cap and insert them both in the filter housing. Screw on the cap and tighten to the specified torque.

3.3 Removing the oil filler cap

> **HAYNES HiNT**
> *As the drain plug releases from the threads, move it away quickly so that the stream of oil running out of the sump goes into the drain pan and not up your sleeve.*

3.8 Using an oil filter removal tool to slacken the canister-type filter – 1.8 litre engines

3.9a Separate the paper-element type filter from the cap . . .

3.9b . . . then remove the O-ring seal – 1.8 litre engines

3.14a Unscrew the filter cap . . .

3.14b . . . and withdraw it together with the element . . .

3.14c . . . then separate the element from the cap – 2.2 litre engines

All engines

17 After all the oil has drained, wipe the drain plug and the sealing washer/O-ring with a clean rag. Examine the condition of the sealing washer/O-ring, and renew it if it shows signs of damage which may prevent an oil-tight seal. Clean the area around the drain plug opening, and refit the plug complete with the washer/O-ring. Tighten the plug to the specified torque, using a torque wrench.

18 Remove the old oil and all tools from under the vehicle then lower the vehicle to the ground.

19 Fill the engine through the filler hole in the camshaft cover, using the correct grade and type of oil (refer to *Weekly checks* for details of topping-up). Pour in half the specified quantity of oil first, then wait a few minutes for the oil to drain into the sump. Continue to add oil, a small quantity at a time, until the level is up to the lower mark on the dipstick. Adding approximately a further 1.0 litre will bring the level up to the upper mark on the dipstick.

20 Start the engine and run it until it reaches normal operating temperature. While the engine is warming-up, check for leaks around the oil filter and the sump drain plug.

21 Stop the engine, and wait at least five minutes for the oil to settle in the sump once more. With the new oil circulated and the filter now completely full, recheck the level on the dipstick, and add more oil as necessary.

22 Dispose of the used engine oil and filter safely, with reference to *General repair procedures* in the Reference Chapter of this manual. Do not discard the old filter with domestic household waste. The facility for waste oil disposal provided by many local council refuse tips and/or recycling centres generally has a filter receptacle alongside.

Every 20 000 miles or 12 months

4 Hose and fluid leak check

Note: *Also refer to Section 8.*

1 Visually inspect the engine joint faces, gaskets and seals for any signs of water or oil leaks. Pay particular attention to the areas around the camshaft cover, cylinder head, oil filter and sump joint faces. Similarly, check the transmission and (where applicable) the air conditioning compressor for oil leakage. Bear in mind that, over a period of time, some very slight seepage from these areas is to be expected; what you are really looking for is any indication of a serious leak. Should a leak be found, renew the offending gasket or oil seal by referring to the appropriate Chapters in this manual.

HAYNES HINT

A leak in the cooling system will usually show up as white- or antifreeze-coloured deposits on the area adjoining the leak.

2 Also check the security and condition of all the engine-related pipes and hoses. Ensure that all cable-ties or securing clips are in place, and in good condition. Clips which are broken or missing can lead to chafing of the hoses pipes or wiring, which could cause more serious problems in the future.

3 Carefully check the radiator hoses and heater hoses along their entire length. Renew any hose which is cracked, swollen or deteriorated. Cracks will show up better if the hose is squeezed. Pay close attention to the hose clips that secure the hoses to the cooling system components. Hose clips can pinch and puncture hoses, resulting in cooling system leaks. If wire-type hose clips are used, it may be a good idea to update them with screw-type clips.

4 Inspect all the cooling system components (hoses, joint faces, etc) for leaks. Where any problems of this nature are found on system components, renew the component or gasket with reference to Chapter 3 **(see Haynes Hint)**.

5 Where applicable, inspect the automatic transmission fluid cooler hoses for leaks or deterioration.

6 With the vehicle raised, inspect the petrol tank and filler neck for punctures, cracks and other damage. The connection between the filler neck and tank is especially critical. Sometimes, a rubber filler neck or connecting hose will leak due to loose retaining clamps or deteriorated rubber.

7 Carefully check all rubber hoses and metal fuel lines leading away from the petrol tank. Check for loose connections, deteriorated hoses, crimped lines and other damage. Pay particular attention to the vent pipes and hoses, which often loop up around the filler neck and can become blocked or crimped. Follow the lines to the front of the vehicle, carefully inspecting them all the way. Renew damaged sections as necessary. Similarly, whilst the vehicle is raised, take the opportunity to inspect all underbody brake fluid pipes and hoses.

8 From within the engine compartment, check the security of all fuel hose attachments and pipe unions, and inspect the fuel hoses and vacuum hoses for kinks, chafing and deterioration.

5 Power steering fluid level check

Refer to Chapter 10, Section 21.

6 Clutch hydraulic fluid level check – Easytronic models

Note: *The fluid level check on manual transmission models is in 'Weekly checks'.*

1 The clutch hydraulic fluid level markings are on the side of the fluid reservoir located on the front of the transmission. The use of a mirror will be helpful.

2 Check that the level of the fluid is at or near

the MAX marking on the side of the reservoir **(see illustration)**.

3 If topping-up is required, unscrew the filler cap and pour in fresh fluid of the specified type (see *Lubricants and fluids*), until the level is at the MAX marking. Retighten the cap on completion.

7 Brake pad, caliper and disc check

1 Firmly apply the handbrake, then jack up the front and rear of the vehicle and support it securely on axle stands (see *Jacking and vehicle support*). Remove the roadwheels.
2 For a quick check, the pad thickness can be carried out via the inspection hole on the caliper **(see Haynes Hint)**. Using a steel rule, measure the thickness of the pad lining including the backing plate. This must not be less than that indicated in the Specifications.
3 The view through the caliper inspection hole gives a rough indication of the state of the brake pads. For a comprehensive check, the brake pads should be removed and cleaned. The operation of the caliper can then also be checked, and the condition of the brake disc itself can be fully examined on both sides. Chapter 9 contains a detailed description of how the brake disc should be checked for wear and/or damage.
4 If any pad's friction material is worn to the specified thickness or less, *all four pads must be renewed as a set*. Refer to Chapter 9 for details.
5 On completion, refit the roadwheels and lower the vehicle to the ground.

8 Brake fluid pipe and hose check

1 The brake hydraulic system includes a number of metal pipes, which run from the master cylinder to the hydraulic modulator of the anti-lock braking system (ABS) and then to the front and rear brake assemblies. Flexible hoses are fitted between the pipes and the front and rear brake assemblies, to allow for steering and suspension movement.
2 When checking the system, first look for signs of leakage at the pipe or hose unions, then examine the flexible hoses for signs of cracking, chafing or deterioration of the rubber. Bend the hoses sharply between the fingers (but do not actually bend them double, or the casing may be damaged) and check that this does not reveal previously-hidden cracks, cuts or splits. Check that the pipes and hoses are securely fastened in their clips.
3 Carefully working along the length of the metal pipes, look for dents, kinks, damage of any sort, or corrosion. Light corrosion can be polished off, but if the depth of pitting is significant, the pipe must be renewed.

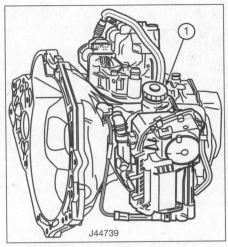

6.2 Clutch fluid reservoir (1) on Easytronic models

9 Front suspension and steering check

1 Apply the handbrake, then raise the front of the vehicle and securely support it on axle stands (see *Jacking and vehicle support*).
2 Inspect the balljoint dust covers and the steering gear gaiters for splits, chafing or deterioration.
3 Any wear of these components will cause loss of lubricant, and may allow water to enter the components, resulting in rapid deterioration of the balljoints or steering gear.
4 Grasp each roadwheel at the 12 o'clock and 6 o'clock positions, and try to rock it **(see illustration)**. Very slight free play may be felt, but if the movement is appreciable, further investigation is necessary to determine the source. Continue rocking the wheel while an assistant depresses the footbrake. If the movement is now eliminated or significantly reduced, it is likely that the hub bearings are at fault. If the free play is still evident with the footbrake depressed, then there is wear in the suspension joints or mountings.
5 Now grasp each wheel at the 9 o'clock and 3 o'clock positions, and try to rock it as before. Any movement felt now may again

9.4 Check for wear in the hub bearings by grasping the wheel and trying to rock it

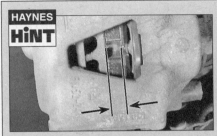

For a quick check, the thickness of friction material remaining on the inner brake pad can be measured through the aperture in the caliper body.

be caused by wear in the hub bearings or the steering track rod end balljoints. If the track rod end balljoint is worn, the visual movement will be obvious.
6 Using a large screwdriver or flat bar, check for wear in the suspension mounting bushes by levering between the relevant suspension component and its attachment point. Some movement is to be expected, as the mountings are made of rubber, but excessive wear should be obvious. Also check the condition of any visible rubber bushes, looking for splits, cracks or contamination of the rubber.
7 Check for any signs of fluid leakage around the suspension struts, or from the rubber gaiters around the piston rods. Should any fluid be noticed, the suspension strut is defective internally, and should be renewed. **Note:** *Suspension struts should always be renewed in pairs on the same axle.*
8 With the vehicle standing on its wheels, have an assistant turn the steering wheel back-and-forth about an eighth of a turn each way. There should be very little, if any, lost movement between the steering wheel and roadwheels. If this is not the case, closely observe the joints and mountings previously described. In addition, check the steering column universal joints for wear, and also check the rack-and-pinion steering gear itself.
9 The efficiency of each suspension strut may be checked by bouncing the vehicle at each front corner. Generally speaking, the body will return to its normal position and stop after being depressed. If it rises and returns on a rebound, the suspension strut is probably suspect. Also examine the suspension strut upper mountings for any signs of wear.

10 Driveshaft check

1 Firmly apply the handbrake, then jack up the front of the car and support it securely on axle stands (see *Jacking and vehicle support*).
2 Turn the steering onto full lock then slowly rotate the roadwheel. Inspect the condition of the outer constant velocity (CV) joint rubber gaiters while squeezing the gaiters to open

10.2 Check the condition of the driveshaft gaiters (1) and the retaining clips (2)

11.3 Exhaust mountings

out the folds **(see illustration)**. Check for signs of cracking, splits or deterioration of the rubber which may allow the grease to escape and lead to water and grit entry into the joint. Also check the security and condition of the retaining clips. Repeat these checks on the inner CV joints. If any damage or deterioration is found, the gaiters should be renewed as described in Chapter 8.

3 At the same time, check the general condition of the CV joints themselves by first holding the driveshaft and attempting to rotate the wheel. Repeat this check by holding the inner joint and attempting to rotate the driveshaft. Any appreciable movement indicates wear in the joints, wear in the driveshaft splines or loose driveshaft retaining nut.

11 Exhaust system check

1 With the engine cold (at least an hour after the vehicle has been driven), check the complete exhaust system from the engine to the end of the tailpipe. The exhaust system is most easily checked with the vehicle raised on a hoist, or suitably-supported on axle stands, so that the exhaust components are readily visible and accessible (see *Jacking and vehicle support*).

2 Check the exhaust pipes and connections for evidence of leaks, severe corrosion and damage. Make sure that all brackets and mountings are in good condition, and that all relevant nuts and bolts are tight. Leakage at any of the joints or in other parts of the system will usually show up as a black sooty stain in the vicinity of the leak.

3 Rattles and other noises can often be traced to the exhaust system, especially the brackets and mountings **(see illustration)**. Try to move the pipes and silencers. If the components are able to come into contact with the body or suspension parts, secure the system with new mountings. Otherwise separate the joints (if possible) and twist the pipes as necessary to provide additional clearance.

12 Rear suspension check

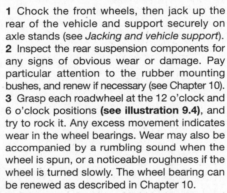

1 Chock the front wheels, then jack up the rear of the vehicle and support securely on axle stands (see *Jacking and vehicle support*).

2 Inspect the rear suspension components for any signs of obvious wear or damage. Pay particular attention to the rubber mounting bushes, and renew if necessary (see Chapter 10).

3 Grasp each roadwheel at the 12 o'clock and 6 o'clock positions **(see illustration 9.4)**, and try to rock it. Any excess movement indicates wear in the wheel bearings. Wear may also be accompanied by a rumbling sound when the wheel is spun, or a noticeable roughness if the wheel is turned slowly. The wheel bearing can be renewed as described in Chapter 10.

4 Check for any signs of fluid leakage around the shock absorber bodies. Should any fluid be noticed, the shock absorber is defective internally, and should be renewed. **Note:** *Shock absorbers should always be renewed in pairs on the same axle.*

5 With the vehicle standing on its wheels, the efficiency of each shock absorber may be checked by bouncing the vehicle at each rear corner. Generally speaking, the body will return to its normal position and stop after being depressed. If it rises and returns on a rebound, the shock absorber is probably suspect.

13 Bodywork and underbody condition check

Note: *This work should be carried out by a Vauxhall/Opel dealer in order to validate the vehicle warranty. The work includes a thorough inspection of the vehicle paintwork and underbody for damage and corrosion.*

Bodywork damage/ corrosion check

1 Once the car has been washed, and all tar spots and other surface blemishes have been cleaned off, carefully check all paintwork, looking closely for chips or scratches. Pay particular attention to vulnerable areas such as the front panels (bonnet and spoiler), and around the wheel arches. Any damage to the paintwork must be rectified as soon as possible, to comply with the terms of the manufacturer's anti-corrosion warranties; check with a Vauxhall/Opel dealer for details.

2 If a chip or light scratch is found which is recent and still free from rust, it can be touched-up using the appropriate touch-up stick which can be obtained from Vauxhall/ Opel dealers. Any more serious damage, or rusted stone chips, can be repaired as described in Chapter 11, but if damage or corrosion is so severe that a panel must be renewed, seek professional advice as soon as possible.

3 Always check that the door and ventilation opening drain holes and pipes are completely clear, so that water can drain out.

Corrosion protection check

4 The wax-based underbody protective coating should be inspected annually, preferably just prior to Winter, when the underbody should be washed down as thoroughly as possible without disturbing the protective coating. Any damage to the coating should be repaired using a suitable wax-based sealer. If any of the body panels are disturbed for repair or renewal, do not forget to re-apply the coating. Wax should be injected into door cavities, sills and box sections, to maintain the level of protection provided by the vehicle manufacturer – seek the advice of a Vauxhall/ Opel dealer.

14 Roadwheel bolt tightness check

1 Where applicable, remove the wheel trims from the wheels.

2 Using a torque wrench on each wheel bolt in turn, ensure that the bolts are tightened to the specified torque.

3 Where applicable, refit the wheel trims on completion, making sure they are fitted correctly.

15 Hinge and lock lubrication

1 Work around the vehicle and lubricate the hinges of the bonnet, doors, boot lid and tailgate with a light machine oil.
2 Lightly lubricate the bonnet release mechanism and exposed section of inner cable with a smear of grease.
3 Check the security and operation of all hinges, latches and locks, adjusting them where required. Check the operation of the central locking system.
4 Check the condition and operation of the tailgate struts, renewing them both if either is leaking or no longer able to support the tailgate securely when raised.

16 Electrical systems check

1 Check the operation of all the electrical equipment, ie, lights, direction indicators, horn, etc. Refer to the appropriate sections of Chapter 12 for details if any of the circuits are found to be inoperative.
2 Note that the stop-light switch is described in Chapter 9.
3 Check all accessible wiring connectors, harnesses and retaining clips for security, and for signs of chafing or damage. Rectify any faults found.

17 Headlight beam alignment check

1 Accurate adjustment of the headlight beam is only possible using optical beam-setting equipment, and this work should therefore be carried out by a Vauxhall/Opel dealer or service station with the necessary facilities. Refer to Chapter 12 for further information.

Every 40 000 miles or 2 years

20 Pollen filter renewal

1 Open the bonnet, and pull up the rubber weatherseal from the flange at the rear of the engine compartment **(see illustration)**.
2 Open the cover in the water deflector for access to the pollen filter **(see illustration)**.

18 Road test

Instruments and electrical equipment
1 Check the operation of all instruments, warning lights and electrical equipment.
2 Make sure that all instruments read correctly, and switch on all electrical equipment in turn, to check that it functions properly.

Steering and suspension
3 Check for any abnormalities in the steering, suspension, handling or road 'feel'.
4 Drive the vehicle, and check that there are no unusual vibrations or noises.
5 Check that the steering feels positive, with no excessive 'sloppiness', or roughness, and check for any suspension noises when cornering and driving over bumps.

Drivetrain
6 Check the performance of the engine, clutch, transmission and driveshafts.
7 Listen for any unusual noises from the engine, clutch and transmission.
8 Make sure that the engine runs smoothly when idling, and that there is no hesitation when accelerating.
9 Check that, where applicable, the clutch action is smooth and progressive, that the drive is taken up smoothly, and that the pedal travel is not excessive. Also listen for any noises when the clutch pedal is depressed.
10 Check that all gears can be engaged smoothly without noise, and that the gear lever action is smooth and not abnormally vague or 'notchy'.
11 On automatic transmission models, make sure that all gearchanges occur smoothly, without snatching, and without an increase in engine speed between changes. Check that all of the gear positions can be selected with the vehicle at rest. If any problems are found, they should be referred to a Vauxhall/Opel dealer.
12 Listen for a metallic clicking sound from

the front of the vehicle, as the vehicle is driven slowly in a circle with the steering on full-lock. Carry out this check in both directions. If a clicking noise is heard, this indicates wear in a driveshaft joint (see Chapter 8).

Braking system
13 Make sure that the vehicle does not pull to one side when braking, and that the wheels do not lock when braking hard.
14 Check that there is no vibration through the steering when braking.
15 Check that the handbrake operates correctly, without excessive movement of the lever, and that it holds the vehicle stationary on a slope.
16 Test the operation of the brake servo unit as follows. Depress the footbrake four or five times to exhaust the vacuum, then start the engine. As the engine starts, there should be a noticeable 'give' in the brake pedal as vacuum builds-up. Allow the engine to run for at least two minutes, and then switch it off. If the brake pedal is now depressed again, it should be possible to detect a hiss from the servo as the pedal is depressed. After about four or five applications, no further hissing should be heard, and the pedal should feel considerably harder.

19 Service interval indicator reset

1 With the ignition switched off, the display on the instrument panel must show the trip odometer.
2 With the ignition still switched off, depress and hold the trip odometer reset button located on the instrument panel.
3 With the reset button depressed, switch on the ignition, wait until the service interval display changes (approximately 10 seconds).
4 After approximately 10 seconds the display will show the service symbol and the maximum mileage before the next required service, followed by 'InSP'. When '- - -' appears in the display, release the reset button and switch off the ignition. When the button is released, the odometer reading will appear again.

20.1 Pull up the rubber weatherseal . . .

20.2 . . . then open the cover

20.3a Release the clips at each end . . .

3 Release the clips from each end, then lift out the filter (**see illustrations**).
4 Fit the new filter using a reversal of the removal procedure; make sure that the filter is fitted the correct way up as indicated on the edge of the filter.

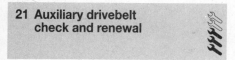

21 Auxiliary drivebelt check and renewal

Note: *The manufacturers recommend that the tensioner pulley is checked and if necessary renewed at the same time as the drivebelt.*

Checking

1 Due to their function and material make-up, drivebelts are prone to failure after a long period of time and should therefore be inspected regularly.
2 Apply the handbrake, then jack up the front of the vehicle and support it on axle stands (see *Jacking and vehicle support*). Remove the right-hand front roadwheel and the wheel arch liner inner cover for access to the right-hand side of the engine.

20.3b . . . and lift out the pollen filter

3 With the engine stopped, inspect the full length of the drivebelt for cracks and separation of the belt plies. It will be necessary to turn the engine (using a spanner or socket and bar on the crankshaft pulley bolt) so that the belt can be inspected thoroughly. Twist the belt between the pulleys so that both sides can be viewed. Also check for fraying, and glazing which gives the belt a shiny appearance. Check the pulleys for nicks, cracks, distortion and corrosion. If the belt shows signs of wear or damage, it should be renewed as a precaution against breakage in service.
4 On 2.2 litre engines also check the position of the drivebelt tensioner assembly arm. The mark on the underside of the moveable arm should be in between the two marks on the tensioner body, and the arm should be free to move.

Renewal

5 If not already done, apply the handbrake, then jack up the front of the vehicle and support it on axle stands (see *Jacking and vehicle support*). Remove the right-hand front

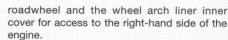

roadwheel and the wheel arch liner inner cover for access to the right-hand side of the engine.
6 For additional working clearance, remove the air cleaner housing as described in Chapter 4A.
7 If the drivebelt is to be re-used, mark it to indicate its normal running direction.

1.8 litre models

8 Note the routing of the drivebelt, then, using a Torx key or spanner (as applicable) on the pulley centre bolt, or the raised projection on the tensioner arm, turn the tensioner anti-clockwise against the spring tension. Hold the tensioner in this position by inserting a suitable locking pin/bolt through the special hole provided (**see illustrations**).
9 Locate the auxiliary drivebelt onto the pulleys in the correct routing. If the drivebelt is being re-used, make sure it is fitted the correct way around.
10 Turn back the tensioner and remove the locking pin/bolt then release it, making sure that the drivebelt ribs locate correctly on each of the pulley grooves.
11 Refit the air cleaner housing (if removed), then refit the wheel arch liner inner cover and roadwheel, and lower the vehicle to the ground.

2.2 litre models

12 Note the routing of the drivebelt, then insert a socket bar or similar tool into the square hole on the tensioner arm. Turn the tensioner anti-clockwise against the spring tension and slip the auxiliary drivebelt off of the pulleys (**see illustration**). Release the tensioner arm.
13 Turn the tensioner anti-clockwise and locate the auxiliary drivebelt onto the pulleys in the correct routing. If the drivebelt is being

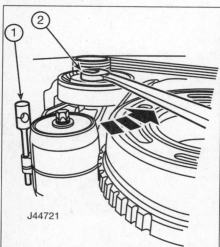

21.8a Auxiliary drivebelt tensioner on 1.8 litre Z18XE engines

1 Locking pin/bolt
2 Turn the tensioner as indicated to release the tension

21.8b Auxiliary drivebelt tensioner on 1.8 litre Z18XER engines

1 Raised projection on tensioner arm
2 Locking pin/bolt hole

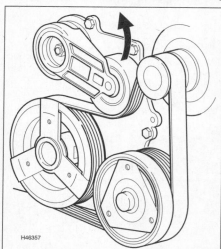

21.12 Auxiliary drivebelt tensioner on 2.2 litre engines

Turn the tensioner as indicated to release the tension

re-used, make sure it is fitted the correct way around. With the belt in position, slowly release the tensioner arm making sure that the drivebelt ribs locate correctly on each of the pulley grooves.

14 Refit the air cleaner housing (if removed), then refit the wheel arch liner inner cover and roadwheel, and lower the vehicle to the ground.

Every 2 years, regardless of mileage

22 Remote control battery renewal

1 Using a screwdriver, prise the battery cover from the ignition key fob (see illustrations).
2 Note how the circular battery is fitted, then carefully remove it from the contacts.
3 Fit the new battery (type CR 20 32) and refit the cover, making sure that it clips fully onto the base.
4 After changing the battery, lock and unlock the driver's door with the key in the lock to synchronise the remote control unit.

23 Hydraulic fluid renewal

Note: *It is not possible for the home mechanic to bleed the clutch hydraulic system on Easytronic models. Refer to Chapter 7C for additional information.*

 Warning: Hydraulic fluid can harm your eyes and damage painted surfaces, so use extreme caution when handling and pouring it. Do not use fluid that has been standing open for some time, as it absorbs moisture from the air. Excess moisture can cause a dangerous loss of braking effectiveness.

1 The procedure is similar to that for the bleeding of the hydraulic system as described in Chapters 9 (brake) and 6 (clutch).
2 Working as described in Chapter 9, open the first bleed screw in the sequence, and pump the brake pedal gently until nearly all the old fluid has been emptied from the master cylinder reservoir. Top-up to the MAX level with new fluid, and continue pumping until only the new fluid remains in the reservoir, and new fluid can be seen emerging from the

bleed screw. Tighten the screw, and top the reservoir level up to the MAX level line.

 Old hydraulic fluid is invariably much darker in colour than the new, making it easy to distinguish the two.

3 Work through all the remaining bleed screws in the sequence until new fluid can be seen at all of them. Be careful to keep the master cylinder reservoir topped-up to above the MIN level at all times, or air may enter the system and greatly increase the length of the task.
4 Bleed the fluid from the clutch hydraulic system as described in Chapter 6.
5 When the operation is complete, check that all bleed screws are securely tightened, and that their dust caps are refitted. Wash off all traces of spilt fluid, and recheck the master cylinder reservoir fluid level.
6 Check the operation of the brakes and clutch before taking the car on the road.

24 Coolant renewal

Note: *Vauxhall/Opel do not specify renewal intervals for the antifreeze mixture, as the mixture used to fill the system when the vehicle is new is designed to last the lifetime of the vehicle. However, it is strongly recommended that the coolant is renewed at the intervals specified in the 'Maintenance schedule', as a precaution against possible engine corrosion problems. This is particularly advisable if the coolant has been renewed using an antifreeze other than that specified by Vauxhall/Opel. With many antifreeze types, the corrosion inhibitors become progressively less effective with age. It is up to the individual owner whether or not to follow this advice.*

 Warning: Wait until the engine is cold before starting this procedure. Do not allow antifreeze to come in contact with your skin, or with the painted surfaces of the vehicle. Rinse off spills immediately with plenty of water. Never leave antifreeze lying around in an open container, or in a puddle in the driveway or on the garage floor. Children and pets are attracted by its sweet smell, but antifreeze can be fatal if ingested.

Cooling system draining

1 To drain the cooling system, first cover the expansion tank cap with a wad of rag, and slowly turn the cap anti-clockwise to relieve the pressure in the cooling system (a hissing sound will normally be heard). Wait until any pressure remaining in the system is released, then continue to turn the cap until it can be removed.
2 The coolant drain plug is located at the bottom of the radiator left-hand or right-hand end tank, according to engine. Position a container beneath the radiator then unscrew the drain plug and allow the coolant to drain. On 2.2 litre engines, also unscrew the drain plug from under the coolant pump housing (see illustration).
3 When the flow of coolant stops, refit and tighten the drain plug(s).
4 As no cylinder block drain plug is fitted, it is not possible to drain all of the coolant. Due consideration must be made for this when refilling the system, in order to maintain the correct concentration of antifreeze.
5 If the coolant has been drained for a reason other than renewal, then provided it is clean and less than two years old, it can be re-used.

Cooling system flushing

6 If coolant renewal has been neglected, or if the antifreeze mixture has become diluted,

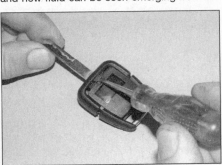
22.1a Prise off the battery cover . . .

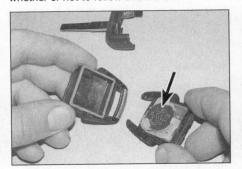
22.1b . . . and remove the circular battery

24.2 Removing the coolant drain plug located under the coolant pump housing – 2.2 litre engines

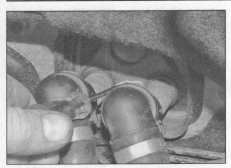

24.17 Lift up the wire clip and disconnect the left-hand heater hose from the heater matrix pipe stub

then in time, the cooling system may gradually lose efficiency, as the coolant passages become restricted due to rust, scale deposits, and other sediment. The cooling system efficiency can be restored by flushing the system clean.

7 The radiator should be flushed independently of the engine, to avoid unnecessary contamination.

Radiator flushing

8 Disconnect the top and bottom hoses and any other relevant hoses from the radiator, with reference to Chapter 3.

9 Insert a garden hose into the radiator top inlet. Direct a flow of clean water through the radiator, and continue flushing until clean water emerges from the radiator bottom outlet.

10 If after a reasonable period, the water still does not run clear, the radiator can be flushed with a good proprietary cleaning agent. It is important that the manufacturer's instructions are followed carefully. If the contamination is particularly bad, remove the radiator, insert the hose in the radiator bottom outlet, and reverse-flush the radiator.

Engine flushing

11 To flush the engine, the thermostat must be removed, because it will be shut, and would otherwise prevent the flow of water around the engine. The thermostat can be removed as described in Chapter 3. Take care

not to introduce dirt or debris into the system if this approach is used.

12 With the bottom hose disconnected from the radiator, insert a garden hose into the thermostat opening. Direct a clean flow of water through the engine, and continue flushing until clean water emerges from the radiator bottom hose.

13 On completion of flushing, refit the thermostat with reference to Chapter 3, and reconnect the hoses.

Cooling system filling

14 Before attempting to fill the cooling system, make sure that all hoses and clips are in good condition, and that the clips are tight. Note that an antifreeze mixture must be used all year round, to prevent corrosion of the engine components.

15 Remove the expansion tank filler cap.

16 Fill the system by slowly pouring the coolant into the expansion tank until it is up to the filler neck.

17 Using a small screwdriver, lift up the wire clip securing the left-hand heater hose to the heater matrix pipe stub, and disconnect the hose from the stub (see illustration).

18 As soon as coolant begins to run from the heater matrix, push the securing wire clip back into position on the heater hose end fitting, then push the hose back onto the matrix pipe stub. Ensure that the wire clip securely locks the hose in position.

19 Top-up the expansion tank until the coolant level is up to the KALT/COLD mark on the side of the tank.

20 Refit and tighten the expansion tank filler cap.

21 Start the engine and run it at 2000 to 2500 rpm for 30 seconds, allow it to idle for 5 seconds, then run it at 2000 to 2500 rpm again for a further 30 seconds.

22 Continue running the engine at idling speed and allow it to warm-up. When the cooling fan cuts-in, run the engine again at 2000 to 2500 rpm for 30 seconds, allow it to idle for 5 seconds, then run it at 2000 to 2500 rpm again for a further 30 seconds.

23 Stop the engine, and allow it to cool, then recheck the coolant level with reference to *Weekly checks*. Top-up the level if necessary and refit the expansion tank filler cap.

Antifreeze mixture

24 Always use an ethylene-glycol based antifreeze which is suitable for use in mixed-metal cooling systems. **Note:** *Vauxhall/ Opel recommend the use of silicate-free 'red' coolant (09 194 431).* The quantity of antifreeze and levels of protection are given in the Specifications.

25 Before adding antifreeze, the cooling system should be completely drained, preferably flushed, and all hoses checked for condition and security.

26 After filling with antifreeze, a label should be attached to the expansion tank, stating the type and concentration of antifreeze used, and the date installed. Any subsequent topping-up should be made with the same type and concentration of antifreeze.

Caution: Do not use engine antifreeze in the windscreen/tailgate washer system, as it will cause damage to the vehicle paintwork. A screenwash additive should be added to the washer system in the quantities stated on the bottle.

25 Exhaust emission check

1 The exhaust emission check is carried out initially after 3 years, then every 2 years, however, on vehicles which are subject to intensive use (eg, taxis/hire cars/ambulances) it must be carried out annually. The check involves checking the engine management system operation by plugging an electronic tester into the system diagnostic socket to check the electronic control unit (ECU) memory for faults (see Chapter 4A).

2 In reality, if the vehicle is running correctly and the engine management warning light in the instrument panel is functioning normally, then this check need not be carried out.

Every 40 000 miles or 4 years

26.2 Slacken the retaining clip and disconnect the air intake duct from the airflow meter

26.3 Disconnect the wiring connector from the airflow meter

26 Air cleaner element renewal

1 The air cleaner is located in the front right-hand corner of the engine compartment.

2 Slacken the retaining clip and disconnect the air intake duct from the airflow meter (see illustration).

3 Disconnect the wiring connector from the side of the airflow meter (see illustration).

4 Undo the screws and lift off the air cleaner cover, then lift out the filter element (see illustrations).

26.4a Undo the retaining screws . . .

26.4b . . . lift off the air cleaner cover . . .

26.4c . . . then lift out the filter element

5 Wipe out the casing and the cover.
6 Fit the new filter, noting that the rubber locating flange should be uppermost, and secure the cover with the screws.
7 Reconnect the airflow meter wiring connector and the air intake duct.

27 Spark plug renewal

1 The correct functioning of the spark plugs is vital for the correct running and efficiency of the engine. It is essential that the plugs fitted are appropriate for the engine; suitable types are specified at the beginning of this Chapter, or in the vehicle's Owner's Handbook. If the correct type is used and the engine is in good condition, the spark plugs should not need attention between scheduled renewal intervals. Spark plug cleaning is rarely necessary, and should not be attempted unless specialised equipment is available, as damage can easily be caused to the firing ends.
2 Where applicable, remove the engine top cover after removing the oil filler cap. Refit the cap.
3 Remove the ignition module from the spark plugs with reference to Chapter 5B.
4 It is advisable to remove the dirt from the spark plug recesses using a clean brush, vacuum cleaner or compressed air before removing the plugs, to prevent dirt dropping into the cylinders.
5 Unscrew the spark plugs from the cylinder head using a spark plug spanner, suitable box spanner or a deep socket and extension bar (see illustration). Keep the socket aligned with the spark plug – if it is forcibly moved to one side, the ceramic insulator may be broken off.
6 Examination of the spark plugs will give a good indication of the condition of the engine. As each plug is removed, examine it as follows. If the insulator nose of the spark plug is clean and white, with no deposits, this is indicative of a weak mixture or too hot a plug (a hot plug transfers heat away from the electrode slowly, a cold plug transfers heat away quickly).
7 If the tip and insulator nose are covered with hard black-looking deposits, then this is indicative that the mixture is too rich. Should the plug be black and oily, then it is likely that the engine is fairly worn, as well as the mixture being too rich.
8 If the insulator nose is covered with light tan to greyish-brown deposits, then the mixture is correct and it is likely that the engine is in good condition.
9 Some engines are fitted with multi-electrode plugs as standard (see illustration). On these plugs, the electrode gaps are all preset and no attempt should be made to bend the electrodes.
10 If single electrode plugs are to be installed, the spark plug electrode gap is of considerable importance. If the gap is too large or too small, the size of the spark and its efficiency will be seriously impaired and it will not perform correctly under all engine speed and load conditions. For the best results, the spark plug gap should be set in accordance with the Specifications at the beginning of this Chapter.
11 To set the gap, measure it with a feeler blade or spark plug gap gauge and then carefully bend the outer plug electrode until the correct gap is achieved. The centre electrode should never be bent, as this may crack the insulator and cause plug failure, if nothing worse. If using feeler blades, the gap is correct when the appropriate-size blade is a firm sliding fit (see illustrations).
12 Special spark plug electrode gap adjusting tools are available from most motor accessory shops, or from some spark plug manufacturers (see illustration).
13 Before fitting the spark plugs, check that the threaded connector sleeves on the top of

**27.5 Removing the spark plugs –
2.2 litre engines**

**27.9 The gap of the multi-electrode plugs
(where fitted) should not be adjusted**

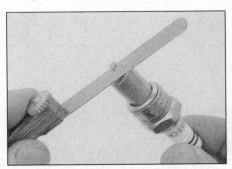
**27.11a If single electrode plugs are fitted,
check the electrode gap using a feeler
gauge . . .**

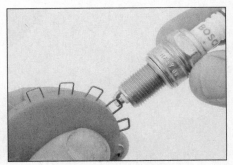
27.11b . . . or a wire gauge . . .

27.12 . . . and if necessary adjust the gap by bending the electrode

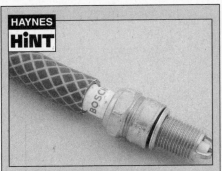

29.1 The fuel filter is clipped to the side of the fuel tank

the plug are tight, and that the plug exterior surfaces and threads are clean.

14 Screw in the spark plugs by hand where possible, then tighten them to the specified torque. Take extra care to enter the plug threads correctly, as the cylinder head is of light alloy construction **(see Haynes Hint)**.

15 On completion, refit the ignition module as described in Chapter 5B then, where applicable, refit the engine top cover.

28 Timing belt, tensioner and idler pulley renewal – 1.8 litre engines

Refer to the procedures contained in Chapter 2A.

29 Fuel filter renewal

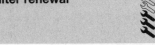

1 The fuel filter is located under the rear of the

It is very often difficult to insert spark plugs into their holes without cross-threading them. To avoid this possibility, fit a short length of rubber hose over the end of the spark plug. The flexible hose acts as a universal joint to help align the plug with the plug hole. Should the plug begin to cross-thread, the hose will slip on the spark plug, preventing thread damage to the aluminium cylinder head.

vehicle where it is clipped onto the side of the fuel tank **(see illustration)**.

2 Depressurise the fuel system as described in Chapter 4A.

3 Chock the front wheels, then jack up the rear of the vehicle and support on axle stands (see *Jacking and vehicle support*).

4 Position a suitable container below the fuel filter, to catch spilt fuel.

5 Disconnect the quick-release fittings and remove the fuel hoses from the fuel filter, noting their locations to ensure correct refitting. A Vauxhall/Opel special tool is

available to disconnect the hose connectors, but provided care is taken, the connections can be released using a pair of long-nosed pliers, or a similar tool, to depress the retaining tangs. Be prepared for fuel spillage, and take adequate precautions. Vauxhall/Opel recommend that the connecting clips of the quick-release connectors are renewed whenever removed.

6 Lift the retaining tab and push the filter forwards, out of the mounting bracket. Note the orientation of the fuel flow direction arrow.

7 Fitting the new filter is a reversal of removal, bearing in mind the following points.

a) *Ensure that the filter is fitted with the flow direction arrow on the filter body pointing in the direction of fuel flow.*

b) *Ensure that the hoses are reconnected to their correct locations, as noted before removal.*

c) *On completion, run the engine and check for leaks. If leakage is evident, stop the engine immediately and rectify the problem without delay.*

Every 100 000 miles or 10 years

30 Valve clearance check and adjustment – 1.8 litre Z18XER engines

Refer to the procedures contained in Chapter 2A.

Lubricants and fluids .... Refer to *Weekly checks* on page 0•17

Capacities
Engine oil (including oil filter) .... 4.3 litres
Difference between MIN and MAX dipstick marks .... 1.0 litre
Cooling system .... 7.5 litres

Transmission
Manual transmission .... 2.2 litres
Automatic transmission (at fluid change) .... 3.0 litres (approximately)

Washer fluid reservoir
Without headlight washers .... 2.9 litres
With headlight washers .... 5.6 litres

Fuel tank
Saloon and Hatchback models .... 60 litres
Estate models .... 61 litres

Cooling system
Antifreeze mixture:
    40% antifreeze .... Protection down to -28°C
    50% antifreeze .... Protection down to -40°C

Brakes
Friction material minimum thickness (including backing plate):
    Front brake pads .... 9.0 mm
    Rear brake pads .... 8.0 mm

Torque wrench settings

	Nm	lbf ft
Engine oil filter	15	11
Fuel filter housing cover retaining ring	30	22
Roadwheel bolts	110	81
Sump drain plug	20	15

The maintenance intervals in this manual are provided with the assumption that you, not the dealer, will be carrying out the work. These are the minimum maintenance intervals based on the standard service schedule recommended by the manufacturer for vehicles driven daily. If you wish to keep your vehicle in peak condition at all times, you may wish to perform some of these procedures more often. We encourage frequent maintenance, because it enhances the efficiency, performance and resale value of your vehicle.

If the vehicle is driven in dusty areas, used to tow a trailer, or driven frequently at slow speeds (idling in traffic) or on short journeys, more frequent maintenance intervals are recommended.

When the vehicle is new, it should be serviced by a dealer service department (or other workshop recognised by the vehicle manufacturer as providing the same standard of service) in order to preserve the warranty. The vehicle manufacturer may reject warranty claims if you are unable to prove that servicing has been carried out as and when specified, using only original equipment parts or parts certified to be of equivalent quality.

Every 250 miles or weekly

☐ Refer to *Weekly checks*

Every 10 000 miles or 6 months – whichever comes first

☐ Renew the engine oil and filter (Section 3)

Note: *Vauxhall/Opel recommend that the engine oil and filter are changed every 20 000 miles or 12 months if the vehicle is being operated under the standard service schedule. However, oil and filter changes are good for the engine and we recommend that the oil and filter are renewed more frequently, especially if the vehicle is used on a lot of short journeys.*

Every 20 000 miles or 12 months – whichever comes first

☐ Check all underbonnet and underbody components, pipes and hoses for leaks (Section 4)
☐ Drain the water from the fuel filter (Section 5)
☐ Check the power steering fluid level (Section 6)
☐ Check the condition of the brake pads (renew if necessary), the calipers and discs (Section 7)
☐ Check the condition of all brake fluid pipes and hoses (Section 8)
☐ Check the condition of the front suspension and steering components, particularly the rubber gaiters and seals (Section 9)
☐ Check the condition of the driveshaft joint gaiters, and the driveshaft joints (Section 10)
☐ Check the condition of the exhaust system components (Section 11)
☐ Check the condition of the rear suspension components (Section 12)
☐ Check the bodywork and underbody for damage and corrosion, and check the condition of the underbody corrosion protection (Section 13)
☐ Check the tightness of the roadwheel bolts (Section 14)
☐ Lubricate all door, bonnet, boot lid and tailgate hinges and locks (Section 15)
☐ Check the operation of the horn, all lights, and the wipers and washers (Section 16)
☐ Check the headlight beam alignment (Section 17)
☐ Carry out a road test (Section 18)
☐ Reset the service interval indicator (Section 19)

Every 40 000 miles or 2 years – whichever comes first

☐ Renew the pollen filter (Section 20)
☐ Renew the fuel filter (Section 21)
☐ Check the auxiliary drivebelt and tensioner (Section 22)
☐ Check, and if necessary adjust, the valve clearances – Z19DT engines (Section 23)

Every 2 years, regardless of mileage

☐ Renew the battery for the remote control handset (Section 24)
☐ Renew the brake and clutch fluid (Section 25)
☐ Renew the coolant (Section 26)*
☐ Exhaust emission test (Section 27)

* **Note:** *Vehicles using Vauxhall/Opel silicate-free coolant do not need the coolant renewed on a regular basis.*

Every 40 000 miles or 4 years – whichever comes first

☐ Renew the air cleaner filter element (Section 28)
☐ Renew the timing belt, tensioner and idler pulleys (Section 29)*

* **Note:** *The normal interval for timing belt renewal is 100 000 miles or 10 years. However, it is strongly recommended that the interval used is 40 000 miles on vehicles which are subjected to intensive use, ie, mainly short journeys or a lot of stop-start driving. The actual belt renewal interval is therefore very much up to the individual owner, but bear in mind that severe engine damage will result if the belt breaks.*

Underbonnet view of an SOHC engine model

1   Engine oil level dipstick
2   Engine oil filler cap
3   Air cleaner assembly
4   Front suspension strut
    upper mounting
5   Screen washer fluid
    reservoir
6   Airflow meter
7   Brake (and clutch) fluid
    reservoir
8   Fuel filter
9   Coolant expansion tank
10 Battery
11 Fuse/relay box
12 ABS hydraulic modulator

Underbonnet view of a DOHC engine model

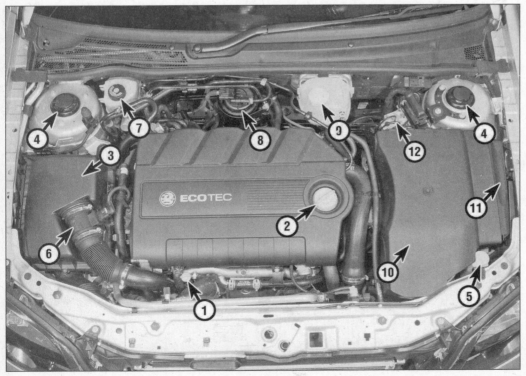

1   Engine oil level dipstick
2   Engine oil filler cap
3   Air cleaner assembly
4   Front suspension strut
    upper mounting
5   Screen washer fluid
    reservoir
6   Airflow meter
7   Brake (and clutch) fluid
    reservoir
8   Fuel filter
9   Coolant expansion tank
10 Battery
11 Fuse/relay box
12 ABS hydraulic modulator

Front underbody view

1 Exhaust front pipe
2 Steering track rods
3 Front suspension lower arms
4 Front brake calipers
5 Engine mounting front torque link
6 Engine mounting rear torque link
7 Right-hand driveshaft
8 Manual transmission
9 Engine oil drain plug
10 Air conditioning compressor
11 Electric cooling fan
12 Front subframe

Rear underbody view

1 Handbrake cable
2 Exhaust tailpipe and silencer
3 Exhaust heat shield
4 Rear axle body
5 Rear hub carrier
6 Lower control arm
7 Upper control arm
8 Auxiliary control arm
9 Shock absorber
10 Rear anti-roll bar
11 Rear suspension trailing arm
12 Fuel tank

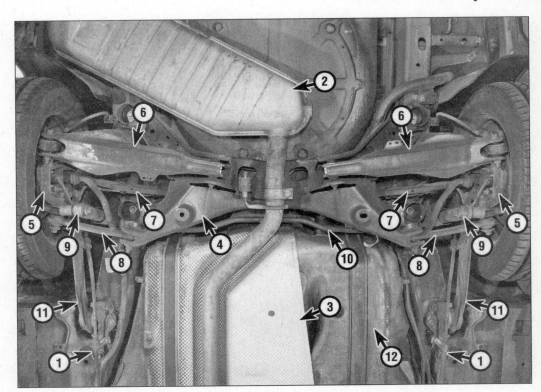

1 General information

1 This Chapter is designed to help the home mechanic maintain his/her vehicle for safety, economy, long life and peak performance.

2 The Chapter contains a master maintenance schedule, followed by Sections dealing specifically with each task in the schedule. Visual checks, adjustments, component renewal and other helpful items are included. Refer to the accompanying illustrations of the engine compartment and the underside of the vehicle for the locations of the various components.

3 Servicing your vehicle in accordance with the mileage/time maintenance schedule and the following Sections will provide a planned maintenance programme, which should result in a long and reliable service life. This is a comprehensive plan, so maintaining some items but not others at the specified service intervals will not produce the same results.

4 As you service your vehicle, you will discover that many of the procedures can – and should – be grouped together, because of the particular procedure being performed, or because of the proximity of two otherwise-unrelated components to one another. For example, if the vehicle is raised for any reason, the exhaust can be inspected at the same time as the suspension and steering components.

5 The first step in this maintenance programme is to prepare yourself before the actual work begins. Read through all the Sections relevant to the work to be carried out, then make a list and gather all the parts and tools required. If a problem is encountered, seek advice from a parts specialist, or a dealer service department.

2 Regular maintenance

1 If, from the time the vehicle is new, the routine maintenance schedule is followed closely, and frequent checks are made of fluid levels and high-wear items, as suggested throughout this manual, the engine will be kept in relatively good running condition, and the need for additional work will be minimised.

2 It is possible that there will be times when the engine is running poorly due to the lack of regular maintenance. This is even more likely if a used vehicle, which has not received regular and frequent maintenance checks, is purchased. In such cases, additional work may need to be carried out, outside of the regular maintenance intervals.

3 If engine wear is suspected, a compression test (refer to the appropriate part of Chapter 2) will provide valuable information regarding the overall performance of the main internal components. Such a test can be used as a basis to decide on the extent of the work to be carried out. If, for example, a compression test indicates serious internal engine wear, conventional maintenance as described in this Chapter will not greatly improve the performance of the engine, and may prove a waste of time and money, unless extensive overhaul work is carried out first.

4 The following series of operations are those most often required to improve the performance of a generally poor-running engine:

Primary operations

a) Clean, inspect and test the battery (refer to Weekly checks).
b) Check all the engine-related fluids (refer to Weekly checks).
c) Check the condition and tension of the auxiliary drivebelt (Section 22).
d) Check the condition of the air filter, and renew if necessary (Section 28).
e) Renew the fuel filter (Section 21).
f) Check the condition of all hoses, and check for fluid leaks (Section 4).

5 If the above operations do not prove fully effective, carry out the following secondary operations:

Secondary operations

All items listed under Primary operations, plus the following:

a) Check the charging system (refer to Chapter 5A).
b) Check the pre/post-heating system (refer to Chapter 5A).
c) Check the fuel, exhaust and emission control systems (refer to the appropriate Parts of Chapter 4).

Every 10 000 miles or 6 months

3 Engine oil and filter renewal

HAYNES HiNT *Frequent oil and filter changes are the most important preventative maintenance procedures which can be undertaken by the DIY owner. As engine oil ages, it becomes diluted and contaminated, which leads to premature engine wear.*

1 Before starting this procedure, gather together all the necessary tools and materials. Also make sure that you have plenty of clean rags and newspapers handy, to mop-up any spills. Ideally, the engine oil should be warm, as it will drain more easily, and more built-up sludge will be removed with it. Take care not to touch the exhaust or any other hot parts of the engine when working under the vehicle. To avoid any possibility of scalding, and to protect yourself from possible skin irritants and other harmful contaminants in used engine oils, it is advisable to wear gloves when carrying out this work.

2 Access to the underside of the vehicle will be greatly improved if it can be raised on a lift, driven onto ramps, or jacked up and supported on axle stands (see Jacking and vehicle support). Whichever method is chosen, make sure that the vehicle remains level, or if it is at an angle, that the drain plug is at the lowest point. Remove the engine undertray for access.

3 Remove the oil filler cap from the camshaft cover or oil filler housing, as applicable (twist it through a quarter-turn anti-clockwise and withdraw it) (see illustration).

4 Using a spanner, or preferably a suitable socket and bar, slacken the drain plug about half a turn (see illustration). Position the draining container under the drain plug, then remove the plug completely (see Haynes Hint).

5 Allow some time for the oil to drain, noting

3.3 Removing the oil filler cap – Z19DT engines

3.4 Engine oil drain plug location (arrowed)

HAYNES HiNT

As the drain plug releases from the threads, move it away quickly so that the stream of oil running out of the sump goes into the drain pan and not up your sleeve.

3.7a Unscrew the filter cap and withdraw it together with the element . . .

3.7b . . . then separate the element from the cap . . .

3.7c . . . and remove the two O-ring seals

that it may be necessary to reposition the container as the oil flow slows to a trickle.

6 Position another container under the oil filter. The filter is located at the rear of the engine and is accessible from under the car.

7 Unscrew the filter housing cap and withdraw it, together with the element, then separate the element, and remove the two O-ring seals from the cap **(see illustrations)**.

8 Use a clean rag to remove all oil, dirt and sludge from the oil filter housing and cap.

9 Locate the new O-ring seals in their grooves on the housing cap, then locate the new element in the cap and insert them both in the filter housing. Screw on the cap and tighten to the specified torque.

10 After all the oil has drained, wipe the drain plug and the sealing washer/O-ring with a clean rag. Examine the condition of the sealing washer/O-ring, and renew it if it shows signs of damage which may prevent an oil-tight seal. Clean the area around the drain plug opening, and refit the plug complete with the washer/O-ring. Tighten the plug to the specified torque, using a torque wrench.

11 Remove the old oil and all tools from under the vehicle then lower the vehicle to the ground.

12 Fill the engine through the filler hole in the camshaft cover or oil filler housing, as applicable, using the correct grade and type of oil (refer to *Weekly checks* for details of topping-up). Pour in half the specified quantity of oil first, then wait a few minutes for the oil to drain into the sump. Continue to add oil, a small quantity at a time, until the level is up to the lower mark on the dipstick. Adding approximately a further 1.0 litre will bring the level up to the upper mark on the dipstick.

13 Start the engine and run it until it reaches normal operating temperature. While the engine is warming-up, check for leaks around the oil filter and the sump drain plug.

14 Stop the engine, and wait at least five minutes for the oil to settle in the sump once more. With the new oil circulated and the filter now completely full, recheck the level on the dipstick, and add more oil as necessary.

15 Dispose of the used engine oil and filter safely, with reference to *General repair*

procedures in the Reference Chapter of this manual. Do not discard the old filter with domestic household waste. The facility for waste oil disposal provided by many local council refuse tips and/or recycling centres generally has a filter receptacle alongside.

Every 20 000 miles or 12 months

4 Hose and fluid leak check

Refer to Chapter 1A, Section 4.

5 Fuel filter water draining

Caution: Before starting any work on the fuel filter, wipe clean the filter assembly and the area around it; it is essential that no dirt or other foreign matter is allowed into the system. Obtain a suitable container into which the filter can be drained and place rags or similar material under the filter assembly to catch any spillages. Do not allow diesel fuel to contaminate components such as the

alternator and starter motor, the coolant hoses and engine mountings, and any wiring.

1 The fuel filter is located at the rear of the engine compartment, in the centre of the bulkhead.

2 Disconnect the heater element wiring

connector from the fuel filter cover, and the water level sensor wiring connector from the base of the filter housing **(see illustrations)**.

3 Using a screwdriver inserted from the right-hand side, depress the retaining clip and lift the filter from the crash box **(see illustration)**.

5.2a Disconnect the heater element wiring connector from the fuel filter cover . . .

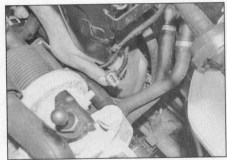

5.2b . . . and the water level sensor wiring connector from the base of the filter housing

5.3 Depress the retaining clip and lift the filter from the crash box

4 In addition to taking the precautions noted above to catch any fuel spillages, connect a tube to the drain screw on the base of the fuel filter **(see illustration)**. Place the other end of the tube in a clean jar or can.
5 Loosen the drain screw approximately one complete turn and allow the filter to drain until clean fuel, free of dirt or water, emerges from the tube (approximately 100 cc is usually sufficient).
6 Remove the drain tube, then tighten the drain screw securely.
7 Insert the filter in the crash box making sure that the retaining clip engages.
8 Reconnect the wiring.
9 On completion, dispose of the drained fuel safely. Check all disturbed components to ensure that there are no leaks (of air or fuel) when the engine is restarted.

6 Power steering fluid level check

Refer to Chapter 10, Section 21.

7 Brake pad, caliper and disc check

Refer to Chapter 1A, Section 7.

8 Brake fluid pipe and hose check

Refer to Chapter 1A, Section 8.

5.4 Fuel filter drain screw (arrowed)

9 Front suspension and steering check

Refer to Chapter 1A, Section 9.

10 Driveshaft check

Refer to Chapter 1A, Section 10.

11 Exhaust system check

Refer to Chapter 1A, Section 11.

12 Rear suspension check

Refer to Chapter 1A, Section 12.

13 Bodywork and underbody condition check

Refer to Chapter 1A, Section 13.

14 Roadwheel bolt tightness check

Refer to Chapter 1A, Section 14.

15 Hinge and lock lubrication

Refer to Chapter 1A, Section 15.

16 Electrical systems check

Refer to Chapter 1A, Section 16.

17 Headlight beam alignment check

Refer to Chapter 1A, Section 17.

18 Road test

Refer to Chapter 1A, Section 18.

19 Service interval indicator reset

1 With the ignition switched off, the display on the instrument panel must show the trip odometer.
2 With the ignition still switched off, depress and hold the trip odometer reset button located on the instrument panel. After approximately 3 seconds the display will show the service symbol.
3 With the reset button depressed, also depress the brake pedal and switch on the ignition. 'InSP - - -' will appear in the display.
4 After approximately 10 seconds the display will show 'InSP' followed by the maximum mileage before the next required service indicating that the service interval indicator has been reset. Release the reset button and brake pedal, then switch off the ignition.

Every 40 000 miles or 2 years

20 Pollen filter renewal

Refer to Chapter 1A, Section 20.

21 Fuel filter renewal

Caution: Before starting any work on the fuel filter, wipe clean the filter assembly and the area around it; it is essential that no dirt or other foreign matter is allowed into the system. Obtain a suitable container into which the filter can be drained and place rags or similar material under the

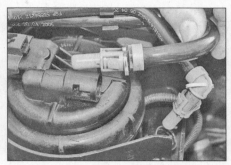

21.3a Depress the quick-release connector retaining tangs . . .

21.3b . . . and remove the hoses from the fuel filter housing cover

21.7 Using a home-made tool to slacken the filter housing cover retaining ring

21.9a Unscrew and remove the cover retaining ring . . .

21.9b . . . then lift the cover together with the filter element . . .

21.9c . . . and recover the O-ring seal

filter assembly to catch any spillages. Do not allow diesel fuel to contaminate components such as the starter motor, the coolant hoses and engine mountings, and any wiring.

Note: Vauxhall/Opel special tool EN-46784-010, or a suitable alternative will be required to unscrew the filter housing cover retaining ring.

1 The fuel filter is located at the rear of the engine compartment, in the centre of the bulkhead.

2 Disconnect the heater element wiring connector from the fuel filter cover, and the water level sensor wiring connector from the base of the filter housing (see illustrations 5.2a and 5.2b).

3 Detach the two fuel hose quick-release connectors and remove the hoses from the fuel filter housing and cover. A Vauxhall/

Opel special tool (KM-796-A) is available to disconnect the hose connectors, but provided care is taken, the connections can be released using two screwdrivers, a pair of long-nosed pliers, or similar, to depress the retaining tangs (see illustrations). Suitably cover or plug the open hose connections to prevent dirt entry.

4 Using a screwdriver inserted from the right-hand side, depress the retaining clip and lift the filter housing from the crash box.

5 Loosen the drain screw on the base of the filter housing one complete turn and drain the fuel into a suitable container. Tighten the drain screw securely once the filter has drained.

6 Lay the filter on its side and clamp the two filter housing mounting lugs in a soft-jawed vice. Take great care not to damage the lugs and only tighten the vice sufficiently to hold the housing while the cover retaining ring is slackened.

7 Slacken the filter housing cover retaining ring using the Vauxhall/Opel special tool or a suitable alternative (see illustration).

8 Reposition the filter housing vertically in the vice and tighten the vice lightly.

9 Fully unscrew the cover retaining ring, then lift the cover together with the filter element from the housing. Recover the O-ring seal (see illustrations).

10 Turn the filter element approximately 50° anti-clockwise to release it from the cover (see illustration).

11 Empty the fuel from the filter housing, then thoroughly clean the housing and cover with a lint-free cloth.

12 Align the arrow on the new filter element with the corresponding arrow on the cover then push the filter onto the cover until it locks in position (see illustrations).

13 Locate a new O-ring seal on the filter

21.10 Turn the filter element approximately 50° anti-clockwise to release it from the cover

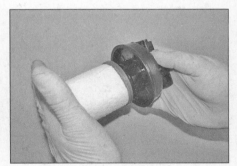

21.12a Align the arrow on the new filter element with the corresponding arrow on the cover . . .

21.12b . . . then push the filter onto the cover until it locks in position

21.13a Locate a new O-ring seal on the filter housing . . .

21.13b . . . then fit the element and cover to the housing

22.7a Turn the drivebelt tensioner clockwise using a spanner on the pulley centre bolt (arrowed) . . .

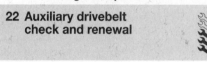

22.7b . . . then lock the tensioner by inserting a locking pin or drill bit (arrowed) through the special hole

housing, then fit the element and cover to the housing **(see illustrations)**.

14 Lubricate the threads of the retaining ring with a little diesel fuel then screw the ring onto the housing. Reposition the housing horizontally in the vice as before, and tighten the retaining ring to the specified torque using the special tool or alternative.

15 Insert the filter assembly into the crash box, making sure that the retaining clip engages. Reconnect the fuel hoses and the wiring connectors.

16 Bleed the fuel system as described in Chapter 4B and check all disturbed components to ensure that there are no leaks (of air or fuel) when the engine is restarted.

17 On completion, safely dispose of the drained fuel.

22 Auxiliary drivebelt check and renewal

Checking

1 Due to their function and material make-up, drivebelts are prone to failure after a long period of time and should therefore be inspected regularly.

2 Apply the handbrake, then jack up the front of the vehicle and support it on axle stands (see *Jacking and vehicle support*). Remove the right-hand front roadwheel and the engine undertray.

3 With the engine stopped, inspect the full length of the drivebelt for cracks and

separation of the belt plies. It will be necessary to turn the engine (using a spanner or socket and bar on the crankshaft pulley bolt) so that the belt can be inspected thoroughly. Twist the belt between the pulleys so that both sides can be viewed. Also check for fraying, and glazing which gives the belt a shiny appearance. Check the pulleys for nicks, cracks, distortion and corrosion. If the belt shows signs of wear or damage, it should be renewed as a precaution against breakage in service.

Renewal

4 If not already done, apply the handbrake, then jack up the front of the vehicle and support it on axle stands (see *Jacking and vehicle support*). Remove the right-hand front roadwheel and the engine undertray.

5 For additional working clearance, remove the air cleaner housing as described in Chapter 4B.

6 If the drivebelt is to be re-used, mark it to indicate its normal running direction.

7 Using a spanner on the pulley centre bolt, turn the tensioner clockwise against the spring tension. Hold the tensioner in this position by inserting a suitable locking pin or drill bit through the special hole provided **(see illustrations)**.

8 Slip the drivebelt from the pulleys.

9 Locate the new drivebelt on the pulleys in the correct routing **(see illustrations)**. If the drivebelt is being re-used, make sure it is fitted the correct way around.

10 Turn back the tensioner and remove the locking pin/drill bit, then release it, making sure that the drivebelt ribs locate correctly on each of the pulley grooves.

11 Refit the air cleaner housing (if removed), then refit the engine undertray and roadwheel, and lower the vehicle to the ground.

23 Valve clearance check and adjustment – Z19DT engines

Refer to the procedures contained in Chapter 2C.

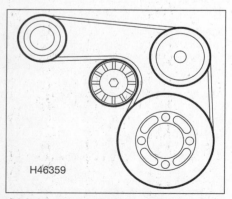

22.9a Auxiliary drivebelt configuration on models without air conditioning . . .

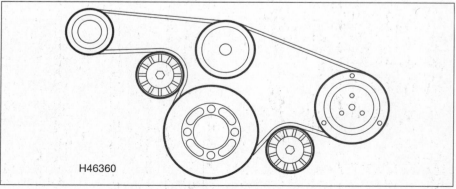

22.9b . . . and on models with air conditioning

Every 2 years, regardless of mileage

24 Remote control battery renewal

Refer to Chapter 1A, Section 22.

25 Hydraulic fluid renewal

⚠️ *Warning: Hydraulic fluid can harm your eyes and damage painted surfaces, so use extreme caution when handling and pouring it. Do not use fluid that has been standing open for some time, as it absorbs moisture from the air. Excess moisture can cause a dangerous loss of braking effectiveness.*

Note: *The brake and clutch hydraulic systems share a common reservoir.*

1 The procedure is similar to that for the bleeding of the hydraulic system as described in Chapters 9 (brake) and 6 (clutch).

2 Working as described in Chapter 9, open the first bleed screw in the sequence, and pump the brake pedal gently until nearly all the old fluid has been emptied from the master cylinder reservoir. Top-up to the MAX level with new fluid, and continue pumping until only the new fluid remains in the reservoir, and new fluid can be seen emerging from the bleed screw. Tighten the screw, and top the reservoir level up to the MAX level line.

 HAYNES HiNT *Old hydraulic fluid is invariably much darker in colour than the new, making it easy to distinguish the two.*

3 Work through all the remaining bleed screws in the sequence until new fluid can be seen at all of them. Be careful to keep the master cylinder reservoir topped-up to above the MIN level at all times, or air may enter the system and greatly increase the length of the task.

4 Bleed the fluid from the clutch hydraulic system as described in Chapter 6.

5 When the operation is complete, check that all bleed screws are securely tightened, and that their dust caps are refitted. Wash off all traces of spilt fluid, and recheck the master cylinder reservoir fluid level.

6 Check the operation of the brakes and clutch before taking the car on the road.

26 Coolant renewal

Note: *Vauxhall/Opel do not specify renewal intervals for the antifreeze mixture, as the mixture used to fill the system when the vehicle is new is designed to last the lifetime of the vehicle. However, it is strongly recommended that the coolant is renewed at the intervals specified in the 'Maintenance schedule', as a precaution against possible engine corrosion problems. This is particularly advisable if the coolant has been renewed using an antifreeze other than that specified by Vauxhall/Opel. With many antifreeze types, the corrosion inhibitors become progressively less effective with age. It is up to the individual owner whether or not to follow this advice.*

⚠️ *Warning: Wait until the engine is cold before starting this procedure. Do not allow antifreeze to come in contact with your skin, or with the painted surfaces of the vehicle. Rinse off spills immediately with plenty of water. Never leave antifreeze lying around in an open container, or in a puddle in the driveway or on the garage floor. Children and pets are attracted by its sweet smell, but antifreeze can be fatal if ingested.*

Cooling system draining

1 To drain the cooling system, first cover the expansion tank cap with a wad of rag, and slowly turn the cap anti-clockwise to relieve the pressure in the cooling system (a hissing sound will normally be heard). Wait until any pressure remaining in the system is released, then continue to turn the cap until it can be removed.

2 Remove the engine undertray, then position a suitable container beneath the right-hand side of the radiator.

3 The coolant drain plug is located at the bottom of the radiator left-hand end tank. Unscrew the drain plug and allow the coolant to drain.

4 When the flow of coolant stops, refit and tighten the drain plugs.

5 As no cylinder block drain plug is fitted, it is not possible to drain all of the coolant. Due consideration must be made for this when refilling the system, in order to maintain the correct concentration of antifreeze.

6 If the coolant has been drained for a reason other than renewal, then provided it is clean and less than two years old, it can be re-used.

26.18a Lift up the wire clip and disconnect the left-hand heater hose from the heater matrix pipe stub . . .

Cooling system flushing

7 If coolant renewal has been neglected, or if the antifreeze mixture has become diluted, then in time, the cooling system may gradually lose efficiency, as the coolant passages become restricted due to rust, scale deposits, and other sediment. The cooling system efficiency can be restored by flushing the system clean.

8 The radiator should be flushed independently of the engine, to avoid unnecessary contamination.

Radiator flushing

9 Disconnect the top and bottom hoses and any other relevant hoses from the radiator, with reference to Chapter 3.

10 Insert a garden hose into the radiator top inlet. Direct a flow of clean water through the radiator, and continue flushing until clean water emerges from the radiator bottom outlet.

11 If after a reasonable period, the water still does not run clear, the radiator can be flushed with a good proprietary cleaning agent. It is important that the manufacturer's instructions are followed carefully. If the contamination is particularly bad, remove the radiator, insert the hose in the radiator bottom outlet, and reverse-flush the radiator.

Engine flushing

12 To flush the engine, the thermostat must be removed, because it will be shut, and would otherwise prevent the flow of water around the engine. The thermostat can be removed as described in Chapter 3. Take care not to introduce dirt or debris into the system if this approach is used.

13 With the bottom hose disconnected from the radiator, insert a garden hose into the thermostat opening. Direct a clean flow of water through the engine, and continue flushing until clean water emerges from the radiator bottom hose.

14 On completion of flushing, refit the thermostat with reference to Chapter 3, and reconnect the hoses.

Cooling system filling

15 Before attempting to fill the cooling system, make sure that all hoses and clips are in good condition, and that the clips are tight. Note that an antifreeze mixture must be used all year round, to prevent corrosion of the engine components.

16 Remove the expansion tank filler cap.

17 Fill the system by slowly pouring the coolant into the expansion tank until it is up to the filler neck.

18 Using a small screwdriver, lift up the wire clip securing the left-hand heater hose to the heater matrix pipe stub, and disconnect the hose from the stub. Additionally, open the bleed screw in the coolant pipe above the exhaust manifold (see illustrations).

19 As soon as coolant begins to run from the

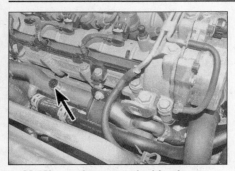

26.18b . . . then open the bleed screw (arrowed) in the coolant pipe above the exhaust manifold

heater matrix, push the securing wire clip back into position on the heater hose end fitting, then push the hose back onto the matrix pipe stub. Ensure that the wire clip securely locks the hose in position. Close the coolant pipe bleed screw as soon as coolant emerges.

20 Top-up the expansion tank until the coolant level is up to the KALT/COLD mark on the side of the tank.

21 Refit the expansion tank filler cap.

22 Start the engine and run it at 2000 to 2500 rpm for 30 seconds, allow it to idle for 5 seconds, then run it at 2000 to 2500 rpm again for a further 30 seconds.

23 Continue running the engine at idling speed and allow it to warm-up. When the cooling fan cuts-in, run the engine again at 2000 to 2500 rpm for 30 seconds, allow it to idle for 5 seconds, then run it at 2000 to 2500 rpm again for a further 30 seconds.

24 Stop the engine, and allow it to cool, then recheck the coolant level with reference to *Weekly checks*. Top-up the level if necessary and refit the expansion tank filler cap. Refit the engine undertray.

Antifreeze mixture

25 Always use an ethylene-glycol based antifreeze which is suitable for use in mixed-metal cooling systems. **Note:** *Vauxhall/ Opel recommend the use of silicate-free 'red' coolant (09 194 431).* The quantity of antifreeze and levels of protection are given in the Specifications.

26 Before adding antifreeze, the cooling system should be completely drained, preferably flushed, and all hoses checked for condition and security.

27 After filling with antifreeze, a label should be attached to the expansion tank, stating the type and concentration of antifreeze used, and the date installed. Any subsequent topping-up should be made with the same type and concentration of antifreeze.

Caution: Do not use engine antifreeze in the windscreen/tailgate washer system, as it will cause damage to the vehicle paintwork. A screenwash additive should be added to the washer system in the quantities stated on the bottle.

27 Exhaust emission check

Refer to Chapter 1A, Section 25, and Chapter 4B.

Every 40 000 miles or 4 years

28 Air cleaner element renewal

Refer to Chapter 1A, Section 26.

29 Timing belt, tensioner and idler pulley renewal

Refer to the procedures contained in Chapter 2C or 2D.

Chapter 2 Part A:
1.8 litre petrol engine in-car repair procedures

Contents

Degrees of difficulty

| Easy, suitable for novice with little experience 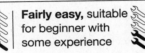 | Fairly easy, suitable for beginner with some experience 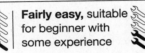 | Fairly difficult, suitable for competent DIY mechanic 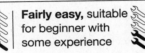 | Difficult, suitable for experienced DIY mechanic 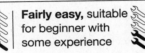 | Very difficult, suitable for expert DIY or professional |

Specifications

General
Engine type	Four-cylinder, in-line, water-cooled. Double overhead camshafts, belt-driven
Manufacturer's engine code*	Z18XE and Z18XER
Bore	80.5 mm
Stroke	88.2 mm
Capacity	1796 cc
Compression ratio	10.5:1
Firing order	1-3-4-2 (No 1 cylinder at timing belt end)
Direction of crankshaft rotation	Clockwise (viewed from timing belt end of engine)

* For details of engine code location, see 'Vehicle identification' in the Reference Chapter.

Compression pressures
Standard	14 to 16 bar
Maximum difference between any two cylinders	1 bar

Valve clearances (Z18XER engines)
Engine cold:
Inlet	0.21 to 0.29 mm
Exhaust	0.27 to 0.35 mm

Lubrication system
Minimum oil pressure at 80ºC	1.3 bar at idle speed
Oil pump type	Rotor-type, driven directly from crankshaft

Rotor-to-housing clearance (endfloat):
Z18XE engines	0.03 to 0.10 mm
Z18XER engines	0.02 to 0.058 mm

Torque wrench settings

	Nm	lbf ft
Z18XE engines		
Auxiliary drivebelt tensioner bolt	35	26
Camshaft bearing cap bolts	8	6
Camshaft cover bolts	8	6
Camshaft sprocket bolt:*		
Stage 1	50	37
Stage 2	Angle-tighten a further 60°	
Stage 3	Angle-tighten a further 15°	
Connecting rod big-end bearing cap bolt:*		
Stage 1	25	18
Stage 2	Angle-tighten a further 30°	
Crankshaft pulley bolt:*		
Stage 1	95	70
Stage 2	Angle-tighten a further 30°	
Stage 3	Angle-tighten a further 15°	
Crankshaft sensor mounting bracket bolt	8	6
Cylinder head bolts:*		
Stage 1	25	18
Stage 2	Angle-tighten a further 90°	
Stage 3	Angle-tighten a further 90°	
Stage 4	Angle-tighten a further 90°	
Stage 5	Angle-tighten a further 45°	
Engine mountings:		
Front mounting/torque link:		
Mounting to transmission	80	59
Mounting to subframe	80	59
Left-hand mounting:		
Mounting-to-body bolts	20	15
Mounting bracket to transmission bracket	55	41
Transmission bracket to transmission	80	59
Rear mounting/torque link:		
Mounting bracket to transmission	80	59
Mounting to subframe	60	44
Mounting to transmission bracket	80	59
Right-hand mounting:		
Engine bracket-to-engine bolts:*		
Stage 1	65	48
Stage 2	Angle-tighten a further 45°	
Mounting-to-body bolts/nut	55	41
Mounting-to-engine bracket bolts	55	41
Engine-to-transmission bolts	60	44
Flywheel bolts:*		
Stage 1	35	26
Stage 2	Angle-tighten a further 30°	
Stage 3	Angle-tighten a further 15°	
Main bearing cap bolts:*		
Stage 1	50	37
Stage 2	Angle-tighten a further 45°	
Stage 3	Angle-tighten a further 15°	
Oil pump:		
Retaining bolts	10	7
Pump cover screws	6	4
Oil pressure relief valve bolt	50	37
Oil pump pick-up/strainer and baffle bolts	8	6
Roadwheel bolts	110	81
Sump bolts:		
Sump-to-cylinder block/oil pump bolts	10	7
Sump flange-to-transmission bolts	40	30
Drain plug	14	10
Timing belt cover bolts:		
Upper and lower covers	4	3
Rear cover	6	4
Timing belt idler pulley bolt	25	18
Timing belt tensioner bolt	20	15

* Use new fasteners

Torque wrench settings

Z18XER engines

	Nm	lbf ft
Auxiliary drivebelt tensioner bolt*	50	37
Camshaft bearing cap bolts	8	6
Camshaft bearing support bolts	8	6
Camshaft cover bolts	8	6
Camshaft sprocket closure bolt	30	22
Camshaft sprocket retaining bolt:*		
Stage 1	65	48
Stage 2	Angle-tighten a further 125°	
Stage 3	Angle-tighten a further 15°	
Connecting rod big-end bearing cap bolt:*		
Stage 1	35	26
Stage 2	Angle-tighten a further 45°	
Stage 3	Angle-tighten a further 15°	
Crankshaft pulley bolt:*		
Stage 1	95	70
Stage 2	Angle-tighten a further 30°	
Stage 3	Angle-tighten a further 15°	
Cylinder head bolts:*		
Stage 1	25	18
Stage 2	Angle-tighten a further 90°	
Stage 3	Angle-tighten a further 90°	
Stage 4	Angle-tighten a further 90°	
Stage 5	Angle-tighten a further 45°	
Engine mountings:		
Front mounting/torque link:		
Mounting to transmission	80	59
Mounting to subframe	80	59
Left-hand mounting:		
Mounting-to-body bolts	20	15
Mounting bracket to transmission bracket	55	41
Rubber mounting through bolt	55	41
Transmission bracket to transmission	55	41
Rear mounting/torque link:		
Mounting bracket to transmission	80	59
Mounting to subframe	60	44
Mounting to transmission bracket	80	59
Right-hand mounting:		
Engine bracket-to-engine bolts	55	41
Mounting-to-body bolts	35	26
Mounting-to-engine bracket bolts	55	41
Rubber mounting through bolt	55	41
Engine-to-transmission bolts	60	44
Exhaust front pipe-to-manifold nuts	20	15
Flywheel bolts:*		
Stage 1	35	26
Stage 2	Angle-tighten a further 30°	
Stage 3	Angle-tighten a further 15°	
Main bearing cap bolts:*		
Stage 1	50	37
Stage 2	Angle-tighten a further 45°	
Stage 3	Angle-tighten a further 15°	
Oil pump:		
Retaining bolts	20	15
Pump cover screws	8	6
Oil pressure relief valve cap	20	15
Oil pump pick-up/strainer and baffle plate bolts	8	6
Roadwheel bolts	110	81
Sump bolts:		
Sump-to-cylinder block/oil pump bolts	10	7
Sump flange-to-transmission bolts	40	30
Timing belt cover bolts	6	4
Timing belt idler pulley bolt*	25	18
Timing belt tensioner bolt*	20	15
VVT oil control valve bolts	6	4

* Use new fasteners

1 General information

How to use this Chapter

This Part of Chapter 2 describes the repair procedures which can reasonably be carried out on the engine while it remains in the vehicle. If the engine has been removed from the vehicle and is being dismantled as described in Chapter 2E, any preliminary dismantling procedures can be ignored.

Note that, while it may be possible physically to overhaul items such as the piston/connecting rod assemblies while the engine is in the vehicle, such tasks are not usually carried out as separate operations, and usually require the execution of several additional procedures (not to mention the cleaning of components and of oilways); for this reason, all such tasks are classed as major overhaul procedures, and are described in Chapter 2E.

Chapter 2E describes the removal of the engine/transmission unit from the vehicle, and the full overhaul procedures which can then be carried out.

Engine description

The engine is a double overhead camshaft, four-cylinder, in-line unit, mounted transversely at the front of the car, with the transmission attached to its left-hand end.

The crankshaft is supported within the cylinder block on five shell-type main bearings. Thrustwashers are fitted to number 3 main bearing, to control crankshaft endfloat.

The connecting rods are attached to the crankshaft by horizontally-split shell-type big-end bearings, and to the pistons by interference-fit gudgeon pins. The aluminium alloy pistons are of the slipper type, and are fitted with three piston rings, comprising two compression rings and a scraper-type oil control ring.

The camshafts run directly in the cylinder head, and are driven by the crankshaft via a toothed composite rubber timing belt (which also drives the coolant pump on Z18XE engines). One camshaft operates the inlet valves, and the other operates the exhaust valves.

On Z18XE engines, the camshafts operate each valve via a hydraulic self-adjusting camshaft follower. On Z18XER engines, the camshafts operate each valve via a solid camshaft follower. The camshaft followers are available in various thicknesses to facilitate valve clearance adjustment.

On Z18XER engines, a variable valve timing (VVT) system is employed. The VVT system allows the inlet and exhaust camshaft timing to be varied under the control of the engine management system, to boost both low-speed torque and top-end power, as well as reducing exhaust emissions. The VVT camshaft adjuster

is integral with each camshaft timing belt sprocket, and is supplied with two pressurised oil feeds through passages in the camshaft itself. Two electro-magnetic oil control valves, one for each camshaft and operated by the engine management system, are fitted to the cylinder head, and are used to supply the pressurised oil to each camshaft adjuster through the two oil feeds. Each adjuster contains two chambers – depending on which of the two oil feeds is enabled by the control valve, the oil pressure will turn the camshaft clockwise (advance) or anti-clockwise (retard) to adjust the valve timing as required. If pressure is removed from both feeds, this induces a timing 'hold' condition. Thus the valve timing is infinitely variable within a given range.

Lubrication is by pressure-feed from a rotor-type oil pump, which is mounted on the right-hand end of the crankshaft. The pump draws oil through a strainer located in the sump, and then forces it through an externally mounted full-flow oil filter. The oil flows into galleries in the cylinder block/crankcase, from where it is distributed to the crankshaft (main bearings) and camshafts. The big-end bearings are supplied with oil via internal drillings in the crankshaft, while the camshaft bearings also receive a pressurised supply. The camshaft lobes and valves are lubricated by splash, as are all other engine components.

A semi-closed crankcase ventilation system is employed; crankcase fumes are drawn from camshaft cover, and passed via a hose to the inlet manifold.

Operations with engine in car

The following operations can be carried out without having to remove the engine from the car.

a) Removal and refitting of the camshaft cover.
b) Adjustment of the valve clearances (Z18XER engines).
c) Removal and refitting of the VVT oil control valves (Z18XER engines).
d) Removal and refitting of the cylinder head.
e) Removal and refitting of the timing belt, tensioner and sprockets.
f) Renewal of the camshaft oil seals.
g) Removal and refitting of the camshafts and followers.
h) Removal and refitting of the sump.
i) Removal and refitting of the connecting rods and pistons.*
j) Removal and refitting of the oil pump.
k) Renewal of the crankshaft oil seals.
l) Renewal of the engine mountings.
m) Removal and refitting of the flywheel.

* Although the operation marked with an asterisk can be carried out with the engine in the car (after removal of the sump), it is preferable for the engine to be removed, in the interests of cleanliness and improved access. For this reason, the procedure is described in Chapter 2E.

2 Compression test – general information

1 When engine performance is down, or if misfiring occurs which cannot be attributed to the ignition or fuel systems, a compression test can provide diagnostic clues as to the engine's condition. If the test is performed regularly, it can give warning of trouble before any other symptoms become apparent.

2 Due to the electronic throttle control system used on these engines, a compression test can only be carried out with the engine management electronic control unit connected to Vauxhall/Opel diagnostic test equipment, or a compatible alternative unit. Without the test equipment, the throttle valve cannot be opened (as there is no accelerator cable) and the test will be inconclusive. Note that even with the accelerator pedal fully depressed, the engine management ECU will only control the throttle valve position when the engine is actually running. The test equipment independently actuates the throttle valve (irrespective of ECU commands) and opens the throttle valve fully.

3 As the equipment needed for the compression test is unlikely to be available to the home mechanic, it is recommended that the test is performed by a Vauxhall/Opel dealer, or suitably-equipped garage.

3 Top dead centre (TDC) for No 1 piston – locating

1 Top dead centre (TDC) is the highest point in the cylinder that a piston reaches as the crankshaft turns. Each piston reaches TDC at the end of the compression stroke, and again at the end of the exhaust stroke. For the purpose of timing the engine, TDC refers to the position of No 1 piston at the end of its compression stroke. No 1 piston and cylinder are at the timing belt end of the engine.

2 Disconnect the battery negative terminal (refer to *Disconnecting the battery* in the Reference Chapter). If necessary, remove all the spark plugs as described in Chapter 1A to enable the engine to be easily turned over.

3 Remove the timing belt upper cover as described in Section 6.

4 Apply the handbrake, then jack up the front of the vehicle and support it on axle stands (see *Jacking and vehicle support*). Remove the right-hand front roadwheel, then remove the wheel arch liner inner cover for access to the crankshaft pulley.

5 Using a socket and extension bar on the crankshaft pulley bolt, rotate the crankshaft until the timing marks on the camshaft sprockets are facing towards each other, and an imaginary straight line can be drawn through the camshaft sprocket bolts and the timing marks. With the camshaft sprocket marks correctly positioned, align the notch

3.5a Align the camshaft timing marks . . .

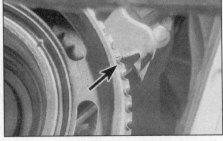

3.5b . . . and the notch on the crankshaft pulley rim with the mark on the timing belt lower cover – Z18XE engines

3.5c Align the camshaft timing marks (arrowed) . . .

on the crankshaft pulley rim with the mark on the timing belt lower cover (see illustrations). The engine is now positioned with No 1 piston at TDC on its compression stroke.

6 If the crankshaft pulley and lower timing belt cover have been removed, the timing mark on the crankshaft sprocket can be used instead of the mark on the pulley. The mark on the crankshaft sprocket must align with the corresponding mark on the timing belt rear cover, or oil pump housing (see illustration).

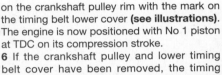

4 Camshaft cover –
removing and refitting

3.5d . . . and the notch on the crankshaft pulley rim with the mark on the timing belt lower cover (arrowed) – Z18XER engines

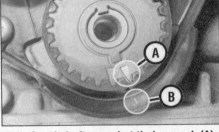

3.6 Crankshaft sprocket timing mark (A) aligned with mark (B) on timing belt rear cover (crankshaft pulley removed)

10 Apply a smear of suitable sealant to areas of the cylinder head surface around the right-hand end inlet and exhaust camshaft bearing caps.

11 Carefully manoeuvre the camshaft cover into position, taking great care to ensure the seal remains correctly seated. Refit the cover retaining bolts and tighten the retaining bolts to the specified torque, working in a spiral pattern from the centre outwards.

12 Reconnect the coolant pipe to the thermostat housing, making sure it is secured by the retaining bracket on the camshaft cover and inlet manifold.

13 Refit the wiring plugs to the coolant temperature sensor and camshaft sensor. Clip the oxygen sensor wiring back into position in the camshaft cover.

14 Reconnect the breather hoses, securing them in position with the retaining clips.

15 Refit the ignition module with reference to Chapter 5B.

16 Refit the engine cover, then top-up the cooling system as described in Chapter 1A.

Z18XER engines

Removal

17 Remove the ignition module from the spark plugs as described in Chapter 5B.

18 Lift the wiring harness up and out of the support on the right-hand end of the camshaft cover (see illustration).

19 Unclip the wiring harness trough from the rear of the camshaft cover (see illustration).

20 Pull out the retaining wire clip and disconnect the breather hose from the camshaft cover (see illustration).

21 Unscrew the eleven bolts securing the camshaft cover to the cylinder head.

22 Lift the camshaft cover away from the

Z18XE engines

Removal

1 Remove the oil filler cap, then undo the retaining screws, and remove the plastic cover from the top of the engine. Refit the oil filler cap.

2 Remove the ignition module from the spark plugs with reference to Chapter 5B.

3 Slacken the retaining clips and disconnect the breather hoses from the left-hand rear of the cover (see illustration).

4 Disconnect the wiring plug from the coolant temperature sensor and camshaft sensor, then release the wiring harness from the camshaft cover.

5 Disconnect the coolant pipe from the thermostat housing. Unbolt the retaining bracket from the camshaft cover and inlet manifold, release the retaining clips and move the pipe to one side. Be prepared for coolant spillage.

6 Unclip the oxygen sensor wiring from the camshaft cover.

7 Evenly and progressively slacken and remove the camshaft cover retaining bolts.

8 Lift the camshaft cover away from the cylinder head and recover the rubber seal. Examine the seal for signs of wear or damage and renew if necessary.

Refitting

9 Ensure the cover and cylinder head surfaces are clean and dry then fit the rubber seal securely to the cover groove (see illustration).

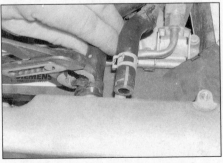

4.3 Disconnect the breather hoses from the camshaft cover – Z18XE engines

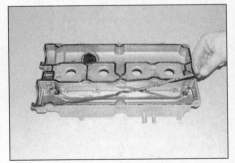

4.9 Carefully fit the camshaft cover seal – Z18XE engines

4.18 Lift the wiring harness out of the support on the camshaft cover – Z18XER engines

4.19 Unclip the wiring harness trough from the rear of the camshaft cover – Z18XER engines

4.20 Pull out the retaining wire clip and disconnect the breather hose from the camshaft cover – Z18XER engines

4.25 Locate the rubber seal into the grooves of the camshaft cover – Z18XER engines

cylinder head and recover the rubber seal. Examine the seal for signs of wear or damage and renew if necessary.

Refitting

23 Ensure that the camshaft cover grove and rubber seal are clean and dry with all traces of oil removed. If necessary, degrease the seal and cover groove with brake cleaner or a similar product.

24 Clean the mating surface of the cylinder head and the area around the camshaft bearing caps at the timing belt end, ensuring that all traces of oil are removed.

25 Locate the rubber seal into the grooves of the camshaft cover, ensuring that it is fully seated, with no chance of it falling out as the cover is fitted (see illustration).

26 Carefully manoeuvre the camshaft cover

5.3 Engage a strip of metal with the flywheel ring gear teeth through the access slot (arrowed) – Z18XER engines

into position, taking great care to ensure the seal remains correctly seated. Screw in all the cover retaining bolts and tighten them to the specified torque, working in a spiral pattern from the centre outwards.

27 Reconnect the engine breather hose, then clip the wiring harness trough back into position. Engage the wiring harness with the support on cover.

28 Refit the ignition module to the spark plugs as described in Chapter 5B.

5 Crankshaft pulley – removal and refitting

Note: A new pulley retaining bolt will be required on refitting.

5.5 Align the pulley cut-out with the raised notch

Removal

1 Firmly apply the handbrake, then jack up the front of the car and support it securely on axle stands (see Jacking and vehicle support). Remove the right-hand roadwheel, then remove the wheel arch liner inner cover for access to the crankshaft pulley.

2 Remove the auxiliary drivebelt as described in Chapter 1A. Prior to removal, mark the direction of rotation on the belt to ensure the belt is refitted the same way around.

3 Slacken the crankshaft pulley retaining bolt. To prevent crankshaft rotation, have an assistant select top gear and apply the brakes firmly. Alternatively, on Z18XER engines, engage a strip of metal with the flywheel ring gear teeth through the access slot located just above the front engine mounting/torque link (see illustration).

4 Unscrew the retaining bolt and washer and remove the crankshaft pulley from the end of the crankshaft.

Refitting

5 Refit the crankshaft pulley, aligning the pulley cut-out with the raised notch on the timing belt sprocket, then fit the washer and new retaining bolt (see illustration).

6 Lock the crankshaft by the method used on removal, and tighten the pulley retaining bolt to the specified Stage 1 torque setting, then angle-tighten the bolt through the specified Stage 2 angle, using a socket and extension bar, and finally through the specified Stage 3 angle. It is recommended that an angle-measuring gauge is used during the final stages of the tightening, to ensure accuracy. If a gauge is not available, use white paint to make alignment marks between the bolt head and pulley prior to tightening; the marks can then be used to check that the bolt has been rotated through the correct angle.

7 Refit the auxiliary drivebelt as described in Chapter 1A using the mark made prior to removal to ensure the belt is fitted the correct way around.

8 Refit the wheel arch liner inner cover and the roadwheel. Lower the car to the ground and tighten the wheel bolts to the specified torque.

6 Timing belt covers – removal and refitting

Z18XE engines

Upper cover

1 Remove the oil filler cap, then undo the retaining screws, and remove the plastic cover from the top of the engine. Refit the oil filler cap.

2 Remove the air cleaner assembly and intake ducts as described in Chapter 4A.

3 Undo the three retaining screws then unclip the upper cover from the rear cover and

6.3 Undo the three screws and remove the timing belt upper cover – Z18XE engines

6.7 Remove the auxiliary drivebelt tensioner – Z18XE engines

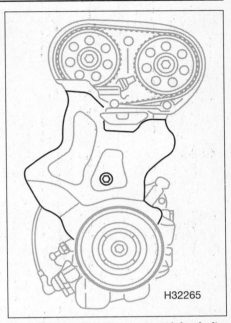

6.8 Timing belt lower cover retaining bolt – Z18XE engines

remove it from the engine compartment **(see illustration)**.

4 Refitting is the reverse of removal, tighten the retaining bolts to the specified torque.

Lower cover

5 Remove the upper cover as described in paragraphs 1 to 3.

6 Remove the crankshaft pulley as described in Section 5.

7 Undo the retaining bolt and remove the auxiliary drivebelt tensioner **(see illustration)**.

8 Undo the retaining bolt then unclip the lower cover from the rear cover and manoeuvre it out of position **(see illustration)**.

9 Refitting is the reverse of removal, clip the cover into position and tighten the cover bolts and auxiliary drivebelt tensioner bolt to the specified torque.

Rear cover

10 Remove the timing belt as described in Section 7.

11 Remove the camshaft sprockets, crankshaft sprocket, timing belt tensioner, front idler pulley and the rear idler pulley as described in Section 8.

12 Slacken and remove the three retaining bolts, and withdraw the engine mounting bracket bolted to the cylinder block **(see illustration)**.

13 Undo the four retaining bolts and remove the rear cover upwards and away from the engine **(see illustration)**.

14 Refitting is the reverse of removal. Refit and tighten the cover bolts to the specified torque.

Z18XER engines

Upper cover

15 Remove the air cleaner assembly and intake ducts as described in Chapter 4A.

16 Undo the two retaining bolts then withdraw the upper cover from the rear cover and remove it from the engine compartment **(see illustration)**.

17 Refitting is the reverse of removal, tightening the cover retaining bolts to the specified torque.

Lower cover

18 Remove the crankshaft pulley as described in Section 5.

19 Undo the retaining bolt and remove the auxiliary drivebelt tensioner **(see illustration)**.

20 Undo the four retaining bolts then manoeuvre the lower cover off the engine.

21 Refitting is the reverse of removal, tightening the cover retaining bolts and auxiliary drivebelt tensioner bolt to the specified torque.

Centre cover

22 Remove the upper and lower covers as described previously.

23 Remove the right-hand engine mounting as described in Section 18, then undo the three retaining bolts and remove the mounting bracket bolted to the cylinder block.

24 Release the two clips securing the centre cover to the rear cover and manoeuvre the centre cover off the engine.

25 Refitting is the reverse of removal, tightening the engine mounting bracket retaining bolts to the specified torque.

6.12 Engine mounting bracket-to-cylinder block retaining bolts – Z18XE engines

6.16 Undo the two retaining bolts (arrowed) and withdraw the upper cover from the rear cover – Z18XER engines

Rear cover

26 Remove the timing belt as described in Section 7.

27 Remove the camshaft sprockets, crankshaft sprocket, timing belt tensioner and idler pulley as described in Section 8.

28 Unclip the wiring harness from the

6.13 Lift the rear cover away from the engine – Z18XE engines

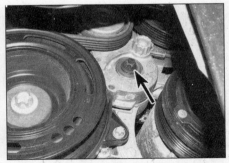

6.19 Undo the retaining bolt and remove the auxiliary drivebelt tensioner – Z18XER engines

7.3 **Unbolt the camshaft sensor and position it clear of the timing belt – Z18XE engines**

7.5 **Slacken the timing belt tensioner bolt (1) and rotate the tensioner clockwise using an Allen key in the arm cut-out (2) – Z18XE engines**

cover, then undo the four retaining bolts and manoeuvre the rear cover off the engine.

29 Refitting is the reverse of removal, tightening the cover retaining bolts to the specified torque.

7 Timing belt – removal and refitting

Note: *The timing belt must be removed and refitted with the engine cold.*

Z18XE engines

Removal

1 Position No 1 cylinder at TDC on its compression stroke as described in Section 3.

2 Remove the timing belt lower cover as described in Section 6.

3 Check that the timing marks on the camshaft sprockets are still correctly aligned and facing towards each other and the crankshaft sprocket timing mark is aligned with the mark on the rear timing belt cover (see Section 3). Undo the two bolts securing the camshaft sensor to the cylinder head and position it clear of the engine (see illustration).

4 Remove the right-hand engine mounting as described in Section 18.

7.6 **Removing the timing belt – Z18XE engines**

5 Slacken the timing belt tensioner bolt. Using an Allen key, rotate the tensioner arm clockwise to its stop, to relieve the tension in the timing belt, hold it in position and securely tighten the retaining bolt **(see illustration).**

6 Slide the timing belt from its sprockets and remove it from the engine **(see illustration).** If the belt is to be re-used, use white paint or similar to mark the direction of rotation on the belt. **Do not** rotate the crankshaft or camshafts until the timing belt has been refitted.

7 Check the timing belt carefully for any signs of uneven wear, splitting or oil contamination, and renew it if there is the slightest doubt about its condition. If the engine is undergoing an overhaul and is approaching the specified interval for belt renewal (see Chapter 1A) renew the belt as a matter of course, regardless of its apparent condition. If signs of oil contamination are found, trace the source of the oil leak and rectify it, then wash down the engine timing belt area and all related components to remove all traces of oil.

Refitting

8 On reassembly, thoroughly clean the timing belt sprockets and tensioner/idler pulleys.

9 Check that the camshaft and crankshaft sprocket timing marks are still correctly aligned as described in Section 3.

10 Fit the timing belt over the crankshaft and camshaft sprockets and around the idler pulleys, ensuring that the belt front run is taut (ie, all slack is on the tensioner side of the belt), then fit the belt over the coolant pump sprocket and tensioner pulley. Do not twist the belt sharply while refitting it. Ensure that the belt teeth are correctly seated centrally in the sprockets, and that the timing marks remain in alignment. If a used belt is being refitted, ensure that the arrow mark made on removal points in the normal direction of rotation, as before.

11 Slacken the timing belt tensioner bolt to release the tensioner spring. Rotate the tensioner arm anti-clockwise until the

tensioner pointer is positioned just before the left stop, without exerting any excess strain on the belt. Hold the tensioner in position and securely tighten its retaining bolt.

12 Check the sprocket timing marks are still correctly aligned. If adjustment is necessary, release the tensioner again then disengage the belt from the sprockets and make any necessary adjustments.

13 Using a socket on the crankshaft pulley bolt, rotate the crankshaft smoothly through two complete turns (720°) in the normal direction of rotation to settle the timing belt in position.

14 Check that both the camshaft and crankshaft sprocket timing marks are correctly realigned then slacken the tensioner bolt again.

15 If a new timing belt is being fitted, adjust the tensioner so that the pointer is aligned with the cut-out on the backplate **(see illustration).** Hold the tensioner in the correct position and tighten its retaining bolt to the specified torque. Rotate the crankshaft smoothly through another two complete turns in the normal direction of rotation, to bring the sprocket timing marks back into alignment. Check that the tensioner pointer is still aligned with the backplate cut-out.

16 If the original belt is being refitted, adjust the tensioner so that the pointer is positioned 4 mm to the left of the cut-out on the backplate **(see illustration 7.15).** Hold the tensioner in the correct position and tighten its retaining bolt to the specified torque. Rotate the crankshaft smoothly through another two complete turns in the normal direction of rotation, to bring the sprocket timing marks back into alignment. Check that the tensioner pointer is still correctly positioned in relation to the backplate cut-out.

17 If the tensioner pointer is not correctly positioned in relation to the backplate, repeat the procedure in paragraph 15 (new belt) or 16 (original belt).

18 Once the tensioner pointer and backplate remain correctly aligned, refit the camshaft sensor, then refit the timing belt covers as described in Section 6.

19 Refit the right-hand engine mounting as described in Section 18, then refit the crankshaft pulley as described in Section 5.

Z18XER engines

Removal

20 Position No 1 cylinder at TDC on its compression stroke as described in Section 3.

21 Remove the timing belt lower and centre covers as described in Section 6.

22 Check that the timing marks on the camshaft sprockets are still correctly aligned and facing towards each other, and the timing mark on the crankshaft sprocket is aligned with the corresponding mark on the oil pump housing (Section 3).

23 Using an Allen key inserted in the slot on the face of the timing belt tensioner, rotate the tensioner clockwise to relieve the tension in the timing belt. Insert a small drill bit or similar into the slot on the inner edge of the tensioner body to lock the tensioner in the released position.

24 Slide the timing belt from its sprockets and remove it from the engine. If the belt is to be re-used, use white paint or similar to mark the direction of rotation on the belt. **Do not** rotate the crankshaft or camshafts until the timing belt has been refitted.

25 Check the timing belt carefully for any signs of uneven wear, splitting or oil contamination, and renew it if there is the slightest doubt about its condition. If the engine is undergoing an overhaul and is approaching the specified interval for belt renewal (see Chapter 1A) renew the belt as a matter of course, regardless of its apparent condition. If signs of oil contamination are found, trace the source of the oil leak and rectify it, then wash down the engine timing belt area and all related components to remove all traces of oil.

Refitting

26 On reassembly, thoroughly clean the timing belt sprockets and tensioner/idler pulleys.

27 Check that the camshaft and crankshaft sprocket timing marks are still correctly aligned as described in Section 3.

28 Fit the timing belt over the crankshaft and camshaft sprockets and around the idler pulley, ensuring that the belt front run is taut (ie, all slack is on the tensioner side of the belt), then fit the belt over the tensioner pulley. Do not twist the belt sharply while refitting it. Ensure that the belt teeth are correctly seated centrally in the sprockets, and that the timing marks remain in alignment. If a used belt is being refitted, ensure that the arrow mark made on removal points in the normal direction of rotation, as before.

29 Using the Allen key, turn the tensioner clockwise slightly and remove the drill bit or similar tool used to lock the tensioner. Slowly release the tensioner and allow it to turn anti-

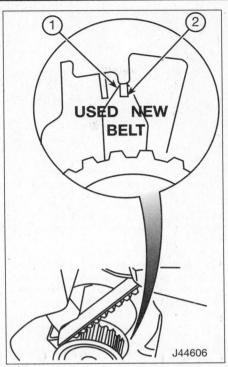

7.15 Align the pointer (1) with the relevant mark on the tensioner backplate (2) – Z18XE engines

clockwise and automatically tension the timing belt.

30 Check the sprocket timing marks are still correctly aligned. If adjustment is necessary, release the tensioner again then disengage the belt from the sprockets and make any necessary adjustments.

31 Using a socket on the temporarily refitted crankshaft pulley bolt, rotate the crankshaft smoothly through two complete turns (720º) in the normal direction of rotation to settle the timing belt in position.

32 Set the crankshaft back in the timing position and check that all the sprocket timing marks are still correctly aligned. If this is not the case, repeat the timing belt refitting procedure.

33 If everything is satisfactory, refit the timing belt covers as described in Section 6.

8.3 Counterholding the inlet camshaft using a spanner on the flats in front of No 1 cam lobe – Z18XE engines

8 Timing belt sprockets, tensioner and idler pulleys – removal and refitting

Z18XE engines

Camshaft sprockets

Note: *New sprocket retaining bolt(s) will be required for refitting.*

1 Remove the camshaft cover as described in Section 4.

2 Remove the timing belt as described in Section 7.

3 The camshaft must be prevented from turning as the sprocket bolt is unscrewed, and this can be achieved in one of two ways as follows:

a) *Make up a sprocket-holding tool using two lengths of steel strip (one long, the other short), and three nuts and bolts; one nut and bolt forms the pivot of a forked tool, with the remaining two nuts and bolts at the tips of the 'forks' to engage with the sprocket holes.*

b) *Hold the camshaft with an open-ended spanner on the flats provided* **(see illustration)**.

4 Unscrew the retaining bolt and washer and remove the sprocket from the end of the camshaft. If the sprocket locating pin is a loose fit in the camshaft end, remove it and store it with the sprocket for safe-keeping.

5 If necessary, remove the remaining sprocket using the same method. The inlet and exhaust sprockets are different; the exhaust camshaft sprocket can be easily identified by the lugs which activate the camshaft position sensor.

6 Prior to refitting, check the oil seal(s) for signs of damage or leakage. If necessary, renew as described in Section 10.

7 Ensure the locating pin is in position in the camshaft end.

8 Refit the sprocket to the camshaft end, aligning its cut-out with the locating pin, and fit the washer and new retaining bolt **(see illustration)**. If both sprockets have been removed, ensure each sprocket is fitted to the correct shaft; the exhaust camshaft sprocket can be identified by the lugs on the sprocket outer face which trigger the camshaft position sensor.

8.8 Ensure the camshaft sprocket cut-out (arrowed) is correctly engaged with the locating pin – Z18XE engines

8.13 Refit the crankshaft sprocket with the locating flange and pulley locating lug outermost – Z18XE engines

8.17 Engage the tensioner backplate lug with the locating hole in the oil pump housing – Z18XE engines

8.20 Idler pulley retaining bolt – Z18XE engines

9 Retain the sprocket by the method used on removal, and tighten the sprocket retaining bolt to the specified Stage 1 torque setting then angle-tighten the bolt through the specified Stage 2 angle, using a socket and extension bar, and finally through the specified Stage 3 angle. It is recommended that an angle-measuring gauge is used during the final stages of the tightening, to ensure accuracy. If a gauge is not available, use white paint to make alignment marks between the bolt head and sprocket prior to tightening; the marks can then be used to check that the bolt has been rotated through the correct angle.
10 Refit the timing belt as described in Section 7, then refit the camshaft cover as described in Section 4.

Crankshaft sprocket

11 Remove the timing belt as described in Section 7.
12 Slide the sprocket off from the end of the crankshaft, noting which way around it is fitted.
13 Align the sprocket locating key with the crankshaft groove then slide the sprocket into position, making sure its timing mark is facing outwards **(see illustration)**.
14 Refit the timing belt as described in Section 7.

Tensioner assembly

15 Remove the timing belt as described in Section 7.

16 Slacken and remove the retaining bolt and remove the tensioner assembly from the engine.
17 Fit the tensioner to the engine, making sure that the lug on the backplate is correctly located in the oil pump housing hole **(see illustration)**. Ensure the tensioner is correctly seated then refit the retaining bolt. Using an Allen key, rotate the tensioner arm clockwise to its stop then securely tighten the retaining bolt.
18 Refit the timing belt as described in Section 7.

Idler pulleys

19 Remove the timing belt as described in Section 7.
20 Slacken and remove the retaining bolt(s) and remove the idler pulley(s) from the engine **(see illustration)**.
21 Refit the idler pulley(s) and tighten the retaining bolt(s) to the specified torque.
22 Refit the timing belt as described in Section 7.

Z18XER engines

Camshaft sprockets

Note 1: *Vauxhall/Opel special tools KM-6340 and KM-6628 or suitable alternatives will be required for this procedure.*
Note 2: *New sprocket retaining bolt(s) and a new sprocket closure bolt seal will be required for refitting.*

23 Remove the camshaft cover as described in Section 4.
24 Remove the timing belt as described in Section 7.
25 Insert Vauxhall/Opel special tool KM-6628 into the slots on the end of the camshafts to lock the camshafts in the TDC position. In the absence of the special tool, a suitable alternative can be fabricated from a steel strip **(see Tool Tip and illustration)**. It may be necessary to turn the camshafts slightly using an open-ended spanner on the flats provided, to allow the tool to fully engage with the slots.
26 Unscrew the closure bolt from the relevant camshaft sprocket **(see illustration)**. Note that a new closure bolt seal will be required for refitting.
27 Hold the camshaft using an open-ended spanner on the flats provided, and unscrew the camshaft sprocket retaining bolt. Withdraw the sprocket from the end of the camshaft.
28 If necessary, remove the remaining sprocket using the same method.
29 Prior to refitting check the oil seal(s) for signs of damage or leakage. If necessary, renew as described in Section 10.
30 Refit the sprocket to the camshaft end and fit the new retaining bolt. Tighten the bolt finger-tight only at this stage. If both sprockets have been removed, ensure each sprocket is fitted to the correct shaft; the exhaust camshaft sprocket has the timing belt guide flange on its inner face and the inlet sprocket has the guide flange on its outer face.

8.25 Insert the special tool into the slots on the end of the camshafts to lock the camshafts in the TDC position – Z18XER engines

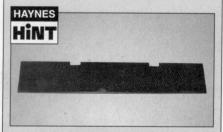

HAYNES HiNT

A camshaft locking tool can be made from a steel strip approximately 4.5 mm thick, with two grooves filed in the strip to clear the camshaft sensor trigger lugs.

8.26 Camshaft sprocket closure bolts (arrowed) – Z18XER engines

31 Turn the camshaft sprocket(s) until the timing marks are facing towards each other and aligned. It will now be necessary to retain the sprockets in the timing position while the sprocket retaining bolt is tightened. Engage Vauxhall/Opel special tool KM-6340 or a suitable alternative with the teeth on both sprockets to lock the sprockets together.

32 With the camshafts and sprockets locked in the timing position with the special tools, hold the camshaft using an open-ended spanner on the flats provided and tighten the sprocket retaining bolt to the specified Stage 1 torque setting. Now angle-tighten the bolt through the specified Stage 2 angle, using a socket and extension bar, and finally through the specified Stage 3 angle. It is recommended that an angle-measuring gauge is used during the final stages of the tightening, to ensure accuracy. If a gauge is not available, use white paint to make alignment marks between the bolt head and sprocket prior to tightening; the marks can then be used to check that the bolt has been rotated through the correct angle.

33 Fit a new seal to the camshaft sprocket closure bolt, then refit the closure bolt and tighten to the specified torque.

34 Remove the special tools, then refit the timing belt as described in Section 7, and the camshaft cover as described in Section 4.

Crankshaft sprocket

35 Remove the timing belt as described in Section 7.

36 Slide the sprocket off from the end of the crankshaft, noting which way around it is fitted.

37 Align the sprocket locating key with the crankshaft groove then slide the sprocket into position, making sure its timing mark is facing outwards.

38 Refit the timing belt as described in Section 7.

Tensioner assembly

Note: *A new tensioner retaining bolt will be required for refitting.*

39 Remove the timing belt as described in Section 7.

40 Slacken and remove the retaining bolt and remove the tensioner assembly from the engine.

41 Clean the tensioner retaining bolt threads in the oil pump housing, ensuring that all traces of sealant, oil or grease are removed.

42 Fit the tensioner to the engine, making sure that the lug on the backplate is correctly located in the oil pump housing hole. On later models, also ensure that the projecting end of the tensioner spring engages with the slot on the oil pump housing. Ensure the tensioner is correctly seated then refit the new retaining bolt and tighten it to the specified torque.

43 Refit the timing belt as described in Section 7.

Idler pulley

Note: *A new idler pulley retaining bolt will be required for refitting.*

9.2 Disconnect the wiring connector (arrowed) from the VVT oil control valve

44 Remove the timing belt as described in Section 7.

45 Slacken and remove the retaining bolt and remove the idler pulley from the engine.

46 Refit the idler pulley and tighten the new retaining bolt to the specified torque.

47 Refit the timing belt as described in Section 7.

9 VVT oil control valves (Z18XER engines) – removal and refitting

Removal

1 The VVT oil control valves are fitted to the camshaft bearing support, adjacent to the camshaft sprockets. Two oil control valves are used, one for each camshaft.

2 Disconnect the wiring connector from the relevant oil control valve **(see illustration)**.

3 Undo the retaining bolt located below the valve, and withdraw the valve from the camshaft bearing support. Be prepared for oil spillage.

Refitting

4 Lubricate the valve sealing rings with clean engine oil and insert the valve into the camshaft bearing support.

5 Refit and tighten the retaining bolt and reconnect the wiring connector.

6 On completion, check and if necessary top-up the engine oil as described in *Weekly checks*.

10.2 Camshaft oil seal removal method

10 Camshaft oil seals – renewal

1 Remove the relevant camshaft sprocket as described in Section 8.

2 Carefully punch or drill two small holes opposite each other in the oil seal. Screw a self-tapping screw into each, and pull on the screws with pliers to extract the seal **(see illustration)**.

3 Clean the seal housing, and polish off any burrs or raised edges which may have caused the seal to fail in the first place.

4 Press the new seal into position using a suitable tubular drift (such as a socket) which bears only on the hard outer edge of the seal **(see illustration)**. Take care not to damage the seal lips during fitting; note that the seal lips should face inwards.

5 Refit the camshaft sprocket as described in Section 8.

11 Valve clearances (Z18XER engines) – checking and adjustment

Note: *Z18XE engines are equipped with hydraulic self-adjusting camshaft followers and valve clearance adjustment is not required.*

Checking

1 The importance of having the valve clearances correctly adjusted cannot be over stressed, as they vitally affect the performance of the engine. The engine must be cold for the check to be accurate. The clearances are checked as follows.

2 Firmly apply the handbrake, then jack up the front of the car and support it securely on axle stands (see *Jacking and vehicle support*). Remove the right-hand front roadwheel then remove the wheel arch liner inner cover for access to the crankshaft pulley.

3 Remove the camshaft cover as described in Section 4.

4 Position No 1 cylinder at TDC on its compression stroke as described in Section 3.

5 With the engine at TDC on compression for No 1 cylinder, the inlet camshaft lobes for No 2 cylinder and the exhaust camshaft lobes

10.4 Using the old camshaft sprocket bolt and a socket to fit the new camshaft oil seal

11.7a Using feeler blades, measure the clearance between the base of both No 2 cylinder inlet cam lobes . . .

11.7b . . . and No 3 cylinder exhaust cam lobes and their followers

for No 3 cylinder are pointing upwards and slightly towards the centre. This indicates that these valves are completely closed, and the clearances can be checked.

6 On a piece of paper, draw the outline of the engine with the cylinders numbered from the timing belt end. Show the position of each valve, together with the specified valve clearance.

7 With the cam lobes positioned as described in paragraph 5, using feeler blades, measure the clearance between the base of both No 2 cyl- inder inlet cam lobes and No 3 cylinder exhaust cam lobes and their followers. Record the clearances on the paper **(see illustrations)**.

8 Rotate the crankshaft pulley in the normal direction of rotation through a half a turn (180°) to position No 1 cylinder inlet camshaft lobes and No 4 cylinder exhaust camshaft lobes pointing upwards and slightly towards the centre. Measure the clearance between the base of the camshaft lobes and their followers and record the clearances on the paper.

9 Rotate the crankshaft pulley through a half a turn (180°) to position No 3 cylinder inlet camshaft lobes and No 2 cylinder exhaust camshaft lobes pointing upwards and slightly towards the centre. Measure the clearance between the base of the camshaft lobes and their followers and record the clearances on the paper.

10 Rotate the crankshaft pulley through a half a turn (180°) to position No 4 cylinder inlet camshaft lobes and No 1 cylinder exhaust camshaft lobes pointing upwards and slightly towards the centre. Measure the clearance between the base of the camshaft lobes and their followers and record the clearances on the paper.

11 If all the clearances are correct, refit the camshaft cover (see Section 4), then refit the wheel arch liner inner cover and the roadwheel. Lower the vehicle to the ground and tighten the wheel bolts to the specified torque. If any clearance measured is not correct, adjustment must be carried out as described in the following paragraphs.

Adjustment

12 If adjustment is necessary, remove the relevant camshaft(s) and camshaft followers as described in Section 12.

13 Clean the followers of the valves that require clearance adjustment and note the thickness marking on the follower. The thickness marking is stamped on the underside of each follower. For example, a 3.20 mm thick follower will have a 20 thickness marking, a 3.21 mm thick follower will have a 21 thickness marking, etc.

14 Add the measured clearance of the valve to the thickness of the original follower then subtract the specified valve clearance from this figure. This will give you the thickness of the follower required. For example:

Clearance measured of inlet valve	*0.31 mm*
Plus thickness of the original follower	*3.20 mm*
Equals	*3.51 mm*
Minus clearance required	*0.25 mm*
Thickness of follower required	*3.26 mm*

15 Repeat this procedure on the remaining valves which require adjustment, then obtain the correct thickness of follower(s) required.

16 Refit the camshaft followers and the relevant camshaft(s) as described in Section 12. Rotate the crankshaft a few times to settle all the components, then recheck the valve clearances before refitting the camshaft cover (Section 4).

17 Refit the wheel arch liner inner cover and roadwheel then lower the vehicle to the ground and tighten the wheel bolts to the specified torque.

---

12 Camshaft and followers – removal, inspection and refitting

Note: *New timing belt end oil seals, and a tube of suitable sealant will be required when refitting.*

Z18XE engines

Removal

1 Remove the timing belt as described in Section 7.

2 Remove the camshaft sprockets as described in Section 8.

3 Remove the timing belt rear cover as described in Section 6.

4 Starting on the inlet camshaft, working in a spiral pattern from the outside inwards, slacken the camshaft bearing cap retaining bolts by half a turn at a time, to relieve the pressure of the valve springs on the bearing caps gradually and evenly **(the reverse of**

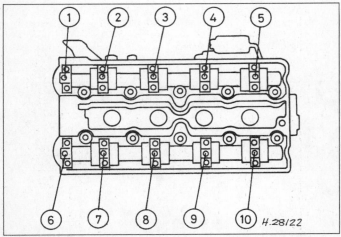

12.4a Camshaft bearing cap numbering sequence (No 1 at timing belt end) – Z18XE engines

12.4b Camshaft bearing cap numbers (exhaust camshaft shown) – Z18XE engines

illustration 12.16). Once the valve spring pressure has been relieved, the bolts can be fully unscrewed and removed along with the caps; the bearing caps and the cylinder head locations are numbered (inlet camshaft 1 to 5, exhaust camshaft 6 to 10) to ensure the caps are correctly positioned on refitting **(see illustrations)**. Take care not to lose the locating dowels (where fitted).

Caution: If the bearing cap bolts are carelessly slackened, the bearing caps might break. If any bearing cap breaks then the complete cylinder head assembly must be renewed; the bearing caps are matched to the head and are not available separately.

5 Lift the camshaft out of the cylinder head and slide off the oil seal.

6 Repeat the operations described in paragraphs 4 and 5 and remove the exhaust camshaft.

7 Obtain sixteen small, clean plastic containers, and label them for identification. Alternatively, divide a larger container into compartments. Using a rubber sucker tool, lift the followers out from the top of the cylinder head and store each one in its respective fitted position **(see illustration)**. Note: *Store all the followers the correct way up, with the oil groove at the bottom, to prevent the oil draining from the hydraulic valve adjustment mechanisms.*

Inspection

8 Examine the camshaft bearing surfaces and cam lobes for signs of wear ridges and scoring. Renew the camshaft if any of these conditions are apparent. Examine the condition of the bearing surfaces both on the camshaft journals and in the cylinder head. If the head bearing surfaces are worn excessively, the cylinder head will need to be renewed.

9 Examine the follower bearing surfaces which contact the camshaft lobes for wear ridges and scoring. Check the followers and their bores in the cylinder head for signs of

12.7 Remove the followers from the cylinder head, and store with the oil groove (arrowed) at the bottom – Z18XE engines

wear or damage. If any follower is thought to be faulty or is visibly worn it should be renewed.

Refitting

10 Commence refitting by turning the crankshaft anti-clockwise by 60°. This will position Nos 1 and 4 pistons a third of the way down the bore, and prevent any chance of the valves touching the piston crowns as the camshafts are being fitted. This could happen if any of the cam followers have excessive oil in them before the pressure of the valve springs forces it out.

11 Where removed, lubricate the followers with clean engine oil and carefully insert each one into its original location in the cylinder head.

12 Lubricate the camshaft followers with molybdenum disulphide paste (or clean engine oil) then lay the camshafts in position.

13 Ensure the mating surfaces of the bearing caps and cylinder head are clean and dry and lubricate the camshaft journals and lobes with clean engine oil.

14 Apply a smear of sealant to the mating surfaces of both the inlet (No 1) and exhaust (No 6) camshaft right-hand bearing caps **(see illustration)**.

15 Ensure the locating dowels (where fitted)

are in position then refit the camshaft bearing caps and the retaining bolts in their original locations on the cylinder head. The caps are numbered (inlet camshaft 1 to 5, exhaust camshaft 6 to 10) from the timing belt end, and the corresponding numbers are marked on the cylinder head upper surface. All bearing cap numbers should be the right way up when viewed from the front of the engine.

16 Working on the inlet camshaft, tighten the bearing cap bolts by hand only then, working in a spiral pattern from the centre outwards, tighten the bolts by half a turn at a time to gradually impose the pressure of the valve springs on the bearing caps **(see illustration)**. Repeat this sequence until all bearing caps are in contact with the cylinder head then go around and tighten the camshaft bearing cap bolts to the specified torque.

Caution: If the bearing cap bolts are carelessly tightened, the bearing caps might break. If any bearing cap breaks then the complete cylinder head assembly must be renewed; the bearing caps are matched to the head and are not available separately.

17 Tighten the exhaust camshaft bearing cap bolts as described in paragraph 16.

18 Fit new camshaft oil seals as described in Section 10.

19 Refit and tighten the timing belt rear cover bolts.

20 Refit the camshaft sprockets as described in Section 8.

21 Align all the sprocket timing marks to bring the camshafts and crankshaft back to TDC then refit the timing belt as described in Section 7.

Z18XER engines

Removal

22 Remove the camshaft cover as described in Section 4.

23 Remove the timing belt as described in Section 7.

12.14 Apply a smear of sealant to the right-hand bearing caps – Z18XE engines

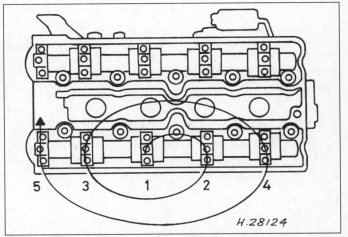

12.16 Camshaft bearing cap tightening sequence (exhaust camshaft shown – inlet identical) – Z18XE engines

12.28 Camshaft bearing support retaining bolts (arrowed) – Z18XER engines

24 Remove the camshaft sprockets as described in Section 8.
25 Remove the timing belt rear cover as described in Section 6.
26 Remove the special tool used to lock the camshafts in the TDC position.
27 Disconnect the wiring connector at the inlet camshaft and exhaust camshaft VVT oil control valves **(see illustration 9.2)**.
28 Undo the four bolts securing the camshaft bearing support at the timing belt end of the engine **(see illustration)**. Undo the two outer bolts first, followed by the two inner bolts. Using a plastic mallet, gently tap the bearing support free and remove it from the cylinder head.
29 Starting on the inlet camshaft, working in a spiral pattern from the outside inwards, slacken the camshaft bearing cap retaining bolts by half a turn at a time, to relieve the pressure of the valve springs on the bearing caps gradually and evenly **(the reverse of illustration 12.40)**. Once the valve spring pressure has been relieved, the bolts can be fully unscrewed and removed along with the caps; the bearing caps are numbered inlet camshaft 2 to 5, exhaust camshaft 6 to 9 to ensure the caps are correctly positioned on refitting **(see illustration)**. Take care not to lose the locating dowels (where fitted).
Caution: If the bearing cap bolts are carelessly slackened, the bearing caps might break. If any bearing cap breaks then the complete cylinder head assembly must be renewed; the bearing caps are matched to the head and are not available separately.

12.40 Camshaft bearing cap tightening sequence (inlet camshaft shown – exhaust identical) – Z18XER engines

12.29 Camshaft bearing cap numbers (inlet camshaft shown) – Z18XER engines

30 Lift the camshaft out of the cylinder head and slide off the oil seal.
31 Repeat the operations described in paragraphs 29 and 30 and remove the exhaust camshaft.
32 Obtain sixteen small, clean plastic containers, and label them for identification. Alternatively, divide a larger container into compartments. Using a rubber sucker tool, lift the followers out from the top of the cylinder head and store each one in its respective fitted position **(see illustration)**.

Inspection

33 Refer to the information contained in paragraphs 8 and 9.

Refitting

34 Commence refitting by turning the crankshaft anti-clockwise by 60°. This will position Nos 1 and 4 pistons a third of the way down the bore, and prevent any chance of the valves touching the piston crowns as the camshafts are being fitted.
35 Thoroughly clean the mating surfaces of the camshaft bearing support and cylinder head, ensuring all traces of old sealant are removed.
36 Where removed, lubricate the followers with clean engine oil and carefully insert each one into its original location in the cylinder head.
37 Lubricate the camshaft followers with molybdenum disulphide paste (or clean engine oil) then lay the camshafts in position.
38 Ensure the mating surfaces of the bearing caps and cylinder head are clean and dry and lubricate the camshaft journals and lobes with clean engine oil.
39 Ensure the locating dowels (where fitted) are in position then refit camshaft bearing caps 2 to 9 and the retaining bolts in their original locations on the cylinder head.
40 Working on the inlet camshaft, tighten the bearing cap bolts by hand only then, working in a spiral pattern from the centre outwards, tighten the bolts by half a turn at a time to gradually impose the pressure of the valve springs on the bearing caps **(see illustration)**. Repeat this sequence until all bearing caps are in contact with the cylinder head then go around and tighten the camshaft bearing cap bolts to the specified torque.

12.32 Use a valve lapping tool to remove the cam followers – Z18XER engines

Caution: If the bearing cap bolts are carelessly tightened, the bearing caps might break. If any bearing cap breaks then the complete cylinder head assembly must be renewed; the bearing caps are matched to the head and are not available separately.

41 Tighten the exhaust camshaft bearing cap bolts as described in paragraph 40.
42 Apply a smear of sealant to the mating surface of the camshaft bearing support, ensuring that the oil grooves remain free of sealant. Do not apply sealant to the area immediately adjacent to the bearing surface on the inside of the oil groove.
43 Place the camshaft bearing support in position and refit the four retaining bolts. Tighten the bolts to the specified torque, starting with the two inner bolts, then the two outer bolts.
44 If new components have been fitted, the valve clearances should now be checked and, if necessary adjusted, before proceeding with the refitting procedure. Temporarily refit the camshaft sprockets and secure with their retaining bolts, to allow the camshafts to be turned for the check. Refer to the procedure contained in Section 11, but as the timing belt is not fitted, check the clearances of each camshaft individually. Use the sprocket retaining bolt to turn the camshafts as necessary until the cam lobes for each pair of valves are pointing upward, away from the valves.
45 Once the valve clearances have been checked and if necessary adjusted, position the camshafts so that their timing slots are parallel with the cylinder head surface and refit the locking tool to the slots. Undo the retaining bolts and remove the camshaft sprockets.
46 Reconnect the wiring connector at the inlet camshaft and exhaust camshaft VVT oil control valves.
47 Refit the timing belt rear cover as described in Section 6.
48 Fit new camshaft oil seals as described in Section 10.
49 Refit the camshaft sprockets as described in Section 8.
50 Align all the sprocket timing marks to bring the camshafts and crankshaft back to TDC then refit the timing belt as described in Section 7.
51 Refit the camshaft cover as described in Section 4.

13 Cylinder head – removal and refitting

Note: *The engine must be cold when removing the cylinder head. A new cylinder head gasket and new cylinder head bolts must be used on refitting.*

Removal

1 Depressurise the fuel system as described in Chapter 4A.

2 Disconnect the battery negative terminal (refer to *Disconnecting the battery* in the Reference Chapter).

3 Apply the handbrake, then jack up the front of the vehicle and support it on axle stands (see *Jacking and vehicle support*). Remove the right-hand front roadwheel and the wheel arch liner inner cover for access to the right-hand side of the engine.

4 Drain the cooling system as described in Chapter 1A.

5 Remove the spark plugs as described in Chapter 1A.

6 Remove the camshaft cover as described in Section 4.

7 Remove the timing belt as described in Section 7.

8 Remove the camshaft sprockets, timing belt tensioner, and the timing belt idler pulleys, as described in Section 8.

9 Remove the rear timing belt cover with reference to Section 6.

10 Refer to Chapter 4A and unbolt the exhaust front pipe from the exhaust manifold, taking care to support the flexible section.
Note: *Angular movement in excess of 10° can cause permanent damage to the flexible section.* Release the mounting rubbers and support the front of the exhaust pipe to one side.

11 Disconnect the engine management wiring loom from the following, noting its routing:
  a) *Crankshaft speed/position sensor.*
  b) *Oil pressure switch.*
  c) *Oil level sensor.*

12 Release the cable-ties and place the wiring loom to one side.

13 On Z18XE engines, unscrew the securing bolts, and remove the upper alternator mounting bracket. Pivot the alternator rearwards away from the manifold as far as it will go.

14 Remove the inlet and exhaust manifolds as described in Chapter 4A.

15 Referring to Chapter 3, unclip the coolant hoses from the heater matrix unions on the engine compartment bulkhead to drain the coolant from the cylinder block. Once the flow of coolant has stopped, reconnect both hoses and mop up any spilt coolant.

16 Loosen the clips and remove the upper hose from the radiator and thermostat housing.

17 Loosen the clips and disconnect the heater hoses from the left-hand end of the cylinder head or thermostat housing.

18 Undo the bolt and free the oil dipstick guide tube from the cylinder head.

19 Make a final check to ensure that all relevant hoses, pipes and wires have been disconnected.

20 Working in the sequence shown, progressively loosen the cylinder head bolts **(see illustration)**. First loosen all the bolts by quarter of a turn, then loosen all the bolts by half a turn, then finally slacken all the bolts fully and withdraw them from the cylinder head. Recover the washers.

21 Lift the cylinder head from the cylinder block. If necessary, tap the cylinder head gently with a soft-faced mallet to free it from the block, but **do not** lever at the mating faces. Note that the cylinder head is located on dowels.

22 Recover the cylinder head gasket, and discard it.

Preparation for refitting

23 The mating faces of the cylinder head and block must be perfectly clean before refitting the head. Use a scraper to remove all traces of gasket and carbon, and also clean the tops of the pistons. Take particular care with the aluminium surfaces, as the soft metal is damaged easily. Also, make sure that debris is not allowed to enter the oil and water channels – this is particularly important for the oil circuit, as carbon could block the oil supply to the camshaft or crankshaft bearings. Using adhesive tape and paper, seal the water, oil and bolt holes in the cylinder block. To prevent carbon entering the gap between the pistons and bores, smear a little grease in the gap. After cleaning the piston, rotate the crankshaft so that the piston moves down the bore, then wipe out the grease and carbon with a cloth rag. Clean the other piston crowns in the same way.

24 Check the block and head for nicks, deep scratches and other damage. If slight, they may be removed carefully with a file. More serious damage may be repaired by machining, but this is a specialist job.

25 If warpage of the cylinder head is suspected, use a straight-edge to check it for distortion. Refer to Chapter 2E if necessary.

26 Ensure that the cylinder head bolt holes in the crankcase are clean and free of oil. Syringe or soak up any oil left in the bolt holes. This is most important in order that the correct bolt tightening torque can be applied and to prevent the possibility of the block being cracked by hydraulic pressure when the bolts are tightened.

27 Renew the cylinder head bolts regardless of their apparent condition.

Refitting

28 Ensure that the two locating dowels are in position at each end of the cylinder block/crankcase surface.

29 Fit the new cylinder head gasket to the block, making sure it is fitted with the correct way up with its OBEN/TOP mark uppermost **(see illustration)**.

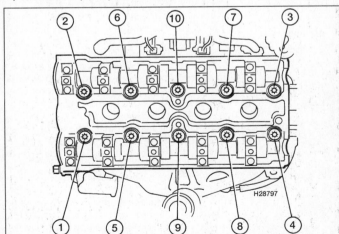

13.20 Cylinder head bolt loosening sequence

13.29 Ensure the head gasket is fitted with its OBEN/TOP marking uppermost

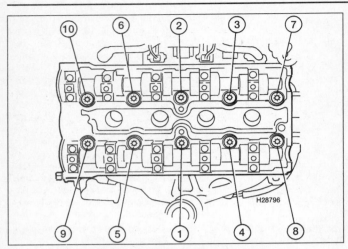

13.32a Cylinder head bolt tightening sequence

13.32b Tighten the cylinder head bolts to the specified Stage 1 torque setting . . .

30 Carefully refit the cylinder head, locating it on the dowels.

31 Fit the washers to the new cylinder head bolts then carefully insert them into position **(do not drop)**, tightening them finger-tight only at this stage.

32 Working progressively and in the sequence shown, first tighten all the cylinder head bolts to the Stage 1 torque setting **(see illustrations)**.

33 Once all bolts have been tightened to the Stage 1 torque, again working in the sequence shown, tighten each bolt through its specified Stage 2 angle, using a socket and extension bar. It is recommended that an angle-measuring gauge is used during this stage of the tightening, to ensure accuracy **(see illustration)**.

34 Working in the specified sequence, go around again and tighten all bolts through the specified Stage 3 angle.

35 Working again in the specified sequence, go around and tighten all bolts through the specified Stage 4 angle.

36 Finally go around in the specified sequence again and tighten all bolts through the specified Stage 5 angle.

37 Refit the exhaust manifold as described in Chapter 4A.

38 Reconnect the heater hoses to the left-hand end of the cylinder head or thermostat housing and tighten the clips.

39 Refit the upper hose to the radiator and thermostat housing and tighten the clips.

40 Refit the inlet manifold as described in Chapter 4A.

41 Where applicable, refit the alternator upper mounting bracket and tighten the bolts.

42 Reconnect the wiring to the components listed in paragraph 11, then secure the wiring with cable-ties.

43 Refer to Chapter 4A and refit the exhaust front pipe to the exhaust manifold. Refit the mounting rubbers.

44 Refit the rear timing belt cover with reference to Section 6.

45 Refit the camshaft sprockets, timing belt tensioner, and the timing belt idler pulleys, with reference to Section 8.

46 Refit the timing belt as described in Section 7.

47 Refit the spark plugs as described in Chapter 1A.

48 Refit the camshaft cover as described in Section 4.

49 Refit the wheel arch liner inner cover and front roadwheel, then lower the vehicle to the ground.

50 Reconnect the battery negative terminal.

51 Check that all relevant hoses, pipes and wires, etc, have been reconnected. Check the security of the fuel hose connections.

52 Refill and bleed the cooling system with reference to Chapter 1A.

53 When the engine is started, check for signs of oil or coolant leakage.

14 Sump – removal and refitting

Removal

1 Disconnect the battery negative terminal (refer to *Disconnecting the battery* in the Reference Chapter).

2 Apply the handbrake, then jack up the front

13.33 . . . and then through the various specified angles as described in the text

of the vehicle and support it on axle stands (see *Jacking and vehicle support*). Remove the right-hand front roadwheel and the wheel arch liner inner cover for access to the right-hand side of the engine.

3 Drain the engine oil as described in Chapter 1A, then fit a new sealing washer and refit the drain plug, tightening it to the specified torque.

4 Remove the exhaust system as described in Chapter 4A.

5 Disconnect the wiring connector from the oil level sensor.

6 On Z18XER engines, undo the retaining bolt and remove the oil dipstick guide tube.

7 Slacken and remove the bolts securing the sump flange to the transmission housing.

8 On Z18XE engines, remove the rubber plugs from the transmission end of the sump flange to gain access to the sump end retaining bolts.

9 Progressively slacken and remove the bolts securing the sump to the base of the cylinder block/oil pump. Using a wide-bladed scraper or similar tool inserted between the sump and cylinder block, carefully break the joint, then remove the sump from under the car.

10 While the sump is removed, take the opportunity to check the oil pump pick-up/strainer for signs of clogging or splitting. On Z18XE engines, unbolt the pick-up/strainer and remove it from the engine along with its sealing ring. On Z18XER engines, undo the two bolts and remove the baffle plate from the sump. Unbolt the pick-up/strainer flange and strainer base and remove it from the sump along with its sealing ring. The strainer can then be cleaned easily in solvent or renewed.

Refitting

11 Thoroughly clean the sump, baffle plate and pick-up/strainer, then remove all traces of sealer and oil from the mating surfaces of the sump and cylinder block and (where removed) the pick-up/strainer. Also remove all traces of locking compound from the pick-up bolts (where removed).

14.12 Fit new seal/gasket to the oil pump pick-up pipe – Z18XE engines

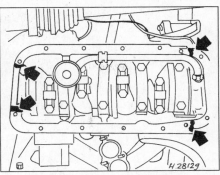

14.15 Apply sealant to the oil pump and main bearing cap joints (arrowed) before the sump is refitted

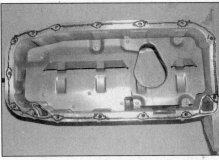

14.16 Apply a 2.5mm thick bead of sealant to the sump sealing surface – increase the thickness to 3.5mm around the No 5 main bearing cap area

12 On Z18XE engines, where necessary, position a new gasket/seal on top of the oil pump pick-up/strainer and fit the strainer (see illustration). Apply locking compound to the threads of the retaining bolts then fit the bolts and tighten to the specified torque.

13 On Z18XER engines, where necessary, position a new gasket/seal on the oil pump pick-up/strainer flange and fit the strainer. Refit the flange and base retaining bolts and tighten to the specified torque.

14 Ensure the sump and cylinder block mating surfaces are clean and dry and remove all traces of locking compound from the sump bolts.

15 Apply a smear of suitable sealant (available from Vauxhall/Opel dealers) to the areas of the cylinder block mating surface around the areas of the of the oil pump housing and main bearing cap joints (see illustration).

16 Apply a bead of suitable sealant (available from Vauxhall/Opel dealers) approximately 2.5 mm thick to the sealing surface of the sump. Around the No 5 main bearing cap area, increase the thickness of the bead to 3.5 mm (see illustration).

17 Offer up the sump, and loosely refit all the retaining bolts. Working out from the centre in a diagonal sequence, progressively tighten the bolts securing the sump to the cylinder block/oil pump to their specified torque setting.

18 Tighten the bolts securing the sump flange to the transmission housing to their specified

torque settings. Where fitted, refit the rubber plugs to the sump flange cut-outs.

19 Refit the exhaust system (see Chapter 4A) and reconnect the oil level sensor wiring connector.

20 Refit the wheel arch liner inner cover and front roadwheel, then lower the vehicle to the ground. Fill the engine with fresh oil, with reference to Chapter 1A.

15 Oil pump – removal, overhaul and refitting

Z18XE engines

Note: The pressure relief valve can be removed with pump in position on the engine unit, although on some models it will be necessary to unbolt the mounting bracket assembly from the block to allow the valve to be removed.

Removal

1 Remove the timing belt as described in Section 7.

2 Remove the rear timing belt cover as described in Section 6.

3 Remove the sump and oil pump pick-up/strainer as described in Section 14.

4 Disconnect the wiring connector from the oil pressure switch.

5 Slacken and remove the retaining bolts then slide the oil pump housing assembly off of the

end of the crankshaft, taking great care not to lose the locating dowels.

6 Remove the housing gasket and discard it.

Overhaul

7 Undo the retaining screws and lift off the pump cover from the rear of the housing.

8 Check the inner and outer rotors for identification dots indicating which way round they are fitted. If no marks are visible, use a suitable marker pen to mark the surface of both the pump inner and outer rotors.

9 Lift out the inner and outer rotors from the pump housing (see illustration).

10 Unscrew the oil pressure relief valve bolt from the front of the housing and withdraw the spring and plunger from the housing, noting which way around the plunger is fitted. Remove the sealing washer from the valve bolt (see illustration).

11 Clean the components, and carefully examine the rotors, pump body and relief valve plunger for any signs of scoring or wear. Renew any component which shows signs of wear or damage; if the rotors or pump housing are marked then the complete pump assembly should be renewed.

12 If the components appear serviceable, measure the rotor endfloat using feeler blades, and check the flatness of the end cover (see illustration). If the clearances exceed the specified tolerances the pump must be renewed.

15.9 Removal of the pump outer rotor – outer face identification punch mark arrowed – Z18XE engines

15.10 Oil pressure relief valve components – Z18XE engines

1 Plunger 3 Sealing washer
2 Spring 4 Valve bolt

15.12 Using a straight-edge and feeler blade to measure rotor endfloat – Z18XE engines

15.14 Fitting a new crankshaft oil seal to the oil pump housing – Z18XE engines

13 If the pump is satisfactory, reassemble the components in the reverse order of removal, noting the following.
  a) *Ensure both rotors are fitted the correct way around.*
  b) *Fit a new sealing ring to the pressure relief valve bolt and tighten the bolt to the specified torque.*
  c) *Apply a little locking compound to the threads, and tighten the pump cover screws to the specified torque.*
  d) *On completion prime the oil pump by filling it with clean engine oil whilst rotating the inner rotor.*

Refitting

14 Prior to refitting, carefully lever out the crankshaft oil seal using a flat-bladed screwdriver. Fit the new oil seal, ensuring its sealing lip is facing inwards, and press

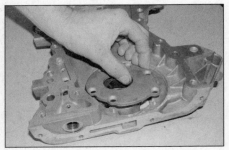

15.35 Remove the securing screws and withdraw the oil pump cover from the rear of the housing – Z18XER engines

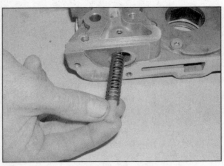

15.37b ... then withdraw the spring ...

15.17 Take care not to damage the oil seal on the crankshaft lip (1) and engage the inner rotor with the crankshaft flats (2) – Z18XE engines

it squarely into the housing using a tubular drift which bears only on the hard outer edge of the seal **(see illustration)**. Press the seal into position so that it is flush with the housing.
15 Ensure the mating surfaces of the oil pump and cylinder block are clean and dry and the locating dowels are in position.
16 Fit a new gasket to the cylinder block.
17 Carefully manoeuvre the oil pump into position and engage the inner rotor with the crankshaft end **(see illustration)**. Locate the pump on the dowels, taking great care not damage the oil seal lip.
18 Refit the pump housing retaining bolts in their original locations and tighten them to the specified torque.
19 Reconnect the oil pressure sensor wiring connector.

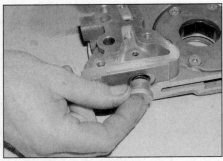

15.37a Unscrew the oil pressure relief valve cap ...

15.37c ... and the plunger – Z18XER engines

20 Refit the oil pump pick-up/strainer and sump as described in Section 14.
21 Refit the rear timing belt cover to the engine, tightening its retaining bolts to the specified torque.
22 Refit the timing belt sprockets, idler pulleys and tensioner then refit the belt as described in Sections 8 and 7.
23 On completion, fit a new oil filter and fill the engine with clean oil as described in Chapter 1A.

Z18XER engines

Removal

24 Drain the cooling system as described in Chapter 1A.
25 Remove the alternator as described in Chapter 5A.
26 Remove the exhaust manifold as described in Chapter 4A.
27 Remove the timing belt as described in Section 7.
28 Remove the timing belt tensioner and idler pulley, and the crankshaft sprocket as described in Section 8.
29 Remove the sump as described in Section 14.
30 Release the clamp and disconnect the coolant hose from the coolant pump.
31 Undo the two bolts securing the upper metal coolant pipe to the rear of the coolant pump.
32 Undo the support bracket bolt securing the lower metal coolant pipe to the oil filter housing.
33 Slacken and remove the eight retaining bolts (noting their different lengths) then slide the oil pump housing assembly off of the end of the crankshaft, taking great care not to lose the locating dowels. Remove the housing gasket and discard it.
34 Remove the metal coolant pipes and renew the four seals.

Overhaul

35 Remove the securing screws/bolts and withdraw the oil pump cover from the rear of the oil pump housing **(see illustration)**.
36 Remove the inner and outer rotor from the pump housing, noting which way round they are fitted, and wipe them clean. Also clean the rotor location in the oil pump housing.
37 The oil pressure relief valve components can also be removed from the oil pump housing by unscrewing the cap. Withdraw the cap, spring and plunger **(see illustrations)**.
38 Locate the inner and outer rotor back in the oil pump housing, ensuring they are fitted the right way round as noted during removal.
39 Check the clearance between the end faces of the rotors and the housing (endfloat) using a straight-edge and a feeler gauge **(see illustration)**.
40 If the clearance is outside the specified limits, renew the components as necessary.
41 Examine the pressure relief valve spring and plunger, and renew if any sign of damage or wear is evident.

42 Ensure that the rotor location in the interior of the oil pump housing is scrupulously clean before commencing reassembly.

43 Thoroughly clean the pressure relief valve components, and lubricate them with clean engine oil before refitting. Insert the plunger and spring, then refit the cap and tighten to the specified torque.

44 Ensure that the rotors are clean, then lubricate them with clean engine oil, and refit them to the pump body ensuring they are fitted the right way round as noted during removal.

45 Wipe clean the mating faces of the rear cover and the pump housing, then refit the rear cover. Refit and tighten the securing screws securely. Prime the oil pump by filling it with clean engine oil whilst rotating the inner rotor

Refitting

46 Prior to refitting, carefully lever out the crankshaft oil seal using a flat-bladed screwdriver. Fit the new oil seal, ensuring its sealing lip is facing inwards, and press it squarely into the housing using a tubular drift which bears only on the hard outer edge of the seal. Press the seal into position so that it is flush with the housing.

47 Refit the two previously-removed metal coolant pipes.

48 Ensure the mating surfaces of the oil pump housing and cylinder block are clean and dry and the locating dowels are in position.

49 Fit a new gasket to the cylinder block.

50 Carefully manoeuvre the oil pump into position and engage the inner rotor with the crankshaft end. Engage the coolant pipes, then locate the pump on the dowels, taking great care not damage the oil seal lip.

51 Refit the pump housing retaining bolts in their original locations and tighten them to the specified torque.

52 Refit the metal coolant pipe retaining bolts and tighten securely.

53 Reconnect the coolant hose to the pump and secure with the retaining clip.

54 Refit the sump as described in Section 14.

55 Refit the timing belt tensioner and idler pulley and the crankshaft sprocket, then refit the timing belt as described in Sections 8 and 7.

56 Refit the exhaust manifold as described in Chapter 4A.

57 Refit the alternator as described in Chapter 5A.

58 On completion, refer to Chapter 1A and fit a new oil filter and fill the engine with clean oil, then refill the cooling system.

16 Flywheel – removal, inspection and refitting

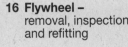

Note: *New flywheel retaining bolts will be required on refitting.*

Removal

1 Remove the transmission as described in Chapter 7A or 7C as applicable, then remove the clutch assembly as described in Chapter 6.

15.39 Check the oil pump rotor endfloat using a straight-edge and feeler gauge – Z18XER engines

16.8a Tighten the flywheel bolts to the specified torque using a torque wrench . . .

2 Prevent the flywheel from turning by locking the ring gear teeth with a similar arrangement to that shown **(see illustration)**. Alternatively, bolt a strap between the flywheel and the cylinder block/crankcase. Make alignment marks between the flywheel and crankshaft using paint or a suitable marker pen.

3 Slacken and remove the retaining bolts and remove the flywheel. Do not drop it, as it is very heavy.

Inspection

4 Examine the flywheel for scoring of the clutch face. If the clutch face is scored, the flywheel may be surface-ground, but renewal is preferable. Also check for wear or chipping of the ring gear teeth.

5 If there is any doubt about the condition of the flywheel, seek the advice of a Vauxhall/Opel dealer or engine reconditioning specialist. They will be able to advise if it is possible to recondition it or whether renewal is necessary.

Refitting

6 Clean the mating surfaces of the flywheel and crankshaft.

7 Offer up the flywheel and fit the new retaining bolts. If the original is being refitted align the marks made prior to removal.

8 Lock the flywheel by the method used on removal, and tighten the retaining bolts to the specified Stage 1 torque setting then angle-tighten the bolts through the specified Stage 2 angle, using a socket and extension bar, and finally through the specified Stage 3 angle. It is recommended that an angle-measuring gauge is used during the final

16.2 Prevent the flywheel from turning by locking the ring gear teeth with a suitable tool

16.8b . . . then through the specified angle using an angle tightening gauge

stages of the tightening, to ensure accuracy **(see illustrations)**. If a gauge is not available, use white paint to make alignment marks between the bolt head and flywheel prior to tightening; the marks can then be used to check that the bolt has been rotated through the correct angle.

9 Refit the clutch as described in Chapter 6 then remove the locking tool, and refit the transmission as described in Chapter 7A, or 7C.

17 Crankshaft oil seals – renewal

Right-hand (timing belt end)

1 Remove the crankshaft sprocket as described in Section 8.

2 Carefully punch or drill two small holes opposite each other in the oil seal. Screw a

17.2 Removing the crankshaft oil seal

self-tapping screw into each and pull on the screws with pliers to extract the seal **(see illustration)**.
Caution: Great care must be taken to avoid damage to the oil pump.
3 Clean the seal housing and polish off any burrs or raised edges which may have caused the seal to fail in the first place.
4 Ease the new seal into position on the end of the crankshaft. Press the seal squarely into position until it is flush with the housing. If necessary, a suitable tubular drift, such as a socket, which bears only on the hard outer edge of the seal can be used to tap the seal into position **(see illustration)**. Take great care not to damage the seal lips during fitting and ensure that the seal lips face inwards.
5 Wash off any traces of oil, then refit the crankshaft sprocket as described in Section 8.

Left-hand (flywheel end)

6 Remove the flywheel as described in Section 16.
7 Renew the seal as described in paragraphs 2 to 4 **(see illustration)**.
8 Refit the flywheel as described in Section 16.

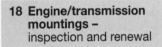

18 Engine/transmission mountings – inspection and renewal

Inspection

1 If improved access is required, firmly apply the handbrake, then jack up the front of the car and support it securely on axle stands (see *Jacking and vehicle support*).
2 Check the mounting rubber to see if it is cracked, hardened or separated from the metal at any point; renew the mounting if any such damage or deterioration is evident.
3 Check that all the mounting's fasteners are securely tightened; use a torque wrench to check if possible.

17.4 Fitting a new crankshaft oil seal

4 Using a large screwdriver or a pry bar, check for wear in the mounting by carefully levering against it to check for free play; where this is not possible, enlist the aid of an assistant to move the engine/transmission unit back-and-forth, or from side-to-side, while you watch the mounting. While some free play is to be expected even from new components, excessive wear should be obvious. If excessive free play is found, check first that the fasteners are correctly secured, then renew any worn components as described below.

Renewal

Note: *Before slackening any of the engine mounting bolts/nuts, the relative positions of the mountings to their various brackets should be marked to ensure correct alignment upon refitting.*

Front mounting/torque link

5 Apply the handbrake, then jack up the front of the vehicle and support it on axle stands (see *Jacking and vehicle support*).
6 Slacken and remove the nut securing the mounting to the subframe bracket. Withdraw the through-bolt **(see illustration)**.
7 Undo the bolts securing the mounting bracket to the transmission, then manoeuvre the mounting and bracket out of position.

17.7 Left-hand crankshaft oil seal – transmission and flywheel removed

8 Check all components for signs of wear or damage, and renew as necessary.
9 Locate the mounting in the subframe, refit the through-bolt and nut, then tighten the nut finger-tight at this stage.
10 Refit the mounting bracket to the transmission and tighten its bolts to the specified torque.
11 Tighten the through-bolt nut to the specified torque.
12 On completion, lower the vehicle to the ground.

Rear mounting/torque link

13 Apply the handbrake, then jack up the front of the vehicle and support it on axle stands (see *Jacking and vehicle support*).
14 Undo the three bolts securing the mounting bracket to the transmission and the through-bolt securing the mounting to the bracket **(see illustration)**.
15 Undo the nuts and remove the two bolts securing the mounting to the subframe **(see illustration)**. Manoeuvre the mounting and bracket out from under the car.
16 Refit the bracket to the transmission and tighten the bolts to the specified torque.
17 Locate the new mounting in position. Insert the bolts and tighten the bolt/nuts to the specified torque.
18 On completion, lower the vehicle to the ground.

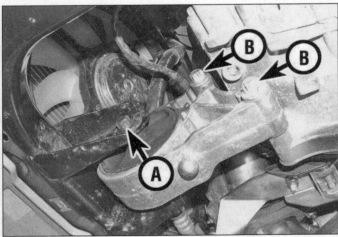

18.6 Front mounting/torque link through-bolt (A) and mounting bracket-to-transmission bolts (B)

18.14 Rear mounting/torque link through-bolt (arrowed)

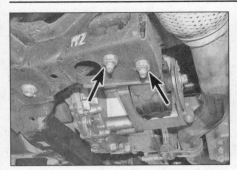

18.15 Rear mounting/torque link bracket-to-subframe mounting bolt nuts (arrowed)

18.22a Right-hand mounting bracket-to-engine bracket bolts (arrowed) . . .

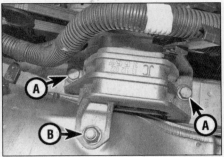

18.22b . . . and mounting-to-body retaining bolts (A) and nut (B)

Right-hand mounting

19 Apply the handbrake, then jack up the front of the vehicle and support it on axle stands (see *Jacking and vehicle support*).

20 Remove the air cleaner as described in Chapter 4A.

21 Attach a suitable hoist and lifting tackle to the engine lifting brackets on the cylinder head, and support the weight of the engine.

22 Mark the position of the three bolts securing the mounting bracket to the engine bracket and undo the bolts. Undo the two bolts and one nut securing the mounting to the body and remove the mounting assembly **(see illustrations)**.

23 Place the mounting assembly in position and refit the two bolts and the nut securing the mounting to the body. Tighten the bolts/nut to the specified torque. Align the mounting in its original position, then tighten the three mounting bracket bolts to the specified torque.

24 Remove the hoist, then refit the air cleaner as described in Chapter 4A.

25 On completion, lower the vehicle to the ground.

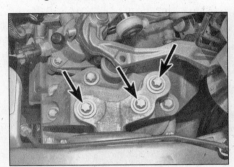

18.28 Left-hand mounting bracket-to-transmission bracket retaining bolts (arrowed) – diesel model shown, petrol similar

Left-hand mounting

26 Remove the battery and battery box as described in Chapter 5A.

27 Attach a suitable hoist and lifting tackle to the engine lifting brackets on the cylinder head, and support the weight of the engine.

28 Using a Torx socket, unscrew the three bolts securing the mounting bracket to the transmission bracket **(see illustration)**.

29 Undo the four bolts securing the mounting

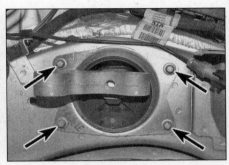

18.29 Left-hand mounting-to-body retaining bolts (arrowed) – shown with engine/transmission removed

to the body and the three bolts securing the transmission bracket to the transmission **(see illustration)**. Remove the mounting assembly from the car.

30 Locate the mounting brackets in position then insert the bolts and tighten them to the specified torque.

31 Disconnect the hoist and lifting tackle.

32 Refit the battery box and battery as described in Chapter 5A.

Notes

Chapter 2 Part B:
2.2 litre petrol engine in-car repair procedures

Contents

Degrees of difficulty

Easy, suitable for novice with little experience 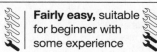 | **Fairly easy,** suitable for beginner with some experience | **Fairly difficult,** suitable for competent DIY mechanic | **Difficult,** suitable for experienced DIY mechanic | **Very difficult,** suitable for expert DIY or professional

Specifications

General

Engine type.	Four-cylinder, in-line, water-cooled. Double overhead camshafts, chain-driven
Manufacturer's engine code*	Z22YH
Bore	86.0 mm
Stroke.	94.6 mm
Capacity	2198 cc
Compression ratio	12.0:1
Firing order.	1-3-4-2 (No 1 cylinder at timing chain end of engine)
Direction of crankshaft rotation	Clockwise (viewed from timing chain end of engine)

* For details of engine code location, see 'Vehicle identification' in the Reference Chapter.

Compression pressures

Standard.	16 to 20 bar
Maximum difference between any two cylinders.	1 bar

Lubrication system

Minimum oil pressure at 80°C	1.5 bar at idle speed
Oil pump type.	Rotor-type, driven by crankshaft pulley/vibration damper from crankshaft
Oil pump clearances:	
Between inner and outer rotor	0.150 mm (max)
Between outer rotor and oil pump housing	0.350 mm (max)
Indentation/endfloat (rotor-to-upper edge of timing case cover)	0.080 mm (max)

Torque wrench settings

	Nm	lbf ft
Auxiliary drivebelt tensioner mounting bolt	42	31
Balance shaft retaining bracket bolts	10	7
Balance shaft sprocket bolts:*		
Stage 1	8	6
Stage 2	Angle-tighten a further 30°	
Camshaft bearing cap bolts:		
Bearing caps 1 to 10	10	7
Bearing cap 11 (intake camshaft, flywheel/driveplate end)	22	16
Bearing cap 11 cover plate	23	17
Camshaft cover bolts	10	7
Camshaft sprocket bolt:*		
Stage 1	85	63
Stage 2	Angle-tighten a further 30°	
Stage 3	Angle-tighten a further 15°	
Connecting rod big-end bearing cap bolt:*		
Stage 1	25	18
Stage 2	Angle-tighten a further 50°	
Stage 3	Angle-tighten a further 50°	
Stage 4	Angle-tighten a further 15°	
Coolant drain bolt in coolant pump	20	15
Coolant pump sprocket access cover bolts	7	5
Coolant pump sprocket bolts	8	6
Coolant pump-to-cylinder block bolts	23	17
Crankshaft pulley/vibration damper bolt:*		
Stage 1	100	74
Stage 2	Angle-tighten a further 75°	
Stage 3	Angle-tighten a further 15°	
Cylinder block lower casing to cylinder block :		
M8 bolts	25	18
M10 bolts (main bearing bolts):*		
Stage 1	20	15
Stage 2	Angle-tighten a further 70°	
Stage 3	Angle-tighten a further 15°	
Cylinder head x10 (main) bolts:*		
Stage 1	30	22
Stage 2	Angle-tighten a further 90°	
Stage 3	Angle-tighten a further 60°	
Stage 4	Angle-tighten a further 15°	
Cylinder head x4 (timing chain end) bolts	35	26
Driveplate bolts:*		
Stage 1	53	39
Stage 2	Angle-tighten a further 25°	
Engine mountings:		
Front mounting/torque link:		
Mounting to transmission	80	59
Mounting to subframe	80	59
Left-hand mounting:		
Mounting-to-body bolts	20	15
Mounting bracket to transmission bracket	55	41
Transmission bracket to transmission	55	41
Rear mounting/torque link:		
Mounting bracket to transmission	80	59
Mounting to subframe	60	44
Mounting to transmission bracket	80	59
Right-hand mounting:		
Engine bracket-to-engine bolts	55	41
Mounting-to-body bolts/nut	55	41
Mounting-to-engine bracket bolts	55	41
Engine-to-transmission bolts	60	44
Exhaust system front pipe to catalytic converter	20	15
Flywheel bolts:*		
Stage 1	60	44
Stage 2	Angle-tighten a further 30°	
Stage 3	Angle-tighten a further 15°	
Oil dipstick tube to inlet manifold	10	7
Oil level sensor bolts	10	7

Torque wrench settings (continued)

	Nm	lbf ft
Oil pump:		
Oil pressure control valve plug	40	30
Oil pump cover plate-to-timing cover bolts	6	4
Roadwheel bolts	110	81
Sump drain plug	25	18
Sump-to-cylinder block lower casing bolts	23	17
Sump-to-transmission bolts	40	30
Timing chain cover bolts	21	15
Timing chain guide rail bolt access plug	65	48
Timing chain guide rail bolts	10	7
Timing chain oil spray/injector nozzle	10	7
Timing chain sliding rail bolt*	10	7
Timing chain tensioner:		
Balance shafts	10	7
Camshaft	75	55
Timing chain tensioner rail pivot bolt	10	7

* Use new fasteners

1 General information

This Part of Chapter 2 describes the repair procedures which can reasonably be carried out on the engine while it remains in the vehicle. If the engine has been removed from the vehicle and is being dismantled as described in Chapter 2E, any preliminary dismantling procedures can be ignored.

Note that, while it may be possible physically to overhaul items such as the piston/connecting rod assemblies while the engine is in the vehicle, such tasks are not usually carried out as separate operations, and usually require the execution of several additional procedures (not to mention the cleaning of components and of oilways); for this reason, all such tasks are classed as major overhaul procedures, and are described in Chapter 2E.

Chapter 2E describes the removal of the engine/transmission unit from the vehicle, and the full overhaul procedures which can then be carried out.

Engine description

The engine is of the sixteen-valve, in-line four-cylinder, double overhead camshaft (DOHC) type, mounted transversely at the front of the car with the transmission attached to its left-hand end.

The aluminium alloy cylinder block is of the dry-liner type. The crankshaft is supported within the cylinder block on five shell-type main bearings. Thrustwashers are fitted to number 2 main bearing, to control crankshaft endfloat.

The connecting rods rotate on horizontally-split bearing shells at their big-ends. The pistons are attached to the connecting rods by gudgeon pins, which are retained by circlips. The aluminium-alloy pistons are fitted with three piston rings – two compression rings and scraper-type oil control ring.

The inlet and exhaust valves are each closed by coil springs, and operate in guides pressed into the cylinder head.

The camshafts are driven by the crankshaft via a timing chain arrangement; there is also a lower timing chain which links the crankshaft to the balance shafts and coolant pump. The camshafts rotate directly in the head and operate the sixteen valves via followers and hydraulic tappets. The followers are situated directly below the camshafts, each one operating a separate valve. Valve clearances are automatically adjusted by the hydraulic tappets.

Lubrication is by means of an oil pump, which is driven off the right-hand end of the crankshaft. It draws oil from the sump, and then forces it through an externally-mounted filter into galleries in the cylinder block/crankcase. From there, the oil is distributed to the crankshaft (main bearings) and camshafts. The big-end bearings are supplied with oil via internal drillings in the crankshaft, while the camshaft bearings also receive a pressurised supply. The camshaft lobes and valves are lubricated by splash, as are all other engine components. The timing chain is lubricated by an oil spray nozzle.

A semi-closed crankcase ventilation system is employed; crankcase fumes are drawn from camshaft cover, and passed via a hose to the inlet manifold.

Operations with engine in car

The following operations can be carried out without having to remove the engine from the car.

a) *Compression pressure – testing.*
b) *Camshaft cover – removal and refitting.*
c) *Timing chain cover – removal and refitting.*
d) *Timing chains – removal and refitting.*
e) *Timing chain tensioners, guides and sprockets – removal and refitting.*
f) *Camshaft and followers – removal, inspection and refitting.*
g) *Cylinder head – removal and refitting.*
h) *Connecting rods and pistons – removal and refitting.**
i) *Sump – removal and refitting.*
j) *Oil pump – removal, overhaul and refitting.*
k) *Crankshaft oil seals – renewal.*
l) *Engine/transmission mountings – inspection and renewal.*
m) *Flywheel/driveplate – removal, inspection and refitting.*
* Although the operation marked with an asterisk can be carried out with the engine in the car (after removal of the sump), it is better for the engine to be removed, in the interests of cleanliness and improved access. For this reason, the procedure is described in Chapter 2E.

2 Compression test – general information

Refer to Chapter 2A, Section 2.

3 Valve timing – checking and adjustment

Note: *To check the valve timing, it will be necessary to use a Vauxhall/Opel special tool (or suitable equivalent); the camshaft locking tool number is KM-6148. If access to this tool cannot be gained, this task must be entrusted to a Vauxhall/Opel dealer. The camshaft locking tool has locating pins that locate in the holes in the camshaft sprockets, to ensure that the camshafts remain correctly positioned.*

1 The valve timing is checked and, if necessary adjusted, with No 4 piston at top dead centre (TDC) on its compression stroke. No 4 piston and cylinder are at the flywheel/driveplate end of the engine.

2 Remove the camshaft cover as described in Section 4.

3 Apply the handbrake, then jack up the front of the vehicle and support it on axle stands (see *Jacking and vehicle support*). Remove the right-hand front roadwheel and the wheel arch liner inner cover for access to the crankshaft pulley.

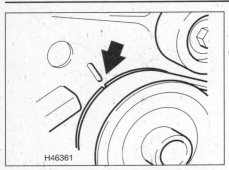

3.4 Crankshaft pulley and timing chain cover timing marks (1)

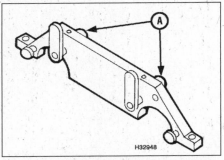

3.6a Vauxhall/Opel camshaft locking tool (KM-6148)

A Camshaft sprocket locating pins

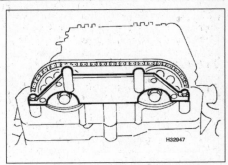

3.6b Locking the camshaft sprockets in position using the Vauxhall/Opel tool

4 Using a socket and extension bar on the crankshaft pulley bolt, rotate the crankshaft clockwise (when viewed from the right-hand side of the car) until the notch on the crankshaft pulley rim is aligned with the pointer on the timing chain cover **(see illustration)**. The engine is now positioned with No 1 and 4 pistons at TDC.

5 To determine which piston is on its compression stroke, check the position of the camshaft lobes. When No 4 piston is at TDC on its compression stroke, No 4 cylinder camshaft lobes will be pointing upwards. If No 4 cylinder camshaft lobes are pointing downwards, rotate the crankshaft through a further complete turn (360°) to bring No 4 cylinder to TDC on its compression stroke.

6 With the notch on the crankshaft pulley rim aligned with the pointer on the timing chain cover, insert the camshaft locking tool into position on the camshaft sprockets **(see illustrations)**.

7 If the locking tool can be correctly fitted the valve timing is correctly set and no adjustment is necessary.

8 Refit the camshaft cover as described In Section 4, then refit the wheel arch liner inner cover and roadwheel, and lower the vehicle to the ground.

9 If the camshaft tool cannot be inserted correctly into the camshaft sprockets, the timing will need to be reset. Refer to Section 8 for the removal, inspection and refitting of the timing chain and sprockets.

4.1 Remove the plastic cover from the top of the engine

4 Camshaft cover – removal and refitting

Removal

1 Unclip and remove the plastic cover from the top of the engine **(see illustration)**.

2 Remove the air cleaner assembly and air intake duct as described in Chapter 4A.

3 Remove the ignition module as described in Chapter 5B.

4 Disconnect the breather hose from the front of the camshaft cover **(see illustration)**.

5 Unscrew the nut securing the coolant pipe to the stud at the left-hand end of the camshaft cover.

6 Disconnect the wiring connectors from the EGR (exhaust gas recirculation) valve and the oxygen sensors.

7 Undo the two retaining bolts and release the wiring bracket from the left-hand side of the camshaft cover. With the bracket removed, undo the right-hand stud to release the earth strap.

8 Undo the two retaining bolts from the timing chain end of the camshaft cover to release the hoses and pipe supports.

9 Free the wiring harness from its clips/ brackets at the front and side of the camshaft cover as necessary.

10 Slacken and remove the camshaft cover retaining bolts along with their sealing washers (where fitted) then lift the camshaft cover and gasket/seals away from the cylinder head. Renew the cover gasket/seals and retaining bolt sealing washers, as applicable.

Refitting

11 Refitting is a reversal of removal noting the following points:
  a) Use new camshaft cover gasket/seals.
  b) Once the cover is in position, first tighten all the bolts hand-tight, then go around and tighten them all to the specified torque setting.
  c) Refit the ignition module as described in Chapter 5B.
  d) Refit the air cleaner and intake duct as described in Chapter 4A.

5 Crankshaft pulley/ vibration damper – removal and refitting

Note 1: *Vauxhall/Opel special tools KM-956-1 and KM-J-38122 or suitable alternative will be required to prevent crankshaft rotation whilst the retaining bolt is slackened/tightened.*

Note 2: *A new pulley retaining bolt will be required on refitting.*

Removal

1 Apply the handbrake, then jack up the front of the vehicle and support it on axle stands (see *Jacking and vehicle support*). Remove the right-hand front roadwheel and the wheel arch liner inner cover for access to the crankshaft pulley.

2 Remove the auxiliary drivebelt as described in Chapter 1A. Prior to removal, mark the direction of rotation on the belt to ensure the belt is refitted the same way around.

3 Slacken the crankshaft pulley retaining bolt. To prevent crankshaft rotation whilst the retaining bolt is slackened, it will be necessary to hold the crankshaft pulley with the Vauxhall/Opel tool or a suitable alternative **(see illustration 5.6)**.

4 Unscrew the retaining bolt and washer and remove the crankshaft pulley from the end of the crankshaft. Whilst the pulley is removed check the oil seal for signs of wear or damage and, if necessary, renew as described in Section 14.

4.4 Disconnect the breather hose (arrowed) from the camshaft cover

5.5a Turn the pulley until the flat on the centre hub locates with the oil pump drive . . .

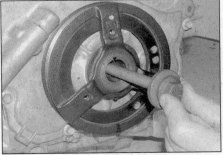

5.5b . . . then fit a new securing bolt to the pulley

5.6 Using an angle-measuring gauge to tighten the crankshaft pulley whilst preventing pulley rotation with a suitable tool

Refitting

5 Carefully locate the crankshaft pulley on the crankshaft end. Align the flats on the pulley with the oil pump, then turn the pulley to align the slot in the pulley with the crankshaft key. Slide the pulley fully into position, taking great care not to damage the oil seal, then fit the washer and new retaining bolt (see illustrations).

6 Lock the crankshaft by the method used on removal, and tighten the pulley retaining bolt to the specified Stage 1 torque setting then angle-tighten the bolt through the specified Stage 2 angle, using a socket and extension bar, and finally through the specified Stage 3 angle. It is recommended that an angle-measuring gauge is used during the final stages of the tightening, to ensure accuracy (see illustration). If a gauge is not available, use white paint to make alignment marks between the bolt head and pulley prior to tightening; the marks can then be used to check that the bolt has been rotated through the correct angle.

7 Refit the auxiliary drivebelt as described in Chapter 1A using the mark made prior to removal to ensure the belt is fitted the correct way around.

8 Refit the wheel arch liner inner cover and roadwheel, and lower the vehicle to the ground.

6 Timing chain cover – removal and refitting

Removal

1 Unclip and remove the plastic cover from the top of the engine (see illustration 4.1).

2 Disconnect the battery negative terminal (refer to Disconnecting the battery in the Reference Chapter).

3 Remove the air cleaner assembly and air intake duct as described in Chapter 4A.

4 Apply the handbrake, then jack up the front of the vehicle and support it on axle stands (see Jacking and vehicle support).

5 Remove the right-hand front roadwheel and the wheel arch liner inner cover.

6 Drain the engine oil as described in Chapter 1A. When the oil has completely drained, refit the drain plug with new sealing washer, and tighten to the specified torque.

7 Remove the crankshaft pulley/vibration damper as described in Section 5.

8 Undo the three nuts securing the exhaust system front pipe to the catalytic converter, taking care to support the flexible section. Note: Angular movement in excess of 10° can cause permanent damage to the flexible section. Separate the flange joint and recover the gasket.

9 Undo the through-bolt securing the rear engine mounting/torque link to the mounting bracket, and the three bolts securing the mounting bracket to the transmission (see illustration). Remove the mounting bracket from under the car.

10 Unscrew the nut and remove the

through-bolt securing the front engine mounting/torque link to the subframe (see illustration).

11 Connect a suitable hoist and lifting tackle to the right-hand end of the engine and support its weight. If available, the type of support bar which locates in the engine compartment side channels is to be preferred.

12 Mark the bolt positions for correct refitting, then undo the three bolts securing the right-hand engine mounting to the engine bracket, and the two bolts and one nut securing the mounting to the body (see illustrations). Remove the mounting.

13 Using the hoist, carefully raise the right-hand end of the engine until the bolts securing the engine mounting bracket to the cylinder head are accessible. Undo the three bolts and remove the engine bracket.

14 Reposition the hoist as necessary, then

6.9 Rear engine mounting/torque link through-bolt (arrowed)

6.10 Front engine mounting/torque link through-bolt (arrowed)

6.12a Undo the three bolts (arrowed) securing the right-hand engine mounting to the engine bracket . . .

6.12b . . . and the two bolts (A) and one nut (B) securing the mounting to the body

6.14 Undo the central mounting bolt and remove the auxiliary drivebelt tensioner

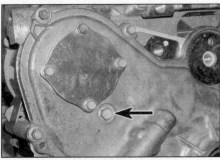

6.15 Note retaining bolt (arrowed) on the inner part of the timing chain cover casing

6.18a Carefully lever the old crankshaft oil seal out of the cover . . .

6.18b . . . then using a suitable drift tap in the new oil seal

undo the drivebelt tensioner central mounting bolt. Remove the tensioner assembly from the engine **(see illustration)**.

15 Noting each bolt's correct fitted location (one bolt is also securing the coolant pump), slacken and remove all the bolts securing the timing chain cover to the cylinder block **(see illustration)**. It may be necessary to raise or lower the engine using the hoist to enable all the bolts to be removed.

16 Carefully ease the timing cover squarely away from the cylinder block and manoeuvre it out of position, noting the correct fitted positions of its locating dowels. If the locating dowels are a loose fit, remove them and store with the cover for safe-keeping.

17 Remove the gasket and ensure the mating surfaces are clean. Obtain a new gasket for refitting.

Refitting

18 Prior to refitting the cover, it is recommended that the crankshaft oil seal should be renewed. Carefully lever the old seal out of the cover using a large flat-bladed screwdriver. Fit the new seal to the cover, making sure its sealing lip is facing inwards. Press/tap the seal into position until it is flush with the cover, using a suitable tubular drift, such as a socket, which bears only on the hard outer edge of the seal **(see illustrations)**.

19 Ensure the mating surfaces of the cover and cylinder block are clean and dry and the locating dowels are in position.

20 Manoeuvre the new gasket into position and locate it on the dowels.

21 Manoeuvre the timing cover into position, locating it on the dowels. Refit the cover retaining bolts, ensuring each one is fitted in its original location, and tighten them evenly and progressively to the specified torque.

22 Place the auxiliary drivebelt tensioner assembly in position ensuring that the locating peg on the tensioner mounting surface engages correctly with the corresponding hole in the timing chain cover. Tighten the tensioner central mounting bolt to the specified torque.

23 Refit the engine mounting bracket to the cylinder head and tighten the three retaining bolts to the specified torque.

24 Locate the right-hand engine mounting in position, then refit the three bolts securing the mounting to the engine bracket and the two bolts and one nut securing the mounting to the body. Align the mounting in its original position, then tighten the bolts and nut to the specified torque.

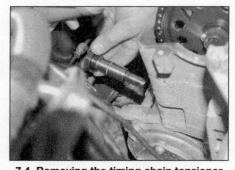

7.4 Removing the timing chain tensioner assembly

25 Remove the hoist and lifting tackle from the engine.

26 Refit the through-bolt and nut securing the front engine mounting/torque link to the subframe. Tighten the nut to the specified torque.

27 Place the rear engine mounting/torque link mounting bracket in position and refit the three bolts securing the bracket to the transmission. Tighten the bolts to the specified torque.

28 Refit the rear engine mounting/torque link through-bolt and tighten the bolt to the specified torque.

29 Using a new gasket, refit the exhaust front pipe flange joint to the catalytic converter and tighten the three retaining nuts to the specified torque.

30 Refit the crankshaft pulley/vibration damper as described in Section 5.

31 Refit the auxiliary drivebelt as described in Chapter 1A.

32 Refit the wheel arch liner inner cover and roadwheel, and lower the vehicle to the ground.

33 Refer to Chapter 4A if necessary and refit the air cleaner assembly and air intake duct.

34 Refill the engine with oil as described in Chapter 1A.

35 On completion, reconnect the battery negative terminal and refit the engine cover. Start the engine and check for signs of oil leaks.

7 Timing chain tensioners – removal and refitting

Camshaft chain tensioner

Note: *If a new camshaft timing chain tensioner is being fitted, then a new tension rail should be fitted at the same time. Under no circumstances should the old tension rail be fitted with a new tensioner.*

Removal

1 Remove the camshaft cover as described in Section 4.

2 Apply the handbrake, then jack up the front of the vehicle and support it on axle stands (see *Jacking and vehicle support*). Remove the right-hand front roadwheel and the wheel arch liner inner cover.

3 Refer to the information contained in Section 3, and set No 4 piston at approximately 10° BTDC on its compression stroke.

4 Unscrew the camshaft timing chain tensioner from the rear of the cylinder head, and remove the inner piston assembly **(see illustration)** Remove the sealing rings and discard them, new ones should be used on refitting.

Caution: Do not rotate the engine whilst the tensioner is removed.

5 Dismantle the tensioner, and inspect the tensioner piston for signs of wear or damage and renew if necessary **(see illustration)**.

7.5 Inner piston removed to check for wear or damage

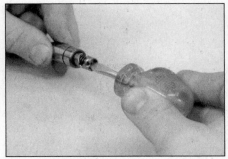

7.6a Turn the inner piston screw clockwise until it locks in position . . .

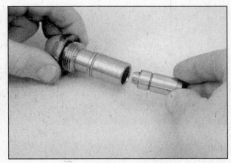

7.6b . . . then fit the inner piston to the outer tensioner assembly

Refitting

6 Pretension the timing chain tensioner, by turning the inner piston clockwise **(see illustrations)** and allow it to lock in position. Lubricate the inner piston, then reassemble the timing chain tensioner.

7 Fit the sealing rings, then lubricate the timing chain tensioner/piston with clean engine oil and insert it into the cylinder head. **Note:** *Check the threads are clean on the tensioner and in the cylinder head before refitting.*

8 Tighten the tensioner to the specified torque.

9 Release the tensioner, by pressing on the tension rail/timing chain with a rounded bar **(see illustration)**. This will press against the inner piston of the tensioner to unlock it, when it releases, the spring-loaded piston will take up the slack in the timing chain.

Caution: This procedure must be carried out correctly, otherwise the chain may be left slack and skip a tooth on the sprockets. This will result in engine damage.

10 Rotate the crankshaft through two complete rotations (720°) in the correct direction of rotation and recheck the valve timing as described in Section 3.

11 Refit the camshaft cover as described in Section 4.

12 Refit the wheel arch liner inner cover and roadwheel, and lower the vehicle to the ground.

Balance shaft chain tensioner

Removal

13 Remove the timing chain cover as described in Section 6.

14 Undo the two retaining bolts and remove the balance shaft chain tensioner from the cylinder block.

Caution: Do not rotate the engine whilst the tensioner is removed.

15 Inspect the tensioner piston for signs of wear or damage and renew if necessary.

Refitting

16 Pretension the balance shaft chain tensioner, by turning the piston clockwise approximately 45° and push it back into the tensioner housing. Insert a 1.0 mm locking pin or drill bit into the hole in the piston housing,

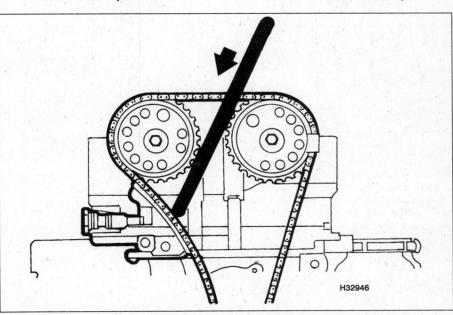

7.9 Press the bar against the tension rail to release the tensioner inner piston

which will lock the piston in position **(see illustration)**.

17 Lubricate the tensioner piston with clean engine oil, then refit it onto the cylinder block tightening the bolts to there specified torque.

18 Once the tensioner is in position, remove the locking pin to release the tensioner piston **(see illustration)**. Make sure the piston engages with the tension rail correctly and

takes up any slack in the balancer shaft timing chain.

Caution: This procedure must be carried out correctly, otherwise the chain may be left slack and skip a tooth on the sprockets. This could result in engine vibration or damage.

19 Refit the timing chain cover as described in Section 6.

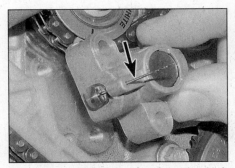

7.16 1.0 mm drill bit (arrowed) used to lock the tensioner piston in place

7.18 Removing the locking pin to release the tensioner

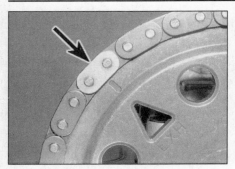

8.0a Align the silver link (arrowed) with the triangular timing mark on the exhaust sprocket . . .

8.0b . . . the copper-coloured link (arrowed) with the diamond timing mark on the intake sprocket . . .

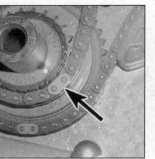

8.0c . . . and the second silver-coloured link (arrowed) with the timing mark (white dot) on the crankshaft sprocket

8.6 Undo the two retaining bolts (arrowed) from the chain sliding rail

Chain tensioner and guide rails

20 Tensioner and guide rail removal and refitting is part of the timing chain and sprockets

removal and refitting procedure (see Section 8). They must be renewed if they show signs of wear or damage on their chain surfaces.

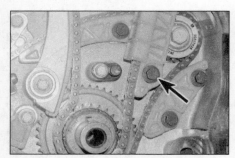

8.7a Remove the access plug from the cylinder head . . .

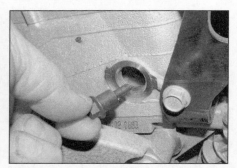

8.7b . . . and remove the guide rail upper securing bolt

8.8 Undo the lower guide rail securing bolt (arrowed) and remove the guide rail downwards

8.9 Undo the camshaft sprocket retaining bolts – hold the camshafts using an open-ended spanner

8 Timing chains and sprockets
– removal, inspection and refitting

Note: *In order to set the valve timing accurately at TDC, a Vauxhall/Opel special tool (or suitable alternative) is required (see Section 3). If the timing chain and sprockets are to be completely removed or refitted, then this task can be carried out without the tool. The timing can be re-aligned using the coloured links on the timing chain and the alignment marks on the sprockets (see illustrations).*
Caution: Prior to removal, ensure the camshaft sprockets are suitably marked as they are identical and can be refitted to either camshaft.

Removal

Camshaft chain and sprockets

Note: *If there is any wear on the camshaft timing chain, tension rails, guides and crankshaft sprocket the components must always be renewed as a complete assembly.*
Note: *New camshaft sprocket retaining bolts and new timing chain sliding rail retaining bolts will be required on refitting.*
1 Disconnect the battery negative terminal (refer to *Disconnecting the battery* in the Reference Chapter), then remove the camshaft cover (see Section 4).
2 Position No 4 piston at TDC on its compression stroke, as described in Section 3.
3 Remove the timing chain cover as described in Section 6.
4 Remove the camshaft timing chain tensioner as described in Section 7.
5 Disconnect the wiring plug, then undo the retaining bolt and remove the camshaft position sensor from the cylinder head.
6 Undo the two retaining bolts from the camshaft timing chain sliding rail on the top of the cylinder head **(see illustration)**.
7 Remove the access plug from the cylinder head and undo the upper securing bolt for the timing chain guide rail **(see illustrations)**.
8 Undo the lower securing bolt for the timing chain guide rail and remove downwards out from the engine **(see illustration)**.
9 Hold the camshafts in turn using an open-ended spanner on the flats provided, then slacken and remove the camshaft sprocket retaining bolts **(see illustration)**.
10 Remove the exhaust camshaft sprocket, making sure it is marked for refitting as they are both identical.
11 Undo the lower securing bolt from the timing chain tension rail, then remove it downwards and out from the engine **(see illustration)**.
12 Lift the timing chain off the crankshaft sprocket and remove the intake camshaft sprocket complete with timing chain out through the top of the cylinder head.
13 Slide the crankshaft drivegear/sprocket (and spring washer, where fitted) off the

8.11 Undo the retaining bolt and remove the tension rail from the engine

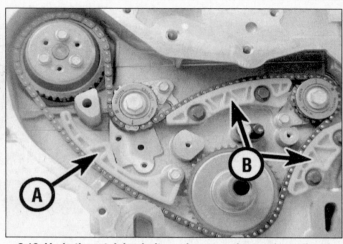

8.16 Undo the retaining bolts and remove the tension rail and guide rails

A Tension rail   B Guide rails

Woodruff key on the crankshaft. **Note:** *FRONT is marked on the outer face of the gear.*

Balance shaft chain and sprockets

Note: *If there is any wear on the balance shaft timing chain, tension rail and guides, balance shaft chain tensioner and all the drivegears/sprockets the components must always be renewed as a complete assembly.*

14 Remove the camshaft timing chain and sprockets as described in paragraphs 1 to 13.

15 Undo the two retaining bolts and remove the balance shaft chain tensioner from the cylinder block.

16 Undo the securing bolts and remove the tension rail and the two guide rails from the cylinder block **(see illustration)**.

17 Lift the balance shaft timing chain from the sprockets and remove.

18 Using a suitable drift, lock the balance shaft sprockets and undo the retaining bolts, then remove the sprocket from the balance shaft **(see illustration)**. Use new bolts when refitting.

19 Slide the crankshaft drivegear/sprocket (and spring washer, where fitted) off the Woodruff key on the crankshaft. **Note:** *FRONT is marked on the outer face of the gear.*

20 Lock the coolant pump drivegear with a suitable screwdriver, and undo the three securing bolts. Remove the drivegear from the coolant pump.

Inspection

21 Examine the teeth on the sprockets for any sign of wear or damage such as chipped, hooked or missing teeth. If there is any sign of wear or damage on any sprocket/gear, all the sprockets/gears and the relevant chain should be renewed as a set.

22 Inspect the links of each timing chain for signs of wear or damage on the rollers. The extent of wear can be judged by checking the amount by which the chain can be bent sideways; a new chain will have very little

sideways movement. If there is an excessive amount of side play in a timing chain, it must be renewed.

23 Note that it is a sensible precaution to renew the timing chains, regardless of their apparent condition, if the engine has covered a high mileage, or if it has been noted that the chain(s) have sounded noisy when the engine running. It is advised renewing the chains and sprockets as a matched set, since it is false economy to run a new chain on worn sprockets and *vice-versa*. If there is any doubt about the condition of the timing chains and sprockets, seek the advice of a Vauxhall/Opel dealer service department, who will be able to advise you as to the best course of action, based on their previous knowledge of the engine.

24 Examine the chain guide(s) and tensioner rail(s) for signs of wear or damage to their chain contact faces, renewing any which are badly marked.

Refitting

Camshaft chain and sprockets

25 If any new components are being fitted, transfer any alignment marks you have made

8.18 Using a drift to lock the balance shaft sprocket

from the original components to aid refitting. Ensure the crankshaft is still at the TDC position.

26 If not already fitted, refit the balance shaft timing chain and sprockets as described in paragraphs 42 to 49.

27 Slide the crankshaft drive sprocket (and spring washer, where fitted) onto the Woodruff key on the crankshaft. **Note:** *FRONT is marked on the outer face of the sprocket* **(see illustration)**.

28 Refit the intake camshaft sprocket complete with timing chain down through the top of the cylinder head. The copper coloured link should line up with the INT mark on the intake sprocket (a cable-tie can be used to keep the chain in position – **see illustration 8.0b**). Attach the sprocket to the camshaft using a new securing bolt, tightening it hand-tight at this stage.

29 Insert the timing chain tension rail up through the engine casing into position for the tensioner. (Do not refit the lower securing bolt until the timing chain is in position.)

30 Insert the exhaust camshaft sprocket into the timing chain, making sure the silver link on the timing chain lines up with the EXH mark on the sprocket (a cable-tie can be used to keep the chain in position – **see illustration 8.0a**).

8.27 Refit the timing chain crankshaft sprocket, noting FRONT is marked on the outer face

8.30 Turning the camshaft slightly using an open-ended spanner to locate the sprocket in the correct position

8.37 Use new retaining bolts when refitting the sliding rail

8.43 Refit the balance shaft crankshaft sprocket, noting FRONT is marked on the outer face

Attach the sprocket to the camshaft using a new securing bolt, tightening it hand-tight at this stage. **Note:** *One or both of the camshafts may have moved slightly, due to valve spring pressure. It may be necessary to turn the camshafts slightly to locate the sprockets in the correct position, use an open-ended spanner on the camshaft if required (see illustration). Do not turn the camshafts too far as the engine is set at TDC and the valves could hit the pistons.*

31 Locate the timing chain onto the crankshaft drive sprocket, aligning the silver link with the mark on the sprocket **(see illustration 8.0c)**.

8.44 Refit the balance shaft sprockets using new securing bolts

32 The lower securing bolt can now be fitted to the tension rail and tightened to its specified torque.

33 Insert the guide rail and fit lower securing bolt, tightening it to its specified torque.

34 Refit the guide rail upper securing bolt and access bolt in the cylinder head, tightening them to their specified torque.

Caution: All the timing marks (coloured chain links) must be aligned with the corresponding marks on the sprockets. This procedure must be carried out correctly, otherwise the timing being offset by one tooth will result in engine damage.

35 Refit the timing chain cover as described in Section 6.

36 Remove the cable-ties from camshaft sprockets. Hold the camshafts in turn with an open-ended spanner on the flats provided and tighten the sprocket bolts to the specified Stage 1 torque setting, then tighten the bolts through the specified Stage 2 and Stage 3 angles. It is recommended that an angle-measuring gauge is used during the final stages of the tightening, to ensure accuracy. If a gauge is not available, use white paint to make alignment marks prior to tightening; the marks can then be used to check that the bolts have been rotated through the correct angle.

37 Attach the sliding rail for the camshaft timing chain to the top of the cylinder head, using new retaining bolts tighten them to the specified torque **(see illustration)**.

38 Refit the camshaft timing chain tensioner as described in Section 7.

39 Refit the camshaft position sensor and reconnect the wiring plug.

40 Rotate the crankshaft through two complete revolutions (720°) in the correct direction of rotation (to bring number 4 piston back to TDC on its compression stroke). If the special tool is available, check the valve timing as described in Section 3.

41 Refit the camshaft cover as described in Section 4, then reconnect the battery negative terminal.

Balance shaft chain and sprockets

42 Refit the drivegear to the coolant pump, and tighten the three securing bolts to the specified torque.

43 Slide the crankshaft drivegear/sprocket (and spring washer, where fitted) onto the Woodruff key on the crankshaft. **Note:** *FRONT is marked on the outer face of the gear (see illustration)*. The timing mark on the drivegear should be pointing downwards to align with the silver-coloured link on the timing chain.

44 Refit the exhaust sprocket to the balance

8.45 The arrow points upwards on the intake sprocket

8.46 Balance shaft timing chain layout

A   *Silver-coloured chain links aligned with timing marks*

B   *Copper-coloured chain link aligned with timing mark*

9.6 Alignment marks made on camshaft sprockets for refitting

9.15 Use a container used to keep the followers and hydraulic tappets in order

9.16 Keep the hydraulic tappets in labelled containers with clean engine oil

shaft, using a new securing bolt **(see illustration)**. The sprocket is marked EXHAUST and has an arrow which points downwards to align with the silver-coloured link on the timing chain. Tighten the bolts to the specified torque, locking the balance shaft sprockets as on removal.

45 Refit the intake sprocket to the balance shaft, using a new securing bolt. The sprocket is marked INTAKE and has an arrow which points upwards to align with the copper-coloured link on the timing chain **(see illustration)**. Tighten the bolts to the specified torque, locking the balance shaft sprockets as on removal.

46 Refit the balance shaft timing chain to the sprockets/gears and align the timing marks (coloured chain links) with the marks on the appropriate sprockets as described above **(see illustration)**.

47 Refit the tension rail and two guide rails to the cylinder block, tightening the securing bolts to the specified torque.

48 Refit the balance shaft chain tensioner as described in Section 7.

49 Refit the camshaft timing chain and sprockets as described above.

9 Camshaft and followers –
removal, inspection and refitting

Note: *New camshaft sprocket retaining bolts and new timing chain sliding rail retaining bolts will be required on refitting.*

Removal

1 Disconnect the battery negative terminal (refer to *Disconnecting the battery* in the Reference Chapter).

2 Remove the high-pressure fuel pump as described in Chapter 4A.

3 Remove the camshaft cover as described in Section 4.

4 Position No 4 piston at TDC on its compression stroke, as described in Section 3.

5 Undo the two retaining bolts and remove the camshaft timing chain sliding rail on the top of the cylinder head **(see illustration 8.6)**.

6 Check that No 4 piston is still positioned at TDC on its compression stroke then cable-tie the timing chain to the camshaft sprockets and mark the sprockets in relation to the cylinder head **(see illustration)**.

7 If the vehicle is still on axle stands, lower it back onto the ground making sure the handbrake is on and 1st gear is engaged. This is to prevent the engine being turned once TDC has been aligned.

8 Remove the camshaft timing chain tensioner as described in Section 7.

9 Disconnect the wiring plug, then undo the retaining bolt and remove the camshaft position sensor from the cylinder head.

10 Hold the camshafts, using an open-ended spanner on the flats provided, then slacken and remove the camshaft sprocket retaining bolts **(see illustration 8.9)**.

11 Disengage the camshaft sprockets (complete with chain) from the camshafts, keeping the chain under tension. Use a suitable screwdriver, bar or bolt to pass through the sprockets and rest on the upper surface of the cylinder head, to prevent the timing chain falling down and coming off the crankshaft drivegear/sprocket.

12 Note the identification markings on the camshaft bearing caps. The caps are numbered 1 to 10 with all numbers being the right way up when viewed from the driver's seat; numbers 1 to 5 on the exhaust camshaft starting from the timing chain end of the engine, and numbers 6 to 10 on the intake camshaft starting at the timing chain end. **Note:** *There is also an 11th cap on the intake camshaft, at the flywheel/driveplate end of the cylinder head.* If the markings are not clearly visible, make identification marks to ensure each cap is fitted correctly on refitting.

13 Where fitted, undo the two bolts and remove the cover plate from No 11 bearing cap.

14 Working in a spiral pattern from the outside inwards, slacken the camshaft bearing cap retaining bolts by half a turn at a time, to relieve the pressure of the valve springs on the bearing caps gradually and evenly. Once the valve spring pressure has been relieved, the bolts can be fully unscrewed and removed, along with the caps. Take care not to loose any locating dowels which may be fitted to some of the bearing caps and lift the camshaft out from the head.

Caution: If the bearing cap bolts are carelessly slackened, the bearing caps might break. If any bearing cap breaks then the complete cylinder head assembly must be renewed; the bearing caps are

matched to the head and are not available separately.

15 Obtain 16 small, clean plastic containers, and label them for identification. Alternatively, divide a larger container into compartments. Lift the followers out from the top of the cylinder head and store each one in its respective fitted position **(see illustration)**.

16 If the hydraulic tappets are also to be removed, withdraw each hydraulic tappet and place them in small containers with clean engine oil. This will keep them primed ready for refitting **(see illustration)**.

Inspection

17 Examine the camshaft bearing surfaces and cam lobes for signs of wear ridges and scoring. Renew the camshaft if any of these conditions are apparent. Examine the condition of the bearing surfaces both on the camshaft journals and in the cylinder head. If the head bearing surfaces are worn excessively, the cylinder head will need to be renewed.

18 Examine the follower bearing surfaces which contact the camshaft lobes for wear ridges and scoring. Renew any followers on which these conditions are apparent.

19 Check the hydraulic tappets (where removed) and their bores in the cylinder head for signs of wear or damage. If any tappet is thought to be faulty it should be renewed.

Refitting

20 Where removed, lubricate the hydraulic tappets with clean engine oil and carefully insert each one into its original location in the cylinder head **(see illustration)**.

9.20 Lubricate the tappets with clean engine oil before refitting

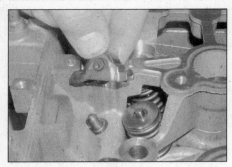

9.21 Refit the camshaft followers in their original position

9.24 Apply silicone sealing compound thinly to the surface areas arrowed

9.25 Refitting No 11 cap to the flywheel/driveplate end of the intake camshaft

9.27 Refit new retaining bolts to the camshaft sprockets

21 Refit the camshaft followers to the cylinder head, ensuring each follower is fitted in its original location **(see illustration)**.

22 Lubricate the camshaft followers with clean engine oil then lay the camshafts into position. Ensure the crankshaft is still set at TDC, and position the camshafts so that the lobes of No 4 cylinder are pointing upward.

23 Ensure the mating surfaces of the bearing caps and cylinder head are clean and dry and lubricate the camshaft journals and lobes with clean engine oil.

24 Apply a smear of sealant to the cylinder head mating surface at the flywheel/driveplate end of the intake camshaft (No 11) bearing cap **(see illustration)**. Refit the cap locating dowels to the cap if they have been removed.

25 Refit the camshaft bearing caps and the retaining bolts in their original locations on the cylinder head. The caps are numbered 1 to 10 with all numbers being the right way up when viewed from the driver's seat; numbers 1 to 5 on the exhaust camshaft starting from the timing chain end of the engine, and numbers 6 to 10 on the intake camshaft starting at the timing chain end. Refit the 11th cap on the intake camshaft, at the flywheel/driveplate end of the cylinder head **(see illustration)**.

26 Tighten all bolts by hand only then, working in a spiral pattern from the centre outwards, tighten the bolts by half a turn at a time to gradually impose the pressure of the valve springs on the bearing caps. Repeat this sequence until all bearing caps are in contact with the cylinder head then go around and tighten the camshaft bearing cap bolts

to the specified torque. When all the caps have been tightened, where applicable, refit the cover plate to No 11 bearing cap using a new gasket, and tighten the two bolts to the specified torque.

Caution: If the bearing cap bolts are carelessly tightened, the bearing caps might break. If any bearing cap breaks then the complete cylinder head assembly must be renewed; the bearing caps are matched to the head and are not available separately.

27 Using the marks made on removal, ensure that the timing chain is still correctly engaged with the sprockets then refit the camshaft sprockets to the camshafts. It may be necessary to turn the camshafts slightly to locate the sprockets in the correct position, use an open-ended spanner on the camshaft if required. Fit the new retaining bolts hand-tight at this stage **(see illustration)**.

10.4 Remove the two coolant hoses (arrowed) from the front of the cylinder head

Remove the cable-ties from the timing chain and sprockets.

28 Refit the camshaft timing chain tensioner as described in Section 7.

29 If the special tool is available, check that No 4 cylinder is correctly set at TDC on compression as described in Section 3. If the special tool is not available, make sure the marks made on the sprockets prior to removal are correctly aligned.

30 Hold the camshafts in turn with an open-ended spanner on the flats provided and tighten the sprocket bolts to the specified Stage 1 torque setting, then tighten the bolts through the specified Stage 2 and Stage 3 angles. It is recommended that an angle-measuring gauge is used during the final stages of the tightening, to ensure accuracy. If a gauge is not available, use white paint to make alignment marks prior to tightening; the marks can then be used to check that the bolts have been rotated through the correct angle.

31 Refit the camshaft timing chain sliding rail using new retaining bolts, then tighten to the specified torque.

32 Rotate the crankshaft through two complete revolutions (720°) in the correct direction of rotation (to bring number 4 piston back to TDC on its compression stroke). If the special tool is available, check the valve timing as described in Section 4. If the special tool is not available, check that the marks made on the sprockets prior to removal are correctly aligned.

33 Refit the camshaft position sensor and reconnect the wiring plug.

34 Refit the camshaft cover as described in Section 4.

35 Refit the high-pressure fuel pump as described in Chapter 4A.

36 Reconnect the battery negative terminal and lower the vehicle to the ground (where applicable)

10 Cylinder head – removal and refitting

Note: *New cylinder head bolts, camshaft timing chain sliding rail bolts and camshaft sprocket retaining bolts will be required on refitting.*

Removal

1 Drain the cooling system as described in Chapter 1A.

2 Remove the camshaft timing chain and sprockets as described in Section 8.

3 Remove the inlet and exhaust manifolds as described in Chapter 4A.

4 Release the retaining clips and disconnect the coolant hoses from the front of the right-hand end of the cylinder head **(see illustration)**.

5 Slacken and remove the four retaining bolts from the timing chain end of the cylinder head **(see illustrations 10.25a and 10.25b)**.

10.16 Using a tap to clean out the threads in the cylinder block

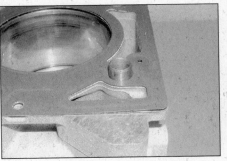

10.17a Check the dowels are in position to locate the cylinder head gasket . . .

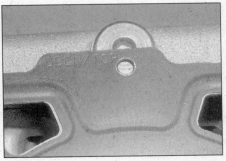

10.17b . . . ensuring the gasket is fitted with its OBEN/TOP marking uppermost

6 Working in the **reverse** of the tightening sequence shown in illustration 10.21, progressively slacken the ten main cylinder head bolts by half a turn at a time, until all bolts can be unscrewed by hand.

7 Lift out the cylinder head bolts and where applicable recover the washers.

8 Lift the cylinder head away; seek assistance if possible, as it is a heavy assembly.

9 Remove the gasket, noting the locating dowels fitted to the top of the cylinder block. If they are a loose fit, remove the locating dowels and store them with the head for safe-keeping.

Caution: Do not lay the head on its lower mating surface; support the head on wooden blocks as it may be damaged if the head is placed directly onto a bench.

10 If the cylinder head is to be dismantled for overhaul, then refer to Part E of this Chapter.

Preparation for refitting

11 The mating faces of the cylinder head and cylinder block/crankcase must be perfectly clean before refitting the head. Use a hard plastic or wood scraper to remove all traces of gasket and carbon; also clean the piston crowns. Take particular care, as the surfaces are damaged easily. Also, make sure that the carbon is not allowed to enter the oil and water passages – this is particularly important for the lubrication system, as carbon could block the oil supply to any of the engine's components. Using adhesive tape and paper, seal the water, oil and bolt holes in the cylinder block/crankcase. To prevent carbon entering the gap between the pistons and bores, smear a little grease in the gap. After cleaning each piston, use a small brush to remove all traces of grease and carbon from the gap, then wipe away the remainder with a clean rag. Clean all the pistons in the same way.

12 Check the mating surfaces of the cylinder block/crankcase and the cylinder head for nicks, deep scratches and other damage. If slight, they may be removed carefully with a file, but if excessive, machining may be the only alternative to renewal (see your local specialist for machining).

13 Ensure that the cylinder head bolt holes in the crankcase are clean and free of oil. Syringe or soak up any oil left in the bolt holes. This is most important in order that the correct

bolt tightening torque can be applied and to prevent the possibility of the block being cracked by hydraulic pressure when the bolts are tightened.

14 The cylinder head bolts must be discarded and renewed, regardless of their apparent condition.

15 If warpage of the cylinder head gasket surface is suspected, use a straight-edge to check it for distortion. Refer to Part E of this Chapter if necessary.

Refitting

16 Using a tap, clean out the thread in the four bolt holes at the timing chain end of the cylinder block **(see illustration)**. Wipe clean the mating surfaces of the cylinder head and cylinder block/crankcase.

17 Check that the locating dowels are in position then fit the new gasket to the cylinder block **(see illustrations)**.

18 Ensure the crankshaft is positioned approx 60° BTDC (this is to prevent any damage to the valves or pistons when refitting the cylinder head).

19 With the aid of an assistant, carefully refit the cylinder head assembly to the block, aligning it with the locating dowels.

20 Apply a smear of oil to the threads and the underside of the heads of the new cylinder head bolts and carefully enter each bolt into its relevant hole (*do not drop them in*). Screw all bolts in, by hand only, until finger-tight.

21 Working progressively and in the sequence shown, tighten the cylinder head bolts to their Stage 1 torque setting, using a torque wrench and suitable socket **(see illustration)**.

22 Once all bolts have been tightened to the Stage 1 torque, working again in the specified sequence, go around and tighten all bolts through the specified Stage 2 angle. It is

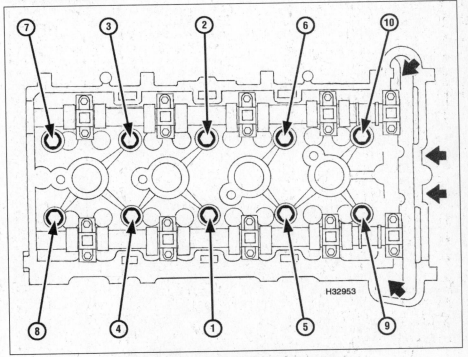

H32953

10.21 Cylinder head bolt tightening sequence

10.22 Tightening the cylinder head down through its stages, using an angle gauge

10.25a Fit four new retaining bolts to the timing chain end of the cylinder head . . .

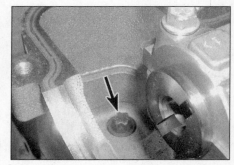

10.25b . . . two of the bolts are inside the timing chain housing (bolt arrowed on exhaust side of head)

recommended that an angle-measuring gauge is used to ensure accuracy **(see illustration)**. If a gauge is not available, use white paint to make alignment marks prior to tightening; the marks can then be used to check that the bolt has been rotated through the correct angle.

23 Go around again in the specified sequence and angle tighten the bolts through the specified Stage 3 angle.

24 Finally go around in the specified sequence and angle tighten the bolts through the specified Stage 4 angle.

25 Refit the four bolts securing the right-hand end of the cylinder head to the block (timing chain end) and tighten them to the specified torque setting **(see illustrations)**.

26 Turn the crankshaft carefully in the direction of engine rotation, to bring No 4 cylinder back to TDC.

27 Reconnect the coolant hoses to the cylinder head and secure them in position with the retaining clips.

28 Refit the inlet and exhaust manifolds and associated components as described in Chapter 4A.

29 Refit the camshaft timing chain and sprockets as described in Section 8.

30 On completion, refill the cooling system and refill the engine with oil as described in Chapter 1A.

11 Sump – removal and refitting

Removal

1 Disconnect the battery negative terminal (refer to *Disconnecting the battery* in the Reference Chapter).

2 Apply the handbrake, then jack up the front of the vehicle and support it on axle stands (see *Jacking and vehicle support*). Remove the right-hand front roadwheel and the wheel arch liner inner cover.

3 Remove the auxiliary drivebelt as described in Chapter 1A. Prior to removal, mark the direction of rotation on the belt to ensure the belt is refitted the same way around.

4 Drain the engine oil as described in Chapter 1A. When the oil has completely drained, refit the drain plug with new sealing washer, and tighten to the specified torque.

5 Disconnect the wiring connector from the oil level sensor (see Chapter 5A).

6 Undo the bolt securing the oil dipstick guide tube to the inlet manifold, then withdraw the guide tube from the sump.

7 Remove the lower mounting bolt for the

air conditioning compressor. Slacken (do not remove) the upper two mounting bolts and use a block of wood (or similar) to wedge the compressor away from the sump. **Note:** *Take care not to damage the bolts or alloy mounting point when inserting the wedge; do not use excessive force.*

8 Slacken and remove the bolts securing the sump flange to the transmission housing **(see illustration)**.

9 Progressively slacken and remove the bolts securing the sump to the base of the cylinder block lower casing (there is one long bolt at the transmission end of the sump – **see illustration 11.8**). To break the sump joint it may be necessary to cut the silicone sealer using a suitable knife, taking care not to damage any surfaces. Lower the sump away from the engine.

10 While the sump is removed, take the opportunity to check the oil pump pick-up/strainer (if possible) for signs of clogging or splitting. **Note:** *The pick-up/strainer cannot be removed from the sump as it is riveted in position.*

Refitting

11 Remove all traces of silicone sealer and oil from the mating surfaces of the sump and cylinder block.

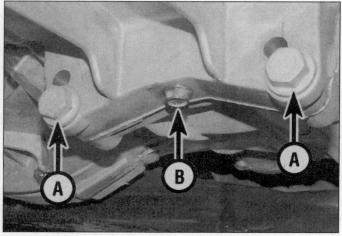

11.8 Undo the two sump to transmission bolts (A) and also the sump-to-lower cylinder block bolt (B)

11.12a Apply a continuous bead of silicone sealer around the sump . . .

12 Apply a continuous bead of silicone sealing compound (available from your Vauxhall/Opel dealer) at approximately 1.0 mm from the inner edge of the sump. The bead of sealant should be between 2.0 and 2.5 mm in diameter. Also apply a bead of sealant (2.0 to 2.5 mm) around the oil intake pipe area of the sump mating surface **(see illustrations)**.

13 Offer up the sump to the cylinder block and loosely refit all the retaining bolts.

14 Working out from the centre in a diagonal sequence, progressively tighten the bolts securing the sump to the cylinder block lower casing. Tighten all the bolts to their specified torque setting.

15 Tighten the bolts securing the sump flange to the transmission housing to their specified torque settings.

16 Remove the wedge-shaped block from the air conditioning compressor and refit the lower mounting bolt. Tighten the three compressor mounting bolts to their specified torque (see Chapter 3).

17 Refit the oil dipstick guide tube and securely tighten the retaining bolt.

18 Reconnect the oil level sensor wiring connector.

19 Refit the auxiliary drivebelt as described in Chapter 1A using the mark made prior to removal to ensure the belt is fitted the correct way around.

20 Refit the wheel arch liner inner cover and roadwheel, and lower the vehicle to the ground.

21 Fill the engine with fresh engine oil as described in Chapter 1A.

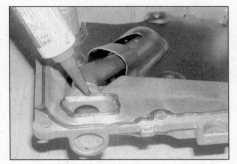

11.12b . . . and also around the oil intake pipe area

12 Oil pump –
removal, inspection and refitting

Note: *The oil pump pressure control valve can be removed with the timing chain cover in position on the engine (see paragraph 5 below).*

Removal

1 The oil pump assembly is built into the timing chain cover. Removal and refitting of the cover is as described in Section 6.

Inspection

2 Undo the retaining screws and lift off the pump cover plate from the inside of the timing chain cover **(see illustration)**.

3 Note any marks identifying the outer faces of the pump rotors. If none can be seen, use a suitable marker pen and mark the surface of both the pump inner and outer rotors; the marks can then be used to ensure the rotors are refitted the correct way around.

4 Lift out the inner and outer rotors from the cover **(see illustration)**.

5 Unscrew the oil pressure control valve plug from the timing chain cover and withdraw the spring and plunger, noting which way around the plunger is fitted. Remove the sealing ring from the valve bolt **(see illustrations)**.

6 Clean the components, and carefully examine the rotors, pump body and valve plungers for any signs of scoring or wear. Renew any component which shows signs of wear or damage; if the rotors or pump housing are marked then the complete pump assembly should be renewed.

7 If the components appear serviceable, measure the clearances (using feeler blades) between:

- a) The inner rotor and the outer rotor.
- b) The outer rotor and oil pump housing.
- c) The rotor endfloat.
- d) The flatness of the end cover.

If the clearances exceed the specified tolerances (see Specifications at the beginning of this Chapter), the pump must be renewed **(see illustrations)**.

8 If the pump is satisfactory, reassemble the components in the reverse order of removal, noting the following.

- a) Ensure both rotors and the valve plunger are fitted the correct way around.
- b) Fit new sealing rings to the pressure control valve and tighten to the specified torque setting.

12.2 Undo the retaining screws and remove the pump cover plate

12.4 Removing the inner and outer rotors

12.5a Undo and remove the oil pressure control valve plug . . .

12.5b . . . and remove the oil pressure valve spring and plunger

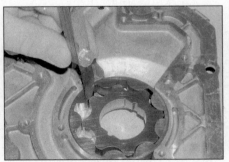

12.7a Using a feeler blade to check the inner-to-outer rotor clearance . . .

12.7b . . . the outer rotor-to-oil pump housing . . .

12.7c . . . and also using a straight-edge to check the endfloat

13.3a Undo the retaining bolt (arrowed) . . .

13.3b . . . and withdraw the balance shaft assembly

c) Refit the pump cover tightening the cover screws to the specified torque.

d) On completion prime the oil pump by filling it with clean engine oil whilst rotating the inner rotor.

Refitting

9 Refit the timing chain cover as described in Section 6.

13 Balance shaft – removal and refitting

Removal

1 Remove the balance shaft timing chain and sprockets as described in Section 8.

2 If the balance shaft sprockets are removed, mark the shafts to identify the intake shaft from the exhaust shaft for refitting.

3 Undo the securing bolt from the balance shaft retaining plate and slide the balance shaft out from the cylinder block (see illustrations).

Refitting

4 Refitting is the reverse of removal, tighten the retaining plate bolts to their specified torque.

5 Refit the balance shaft timing chain and sprockets as described in Section 8.

14 Crankshaft oil seals – renewal

Right-hand (timing chain end)

1 Remove the crankshaft pulley as described in Section 5.

2 Using a large flat-bladed screwdriver, carefully lever the seal out from the timing chain cover.

3 Clean the seal housing and polish off any burrs or raised edges which may have caused the seal to fail in the first place.

4 Press/tap the new seal squarely into position until it sits into the recess in the cover (see illustration). If necessary, a suitable tubular drift, such as a socket, which bears only on the hard outer edge of the seal can be used to tap the seal into position. Take great care not to damage the seal lips during fitting and ensure that the seal lips face inwards.

5 Wash off any traces of oil, then refit the crankshaft pulley as described in Section 5.

Left-hand (flywheel/driveplate end)

6 Remove the flywheel/driveplate as described in Section 15.

7 Carefully punch or drill two small holes opposite each other in the oil seal. Screw a self-tapping screw into each and pull on the screws with pliers to extract the seal (see illustration).

8 Clean the seal housing and polish off any burrs or raised edges which may have caused the seal to fail in the first place. **Note:** *Insulation tape can be put around the crankshaft flange to help fit the oil seal.*

9 Ease the new seal into position on the end of the crankshaft. Press the seal squarely into position until it is flush with the bearing cap. If necessary, a suitable tubular drift, such as a socket, which bears only on the hard outer edge of the seal can be used to tap the seal into position. Take great care not to damage the seal lips during fitting and ensure that the seal lips face inwards (see illustration).

10 If insulation tape was used around the crankshaft flange, remove it, taking care not to damage the oil seal. Refit the flywheel as described in Section 15.

15 Flywheel/driveplate – removal, inspection and refitting

Note: *New flywheel/driveplate retaining bolts will be required on refitting.*

Removal

Manual transmission models

1 Remove the transmission as described in Chapter 7A then remove the clutch assembly as described in Chapter 6.

2 Prevent the flywheel from turning by locking the ring gear teeth with a similar arrangement

14.4 Make sure the seal seats squarely into the timing chain cover

14.7 Removing a crankshaft left-hand oil seal, using a pair of pliers and a screw

14.9 Carefully ease the oil seal over the end of the crankshaft and tap/press it squarely into position

to that shown **(see illustration)**. Alternatively, bolt a strap between the flywheel and the cylinder block/crankcase. Make alignment marks between the flywheel and crankshaft using paint or a suitable marker pen.

3 Slacken and remove the retaining bolts and remove the flywheel. Do not drop it, as it is very heavy.

Automatic transmission models

4 Remove the transmission as described in Chapter 7B then remove the driveplate as described in paragraphs 2 and 3.

Inspection

5 On manual transmission models, examine the flywheel for scoring of the clutch face. If the clutch face is scored, the flywheel may be surface-ground, but renewal is preferable.

6 On automatic transmission models closely examine the driveplate and ring gear teeth for signs of wear or damage and check the driveplate surface for any signs of cracks.

7 If there is any doubt about the condition of the flywheel/driveplate, seek the advice of a Vauxhall/Opel dealer or engine reconditioning specialist. They will be able to advise if it is possible to recondition it or whether renewal is necessary.

Refitting

Manual transmission models

8 Clean the mating surfaces of the flywheel and crankshaft.

9 Apply a drop of locking compound to each of the new retaining bolt threads then offer up the flywheel, if the original is being refitted, align the marks made prior to removal. Screw in the retaining bolts.

10 Lock the flywheel by the method used on removal, and tighten the retaining bolts to the specified Stage 1 torque setting then angle-tighten the bolts through the specified Stage 2 angle, using a socket and extension bar, and finally through the specified Stage 3 angle. It is recommended that an angle-measuring gauge is used during the final stages of the tightening, to ensure accuracy. If a gauge is not available, use white paint to make alignment marks between the bolt head and flywheel prior to tightening; the marks can then be used to check that the bolt has been rotated through the correct angle.

11 Refit the clutch as described in Chapter 6 then remove the locking tool, and refit the transmission as described in Chapter 7A.

Automatic transmission models

12 Clean the mating surfaces of the driveplate and crankshaft and remove all traces of locking compound from the driveplate retaining bolt threads.

13 Apply a drop of locking compound to each of the new retaining bolt threads then offer up the driveplate, if the original is being refitted align the marks made prior to removal. Screw in the retaining bolts.

14 Lock the driveplate by the method used

15.2 Lock the flywheel/driveplate ring gear

on removal, and tighten the retaining bolts to the specified Stage 1 torque setting then angle-tighten the bolts through the specified Stage 2 angle, using a socket and extension bar. It is recommended that an angle-measuring gauge is used during the final stages of the tightening, to ensure accuracy. If a gauge is not available, use white paint to make alignment marks between the bolt head and flywheel prior to tightening; the marks can then be used to check that the bolt has been rotated through the correct angle.

15 Remove the locking tool and refit the transmission as described in Chapter 7B.

16 Engine/transmission mountings – inspection and renewal

Inspection

1 If improved access is required, firmly apply the handbrake, then jack up the front of the car and support it securely on axle stands (see *Jacking and vehicle support*).

2 Check the mounting rubber to see if it is cracked, hardened or separated from the metal at any point; renew the mounting if any such damage or deterioration is evident.

3 Check that all the mounting's fasteners are securely tightened; use a torque wrench to check if possible.

4 Using a large screwdriver or a pry bar, check for wear in the mounting by carefully levering against it to check for free play; where this

is not possible, enlist the aid of an assistant to move the engine/transmission unit back-and-forth, or from side-to-side, while you watch the mounting. While some free play is to be expected even from new components, excessive wear should be obvious. If excessive free play is found, check first that the fasteners are correctly secured, then renew any worn components as described below.

Renewal

Note: *Before slackening any of the engine mounting bolts/nuts, the relative positions of the mountings to their various brackets should be marked to ensure correct alignment upon refitting.*

Front mounting/torque link

5 Apply the handbrake, then jack up the front of the vehicle and support it on axle stands (see *Jacking and vehicle support*).

6 Slacken and remove the nut securing the mounting to the subframe bracket. Withdraw the through-bolt **(see illustration)**.

7 Undo the bolts securing the mounting bracket to the transmission, then manoeuvre the mounting and bracket out of position.

8 Check all components for signs of wear or damage, and renew as necessary.

9 Locate the mounting in the subframe, refit the through bolt and nut, then tighten the nut finger-tight at this stage.

10 Refit the mounting bracket to the transmission and tighten its bolts to the specified torque.

11 Tighten the through-bolt nut to the specified torque then on completion, lower the vehicle to the ground.

Rear mounting/torque link

12 Apply the handbrake, then jack up the front of the vehicle and support it on axle stands (see *Jacking and vehicle support*).

13 Undo the three nuts securing the exhaust system front pipe to the catalytic converter, taking care to support the flexible section. **Note:** *Angular movement in excess of 10° can cause permanent damage to the flexible section.* Separate the flange joint and recover the gasket.

14 Undo the three bolts securing the mounting bracket to the transmission and

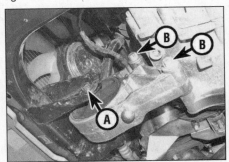

16.6 Front mounting/torque link through-bolt (A) and mounting bracket-to-transmission bolts (B)

16.14 Rear mounting/torque link through-bolt (arrowed)

16.15 Rear mounting/torque link bracket-to-subframe mounting bolt nuts (arrowed)

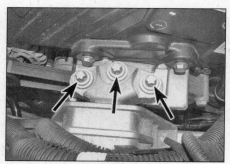

16.22a Right-hand mounting bracket-to-engine bracket bolts (arrowed) . . .

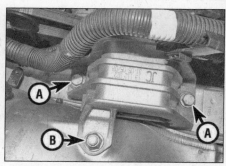

16.22b . . . and mounting-to-body retaining bolts (A) and nut (B)

the through-bolt securing the mounting to the bracket (see illustration).

15 Undo the nuts and remove the two bolts securing the mounting to the subframe (see illustration). Manoeuvre the mounting and bracket out from under the car.

16 Refit the bracket to the transmission and tighten the bolts to the specified torque.

17 Locate the new mounting in position. Insert the bolts and tighten the bolt/nuts to the specified torque.

18 Using a new gasket, refit the exhaust front pipe flange joint to the catalytic converter and tighten the three retaining nuts to the specified torque. On completion, lower the vehicle to the ground.

Right-hand mounting

19 Apply the handbrake, then jack up the front of the vehicle and support it on axle stands (see *Jacking and vehicle support*).

20 Remove the air cleaner as described in Chapter 4A.

21 Attach a suitable hoist and lifting tackle to the engine lifting brackets on the cylinder head, and support the weight of the engine.

22 Mark the position of the three bolts securing the mounting bracket to the engine bracket and undo the bolts. Undo the two bolts and one nut securing the mounting to the body and remove the mounting assembly (see illustrations).

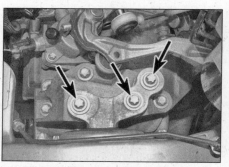

16.28 Left-hand mounting bracket-to-transmission bracket retaining bolts (arrowed) – diesel model shown, petrol similar

23 Place the mounting assembly in position and refit the two bolts and the nut securing the mounting to the body. Tighten the bolts/nut to the specified torque. Align the mounting in its original position, then tighten the three mounting bracket bolts to the specified torque.

24 Remove the hoist, then refit the air cleaner as described in Chapter 4A.

25 On completion, lower the vehicle to the ground.

Left-hand mounting

26 Remove the battery and battery box as described in Chapter 5A.

27 Attach a suitable hoist and lifting tackle

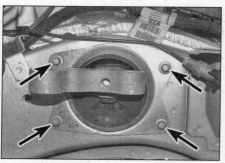

16.29 Left-hand mounting-to-body retaining bolts (arrowed) – shown with engine/transmission removed

to the engine lifting brackets on the cylinder head, and support the weight of the engine.

28 Using a Torx socket, unscrew the three bolts securing the mounting bracket to the transmission bracket (see illustration).

29 Undo the four bolts securing the mounting to the body and the three bolts securing the transmission bracket to the transmission (see illustration). Remove the mounting assembly from the car.

30 Locate the mounting brackets in position then insert the bolts and tighten them to the specified torque.

31 Disconnect the hoist and lifting tackle.

32 Refit the battery box and battery as described in Chapter 5A.

Torque wrench settings

	Nm	lbf ft
Air conditioning compressor mounting bracket to cylinder block/sump .	50	37
Auxiliary drivebelt idler pulley bolt	50	37
Auxiliary drivebelt tensioner assembly bolts	50	37
Camshaft bearing cap bolts.	15	11
Camshaft cover bolts.	10	7
Camshaft sprocket bolt*.	120	89
Connecting rod big-end bearing cap bolt:*		
Stage 1	25	18
Stage 2	Angle-tighten a further 60°	
Crankshaft oil seal housing	9	7
Crankshaft pulley/vibration damper bolts	25	18
Crankshaft sprocket bolt*†	340	251
Cylinder head bolts:*		
Stage 1	20	15
Stage 2	65	48
Stage 3	Angle-tighten a further 90°	
Stage 4	Angle-tighten a further 90°	
Stage 5	Angle-tighten a further 90°	
Engine mountings:		
Front mounting/torque link:		
Mounting to transmission.	80	59
Mounting to subframe	80	59
Left-hand mounting:		
Mounting-to-body bolts	20	15
Mounting bracket to transmission bracket.	55	41
Transmission bracket to transmission	55	41
Rear mounting/torque link:		
Mounting bracket to transmission	80	59
Mounting to subframe	60	44
Mounting to transmission bracket	80	59
Right-hand mounting:		
Engine bracket-to-engine bolts:		
Lower bolts (M8)	25	18
Upper bolts (M10)	50	37
Mounting-to-body bolts/nut	55	41
Mounting-to-engine bracket bolts	55	41
Engine-to-transmission unit bolts:		
M10 bolts	40	30
M12 bolts	60	44
Flywheel bolts*	160	118
High-pressure fuel pump sprocket nut*	50	37
Intermediate shaft bearing housing support bracket bolts	55	41
Main bearing cap bolts:*		
Stage 1	25	18
Stage 2	Angle-tighten a further 100°	
Oil filter housing to cylinder block	50	37
Oil pump housing to cylinder block	9	7
Oil pump pick-up/strainer bolts	9	7
Roadwheel bolts.	110	81
Sump bolts:		
M6 bolts	9	7
M8 bolts	25	18
M10 bolts	40	30
Sump drain plug	20	15
Timing belt idler pulley bolt	50	37
Timing belt tensioner bolt.	30	22
Timing belt upper cover bolts:		
M6 bolts	9	7
M8 bolts	25	18

Use new nuts/bolts
† *Left-hand thread*

1 General information

How to use this Chapter

This Part of Chapter 2 describes the repair procedures which can reasonably be carried out on the engine while it remains in the vehicle. If the engine has been removed from the vehicle and is being dismantled as described in Chapter 2E, any preliminary dismantling procedures can be ignored.

Note that, while it may be possible physically to overhaul items such as the piston/connecting rod assemblies while the engine is in the vehicle, such tasks are not usually carried out as separate operations, and usually require the execution of several additional procedures (not to mention the cleaning of components and of oilways); for this reason, all such tasks are classed as major overhaul procedures, and are described in Chapter 2E.

Chapter 2E describes the removal of the engine/transmission unit from the vehicle, and the full overhaul procedures which can then be carried out.

Engine description

The 1.9 litre SOHC diesel engine is of the eight-valve, in-line four-cylinder, single overhead camshaft type, mounted transversely at the front of the car, with the transmission on its left-hand end.

The crankshaft is supported within the cylinder block on five shell-type main bearings. Thrustwashers are fitted to number 3 main bearing, to control crankshaft endfloat.

The connecting rods rotate on horizontally-split bearing shells at their big-ends. The pistons are attached to the connecting rods by gudgeon pins, which are retained by circlips. The aluminium-alloy pistons are fitted with three piston rings – two compression rings and scraper-type oil control ring.

The camshaft runs directly in the cylinder head, and is driven by the crankshaft via a toothed composite rubber timing belt (which also drives the high-pressure fuel pump and the coolant pump). The camshaft operates each valve via a camshaft follower with adjustment shim.

Lubrication is by pressure-feed from a rotor-type oil pump, which is mounted on the right-hand end of the crankshaft. The pump draws oil through a strainer located in the sump, and then forces it through an externally mounted full-flow cartridge-type filter. The oil flows into galleries in the cylinder block/crankcase, from where it is distributed to the crankshaft (main bearings) and camshaft. The big-end bearings are supplied with oil via internal drillings in the crankshaft, while the camshaft bearings also receive a pressurised supply. The camshaft lobes and valves are lubricated by splash, as are all other engine components.

A semi-closed crankcase ventilation system is employed; crankcase fumes are drawn from the oil separator (integral with the camshaft cover), and passed via a hose to the inlet manifold.

Operations with engine in car

The following operations can be carried out without having to remove the engine from the car.
a) Removal and refitting of the camshaft cover.
b) Adjustment of the valve clearances.
c) Removal and refitting of the cylinder head.
d) Removal and refitting of the timing belt, tensioner, idler pulleys and sprockets.
e) Renewal of the camshaft oil seal.
f) Removal and refitting of the camshaft and followers.
g) Removal and refitting of the sump.
h) Removal and refitting of the connecting rods and pistons.*
i) Removal and refitting of the oil pump.
j) Removal and refitting of the oil filter housing.
k) Renewal of the crankshaft oil seals.
l) Renewal of the engine mountings.
m)Removal and refitting of the flywheel.
* Although the operation marked with an asterisk can be carried out with the engine in the car (after removal of the sump), it is preferable for the engine to be removed, in the interests of cleanliness and improved access. For this reason, the procedure is described in Chapter 2E.

2 Compression and leakdown tests – description and interpretation

Compression test

Note 1: *A compression tester specifically designed for diesel engines must be used for this test.*
Note 2: *The battery must be in a good state of charge, the air filter must be clean, and the engine should be at normal operating temperature.*

1 When engine performance is down, or if misfiring occurs which cannot be attributed to the fuel system, a compression test can provide diagnostic clues as to the engine's condition. If the test is performed regularly, it can give warning of trouble before any other symptoms become apparent.
2 The tester is connected to an adapter which screws into the injector holes. It is unlikely to be worthwhile buying such a tester for occasional use, but it may be possible to borrow or hire one – if not, have the test performed by a Vauxhall/Opel dealer, or suitably-equipped garage. If the necessary equipment is available, proceed as follows.

3 Remove the fuel injectors as described in Chapter 4B.
4 Screw the compression tester adapter in to the fuel injector hole of No 1 cylinder.
5 With the help of an assistant, crank the engine on the starter motor; after one or two revolutions, the compression pressure should build-up to a maximum figure, and then stabilise. Record the highest reading obtained.
6 Repeat the test on the remaining cylinders, recording the pressure in each.
7 All cylinders should produce very similar pressures; any difference greater than the maximum figure given in the Specifications indicates the existence of a fault. Note that the compression should build-up quickly in a healthy engine; low compression on the first stroke, followed by gradually-increasing pressure on successive strokes, indicates worn piston rings. A low compression reading on the first stroke, which does not build-up during successive strokes, indicates leaking valves or a blown head gasket (a cracked head could also be the cause). **Note:** *The cause of poor compression is less easy to establish on a diesel engine than on a petrol one. The effect of introducing oil into the cylinders ('wet' testing) is not conclusive, because there is a risk that the oil will sit in the recess on the piston crown instead of passing to the rings.*
8 On completion of the test, refit the fuel injectors as described in Chapter 4B.

Leakdown test

9 A leakdown test measures the rate at which compressed air fed into the cylinder is lost. It is an alternative to a compression test, and in many ways it is better, since the escaping air provides easy identification of where pressure loss is occurring (piston rings, valves or head gasket).
10 The equipment needed for leakdown testing is unlikely to be available to the home mechanic. If poor compression is suspected, have the test performed by a Vauxhall/Opel dealer, or suitably-equipped garage.

3 Top dead centre (TDC) for No 1 piston – locating

Note: *To accurately determine the TDC position for No 1 piston, it will be necessary to use Vauxhall/Opel special tool EN-46788 (or suitable equivalents) to set the crankshaft at the TDC position* (see illustration).

1 In its travel up and down its cylinder bore, Top Dead Centre (TDC) is the highest point that each piston reaches as the crankshaft rotates. While each piston reaches TDC both at the top of the compression stroke and again at the top of the exhaust stroke, for the purpose of timing the engine, TDC refers to the piston position of No 1 cylinder at the top of its compression stroke.
2 Number 1 piston (and cylinder) is at the

3.0 Vauxhall/Opel special tool EN-46788 (or equivalent) is required to set the TDC position for No 1 piston

3.3a Remove the engine oil filler cap . . .

3.3b . . . undo the two retaining bolts (arrowed) . . .

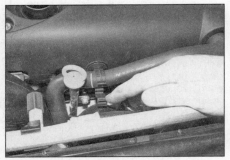

3.3c . . . release the hose support clip . . .

3.3d . . . then lift off the plastic cover over the top of the engine

3.5 Undo the central mounting bolt (arrowed), and remove the auxiliary drivebelt tensioner assembly

right-hand (timing belt) end of the engine, and its TDC position is located as follows. Note that the crankshaft rotates clockwise when viewed from the right-hand side of the car.

3 Remove the engine oil filler cap, undo the two retaining bolts, release the hose support clip, then lift off the plastic cover over the top of the engine (see illustrations). Refit the oil filler cap.

4 Remove the crankshaft pulley/vibration damper as described in Section 6.

5 Undo the central mounting bolt, and remove

the auxiliary drivebelt tensioner assembly from the engine (see illustration).

6 Remove the air cleaner assembly and air intake duct as described in Chapter 4B.

7 Place a trolley jack beneath the right-hand end of the engine with a block of wood on the jack head. Raise the jack until it is supporting the weight of the engine.

8 Mark the bolt positions for correct refitting, then undo the three bolts securing the right-hand engine mounting to the engine bracket, and the two bolts and one nut securing the

mounting to the body. Remove the mounting (see illustration).

9 Unclip the wiring harness from the top and side of the upper timing belt cover. Unscrew the six retaining bolts and lift off the upper timing belt cover (see illustration).

10 Using a socket and extension bar on the crankshaft sprocket bolt, rotate the crankshaft in the normal direction of rotation until the mark on the camshaft sprocket is aligned with the pointer on the camshaft cover (see illustration).

3.8 Undo the retaining nut and bolts and remove the right-hand engine mounting

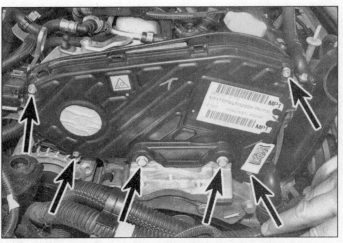

3.9 Upper timing belt cover retaining bolts (arrowed)

3.10 Rotate the crankshaft to align the mark on the camshaft sprocket (arrowed) with the pointer on the camshaft cover

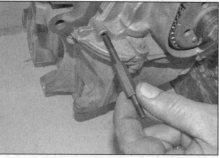

3.11 Screw the fastening stud of special tool EN-46788 into the oil pump housing

3.12 Positioning ring of tool EN-46788 (arrowed) attached to the fastening stud and crankshaft sprocket

11 Unscrew the bolt from the lower left-hand side of the oil pump housing and screw in the fastening stud of Vauxhall/Opel special tool EN-46788 **(see illustration)**.

12 Fit the positioning ring of tool EN-46788 over the fastening stud and engage it with the crankshaft sprocket. Ensure that the hole in the positioning ring engages with the lug on the sprocket. Secure the tool in position with the retaining bolt and nut **(see illustration)**.

13 With the crankshaft positioning ring in place and the mark on the camshaft sprocket aligned with the pointer on the camshaft cover, the engine is positioned with No 1 piston at TDC on compression.

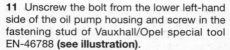

4 Valve timing –
checking and adjustment

1 Position No 1 cylinder at TDC on its compression stroke as described in Section 3.
2 With the crankshaft positioning ring in place, check that the mark on the camshaft sprocket is aligned with the pointer on the camshaft cover; if so, the valve timing is correct.
3 If the mark on the camshaft sprocket is not aligned with the pointer on the camshaft cover, readjust the timing belt position as described in Section 7.

5.2 Undo the retaining bolt(s) to release the vacuum lines from the camshaft cover

5 Camshaft cover –
removal and refitting

Removal

1 Remove the engine oil filler cap, undo the two retaining bolts, release the hose support clip, then undo the two bolts and lift off the plastic cover over the top of the engine **(see illustrations 3.3a to 3.3d)**. Refit the oil filler cap.
2 Undo the retaining bolt(s) to release the

5.3a Release the retaining clips and disconnect the breather hoses from the front . . .

vacuum lines running over the top of the camshaft cover **(see illustration)**.
3 Release the retaining clips and disconnect the breather hoses from the front and rear of the camshaft cover **(see illustrations)**.
4 Disconnect the fuel leak-off hose connection at No 2 and No 3 injector by extracting the locking clip and lifting out the hose fitting. Refit the locking clips to the injectors after disconnecting the hose fitting.
5 Undo the seven retaining bolts securing the camshaft cover to the cylinder head **(see illustration)**.

5.3b . . . and rear of the camshaft cover

5.5 Undo the seven bolts (arrowed) securing the camshaft cover to the cylinder head

5.6 Move the leak-off hose assembly rearward, then lift the camshaft cover from the cylinder head

6 Carefully move the disconnected leak-off hose assembly rearward, then lift the camshaft cover from the cylinder head **(see illustration)**.

Refitting

7 Ensure the cover and cylinder head surfaces are clean and dry then fit the seal to the cover groove **(see illustration)**.

8 Move the leak-off hose assembly to the rear and carefully lower the cover into position. Screw in the retaining bolts and lightly tighten them. Once all bolts are hand-tight, go around and tighten them all to the specified torque setting.

9 Reconnect the leak-off hose fittings to the injectors by pushing in the locking clip, attaching the fitting, then releasing the locking clip. Ensure that each fitting is securely connected and retained by the clip.

7.2 Undo the bolt (arrowed) and remove the auxiliary drivebelt idler pulley from the engine bracket

7.3b . . . and the three upper bolts (arrowed) . . .

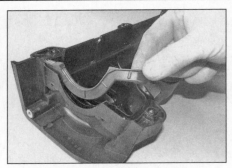

5.7 Fit the seal to the camshaft cover groove

10 Reconnect the breather hoses to the cover.

11 Refit and tighten the bolts securing the vacuum lines.

12 Refit the plastic cover to the top of the engine, tighten the two retaining bolts and resecure the hose.

6 Crankshaft pulley/ vibration damper – removal and refitting

Removal

1 Apply the handbrake, then jack up the front of the vehicle and support it on axle stands (see *Jacking and vehicle support*). Remove the right-hand front roadwheel, then undo the retaining bolts and screws and remove the engine undertray for access to the crankshaft pulley.

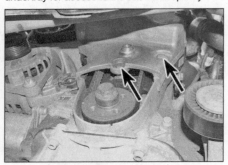

7.3a Undo the two lower bolts (arrowed) . . .

7.3c . . . and remove the engine bracket from the engine

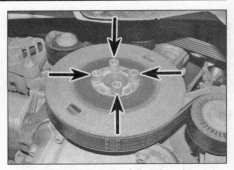

6.3 Crankshaft pulley/vibration damper retaining bolts (arrowed)

2 Remove the auxiliary drivebelt as described in Chapter 1B. Prior to removal, mark the direction of rotation on the belt to ensure the belt is refitted the same way around.

3 Undo the four bolts securing the pulley to the crankshaft sprocket and remove the pulley from the sprocket **(see illustration)**.

Refitting

4 Locate the crankshaft pulley on the sprocket, ensuring that the hole on the rear face of the pulley engages with the lug on the sprocket.

5 Refit the four retaining bolts and tighten them progressively to the specified torque.

6 Refit the auxiliary drivebelt as described in Chapter 1B using the mark made prior to removal to ensure the belt is fitted the correct way around.

7 Refit the roadwheel and engine undertray, then lower the car to the ground and tighten the wheel bolts to the specified torque.

7 Timing belt – removal and refitting

Note: *The timing belt must be removed and refitted with the engine cold.*

Removal

1 Position No 1 cylinder at TDC on its compression stroke as described in Section 3.

2 Undo the retaining bolt and remove the auxiliary drivebelt idler pulley from the engine bracket **(see illustration)**.

3 Undo the two lower bolts, and the three upper bolts, and remove the engine bracket from the engine **(see illustrations)**.

4 Undo the nut and bolt and remove the crankshaft positioning tool (EN-46788) from the crankshaft sprocket.

5 Slacken the timing belt tensioner retaining bolt and allow the tensioner to retract, relieving the tension on the timing belt.

6 Slide the timing belt from its sprockets and remove it from the engine. If the belt is to be re-used, use white paint or similar to mark the direction of rotation on the belt. **Do not** rotate the crankshaft or camshafts until the timing belt has been refitted.

7 Check the timing belt carefully for any signs of uneven wear, splitting or oil contamination, and renew it if there is the slightest doubt about its condition. If the engine is undergoing an overhaul and is approaching the specified interval for belt renewal (see Chapter 1B) renew the belt as a matter of course, regardless of its apparent condition. If signs of oil contamination are found, trace the source of the oil leak and rectify it, then wash down the engine timing belt area and all related components to remove all traces of oil.

Refitting

8 On reassembly, thoroughly clean the timing belt sprockets and tensioner/idler pulleys.
9 Place the timing belt in position over the crankshaft sprocket. If the original belt is being refitted, ensure that the arrow mark made on removal points in the normal direction of rotation, as before.
10 Check that the camshaft and crankshaft are still correctly positioned with No 1 piston at TDC on compression as described in Section 3, and refit the crankshaft positioning tool.
11 Fit the timing belt over the crankshaft, camshaft and fuel pump sprockets and around the idler pulleys, ensuring that the belt front run is taut (ie, all slack is on the tensioner side of the belt), then fit the belt over the coolant pump sprocket and tensioner pulley. Do not twist the belt sharply while refitting it. Ensure that the belt teeth are correctly seated centrally in the sprockets, and that the timing mark on the camshaft sprocket remain in alignment.
12 Screw in a suitable bolt, approximately 50 mm in length, into the threaded hole directly below the timing belt tensioner. Using a screwdriver resting on the bolt as a pivot, move the adjusting lever on the tensioner until the tensioner pointer is aligned with the mark on the backplate. Hold the tensioner in this position and tighten the tensioner retaining bolt **(see illustrations)**.
13 Remove the crankshaft positioning tool.
14 Using a socket on the crankshaft sprocket bolt, rotate the crankshaft smoothly through two complete turns (720°) in the normal direction of rotation to settle the timing belt in position. At the end of the second turn, align the mark on the camshaft sprocket with the pointer on the camshaft cover.
15 Refit the positioning ring of tool EN-46788 over the fastening stud and engage it with the crankshaft sprocket. Ensure that the hole in the positioning ring engages with the lug on the sprocket. Secure the tool in position with the retaining bolt and nut.
16 Slacken the timing belt tensioner retaining bolt and, using a screwdriver resting on the pivot bolt as before, move the adjusting lever on the tensioner until the tensioner pointer is once again aligned with the mark on the backplate. Hold the tensioner in this position and tighten the tensioner retaining bolt to the specified torque.
17 Remove all the positioning tools and

7.12a Using a screwdriver resting on a pivot bolt (arrowed), move the adjusting lever on the tensioner . . .

again rotate the crankshaft smoothly through two complete turns (720°) in the normal direction of rotation. Check that the timing belt tensioner pointer is still aligned with the mark on the backplate. If not, repeat the procedure described in paragraph 16.
18 When all is correct, remove the tensioner position pivot bolt. Refit the bolt removed from the oil pump housing and tighten it to the specified torque.
19 Place the engine bracket in position and refit the two lower bolts, and the three upper bolts. Tighten the bolts to the specified torque. Refit the auxiliary drivebelt idler pulley to the engine bracket and tighten the retaining bolt to the specified torque.
20 Refit the upper timing belt cover and tighten the retaining bolts to the specified torque. Clip the wiring harness back into position.
21 Place the right-hand engine mounting assembly in position and refit the two bolts and the nut securing the mounting to the body. Tighten the bolts/nut to the specified torque.

To make a sprocket holding tool, obtain two lengths of steel strip about 6 mm thick by about 30 mm wide or similar, one 600 mm long, the other 200 mm long (all dimensions are approximate). Bolt the two strips together to form a forked end, leaving the bolt slack so that the shorter strip can pivot freely. At the other end of each 'prong' of the fork, drill a suitable hole and fit a nut and bolt to allow the tool to engage with the spokes in the sprocket.

7.12b . . . until the tensioner pointer (arrowed) is aligned with the mark on the backplate

Align the mounting in its original position, then tighten the three mounting bracket bolts to the specified torque. Remove the jack from under the engine.
22 Refit the air cleaner assembly and air intake duct as described in Chapter 4B.
23 Place the auxiliary drivebelt tensioner assembly in position ensuring that the locating peg on the tensioner mounting surface engages correctly with the corresponding hole in the mounting bracket. Tighten the tensioner central mounting bolt to the specified torque.
24 Refit the crankshaft pulley/vibration damper as described in Section 6, then refit the auxiliary drivebelt as described in Chapter 1B.
25 Refit the plastic cover to the top of the engine and tighten the retaining bolts.
26 Refit the roadwheel and engine undertray, then lower the car to the ground and tighten the wheel bolts to the specified torque.

8 Timing belt sprockets, tensioner and idler pulley – removal and refitting

Note: *Certain special tools will be required for the removal and refitting of the sprockets. Read through the entire procedure to familiarise yourself with the work involved, then either obtain the manufacturer's special tools, or use the alternatives described.*

Camshaft sprocket

Note: *A new sprocket retaining bolt will be required for refitting.*

Removal

1 Remove the timing belt as described in Section 7.
2 It will now be necessary to hold the camshaft sprocket to enable the retaining bolt to be removed. Vauxhall/Opel special tools EN-46787 and KM-956-1 are available for this purpose, however, a home-made tool can easily be fabricated **(see Tool Tip)**.
3 Engage the tool with the holes in the camshaft sprocket, taking care not to damage the camshaft sensor located behind the sprocket
4 Unscrew the retaining bolt and remove the sprocket from the end of the camshaft.

8.12a Remove the bolt and washer . . .

8.12b . . . and slide the sprocket off the end of the crankshaft

8.18 Engage the holding tool with the holes in the fuel pump sprocket and undo the retaining nut

Refitting

5 Prior to refitting check the oil seal for signs of damage or leakage. If necessary, renew as described in Section 9.

6 Refit the sprocket to the camshaft end, aligning its cut-out with the locating peg, and fit the new retaining bolt.

7 Retain the sprocket using the holding tool, and tighten the retaining bolt to the specified torque.

8 Refit the timing belt as described in Section 7.

Crankshaft sprocket

Note 1: *The crankshaft sprocket retaining bolt is extremely tight. Ensure that the holding tool used to prevent rotation as the bolt is slackened is of sturdy construction and securely attached.*

Note 2: *A new sprocket retaining bolt will be required for refitting.*

Removal

9 Remove the timing belt as described in Section 7.

10 It will now be necessary to hold the crankshaft sprocket to enable the retaining bolt to be removed. Vauxhall special tools EN-47630 and KM-956-1 are available for this purpose, however, a home-made tool similar to that described in paragraph 2 can easily be fabricated.

11 Using the crankshaft pulley retaining bolts, securely attach the tool to the crankshaft sprocket. With the help of an assistant, hold

the sprocket stationary and unscrew the retaining bolt. **Note:** *The sprocket retaining bolt has a **left-hand thread** and is unscrewed by turning it clockwise.*

12 Remove the bolt and washer and slide the sprocket off the end of the crankshaft **(see illustrations)**. Note that a new bolt will be required for refitting.

Refitting

13 Align the sprocket location key with the crankshaft groove and slide the sprocket into position. Fit the new retaining bolt and washer.

14 Hold the sprocket stationary using the holding tool and tighten the retaining bolt to the specified torque. Remove the holding tool.

15 Refit the timing belt as described in Section 7.

High-pressure pump sprocket

Note: *A new sprocket retaining nut will be required for refitting.*

Removal

16 Remove the timing belt as described in Section 7.

17 It will now be necessary to hold the fuel pump sprocket to enable the retaining nut to be removed. Vauxhall special tools KM-6347 and KM-956-1 are available for this purpose, however, a home-made tool similar to that described in paragraph 2 can easily be fabricated.

18 Engage the tool with the holes in the

fuel pump sprocket and undo the sprocket retaining nut **(see illustration)**. Note that a new nut will be required for refitting.

19 Attach a suitable puller to the threaded holes in the fuel pump sprocket using bolts and washers similar to the arrangement shown **(see illustration)**.

20 Tighten the puller centre bolt to release the sprocket from the taper on the pump shaft. Once the taper releases, remove the puller and withdraw the sprocket. Collect the Woodruff key from the pump shaft **(see illustrations)**.

Refitting

21 Clean the fuel pump shaft and the sprocket hub ensuring that all traces of oil or grease are removed.

22 Refit the Woodruff key to the pump shaft, then locate the sprocket in position. Fit the new retaining nut.

23 Hold the sprocket stationary using the holding tool and tighten the retaining nut to the specified torque. Remove the holding tool.

24 Refit the timing belt as described in Section 7.

Tensioner assembly

Removal

25 Remove the timing belt as described in Section 7.

26 Slacken and remove the retaining bolt and remove the tensioner assembly from the engine **(see illustration)**.

8.19 Use a suitable puller to release the fuel pump sprocket taper

8.20a Once the taper releases, withdraw the sprocket . . .

8.20b . . . and collect the Woodruff key from the pump shaft

Refitting

27 Fit the tensioner to the engine, making sure that the slot on the tensioner backplate is correctly located over the peg on the engine bracket **(see illustration)**.

28 Clean the threads of the retaining bolt and apply thread locking compound to the bolt threads. Screw in the retaining bolt, set the tensioner in the retracted position and tighten the retaining bolt.

29 Refit the timing belt as described in Section 7.

Idler pulley

Removal

30 Remove the timing belt as described in Section 7.

31 Slacken and remove the retaining bolt and remove the idler pulley from the engine.

Refitting

32 Refit the idler pulley and tighten the retaining bolt to the specified torque.

33 Refit the timing belt as described in Section 7.

9 Camshaft oil seal – renewal

1 Remove the camshaft sprocket as described in Section 8.

2 Carefully punch or drill a small hole in the oil seal. Screw in a self-tapping screw, and pull on the screw with pliers to extract the seal.

3 Clean the seal housing, and polish off any burrs or raised edges which may have caused the seal to fail in the first place.

4 Press the new oil seal into position using a suitable tubular drift (such as a socket) which bears only on the hard outer edge of the seal. Take care not to damage the seal lips during fitting; note that the seal lips should face inwards.

5 Refit the camshaft sprocket as described in Section 8.

10 Valve clearances – checking and adjustment

Note: *Vauxhall/Opel special tools EN-46797 and EN-46799 (or suitable equivalents) will be required if adjustment is necessary.*

Checking

1 The importance of having the valve clearances correctly adjusted cannot be overstressed, as they vitally affect the performance of the engine. The engine must be cold for the check to be accurate. The clearances are checked as follows.

2 Apply the handbrake, then jack up the front of the vehicle and support it on axle stands (see *Jacking and vehicle support*). Remove

8.26 Slacken and remove the retaining bolt and remove the timing belt tensioner assembly

the right-hand front roadwheel, then undo the ten bolts and remove the engine undertray for access to the crankshaft pulley.

3 Remove the camshaft cover as described in Section 5.

4 Using a socket and extension on the crankshaft pulley bolt, rotate the crankshaft in the normal direction of rotation (clockwise when viewed from the right-hand end of the engine) until camshaft lobes 1 and 6 are pointing upward **(see illustration)**.

5 On a piece of paper, draw the outline of the engine with the cylinders numbered from the timing belt end. Show the position of each valve, together with the specified valve clearance. Note that the clearance for both the inlet and exhaust valves is the same.

6 With the cam lobes positioned as described in paragraph 4, using feeler blades, measure the clearance between the base of camshaft lobes 1 and 6 and the adjustment shim located on the top of the camshaft follower **(see illustration)**. Record the clearances on the paper.

7 Rotate the crankshaft until camshaft lobes 5 and 8 are pointing upward. Measure the clearance between the base of the camshaft lobes and the shims on their followers and record the clearances on the paper.

8 Rotate the crankshaft until camshaft lobes 4 and 7 are pointing upward. Measure the clearance between the base of the camshaft lobes and the shims on their followers and record the clearances on the paper.

9 Rotate the crankshaft until camshaft lobes 2 and 3 are pointing upward. Measure the clearance between the base of the camshaft

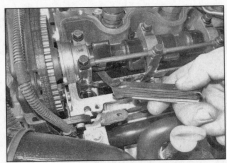

10.6 Valve clearance measurement

lobes and the shims on their followers and record the clearances on the paper.

10 If all the clearances are correct, refit the camshaft cover as described in Section 5. Refit the roadwheel and engine undertray, then lower the car to the ground and tighten the wheel bolts to the specified torque.

11 If any clearance measured is not correct, adjustment must be carried out as described in the following paragraphs.

Adjustment

12 Rotate the crankshaft clockwise until camshaft lobes 1 and 6 are once again pointing upward. With the camshaft in this position, valve No 1 and valve No 6 can be adjusted as follows.

13 Rotate the follower until the groove on its upper edge is facing towards the front of the engine **(see illustration)**.

14 Insert Vauxhall/Opel special tool EN-46797

8.27 The slot on the tensioner backplate must locate over the peg (arrowed) on the engine bracket

10.4 Camshaft positioned with No 1 and No 6 cam lobes (arrowed) pointing upward

10.13 Rotate the follower until the groove (arrowed) is facing towards the front of the engine

10.16 The thickness of each shim should be stamped on one of its surfaces

between the base of the camshaft lobe and the shim and lever downward to open the valve. Now insert Vauxhall/Opel special tool EN-46799 between the edge of the follower and the base of the camshaft to hold the valve open. Take care when doing this as it is possible for the valve to contact the piston. If any resistance is felt as the valve is opened, remove the tool and rotate the crankshaft slightly to move the piston down its bore.

15 Using a small screwdriver inserted in the groove on the edge of the follower, lift up the shim, then slide it out from between the follower and camshaft.

16 Clean the shim, and measure its thickness with a micrometer. The shims carry thickness markings, but wear may have reduced the original thickness, so be sure to double-check **(see illustration)**.

17 Add the measured clearance of the valve to the thickness of the original shim then subtract the specified valve clearance from this figure. This will give you the thickness of the shim required. For example:

Measured valve clearance	0.45 mm
Plus thickness of the original shim	2.70 mm
Equals	3.15 mm
Minus clearance required	0.40 mm
Thickness of shim required	2.75 mm

18 Obtain the correct thickness of shim required and lubricate it with clean engine oil. With the valve still held open with the special tool, slide the shim into position, with the thickness number downwards, ensuring it is correctly located.

19 Using the first special tool, lever down on the shim and remove the second special tool.

Allow the valve to close and remove the first special tool. Check that the valve clearance is within limits.

> **HAYNES HiNT** *It may be possible to correct the clearances by moving the shims around between the valves, but don't rotate the crankshaft with any shims missing. Keep a note of all the shim thicknesses to assist valve clearance adjustment when they need to be done again.*

20 Rotate the crankshaft clockwise until camshaft lobes 5 and 8 are once again pointing upward. Adjust No 5 and No 8 valve clearances as described in paragraphs 13 to 19.

21 Rotate the crankshaft clockwise until camshaft lobes 4 and 7 are once again pointing upward. Adjust No 4 and No 7 valve clearances as described in paragraphs 13 to 19.

22 Rotate the crankshaft clockwise until camshaft lobes 2 and 3 are once again pointing upward. Adjust No 2 and No 3 valve clearances as described in paragraphs 13 to 19.

23 On completion, refit the camshaft cover as described in Section 5. Refit the roadwheel and engine undertray, then lower the car to the ground and tighten the wheel bolts to the specified torque.

11 Camshaft and followers – removal, inspection and refitting

Removal

1 Remove the timing belt as described in Section 7.

2 Remove the camshaft sprocket as described in Section 8.

3 Remove the camshaft cover as described in Section 5.

4 Remove the braking system vacuum pump as described in Chapter 9.

5 Check for identification markings on the camshaft bearing caps. If no markings can be seen, make suitable identification marks on the caps, to indicate their number and which way round they are fitted.

6 Working in a spiral pattern from the outside

inwards, slacken the twelve camshaft bearing cap retaining bolts by half a turn at a time, to relieve the pressure of the valve springs on the bearing caps gradually and evenly **(see illustration)**. Once the valve spring pressure has been relieved, the bolts can be fully unscrewed and removed.

Caution: If the bearing cap bolts are carelessly slackened, the bearing caps might break. If any bearing cap breaks then the complete cylinder head assembly must be renewed; the bearing caps are matched to the head and are not available separately.

7 Carefully release the oil supply pipe from its location in the cylinder head, then lift the pipe off the bearing caps **(see illustration)**.

8 Remove the bearing caps, then lift the camshaft out of the cylinder head and slide off the oil seal.

9 Obtain eight small, clean plastic containers, and label them for identification. Alternatively, divide a larger container into compartments. Lift the followers and shims out from the top of the cylinder head and store each one in its respective fitted position. Make sure the followers and shims are not mixed up, to ensure the valve clearances remain correct on refitting.

Inspection

10 Examine the camshaft bearing surfaces and cam lobes for signs of wear ridges and scoring. Renew the camshaft if any of these conditions are apparent. Examine the condition of the bearing surfaces both on the camshaft journals and in the cylinder head. If the head bearing surfaces are worn excessively, the cylinder head will need to be renewed.

11 Check the camshaft followers and their bores in the cylinder head for signs of wear or damage. If any follower is thought to be faulty or is visibly worn it should be renewed.

Refitting

12 Commence refitting by turning the crankshaft anti-clockwise by 90°. This will position all the pistons half-way down their bores, and prevent any chance of the valves touching the piston crowns as the camshaft is being fitted.

13 Lubricate the camshaft followers with clean engine oil and carefully insert each one (together with its adjusting shim) into its original location in the cylinder head.

14 Lubricate the camshaft follower shims, and the bearing journals with clean engine oil, then lay the camshaft in position.

15 Apply a smear of sealant to the mating surfaces of both the No 1 and No 5 camshaft bearing caps. Using the marks made on removal as a guide, refit the camshaft bearing caps in their original locations on the cylinder head.

16 Carefully engage the oil supply pipe into its location in the cylinder head, then place the pipe in position on the bearing caps.

17 Refit the bearing cap retaining bolts and

11.6 Camshaft bearing cap retaining bolts (arrowed)

11.7 Carefully release the oil pipe (arrowed) from its location in the cylinder head

tighten them by hand until they just contact the bearing caps.

18 Working in a spiral pattern from the centre outwards, tighten the bolts by half a turn at a time to gradually impose the pressure of the valve springs on the bearing caps. Repeat this sequence until all bearing caps are in contact with the cylinder head then go around and tighten the camshaft bearing cap bolts to the specified torque.

Caution: If the bearing cap bolts are carelessly tightened, the bearing caps might break. If any bearing cap breaks then the complete cylinder head assembly must be renewed; the bearing caps are matched to the head and are not available separately.

19 Fit a new camshaft oil seal as described in Section 9.

20 Refit the braking system vacuum pump as described in Chapter 9.

21 Refit the camshaft cover as described in Section 5.

22 Refit the camshaft sprocket as described in Section 8. Rotate the camshaft until the mark on the camshaft sprocket is aligned with the pointer on the camshaft cover (see Section 3).

23 Turn the crankshaft clockwise by 90° to bring No 1 and 4 pistons to approximately the TDC position.

24 Refit the timing belt as described in Section 7.

25 If any new components have been fitted, check, and if necessary adjust, the valve clearances as described in Section 10.

12 Cylinder head – removal and refitting

Note: *New cylinder head bolts will be required on refitting.*

Removal

1 Disconnect the battery negative terminal (refer to *Disconnecting the battery* in the Reference Chapter).

2 Drain the cooling system as described in Chapter 1B.

3 Remove the timing belt as described in Section 7.

4 Disconnect the wiring harness connectors from the following components with reference to the Chapters indicated:
 a) *Coolant temperature sensor (Chapter 3).*
 b) *Fuel pressure sensor (Chapter 4B).*
 c) *Fuel pressure regulating valve (Chapter 4B).*
 d) *Throttle housing (Chapter 4B).*
 e) *Fuel injectors (Chapter 4B).*
 f) *Air conditioning compressor (Chapter 3).*
 g) *EGR valve (Chapter 4C).*
 h) *Charge (boost) pressure sensor (Chapter 4B).*
 i) *High-pressure fuel pump (Chapter 4B).*
 j) *Camshaft sensor (Chapter 4B).*

5 Undo the wiring harness support bracket bolts, release the retaining clips and move the harness to one side **(see illustration)**.

6 Remove the inlet and exhaust manifolds as described in Chapter 4B.

7 Remove the camshaft cover as described in Section 5.

8 Remove the braking system vacuum pump as described in Chapter 9.

9 Make a final check to ensure that all relevant hoses, pipes and wires have been disconnected.

10 Working in the **reverse** of the tightening sequence **(see illustration 12.28)**, progressively slacken the cylinder head bolts by half a turn at a time, until all bolts can be unscrewed by hand. Note that an M14 RIBE socket bit will be required to unscrew the bolts. Remove the cylinder head bolts and recover the washers.

11 Engage the help of an assistant and lift the cylinder head from the cylinder block. Take care as it is a bulky and heavy assembly.

Caution: Do not lay the head on its lower mating surface; support the head on wooden blocks, ensuring each block only contacts the head mating surface.

12 Remove the gasket and keep it for identification purposes (see paragraph 19).

13 If the cylinder head is to be dismantled for overhaul, then refer to Part E of this Chapter.

Preparation for refitting

14 The mating faces of the cylinder head and cylinder block/crankcase must be perfectly clean before refitting the head. Use a hard plastic or wood scraper to remove all traces of gasket and carbon; also clean the piston crowns. Take particular care, as the surfaces are damaged easily. Also, make sure that the carbon is not allowed to enter the oil and water passages – this is particularly important for the lubrication system, as carbon could block the oil supply to any of the engine's components. Using adhesive tape and paper, seal the water, oil and bolt holes in the cylinder block/crankcase. To prevent carbon entering the gap between the pistons and bores, smear a little grease in the gap. After cleaning each piston, use a small brush to remove all traces of grease and carbon from the gap, then wipe away the remainder with a clean rag. Clean all the pistons in the same way.

15 Check the mating surfaces of the cylinder block/crankcase and the cylinder head for nicks, deep scratches and other damage. If slight, they may be removed carefully with a file, but if excessive, machining may be the only alternative to renewal.

16 Ensure that the cylinder head bolt holes in the crankcase are clean and free of oil. Syringe or soak up any oil left in the bolt holes. This is most important in order that the correct bolt tightening torque can be applied and to prevent the possibility of the block being cracked by hydraulic pressure when the bolts are tightened.

17 The cylinder head bolts must be discarded and renewed, regardless of their apparent condition.

12.5 Undo the support bracket bolts (arrowed), release the retaining clips and move the wiring harness to one side

18 If warpage of the cylinder head gasket surface is suspected, use a straight-edge to check it for distortion. Refer to Part E of this Chapter if necessary.

19 On this engine, the cylinder head-to-piston clearance is controlled by fitting different thickness head gaskets. The gasket thickness can be determined by looking at the holes stamped on the edge of the gasket **(see illustration)**.

Number of holes	Gasket thickness
No holes	0.77 to 0.87 mm
One hole	0.87 to 0.97 mm
Two holes	0.97 to 1.07 mm

The correct thickness of gasket required is selected by measuring the piston protrusions as follows.

20 Mount a dial test indicator securely on the block so that its pointer can be easily pivoted between the piston crown and block mating surface. Turn the crankshaft to bring No 1 piston roughly to the TDC position. Move the dial test indicator probe over and in contact with No 1 piston. Turn the crankshaft back and forth slightly until the highest reading is shown on the gauge, indicating that the piston is at TDC.

21 Zero the dial test indicator on the gasket surface of the cylinder block then carefully move the indicator over No 1 piston. Measure its protrusion at the highest point between the valve cut-outs, and then again at its highest point between the valve cut-outs at 90° to the first measurement **(see illustration)**. Repeat this procedure with No 4 piston.

22 Rotate the crankshaft half a turn (180°) to bring No 2 and 3 pistons to TDC. Ensure

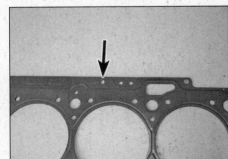

12.19 Cylinder head gasket thickness identification hole (arrowed)

12.21 Using a dial test indicator to measure piston protrusion

the crankshaft is accurately positioned then measure the protrusions of No 2 and 3 pistons at the specified points. Once all pistons have been measured, rotate the crankshaft to position all the pistons at their mid-stroke.

23 Select the correct thickness of head gasket required by determining the largest amount of piston protrusion, and using the following table.

Piston protrusion measurement (mm)	Gasket thickness required (mm)
0.020 to 0.100	0.77 to 0.87 (no holes)
0.101 to 0.200	0.87 to 0.97 (one hole)
0.201 to 0.295	0.97 to 1.07 (two holes)

Refitting

24 Wipe clean the mating surfaces of the cylinder head and cylinder block/crankcase. Place the new gasket in position with the words ALTO/TOP uppermost **(see illustration)**.

25 If not already done, rotate the crankshaft to position all the pistons at their mid-stroke.

26 With the aid of an assistant, carefully refit the cylinder head assembly to the block, aligning it with the locating dowels.

27 Apply a thin film of engine oil to the bolt threads and the underside of the bolt heads. Carefully enter each new cylinder head bolt into its relevant hole (*do not drop them in*). Screw all bolts in, by hand only, until finger-tight.

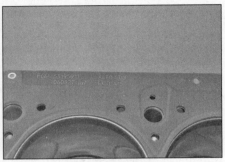

12.24 Place the new gasket in position with the words ALTO/TOP uppermost

28 Working progressively in the sequence shown, tighten the cylinder head bolts to their Stage 1 torque setting, using a torque wrench and suitable socket **(see illustration)**. Working again in the same sequence, go around and tighten all bolts through the specified Stage 2 torque setting.

29 Once all bolts have been tightened to the Stage 2 torque, working again in the same sequence, go around and tighten all bolts through the specified Stage 3 angle, then through the specified Stage 4 angle, and finally through the specified Stage 5 angle using an angle-measuring gauge.

30 Refit the braking system vacuum pump as described in Chapter 9.

31 Refit the camshaft cover as described in Section 5.

32 Refit the inlet and exhaust manifolds as described in Chapter 4B.

33 Reconnect the wiring harness connectors to the components listed in paragraph 4, then refit the wiring harness support bracket bolts, and secure the harness with the retaining clips.

34 Refit the timing belt as described in Section 7.

35 On completion, reconnect the battery negative terminal, then refill the cooling system as described in Chapter 1B.

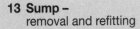

13 Sump –
removal and refitting

Removal

1 Disconnect the battery negative terminal (refer to *Disconnecting the battery* in the Reference Chapter).

2 Apply the handbrake, then jack up the front of the vehicle and support it on axle stands (see *Jacking and vehicle support*). Remove the right-hand front roadwheel, then undo the ten bolts and remove the engine undertray.

3 Remove the right-hand driveshaft and the intermediate shaft as described in Chapter 8.

4 Undo the three bolts securing the intermediate shaft bearing housing support bracket to the cylinder block and remove the support bracket **(see illustration)**.

5 Remove the exhaust system as described in Chapter 4B.

6 Undo the three bolts and remove the support bracket from the catalytic converter and sump.

7 Remove the crankshaft pulley/vibration damper as described in Section 6.

8 Disconnect the wiring connector from the air conditioning compressor. Undo the three bolts securing the air conditioning compressor to the mounting bracket and suitably support the compressor on the front subframe.

9 Undo the four bolts securing the compressor mounting bracket to the cylinder block and sump **(see illustration)**. Unclip the wiring harness and remove the mounting bracket.

10 Drain the engine oil as described in Chapter 1B. When the oil has completely drained, refit the drain plug with new sealing washer, and tighten to the specified torque.

11 Undo the upper bolt securing the oil dipstick guide tube to the coolant pipe. Undo the lower bolt securing the guide tube to the sump flange, then unclip the wiring harness

12.28 Cylinder head bolt tightening sequence

13.4 intermediate shaft bearing housing support bracket retaining bolts (arrowed)

13.9 Air conditioning compressor mounting bracket retaining bolts (arrowed)

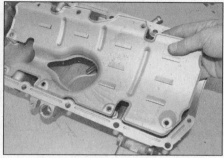

13.17 Removing the oil baffle plate from inside the sump

13.18 Renew the pick-up/strainer sealing ring prior to refitting

and withdraw the tube from the sump flange sealing grommet.

12 Disconnect the wiring connector from the oil level sensor, then release the retaining clip and disconnect the oil return hose.

13 Undo the two bolts securing the sump flange to the transmission bellhousing.

14 Using a socket and extension on the crankshaft pulley bolt, rotate the crankshaft in the normal direction of rotation (clockwise when viewed from the right-hand end of the engine) until the opening in the flywheel is positioned to allow access to one of the rear sump retaining bolts. Undo and remove the bolt, then rotate the crankshaft again until the flywheel allow access to the second rear retaining bolt. Undo and remove the bolt.

15 Progressively slacken and remove the remaining twelve bolts securing the sump to the base of the cylinder block and oil pump housing. Using a wide-bladed scraper or similar tool inserted between the sump and cylinder block, carefully break the joint to release the sump.

16 Manoeuvre the sump out from under the car. Clearance is extremely limited between the sump and subframe, and it may be necessary to release the oil pump pick-up/ strainer, by undoing its two retaining bolts, to enable the sump to be removed.

17 If required, undo the retaining bolts and remove the oil baffle plate from inside the sump **(see illustration)**.

18 While the sump is removed, take the opportunity to check the oil pump pick-up/ strainer for signs of clogging or splitting. If not already done, unbolt the oil pump pick-up/ strainer and remove it from the engine along with its sealing ring. The strainer can then be cleaned easily in solvent or renewed. Renew the pick-up/strainer sealing ring prior to refitting **(see illustration)**.

Refitting

19 Thoroughly clean the sump and remove all traces of silicone sealer and oil from the mating surfaces of the sump and cylinder block. If removed, refit the oil baffle plate and tighten its retaining bolts securely.

20 If clearance allows, refit the oil pump pick-up/strainer using a new sealing ring, and tighten its two retaining bolts securely.

If it was necessary to unbolt the pick-up/ strainer to allow the sump to be removed, place the unit in position and loosely screw in the bolt securing it to the main bearing cap. It must still be possible for the forward end of the pipe to be moved to the rear as the sump is refitted.

21 Apply a continuous bead of silicone sealing compound (available from your Vauxhall/Opel dealer) at approximately 1.0 mm from the inner edge of the sump **(see illustration)**. The bead of sealant should be between 2.0 and 2.5 mm in diameter.

22 Locate the sump over the pick-up/strainer then, where applicable, fit the forward end of the pick-up/strainer to the oil pump housing and fit the retaining bolt. Tighten both retaining bolts securely.

23 Engage the sump with the cylinder block and loosely refit all the retaining bolts.

24 Working out from the centre in a diagonal sequence, progressively tighten the bolts securing the sump to the cylinder block and oil pump housing. Tighten all the bolts to their specified torque setting.

25 Tighten the two bolts securing the sump flange to the transmission bellhousing to their specified torque settings.

26 Reconnect the wiring connector to the oil level sensor, then refit the oil return hose and secure with the retaining clip.

27 Refit the oil dipstick guide tube and secure with the two bolts tightened securely.

28 Locate the air conditioning compressor mounting bracket in position and refit the four retaining bolts. Tighten the bolts to the

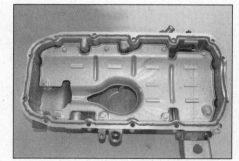

13.21 Apply a continuous bead of silicone sealing compound to the sump flange

specified torque. Clip the wiring harness back into position on the bracket.

29 Position the air conditioning compressor on the mounting bracket. Fit and tighten the three retaining bolts to the specified torque (see Chapter 3), then reconnect the compressor wiring connector.

30 Refit the crankshaft pulley/vibration damper as described in Section 6.

31 Refit the catalytic converter support bracket and securely tighten the three bolts.

32 Refit the exhaust system as described in Chapter 4B.

33 Position the intermediate shaft bearing housing support bracket on the cylinder block and secure with the three retaining bolts tightened to the specified torque.

34 Refit the intermediate shaft and right-hand driveshaft as described in Chapter 8.

35 Refit the roadwheel and engine undertray, then lower the car to the ground and tighten the wheel bolts to the specified torque.

36 Fill the engine with fresh engine oil as described in Chapter 1B.

37 On completion, reconnect the battery negative terminal.

14 Oil pump – removal, overhaul and refitting

Removal

1 Remove the timing belt as described in Section 7.

2 Remove the crankshaft sprocket as described In Section 8.

3 Remove the sump and oil pump pick-up/ strainer as described in Section 13.

4 Slacken and remove the seven retaining bolts then slide the oil pump housing assembly off of the end of the crankshaft **(see illustration)**. Remove the housing gasket and discard it.

Overhaul

5 Undo the retaining screws and lift off the pump cover from the rear of the housing **(see illustration)**.

6 Check the inner and outer rotors for identification dots indicating which way round they are fitted **(see illustration)**. If no marks

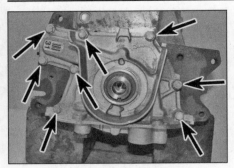

14.4 Oil pump housing retaining bolts (arrowed)

14.5 Undo the retaining screws and lift off the oil pump cover

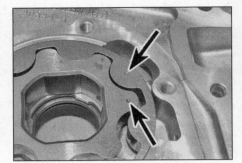

14.6 Oil pump inner and outer rotor identification dots (arrowed)

14.8a Unscrew the oil pressure relief valve bolt . . .

14.8b . . . and withdraw the spring . . .

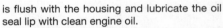

14.8c . . . and plunger

are visible, use a suitable marker pen to mark the surface of both the pump inner and outer rotors.

7 Lift out the inner and outer rotors from the pump housing.

8 Unscrew the oil pressure relief valve bolt from the base of the housing and withdraw the spring and plunger, noting which way around the plunger is fitted **(see illustrations)**. Remove the sealing washer from the valve bolt.

9 Clean the components, and carefully examine the rotors, pump body and relief valve plunger for any signs of scoring or wear. If any damage or wear is noticed, it will be necessary to renew the complete pump assembly.

10 If the pump is satisfactory, reassemble the components in the reverse order of removal, noting the following.

a) *Ensure both rotors are fitted the correct way around.*

b) *Fit a new sealing ring to the pressure relief valve bolt and securely tighten the bolt.*

c) *Apply a little locking compound to the threads, and securely tighten the pump cover screws.*

d) *On completion prime the oil pump by filling it with clean engine oil whilst rotating the inner rotor **(see illustration)**.*

Refitting

11 Prior to refitting, carefully lever out the crankshaft oil seal using a flat-bladed screwdriver. Fit the new oil seal, ensuring its sealing lip is facing inwards, and press it squarely into the housing using a tubular drift which bears only on the hard outer edge of the seal. Press the seal into position so that it

is flush with the housing and lubricate the oil seal lip with clean engine oil.

12 Ensure the mating surfaces of the oil pump and cylinder block are clean and dry.

13 Fit a new gasket to the oil pump housing and bend down the tabs on the edge of the gasket to retain it on the pump housing **(see illustration)**.

14 Locate the pump housing over the end of the crankshaft and into position on the cylinder block.

15 Refit the pump housing retaining bolts and tighten them to the specified torque.

16 Refit the oil pump pick-up/strainer and sump as described in Section 13.

17 Refit the crankshaft sprocket as described in Section 8.

18 Refit the timing belt as described in Section 7.

19 On completion, fit a new oil filter and fill the engine with clean oil as described in Chapter 1B.

15 Oil filter housing – removal and refitting

Removal

1 The oil filter housing with integral oil cooler is located at the rear of the cylinder block, above the right-hand driveshaft.

2 Disconnect the battery negative terminal (refer to *Disconnecting the battery* in the Reference Chapter).

3 Apply the handbrake, then jack up the front

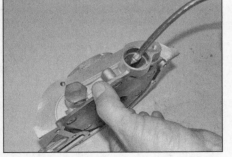

14.10 Prime the oil pump by filling it with clean engine oil whilst rotating the inner rotor

14.13 Bend down the tabs on the edge of the gasket to retain it on the oil pump housing

15.10 Oil filter housing retaining bolts (arrowed)

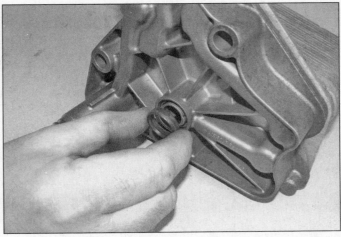

15.11a Fit a new sealing ring to the oil filter housing supply channel . . .

of the vehicle and support it on axle stands (see *Jacking and vehicle support*). Remove the right-hand front roadwheel, then undo the ten bolts and remove the engine undertray.

4 Drain the cooling system as described in Chapter 1B.

5 Remove the engine oil filter element as described in Chapter 1B.

6 Remove the right-hand driveshaft and the intermediate shaft as described in Chapter 8.

7 Undo the three bolts securing the intermediate shaft bearing housing support bracket to the cylinder block and remove the support bracket **(see illustration 13.4)**.

8 Disconnect the wiring connector from the oil pressure switch.

9 Release the retaining clips and disconnect the two coolant hoses from the oil cooler on the oil filter housing.

10 Undo the three retaining bolts and remove the oil filter housing from the cylinder block **(see illustration)**. Recover the two rubber seals from the rear of the housing. Note that new seals will be required for refitting.

Refitting

11 Thoroughly clean the oil filter housing, then fit the two new sealing rings **(see illustrations)**.

12 Position the oil filter housing on the cylinder block and refit the retaining bolts. Tighten the bolts to the specified torque.

13 Refit the two coolant hoses and secure with their retaining clips. Reconnect the oil pressure switch wiring connector.

14 Position the intermediate shaft bearing housing support bracket on the cylinder block and secure with the three retaining bolts tightened to the specified torque.

15 Refit the intermediate shaft and right-hand driveshaft as described in Chapter 8.

16 Fit a new oil filter element as described in Chapter 1B.

17 Refit the roadwheel and engine undertray, then lower the car to the ground and tighten the wheel bolts to the specified torque.

18 Refill the cooling system as described in Chapter 1B.

19 Check, and if necessary, top-up the engine oil as described in *Weekly checks*.

20 On completion, reconnect the battery negative terminal.

16 Crankshaft oil seals – renewal

Right-hand (timing belt end)

1 Remove the crankshaft sprocket as described in Section 8.

2 Carefully punch or drill a small hole in the oil seal. Screw in a self-tapping screw and pull on the screw with pliers to extract the seal **(see illustration)**.

3 Clean the seal housing and polish off any burrs or raised edges which may have caused the seal to fail in the first place.

4 Ease the new oil seal into position on the end of the crankshaft. Press the seal squarely into position until it is flush with the housing. If necessary, a suitable tubular drift which bears only on the hard outer edge of the seal can be used to tap the seal into position **(see illustration)**. Take great care not to damage

15.11b . . . and to the return channel

the seal lips during fitting and ensure that the seal lips face inwards.

5 Wash off any traces of oil, then refit the crankshaft sprocket as described in Section 8.

Left-hand (flywheel end)

6 Remove the flywheel as described in Section 17.

7 Remove the sump as described in Section 13.

8 Undo the five bolts and remove the oil seal housing. Note that the oil seal and the housing are a single assembly.

9 Clean the crankshaft and polish off any

16.2 Screw in a self-tapping screw and pull on the screw with pliers to extract the oil seal

16.4 Using a socket as a tubular drift to fit the new oil seal

16.10 Fitting the new oil seal housing, with integral oil seal, over the crankshaft

burrs or raised edges which may have caused the seal to fail in the first place.

10   Position the new oil seal housing, complete with seal, over the crankshaft and into position on the cylinder block **(see illustration)**. Note that the new oil seal housing is supplied with a protector sleeve over the oil seal. Leave the sleeve in position as the housing is fitted.

11   Refit the five retaining bolts and tighten to the specified torque.

12   Remove the protector sleeve from the housing **(see illustration)**.

13   Refit the sump as described in Section 13.

14   Refit the flywheel as described in Section 17.

17.2 Prevent the flywheel from turning by locking the ring gear teeth

16.12 After fitting, remove the protector sleeve from the housing

17 Flywheel – removal, inspection and refitting

Note: *New flywheel retaining bolts will be required on refitting.*

Removal

1   Remove the transmission as described in Chapter 7A, then remove the clutch assembly as described in Chapter 6.

2   Prevent the flywheel from turning by locking the ring gear teeth with a similar arrangement to that shown **(see illustration)**.

3   Slacken and remove the retaining bolts and remove the flywheel **(see illustration)**. Do not drop it, as it is very heavy.

Inspection

4   If there is any doubt about the condition of the flywheel, seek the advice of a Vauxhall/Opel dealer or engine reconditioning specialist. They will be able to advise if it is possible to recondition it or whether renewal is necessary.

Refitting

5   Clean the mating surfaces of the flywheel and crankshaft.

6   Offer up the flywheel and engage it over the

positioning dowel on the crankshaft. Apply a drop of locking compound to the threads of each new flywheel retaining bolt (unless they are already precoated) and install the new bolts.

7   Lock the flywheel by the method used on removal then, working in a diagonal sequence, evenly and progressively tighten the retaining bolts to the specified torque.

8   Refit the clutch as described in Chapter 6 then remove the locking tool, and refit the transmission as described in Chapter 7A.

18 Engine/transmission mountings – inspection and renewal

Inspection

1   If improved access is required, firmly apply the handbrake, then jack up the front of the car and support it securely on axle stands (see *Jacking and vehicle support*).

2   Check the mounting rubber to see if it is cracked, hardened or separated from the metal at any point; renew the mounting if any such damage or deterioration is evident.

3   Check that all the mounting's fasteners are securely tightened; use a torque wrench to check if possible.

4   Using a large screwdriver or a pry bar, check for wear in the mounting by carefully levering against it to check for free play; where this is not possible, enlist the aid of an assistant to move the engine/transmission unit back-and-forth, or from side-to-side, while you watch the mounting. While some free play is to be expected even from new components, excessive wear should be obvious. If excessive free play is found, check first that the fasteners are correctly secured, then renew any worn components as described below.

Renewal

Note: *Before slackening any of the engine mounting bolts/nuts, the relative positions of*

17.3 Flywheel retaining bolts (arrowed)

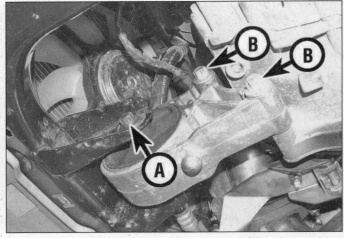

18.6 Front mounting/torque link through-bolt (A) and mounting bracket-to-transmission bolts (B)

18.14 Rear mounting/torque link through-bolt (arrowed)

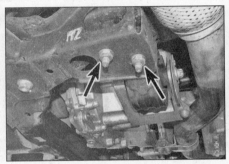

18.15 Rear mounting/torque link bracket-to-subframe mounting bolt nuts (arrowed)

18.22a Right-hand mounting bracket-to-engine bracket bolts (arrowed) . . .

18.22b . . . and mounting-to-body retaining bolts (A) and nut (B)

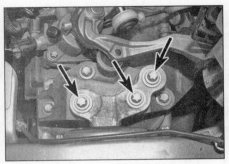

18.28 Left-hand mounting bracket-to-transmission bracket retaining bolts (arrowed)

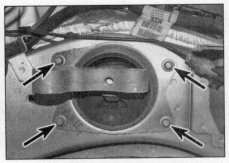

18.29 Left-hand mounting-to-body retaining bolts (arrowed) – shown with engine/transmission removed

the mountings to their various brackets should be marked to ensure correct alignment upon refitting.

Front mounting/torque link

5 Apply the handbrake, then jack up the front of the vehicle and support it on axle stands (see *Jacking and vehicle support*).

6 Slacken and remove the nut securing the mounting to the subframe bracket. Withdraw the through-bolt **(see illustration)**.

7 Undo the bolts securing the mounting bracket to the transmission, then manoeuvre the mounting and bracket out of position.

8 Check all components for signs of wear or damage, and renew as necessary.

9 Locate the mounting in the subframe, refit the through-bolt and nut, then tighten the nut finger-tight at this stage.

10 Refit the mounting bracket to the transmission and tighten its bolts to the specified torque.

11 Tighten the through-bolt nut to the specified torque.

12 On completion, lower the vehicle to the ground.

Rear mounting/torque link

13 Apply the handbrake, then jack up the front of the vehicle and support it on axle stands (see *Jacking and vehicle support*).

14 Undo the three bolts securing the mounting bracket to the transmission and the through-bolt securing the mounting to the bracket **(see illustration)**.

15 Undo the nuts and remove the two bolts securing the mounting to the subframe **(see illustration)**. Manoeuvre the mounting and bracket out from under the car.

16 Refit the bracket to the transmission and tighten the bolts to the specified torque.

17 Locate the new mounting in position. Insert the bolts and tighten the bolt/nuts to the specified torque.

18 On completion, lower the vehicle to the ground.

Right-hand mounting

19 Apply the handbrake, then jack up the front of the vehicle and support it on axle stands (see *Jacking and vehicle support*).

20 Remove the air cleaner as described in Chapter 4B.

21 Place a trolley jack beneath the right-hand end of the engine with a block of wood on the jack head. Raise the jack until it is supporting the weight of the engine.

22 Mark the position of the three bolts securing the mounting bracket to the engine bracket and undo the bolts. Undo the two bolts and one nut securing the mounting to the body and remove the mounting assembly **(see illustrations)**.

23 Place the mounting assembly in position

and refit the two bolts and the nut securing the mounting to the body. Tighten the bolts/nut to the specified torque. Align the mounting in its original position, then tighten the three mounting bracket bolts to the specified torque.

24 Remove the support jack, then refit the air cleaner as described in Chapter 4B.

25 On completion, lower the vehicle to the ground.

Left-hand mounting

26 Remove the battery and battery box as described in Chapter 5A.

27 Place a trolley jack beneath the transmission with a block of wood on the jack head. Raise the jack until it is supporting the weight of the engine/transmission unit.

28 Using a Torx socket, unscrew the three bolts securing the mounting bracket to the transmission bracket **(see illustration)**.

29 Undo the four bolts securing the mounting to the body and the three bolts securing the transmission bracket to the transmission **(see illustration)**. Remove the mounting assembly from the car.

30 Locate the mounting brackets in position then insert the bolts and tighten them to the specified torque.

31 Remove the support jack from under the transmission.

32 Refit the battery box and battery as described in Chapter 5A.

Notes

Chapter 2 Part D:
1.9 litre DOHC diesel engine in-car repair procedures

Degrees of difficulty

| Easy, suitable for novice with little experience | Fairly easy, suitable for beginner with some experience | Fairly difficult, suitable for competent DIY mechanic | Difficult, suitable for experienced DIY mechanic | Very difficult, suitable for expert DIY or professional |

Specifications

General
Engine type................................... Four-cylinder, in-line, water-cooled. Double overhead camshaft, belt-driven
Manufacturer's engine code*.................. Z19DTH
Bore .... 82.0 mm
Stroke....................................... 90.4 mm
Capacity..................................... 1910 cc
Compression ratio 17.5:1
Firing order .... 1-3-4-2 (No 1 cylinder at timing belt end of engine)
Direction of crankshaft rotation .... Clockwise (viewed from timing belt end of engine)
* For details of engine code location, see 'Vehicle identification' in the Reference Chapter.

Compression pressures
Maximum difference between any two cylinders................. 1.5 bar

Lubrication system
Minimum oil pressure at 100°C .... 1.0 bar at idle speed
Oil pump type.. Rotor-type, driven by crankshaft pulley/vibration damper from crankshaft

Torque wrench settings

	Nm	lbf ft
Air conditioning compressor mounting bracket to cylinder block/sump .	50	37
Auxiliary drivebelt idler pulley bolt	50	37
Auxiliary drivebelt tensioner assembly bolts	50	37
Camshaft drivegear bolts	120	89
Camshaft housing closure bolts	16	12
Camshaft sprocket bolt*	120	89
Connecting rod big-end bearing cap bolt:*		
Stage 1	25	18
Stage 2	Angle-tighten a further 60°	
Crankshaft oil seal housing	9	7
Crankshaft pulley/vibration damper bolts	25	18
Crankshaft sprocket bolt*†	340	251
Cylinder head bolts:*		
Stage 1	20	15
Stage 2	65	48
Stage 3	Angle-tighten a further 90°	
Stage 4	Angle-tighten a further 90°	
Stage 5	Angle-tighten a further 90°	
Engine mountings:		
Front mounting/torque link:		
Mounting to transmission	80	59
Mounting to subframe	80	59
Left-hand mounting:		
Mounting-to-body bolts	20	15
Mounting bracket to transmission bracket	55	41
Transmission bracket to transmission	55	41
Rear mounting/torque link:		
Mounting bracket to transmission	80	59
Mounting to subframe	60	44
Mounting to transmission bracket	80	59
Right-hand mounting:		
Engine bracket-to-engine bolts:		
Lower bolts (M8)	25	18
Upper bolts (M10)	50	37
Mounting-to-body bolts/nut	55	41
Mounting-to-engine bracket bolts	55	41
Engine-to-transmission unit bolts:		
M10 bolts	40	30
M12 bolts	60	44
Flywheel/driveplate bolts*	160	118
High-pressure fuel pump sprocket nut*	50	37
Intermediate shaft bearing housing support bracket bolts	55	41
Main bearing cap bolts:*		
Stage 1	25	18
Stage 2	Angle-tighten a further 100°	
Oil filter housing to cylinder block	50	37
Oil pump housing to cylinder block	9	7
Oil pump pick-up/strainer bolts	9	7
Roadwheel bolts	110	81
Sump bolts:		
M6 bolts	9	7
M8 bolts	25	18
M10 bolts	40	30
Sump drain plug	20	15
Timing belt idler pulley bolt	50	37
Timing belt tensioner bolt	30	22
Timing belt upper cover bolts:		
M6 bolts	9	7
M8 bolts	25	18

* *Use new nuts/bolts*

† *Left-hand thread*

1 General information

How to use this Chapter

This Part of Chapter 2 describes the repair procedures which can reasonably be carried out on the engine while it remains in the vehicle. If the engine has been removed from the vehicle and is being dismantled as described in Chapter 2E, any preliminary dismantling procedures can be ignored.

Note that, while it may be possible physically to overhaul items such as the piston/connecting rod assemblies while the engine is in the vehicle, such tasks are not usually carried out as separate operations, and usually require the execution of several additional procedures (not to mention the cleaning of components and of oilways); for this reason, all such tasks are classed as major overhaul procedures, and are described in Chapter 2E.

Chapter 2E describes the removal of the engine/transmission unit from the vehicle, and the full overhaul procedures which can then be carried out.

Engine description

The 1.9 litre DOHC diesel engine is of the sixteen-valve, in-line four-cylinder, double overhead camshaft type, mounted transversely at the front of the car, with the transmission on its left-hand end.

The crankshaft is supported within the cylinder block on five shell-type main bearings. Thrustwashers are fitted to number 3 main bearing, to control crankshaft endfloat.

The connecting rods rotate on horizontally-split bearing shells at their big-ends. The pistons are attached to the connecting rods by gudgeon pins, which are retained by circlips. The aluminium-alloy pistons are fitted with three piston rings – two compression rings and scraper-type oil control ring.

The camshafts are situated in a separate housing bolted to the top of the cylinder head. The exhaust camshaft is driven by the crankshaft via a toothed composite rubber timing belt (which also drives the high-pressure fuel pump and the coolant pump). The exhaust camshaft drives the inlet camshaft via a spur gear. Each cylinder has four valves (two inlet and two exhaust), operated via followers which are supported at their pivot ends by hydraulic self-adjusting tappets. One camshaft operates the inlet valves, and the other operates the exhaust valves.

The inlet and exhaust valves are each closed by a single valve spring, and operate in guides pressed into the cylinder head.

Lubrication is by pressure-feed from a rotor-type oil pump, which is mounted on the right-hand end of the crankshaft. The pump draws oil through a strainer located in the sump, and then forces it through an externally mounted full-flow cartridge-type filter. The oil flows into galleries in the cylinder block/crankcase, from where it is distributed to the crankshaft (main bearings) and camshafts. The big-end bearings are supplied with oil via internal drillings in the crankshaft, while the camshaft bearings also receive a pressurised supply. The camshaft lobes and valves are lubricated by splash, as are all other engine components.

A semi-closed crankcase ventilation system is employed; crankcase fumes are drawn from the oil separator attached to the cylinder block via a hose to the camshaft housing. The fumes are then passed via a hose to the inlet manifold.

Operations with engine in car

The following operations can be carried out without having to remove the engine from the car.

a) Removal and refitting of the cylinder head.
b) Removal and refitting of the timing belt, tensioner, idler pulleys and sprockets.
c) Renewal of the camshaft oil seal.
d) Removal and refitting of the camshaft housing.
e) Removal and refitting of the camshafts and followers.
f) Removal and refitting of the sump.
g) Removal and refitting of the connecting rods and pistons.*
h) Removal and refitting of the oil pump.
i) Removal and refitting of the oil filter housing.
j) Renewal of the crankshaft oil seals.
k) Renewal of the engine mountings.
l) Removal and refitting of the flywheel/driveplate.

* Although the operation marked with an asterisk can be carried out with the engine in the car (after removal of the sump), it is preferable for the engine to be removed, in the interests of cleanliness and improved access. For this reason, the procedure is described in Chapter 2E.

2 Compression and leakdown tests – description and interpretation

Compression test

Note 1: *A compression tester specifically designed for diesel engines must be used for this test.*
Note 2: *The battery must be in a good state of charge, the air filter must be clean, and the engine should be at normal operating temperature.*

1 When engine performance is down, or if misfiring occurs which cannot be attributed to the fuel system, a compression test can provide diagnostic clues as to the engine's condition. If the test is performed regularly, it can give warning of trouble before any other symptoms become apparent.
2 The tester is connected to an adapter which screws into the glow plug holes. It is unlikely to be worthwhile buying such a tester for occasional use, but it may be possible to borrow or hire one – if not, have the test performed by a Vauxhall/Opel dealer, or suitably-equipped garage. If the necessary equipment is available, proceed as follows.
3 Remove the glow plugs as described in Chapter 5A, then disconnect the wiring connector from the fuel pressure regulating valve on the fuel rail (see Chapter 4B) to prevent the engine from running or fuel from being discharged.
4 Screw the compression tester adapter in to the glow plug hole of No 1 cylinder.
5 With the help of an assistant, crank the engine on the starter motor; after one or two revolutions, the compression pressure should build-up to a maximum figure, and then stabilise. Record the highest reading obtained.
6 Repeat the test on the remaining cylinders, recording the pressure in each.
7 All cylinders should produce very similar pressures; any difference greater than the maximum figure given in the Specifications indicates the existence of a fault. Note that the compression should build-up quickly in a healthy engine; low compression on the first stroke, followed by gradually-increasing pressure on successive strokes, indicates worn piston rings. A low compression reading on the first stroke, which does not build-up during successive strokes, indicates leaking valves or a blown head gasket (a cracked head could also be the cause). **Note:** *The cause of poor compression is less easy to establish on a diesel engine than on a petrol one. The effect of introducing oil into the cylinders ('wet' testing) is not conclusive, because there is a risk that the oil will sit in the recess on the piston crown instead of passing to the rings.*
8 On completion of the test refit the glow plugs as described in Chapter 5A, and reconnect the wiring connector to the fuel pressure regulating valve.

Leakdown test

9 A leakdown test measures the rate at which compressed air fed into the cylinder is lost. It is an alternative to a compression test, and in many ways it is better, since the escaping air provides easy identification of where pressure loss is occurring (piston rings, valves or head gasket).
10 The equipment needed for leakdown testing is unlikely to be available to the home mechanic. If poor compression is suspected, have the test performed by a Vauxhall/Opel dealer, or suitably-equipped garage.

3.0a Vauxhall/Opel special tool EN-46788 (or equivalent) is required to set the TDC position for No 1 piston . . .

3 Top dead centre (TDC) for No 1 piston – locating

Note: *To accurately determine the TDC position for No 1 piston, it will be necessary to use Vauxhall/Opel special tool EN-46788 (or suitable equivalent) to set the crankshaft at the TDC position, together with the camshaft positioning tool, Vauxhall/Opel special tool EN-46789 (or suitable equivalent)* **(see illustrations)**.

1 In its travel up and down its cylinder bore, Top Dead Centre (TDC) is the highest point that each piston reaches as the crankshaft rotates. While each piston reaches TDC both at the top of the compression stroke and again at the top of the exhaust stroke, for the purpose of timing the engine, TDC refers to

3.8 Undo the retaining nut and bolts (arrowed) and remove the right-hand engine mounting

3.10 Undo the bolt (arrowed) and release the engine oil dipstick guide tube from the coolant pipe

3.0b . . . together with Vauxhall/Opel special tool EN-46789 (or equivalent) to set the camshaft position

the piston position of No 1 cylinder at the top of its compression stroke.

2 Number 1 piston (and cylinder) is at the right-hand (timing belt) end of the engine, and its TDC position is located as follows. Note that the crankshaft rotates clockwise when viewed from the right-hand side of the car.

3 Disconnect the battery negative terminal (refer to *Disconnecting the battery* in the Reference Chapter), then lift off the plastic cover over the top of the engine.

4 Remove the crankshaft pulley/vibration damper as described in Section 5.

5 Undo the central mounting bolt, and remove the auxiliary drivebelt tensioner assembly from the engine **(see illustration)**.

6 Remove the air cleaner assembly and air intake duct as described in Chapter 4B.

7 Place a trolley jack beneath the right-hand end of the engine with a block of wood on the

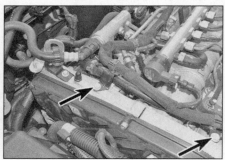

3.9 Engine breather pipe retaining bolts (arrowed)

3.11 Unscrew the closure bolt from the valve timing checking hole in the camshaft housing

3.5 Undo the central mounting bolt (arrowed), and remove the auxiliary drivebelt tensioner assembly

jack head. Raise the jack until it is supporting the weight of the engine.

8 Mark the bolt positions for correct refitting, then undo the three bolts securing the right-hand engine mounting to the engine bracket, and the two bolts and one nut securing the mounting to the body. Remove the mounting **(see illustration)**.

9 Release the retaining clip securing the engine breather hose to the breather pipe adjacent to the engine oil dipstick. Undo the two bolts securing the breather pipe to the cylinder head, and disconnect the pipe from the hose **(see illustration)**.

10 Undo the bolt and release the engine oil dipstick guide tube from the coolant pipe **(see illustration)**.

11 Unscrew the closure bolt from the valve timing checking hole in the camshaft housing **(see illustration)**.

12 Screw the camshaft positioning tool (Vauxhall/Opel special tool EN-46789) into the valve timing checking hole.

13 Using a socket and extension bar on the crankshaft sprocket bolt, rotate the crankshaft in the normal direction of rotation until the spring-loaded plunger of the positioning tool slides into engagement with the slot in the camshaft. There will be an audible click from the tool when this happens.

14 Unscrew the bolt from the lower left-hand side of the oil pump housing and screw in the fastening stud of Vauxhall/Opel special tool EN-46788 **(see illustration)**.

15 Fit the positioning ring of tool EN-46788 over the fastening stud and engage it with the

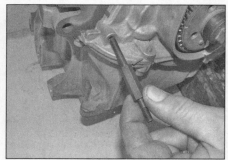

3.14 Screw the fastening stud of special tool EN-46788 into the oil pump housing

crankshaft sprocket. Ensure that the hole in the positioning ring engages with the lug on the sprocket. Secure the tool in position with the retaining bolt and nut **(see illustration)**.

16 With the crankshaft positioning ring in place and the camshaft positioning tool engaged with the slot in the camshaft, the engine is positioned with No 1 piston at TDC on compression.

4 Valve timing – checking and adjustment

Note: *To check and adjust the valve timing, it will be necessary to use Vauxhall/Opel special tool EN-46788 (or suitable equivalent) to set the crankshaft at the TDC position. Additionally, it will be necessary to use Vauxhall/Opel special tools EN-46789 and EN46789-100 (or suitable equivalents) to lock the camshafts in the TDC position.*

Checking

1 Disconnect the battery negative terminal (refer to *Disconnecting the battery* in the Reference Chapter), then lift off the plastic cover over the top of the engine.

2 Release the retaining clip securing the engine breather hose to the breather pipe adjacent to the engine oil dipstick. Undo the two bolts securing the breather pipe to the cylinder head, and disconnect the pipe from the hose **(see illustration 3.9)**.

3 Undo the bolt and release the engine oil dipstick guide tube from the coolant pipe **(see illustration 3.10)**.

4 Unscrew the closure bolt from the valve timing checking hole in the exhaust side of camshaft housing **(see illustration 3.11)**.

5 Screw the exhaust camshaft positioning tool (Vauxhall/Opel special tool EN-46789) into the valve timing checking hole.

6 Unscrew the closure bolt from the valve timing checking hole in the inlet side of the camshaft housing. The closure bolt is located below the fuel pressure regulating valve on the fuel rail.

7 Screw the inlet camshaft positioning tool (Vauxhall/Opel special tool EN-46789-100) into the valve timing checking hole.

8 Using a socket and extension bar on the crankshaft sprocket bolt, rotate the crankshaft in the normal direction of rotation until the spring-loaded plungers of the positioning tools slide into engagement with the slots in the camshafts. There will be an audible click from the tools when this happens.

9 Remove the crankshaft pulley/vibration damper as described in Section 5.

10 Unscrew the bolt from the lower left-hand side of the oil pump housing and screw in the fastening stud of Vauxhall/Opel special tool EN-46788 **(see illustration 3.14)**.

11 Fit the positioning ring of tool EN-46788 over the fastening stud and engage it with the crankshaft sprocket. Ensure that the hole in the positioning ring engages with the lug on the

3.15 Positioning ring of tool EN-46788 (arrowed) attached to the fastening stud and crankshaft sprocket

sprocket. Secure the tool in position with the retaining bolt and nut **(see illustration 3.15)**.

12 If it is not possible to fit the positioning ring of tool EN-46788 as described, or if the camshaft positioning tools did not engage with the camshaft slots, adjust the valve timing as follows.

Adjustment

13 Remove the timing belt as described in Section 6.

14 Using a socket and extension bar on the crankshaft sprocket bolt, rotate the crankshaft anti-clockwise by 90°. This will position all the pistons half-way down their bores, and prevent any chance of the valves touching the piston crowns during the following procedure.

15 Remove the inlet and exhaust camshaft positioning tools from the valve timing checking holes.

16 Using a suitable tool engaged with the timing belt sprocket on the exhaust camshaft, rotate the sprocket approximately 90° clockwise. Vauxhall/Opel special tools EN-46787 and KM-956-1 are available for this purpose, however, a home-made tool can easily be fabricated **(see Tool Tip in Section 7)**. Take care not to damage the camshaft sensor with the tool as the sprocket is rotated.

17 Screw the inlet camshaft positioning tool (Vauxhall/Opel special tool EN-46789-100) into the valve timing checking hole.

18 Rotate the camshaft sprocket clockwise until the spring-loaded plunger of the positioning tool slides into engagement with the slot in the inlet camshaft. There will be an audible click from the tool when this happens.

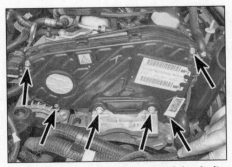

6.2 Upper timing belt cover retaining bolts (arrowed)

19 Release the two retaining clips and disconnect the charge air hose from the throttle body/housing, and intercooler charge air pipe.

20 Release the clip and disconnect the crankcase ventilation hose from the engine oil filler housing.

21 Disconnect the wiring connector from the coolant temperature sensor, then undo the three retaining bolts and remove the oil filler housing.

22 Remove the braking system vacuum pump as described in Chapter 9.

23 Working through the oil filler housing aperture, and using the holding tool to prevent rotation of the camshaft, slacken the inlet camshaft drivegear retaining bolt. Working through the vacuum pump aperture, slacken the exhaust camshaft drivegear retaining bolt in the same way.

24 Screw the exhaust camshaft positioning tool (Vauxhall/Opel special tool EN-46789) into the valve timing checking hole.

25 Rotate the camshaft sprocket clockwise until the spring-loaded plunger of the positioning tool slides into engagement with the slot in the exhaust camshaft. There will be an audible click from the tool when this happens.

26 Hold the camshaft sprocket with the tool and tighten both drivegear retaining bolts to the specified torque.

27 Remove the positioning tool from the inlet camshaft and refit the closure bolt. Tighten the bolt to the specified torque.

28 Refit the oil filler housing to the camshaft housing using a new gasket, refit the retaining bolts and tighten the bolts securely. Reconnect the coolant temperature sensor wiring connector, and reconnect the crankcase ventilation hose.

29 Refit the braking system vacuum pump as described in Chapter 9.

30 Refit the charge air hose to the throttle body/housing, and intercooler charge air pipe and secure with the retaining clips.

31 Refit the timing belt as described in Section 6.

5 Crankshaft pulley/ vibration damper – removal and refitting

Refer to Chapter 2C, Section 6, where necessary using this Chapter's specifications.

6 Timing belt – removal and refitting

Note: *The timing belt must be removed and refitted with the engine cold.*

Removal

1 Position No 1 cylinder at TDC on its compression stroke as described in Section 3.

2 Unclip the wiring harness from the side of the upper timing belt cover. Unscrew the seven retaining bolts and lift off the upper timing belt cover **(see illustration)**.

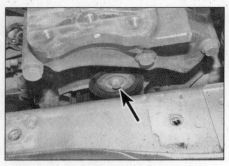

6.3 Undo the bolt (arrowed) and remove the auxiliary drivebelt idler pulley from the engine bracket

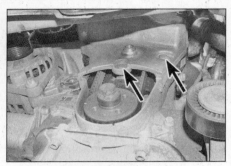

6.4a Undo the two lower bolts (arrowed) . . .

6.4b . . . and the three upper bolts (arrowed) . . .

6.4c . . . and remove the engine bracket from the engine

3 Undo the retaining bolt and remove the auxiliary drivebelt idler pulley from the engine bracket **(see illustration)**.

4 Undo the two lower bolts, and the three upper bolts, and remove the engine bracket from the engine **(see illustrations)**.

5 Undo the nut and bolt and remove the crankshaft positioning tool (EN-46788) from the crankshaft sprocket.

6 Slacken the timing belt tensioner retaining bolt and allow the tensioner to retract, relieving the tension on the timing belt.

7 Slide the timing belt from its sprockets and remove it from the engine. If the belt is to be re-used, use white paint or similar to mark the direction of rotation on the belt. **Do not** rotate the crankshaft or camshafts until the timing belt has been refitted.

8 Check the timing belt carefully for any signs of uneven wear, splitting or oil contamination, and renew it if there is the slightest doubt about its condition. If the engine is undergoing an overhaul and is approaching the specified interval for belt renewal (see Chapter 1B) renew the belt as a matter of course, regardless of its apparent condition. If signs of oil contamination are found, trace the source of the oil leak and rectify it, then wash down the engine timing belt area and all related components to remove all traces of oil.

Refitting

9 On reassembly, thoroughly clean the timing belt sprockets and tensioner/idler pulleys.

10 Place the timing belt in position over the crankshaft sprocket. If the original belt is being refitted, ensure that the arrow mark made on removal points in the normal direction of rotation, as before.

11 Check that the camshaft and crankshaft are still positioned with No 1 piston at TDC on compression as described in Section 3, and with the camshaft positioning tool still in place. Now refit the crankshaft positioning tool.

12 Fit the timing belt over the crankshaft, camshaft and fuel pump sprockets and around the idler pulleys, ensuring that the belt front run is taut (ie, all slack is on the tensioner side of the belt), then fit the belt over the coolant pump sprocket and tensioner pulley. Do not twist the belt sharply while refitting it. Ensure that the belt teeth are correctly seated centrally in the sprockets.

13 Screw in a suitable bolt, approximately 50 mm in length, into the threaded hole directly below the timing belt tensioner. Using a screwdriver resting on the bolt as a pivot, move the adjusting lever on the tensioner until the tensioner pointer is aligned with the mark on the backplate. Hold the tensioner in this position and tighten the tensioner retaining bolt **(see illustrations)**.

14 Remove the crankshaft and camshaft positioning tools.

15 Using a socket on the crankshaft sprocket bolt, rotate the crankshaft smoothly through two complete turns (720°) in the normal direction of rotation to settle the timing belt in position. Stop rotating the crankshaft just before completing the second turn.

16 Refit the camshaft positioning tool and continue turning the crankshaft until the camshaft positioning tool engages.

17 Refit the positioning ring of tool EN-46788 over the fastening stud and engage it with the crankshaft sprocket. Ensure that the hole in the positioning ring engages with the lug on the sprocket. Secure the tool in position with the retaining bolt and nut.

18 Slacken the timing belt tensioner retaining bolt and, using a screwdriver resting on the pivot bolt as before, move the adjusting lever on the tensioner until the tensioner pointer is once again aligned with the mark on the backplate. Hold the tensioner in this position and tighten the tensioner retaining bolt to the specified torque.

19 Remove all the positioning tools and again rotate the crankshaft smoothly through two complete turns (720°) in the normal direction of rotation. Check that the timing belt tensioner pointer is still aligned with the mark on the backplate. If not, repeat the procedure described in paragraph 18.

20 When all is correct, remove the tensioner position pivot bolt. Refit the bolt removed from the oil pump housing and tighten it to the specified torque. Refit the closure plug to the camshaft housing and tighten to the specified torque.

21 Place the engine bracket in position and refit the two lower bolts, and the three upper bolts. Tighten the bolts to the specified torque. Refit the auxiliary drivebelt idler pulley to the

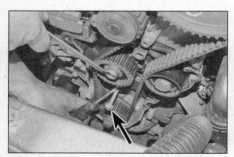

6.13a Using a screwdriver resting on a pivot bolt (arrowed), move the adjusting lever on the tensioner . . .

6.13b . . . until the tensioner pointer (arrowed) is aligned with the mark on the backplate

engine bracket and tighten the retaining bolt to the specified torque.

22 Refit the upper timing belt cover and tighten the retaining bolts to the specified torque. Clip the wiring harness back into position.

23 Place the right-hand engine mounting assembly in position and refit the two bolts and the nut securing the mounting to the body. Tighten the bolts/nut to the specified torque. Align the mounting in its original position, then tighten the three mounting bracket bolts to the specified torque. Remove the jack from under the engine.

24 Refit the air cleaner assembly and air intake duct as described in Chapter 4B.

25 Place the auxiliary drivebelt tensioner assembly in position ensuring that the locating peg on the tensioner mounting surface engages correctly with the corresponding hole in the mounting bracket. Tighten the tensioner central mounting bolt to the specified torque.

26 Refit the crankshaft pulley/vibration damper as described in Section 5, then refit the auxiliary drivebelt as described in Chapter 1B.

27 Move the engine oil dipstick guide tube back into position. Refit the bolt securing the guide tube to the coolant pipe and tighten the bolt securely.

28 Attach the engine breather hose to the breather pipe and secure with the retaining clip. Secure the breather pipe to the cylinder head with the two bolts securely tightened.

29 Refit the plastic cover to the top of the engine.

30 Refit the roadwheel and engine undertray, then lower the car to the ground and tighten the wheel bolts to the specified torque.

---

7 Timing belt sprockets, tensioner and idler pulley – removal and refitting

Note: *Certain special tools will be required for the removal and refitting of the sprockets. Read through the entire procedure to familiarise yourself with the work involved, then either obtain the manufacturer's special tools, or use the alternatives described.*

Camshaft sprocket

Note: *A new sprocket retaining bolt will be required for refitting.*

Removal

1 Remove the timing belt as described in Section 6, then remove camshaft positioning tool from the valve timing checking hole.

2 It will now be necessary to hold the camshaft sprocket to enable the retaining bolt to be removed. Vauxhall/Opel special tools EN-46787 and KM-956-1 are available for this purpose, however, a home-made tool can easily be fabricated (**see Tool Tip**).

3 Engage the tool with the holes in the camshaft sprocket, taking care not to damage

the camshaft sensor located behind the sprocket

4 Unscrew the retaining bolt and remove the sprocket from the end of the camshaft.

Refitting

5 Prior to refitting check the oil seal for signs of damage or leakage. If necessary, renew as described in Section 8.

6 Refit the sprocket to the camshaft end, aligning its cut-out with the locating peg, and fit the new retaining bolt finger-tight only at this stage. Final tightening is carried out after the timing belt has been fitted and tensioned.

7 Refit the camshaft positioning tool to the valve timing checking hole. If necessary, rotate the camshaft slightly, by means of the sprocket, until the tool audibly engages.

8 Proceed with the timing belt refitting procedure as described in Section 6, paragraphs 9 to 14.

9 Retain the camshaft sprocket using the holding tool, and tighten the retaining bolt to the specified torque.

10 Continue with the timing belt refitting procedure as described in Section 6, paragraphs 15 to 30.

Crankshaft sprocket

Note 1: *The crankshaft sprocket retaining bolt is extremely tight. Ensure that the holding tool used to prevent rotation as the bolt is slackened is of sturdy construction and securely attached.*

Note 2: *A new sprocket retaining bolt will be required for refitting.*

Removal

11 Remove the timing belt as described in Section 6.

12 It will now be necessary to hold the crankshaft sprocket to enable the retaining bolt to be removed. Vauxhall special tools EN-47630 and KM-956-1 are available for this purpose, however, a home-made tool similar to that described in paragraph 2, can easily be fabricated.

13 Using the crankshaft pulley retaining bolts, securely attach the tool to the crankshaft sprocket. With the help of an assistant, hold the sprocket stationary and unscrew the retaining bolt. **Note:** *The sprocket retaining*

TOOL TiP

To make a sprocket holding tool, obtain two lengths of steel strip about 6 mm thick by about 30 mm wide or similar, one 600 mm long, the other 200 mm long (all dimensions are approximate). Bolt the two strips together to form a forked end, leaving the bolt slack so that the shorter strip can pivot freely. At the other end of each 'prong' of the fork, drill a suitable hole and fit a nut and bolt to allow the tool to engage with the spokes in the sprocket.

bolt has a **left-hand thread** and is unscrewed by turning it clockwise.

14 Remove the bolt and washer and slide the sprocket off the end of the crankshaft **(see illustrations)**. Note that a new bolt will be required for refitting.

Refitting

15 Align the sprocket location key with the crankshaft groove and slide the sprocket into position. Fit the new retaining bolt and washer.

16 Hold the sprocket stationary using the holding tool and tighten the retaining bolt to the specified torque. Remove the holding tool.

17 Refit the timing belt as described in Section 6.

High-pressure pump sprocket

Note: *A new sprocket retaining nut will be required for refitting.*

Removal

18 Remove the timing belt as described in Section 6.

7.14a Remove the bolt and washer . . .

7.14b . . . and slide the sprocket off the end of the crankshaft

7.20 Engage the holding tool with the holes in the fuel pump sprocket and undo the retaining nut

7.21 Use a suitable puller to release the fuel pump sprocket taper

7.22a Once the taper releases, withdraw the sprocket . . .

7.22b . . . and collect the Woodruff key from the pump shaft

19 It will now be necessary to hold the fuel pump sprocket to enable the retaining nut to

be removed. Vauxhall special tools KM-6347 and KM-956-1 are available for this purpose,

however, a home-made tool similar to that described in paragraph 2, can easily be fabricated.

20 Engage the tool with the holes in the fuel pump sprocket and undo the sprocket retaining nut **(see illustration)**. Note that a new nut will be required for refitting.

21 Attach a suitable puller to the threaded holes in the fuel pump sprocket using bolts and washers similar to the arrangement shown **(see illustration)**.

22 Tighten the puller centre bolt to release the sprocket from the taper on the pump shaft. Once the taper releases, remove the puller and withdraw the sprocket. Collect the Woodruff key from the pump shaft **(see illustrations)**.

Refitting

23 Clean the fuel pump shaft and the sprocket hub ensuring that all traces of oil or grease are removed.

24 Refit the Woodruff key to the pump shaft, then locate the sprocket in position. Fit the new retaining nut.

25 Hold the sprocket stationary using the holding tool and tighten the retaining nut to the specified torque. Remove the holding tool.

26 Refit the timing belt as described in Section 6.

Tensioner assembly

Removal

27 Remove the timing belt as described in Section 6.

28 Slacken and remove the retaining bolt and remove the tensioner assembly from the engine **(see illustrations)**.

Refitting

29 Fit the tensioner to the engine, making sure that the slot on the tensioner backplate is correctly located over the peg on the engine bracket **(see illustration)**.

30 Clean the threads of the retaining bolt and apply thread-locking compound to the bolt threads. Screw in the retaining bolt, set the tensioner in the retracted position and tighten the retaining bolt.

31 Refit the timing belt as described in Section 6.

Idler pulley

Removal

32 Remove the timing belt as described in Section 6.

33 Slacken and remove the retaining bolt and remove the idler pulley from the engine **(see illustration)**.

Refitting

34 Refit the idler pulley and tighten the retaining bolt to the specified torque.

35 Refit the timing belt as described in Section 6.

7.28a Slacken and remove the retaining bolt . . .

7.28b . . . and remove the timing belt tensioner assembly

7.29 The slot on the tensioner backplate must locate over the peg (arrowed) on the engine bracket

7.33 Slacken and remove the retaining bolt and remove the idler pulley from the engine

9.2a Disconnect the wiring connectors at the fuel injectors . . .

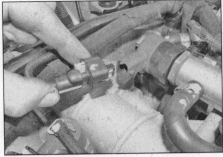

9.2b . . . fuel pressure regulating valve . . .

9.2c . . . fuel pressure sensor . . .

8 Camshaft oil seal – renewal

1 Remove the camshaft sprocket as described in Section 7.
2 Carefully punch or drill a small hole in the oil seal. Screw in a self-tapping screw, and pull on the screw with pliers to extract the seal.
3 Clean the seal housing, and polish off any burrs or raised edges which may have caused the seal to fail in the first place.
4 Press the new oil seal into position using a suitable tubular drift (such as a socket) which bears only on the hard outer edge of the seal. Take care not to damage the seal lips during fitting; note that the seal lips should face inwards.
5 Refit the camshaft sprocket as described in Section 7.

9 Camshaft housing – removal and refitting

Removal

1 Remove the timing belt as described in Section 6.
2 Disconnect the wiring harness connectors from the following components (see illustrations):
 a) Fuel injectors.
 b) Fuel pressure regulating valve.
 c) Fuel pressure sensor.
 d) Camshaft sensor.
 e) Air conditioning compressor.
3 Release the air conditioning compressor wiring harness from the clip on the oil dipstick guide tube. Undo the two bolts securing the plastic wiring harness guide to the camshaft housing and move the disconnected wiring harness to one side (see illustrations).
4 Disconnect the two vacuum hoses from the vacuum pipe assembly on top of the camshaft housing. Undo the two retaining bolts and move the pipe assembly to one side (see illustration).
5 Remove the fuel injectors and the fuel rail as described in Chapter 4B.

9.2d . . . camshaft sensor . . .

9.2e . . . and air conditioning compressor (arrowed)

6 Release the two retaining clips and disconnect the charge air hose from the throttle body/housing, and intercooler charge air pipe (see illustration).

9.3a Undo the two bolts (arrowed) securing the wiring harness guide to the camshaft housing . . .

9.3b . . . and move the disconnected wiring harness to one side

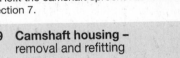

9.4a Disconnect the two vacuum hoses from the vacuum pipe assembly . . .

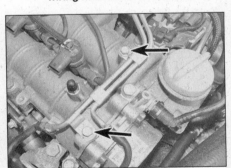

9.4b . . . then undo the two retaining bolts (arrowed) and move the pipe assembly to one side

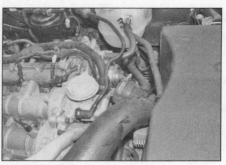

9.6 Release the retaining clips and remove the charge air hose

9.7 Disconnect the vacuum hose quick-release fitting from the braking system vacuum pump

9.8 Disconnect the crankcase ventilation hose from the engine oil filler housing

9.11 Lift the camshaft housing off the cylinder head and recover the gasket

7 Disconnect the vacuum hose quick-release fitting from the braking system vacuum pump **(see illustration)**.

8 Release the clip and disconnect the crankcase ventilation hose from the engine oil filler housing **(see illustration)**.

9 Undo the retaining bolts and remove the two engine lifting brackets from the left-hand end of the camshaft housing. Undo the bolt securing the turbocharger charge air pipe to the right-hand end of the camshaft housing

10 Working in a spiral pattern from the outside inwards, progressively slacken, then remove, the sixteen bolts securing the camshaft housing to the cylinder head. Ensure that the housing releases evenly from the cylinder block.

11 Lift the camshaft housing off the cylinder head and recover the gasket **(see illustration)**.

12 Thoroughly clean the mating faces of the cylinder head, camshaft housing and vacuum pump and obtain a new gasket for refitting.

Refitting

13 Check that all the hydraulic tappets and rocker arms are correctly positioned in the cylinder head and none have been disturbed.

14 Commence refitting by turning the crankshaft anti-clockwise by 90°. This will position all the pistons half-way down their bores, and prevent any chance of the valves touching the piston crowns as the camshaft housing is being fitted.

15 Place a new gasket on the cylinder head, then locate the camshaft housing in position aligning it with the locating dowels.

16 Refit the sixteen camshaft housing retaining bolts. Progressively screw in the bolts to gradually draw the housing down and into contact with the cylinder head.

17 Working in a spiral pattern from the inside outwards, progressively tighten the sixteen bolts securely.

18 Refit the two engine lifting brackets to the left-hand end of the camshaft housing and tighten the retaining bolts securely. Refit and tighten the charge air pipe retaining bolt.

19 Reconnect the crankcase ventilation hose to the engine oil filler housing.

20 Reconnect the vacuum hose quick-release fitting to the braking system vacuum pump ensuring that the fitting audibly engages.

21 Refit the charge air hose to the throttle body/housing, and intercooler charge air pipe and secure with the retaining clips.

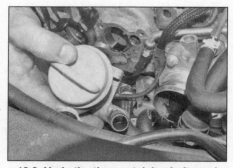

10.3 Undo the three retaining bolts and remove the oil filler housing

22 Refit the fuel rail and fuel injectors as described in Chapter 4B.

23 Place the vacuum pipe assembly in position on the top of the camshaft housing and refit the two retaining bolts. Tighten the bolts securely, then reconnect the two vacuum hoses.

24 Lay the plastic wiring harness guide in position on the camshaft housing, then refit and tighten the two retaining bolts.

25 Reconnect the wiring harness connectors to the components listed in paragraph 2, ensuring that the harness is secured by all the relevant retaining clips.

26 Turn the crankshaft clockwise by 90° to bring No 1 and 4 pistons to approximately the TDC position.

27 Refit the timing belt as described in Section 6.

10 Camshafts – removal, inspection and refitting

Note: *An additional camshaft positioning tool Vauxhall/Opel special tool EN-46789 (or suitable equivalent) will be required for this operation – two in total (see Section 3).*

Removal

1 Carry out the operations described in Section 9, paragraphs 1 to 8.

2 Remove the braking system vacuum pump as described in Chapter 9.

3 Disconnect the wiring connector from the coolant temperature sensor, then undo the three retaining bolts and remove the oil filler housing **(see illustration)**.

4 Undo the retaining bolt and remove the camshaft sensor from the right-hand end of the camshaft housing.

5 Before removing the camshaft housing completely, the retaining bolts for the camshaft drivegears and sprocket should be slackened as follows.

6 Remove the exhaust camshaft positioning tool from the valve timing checking hole.

7 It will be necessary to hold the camshaft sprocket to enable the drivegear and sprocket retaining bolts to be slackened. Vauxhall special tools EN-46787 and KM-956-1 are available for this purpose, however, a home-made tool can easily be fabricated **(see Tool tip in Section 7)**.

8 Working through the oil filler housing aperture, and using the holding tool to prevent rotation of the camshaft, slacken the inlet camshaft drivegear retaining bolt. Working through the vacuum pump aperture, slacken the exhaust camshaft drivegear retaining bolt in the same way **(see illustrations)**.

9 Again, using the holding tool, slacken the camshaft sprocket retaining bolt.

10 Continue with the camshaft housing removal procedure as described in Section 9, paragraphs 9 to 11.

10.8a Slacken the inlet camshaft drivegear retaining bolt . . .

10.8b . . . and the exhaust camshaft drivegear retaining bolt

10.12a Unscrew and remove the two previously-slackened retaining bolts . . .

11 With the camshaft housing placed upside down on the bench, unscrew and remove the previously-slackened retaining bolt, and remove the timing belt sprocket from the exhaust camshaft.

12 At the other end of the housing, unscrew and remove the two previously-slackened retaining bolts, and lift off the drivegears from the inlet and exhaust camshafts **(see illustrations)**.

13 Carefully prise out the exhaust camshaft oil seal with a screwdriver or similar hooked tool. Carefully withdraw the exhaust camshaft out from the timing belt end of the camshaft housing **(see illustration)**.

14 Using a wooden dowel or similar, carefully tap the end of the inlet camshaft toward the timing belt end of the housing to release the blanking cap. Remove the cap, then carefully withdraw the inlet camshaft from the housing **(see illustration)**.

Inspection

15 Examine the camshaft bearing surfaces and cam lobes for signs of wear ridges and scoring. Renew the camshaft(s) if any of these conditions are apparent. Examine the condition of the bearing surfaces in the camshaft housing. If the any wear or scoring is evident, the camshaft housing will need to be renewed.

16 If either camshaft is being renewed, it will be necessary to renew all the rocker arms and tappets for that particular camshaft also (see Section 11).

17 Check the condition of the camshaft

10.12b . . . then lift out the exhaust camshaft drivegear . . .

drivegears and sprocket for chipped or damaged teeth, wear ridges and scoring. Renew any components as necessary.

Refitting

18 Prior to refitting, thoroughly clean all components and dry with a lint-free cloth. Ensure that all traces of oil and grease are removed from the contact faces of the drivegears, sprocket and camshafts.

19 Lubricate the camshaft bearing journals in the camshaft housing and carefully insert the inlet and exhaust camshafts.

20 Ensuring that the contact faces are clean and dry, refit the drivegear to each camshaft. Note that the gear with the vacuum pump drive dogs is fitted to the exhaust camshaft, and the plain gear is fitted to the inlet camshaft.

21 Screw in a new drivegear retaining bolt for each camshaft and tighten both bolts finger-tight only at this stage.

10.12c . . . and the inlet camshaft drivegear

22 Refit the camshaft positioning tool to the valve timing checking hole of the exhaust camshaft. If necessary, rotate the exhaust camshaft slightly until the tool audibly engages **(see illustration)**.

23 Unscrew and remove the closure bolt from the inlet camshaft side of the camshaft housing and fit a second camshaft positioning tool **(see illustrations)**. If necessary, rotate the camshaft slightly until the tool audibly engages.

24 With both camshafts locked by means of the positioning tools, tighten both drivegear retaining bolts to the specified torque **(see illustration)**. It may be beneficial to have an assistant securely support the camshaft housing as the bolts are tightened.

25 Remove the positioning tool from the inlet camshaft and refit the closure bolt. Tighten the bolt to the specified torque.

26 Fit a new inlet camshaft blanking cap to the

10.13 Withdraw the exhaust camshaft . . .

10.14 . . . and inlet camshaft from the camshaft housing

10.22 Refit the camshaft positioning tool to the valve timing checking hole of the exhaust camshaft

10.23a Unscrew the closure bolt from the inlet camshaft side of the camshaft housing . . .

10.23b . . . and fit a camshaft positioning tool for the inlet camshaft

10.24 With both camshafts locked, tighten both drivegear retaining bolts to the specified torque

10.26a Fit a new inlet camshaft blanking cap to the camshaft housing . . .

10.26b . . . and tap it into position until it is flush with the outer face of the housing

10.27 Similarly, fit a new exhaust camshaft oil seal to the camshaft housing

timing belt end of the camshaft housing and tap it into position until it is flush with the outer face of the housing, using a suitable socket or tube, or a wooden block **(see illustrations)**.

27 Similarly, fit a new exhaust camshaft oil seal to the timing belt end of the camshaft housing and tap it into position until it is flush with the outer face of the housing, using a suitable socket or tube, or a wooden block **(see illustration)**.

28 Refit the timing belt sprocket to the exhaust camshaft, aligning its cut-out with the locating peg, and fit the new retaining bolt finger-tight only at this stage. Final tightening is carried out after the timing belt has been fitted and tensioned.

29 Refit the camshaft sensor to the camshaft housing and tighten the retaining bolt securely.

30 Refit the oil filler housing to the camshaft housing using a new gasket, refit the retaining bolts and tighten the bolts securely. Reconnect the coolant temperature sensor wiring connector.

31 Refit the braking system vacuum pump as described in Chapter 9.

32 Thoroughly clean the mating faces of the cylinder head and camshaft housing.

33 Refit the camshaft housing to the cylinder head as described in Section 9, paragraphs 13 to 26.

34 Commence refitting of the timing belt as described in Section 6, paragraphs 9 to 14.

35 Retain the camshaft sprocket using the holding tool, and tighten the retaining bolt to the specified torque.

36 Continue refitting of the timing belt as described in Section 6, paragraphs 15 to 30.

11 Camshaft followers and hydraulic tappets – removal, inspection and refitting

Removal

1 Remove the camshaft housing as described in Section 9.

2 Obtain sixteen small, oil tight clean plastic containers, and number them inlet 1 to 8 and exhaust 1 to 8; alternatively, divide a larger container into sixteen compartments and number each compartment accordingly.

3 Withdraw each camshaft follower and hydraulic tappet in turn, unclip the follower from the tappet, and place them in their respective container **(see illustrations)**. Do not interchange the followers and tappets, or the rate of wear will be much increased. Fill each container with clean engine oil and ensure that the tappet is submerged.

Inspection

4 Examine the followers and hydraulic tappet bearing surfaces for wear ridges and scoring. Renew any follower or tappet on which these conditions are apparent.

5 If any new hydraulic tappets are obtained, they should be immersed in a container of clean engine oil prior to refitting.

Refitting

6 Liberally oil the cylinder head hydraulic tappet bores and the tappets. Working on one

11.3a Withdraw each camshaft follower . . .

11.3b . . . and hydraulic tappet in turn, and place them in their respective container

assembly at a time, clip the follower back onto the tappet, then refit the tappet to the cylinder head, ensuring that it is refitted to its original bore. Lay the follower over its respective valve (see illustrations).

7 Refit the remaining tappets and followers in the same way.

8 With all the tappets and followers in place, refit the camshaft housing as described in Section 9.

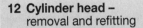

12 Cylinder head –
removal and refitting

Note: *New cylinder head bolts will be required for refitting.*

Removal

1 Disconnect the battery negative terminal (refer to *Disconnecting the battery* in the Reference Chapter).

2 Drain the cooling system as described in Chapter 1B.

3 Remove the camshaft housing as described in Section 9.

4 Remove the camshaft followers and hydraulic tappets as described in Section 11.

5 Remove the inlet and exhaust manifolds as described in Chapter 4B.

6 Release the clips and disconnect the remaining two coolant hoses at the thermostat housing, and the coolant hose at the EGR valve heat exchanger (see illustration).

7 Release the coolant pipe from the stud at the base of the thermostat housing (see illustration).

8 Undo the bolt securing the high-pressure fuel pump mounting bracket to the cylinder head (see illustration).

9 Make a final check to ensure that all relevant hoses, pipes and wires have been disconnected.

10 Working in the **reverse** of the tightening sequence (**see illustration 12.27**), progressively slacken the cylinder head bolts by half a turn at a time, until all bolts can be unscrewed by hand. Note that an M14 RIBE socket bit will be required to unscrew the bolts. Remove the cylinder head bolts and recover the washers.

11 Engage the help of an assistant, if necessary, and lift the cylinder head from the cylinder block (see illustration).

Caution: Do not lay the head on its lower mating surface; support the head on wooden blocks, ensuring each block only contacts the head mating surface.

12 Remove the gasket and keep it for identification purposes (see paragraph 19).

13 If the cylinder head is to be dismantled for overhaul, then refer to Part E of this Chapter.

Preparation for refitting

14 The mating faces of the cylinder head and cylinder block/crankcase must be perfectly clean before refitting the head. Use a hard

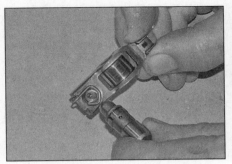

11.6a Clip the follower back onto the tappet . . .

11.6b . . . then refit the tappet to its original bore, and lay the follower over its respective valve

plastic or wood scraper to remove all traces of gasket and carbon; also clean the piston crowns. Take particular care, as the surfaces are damaged easily. Also, make sure that the carbon is not allowed to enter the oil and water passages – this is particularly important for the lubrication system, as carbon could block the oil supply to any of the engine's components. Using adhesive tape and paper, seal the water, oil and bolt holes in the cylinder block/crankcase. To prevent carbon entering the gap between the pistons and bores, smear a little grease in the gap. After cleaning each piston, use a small brush to remove all traces of grease and carbon from the gap, then wipe away the remainder with a clean rag. Clean all the pistons in the same way.

15 Check the mating surfaces of the cylinder block/crankcase and the cylinder head for

nicks, deep scratches and other damage. If slight, they may be removed carefully with a file, but if excessive, machining may be the only alternative to renewal.

16 Ensure that the cylinder head bolt holes in the crankcase are clean and free of oil. Syringe or soak up any oil left in the bolt holes. This is most important in order that the correct bolt tightening torque can be applied and to prevent the possibility of the block being cracked by hydraulic pressure when the bolts are tightened.

17 The cylinder head bolts must be discarded and renewed, regardless of their apparent condition.

18 If warpage of the cylinder head gasket surface is suspected, use a straight-edge to check it for distortion. Refer to Part E of this Chapter if necessary.

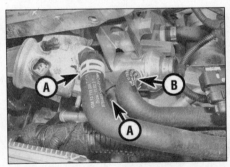

12.6 Disconnect the coolant hoses at the thermostat housing (A), and at the EGR valve heat exchanger (B)

12.7 Release the coolant pipe from the stud (arrowed) at the base of the thermostat housing

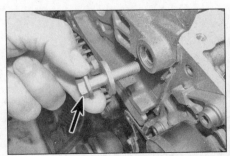

12.8 Undo the bolt (arrowed) securing the high-pressure fuel pump mounting bracket to the cylinder head

12.11 Lift the cylinder head from the cylinder block

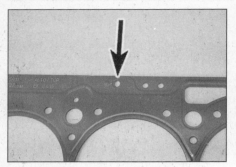

12.19 Cylinder head gasket thickness identification hole (arrowed)

12.21 Using a dial test indicator to measure piston protrusion

19 On this engine, the cylinder head-to-piston clearance is controlled by fitting different thickness head gaskets. The gasket thickness can be determined by looking at the holes stamped on the edge of the gasket (see illustration).

Number of holes	Gasket thickness
No holes	*0.77 to 0.87 mm*
One hole	*0.87 to 0.97 mm*
Two holes	*0.97 to 1.07 mm*

The correct thickness of gasket required is selected by measuring the piston protrusions as follows.

20 Mount a dial test indicator securely on the block so that its pointer can be easily pivoted between the piston crown and block mating surface. Turn the crankshaft to bring No 1 piston roughly to the TDC position. Move the dial test indicator probe over and in contact with No 1 piston. Turn the crankshaft back and forth slightly until the highest reading is shown on the gauge, indicating that the piston is at TDC.

21 Zero the dial test indicator on the gasket surface of the cylinder block then carefully move the indicator over No 1 piston. Measure its protrusion at the highest point between the valve cut-outs, and then again at its highest point between the valve cut-outs at 90° to the first measurement (see illustration). Repeat this procedure with No 4 piston.

22 Rotate the crankshaft half a turn (180°) to bring No 2 and 3 pistons to TDC. Ensure the crankshaft is accurately positioned then measure the protrusions of No 2 and 3 pistons at the specified points. Once all pistons have been measured, rotate the crankshaft to position all the pistons at their mid-stroke.

23 Select the correct thickness of head gasket required by determining the largest amount of piston protrusion, and using the following table.

Piston protrusion measurement (mm)	Gasket thickness required (mm)
0.020 to 0.100	0.77 to 0.87 (no holes)
0.101 to 0.200	0.87 to 0.97 (one hole)
0.201 to 0.295	0.97 to 1.07 (two holes)

Refitting

24 Wipe clean the mating surfaces of the cylinder head and cylinder block/crankcase. Place the new gasket in position with the words ALTO/TOP uppermost (see illustration).

25 Carefully refit the cylinder head assembly to the block, aligning it with the locating dowels.

26 Apply a thin film of engine oil to the bolt threads and the underside of the bolt heads. Carefully enter each new cylinder head bolt into its relevant hole (*do not drop them in*). Screw all bolts in, by hand only, until finger-tight.

27 Working progressively in the sequence shown, tighten the cylinder head bolts to their Stage 1 torque setting, using a torque wrench and suitable socket (see illustration). Working again in the same sequence, go around and tighten all bolts through the specified Stage 2 torque setting.

28 Once all bolts have been tightened to the Stage 2 torque, working again in the same sequence, go around and tighten all bolts through the specified Stage 3 angle, then through the specified Stage 4 angle, and finally through the specified Stage 5 angle using an angle-measuring gauge.

29 Refit the bolt securing the high-pressure fuel pump mounting bracket to the cylinder head and tighten the bolt securely.

30 Engage the coolant pipe with the stud on the thermostat housing, then reconnect the coolant hoses to the thermostat housing and EGR valve heat exchanger.

31 Refit the inlet and exhaust manifolds as described in Chapter 4B.

32 Refit the camshaft followers and hydraulic tappets as described in Section 11.

33 Refit the camshaft housing as described in Section 9.

34 On completion, reconnect the battery negative terminal, then refill the cooling system as described in Chapter 1B.

13 Sump –
removal and refitting

Refer to Chapter 2C, Section 13, but use the torque settings from the beginning of this Chapter.

14 Oil pump –
removal, overhaul and refitting

Refer to Chapter 2C, Section 14, but use

12.24 Place the new gasket in position with the words ALTO/TOP uppermost

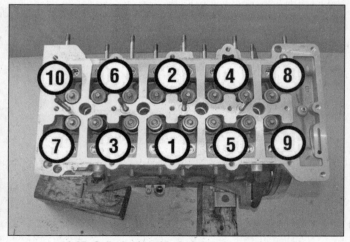

12.27 Cylinder head bolt tightening sequence

the torque settings from the beginning of this Chapter, and the following procedures from this Chapter.

a) Timing belt removal and refitting (Section 6).
b) Crankshaft sprocket removal and refitting (Section 7).

15 Oil filter housing – removal and refitting

Refer to Chapter 2C, Section 15, but use the torque settings from the beginning of this Chapter.

16 Crankshaft oil seals – renewal

Refer to Chapter 2C, Section 16, but use the torque settings from the beginning of this Chapter, and the crankshaft sprocket removal and refitting procedure from Section 7 in this Chapter.

17 Flywheel/driveplate – removal, inspection and refitting

Note: *New flywheel/driveplate retaining bolts will be required on refitting.*

Removal

Manual transmission models

1 Remove the transmission as described in Chapter 7A, then remove the clutch assembly as described in Chapter 6.
2 Prevent the flywheel from turning by locking

17.2 Prevent the flywheel from turning by locking the ring gear teeth

the ring gear teeth with a similar arrangement to that shown **(see illustration)**.
3 Slacken and remove the retaining bolts and remove the flywheel **(see illustration)**. Do not drop it, as it is very heavy.

Automatic transmission models

4 Remove the transmission as described in Chapter 7B then remove the driveplate as described in paragraphs 2 and 3.

Inspection

5 If there is any doubt about the condition of the flywheel/driveplate, seek the advice of a Vauxhall/Opel dealer or engine reconditioning specialist. They will be able to advise if it is possible to recondition it or whether renewal is necessary.

Refitting

Manual transmission models

6 Clean the mating surfaces of the flywheel and crankshaft.
7 Offer up the flywheel and engage it over the positioning dowel on the crankshaft. Apply a

17.3 Flywheel retaining bolts (arrowed)

drop of locking compound to the threads of each new flywheel retaining bolt (unless they are already precoated) and install the new bolts.
8 Lock the flywheel by the method used on removal then, working in a diagonal sequence, evenly and progressively tighten the retaining bolts to the specified torque.
9 Refit the clutch as described in Chapter 6 then remove the locking tool, and refit the transmission as described in Chapter 7A.

Automatic transmission models

10 Refit the driveplate as described in paragraphs 6 to 8.
11 Remove the locking tool, and refit the transmission as described in Chapter 7B.

18 Engine/transmission mountings – inspection and renewal

Refer to Chapter 2C, Section 18, where necessary using this Chapter's specifications.

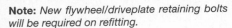

Chapter 2 Part E:
Engine removal and overhaul procedures

Contents

Degrees of difficulty

Easy, suitable for novice with little experience	**Fairly easy,** suitable for beginner with some experience	**Fairly difficult,** suitable for competent DIY mechanic	**Difficult,** suitable for experienced DIY mechanic	**Very difficult,** suitable for expert DIY or professional

Specifications

1.8 litre Z18XE petrol engines

Cylinder head

Maximum gasket face distortion	0.05 mm
Cylinder head height	135.85 to 136.00 mm
Valve seat angle in cylinder head	90° 30'
Valve seat width in cylinder head:	
Inlet.	1.0 to 1.4 mm
Exhaust.	1.4 to 1.8 mm

Valves and guides

Stem diameter:	
Inlet valve	4.955 to 4.970 mm
Exhaust valve	4.935 to 4.950 mm
Valve head diameter:	
Inlet valve	31.10 to 31.30 mm
Exhaust valve	27.40 to 27.60 mm
Valve length:	
Inlet valve	101.20 to 101.60 mm
Exhaust valve	100.56 to 100.96 mm
Maximum permissible valve stem play in guide:	
Inlet.	0.030 to 0.057 mm
Exhaust.	0.050 to 0.077 mm
Valve clearances.	Automatic adjustment by hydraulic cam followers

Cylinder block

Maximum gasket face distortion	0.05 mm
Cylinder bore diameter.	80.485 to 80.555 mm (nominal)
Maximum cylinder bore ovality and taper	0.013 mm

1.8 litre Z18XE petrol engines (continued)

Crankshaft and bearings
Number of main bearings 5
Main bearing journal diameter .... 54.980 to 54.997 mm
Big-end bearing journal diameter .... 42.971 to 42.987 mm
Crankshaft endfloat .... 0.100 to 0.202 mm

Pistons
Piston diameter .... 80.455 to 80.525 mm (nominal)

Piston rings
Number of rings (per piston) .... 2 compression, 1 oil control
Ring end gap:
  Compression .... 0.30 to 0.50 mm
  Oil control .... 0.40 to 1.40 mm

Torque wrench settings
Refer to Chapter 2A Specifications

1.8 litre Z18XER petrol engines
Note: *Where specifications are given as N/A, no information was available at the time of writing. Refer to your Vauxhall/Opel dealer for the latest information available.*

Cylinder head
Maximum gasket face distortion .... 0.05 mm
Cylinder head height .... N/A
Valve seat angle in cylinder head .... 90° 30'
Valve seat width in cylinder head:
  Inlet .... 1.0 to 1.4 mm
  Exhaust .... 1.4 to 1.8 mm

Valves and guides
Stem diameter:
  Inlet valve .... 4.955 to 4.970 mm
  Exhaust valve .... 4.935 to 4.950 mm
Valve head diameter:
  Inlet valve .... 30.70 to 30.80 mm
  Exhaust valve .... 27.10 to 27.20 mm
Valve length:
  Inlet valve .... 117.10 to 117.30 mm
  Exhaust valve .... 116.16 to 116.36 mm
Maximum permissible valve stem play in guide:
  Inlet .... 0.030 to 0.061 mm
  Exhaust .... 0.050 to 0.081 mm
Valve clearances (cold):
  Inlet valve .... 0.21 to 0.29 mm
  Exhaust valve .... 0.27 to 0.35 mm

Cylinder block
Maximum gasket face distortion .... 0.05 mm
Cylinder bore diameter .... 80.492 to 80.558 mm (nominal)
Maximum cylinder bore ovality and taper .... 0.013 mm

Crankshaft and bearings
Number of main bearings 5
Main bearing journal diameter .... 54.980 to 54.997 mm
Big-end bearing journal diameter .... 42.971 to 42.987 mm
Crankshaft endfloat .... 0.100 to 0.202 mm

Pistons
Piston diameter .... 80.455 to 80.515 mm (nominal)

Piston rings
Number of rings (per piston) .... 2 compression, 1 oil control
Ring end gap:
  Top compression .... 0.20 to 0.40 mm
  Second compression .... 0.40 to 0.60 mm
  Oil control .... 0.25 to 0.75 mm

Torque wrench settings
Refer to Chapter 2A Specifications

2.2 litre petrol engines

Cylinder head
Maximum gasket face distortion	0.05 mm
Cylinder head height	129.00 mm
Valve seat angle in cylinder head	90°

Valve seat width in cylinder head:
Inlet valve	1.1 to 1.3 mm
Exhaust valve	1.4 to 1.8 mm

Valves and guides
Stem diameter:
Inlet valve	5.955 to 5.970 mm
Exhaust valve	5.945 to 5.960 mm

Valve head diameter:
Inlet valve	34.95 to 35.25 mm
Exhaust valve	29.95 to 30.25 mm

Valve length:
Inlet valve	101.995 to 102.545 mm
Exhaust valve	100.685 to 101.235 mm

Maximum permissible valve stem play in guide:
Inlet	0.042 to 0.045 mm
Exhaust	0.052 to 0.055 mm
Valve clearances	Automatic adjustment by hydraulic cam followers

Cylinder block
Maximum gasket face distortion	0.05 mm
Cylinder bore diameter	85.992 to 86.008 mm
Maximum cylinder bore ovality and taper	0.013 mm

Crankshaft and bearings
Number of main bearings	5
Main bearing journal diameter	55.994 to 56.008 mm
Big-end bearing journal diameter	49.000 to 49.014 mm
Crankshaft endfloat	0.04 to 0.292 mm

Pistons
Piston diameter	85.967 to 85.982 mm

Piston rings
Number of rings (per piston)	2 compression, 1 oil control

Ring end gap:
Top compression	0.20 to 0.40 mm
Second compression	0.35 to 0.55 mm
Oil control	0.25 to 0.76 mm

Torque wrench settings
Refer to Chapter 2B Specifications

1.9 litre SOHC diesel engines

Note: *Where specifications are given as N/A, no information was available at the time of writing. Refer to your Vauxhall/Opel dealer for the latest information available.*

Cylinder head
Maximum gasket face distortion	0.10 mm
Cylinder head height	140.85 to 141.15 mm
Valve seat angle in cylinder head	N/A
Valve seat width in cylinder head	N/A

Valves and guides
Stem diameter (inlet and exhaust)	7.974 to 7.992 mm
Valve head diameter	N/A
Valve length	N/A
Maximum permissible valve stem play in guide	N/A

Valve clearances (cold):
Inlet valve	0.25 to 0.35 mm
Exhaust valve	0.30 to 0.40 mm

Cylinder block
Maximum gasket face distortion	0.15 mm
Cylinder bore diameter	82.000 to 82.030 mm
Maximum cylinder bore ovality	0.050 mm
Maximum cylinder bore taper	0.005 mm

1.9 litre SOHC diesel engines (continued)

Crankshaft and bearings

Number of main bearings	5
Main bearing journal diameter	59.855 to 60.000 mm
Big-end bearing journal diameter	50.660 to 50.805 mm
Crankshaft endfloat	0.049 to 0.211 mm

Pistons

Piston diameter	81.920 to 81.950 mm

Piston rings

Number of rings (per piston)	2 compression, 1 oil control
Ring end gap:	
Top compression	0.25 to 0.40 mm
Second compression	0.25 to 0.50 mm
Oil control	0.25 to 0.50 mm

Torque wrench settings	Refer to Chapter 2C Specifications

1.9 litre DOHC diesel engines

Note: *Where specifications are given as N/A, no information was available at the time of writing. Refer to your Vauxhall/Opel dealer for the latest information available.*

Cylinder head

Maximum gasket face distortion	0.10 mm
Cylinder head height	106.95 to 107.05 mm
Valve seat angle in cylinder head	N/A
Valve seat width in cylinder head	N/A

Valves and guides

Stem diameter:	
Inlet valve	5.982 to 6.000 mm
Exhaust valve	5.972 to 5.990 mm
Valve head diameter	N/A
Valve length (inlet and exhaust)	107.95 mm
Maximum permissible valve stem play in guide	N/A
Valve clearances	Automatic adjustment by hydraulic cam followers

Cylinder block

Maximum gasket face distortion	0.15 mm
Cylinder bore diameter	82.000 to 82.030 mm
Maximum cylinder bore ovality	0.050 mm
Maximum cylinder bore taper	0.005 mm

Crankshaft and bearings

Number of main bearings	5
Main bearing journal diameter	59.855 to 60.000 mm
Big-end bearing journal diameter	50.660 to 50.805 mm
Crankshaft endfloat	0.049 to 0.211 mm

Pistons

Piston diameter	81.920 to 81.950 mm

Piston rings

Number of rings (per piston)	2 compression, 1 oil control
Ring end gap:	
Top compression	0.20 to 0.35 mm
Second compression	0.60 to 0.80 mm
Oil control	0.25 to 0.50 mm

Torque wrench settings	Refer to Chapter 2D Specifications

1 General information

Included in this Part of Chapter 2 are details of removing the engine/transmission from the car and general overhaul procedures for the cylinder head, cylinder block/crankcase and all other engine internal components.

The information given ranges from advice concerning preparation for an overhaul and the purchase of new parts, to detailed step-by-step procedures covering removal, inspection, renovation and refitting of engine internal components.

After Section 5, all instructions are based on the assumption that the engine has been removed from the car. For information concerning in-car engine repair, as well as the removal and refitting of those external components necessary for full overhaul, refer to Part A, B, C or D of this Chapter (as applicable) and to Section 5. Ignore any preliminary dismantling operations described in Part A, B, C or D that are no longer relevant once the engine has been removed from the car.

Apart from torque wrench settings, which are given at the beginning of Part A, B, C or D (as applicable), all specifications relating to engine overhaul are at the beginning of this Part of Chapter 2.

2 Engine overhaul – general information

It is not always easy to determine when, or if, an engine should be completely overhauled, as a number of factors must be considered.

High mileage is not necessarily an indication that an overhaul is needed, while low mileage does not preclude the need for an overhaul. Frequency of servicing is probably the most important consideration. An engine which has had regular and frequent oil and filter changes, as well as other required maintenance, should give many thousands of miles of reliable service. Conversely, a neglected engine may require an overhaul very early in its life.

Excessive oil consumption is an indication that piston rings, valve seals and/or valve guides are in need of attention. Make sure that oil leaks are not responsible before deciding that the rings and/or guides are worn. Have a compression test performed (refer to Part A or B of this Chapter for petrol engines and to Part C or D for diesel engines), to determine the likely cause of the problem.

Check the oil pressure with a gauge fitted in place of the oil pressure switch, and compare it with that specified. If it is extremely low, the main and big-end bearings, and/or the oil pump, are probably worn out.

Loss of power, rough running, knocking or metallic engine noises, excessive valve gear noise, and high fuel consumption may also point to the need for an overhaul, especially if they are all present at the same time. If a complete service does not cure the situation, major mechanical work is the only solution.

A full engine overhaul involves restoring all internal parts to the specification of a new engine. During a complete overhaul, the pistons and the piston rings are renewed, and the cylinder bores are reconditioned. New main and big-end bearings are generally fitted; if necessary, the crankshaft may be reground, to compensate for wear in the journals. The valves are also serviced as well, since they are usually in less-than-perfect condition at this point. Always pay careful attention to the condition of the oil pump when overhauling the engine, and renew it if there is any doubt as to its serviceability. The end result should be an as-new engine that will give many trouble-free miles.

Critical cooling system components such as the hoses, thermostat and coolant pump should be renewed when an engine is overhauled. The radiator should also be checked carefully, to ensure that it is not clogged or leaking.

Before beginning the engine overhaul, read through the entire procedure, to familiarise yourself with the scope and requirements of the job. Check on the availability of parts and make sure that any necessary special tools and equipment are obtained in advance. Most work can be done with typical hand tools, although a number of precision measuring tools are required for inspecting parts to determine if they must be renewed.

The services provided by an engineering machine shop or engine reconditioning specialist will almost certainly be required, particularly if major repairs such as crankshaft regrinding or cylinder reboring are necessary. Apart from carrying out machining operations, these establishments will normally handle the inspection of parts, offer advice concerning reconditioning or renewal and supply new components such as pistons, piston rings and bearing shells. It is recommended that the establishment used is a member of the Federation of Engine Re-Manufacturers, or a similar society.

Always wait until the engine has been completely dismantled, and until all components (especially the cylinder block/crankcase and the crankshaft) have been inspected, before deciding what service and repair operations must be performed by an engineering works. The condition of these components will be the major factor to consider when determining whether to overhaul the original engine, or to buy a reconditioned unit. Do not, therefore, purchase parts or have overhaul work done on other components until they have been thoroughly inspected. As a general rule, time is the primary cost of an overhaul, so it does not pay to fit worn or sub-standard parts.

As a final note, to ensure maximum life and minimum trouble from a reconditioned engine, everything must be assembled with care, in a spotlessly-clean environment.

3 Engine removal – methods and precautions

If you have decided that the engine must be removed for overhaul or major repair work, several preliminary steps should be taken.

Engine/transmission removal is extremely complicated and involved on these vehicles. It must be stated, that unless the vehicle can be positioned on a ramp, or raised and supported on axle stands over an inspection pit, it will be very difficult to carry out the work involved.

Cleaning the engine compartment and engine/transmission before beginning the removal procedure will help keep tools clean and organised.

An engine hoist will also be necessary. Make sure the equipment is rated in excess of the combined weight of the engine and transmission. Safety is of primary importance, considering the potential hazards involved in removing the engine/transmission from the car.

The help of an assistant is essential. Apart from the safety aspects involved, there are many instances when one person cannot simultaneously perform all of the operations required during engine/transmission removal.

Plan the operation ahead of time. Before starting work, arrange for the hire of or obtain all of the tools and equipment you will need. Some of the equipment necessary to perform engine/transmission removal and installation safely (in addition to an engine hoist) is as follows: a heavy duty trolley jack, complete sets of spanners and sockets as described in the rear of this manual, wooden blocks, and plenty of rags and cleaning solvent for mopping-up spilled oil, coolant and fuel. If the hoist must be hired, make sure that you arrange for it in advance, and perform all of the operations possible without it beforehand. This will save you money and time.

Plan for the car to be out of use for quite a while. An engineering machine shop or engine reconditioning specialist will be required to perform some of the work which cannot be accomplished without special equipment. These places often have a busy schedule, so it would be a good idea to consult them before removing the engine, in order to accurately estimate the amount of time required to rebuild or repair components that may need work.

During the engine/transmission removal procedure, it is advisable to make notes of the locations of all brackets, cable ties, earthing points, etc, as well as how the wiring harnesses, hoses and electrical connections are attached and routed around the engine and engine compartment. An effective way of doing this is to take a series of photographs of the various components before they are disconnected or removed; the resulting photographs will prove invaluable when the engine/transmission is refitted.

Always be extremely careful when removing and refitting the engine/transmission. Serious injury can result from careless actions. Plan ahead and take your time, and a job of this nature, although major, can be accomplished successfully.

On all Vectra models, the engine must be removed complete with the transmission as an assembly. There is insufficient clearance in the engine compartment to remove the engine leaving the transmission in the vehicle. The assembly is removed by raising the front of the vehicle, and lowering the assembly from the engine compartment.

4 Engine and transmission unit – removal, separation and refitting

Note 1: *The engine can be removed from the car only as a complete unit with the transmission; the two are then separated for overhaul. The engine/transmission unit is lowered out of position, and withdrawn from under the vehicle. Bearing this in mind, and*

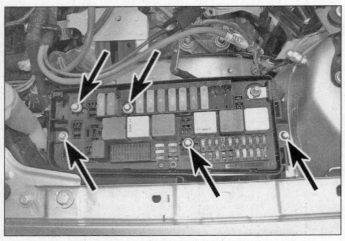

4.8a Unscrew the bolts (arrowed) securing the fuse/relay box upper and lower sections and the wiring harness block connectors . . .

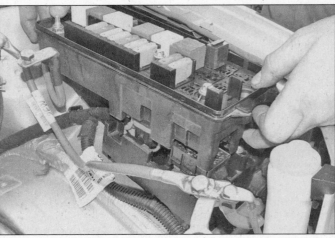

4.8b . . . depress the tabs at each end and lift the upper section off the lower section . . .

also bearing in mind the information contained in Section 3, ensure the vehicle is raised sufficiently so that there is enough clearance between the front of the vehicle and the floor to allow the engine/transmission unit to be slid out once it has been lowered out of position.

Note 2: *Such is the complexity of the power unit arrangement on these vehicles, and the variations that may be encountered according to model and optional equipment fitted, that the following should be regarded as a guide to the work involved, rather than a step-by-step*

procedure. Where differences are encountered, or additional component disconnection or removal is necessary, make notes of the work involved as an aid to refitting.

Removal

1 On models equipped with air conditioning, have the air conditioning system fully discharged by an air conditioning specialist.
2 Position the vehicle as described in Section 3, paragraph 2, and remove both front road-wheels. On petrol engine models, remove the

right-hand wheel arch liner inner cover. On diesel engine models, remove the engine undertray.
3 Remove the bonnet and the front bumper as described in Chapter 11.
4 Remove the plastic cover from the top of the engine.
5 Remove the battery and battery box as described in Chapter 5A.
6 Carry out the following operations as described in Chapter 1A or 1B, as applicable:
a) Drain the engine oil.
b) Drain the cooling system.
c) Remove the auxiliary drivebelt.
7 Remove the air cleaner assembly and intake ducts as described in Chapter 4A or 4B, as applicable.
8 Lift off the cover from the engine compartment fuse/relay box, and unscrew the two bolts securing the upper section of the fuse/relay box to the lower section. Undo the three bolts securing the engine wiring harness block connectors to the fuse/relay box upper section. Depress the tabs at each end and lift the upper section off the lower section, while at the same time disconnecting the three block connectors **(see illustrations)**.

4.8c . . . while at the same time disconnecting the wiring harness block connectors

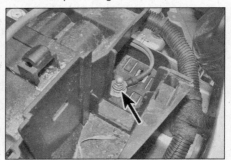

4.9a Undo the nut securing the earth lead to the stud in front of the battery box (arrowed) . . .

9 Undo the nut securing the earth lead to the stud in front of the battery box location. Release the disconnected wiring harness from the fuse/relay box lower section so that it is free to be removed with the engine **(see illustrations)**.
10 Disconnect the wiring block connector from the cooling fan module above the cooling fans **(see illustration)**. Release the wiring harness from the retaining clips so that it is free to be removed with the engine.
11 Remove the air conditioning system compressor as described in Chapter 3.

Petrol engine models

12 Depressurise the fuel system with reference to Chapter 4A, then disconnect the fuel supply pipe from the fuel rail and support bracket. Be prepared for fuel spillage, and take adequate precautions. Clamp or plug the open unions, to minimise further fuel loss.

4.9b . . . then release the disconnected wiring harness from the fuse/relay box lower section so that it is free to be removed with the engine

4.10 Disconnect the wiring block connector from the cooling fan module above the cooling fans

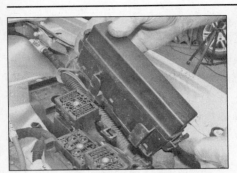

4.14 Detach the additional relay box at the left-hand side of the engine compartment – diesel engines

13 Disconnect the brake vacuum servo hose, and fuel evaporation purge hose.

Diesel engine models

14 Detach the additional relay box at the left-hand side of the engine compartment and free the wiring harness so that it can be removed with the engine **(see illustration)**.
15 Disconnect the brake vacuum servo hose from the vacuum pump.
16 Disconnect the heater element wiring connector from the fuel filter cover, and the water level sensor wiring connector from the base of the filter housing **(see illustrations)**.
17 Detach the two fuel hose quick-release connectors and remove the hoses from the fuel filter housing and cover. A Vauxhall/Opel special tool (KM-796-A) is available to disconnect the hose connectors, but provided care is taken, the connections can be released using two screwdrivers, a pair of long-nosed pliers, or similar, to depress the retaining tangs **(see illustrations)**.
18 Once the two fuel hoses are disconnected, suitably cover or plug the open connections to prevent dirt entry.
19 Working under the front, right-hand side of the car, release the locking lever catch, then lift the locking levers and disconnect the two wiring connectors from the engine management system ECU **(see illustrations)**.

All models

20 Loosen the clips and remove the upper and lower radiator hoses.
21 Release the retaining clips and disconnect the coolant hoses at the cooling system expansion tank. Disconnect the wiring connector then remove the expansion tank from its mounting bracket.
22 Using a small screwdriver, lift up the wire clips securing the two heater hoses to the heater matrix pipe stubs, and disconnect the hoses from the stubs **(see illustration)**.
23 On manual transmission models (except Easytronic), using a suitable forked tool, release the gearchange selector cable end fittings from the transmission selector levers. Pull back the retaining sleeves and detach the outer cables from the mounting bracket on the transmission **(see illustrations)**.
24 On automatic transmission models, use

4.16a Disconnect the heater element wiring connector from the fuel filter cover . . .

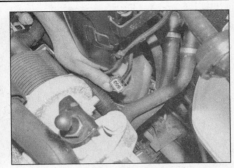

4.16b . . . and the water level sensor wiring connector from the base of the filter housing – diesel engines

4.17a Depress the retaining tangs and detach the two fuel hose quick-release connectors . . .

4.17b . . . then remove the hoses from the fuel filter housing and cover – diesel engines

a forked tool or flat-bladed screwdriver, and carefully lever the gear selector inner cable end fitting off the balljoint on the selector lever

position switch. Pull back the retaining sleeve and detach the outer cable from the mounting bracket on the transmission.

4.19a Release the locking lever catch . . .

4.19b . . . then lift the locking levers . . .

4.19c . . . and disconnect the two wiring connectors from the ECU – diesel engines

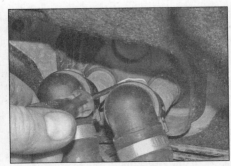

4.22 Lift up the wire clips and disconnect the heater hoses from the matrix pipe stubs

4.23a Release the selector inner cable end fittings from the transmission selector levers . . .

4.23b . . . then pull back the retaining sleeves and detach the outer cables from the transmission mounting bracket

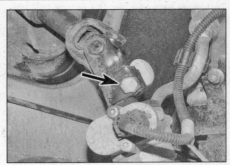

4.28 Unscrew the nut and remove the bolt (arrowed) securing the steering column intermediate shaft to the steering gear pinion shaft

25 Drain the transmission oil fluid as described in the relevant Part of Chapter 7.

26 Remove both driveshafts as described in Chapter 8.

27 Position the steering with the front roadwheels straight-ahead, and lock the steering by removing the ignition key.

28 Unscrew the nut and remove the bolt securing the steering column intermediate shaft to the steering gear pinion shaft. Separate the intermediate shaft from the pinion shaft by pulling the intermediate shaft upwards **(see illustration)**.
Caution: To prevent damage to the airbag wiring contact unit, the steering lock must remain locked until the intermediate shaft is re-attached to the pinion shaft.

29 On manual transmission models (except Easytronic), remove the filler cap from the brake/clutch fluid reservoir on the bulkhead, then tighten it onto a piece of polythene. This will reduce the loss of fluid when the clutch hydraulic hose is disconnected. Alternatively, fit a hose clamp to the flexible hose next to the clutch hydraulic connection on the transmission housing.

30 Place some cloth rags beneath the hose, then prise out the retaining clip securing the clutch hydraulic hose to the end fitting on top of the transmission bellhousing. Detach the hose from the end fitting **(see illustrations)**. Gently squeeze the two legs of the retaining clip together and re-insert the retaining clip back into position in the end fitting. Discard

the sealing ring from the hose end; a new sealing ring must be used on refitting. Plug/cover both the end fitting and hose end to minimise fluid loss and prevent the entry of dirt into the hydraulic system. **Note:** *Whilst the hose is disconnected, do not depress the clutch pedal.*

31 On automatic transmission models, unscrew the central retaining bolt (or nut) and detach the fluid cooler pipes from the transmission. Suitably cover the pipe ends and plug the transmission orifices to prevent dirt entry.

32 Attach a suitable hoist and lifting tackle to the engine lifting brackets on the cylinder head, and support the weight of the engine/transmission.

33 Remove the front subframe as described in Chapter 10.

34 Mark the position of the three bolts securing the right-hand engine mounting bracket to the engine bracket and undo the bolts **(see illustration)**. **Note:** *There is no need to remove the mounting, since the engine/transmission is lowered from the engine compartment.*

35 Mark the position of the three bolts securing the left-hand engine mounting to the transmission bracket **(see illustration)**.

36 Make a final check to ensure that all relevant pipes, hoses, wires, etc, have been disconnected, and that they are positioned clear of the engine and transmission.

37 With the help of an assistant, carefully lower the engine/transmission assembly to the ground. Make sure that the surrounding components in the engine compartment are not damaged. Ideally, the assembly should be lowered onto a trolley jack or low platform with castors, so that it can easily be withdrawn from under the car.

38 Ensure that the assembly is adequately supported, then disconnect the engine hoist and lifting tackle, and withdraw the engine/transmission assembly from under the front of the vehicle.

39 Clean away any external dirt using paraffin or a water-soluble solvent and a stiff brush.

40 With reference to the relevant Part of Chapter 7, unbolt the transmission from the

4.30a Prise out the clip securing the clutch hydraulic hose to the end fitting on the transmission bellhousing . . .

4.30b . . . then detach the hose from the end fitting

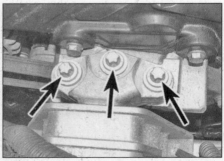

4.34 Right-hand engine mounting bracket-to-engine bracket retaining bolts (arrowed)

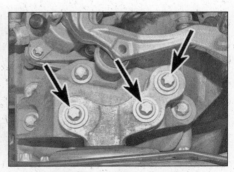

4.35 Left-hand engine mounting-to-transmission bracket retaining bolts (arrowed)

engine. Carefully withdraw the transmission from the engine. On manual transmission models, ensure that its weight is not allowed to hang on the input shaft while engaged with the clutch friction disc. On automatic transmission models, ensure that the torque converter is removed together with the transmission so that it remains engaged with the oil pump. Note that the transmission locates on dowels positioned in the rear of the cylinder block.

Refitting

41 With reference to the relevant Part of Chapter 7, refit the transmission to the engine and tighten the bolts to the specified torque.
42 With the front of the vehicle raised and supported on axle stands, move the engine/transmission assembly under the vehicle, ensuring that the assembly is adequately supported.
43 Reconnect the hoist and lifting tackle to the engine lifting brackets, and carefully raise the engine/transmission assembly up into the engine compartment with the help of an assistant.
44 Reconnect the right- and left-hand engine/transmission mountings and tighten the bolts to the specified torque given in the relevant Part of this Chapter. Ensure that the marks made on removal are correctly aligned when tightening the retaining bolts.
45 Refit the front subframe as described in Chapter 10.
46 Disconnect the hoist and lifting tackle from the engine lifting brackets.
47 Refit the driveshafts as described in Chapter 8.
48 On manual transmission models, refill the transmission with correct quantity and type of oil, as described in Chapter 7A or 7C.
49 Reconnect the steering column intermediate shaft to the steering gear pinion shaft and tighten the bolt and nut with reference to Chapter 10.
50 On automatic transmission models, reconnect the fluid cooler pipes together with new O-ring seals to the transmission.
51 On manual transmission models (except Easytronic), reconnect and bleed the clutch hydraulic connection at the transmission with reference to Chapter 6.
52 Refit the gearchange/selector outer cable(s) to the mounting bracket on the transmission. Engage the inner cable end fitting(s) with the selector lever balljoint, squeezing them together with pliers if necessary.
53 Push the securing wire clip back into position on the heater hose end fittings, then push the hoses back onto the matrix pipe stubs. Ensure that the wire clips securely lock the hoses in position.
54 Refit the cooling system expansion tank, and reconnect the wiring connector and the coolant hoses.
55 Reconnect the upper and lower radiator hoses.

Petrol engine models
56 Reconnect the brake vacuum servo hose, and fuel evaporation purge hose and fuel supply pipe.

Diesel engine models
57 Reconnect the two vacuum hoses at the solenoid valve located above the radiator.
58 Reconnect the brake vacuum servo hose to the vacuum pump, and the fuel hoses and wiring connectors at the fuel filter.
59 Refit the additional relay box to its location at the left-hand side of the engine compartment and secure the wiring harness.
60 Reconnect the two wiring connectors to the engine management system ECU.

All models
61 Refit the air conditioning system compressor as described in Chapter 3, then refit the auxiliary drivebelt as described in Chapter 1A or 1B, as applicable..
62 Reconnect the wiring block connector to the cooling fan module.
63 Locate the engine wiring harness block connectors back into position in the fuse/relay box lower section. Refit the upper section to the lower section ensuring that the block connectors are properly engaged. Refit and tighten the three bolts securing the block connectors, and the two bolts securing the upper section to the lower section.
64 Reconnect the earth lead to the stud in front of the battery box location and secure with the retaining nut.
65 Refit the air cleaner assembly and intake ducts as described in Chapter 4A or 4B, as applicable.
66 Refit the battery box and battery as described in Chapter 5A.
67 Refit the bonnet and the front bumper as described in Chapter 11.
68 Refit the right-hand wheel arch liner inner cover, or engine undertray, and both front roadwheels, then lower the vehicle to the ground.
69 Make a final check to ensure that all relevant hoses, pipes and wires have been correctly reconnected.
70 Refill the engine with oil with reference to Chapter 1A or 1B, as applicable.
71 On automatic transmission models, refill the transmission with correct quantity and type of fluid, as described in Chapter 7B.
72 Refill and bleed the cooling system with reference to Chapter 1A or 1B, as applicable.
73 On models equipped with air conditioning, have the air conditioning system evacuated, charged and leak-tested by the specialist who discharged it.

5 Engine overhaul – dismantling sequence

1 It is much easier to dismantle and work on the engine if it is mounted on a portable engine stand. These stands can often be hired from a tool hire shop. Before the engine is mounted on a stand, the flywheel/driveplate should be removed, so that the stand bolts can be tightened into the end of the cylinder block/crankcase.
2 If a stand is not available, it is possible to dismantle the engine with it blocked up on a sturdy workbench, or on the floor. Be extra careful not to tip or drop the engine when working without a stand.
3 If you are going to obtain a reconditioned engine, all the external components must be removed first, to be transferred to the new engine (just as they will if you are doing a complete engine overhaul yourself). These components include the following:
a) Engine wiring harness and supports.
b) Alternator and air conditioning compressor mounting brackets (as applicable).
c) Coolant pump (where applicable) and inlet/outlet housings.
d) Dipstick tube.
e) Fuel system components.
f) All electrical switches and sensors.
g) Inlet and exhaust manifolds and, where fitted, the turbocharger.
h) Oil filter and oil cooler/heat exchanger.
i) Flywheel/driveplate.
Note: When removing the external components from the engine, pay close attention to details that may be helpful or important during refitting. Note the fitted position of gaskets, seals, spacers, pins, washers, bolts, and other small items.
4 If you are obtaining a 'short' engine (which consists of the engine cylinder block/crankcase, crankshaft, pistons and connecting rods all assembled), then the cylinder head, sump, oil pump, and timing belt/chains (as applicable) will have to be removed also.
5 If you are planning a complete overhaul, the engine can be dismantled, and the internal components removed, in the order given below.

Petrol engines
a) Inlet and exhaust manifolds (see Chapter 4A).
b) Timing belt/chain, sprockets, tensioner and idler pulleys (see Chapter 2A or 2B).
c) Coolant pump (see Chapter 3).
d) Cylinder head (see Chapter 2A or 2B).
e) Flywheel/driveplate (see Chapter 2A or 2B).
f) Sump (see Chapter 2A or 2B).
g) Oil pump (see Chapter 2A or 2B).
h) Pistons/connecting rod assemblies (see Section 9).
i) Crankshaft (see Section 10).

Diesel engines
a) Inlet and exhaust manifolds (see Chapter 4B).

6.2 Using a valve spring compressor, compress the valve spring to relieve the pressure on the collets

6.4 Extract the two split collets by hooking them out using a small screwdriver

6.5a Remove the valve spring cap . . .

6.5b . . . and the spring . . .

6.5c . . . then withdraw the valve through the combustion chamber

6.5d Using pliers, remove the valve stem oil seal, which also incorporates the spring seat on most engines

b) Timing belt, sprockets, tensioner and idler pulleys (see Chapter 2C or 2D).
c) Coolant pump (see Chapter 3).
d) Cylinder head (see Chapter 2C or 2D).
e) Flywheel/driveplate (see Chapter 2C or 2D).
f) Sump (see Chapter 2C or 2D).
g) Oil pump (see Chapter 2C or 2D).
h) Piston/connecting rod assemblies (see Section 9).
i) Crankshaft (see Section 10).

6 Before beginning the dismantling and overhaul procedures, make sure that you have all of the correct tools necessary. See *Tools and working facilities* for further information.

6 Cylinder head – dismantling

Note: *New and reconditioned cylinder heads are available from the manufacturer, and from engine overhaul specialists. Due to the fact that some specialist tools are required for the dismantling and inspection procedures, and new components may not be readily available, it may be more practical and economical for the home mechanic to purchase a reconditioned head rather than to dismantle, inspect and recondition the original head. A valve spring compressor tool will be required for this operation.*

1 With the cylinder head removed as described in the relevant Part of this Chapter,

clean away all external dirt, and remove the following components as applicable, if not already done:
a) Manifolds (see Chapter 4A or 4B).
b) Spark plugs (petrol engines – see Chapter 1A).
c) Glow plugs (diesel engines – see Chapter 5A).
d) Camshafts and and associated valve train components (see Chapter 2A, 2B, 2C or 2D).
e) Fuel injectors (diesel engines – see Chapter 4B).
f) Engine lifting brackets.

2 To remove a valve, fit a valve spring compressor tool. Ensure that the arms of the compressor tool are securely positioned on the head of the valve and the spring cap **(see illustration)**. The valves are deeply-recessed on petrol engines, and a suitable

6.6 Place each valve assembly in a labelled polythene bag or similar container

extension piece may be required for the spring compressor.

3 Compress the valve spring to relieve the pressure of the spring cap acting on the collets.

> **HAYNES HiNT** *If the spring cap sticks to the valve stem, support the compressor tool, and give the end a light tap with a soft-faced mallet to help free the spring cap.*

4 Extract the two split collets by hooking them out using a small screwdriver, then slowly release the compressor tool **(see illustration)**.
5 Remove the valve spring cap and the spring, then withdraw the valve through the combustion chamber. Using pliers, remove the valve stem oil seal, which also incorporates the spring seat on most engines **(see illustrations)**. If the spring seat is not part of the valve stem oil seal, hook it out using a small screwdriver.
6 Repeat the procedure for the remaining valves, keeping all components in strict order so that they can be refitted in their original positions, unless all the components are to be renewed. If the components are to be kept and used again, place each valve assembly in a labelled polythene bag or a similar small container **(see illustration)**. Note that as with cylinder numbering, the valves are normally numbered from the timing chain (or timing belt) end of the engine. Make sure that the valve components are identified as inlet and exhaust, as well as numbered.

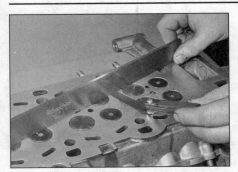

7.6 Using a straight-edge and feeler gauge to check cylinder head surface distortion

7 Cylinder head and valves – cleaning and inspection

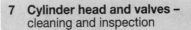

1 Thorough cleaning of the cylinder head and valve components, followed by a detailed inspection, will enable you to decide how much valve service work must be carried out during the engine overhaul. **Note:** *If the engine has been severely overheated, it is best to assume that the cylinder head is warped – check carefully for signs of this.*

Cleaning

2 Scrape away all traces of old gasket material from the cylinder head.

3 Scrape away the carbon from the combustion chambers and ports, then wash the cylinder head thoroughly with paraffin or a suitable solvent.

4 Scrape off any heavy carbon deposits that may have formed on the valves, then use a power-operated wire brush to remove deposits from the valve heads and stems.

Inspection

Note: *Be sure to perform all the following inspection procedures before concluding that the services of a machine shop or engine overhaul specialist are required. Make a list of all items that require attention.*

Cylinder head

5 Inspect the head very carefully for cracks, evidence of coolant leakage, and other damage. If cracks are found, a new cylinder head should be obtained.

6 Use a straight-edge and feeler gauge blade to check that the cylinder head surface is not distorted **(see illustration)**. If it is, it may be possible to resurface it, provided that the cylinder head is not reduced to less than the minimum specified height.

7 Examine the valve seats in each of the combustion chambers. If they are severely pitted, cracked or burned, then they will need to be recut by an engine overhaul specialist. If they are only slightly pitted, this can be removed by grinding-in the valve heads and seats with fine valve-grinding compound, as described below.

8 If the valve guides are worn, indicated by

7.11 Using a micrometer to measure valve stem diameter

a side-to-side motion of the valve, oversize valve guides are available, and valves with oversize stems can be fitted. This work is best carried out by an engine overhaul specialist. A dial gauge may be used to determine whether the amount of side play of a valve exceeds the specified maximum.

9 Check the tappet bores in the cylinder head for wear. If excessive wear is evident, the cylinder head must be renewed. Also check the tappet oil holes in the cylinder head for obstructions.

Valves

10 Examine the head of each valve for pitting, burning, cracks and general wear, and check the valve stem for scoring and wear ridges. Rotate the valve, and check for any obvious indication that it is bent. Look for pitting and excessive wear on the tip of each valve stem. Renew any valve that shows any such signs of wear or damage.

11 If the valve appears satisfactory at this stage, measure the valve stem diameter at several points using a micrometer **(see illustration)**. Any significant difference in the readings obtained indicates wear of the valve stem. Should any of these conditions be apparent, the valve(s) must be renewed.

12 If the valves are in satisfactory condition, they should be ground (lapped) into their respective seats, to ensure a smooth gas-tight seal. If the seat is only lightly pitted, or if it has been recut, fine grinding compound **only** should be used to produce the required finish. Coarse valve-grinding compound should **not** be used unless a seat is badly burned or deeply pitted; if this is the case, the cylinder head and valves should be inspected by an expert to decide whether seat recutting, or even the renewal of the valve or seat insert, is required.

13 Valve grinding is carried out as follows. Place the cylinder head upside-down on a bench, with a block of wood at each end to give clearance for the valve stems.

14 Smear a trace of the appropriate grade of valve-grinding compound on the seat face, and press a suction grinding tool onto the valve head. With a semi-rotary action, grind the valve head to its seat, lifting the valve occasionally to redistribute the grinding compound **(see illustration)**. A light spring

7.14 Grinding-in a valve

placed under the valve head will greatly ease this operation.

15 If coarse grinding compound is being used, work only until a dull, matt even surface is produced on both the valve seat and the valve, then wipe off the used compound and repeat the process with fine compound. When a smooth unbroken ring of light grey matt finish is produced on both the valve and seat, the grinding operation is complete. **Do not** grind in the valves any further than absolutely necessary, or the seat will be prematurely sunk into the cylinder head.

16 When all the valves have been ground-in, carefully wash off all traces of grinding compound using paraffin or a suitable solvent before reassembly of the cylinder head.

Valve components

17 Examine the valve springs for signs of damage and discoloration; if possible; also compare the existing spring free length with new components.

18 Stand each spring on a flat surface, and check it for squareness. If any of the springs are damaged, distorted or have lost their tension, obtain a complete new set of springs.

8 Cylinder head – reassembly

1 Lubricate the stems of the valves, and insert them into their original locations **(see illustration)**. If new valves are being fitted, insert them into the locations to which they have been ground.

8.1 Lubricate the valve stem with engine oil and insert the valve into the correct guide

8.2a Fit the spring seat . . .

8.2b . . . then fit the seal protector (where supplied) to the valve . . .

8.2c . . . and install the new valve stem oil seal . . .

8.2d . . . pressing it onto the valve guide with a suitable socket

8.3 Refit the valve spring and fit the spring cap

8.4 Compress the valve and locate the collets in the recess on the valve stem

2 Working on the first valve, refit the spring seat if it is not an integral part of the valve stem oil seal. Dip the new valve stem seal in fresh engine oil, then carefully locate it over the valve and onto the guide. Take care not to damage the seal as it is passed over the valve stem. Use a suitable socket or metal tube to press the seal firmly onto the guide. **Note:** *If genuine seals are being fitted, use the oil seal protector which is supplied with the seals; the protector fits over the valve stem and prevents the oil seal lip being damaged on the valve* (**see illustrations**).

3 Locate the spring on the seat and fit the spring cap (**see illustration**).

4 Compress the valve spring, and locate the split collets in the recess in the valve stem

Use a little dab of grease to hold the collets in position on the valve stem while the spring compressor is released.

(**see illustration and Haynes Hint**). Release the compressor, then repeat the procedure on the remaining valves.

5 With all the valves installed, support the cylinder head on blocks on the bench and, using a hammer and interposed block of wood, tap the end of each valve stem to settle the components.

6 Refit the components removed in Section 6, paragraph 1.

9 Pistons/connecting rods – removal

Note: *New connecting rod big-end cap bolts will be needed on refitting.*

1 Referring to the relevant Part of this Chapter, remove the cylinder head and sump. Where fitted, unbolt the pick-up/strainer from the base of the oil pump.

2 If there is a pronounced wear ridge at the top of any bore, it may be necessary to remove it with a scraper or ridge reamer, to avoid piston damage during removal. Such a ridge indicates excessive wear of the cylinder bore.

3 If the connecting rods and big-end caps are not marked to indicate their positions in the cylinder block (ie, marked with cylinder numbers), suitably mark both the rod and cap with quick-drying paint or similar. Note which side of the engine the marks face and accurately record this also. There may not be any other way of identifying which

way round the cap fits on the rod, when refitting.

4 Turn the crankshaft to bring pistons 1 and 4 to BDC (bottom dead centre).

5 Unscrew the bolts from No 1 piston big-end bearing cap, then take off the cap and recover the bottom half-bearing shell. If the bearing shells are to be re-used, tape the cap and the shell together.

Caution: On some engines, the connecting rod/bearing cap mating surfaces are not machined flat; the big-end bearing caps are 'cracked' off from the rod during production and left untouched to ensure the cap and rod mate perfectly. Where this type of connecting rod is fitted, great care must be taken to ensure the mating surfaces of the cap and rod are not marked or damaged in anyway. Any damage to the mating surfaces will adversely affect the strength of the connecting rod and could lead to premature failure.

6 Using a hammer handle, push the piston up through the bore, and remove it from the top of the cylinder block. Recover the bearing shell, and tape it to the connecting rod for safe-keeping.

7 Loosely refit the big-end cap to the connecting rod, and secure with the nuts/bolts – this will help to keep the components in their correct order.

8 Remove No 4 piston assembly in the same way.

9 Turn the crankshaft through 180° to bring pistons 2 and 3 to BDC, and remove them in the same way.

10.3 Check the crankshaft endfloat using a dial gauge . . .

10.4 . . . or a feeler gauge

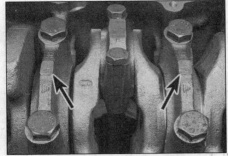

10.5 Main bearing cap identification markings (arrowed) – 1.8 litre petrol engines

10 Crankshaft – removal

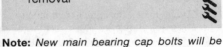

Note: *New main bearing cap bolts will be required on refitting.*

1.8 litre petrol engines

1 Working as described in Part A of this Chapter, remove the flywheel and the oil pump.

2 Remove the piston and connecting rod assemblies as described in Section 9. If no work is to be done on the pistons and connecting rods, unbolt the caps and push the pistons far enough up the bores that the connecting rods are positioned clear of the crankshaft journals.

3 Before removing the crankshaft, check the endfloat using a dial gauge in contact with the end of the crankshaft. Push the crankshaft fully one way, and then zero the gauge. Push the crankshaft fully the other way, and check the endfloat **(see illustration)**. The result should be compared with the specified limit, and will give an indication as to the size of the main bearing shell thrust journal width which will be required for reassembly.

4 If a dial gauge is not available, a feeler gauge can be used to measure crankshaft endfloat. Push the crankshaft fully towards one end of the crankcase, and insert a feeler gauge between the thrust flange of the main bearing shell and the machined surface of the crankshaft web **(see illustration)**. Before measuring, ensure that the crankshaft is fully forced towards one end of the crankcase, to give the widest possible gap at the measuring location. **Note:** *Measure at the bearing with the thrustwasher (see Section 1 in Chapter 2A, 2B 2C or 2D).*

5 The main bearing caps should be numbered 1 to 5 from the timing belt end of the engine and all identification numbers should be the right way up when read from the rear of the cylinder block **(see illustration)**. If the bearing caps are not marked, using a hammer and punch or a suitable marker pen, number the caps from 1 to 5 from the timing belt end of the engine and mark each cap to indicate its correct fitted direction to avoid confusion on refitting.

6 Working in a diagonal sequence, evenly and progressively slacken the ten main bearing cap retaining bolts by half a turn at a time until all bolts are loose. Remove all the bolts.

7 Carefully remove each cap from the cylinder block, ensuring that the lower main bearing shell remains in position in the cap.

8 Carefully lift out the crankshaft, taking care not to displace the upper main bearing shells **(see illustration)**. Remove the oil seal and discard it.

9 Recover the upper bearing shells from the cylinder block, and tape them to their respective caps for safe-keeping.

2.2 litre petrol engines

10 Working as described in Part B of this Chapter, remove the flywheel/driveplate and the timing chains and sprockets.

11 Remove the piston and connecting rod assemblies as described in Section 9. If no work is to be done on the pistons and connecting rods, unbolt the caps and push the pistons far enough up the bores that the connecting rods are positioned clear of the crankshaft journals.

12 Before removing the crankshaft, check the endfloat as described in paragraphs 3 and 4.

13 Evenly and progressively slacken the cylinder block lower casing retaining bolts and remove the casing from the cylinder block **(see illustration)**. If the locating dowels are a loose fit, remove them and store them with the casing for safe-keeping.

14 Carefully lift out the crankshaft, taking care not to displace the upper main bearing shells. Remove the oil seal and discard it.

15 Recover the upper bearing shells from the cylinder block, and tape them to their respective positions in the lower casing for safe-keeping.

Diesel engines

16 Working as described in Part C or D of this Chapter (as applicable), remove the flywheel/driveplate, oil pump and the crankshaft left-hand oil seal housing.

17 Remove the piston and connecting rod assemblies as described in Section 9. If no work is to be done on the pistons and connecting rods, unbolt the caps and push the pistons far enough up the bores that the connecting rods are positioned clear of the crankshaft journals.

18 Before removing the crankshaft, check the endfloat as described in paragraphs 3 and 4.

19 Check the main bearing caps for identification markings. Normally, No 1 bearing cap (timing belt end) is not marked and the remaining caps are numbered I, II, III, IIII. The lug at the base of the cap is used to identify the inlet manifold side of the engine **(see illustrations)**. If the bearing caps are not marked, using a hammer and punch or a suitable marker pen, number the caps from 1 to 5 from the timing belt end of the engine and mark each cap to indicate its correct fitted direction to avoid confusion on refitting.

20 Working in a diagonal sequence, evenly and progressively slacken the ten main bearing cap retaining bolts by half a turn at a time until all bolts are loose. Remove all the bolts.

10.8 Removing the crankshaft – 1.8 litre petrol engines

10.13 Lifting the cylinder block lower casing from the cylinder block – 2.2 litre petrol engines

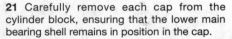

10.19a Main bearing cap identification marks (arrowed) . . .

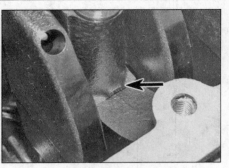

10.19b . . . and the lug at the base of the cap (arrowed) is used to identify the inlet manifold side of the engine – diesel engines

11.3 On diesel engines unscrew the retaining bolts and remove the piston oil spray nozzles from the cylinder block

21 Carefully remove each cap from the cylinder block, ensuring that the lower main bearing shell remains in position in the cap.

22 Carefully lift out the crankshaft, taking care not to displace the upper main bearing shells.

23 Recover the upper bearing shells and the thrustwashers from the cylinder block, and tape them to their respective caps for safe-keeping.

11 Cylinder block – cleaning and inspection

Cleaning

1 For complete cleaning, remove all external components (senders, sensors, brackets, oil pipes, coolant pipes, etc) from the cylinder block.

2 Scrape all traces of gasket and/or sealant from the cylinder block and lower casing (where applicable), taking particular care not to damage the cylinder head and sump mating faces.

3 Remove all oil gallery plugs, where fitted. The plugs are usually very tight – they may have to be drilled out and the holes retapped. Use new plugs when the engine is reassembled. On diesel engines, undo the retaining bolts and remove the piston oil spray nozzles from inside the cylinder block **(see illustration).**

12.2 Using a feeler blade to remove a piston ring

4 If the block and lower casing (where applicable) are extremely dirty, they should be steam-cleaned.

5 If the components have been steam-cleaned, clean all oil holes and oil galleries one more time on completion. Flush all internal passages with warm water until the water runs clear. Dry the block and, where necessary, the lower casing thoroughly and wipe all machined surfaces with a light oil. If you have access to compressed air, use it to speed-up the drying process, and to blow out all the oil holes and galleries.

 Warning: Wear eye protection when using compressed air.

6 If the block and lower casing are relatively clean, an adequate cleaning job can be achieved with hot soapy water and a stiff brush. Take plenty of time, and do a thorough job. Regardless of the cleaning method used, be sure to clean all oil holes and galleries very thoroughly, dry everything completely, and coat all cast-iron machined surfaces with light oil.

7 The threaded holes in the cylinder block must be clean, to ensure accurate torque readings when tightening fixings during reassembly. Run the correct-size tap (which can be determined from the size of the relevant bolt) into each of the holes to remove rust, corrosion, thread sealant or other contamination, and to restore damaged threads. If possible, use compressed air to clear the holes of debris produced by this operation. Do not forget to clean the threads of all bolts and nuts which are to be re-used, as well.

8 Where applicable, apply suitable sealant to the new oil gallery plugs, and insert them into the relevant holes in the cylinder block. Tighten the plugs securely. On diesel engines, refit the oil spray nozzles into the block and secure with the retaining bolts tightened securely.

9 If the engine is to be left dismantled for some time, cover the cylinder block with a large plastic bag to keep it clean and prevent corrosion. Where applicable, refit the lower casing and tighten the bolts finger-tight.

Inspection

10 Visually check the block for cracks, rust and corrosion. Look for stripped threads in the threaded holes. It's also a good idea to have the block checked for hidden cracks by an engine reconditioning specialist who has the equipment to do this type of work, especially if the vehicle had a history of overheating or using coolant. If defects are found, have the block repaired, if possible, or renewed.

11 If in any doubt as to the condition of the cylinder block, have it inspected and measured by an engine reconditioning specialist. If the bores are worn or damaged, they will be able to carry out any necessary reboring (where possible), and supply appropriate oversized pistons, etc.

12 Pistons/connecting rods – inspection

1 Before the inspection process can begin, the piston/connecting rod assemblies must be cleaned, and the original piston rings removed from the pistons. **Note:** *Always use new piston rings when the engine is reassembled.*

2 Carefully expand the old rings over the top of the pistons. The use of two or three old feeler gauges will be helpful in preventing the rings dropping into empty grooves **(see illustration)**. Take care, however, as piston rings are sharp.

3 Scrape away all traces of carbon from the top of the piston. A hand-held wire brush, or a piece of fine emery cloth, can be used once the majority of the deposits have been scraped away.

4 Remove the carbon from the ring grooves in the piston, using an old ring. Break the ring in half to do this (be careful not to cut your fingers – piston rings are sharp). Be very careful to remove only the carbon deposits – do not remove any metal, and do not nick or scratch the sides of the ring grooves.

5 Once the deposits have been removed, clean the piston/connecting rod assembly with paraffin or a suitable solvent, and dry thoroughly. Make sure that the oil return holes in the ring grooves are clear.

6 If the pistons and cylinder bores are not damaged or worn excessively, and if the cylinder block does not need to be rebored, the original pistons can be refitted. Normal piston wear shows up as even vertical wear on the piston thrust surfaces, and slight looseness of the top ring in its groove. New piston rings should always be used when the engine is reassembled.

7 Carefully inspect each piston for cracks around the skirt, at the gudgeon pin bosses, and at the piston ring lands (between the ring grooves).

8 Look for scoring and scuffing on the thrust faces of the piston skirt, holes in the piston crown, and burned areas at the edge of the crown. If the skirt is scored or scuffed, the engine may have been suffering from overheating, and/or abnormal combustion ('pinking') which caused excessively-high operating temperatures. The cooling and lubrication systems should be checked thoroughly. A hole in the piston crown, or burned areas at the edge of the piston crown indicates that abnormal combustion (pre-ignition, 'pinking', knocking or detonation) has been occurring. If any of the above problems exist, the causes must be investigated and corrected, or the damage will occur again.

9 Corrosion of the piston, in the form of pitting, indicates that coolant has been leaking into the combustion chamber and/or the crankcase. Again, the cause must be corrected, or the problem may persist in the rebuilt engine.

10 If in any doubt as to the condition of the pistons and connecting rods, have them inspected and measured by an engine reconditioning specialist. If new parts are required, they will be able to supply and fit appropriate-sized pistons/rings, and rebore (where possible) or hone the cylinder block.

13 Crankshaft – inspection

1 Clean the crankshaft using paraffin or a suitable solvent, and dry it, preferably with compressed air if available. Be sure to clean the oil holes with a pipe cleaner or similar probe, to ensure that they are not obstructed.

⚠️ *Warning: Wear eye protection when using compressed air.*

2 Check the main and big-end bearing journals for uneven wear, scoring, pitting and cracking.

3 Big-end bearing wear is accompanied by distinct metallic knocking when the engine is running (particularly noticeable when the engine is pulling from low revs), and some loss of oil pressure.

4 Main bearing wear is accompanied by severe engine vibration and rumble – getting progressively worse as engine revs increase – and again by loss of oil pressure.

5 Check the bearing journal for roughness by running a finger lightly over the bearing surface. Any roughness (which will be accompanied by obvious bearing wear) indicates that the crankshaft requires regrinding.

6 If the crankshaft has been reground, check for burrs around the crankshaft oil holes (the holes are usually chamfered, so burrs should not be a problem unless regrinding has been carried out carelessly). Remove any burrs with a fine file or scraper, and thoroughly clean the oil holes as described previously.

7 Have the crankshaft journals measured by an engine reconditioning specialist. If the crankshaft is worn or damaged, they may be able to regrind the journals and supply suitable undersize bearing shells. If no undersize shells are available and the crankshaft has worn beyond the specified limits, it will have to be renewed. Consult your Vauxhall/Opel dealer or engine reconditioning specialist for further information on parts availability.

8 If a new crankshaft is to be fitted, undo the screws securing the crankshaft speed/position sensor pulse pick-up ring to the crankshaft, and transfer the ring to the new crankshaft **(see illustration)**.

14 Main and big-end bearings – inspection

1 Even though the main and big-end bearings should be renewed during the engine overhaul, the old bearings should be retained for close examination, as they may reveal valuable information about the condition of the engine.

2 Bearing failure occurs because of lack of lubrication, the presence of dirt or other foreign particles, overloading the engine, or corrosion **(see illustration)**. If a bearing fails, the cause must be found and eliminated before the engine is reassembled, to prevent the failure from happening again.

3 To examine the bearing shells, remove them from the cylinder block, the main bearing caps or cylinder block lower casing, the connecting rods and the big-end bearing caps, and lay them out on a clean surface in the same order as they were fitted to the engine. This will enable any bearing problems to be matched with the corresponding crankshaft journal.

4 Dirt and other foreign particles can enter the engine in a variety of ways. Contamination may be left in the engine during assembly, or it may pass through filters or the crankcase ventilation system. Normal engine wear produces small particles of metal, which can eventually cause problems. If particles find their way into the lubrication system, it is likely that they will eventually be carried to the bearings. Whatever the source, these foreign particles often end up embedded in the soft bearing material, and are easily recognised. Large particles will not embed in the bearing,

13.8 Transfer the crankshaft speed/position sensor pulse pick-up ring to the new crankshaft

and will score or gouge the bearing and journal. To prevent possible contamination, clean all parts thoroughly, and keep everything spotlessly-clean during engine assembly. Once the engine has been installed in the vehicle, ensure that engine oil and filter changes are carried out at the recommended intervals.

5 Lack of lubrication (or lubrication breakdown) has a number of interrelated causes. Excessive heat (which thins the oil), overloading (which squeezes the oil from the bearing face), and oil leakage (from excessive bearing clearances, worn oil pump or high engine speeds) all contribute to lubrication breakdown. Blocked oil passages, which may be the result of misaligned oil holes in a bearing shell, will also starve a bearing of oil and destroy it. When lack of lubrication is the cause of bearing failure, the bearing material is wiped or extruded from the steel backing of the bearing. Temperatures may increase to the point where the steel backing turns blue from overheating.

6 Driving habits can have a definite effect on bearing life. Full-throttle, low-speed operation (labouring the engine) puts very high loads on

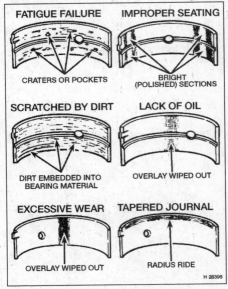

14.2 Typical bearing failures

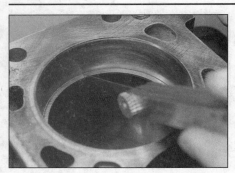

16.4 Measuring a piston ring end gap using a feeler gauge

bearings, which tends to squeeze out the oil film. These loads cause the bearings to flex, which produces fine cracks in the bearing face (fatigue failure). Eventually the bearing material will loosen in places, and tear away from the steel backing. Regular short journeys can lead to corrosion of bearings, because insufficient engine heat is produced to drive off the condensed water and corrosive gases which form inside the engine. These products collect in the engine oil, forming acid and sludge. As the oil is carried to the bearings, the acid attacks and corrodes the bearing material.

7 Incorrect bearing installation during engine assembly will also lead to bearing failure. Tight-fitting bearings leave insufficient bearing lubrication clearance, and will result in oil starvation. Dirt or foreign particles trapped behind a bearing shell results in high spots on the bearing which can lead to failure.

8 *Do not* touch any shell's bearing surface with your fingers during reassembly; there is a risk of scratching the delicate surface, or of depositing particles of dirt on it.

9 As mentioned at the beginning of this Section, the bearing shells should be renewed as a matter of course during engine overhaul; to do otherwise is false economy.

15 Engine overhaul –
reassembly sequence

1 Before reassembly begins, ensure that

16.9 Fitting the oil control spreader ring

all necessary new parts have been obtained (particularly gaskets, and various bolts which must be renewed), and that all the tools required are available. Read through the entire procedure to familiarise yourself with the work involved, and to ensure that all items necessary for reassembly of the engine are to hand. In addition to all normal tools and materials, a thread-locking compound will be required. A tube of suitable sealant will be required to seal certain joint faces which are not fitted with gaskets.

2 In order to save time and avoid problems, engine reassembly can be carried out in the following order:

1.8 litre petrol engines

a) Piston rings (see Section 16).
b) Crankshaft (see Section 17).
c) Piston/connecting rod assemblies (see Section 18).
d) Oil pump (see Chapter 2A).
e) Sump (see Chapter 2A).
f) Flywheel (see Chapter 2A).
g) Cylinder head (see Chapter 2A).
h) Coolant pump (see Chapter 3).
i) Timing belt and sprockets (see Chapter 2A).
j) Inlet and exhaust manifolds (see Chapter 4A).

2.2 litre petrol engines

a) Piston rings (see Section 16).
b) Crankshaft (see Section 17).
c) Piston/connecting rod assemblies (see Section 18).
d) Sump (see Chapter 2B).
e) Flywheel/driveplate (see Chapter 2B).
f) Cylinder head (see Chapter 2B).
g) Coolant pump (see Chapter 3).
h) Timing chains and sprockets (see Chapter 2B).
i) Timing chain cover (see Chapter 2B).
j) Inlet and exhaust manifolds (see Chapter 4A).

Diesel engines

a) Piston rings (see Section 16).
b) Crankshaft (see Section 17).
c) Pistons/connecting rod assemblies (see Section 18).
d) Cylinder head (see Chapter 2C or 2D).
e) Oil pump (see Chapter 2C or 2D).
f) Sump (see Chapter 2C or 2D).
g) Flywheel/driveplate (see Chapter 2C or 2D).
h) Coolant pump (see Chapter 3).
i) Timing belt, sprockets, tensioner and idler pulleys (see Chapter 2C or 2D).
j) Inlet and exhaust manifolds (see Chapter 4B).

3 At this stage, all engine components should be absolutely clean and dry, with all faults repaired. The components should be laid out (or in individual containers) on a completely clean work surface.

16 Piston rings –
refitting

1 Before refitting the new piston rings, the ring end gaps must be checked as follows.

2 Lay out the piston/connecting rod assemblies and the new piston ring sets, so that the ring sets will be matched with the same piston and cylinder during the end gap measurement and subsequent engine reassembly.

3 Insert the top ring into the first cylinder, and push it down the bore slightly using the top of the piston. This will ensure that the ring remains square with the cylinder walls. Push the ring down into the bore until it is positioned 15 to 20 mm down from the top edge of the bore, then withdraw the piston.

4 Measure the end gap using feeler gauges, and compare the measurements with the figures given in the Specifications **(see illustration)**.

5 If the gap is too small (unlikely if genuine Vauxhall/Opel parts are used), it must be enlarged or the ring ends may contact each other during engine operation, causing serious damage. Ideally, new piston rings providing the correct end gap should be fitted, but as a last resort, the end gap can be increased by filing the ring ends very carefully with a fine file. Mount the file in a vice equipped with soft jaws, slip the ring over the file with the ends contacting the file face, and slowly move the ring to remove material from the ends – take care, as piston rings are sharp, and are easily broken.

6 With new piston rings, it is unlikely that the end gap will be too large. If they are too large, check that you have the correct rings for your engine and for the particular cylinder bore size.

7 Repeat the checking procedure for each ring in the first cylinder, and then for the rings in the remaining cylinders. Remember to keep rings, pistons and cylinders matched up.

8 Once the ring end gaps have been checked and if necessary corrected, the rings can be fitted to the pistons.

9 The oil control ring (lowest one on the piston) is composed of three sections, and should be installed first. Fit the lower steel ring, then the spreader ring, followed by the upper steel ring **(see illustration)**.

10 With the oil control ring components installed, the second (middle) ring can be fitted. It is usually stamped with a mark (TOP) which must face up, towards the top of the piston. **Note:** *Always follow the instructions supplied with the new piston ring sets – different manufacturers may specify different procedures. Do not mix up the top and middle rings, as they have different cross-sections.* Using two or three old feeler blades, as for removal of the old rings, carefully slip the ring into place in the middle groove.

11 Fit the top ring in the same manner, ensuring that, where applicable, the mark on the ring is facing up. If a stepped ring is being fitted, fit the ring with the smaller diameter of the step uppermost.

12 Repeat the procedure for the remaining pistons and rings.

17 Crankshaft – refitting

Note: *It is recommended that new main bearing shells are fitted regardless of the condition of the original ones.*

1 Refitting the crankshaft is the first step in the engine reassembly procedure. It is assumed at this point that the cylinder block, cylinder block lower casing (where applicable) and crankshaft have been cleaned, inspected and repaired or reconditioned as necessary.

2 Position the cylinder block with the sump/lower casing mating face uppermost.

3 Clean the bearing shells and the bearing recesses in both the cylinder block, cylinder block lower casing (where applicable) and the caps. If new shells are being fitted, ensure that all traces of the protective grease are cleaned off using paraffin. Wipe the shells dry with a clean lint-free cloth.

4 Note that the crankshaft endfloat is controlled by thrustwashers located on one of the main bearing shells. The thrustwashers may be separate or incorporated into, or attached to, the bearing shells themselves.

5 If the original bearing shells are being re-used, they must be refitted to their original locations in the block or caps.

6 Fit the upper main bearing shells in place in the cylinder block, ensuring that the tab on each shell engages in the notch in the cylinder block **(see illustration)**. Where separate thrustwashers are fitted, use a little grease to stick them to each side of their respective bearing upper location; ensure that the oilway grooves on each thrustwasher face outwards (away from the block).

1.8 litre petrol engines

7 Liberally lubricate each bearing shell in the cylinder block, and lower the crankshaft into position **(see illustration)**.

8 If necessary, seat the crankshaft using light taps from a soft-faced mallet on the crankshaft balance webs.

9 Fit the bearing shells into the bearing caps.

10 Lubricate the bearing shells in the bearing caps, and the crankshaft journals, then fit Nos 1, 2, 3 and 4 bearing caps, and tighten the new bolts as far as possible by hand **(see illustration)**.

11 Ensure No 5 bearing cap is clean and dry then fill the groove on each side of the cap with sealing compound (Vauxhall/Opel recommend the use of sealant, part No 90485251, available from your dealer) **(see illustration)**. Fit the bearing cap to the engine, ensuring it is fitted the correct way around, and tighten the new bolts as far as possible by hand.

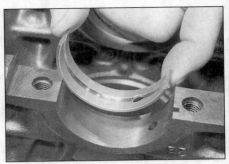

17.6 Fitting a main bearing shell to the cylinder block

12 Working in a diagonal sequence from the centre outwards, tighten the main bearing cap bolts to the specified Stage 1 torque setting **(see illustration)**.

13 Once all bolts are tightened to the specified Stage 1 torque, go around again and tighten all bolts through the specified Stage 2 angle then go around for once more and tighten all bolts through the specified Stage 3 angle. It is recommended that an angle-measuring gauge is used during the final stages of the tightening, to ensure accuracy **(see illustration)**. If a gauge is not available, use white paint to make alignment marks between the bolt head and cap prior to tightening; the marks can then be used to check that the bolt has been rotated through the correct angle.

14 Once all the bolts have been tightened,

17.10 Lubricate the crankshaft journals then refit bearing caps Nos 1 to 4 – 1.8 litre petrol engines

17.12 Tighten the bolts to the specified Stage 1 torque setting . . .

17.7 Lubricate the upper bearing shells with clean engine oil then fit the crankshaft – 1.8 litre petrol engines

inject more sealant down the grooves in the rear main bearing cap until sealant is seen to be escaping through the joints. Once you are sure the cap grooves are full of sealant, wipe off all excess sealant using a clean cloth.

15 Check that the crankshaft is free to rotate smoothly; if excessive pressure is required to turn the crankshaft, investigate the cause before proceeding further.

16 Check the crankshaft endfloat with reference to Section 10.

17 Refit/reconnect the piston connecting rod assemblies to the crankshaft as described in Section 18.

18 Referring to Part A of this Chapter, fit a new left-hand crankshaft oil seal, then refit the oil pump, sump, flywheel, cylinder head, timing belt sprocket(s) and fit a new timing belt.

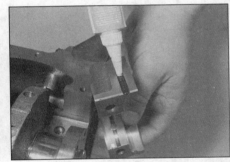

17.11 Fill the side grooves of No 5 bearing cap with sealant prior to refitting it to the engine – 1.8 litre petrol engines

17.13 . . . and then through the specified Stages 2 and 3 angles – 1.8 litre petrol engines

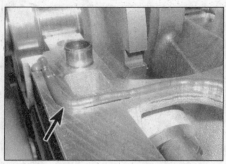

17.22 Apply a continuous bead of sealant (arrowed) to the groove in the cylinder block – 2.2 litre petrol engines

2.2 litre petrol engines

19 Liberally lubricate each bearing shell in the cylinder block, and lower the crankshaft into position.

20 If necessary, seat the crankshaft using light taps from a soft-faced mallet on the crankshaft balance webs.

21 Fit the bearing shells into the cylinder block lower casing.

22 Ensure that the cylinder block and lower casing mating surfaces are clean and dry, then apply a 2 to 5 mm diameter bead of sealant to the groove in the cylinder block **(see illustration)**. Vauxhall/Opel recommend the use of sealant, part No 90543772, available from your dealer.

23 Locate the lower casing over the crankshaft and onto the cylinder block.

24 Fit the twenty new M10 bolts and the ten M8 bolts and tighten the bolts as far as possible by hand.

25 Working in a diagonal sequence from the centre outwards, tighten the twenty M10 lower casing bolts to the specified Stage 1 torque setting.

26 Once all M10 bolts are tightened to the specified Stage 1 torque, go around again and tighten them through the specified Stage 2 angle then go around once more and tighten them through the specified Stage 3 angle. It is recommended that an angle-measuring gauge is used during the final stages of the tightening, to ensure accuracy **(see illustration)**. If a gauge is not available, use white paint to make alignment marks between the bolt head

18.2 Fit the bearing shells making sure their tabs are correctly located in the connecting rod/cap groove (arrowed)

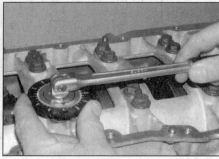

17.26 Tightening the cylinder block lower casing bolts through the specified angles – 2.2 litre petrol engines

and casing prior to tightening; the marks can then be used to check that the bolt has been rotated through the correct angle.

27 After tightening all the M10 bolts, tighten the M8 bolts to the specified torque, working in a diagonal sequence from the centre outwards.

28 Check that the crankshaft is free to rotate smoothly; if excessive pressure is required to turn the crankshaft, investigate the cause before proceeding further.

29 Check the crankshaft endfloat with reference to Section 10.

30 Refit/reconnect the piston connecting rod assemblies to the crankshaft as described in Section 18.

31 Referring to Part B of this Chapter, fit a new left-hand crankshaft oil seal, then refit the sump, flywheel/driveplate, cylinder head, and the timing chains and sprockets.

Diesel engines

32 Liberally lubricate each bearing shell in the cylinder block, and lower the crankshaft into position.

33 If necessary, seat the crankshaft using light taps from a soft-faced mallet on the crankshaft balance webs.

34 Fit the bearing shells into the bearing caps.

35 Lubricate the bearing shells in the bearing caps, and the crankshaft journals, then fit the caps ensuring they are fitted to their correct locations and the right way around. Fit and tighten the new bolts as far as possible by hand.

18.3 Lubricate the piston rings with clean engine oil

36 Working in a spiral pattern from the centre outwards, tighten the main bearing cap bolts to the specified Stage 1 torque setting.

37 Once all bolts are tightened to the specified Stage 1 torque, go around again and tighten all bolts through the specified Stage 2 angle. It is recommended that an angle-measuring gauge is used during the final stages of the tightening, to ensure accuracy. If a gauge is not available, use white paint to make alignment marks between the bolt head and cap prior to tightening; the marks can then be used to check that the bolt has been rotated through the correct angle.

38 Check that the crankshaft is free to rotate smoothly; if excessive pressure is required to turn the crankshaft, investigate the cause before proceeding further.

39 Check the crankshaft endfloat with reference to Section 10.

40 Refit/reconnect the piston connecting rod assemblies to the crankshaft as described in Section 18.

41 Referring to Part C or D of this Chapter, fit a new left-hand crankshaft oil seal/housing, then refit the oil pump, sump, flywheel/driveplate, cylinder head, timing belt sprocket(s) and fit a new timing belt.

18 Pistons/connecting rods – refitting

Note: *It is recommended that new big-end bearing shells are fitted regardless of the condition of the original ones.*

1 Clean the backs of the big-end bearing shells and the recesses in the connecting rods and big-end caps. If new shells are being fitted, ensure that all traces of the protective grease are cleaned off using paraffin. Wipe the shells, caps and connecting rods dry with a lint-free cloth.

2 Press the bearing shells into their locations, ensuring that the tab on each shell engages in the notch in the connecting rod and cap **(see illustration)**. If there is no tab on the bearing shell (and no notch in the rod or cap) position the shell equidistant from each side of the rod and cap. If the original bearing shells are being used ensure they are refitted in their original locations.

3 Lubricate the bores, the pistons and piston rings then lay out each piston/connecting rod assembly in its respective position **(see illustration)**.

Petrol engines

4 Lubricate No 1 piston and piston rings, and check that the ring gaps are correctly positioned. The gaps in the upper and lower steel rings of the oil control ring should be offset by 25 to 50 mm to the right and left of the spreader ring gap. The two upper compression ring gaps should be offset by 180° to each other **(see illustration)**.

5 Fit a ring compressor to No 1 piston, then

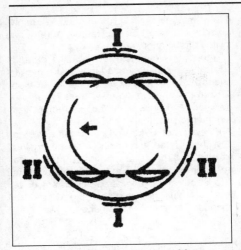

18.4 Piston ring end gap positions – petrol engines

I   Top and second compression rings
II Oil control ring side rails

insert the piston and connecting rod into the cylinder bore so that the base of the compressor stands on the block. With the crankshaft big-end bearing journal positioned at its lowest point, tap the piston carefully into the cylinder bore with the wooden handle of a hammer, and at the same time guide the connecting rod onto the bearing journal. Note that the arrow on the piston crown must point towards the timing chain/belt end of the engine **(see illustrations)**.

6 Liberally lubricate the bearing journals and bearing shells, and fit the bearing cap in its original location (the lug on the bearing cap base should be facing the flywheel/driveplate end of the engine) **(see illustration)**.

7 Screw in the new bearing cap retaining bolts, and tighten both bolts to the specified Stage 1 torque setting then tighten them

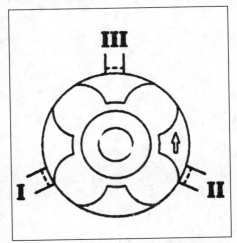

18.11 Piston ring end gap positions – diesel engines

I   Top compression ring
II   Second compression ring
III Oil control ring

18.5a Ensure the piston ring end gaps are correctly spaced then fit the ring compressor – petrol engines

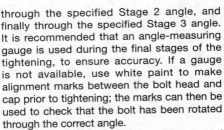

18.5c Tap the piston gently into the bore using handle of a hammer – petrol engines

through the specified Stage 2 angle, and finally through the specified Stage 3 angle. It is recommended that an angle-measuring gauge is used during the final stages of the tightening, to ensure accuracy. If a gauge is not available, use white paint to make alignment marks between the bolt head and cap prior to tightening; the marks can then be used to check that the bolt has been rotated through the correct angle.

8 Refit the remaining three piston and connecting rod assemblies in the same way.

9 Rotate the crankshaft, and check that it turns freely, with no signs of binding or tight spots.

10 Refit the oil pump pick-up/strainer, sump and the cylinder head as described in Part A or B (as applicable) of this Chapter.

Diesel engines

11 Lubricate No 1 piston and piston rings, and space the ring gaps uniformly around the piston at 120° intervals **(see illustration)**.

12 Fit a ring compressor to No 1 piston, then insert the piston and connecting rod into the cylinder bore so that the base of the compressor stands on the block. Ensure that the piston/connecting rod assembly is positioned with the cut-out on the piston skirt on the same side as the the oil spray jet, and the lugs on the cap and rod are be toward the timing belt end of the engine **(see illustration)**.

13 With the crankshaft big-end bearing journal positioned at its lowest point, tap the

18.5b Ensuring the arrow on the piston crown (circled) is pointing towards the timing belt end of the engine – petrol engines

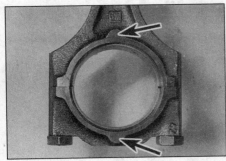

18.6 Make sure the lug (arrowed) is facing the flywheel/driveplate end of the engine – petrol engines

piston carefully into the cylinder bore with the wooden handle of a hammer, and at the same time guide the connecting rod onto the bearing journal.

14 Liberally lubricate the bearing journals and bearing shells, and fit the bearing cap in its original location.

15 Screw in the new bearing cap retaining bolts, and tighten both bolts to the specified Stage 1 torque setting then tighten them

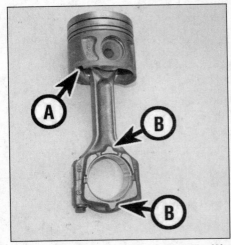

18.12 The cut-out on the piston skirt (A) must be on the same side as the oil spray jet, and the lugs on the cap and rod (B) must be toward the timing belt end of the engine – diesel engines

through the specified Stage 2 angle. It is recommended that an angle-measuring gauge is used during the final stages of the tightening, to ensure accuracy. If a gauge is not available, use white paint to make alignment marks between the bolt head and cap prior to tightening; the marks can then be used to check that the bolt has been rotated through the correct angle.

16 Refit the remaining three piston and connecting rod assemblies in the same way.

17 Rotate the crankshaft, and check that it turns freely, with no signs of binding or tight spots.

18 Refit the oil pump pick-up/strainer, sump and the cylinder head as described in Part C or D (as applicable) of this Chapter.

19 Engine – initial start-up after overhaul

1 With the engine refitted in the vehicle, double-check the engine oil and coolant levels. Make a final check that everything has been reconnected, and that there are no tools or rags left in the engine compartment.

2 Start the engine, noting that this may take a little longer than usual. Make sure that the oil pressure warning light goes out.

3 While the engine is idling, check for fuel, water and oil leaks. Don't be alarmed if there are some odd smells and smoke from parts getting hot and burning off oil deposits.

4 Assuming all is well, run the engine until it reaches normal operating temperature, then switch off the engine.

5 After a few minutes, recheck the oil and coolant levels as described in *Weekly checks*, and top-up as necessary.

6 Note that there is no need to retighten the cylinder head bolts once the engine has first run after reassembly.

7 If new pistons, rings or crankshaft bearings have been fitted, the engine must be treated as new, and run-in for the first 600 miles. Do not operate the engine at full-throttle, or allow it to labour at low engine speeds in any gear. It is recommended that the oil and filter be changed at the end of this period.

Chapter 3
Cooling, heating and air conditioning systems

Contents

Degrees of difficulty

Easy, suitable for novice with little experience	**Fairly easy,** suitable for beginner with some experience	**Fairly difficult,** suitable for competent DIY mechanic	**Difficult,** suitable for experienced DIY mechanic	**Very difficult,** suitable for expert DIY or professional

Specifications

Thermostat
Opening temperatures:
  Petrol engines:
    1.8 litre engines . . . . 92°C
    2.2 litre engines . . . . 82°C
  Diesel engines . . . . 90°C

Air conditioning compressor
Lubricant capacity:
  Petrol engines . . . . 120 cc
  Diesel engines . . . . 135 cc
Lubricant type (synthetic PAG fluid) . . . . Vauxhall part number 90 509 933/19 49 873

Torque wrench settings

	Nm	lbf ft
Petrol engine models		
Air conditioning compressor mounting bolts	20	15
Air conditioning refrigerant pipe block connections	20	15
Coolant pump retaining bolts:		
1.8 litre engines	8	6
2.2 litre engines	23	17
Coolant pump pulley bolts (1.8 litre Z18XER engines)	20	15
Coolant pump sprocket bolts (2.2 litre engines)	8	6
Coolant temperature sensor	20	15
Radiator mounting brackets to subframe	15	11
Thermostat housing/cover:		
1.8 litre engines:		
Z18XE engines	20	15
Z18XER engines	8	6
2.2 litre engines	8	6
Diesel engine models		
Air conditioning compressor mounting bolts	20	15
Air conditioning refrigerant pipe block connections	20	15
Coolant pump retaining bolts	25	18
Coolant temperature sensor	20	15
Radiator mounting brackets to subframe	15	11
Thermostat housing/cover	25	18

1 General information and precautions

The cooling system is of pressurised type, comprising a coolant pump, a crossflow radiator, electric cooling fan, and thermostat.

The coolant pump is driven by the auxiliary drivebelt on 1.8 litre Z18XER petrol engines. On 2.2 litre petrol engines, the coolant pump is driven by the balancer shaft drive chain. On diesel engines and 1.8 litre Z18XE petrol engines the coolant pump is driven by the timing belt.

The system functions as follows. Cold coolant from the radiator passes through the bottom hose to the coolant pump, where it is pumped around the cylinder block, head passages and heater matrix. After cooling the cylinder bores, combustion surfaces and valve seats, the coolant reaches the underside of the thermostat, which is initially closed. The coolant passes through the heater, and is returned to the coolant pump.

When the engine is cold, the coolant circulates only through the cylinder block, cylinder head and heater. When the coolant reaches a predetermined temperature, the thermostat opens and the coolant also passes through to the radiator. As the coolant circulates through the radiator, it is cooled by the inrush of air when the car is in forward motion. Airflow is supplemented by the action of the electric cooling fan when necessary. Once the coolant has passed through the radiator, and has cooled, the cycle is repeated.

On 1.8 litre Z18XER petrol engines, an electrically-assisted thermostat is fitted. Engine coolant temperature is monitored by the engine management system electronic control unit, via the coolant temperature sensor. In conjunction with information received from various other engine sensors, the thermostat opening temperature can be controlled according to engine speed and load. During normal engine operation the thermostat operates conventionally. Under conditions of high engine speed and load, an electric heating element within the thermostat is energised, to cause the thermostat to open at a lower temperature (typically 90°).

The electric cooling fan, mounted on the rear of the radiator, is controlled by the engine management system electronic control unit, in conjunction with a cooling fan module. At a predetermined coolant temperature, the fan is actuated. An auxiliary electric cooling fan is fitted to models with air conditioning.

An expansion tank is fitted to the left-hand side of the engine compartment to accommodate expansion of the coolant when hot.

⚠ **Warning: Do not attempt to remove the expansion tank filler cap, or disturb any part of the cooling system, while the engine is hot; there is a high risk of scalding. If the cap must be** *removed before the engine and radiator have fully cooled (even though this is not recommended) the pressure in the cooling system must first be relieved. Cover the cap with a thick layer of cloth, to avoid scalding, and slowly unscrew the filler cap until a hissing sound can be heard. When the hissing has stopped, indicating that the pressure has reduced, slowly unscrew the filler cap until it can be removed; if more hissing sounds are heard, wait until they have stopped before unscrewing the cap completely. At all times, keep well away from the filler cap opening.*

• Do not allow antifreeze to come into contact with the skin, or with the painted surfaces of the vehicle. Rinse off spills immediately, with plenty of water. Never leave antifreeze lying around in an open container, or in a puddle on the driveway or garage floor. Children and pets are attracted by its sweet smell, but antifreeze can be fatal if ingested.

• If the engine is hot, the electric cooling fan may start rotating even if the engine is not running; be careful to keep hands, hair and loose clothing well clear when working in the engine compartment.

• Refer to Section 10 for precautions to be observed when working on models equipped with air conditioning.

2 Cooling system hoses – disconnection and renewal

Note: *Refer to the warnings given in Section 1 of this Chapter before proceeding. Do not attempt to disconnect any hose while the system is still hot.*

1 If the checks described in Chapter 1A or 1B reveal a faulty hose, it must be renewed as follows.

2 First drain the cooling system (see Chapter 1A or 1B). If the coolant is not due for renewal, it may be re-used if it is collected in a clean container.

3 Before disconnecting a hose, first note its routing in the engine compartment, and whether it is secured by any additional retaining clips or cable-ties. Use a pair of pliers to release the clamp-type clips, or a screwdriver to slacken the screw-type clips,

3.9 Pull out the locking bar and disconnect the wiring harness connector from the cooling fan module

then move the clips along the hose, clear of the relevant inlet/outlet union. Carefully work the hose free.

4 Depending on engine, some of the hose attachments may be of the quick-release type. Where this type of hose is encountered, lift the ends of the wire retaining clip, to spread the clip, then withdraw the hose from the inlet/outlet union.

5 Note that the radiator inlet and outlet unions are fragile; do not use excessive force when attempting to remove the hoses. If a hose proves to be difficult to remove, try to release it by rotating the hose ends before attempting to free it.

6 When fitting a hose, first slide the clips onto the hose, then work the hose into position. If clamp-type clips were originally fitted, it is a good idea to use screw-type clips when refitting the hose. If the hose is stiff, use a little soapy water (washing-up liquid is ideal) as a lubricant, or soften the hose by soaking it in hot water.

7 Work the hose into position, checking that it is correctly routed and secured. Slide each clip along the hose until it passes over the flared end of the relevant inlet/outlet union, before tightening the clips securely.

8 Refill the cooling system with reference to Chapter 1A or 1B.

9 Check thoroughly for leaks as soon as possible after disturbing any part of the cooling system.

3 Radiator – removal, inspection and refitting

Note: *The radiator is removed from below, complete with the cooling fan assembly.*

Removal

Petrol engine models

1 Disconnect the battery negative terminal (refer to *Disconnecting the battery* in the Reference Chapter).

2 Remove the plastic cover from the top of the engine

3 Apply the handbrake, then jack up the front of the vehicle and support it on axle stands (see *Jacking and vehicle support*).

4 Remove the front bumper as described in Chapter 11.

5 Drain the cooling system as described in Chapter 1A.

6 Remove the air cleaner assembly and air intake duct as described in Chapter 4A.

7 Release the retaining clips and disconnect the top hose and expansion tank hose from the radiator.

8 Where fitted, disconnect the wiring connector from the coolant temperature sensor located on the lower left-hand side of the radiator.

9 Pull out the locking bar and disconnect the wiring harness connector from the cooling fan module at the top of the fan housing (**see illustration**). Free the wiring harness from the cable-ties.

3.10a Slacken the bolt (arrowed) securing the radiator left-hand . . .

3.10b . . . and right-hand mounting brackets to the subframe

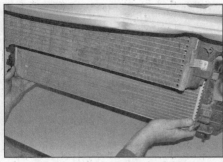

3.16 Carefully lower the radiator down and out from under the car

10 Slacken (but do not remove) the two bolts securing the radiator left-hand and right-hand mounting brackets to the subframe **(see illustrations)**.

11 Release the radiator upper rubber mounting bushes on each side from their guides, and carefully move the top of the radiator forward.

12 Release the clamp and disconnect the bottom hose from the radiator.

13 On models with air conditioning, undo the bolt each side securing the condenser upper mounting brackets to the radiator. Carefully lift up or remove the plastic panels on each side of the radiator for improved access, if necessary. Suitably secure the condenser to the upper body panel using cable-ties or similar, to retain it in place when the radiator is removed.

14 On models with automatic transmission, detach the protective ring (where fitted) over the fluid cooler pipe unions at the radiator. Using a small screwdriver, release the quick-release fitting retaining lugs and disconnect the fitting from the radiator. Suitably cover the open unions after disconnection.

15 Check that all hoses, and connections are released from the radiator in the engine compartment, then engage the help of an assistant to support the radiator.

16 Remove the two bolts securing the radiator left-hand and right-hand mounting brackets to the subframe and carefully lower the radiator down and out from under the car **(see illustration)**. Disengage the condenser lower mounting lugs from the radiator as the radiator is lowered.

Diesel engine models

17 Disconnect the battery negative terminal (refer to *Disconnecting the battery* in the Reference Chapter).

18 Remove the plastic cover from the top of the engine.

19 Apply the handbrake, then jack up the front of the vehicle and support it on axle stands (see *Jacking and vehicle support*). Undo the ten bolts and remove the engine undertray.

20 Remove the front bumper as described in Chapter 11.

21 Remove the headlights as described in Chapter 12.

3.24 Release the retaining clip (arrowed) and disconnect the expansion tank hose from the top of the radiator

22 Drain the cooling system as described in Chapter 1B.

23 Remove the air cleaner assembly and air intake duct as described in Chapter 4B.

24 Release the retaining clip and disconnect the expansion tank hose from the top of the radiator **(see illustration)**.

25 Release the two retaining clips and disconnect the top hose from the radiator and thermostat housing.

26 Pull out the locking bar and disconnect the wiring harness connector from the cooling fan module at the top of the fan housing **(see illustration 3.9)**. Free the wiring harness from the cable-ties.

27 Slacken the two retaining clips and remove the upper charge air hose from the turbo-charger, and intercooler right-hand charge air pipe.

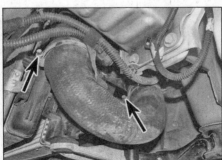

3.30a Slacken the retaining clips (arrowed) and remove the left-hand . . .

3.29 Undo the intercooler left-hand charge air pipe upper retaining bolt (arrowed)

28 Slacken the two retaining clips and disconnect the upper charge air hose from the throttle body/housing, and intercooler left-hand charge air pipe.

29 Undo the intercooler left-hand charge air pipe upper retaining bolt **(see illustration)**.

30 Slacken the retaining clips and remove the left-hand and right-hand lower charge air hoses from the intercooler and charge air pipes **(see illustrations)**.

31 Slacken (but do not remove) the two bolts securing the radiator left-hand and right-hand mounting brackets to the subframe **(see illustrations 3.10a and 3.10b)**.

32 Release the radiator upper rubber mounting bushes on each side from their guides, and carefully move the top of the radiator forward.

33 Undo the bolt securing the intercooler

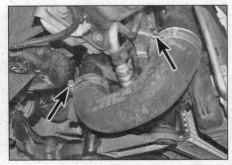

3.30b . . . and right-hand lower charge air hoses from the intercooler and charge air pipes

3.33 Undo the bolt (arrowed) securing the intercooler right-hand charge air pipe upper mounting to the radiator

3.34a Undo the bolt (arrowed) securing the intercooler left-hand . . .

3.34b . . . and right-hand charge air pipe lower moustings to the radiator

right-hand charge air pipe upper mounting to the radiator **(see illustration)**.

34 Undo the bolt each side securing the intercooler left-hand and right-hand charge air pipe lower mountings to the radiator **(see illustrations)**.

35 Release the clamp and disconnect the bottom hose from the radiator.

36 On models with air conditioning, undo the two bolts securing the receiver-dryer to the right-hand side of the radiator **(see illustration)**.

37 Undo the bolt each side securing the intercooler upper mounting brackets to the radiator **(see illustration)**. Carefully lift up or remove the plastic panels on each side of the radiator for improved access, if necessary. Suitably secure the intercooler to the upper body panel using cable-ties or similar, to retain it in place when the radiator is removed.

38 On models with automatic transmission, detach the protective ring (where fitted) over the fluid cooler pipe unions at the radiator. Using a small screwdriver, release the quick-release fitting retaining lugs and disconnect the fitting from the radiator. Suitably cover the open unions after disconnection.

39 Check that all hoses, and connections are released from the radiator in the engine compartment, then engage the help of an assistant to support the radiator.

40 Remove the two bolts securing the radiator left-hand and right-hand mounting brackets to the subframe and carefully lower the radiator down and out from under the car **(see illustration 3.16)**. Disengage the

intercooler lower mounting lugs from the radiator as the radiator is lowered.

Inspection

41 If the radiator has been removed due to suspected blockage, reverse-flush it as described in Chapter 1A or 1B.

42 Clean dirt and debris from the radiator fins, using an airline (in which case, wear eye protection) or a soft brush.
Caution: Be careful, as the fins are easily damaged, and are sharp.

43 If necessary, a radiator specialist can perform a 'flow test' on the radiator, to establish whether an internal blockage exists.

44 A leaking radiator must be referred to a specialist for permanent repair. Do not attempt to weld or solder a leaking radiator.

45 In an emergency, minor leaks from the radiator can be cured by using a suitable radiator sealant (in accordance with its manufacturer's instructions) with the radiator fitted in the vehicle.

46 Inspect the radiator mounting rubbers, and renew them if necessary.

Refitting

47 Refitting is a reversal of removal, bearing in mind the following points.

a) Ensure that the intercooler or condenser (as applicable) lower mountings are correctly engaged with the radiator when refitting.

b) Ensure that all hoses are correctly reconnected, and their retaining clips securely tightened.

c) On completion, refill the cooling system as described in Chapter 1A or 1B.

d) On models with automatic transmission, check and if necessary top-up the automatic transmission fluid level with reference to the 'Automatic transmission fluid – draining and refilling' procedures contained in Chapter 7B.

4 Thermostat – removal and refitting

Removal

1.8 litre Z18XE petrol engine models

1 The thermostat is located on the front right-hand side of the cylinder head, and is integral with its housing.

2 Disconnect the battery negative terminal (refer to *Disconnecting the battery* in the Reference Chapter).

3 Apply the handbrake, then jack up the front of the vehicle and support it on axle stands (see *Jacking and vehicle support*). Remove the plastic cover from the top of the engine.

4 Drain the cooling system as described in Chapter 1A.

5 Loosen the clips and disconnect the top hose and throttle housing coolant hose from the thermostat housing.

6 Disconnect the wiring connector from the coolant temperature sensor on the housing.

7 Unbolt and remove the housing from the cylinder head, then remove the gasket. Thoroughly clean the contact surfaces of the housing and cylinder head.

1.8 litre Z18XER petrol engine models

8 The thermostat is located in a housing attached to the left-hand side of the cylinder head, and is integral with the housing cover.

9 Disconnect the battery negative terminal (refer to *Disconnecting the battery* in the Reference Chapter).

10 Apply the handbrake, then jack up the front of the vehicle and support it on axle stands (see *Jacking and vehicle support*).

11 Drain the cooling system as described in Chapter 1A.

12 Undo the retaining nut and detach the

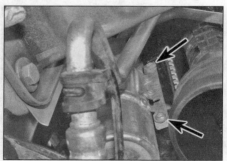

3.36 On models with air conditioning, undo the two bolts (arrowed) securing the receiver-dryer to the radiator

3.37 Undo the bolt (arrowed) each side securing the intercooler upper mounting brackets to the radiator

wiring harness bracket from the thermostat housing.

13 Disconnect the thermostat wiring connector.

14 Release the clips and disconnect the radiator hose from the thermostat cover.

15 Unscrew the four bolts and remove the thermostat cover from the housing.

16 Thoroughly clean the housing and cover contact surfaces.

2.2 litre petrol engine models

17 The thermostat is located on the left-hand rear of the cylinder head, over the transmission.

18 Disconnect the battery negative terminal (refer to *Disconnecting the battery* in the Reference Chapter).

19 Apply the handbrake, then jack up the front of the vehicle and support it on axle stands (see *Jacking and vehicle support*).

20 Drain the cooling system as described in Chapter 1A.

21 Release the clip and disconnect the top hose from the thermostat cover.

22 Unscrew the bolts and remove the cover from the thermostat housing **(see illustration)**.

23 Lift the thermostat from the housing **(see illustration)**. Remove the seal from the rim of the thermostat and discard it. Obtain a new one. Clean the contact surfaces of the cover and housing.

Diesel engine models

24 The thermostat is located on the left-hand end of the cylinder head, and is integral with the housing.

25 Remove the plastic cover over the top of the engine.

26 Remove the battery and battery box as described in Chapter 5A.

27 Apply the handbrake, then jack up the front of the vehicle and support it on axle stands (see *Jacking and vehicle support*).

28 Drain the cooling system as described in Chapter 1B.

29 Release the two retaining clips and disconnect the charge air hose from the throttle housing, and intercooler charge air pipe **(see illustration)**.

30 Release the clips and disconnect the hoses from the thermostat housing.

31 Disconnect the coolant temperature sensor wiring connector.

32 Unscrew the nut and release the coolant pipes from the stud at the base of the thermostat housing.

33 Unbolt the thermostat housing from the cylinder head. Clean away all traces of gasket from the housing and cylinder head.

Refitting

34 Refitting is a reversal of removal, but fit a new gasket/seal (where applicable) and tighten the mounting bolts to the specified torque. Refill the cooling system as described in the relevant Part of Chapter 1.

4.22 Removing the thermostat housing cover

5 Electric cooling fan – removal and refitting

> *Warning: If the engine is hot, the cooling fan may start up at any time. Take extra precautions when working in the vicinity of the fan.*

Removal

1.8 litre Z18XE petrol engine models

1 Disconnect the battery negative terminal (refer to *Disconnecting the battery* in the Reference Chapter).

2 Remove the plastic cover over the top of the engine.

3 Unclip the radiator hose and detach the plastic panel at the front of the battery box.

4 Pull out the locking bar and disconnect the wiring harness connector from the cooling fan module at the side of the fan housing. Free the wiring harness from the cable-ties.

5 Firmly apply the handbrake, then jack up the front of the car and support it securely on axle stands (see *Jacking and vehicle support*).

6 Release the four retaining clips and detach the front bumper lower panel from the subframe.

7 Unscrew the two bolts securing the fan housing to the radiator; one at each upper corner of the housing.

8 Carefully lift the fan housing upwards to disengage it from the lower guides on the radiator, and remove the housing from the engine compartment.

9 To remove the fan motor, disconnect the wiring connector and unclip the wiring harness from the fan housing. Undo the three retaining bolts and remove the fan from the housing.

10 To remove the cooling fan module, undo the retaining screw and unclip the unit from the fan housing.

1.8 litre Z18XER petrol engine models

11 Disconnect the battery negative terminal (refer to *Disconnecting the battery* in the Reference Chapter).

12 Remove the air cleaner assembly as described in Chapter 4A.

13 Undo the bolt securing the resonator to the front upper crossmember. Depress the

4.23 Removing the thermostat from the housing

three retaining lugs and push the resonator rearward. Using a screwdriver, release the locking clip and remove the resonator.

14 Release the retaining clips and detach the coolant hoses from the fan housing.

15 Disconnect the cooling fan wiring harness at the connector on the side of the fan housing.

16 Unscrew the two bolts securing the fan housing to the radiator; one at each upper corner of the housing.

17 Carefully lift the fan housing upwards to disengage it from the lower guides on the radiator, and remove the housing from the engine compartment.

18 To remove the fan motor, undo the bolt securing the wiring connector to the fan housing, then unclip the wiring. Undo the three retaining bolts and remove the fan from the housing.

2.2 litre petrol engine models

19 Remove the battery and battery box as described in Chapter 5A.

20 Undo the retaining bolt and unclip the air intake resonator from above the radiator.

21 Pull out the locking bar and disconnect the wiring harness connector from the cooling fan module at the top of the fan housing. Free the wiring harness from the cable-ties.

22 Unscrew the two bolts securing the fan housing to the radiator; one at each upper corner of the housing.

23 Carefully lift the fan housing upwards to disengage it from the lower guides on the radiator, and remove the housing from the engine compartment.

4.29 Disconnect the charge air hose from the throttle housing, and intercooler charge air pipe

5.24 Undo the three retaining bolts (arrowed) and remove the fan from the housing

5.27 Unscrew the two retaining bolts (arrowed) and lift the fan housing from the lower guides on the radiator

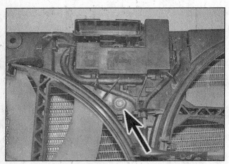

5.29 Undo the retaining screw (arrowed) and unclip the cooling fan module from the fan housing

24 To remove the fan motor(s), disconnect the wiring connector at the relevant motor and unclip the wiring harness from the fan housing. Undo the three retaining bolts and remove the fan from the housing **(see illustration)**.
25 To remove the cooling fan module, undo the retaining screw and unclip the unit from the fan housing.

Diesel engine models

26 Remove the radiator as described in Section 3.
27 Unscrew the two retaining bolts and lift

the fan housing from the lower guides on the radiator **(see illustration)**.
28 To remove the fan motor(s), disconnect the wiring connector at the relevant motor and unclip the wiring harness from the fan housing. Undo the three retaining bolts and remove the fan from the housing **(see illustration 5.24)**.
29 To remove the cooling fan module, undo the retaining screw and unclip the unit from the fan housing **(see illustration)**.

Refitting

30 Refitting is a reversal of removal.

6 Coolant temperature sensor – testing, removal and refitting

Testing

1 Testing of the coolant temperature sensor must be entrusted to a Vauxhall/Opel dealer, who will have the necessary specialist diagnostic equipment.

Removal

2 Partially drain the cooling system with reference to Chapter 1A or 1B. Alternatively, it is possible to change the sensor quickly with

minimal loss of coolant by first releasing any pressure from the cooling system. With the engine cold, temporarily remove the expansion tank cap.
3 Where fitted, remove the plastic cover over the top of the engine.

1.8 litre Z18XE petrol engine models

4 The coolant temperature sensor is located on the thermostat housing on the right-hand end of the cylinder head.
5 Disconnect the wiring connector, then unscrew and remove the sensor from the thermostat housing. If the cooling system has not been drained, either insert the new sensor or fit a blanking plug to prevent further loss of coolant.

1.8 litre Z18XER petrol engine models

6 The coolant temperature sensor is located in the thermostat housing at the left-hand end of the cylinder head **(see illustration)**.
7 Disconnect the wiring connector, then unlock the retaining clamp and remove the sensor from the thermostat housing. If the cooling system has not been drained, either insert the new sensor or fit a blanking plug to prevent further loss of coolant.

2.2 litre petrol engine models

8 The coolant temperature sensor is located on the thermostat housing at the left-hand end of the cylinder head **(see illustration)**.
9 Disconnect the wiring connector, then unscrew and remove the sensor from the thermostat housing. If the cooling system has not been drained, either insert the new sensor or fit a blanking plug to prevent further loss of coolant.

Diesel engine models

10 The coolant temperature sensor is located on the thermostat housing on the left-hand end of the cylinder head **(see illustration)**.
11 Slacken the two retaining clips and disconnect the upper charge air hose from the throttle housing, and intercooler left-hand charge air pipe.

6.6 Coolant temperature sensor location (arrowed) – 1.8 litre Z18XER petrol engine models

6.8 Coolant temperature sensor located on the thermostat housing – 2.2 litre petrol engine models

12 Disconnect the wiring connector, then unscrew and remove the sensor from the thermostat housing. If the cooling system has not been drained, either insert the new sensor or fit a blanking plug to prevent further loss of coolant.

Refitting

13 Fit the new sensor using a reversal of the removal procedure, but tighten the sensor to the specified torque and refill the cooling system with reference to Chapter 1A or 1B.

7 Coolant pump – removal and refitting

Removal

1 Disconnect the battery negative terminal (refer to *Disconnecting the battery* in the Reference Chapter).
2 Where fitted, remove the plastic cover over the top of the engine.

1.8 litre Z18XE petrol engine models

3 Drain the cooling system as described in Chapter 1A.
4 Remove the timing belt as described in Chapter 2A. **Note:** *The timing belt must not come into contact with coolant.*
5 Unscrew and remove the three coolant pump securing bolts **(see illustration)**.
6 Withdraw the coolant pump from the cylinder block, noting that it may be necessary to tap the pump lightly with a soft-faced mallet to free it from the cylinder block.
7 Recover the pump sealing ring, and discard it; a new one must be used on refitting.
8 Note that it is not possible to overhaul the pump. If it is faulty, the unit must be renewed complete.

1.8 litre Z18XER petrol engine models

9 Remove the air cleaner assembly and air intake ducts as described in Chapter 4A.
10 Slacken the three coolant pump pulley retaining bolts.
11 Remove the auxiliary drivebelt as described in Chapter 1A.
12 Drain the cooling system as described in Chapter 1A.
13 Unscrew the previously-slackened coolant pump pulley retaining bolts and remove the pulley from the pump flange.
14 Undo the five retaining bolts and remove the pump from the oil pump housing.
15 Note that it is not possible to overhaul the pump. If it is faulty, the unit must be renewed complete.

2.2 litre petrol engine models

16 Remove the air cleaner assembly and air intake ducts as described in Chapter 4A.
17 Apply the handbrake, then jack up the front of the vehicle and support it on axle stands (see *Jacking and vehicle support*).

18 Disconnect the two oxygen sensor wiring connectors at the right-hand end of the cylinder head. Unclip the wiring harness from the support bracket.
19 Undo the nut and bolt and remove the right-hand engine lifting eye from the cylinder head.
20 Unbolt the heat shield from the exhaust manifold.
21 Drain the cooling system as described in Chapter 1A. Refit and tighten the coolant pump drain plug on completion.
22 Loosen the clip and disconnect the hose from the thermostat housing cover. Also disconnect the heater hoses from the thermostat housing and heater matrix. Remove the hoses.
23 Unclip the coolant temperature sensor wiring from the thermostat housing cover, then disconnect the wiring from the sensor.
24 Unscrew and remove the coolant temperature sensor from the thermostat housing.
25 Unscrew the bolts and remove the thermostat housing and coolant pipe from the cylinder block and coolant pump. Note the lower bolt is a stud bolt, and note the location of the O-ring seal in the pump housing **(see illustrations)**.
26 Unbolt the coolant pump drive sprocket access cover from the timing cover on the right-hand side of the engine **(see illustration)**.
27 Vauxhall/Opel technicians use a special tool (KM-J-43651) to hold the sprocket

6.10 Coolant temperature sensor (arrowed) located on the thermostat housing – diesel engine models

stationary while the coolant pump is being removed. The tool consists of a flanged tube which is bolted to the sprocket and also to the timing housing, with holes to allow removal of the coolant pump bolts. It is possible to fabricate a simple home-made tool from a length of flat metal bar using two threaded rods screwed into the sprocket. First unscrew one of the pump mounting bolts from the sprocket taking care not to drop it into the timing case, then fit the tool into position to hold the sprocket. With the tool in position, unscrew the two remaining bolts from the sprocket **(see illustrations)**. To prevent losing any of the bolts, temporarily place a cloth rag beneath the sprocket in the timing case.

7.5 Unscrew and remove the three coolant pump securing bolts – 1.8 litre Z18XE petrol engine models

7.25a Thermostat housing retaining bolts – 2.2 litre petrol engine models

7.25b Removing the coolant pipe from the pump housing – 2.2 litre petrol engine models

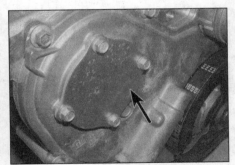

7.26 Coolant pump drive sprocket access cover (arrowed) – 2.2 litre petrol engine models

7.27a Home-made tool holding the coolant pump drive sprocket stationary – 2.2 litre petrol engine models

7.27b Unscrew the two remaining bolts securing the coolant pump to the sprocket – 2.2 litre petrol engine models

28 Unscrew the pump mounting bolts noting that if you are using the Vauxhall/Opel tool, one of the bolts cannot be removed completely. There are two bolts at the front and two at the rear. Remove the pump from the timing housing and withdraw upwards from the engine **(see illustrations)**.
29 Recover the pump sealing ring, and discard it; a new one must be used on refitting.
30 Note that it is not possible to overhaul the pump. If it is faulty, the unit must be renewed complete.

Diesel engine models

31 Drain the cooling system as described in Chapter 1B.
32 Remove the timing belt as described in Chapter 2C or 2D as applicable. **Note:** *The timing belt must not come into contact with coolant.*
33 Unscrew and remove the three coolant pump securing bolts **(see illustration)**.
34 Withdraw the coolant pump from the cylinder block, noting that it may be necessary to tap the pump lightly with a soft-faced mallet to free it from the cylinder block **(see illustration)**.

35 Recover the pump sealing ring, and discard it; a new one must be used on refitting.
36 Note that it is not possible to overhaul the pump. If it is faulty, the unit must be renewed complete.

Refitting

1.8 litre Z18XE petrol engine models

37 Ensure that the pump and cylinder block mating surfaces are clean and dry, and apply a smear of silicone grease to the pump mating surface in the cylinder block.

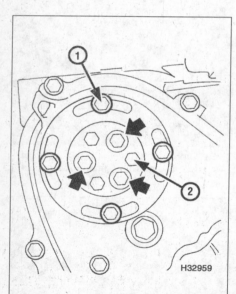

7.27c Vauxhall tool KM-J-43651 retaining the coolant pump sprocket while the pump is being removed – 2.2 litre petrol engine models
1 Bolts holding the tool to the timing housing
2 Bolts holding the sprocket to the tool
Arrows indicate pump mounting bolts

7.28a Unscrew the rear bolts . . .

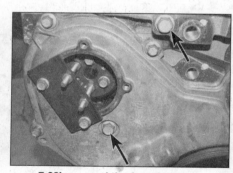

7.28b . . . and the front bolts . . .

7.28c . . . and withdraw the coolant pump from the timing housing – 2.2 litre petrol engine models

7.33 Undo the coolant pump retaining bolts (arrowed) . . .

7.34 . . . and remove the pump from the cylinder head – diesel engine models

9.1a Carefully release the facia decorative strip using a plastic spatula or similar . . .

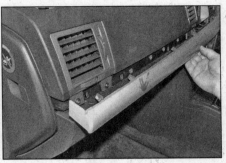

9.1b . . . and remove the strip from the facia

38 Fit a new sealing ring to the pump, and locate the pump in the cylinder block. Make sure that the lug on the oil pump housing engages in the groove of the pump.

39 Insert the securing bolts and tighten to the specified torque.

40 Refit the timing belt as described in Chapter 2A.

41 Reconnect the battery negative terminal, then refill the cooling system as described in Chapter 1A.

1.8 litre Z18XER petrol engine models

42 Ensure that the pump and pump housing mating surfaces are clean and dry.

43 Place the pump in position and refit the retaining bolts. Tighten the bolts to the specified torque.

44 Refit the coolant pump pulley and secure with the three retaining bolts moderately tightened at this stage.

45 Refit the auxiliary drivebelt as described in Chapter 1A.

46 With the drivebelt refitted, tighten the pump pulley retaining bolts to the specified torque.

47 Refit the air cleaner assembly and air intake ducts as described in Chapter 4A.

48 Reconnect the battery negative terminal, then refill the cooling system as described in Chapter 1A.

2.2 litre petrol engine models

49 Ensure that the pump and timing housing mating surfaces are clean and dry, and apply a smear of silicone grease to the pump mating surface.

50 Fit a new sealing ring to the groove in the pump, then locate the pump in the timing housing, making sure that the three bolt holes are aligned with the holes in the sprocket.

51 Insert the pump mounting bolts and two of the sprocket bolts hand-tight to start with, then tighten them to the specified torque.

52 Remove the holding tool and refit the final sprocket bolt, tightening it to the specified torque.

53 Refit the coolant pump drive sprocket access cover to the timing cover together with a new gasket, and tighten the bolts securely.

54 Refit the coolant pipe and thermostat housing together with new sealing rings, and tighten the bolts securely.

55 Refit the coolant temperature sensor to

the thermostat housing and tighten to the specified torque, then reconnect the wiring and secure.

56 Refit the hoses to the thermostat housing cover and heater matrix and tighten the clips.

57 Refit the exhaust manifold heat shield and engine lifting eye.

58 Reconnect the two oxygen sensor wiring connectors at the right-hand end of the cylinder head. secure the wiring harness to the support bracket.

59 Lower the vehicle to the ground, then refit the air cleaner assembly and air intake duct as described in Chapter 4A.

60 Refit the plastic cover to the top of the engine.

61 Reconnect the battery negative terminal, then refill the cooling system as described in Chapter 1A.

Diesel engine models

62 Ensure that the pump and cylinder block mating surfaces are clean and dry, and apply a smear of silicone grease to the pump mating surface in the cylinder block.

63 Fit a new sealing ring to the pump, and locate the pump in the cylinder block.

64 Insert the securing bolts and tighten to the specified torque.

65 Refit the timing belt as described in Chapter 2C or 2D as applicable.

66 Reconnect the battery negative terminal, then refill the cooling system as described in Chapter 1B.

---

8 Heating and ventilation system – general information

The heater/ventilation system consists of a four-speed blower motor (housed behind the facia), face-level vents in the centre and at each end of the facia, and air ducts to the front and rear footwells.

The heater controls are located in the centre of the facia, and the controls operate flap valves to deflect and mix the air flowing through the various parts of the heater/ventilation system. The flap valves are contained in the air distribution housing, which acts as a central distribution unit, passing air to the various ducts and vents.

Cold air enters the system through the grille at the rear of the engine compartment. A pollen filter is fitted to the ventilation intake, to filter out dust, soot, pollen and spores from the air entering the vehicle.

The air (boosted by the blower fan if required) then flows through the various ducts, according to the settings of the controls. Stale air is expelled through ducts at the rear of the vehicle. If warm air is required, the cold air is passed through the heater matrix, which is heated by the engine coolant.

A recirculation switch enables the outside air supply to be closed off, while the air inside the vehicle is recirculated. This can be useful to prevent unpleasant odours entering from outside the vehicle, but should only be used briefly, as the recirculated air inside the vehicle will soon deteriorate.

---

9 Heater/ventilation system components – removal and refitting

Air vents

Removal

1 To remove the air vents from the centre of the facia, carefully release the facia decorative strip using a plastic spatula or similar tool **(see illustrations)**.

2 Undo the four bolts securing the centre vent housing to the facia and withdraw the housing from its location **(see illustrations)**. Lift the locking bar(s) and disconnect the wiring

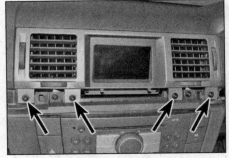

9.2a Undo the four bolts (arrowed) . . .

9.2b . . . and withdraw the centre vent housing from the facia

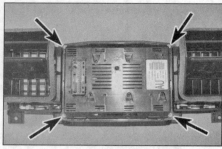

9.3 Undo the four screws (arrowed) and remove the information display unit from the centre vent housing

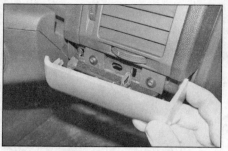

9.4 Carefully release the driver's side facia decorative strip using a plastic spatula or similar

9.5a Undo the two screws (arrowed) . . .

9.5b . . . then pull the vent out at the bottom and disengage the two upper retaining lugs (arrowed)

the vent to the facia. Pull the vent out at the bottom, disengage the two upper retaining lugs, and remove the vent from the facia (see illustrations).

6 To remove the vent from the passenger's side of the facia, release the facia decorative strip as described in paragraph 1, then remove the vent as described in paragraph 5.

7 To remove the rear passenger's air vents, carefully prise them from their locations in the centre console using a plastic spatula inserted at the side of each vent.

Refitting

8 Refitting is a reversal of removal.

Heater blower motor

Removal

9 Remove the glovebox and the facia footwell trim panel on the passenger's side as described in Chapter 11.

10 Undo the retaining bolt and detach the passenger's side footwell air duct (see illustrations).

11 Disconnect the wiring connector at the blower motor, and blower motor resistor at the base of the blower motor housing (see illustration).

12 Undo the seven bolts securing the blower motor housing to the base of the recirculating air valve housing (see illustration).

13 Release the three retaining tabs and remove the blower motor down and out from under the facia (see illustration).

9.10a Undo the retaining bolt (arrowed) . . .

9.10b . . . and detach the passenger's side footwell air duct

connector(s) from the rear of the information display unit.

3 If required, undo the four screws and remove the information display unit from the centre vent housing (see illustration).

4 To remove the vent from the driver's side of the facia, carefully release the facia decorative strip using a plastic spatula or similar tool (see illustration).

5 Undo the two screws securing the base of

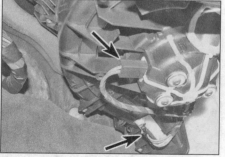

9.11 Disconnect the wiring connectors (arrowed) at the blower motor, and blower motor resistor

9.12 Undo the bolts (arrowed) securing the blower motor to the base of the recirculating air valve housing

9.13 Release the three retaining tabs and remove the blower motor down and out from under the facia

Refitting

14 Refitting is a reversal of removal.

Heater blower motor resistor

Removal

15 Carry out the operations described in paragraphs 9 and 10.
16 Disconnect the wiring connector at the blower motor resistor at the base of the blower motor housing **(see illustration 9.11)**.
17 Slide the resistor towards the centre of the car until its internal lugs align with the slots in the blower motor housing, then withdraw the resistor from the housing.

Refitting

18 Refitting is a reversal of removal.

Recirculating air valve housing

Removal

19 Remove the heater blower motor as described previously.
20 Disconnect the wiring connector from the recirculating air valve servo motor and release the wiring harness from the clip on the air valve housing **(see illustration)**.
21 Undo the retaining bolt and manoeuvre the housing out from under the facia.

Refitting

22 Refitting is a reversal of removal, ensuring that the housing air duct is correctly seated.

Recirculating air valve servo motor

Removal

23 Remove the recirculating air valve housing as described previously.
24 Undo the two retaining bolts and remove the motor from the housing **(see illustration)**. Disengage the servo lever from the air valve lever as the unit is removed.

Refitting

25 Refitting is a reversal of removal. Engage

9.20 Disconnect the wiring connector (arrowed) from the recirculating air valve servo motor

the servo lever with the air valve lever as the unit is refitted.

Mixed air valve servo motor

Removal

26 Remove the glovebox and the facia footwell trim panel on the passenger's side as described in Chapter 11.
27 Disconnect the wiring connector from the servo motor, then undo the two retaining bolts. Disengage the operating lever from the air valve and remove the servo motor **(see illustration)**.

Refitting

28 Refitting is a reversal of removal. Engage the servo lever with the air valve lever as the unit is refitted.

Heater matrix

Removal

29 Working in the engine compartment, use two hose clamps to clamp the hoses leading to the heater matrix. The hoses are located on the bulkhead, just above the steering gear. Alternatively, drain the cooling system completely as described in Chapter 1A or 1B.
30 Using a small screwdriver, lift up the wire

9.24 Recirculating air valve servo motor retaining bolts (arrowed)

clip securing the left-hand and right-hand heater hoses to the heater matrix pipe stubs, and disconnect the hoses from the stubs. Be prepared for some loss of coolant as the hoses are released, by placing cloth rags beneath them.
31 Remove the facia footwell trim panel on the driver's side as described in Chapter 11.
32 Undo the three bolts and remove the heater matrix cover **(see illustration)**.
33 Undo the two bolts and release the clamps securing the heater pipes to the matrix **(see illustration)**. Be prepared for coolant spillage as the pipes are disconnected, and place some cloths or absorbent material over the carpet.
34 Pull the heater matrix from its location and remove it from the car.

Refitting

35 Refitting is a reversal of removal, bearing in mind the following:
a) *Push the securing wire clip back into position on the heater hose end fittings, then push the hoses back onto the matrix pipe stubs. Ensure that the wire clips securely lock the hoses in position.*
b) *If the cooling system was completely drained, refill as described in Chapter 1A*

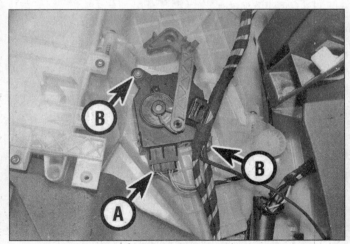

9.27 Mixed air valve servo motor wiring connector (A) and retaining bolts (B)

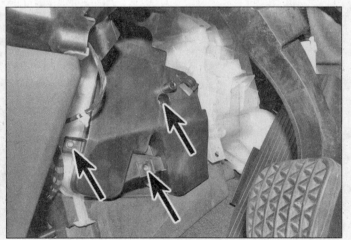

9.32 Undo the three bolts (arrowed) and remove the heater matrix cover

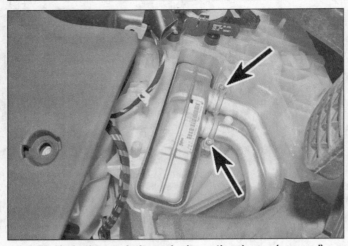

9.33 Undo the two bolts and release the clamps (arrowed) securing the heater pipes to the matrix

9.36 Carefully prise out the heater control assembly from the facia . . .

or 1B. If the heater hoses were clamped prior to removal, top-up the cooling system as described in 'Weekly checks'.

Heater control assembly

Removal

36 Using a small screwdriver, carefully prise out the heater control assembly from the facia **(see illustration)**.
37 Disconnect the wiring from the rear of the control assembly **(see illustration)**.

Refitting

38 Refitting is a reversal of removal.

Air distribution housing

Note: *On models with air conditioning, it is not possible to remove the air distribution housing without opening the refrigerant circuit (see Sections 10 and 11). Have the refrigerant discharged at a dealer service department or an automotive air conditioning repair facility before proceeding.*

Removal

39 Drain the cooling system as described in Chapter 1A or 1B.
40 Remove the complete facia assembly and the facia crossmember as described in Chapter 11.

41 Remove the windscreen wiper arms as described in Chapter 12.
42 Pull up the rubber weatherseal from the flange at the rear of the engine compartment. Carefully release the water deflector by pulling it away from the windscreen to release the retaining clips. Withdraw the water deflector and disconnect the washer hose.
43 Remove the pollen filter as described in Chapter 1A or 1B.
44 Using a small screwdriver, lift up the wire clip securing the left-hand and right-hand heater hoses to the heater matrix pipe stubs, and disconnect the hoses from the stubs. Be prepared for some loss of coolant as the hoses are released by placing cloth rags beneath them.
45 Release the matrix pipe stub rubber seal from the bulkhead by pushing it inward (the seal remains on the pipe stubs).
46 On models with air conditioning, undo the nut securing the refrigerant pipe block connection to the expansion valve and withdraw the refrigerant pipes from the valve **(see illustration)**. Note that new seals for the refrigerant pipes will be required for refitting. Suitably plug or cover the disconnected pipes.
47 Release the expansion valve rubber seal from the bulkhead by pushing it inward (the seal remains on the valve).

48 Disconnect the wiring connectors at the heater blower motor and blower motor resistor.
49 Working inside the vehicle withdraw the air distribution housing from the bulkhead. **Note:** *Keep the matrix unions uppermost as the housing is removed, to prevent coolant spillage.* Mop-up any spilt coolant immediately, and wipe the affected area with a damp cloth to prevent staining.

Refitting

50 Refitting is the reverse of removal. On completion, refill the cooling system as described in Chapter 1A or 1B. On models with air conditioning, have the system evacuated, charged and leak-tested by the specialist who discharged it.

10 Air conditioning system – general information and precautions

General information

1 Air conditioning is standard on top of the range models, and optional on certain other models. It enables the temperature of incoming air to be lowered, and also dehumidifies the air, which makes for rapid demisting and increased comfort.
2 The cooling side of the system works in the same way as a domestic refrigerator. Refrigerant gas is drawn into a belt-driven compressor, and passes into a condenser mounted in front of the radiator, where it loses heat and becomes liquid. The liquid passes through an expansion valve to an evaporator, where it changes from liquid under high pressure to gas under low pressure. This change is accompanied by a drop in temperature, which cools the evaporator. The refrigerant returns to the compressor, and the cycle begins again.
3 Air blown through the evaporator passes to the heater assembly, where it is mixed

9.37 . . . then disconnect the wiring from the rear of the control assembly

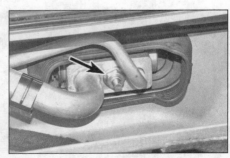

9.46 Undo the nut (arrowed) securing the refrigerant pipe block connection to the expansion valve

with hot air blown through the heater matrix, to achieve the desired temperature in the passenger compartment.

4 The heating side of the system works in the same way as on models without air conditioning (see Section 8).

5 The operation of the system is controlled electronically. Any problems with the system should be referred to a Vauxhall/Opel dealer or an air conditioning specialist.

Air conditioning service ports

6 The high-pressure service port is located just in front of the air cleaner housing (see illustration).

7 The low-pressure service port is located at the front right-hand side of the engine compartment, just behind the body front cross-panel.

Precautions

8 It is necessary to observe special precautions whenever dealing with any part of the system, its associated components, and any items which necessitate disconnection of the system.

⚠️ *Warning: The refrigeration circuit contains a liquid refrigerant. This refrigerant is potentially dangerous, and should only be handled by qualified persons. If it is splashed onto the skin, it can cause frostbite. It is not itself poisonous, but in the presence of a naked flame it forms a poisonous gas; inhalation of the vapour through a lighted cigarette could prove fatal. Uncontrolled discharging of the refrigerant is dangerous, and potentially damaging to the environment. Do not disconnect any part of the system unless it has been discharged by a Vauxhall/Opel dealer or an air conditioning specialist.*
Caution: Do not operate the air conditioning system if it is known to be short of refrigerant, as this may damage the compressor.

11 Air conditioning system components – removal and refitting

⚠️ *Warning: The air conditioning system is under high pressure. Do not loosen any fittings or remove*

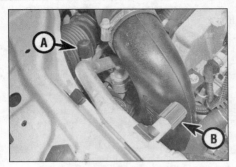

10.6 Air conditioning system high-pressure service port (A) and low-pressure service port (B)

any components until after the system has been discharged. Air conditioning refrigerant should be properly discharged into an approved type of container at a dealer service department or an automotive air conditioning repair facility capable of handling R134a refrigerant. Cap or plug the pipe lines as soon as they are disconnected, to prevent the entry of moisture. Always wear eye protection when disconnecting air conditioning system fittings.

Note: *This Section refers to the components of the air conditioning system itself – refer to Sections 8 and 9 for details of components common to the heating/ventilation system.*

Compressor

Removal

1 Have the refrigerant discharged at a dealer service department or an automotive air conditioning repair facility.

2 Disconnect the battery negative terminal (refer to *Disconnecting the battery* in the Reference Chapter).

3 Firmly apply the handbrake, then jack up the front of the car and support it securely on axle stands (see *Jacking and vehicle support*).

4 Remove the auxiliary drivebelt as described in Chapter 1A or 1B.

5 With the system discharged, undo the retaining bolt(s) and disconnect the refrigerant pipes from the compressor. Discard the O-ring seals – new ones must be used when refitting. Suitably cap the open fittings immediately to keep moisture and contamination out of the system.

6 Disconnect the compressor wiring connector.

7 Unbolt the compressor from the cylinder block/crankcase/sump, then withdraw the compressor downwards from under the vehicle.

Refitting

8 Refit the compressor in the reverse order of removal; renew all seals disturbed.

9 If you are installing a new compressor, refer to the compressor manufacturer's instructions for adding refrigerant oil to the system.

10 Have the system evacuated, charged and leak-tested by the specialist that discharged it.

11 After installing a new compressor, always observe the following running-in procedure:
  1) *Open all instrument panel air outlet flaps.*
  2) *Start vehicle engine and stabilise idle speed for approximately 5 seconds.*
  3) *Switch fan to maximum speed.*
  4) *Switch on the air conditioning and let it run for at least 2 minutes without interruption at engine speed under 1500 rpm.*

Evaporator

Removal

12 Have the refrigerant discharged at a dealer service department or an automotive air conditioning repair facility.

13 Remove the windscreen wiper motor and linkage as described in Chapter 12.

14 Undo the nut securing the refrigerant pipe block connection to the expansion valve and withdraw the refrigerant pipes from the valve (see illustration 9.46). Note that new seals for the refrigerant pipes will be required for refitting. Suitably plug or cover the disconnected pipes.

15 Undo the two retaining bolts and remove the expansion valve (see illustrations).

16 Remove the two seals from the evaporator pipe stubs (see illustration). Note that new seals will be required for refitting.

17 Rotate the evaporator pipe retaining plate to release it from one pipe stub, then slide the plate sideways off the other pipe stub (see illustration).

18 Release the rubber seal from the bulkhead then remove the seal from the pipe stubs (see illustration).

19 Insert a small screwdriver through the slots in the housing and depress the tabs of

11.15a Undo the two retaining bolts (arrowed) . . .

11.15b . . . and remove the expansion valve

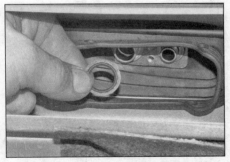

11.16 Remove the two seals from the evaporator pipe stubs

11.17 Rotate the pipe retaining plate to release it from one pipe stub, then slide the plate off the other pipe stub

the evaporator pipe retaining plate. Lift up the retaining plate and remove it from the housing **(see illustrations)**.

20 Remove the recirculating air valve housing as described in Section 9.

21 Undo the eight retaining bolts and remove the evaporator cover from the side of the air distribution housing **(see illustration)**.

22 Carefully pull the evaporator out of the air distribution housing **(see illustration)**.

Refitting

23 Refitting is the reverse of removal ensuring that all disturbed pipe seals are renewed.

24 Have the system evacuated, charged and leak-tested by the specialist who discharged it.

Condenser

Removal – petrol engine models

25 Have the refrigerant discharged at a

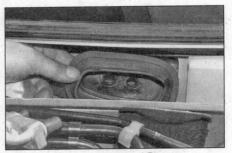

11.18 Release the rubber seal from the bulkhead then remove the seal from the pipe stubs

dealer service department or an automotive air conditioning repair facility.

26 Disconnect the battery negative terminal (refer to *Disconnecting the battery* in the Reference Chapter).

27 Remove the front bumper as described in Chapter 11.

28 Undo the retaining nuts and disconnect the refrigerant pipe connector blocks from the condenser and receiver-dryer. Discard the seals – new ones must be used when refitting. Suitably cap the open fittings immediately to keep moisture and contamination out of the system.

29 Slacken (but do not remove) the two bolts securing the radiator left-hand and right-hand mounting brackets to the subframe **(see illustrations 3.10a and 3.10b)**.

30 Release the radiator upper rubber mounting bushes on each side from their guides, and carefully move the top of the radiator forward.

31 Undo the bolt each side securing the condenser upper mounting brackets to the radiator. Carefully lift up or remove the plastic panels on each side of the radiator for improved access, if necessary.

32 Carefully lift the condenser upwards, disengage the lower mounting lugs from the radiator and remove the condenser from the engine compartment.

33 If required, remove the receiver-dryer from the condenser as described in paragraphs 44 and 45.

Removal – diesel engine models

34 Have the refrigerant discharged at a dealer service department or an automotive air conditioning repair facility.

35 Disconnect the battery negative terminal (refer to *Disconnecting the battery* in the Reference Chapter).

36 Remove the front bumper as described in Chapter 11.

37 Undo the retaining nuts and disconnect the upper and lower refrigerant pipe connector blocks from the condenser **(see illustration)**. Discard the seals – new ones must be used when refitting. Suitably cap the open fittings immediately to keep moisture and contamination out of the system.

38 Undo the bolt each side securing the condenser upper mounting brackets to the intercooler **(see illustration)**.

39 Carefully lift the condenser upwards, disengage the lower mounting lugs from the intercooler and remove the condenser from the engine compartment **(see illustration)**.

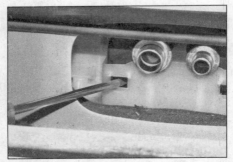

11.19a Depress the tabs of the evaporator pipe retaining plate with a screwdriver . . .

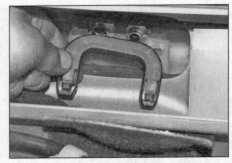

11.19b . . . then lift up the retaining plate and remove it from the housing

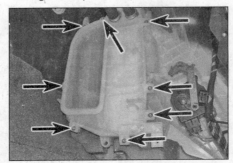

11.21 Undo the retaining bolts (arrowed) and remove the evaporator cover

11.22 Carefully pull the evaporator out of the air distribution housing

11.37 Lower refrigerant pipe connector block retaining nut (arrowed)

11.38 Condenser left-hand upper mounting bracket retaining bolt (arrowed)

Refitting – all models

40 Refitting is the reverse of removal ensuring that all disturbed pipe seals are renewed.
41 Have the system evacuated, charged and leak-tested by the specialist who discharged it.

Receiver-dryer

Removal – petrol engine models

42 Have the refrigerant discharged at a dealer service department or an automotive air conditioning repair facility.
43 Disconnect the battery negative terminal (refer to *Disconnecting the battery* in the Reference Chapter).
44 Remove the front bumper as described in Chapter 11.
45 Undo the retaining nuts and disconnect the refrigerant pipe connector blocks from the condenser and receiver-dryer. Discard the seals – new ones must be used when refitting. Suitably cap the open fittings immediately to keep moisture and contamination out of the system.
46 Undo the two retaining bolts and remove the receiver-dryer from the condenser.

Removal – diesel engine models

47 Have the refrigerant discharged at a dealer service department or an automotive air conditioning repair facility.
48 Disconnect the battery negative terminal (refer to *Disconnecting the battery* in the Reference Chapter).

49 Apply the handbrake, then jack up the front of the vehicle and support it on axle stands (see *Jacking and vehicle support*). Undo the ten bolts and remove the engine undertray.
50 Remove the front bumper as described in Chapter 11.
51 Undo the retaining nut and disconnect the refrigerant pipe upper connector block from the condenser. Discard the seal – a new one must be used when refitting. Suitably cap the open fittings immediately to keep moisture and contamination out of the system.
52 Undo the bolt securing the intercooler right-hand charge air pipe upper mounting to the radiator **(see illustration 3.33)**.
53 Slacken the retaining clips and remove the right-hand lower charge air hose from the intercooler and charge air pipe **(see illustration 3.30b)**.
54 Undo the bolt securing the refrigerant pipe bracket and intercooler right-hand charge air pipe lower mounting to the radiator **(see illustration 3.34b)**.
55 Slacken (but do not remove) the two bolts securing the radiator left-hand and right-hand mounting brackets to the subframe **(see illustrations 3.10a and 3.10b)**.
56 Release the radiator upper rubber mounting bushes on each side from their guides, and carefully move the top of the radiator forward.
57 Undo the retaining nuts and disconnect

11.39 Lift the condenser upwards and disengage the lower mounting lug (arrowed) on each side

the refrigerant pipe connector blocks from the condenser and receiver-dryer. Discard the seals – new ones must be used when refitting. Suitably cap the open fittings immediately to keep moisture and contamination out of the system.
58 Undo the two retaining bolts and remove the receiver-dryer from the radiator. Withdraw the receiver-dryer downwards and remove it from under the car.

Refitting – all models

59 Refitting is the reverse of removal ensuring that all disturbed pipe seals are renewed.
60 Have the system evacuated, charged and leak-tested by the specialist who discharged it.

Notes

Chapter 4 Part A:
Fuel and exhaust systems – petrol engines

Contents

Degrees of difficulty

Easy, suitable for novice with little experience	**Fairly easy,** suitable for beginner with some experience	**Fairly difficult,** suitable for competent DIY mechanic	**Difficult,** suitable for experienced DIY mechanic	**Very difficult,** suitable for expert DIY or professional

Specifications

System type
1.8 litre engines:
Z18XE . . . . Simtec 71.5 multi-point injection
Z18XER . . . . Simtec 75.1 multi-point injection
2.2 litre engines . . . . Simtec 81.1 high-pressure direct injection

Fuel system data
1.8 litre engines:
Fuel supply pump type . . . . Electric, immersed in tank
Fuel pump regulated constant pressure . . . . 3.8 bar
Specified idle speed . . . . Not adjustable – controlled by ECU
Idle mixture CO content . . . . Not adjustable – controlled by ECU
2.2 litre engines:
Fuel pump type:
  Supply pump . . . . Electric, immersed in tank
  High-pressure pump . . . . Mechanical, driven by inlet camshaft
Fuel supply pump delivery pressure . . . . 4.2 bar
Fuel system operating pressure . . . . 40 to 110 bar
Specified idle speed . . . . Not adjustable – controlled by ECU
Idle mixture CO content . . . . Not adjustable – controlled by ECU

Recommended fuel
Minimum octane rating . . . . 95 RON unleaded (UK premium unleaded)
Leaded fuel or LRP must **NOT** be used

Torque wrench settings

	Nm	lbf ft
Accelerator pedal position sensor nuts	9	7
Camshaft sensor*	9	7
Crankshaft sensor bolt:		
1.8 litre engines:		
Z18XE	8	6
Z18XER	5	4
2.2 litre engines	10	7
Exhaust front pipe-to-manifold nuts*	20	15
Exhaust manifold nuts*:		
1.8 litre engines:		
Z18XE	12	9
Z18XER	20	15
2.2 litre engines	12	9
Exhaust manifold heat shield bolts/nuts:		
1.8 litre engines	8	6
2.2 litre engines	23	17
Fuel pressure regulator to fuel rail (2.2 litre engines)	9	7
Fuel pressure sensor to fuel rail (2.2 litre engines)	25	18
Fuel rail bolts:		
1.8 litre engines	9	7
2.2 litre engines:		
Fuel rail stud bolts	9	7
Fuel rail-to-injector bolts:		
Stage 1	4	3
Stage 2	9	7
Fuel tank retaining strap bolts	23	17
High-pressure fuel pipe union nuts (2.2 litre engines)	25	18
High-pressure fuel pump bolts (2.2 litre engines)	9	7
Inlet manifold nuts and bolts:		
1.8 litre engines:		
Z18XE:		
Manifold to cylinder head	22	16
Support bracket to manifold	20	15
Support bracket to cylinder block	35	26
Z18XER	20	15
2.2 litre engines	9	7
Knock sensor bolt:		
1.8 litre engines	20	15
2.2 litre engines	23	17
Manifold absolute pressure sensor bolt	10	7
Throttle housing bolts	10	7

Use new fasteners

1 General information and precautions

The fuel system consists of a fuel tank (which is mounted under the rear of the car, with an electric fuel pump immersed in it), a fuel filter and the fuel feed, and on some engines, return lines. On 1.8 litre engines, the fuel pump supplies fuel to the fuel rail, which acts as a reservoir for the four fuel injectors which inject fuel into the inlet tracts. On 2.2 litre engines, the tank-mounted fuel supply pump supplies fuel to the high-pressure pump mounted on the engine. The high-pressure pump supplies fuel to the fuel rail, which acts as a reservoir for the four fuel injectors which inject fuel directly into the combustion chambers in the cylinder head.

On all engines, the electronic control unit controls both the fuel injection system and the ignition system, integrating the two into a complete engine management system. Refer to Section 10 for further information on the operation of the fuel system and to Chapter 5B for details of the ignition side of the system.

Precautions

Note: *Refer to Part C of this Chapter for general information and precautions relating to the catalytic converter.*

• Before disconnecting any fuel lines, or working on any part of the fuel system, the system must be depressurised (see Section 5).

• Care must be taken when disconnecting the fuel lines. When disconnecting a fuel union or hose, loosen the union or clamp screw slowly, to avoid sudden uncontrolled fuel spillage. Take adequate fire precautions.

• When working on fuel system components, scrupulous cleanliness must be observed, and care must be taken not to introduce any foreign matter into fuel lines or components.

• After carrying out any work involving disconnection of fuel lines, it is advisable to check the connections for leaks; pressurise the system by switching the ignition on and off several times.

• Electronic control units are very sensitive components, and certain precautions must be taken to avoid damage to these units as follows.

a) *When carrying out welding operations on the vehicle using electric welding equipment, the battery and alternator should be disconnected.*

b) *Although the underbonnet-mounted control units will tolerate normal underbonnet conditions, they can be adversely affected by excess heat or moisture. If using welding equipment or pressure-washing equipment in the vicinity of an electronic control unit, take care not to direct heat, or jets of water or steam, at the unit. If this cannot be avoided, remove the control unit from the vehicle, and protect its wiring plug with a plastic bag.*

c) *Before disconnecting any wiring, or removing components, always ensure that the ignition is switched off.*

d) *After working on fuel injection/engine management system components, ensure that all wiring is correctly reconnected before reconnecting the battery or switching on the ignition.*

⚠️ **Warning: Many of the procedures in this Chapter require the removal of fuel lines and connections, which may result in some fuel spillage. Before carrying out any operation on the fuel system, refer to the precautions given in 'Safety first!' at the beginning of this manual, and follow them implicitly. Petrol is a highly-dangerous and volatile liquid, and the precautions necessary when handling it cannot be overstressed.**

Note: *Residual pressure will remain in the fuel lines long after the vehicle was last used. Before disconnecting any fuel line, first depressurise the fuel system as described in Section 5.*

2 Air cleaner assembly and intake ducts – removal and refitting

Removal

1 Slacken the retaining clips securing the air intake duct to the airflow meter and throttle housing. Where applicable, release the clip and disconnect the crankcase ventilation hose from the camshaft cover. Detach the intake duct from the airflow meter and throttle housing, and remove the duct from the engine **(see illustration)**.

2 Disconnect the wiring connector from the side of the airflow meter **(see illustration)**.

3 Unclip the wiring harness from the side of the air cleaner housing.

4 Lift up the inner rear corner of the filter housing to release the mounting grommet. Move the filter housing toward the engine to disengage the front and rear mounting rubbers, then release the air intake duct at the front **(see illustrations)**. Lift the filter housing out from the engine compartment.

5 The various air intake pipes/ducts can be disconnected and removed once the retaining clips have been slackened. In some cases it will be necessary to disconnect breather hoses, vacuum pipes and wiring connectors to allow the pipe/duct to be removed; the pipe/duct may also be bolted to a support bracket

Refitting

6 Refitting is the reverse of removal, making sure all the air intake ducts/hoses are securely reconnected.

3 Accelerator pedal/ position sensor – removal and refitting

Removal

1 Disconnect the battery negative terminal (refer to *Disconnecting the battery* in the Reference Chapter).

2.1 Detach the intake duct from the airflow meter and throttle housing, and remove the duct from the engine

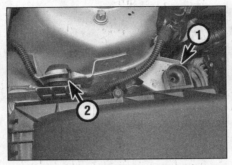

2.4a Lift up the filter housing to release the mounting grommet (1) then move the filter housing toward the engine to disengage the rear mounting rubber (2) . . .

2 Remove the driver's side lower facia panel as described in Chapter 11.

3 Working in the driver's footwell under the facia, disconnect the wiring from the top of the accelerator pedal/position sensor **(see illustration)**.

4 Unscrew the three mounting nuts, and withdraw the sensor from the bulkhead.

Refitting

5 Refitting is a reversal of removal.

4 Unleaded petrol – general information and usage

Note: *The information given in this Chapter is correct at the time of writing. If updated*

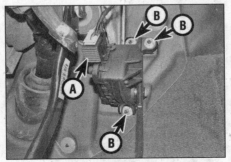

3.3 Accelerator pedal/position sensor wiring connector (A) and mounting nuts (B)

2.2 Disconnect the wiring connector (arrowed) from the side of the airflow meter

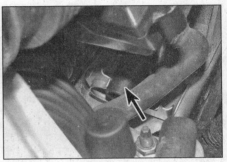

2.4b . . . and front mounting rubber (arrowed)

information is thought to be required, check with a Vauxhall/Opel dealer. If travelling abroad, consult one of the motoring organisations (or a similar authority) for advice on the fuel available.

All petrol models are designed to run on fuel with a minimum octane rating of 95 RON. However, if unavailable, 91 octane may be used on 1.8 litre engines only. 2.2 litre engines must not be run on 91 octane fuel.

All models have a catalytic converter, and so must be run on unleaded fuel only. Under no circumstances should leaded fuel or LRP be used, as this will damage the converter.

Super unleaded petrol can also be used in all models if wished, though there is no advantage in doing so.

5 Fuel injection system – depressurisation

⚠️ **Warning: Refer to the warning note in Section 1 before proceeding. The following procedure will merely relieve the pressure in the fuel system – remember that fuel will still be present in the system components, and take precautions accordingly before disconnecting any of them.**

1 The fuel system referred to in this Section is defined as the tank-mounted fuel pump, the fuel filter, the fuel injectors, and the metal pipes and flexible hoses of the fuel lines between these components. All these contain

5.3a Fuel pressure connection valve (arrowed) – 1.8 litre Z18XER engines

5.3b Fuel pressure connection valve (arrowed) – 2.2 litre engines

fuel which will be under pressure while the engine is running, and/or while the ignition is switched on. The pressure will remain for some time after the ignition has been switched off, and it must be relieved in a controlled fashion when any of these components are disturbed for servicing work.

2 Remove the plastic cover over the top of the engine.

3 Locate the fuel pressure connection valve which is fitted to the fuel rail. On 1.8 litre Z18XE engines it can be found on the top, right-hand end of the fuel rail. On 1.8 litre Z18XER engines it can be found on the top, left-hand end of the fuel rail. On 2.2 litre engines the fuel pressure connection valve is located on the fuel inlet pipe connection on the high-pressure fuel pump **(see illustrations)**.

4 Unscrew the cap from the valve and position

a container beneath the valve. Hold a wad of rag over the valve and relieve the pressure in the fuel system by depressing the valve core with a suitable screwdriver. Be prepared for the squirt of fuel as the valve core is depressed and catch it with the rag. Hold the valve core down until no more fuel is expelled from the valve.

5 Once all pressure is relieved, securely refit the valve cap.

 6 Fuel gauge sender unit – removal and refitting

⚠️ **Warning: Refer to the warning note in Section 1 before proceeding.**

Note 1: *Vauxhall/Opel special tool KM-797 (or suitable alternative) will be required to remove and refit the fuel pump cover locking ring.*
Note 2: *A new fuel pump cover sealing ring will be required on refitting.*

Removal

1 Disconnect the battery negative terminal (refer to *Disconnecting the battery* in the Reference Chapter).

2 Depressurise the fuel system as described in Section 5.

3 Fold the rear seat cushion forwards or alternatively, remove the cushion as described in Chapter 11.

4 Lift up the flap in the carpet to reveal the fuel tank access cover **(see illustration)**.

5 Using a screwdriver, carefully prise the plastic access cover from the floor **(see illustration)**.

6 Disconnect the wiring connector from the fuel supply pump cover, and tape the connector to the vehicle body to prevent it disappearing behind the tank **(see illustration)**.

7 Mark the fuel hoses for identification purposes. The hoses are equipped with quick-release fittings to ease removal. To disconnect each hose, compress the clips located on each side of the fitting and ease the fitting off of its union **(see illustration)**. Plug the hose ends to minimise fuel loss.

8 Using the Vauxhall/Opel special tool, unscrew the locking ring and remove it from the tank **(see illustration)**.

9 Make identification marks on the fuel pump cover and the body to ensure that the cover is refitted in its original position. There may be an arrow stamped on the cover; if so note its direction.

10 Carefully lift the fuel pump cover away from tank until the wiring connectors can be disconnected from its underside **(see illustration)**.

11 Release the retaining clip and disconnect the fuel supply hose from the underside of the fuel pump cover. Where fitted, also disconnect the fuel return hose quick-release fitting from the underside of the cover **(see illustration)**. Remove the fuel pump cover and collect the sealing ring from the top of the tank.

12 The fuel gauge sender unit is clipped to

6.4 Lift up the flap in the carpet to reveal the fuel tank access cover

6.5 Carefully prise the plastic access cover from the floor

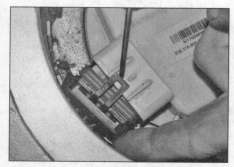

6.6 Disconnect the wiring connector from the fuel pump cover

6.7 Compress the clips located on each side of the fuel hose fitting and ease the fitting off of its union

6.8 Using the Vauxhall/Opel special tool, unscrew the locking ring and remove it from the tank

the side of the fuel supply pump. Depress the retaining clip then slide the sender unit upwards to release it from the pump (see illustrations).

13 Manoeuvre the sender unit through the fuel tank aperture, taking great care not damage the float arm.

Refitting

14 Place a new sealing ring in position on the top of the fuel tank.

15 Manoeuvre the sender unit carefully in through the tank aperture and slide it into position on the side of the fuel supply pump. Ensure the sender unit is clipped securely in position.

16 Reconnect the fuel supply hose and, where fitted, the return hose to the fuel pump cover.

17 Reconnect the fuel pump and sender unit wiring connectors to the fuel pump cover. Locate the cover in position on the tank and align the marks, or direction arrow in the position noted during removal.

18 Refit the locking ring and tighten it with the special tool until it locks in place.

19 Reconnect the fuel hoses to the pump cover, using the marks made on removal, then reconnect the wiring connector.

20 Reconnect the battery then start the engine and check for fuel leaks. If all is well, refit the access cover then refit or fold the seat cushion back into position.

7 Fuel supply pump – removal and refitting

⚠ Warning: Refer to the warning note in Section 1 before proceeding.

Removal

1 Remove the fuel gauge sender unit as described in Section 6.

2 Release the three retaining clips by pressing them inwards then lift the fuel supply pump out of the fuel tank, taking great care not to spill fuel onto the interior of the vehicle (see illustrations).

3 Inspect the fuel filter for signs of damage or deterioration and renew if necessary (see illustration).

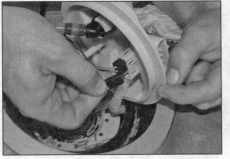
6.10 Lift the fuel pump cover away from tank until the wiring connectors can be disconnected from its underside

6.12a Depress the retaining clip . . .

Refitting

4 Ensure the filter is securely fitted to the base of the pump then carefully manoeuvre the pump assembly into position, making sure it clips securely into position.

5 Refit the fuel gauge sender unit as described in Section 6.

8 Fuel tank – removal and refitting

⚠ Warning: Refer to the warning note in Section 1 before proceeding.

Removal

1 Disconnect the battery negative terminal (refer to *Disconnecting the battery* in the Reference Chapter).

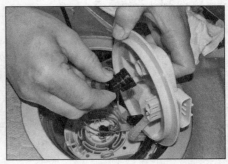
6.11 Disconnect the fuel supply hose from the fuel pump cover and, where fitted, disconnect the fuel return hose

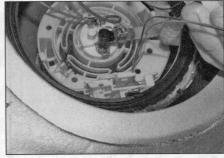
6.12b . . . then slide the sender unit upwards to release it from the fuel supply pump

2 Depressurise the fuel system as described in Section 5.

3 Before removing the fuel tank, all fuel must be drained from the tank. Since a fuel tank drain plug is not provided, it is therefore preferable to carry out the removal operation when the tank is nearly empty. The remaining fuel can then be siphoned or hand-pumped from the tank.

4 Remove the exhaust system and relevant heat shield(s) as described in Section 17.

5 Unclip the handbrake cables from the underbody and fuel tank, then tie them to one side, away from the fuel tank.

6 Disconnect the wiring for the fuel pump and fuel gauge sender at the underbody connector in front of the left-hand side of the tank. Unclip the wiring harness from the two retaining clips.

7 Disconnect the fuel feed line, return line

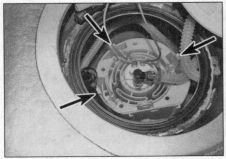
7.2a Release the three retaining clips (arrowed) by pressing them inwards . . .

7.2b . . . then lift the fuel supply pump out of the fuel tank

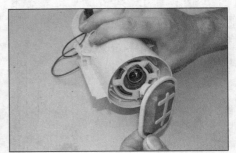
7.3 Inspect the fuel filter for signs of damage or deterioration and renew if necessary

9.4 Disconnect the wiring connector (arrowed) from the throttle housing – 1.8 litre engines

(where applicable) and the evaporative vent line at the underbody quick-release connectors on the right-hand side of the tank. Be prepared for some loss of fuel. A Vauxhall/Opel special tool is available to release the fuel line connectors, but provided care is taken, the connectors can be released using a pair of long-nosed pliers, or a similar tool, to depress the retaining tangs. Suitably plug the disconnected fuel and vent hoses to prevent entry of dust and dirt.

8 Place a suitable container under the tank, then slacken the clip and disconnect the fuel filler hose from the fuel tank. Collect the escaping fuel in the container.

9 Support the weight of the fuel tank on a jack with interposed block of wood.

10 Undo the four bolts and remove the two securing straps from the fuel tank.

11 Taking care not to damage the charcoal canister, slowly lower the tank and move it forwards. When sufficient clearance exists, disconnect the charcoal canister vent hose quick-release fitting.

12 Continue to lower the tank until it can be removed from under the vehicle.

13 If necessary, remove the fuel lines and hoses, heat shield and wiring from the tank for transfer to the new tank. If a new tank is being fitted, it is recommended that the filter is renewed at the same time.

14 If the tank contains sediment or water, it may cleaned out with two or three rinses of clean fuel. Remove the fuel gauge sender unit and fuel supply pump as described in

Sections 6 and 7 respectively. Shake the tank vigorously, and change the fuel as necessary to remove all contamination from the tank.

 Warning: This procedure should be carried out in a well-ventilated area, and it is vital to take adequate fire precautions.

15 Any repairs to the fuel tank should be carried out by a professional. Do not under any circumstances attempt any form of DIY repair to a fuel tank.

Refitting

16 Refitting is the reverse of the removal procedure, noting the following points:

a) *When lifting the tank back into position, take care to ensure that none of the hoses become trapped between the tank and vehicle body. Refit the retaining straps and tighten the bolts to the specified torque.*

b) *Ensure all pipes and hoses are correctly routed and all hoses unions are securely joined.*

c) *On completion, refill the tank with a small amount of fuel, and check for signs of leakage prior to taking the vehicle out on the road.*

9 Throttle housing – removal and refitting

Removal

1.8 litre engines

1 Disconnect the battery negative terminal (refer to *Disconnecting the battery* in the Reference Chapter).

2 Where fitted, remove the plastic cover over the top of the engine.

3 Slacken the retaining clips securing the air intake duct to the airflow meter and throttle housing. Release the clip and disconnect the crankcase ventilation hose from the camshaft cover. Detach the intake duct from the airflow meter and throttle housing, and remove the duct from the engine.

4 Disconnect the wiring connector from the throttle housing **(see illustration)**.

5 Release the retaining clips and disconnect the crankcase ventilation hose and the fuel evaporation hose from the throttle housing.

6 Clamp the two coolant hoses to minimise coolant loss, then release the retaining clips and disconnect the two coolant hoses from the rear of the throttle housing.

7 Undo the four bolts and lift the throttle housing off the inlet manifold **(see illustration)**. Recover the gasket.

8 It is not possible to obtain the throttle valve control motor or throttle valve position sensor separately, so if either is faulty, the complete throttle body must be renewed.

2.2 litre engines

9 Disconnect the battery negative terminal (refer to *Disconnecting the battery* in the Reference Chapter).

10 Remove the plastic cover over the top of the engine.

11 Slacken the retaining clips securing the air intake duct to the airflow meter and throttle housing. Detach the intake duct from the airflow meter and throttle body/housing, and remove the duct from the engine.

12 Disconnect the wiring connector from the throttle housing **(see illustration)**.

13 Undo the four bolts and lift the throttle housing off the inlet manifold **(see illustration)**. Recover the gasket.

14 It is not possible to obtain the throttle valve control motor or throttle valve position sensor separately, so if either is faulty, the complete throttle body must be renewed.

Refitting

15 Refitting is a reversal of removal, but thoroughly clean the mating faces and use a new gasket. Tighten the bolts progressively and securely. On 1.8 litre engines, top-up the coolant level as described in *Weekly checks*.

10 Fuel injection systems – general information

The engine management (fuel injection/ignition) systems incorporate a closed-loop catalytic converter, an evaporative emission control system and an exhaust gas

9.7 Throttle housing retaining bolts (arrowed) – 1.8 litre engines

9.12 Disconnect the wiring connector (arrowed) from the throttle housing – 2.2 litre engines

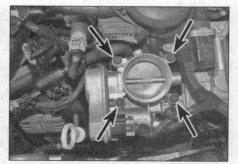

9.13 Undo the four bolts (arrowed) and lift the throttle housing off the inlet manifold – 2.2 litre engines

recirculation system. All the systems operate in a similar manner and comply with the latest emission control standards. The fuel injection side of the systems operate as follows; refer to Chapter 5B for information on the ignition system.

On 1.8 litre engines, the fuel supply pump, immersed in the fuel tank, pumps fuel from the fuel tank to the fuel rail, via a filter mounted underneath the rear of the vehicle. Fuel supply pressure is controlled by the pressure regulator located in the fuel tank.

On 2.2 litre engines, the fuel supply pump, immersed in the fuel tank, pumps fuel from the fuel tank to the high-pressure fuel pump, via a filter mounted underneath the rear of the vehicle. The high-pressure fuel pump is mounted on the left-hand end of the cylinder head and is driven directly by the inlet camshaft. The high-pressure pump supplies fuel at a variable pressure of between 40 and 110 bar to the fuel rail. The fuel pressure at the fuel rail is controlled by means of a fuel pressure sensor and fuel pressure regulator.

The electrical control system consists of the ECU, along with the following sensors.

a) *Throttle potentiometer (integral with the throttle housing) – informs the ECU of the throttle position, and confirms the signals received from the accelerator pedal position sensor.*

b) *Accelerator pedal position sensor – informs the ECU of accelerator pedal position, and the rate of throttle opening/closing.*

c) *Coolant temperature sensor – informs the ECU of engine temperature.*

d) *Airflow meter – informs the ECU of the load on the engine (expressed in terms of the mass of air passing from the air cleaner to the throttle housing).*

e) *Manifold absolute pressure sensor (2.2 litre engines) – informs the ECU of the engine load by monitoring the pressure in the inlet manifold.*

f) *Oxygen sensors (two) – inform the ECU of the oxygen content of the exhaust gases (explained in greater detail in Part C of this Chapter).*

g) *Crankshaft sensor – informs the ECU of engine speed and crankshaft position.*

h) *Camshaft sensor (two sensors on 1.8 litre Z18XER engines) – inform the ECU of speed and position of the camshaft(s).*

i) *Knock sensor – informs the ECU when pre-ignition ('pinking') is occurring.*

j) *ABS control unit – informs the ECU of the vehicle speed, based on wheel speed sensor signals (explained in greater detail in Chapter 9).*

All the above information is analysed by the ECU and, based on this, the ECU determines the appropriate ignition and fuelling requirements for the engine. The ECU controls the fuel injector by varying its pulse width – the length of time the injector is held open – to provide a richer or weaker mixture, as appropriate. The mixture is constantly varied by the ECU, to provide the best setting for cranking, starting (with either a hot or cold engine), warm-up, idle, cruising, and acceleration.

Idle speed and throttle position is controlled by the throttle valve control motor, which is an integral part of the throttle housing. The motor is controlled by the ECU, in conjunction with signals received from the accelerator pedal position sensor.

The systems incorporate a variable tract inlet manifold to help increase torque output at low engine speeds. Each inlet manifold tract is fitted with a valve. The valve is controlled by the ECU via a solenoid valve and vacuum diaphragm unit.

At low engine speeds (below approximately 3600 rpm) the valves remain closed. The air entering the engine is then forced to take the long inlet path through the manifold which leads to an increase in the engine torque output.

At higher engine speeds, the ECU switches the solenoid valve which then allows vacuum to act on the diaphragm unit. The diaphragm unit is linked to the valve assemblies and opens up each of the four valves allowing the air passing through the manifold to take the shorter inlet path which is more suited to higher engine speeds.

The ECU also controls the exhaust and evaporative emission control systems, which are described in detail in Part C of this Chapter.

If certain sensors fail, and send abnormal signals to the ECU, the ECU has a back-up programme. In this event, the abnormal signals are ignored, and a pre-programmed value is substituted for the sensor signal, allowing the engine to continue running, albeit at reduced efficiency. If the ECU enters its back-up mode, a warning light on the instrument panel will illuminate, and a fault code will be stored in the ECU memory. This fault code can be read using suitable specialist test equipment.

11 Fuel injection system components – testing

1 If a fault appears in the engine management system, first ensure that all the system wiring connectors are securely connected and free of corrosion. Ensure that the fault is not due to poor maintenance; ie, check that the air cleaner filter element is clean, the spark plugs are in good condition and correctly gapped, the cylinder compression pressures are correct and that the engine breather hoses are clear and undamaged, referring to Chapters 1A, 2A and 2B for further information.

2 If these checks fail to reveal the cause of the problem, the vehicle should be taken to a suitably-equipped Vauxhall/Opel dealer or engine management diagnostic specialist for testing. A diagnostic socket is located in the centre console, beneath the ashtray

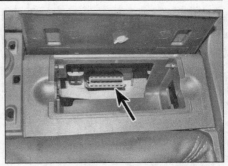

11.2 The diagnostic socket is located beneath the ashtray insert

insert, to which a fault code reader or other suitable test equipment can be connected **(see illustration)**. By using the code reader or test equipment, the engine management ECU can be interrogated, and any stored fault codes can be retrieved. Live data can also be captured from the various system sensors and actuators, indicating their operating parameters. This will allow the fault to be quickly and simply traced, alleviating the need to test all the system components individually, which is a time-consuming operation that carries a risk of damaging the ECU.

12 Simtec 71.5 injection system components – removal and refitting

Fuel rail and injectors

Note: *Refer to the precautions given in Section 1 before proceeding. The seals at both ends of the fuel injectors must be renewed on refitting.*

1 Disconnect the battery negative terminal (refer to *Disconnecting the battery* in the Reference Chapter).

2 Remove the plastic cover over the top of the engine.

3 Depressurise the fuel system as described in Section 5.

4 Slacken the retaining clips securing the air intake duct to the airflow meter and throttle housing. Release the clip and disconnect the crankcase ventilation hose from the camshaft cover. Detach the intake duct from the airflow meter and throttle housing, and remove the duct from the engine.

5 Firmly apply the handbrake, then jack up the front of the car and support it securely on axle stands (see *Jacking and vehicle support*).

6 From under the rear of the engine, disconnect the wiring connectors for the oxygen sensor and oil pressure switch. Release the wiring harness from its clips.

7 From under the front of the engine disconnect the wiring connectors at the oil level sensor and crankshaft sensor. Release the wiring harness from its clips.

8 Working from above, disconnect the camshaft sensor wiring connector, then undo the nut and disconnect the earth lead from the alternator.

12.31 Undo the two retaining bolts and remove the camshaft sensor from the cylinder head

9 Release the clip and disconnect the remaining crankcase ventilation hose from the camshaft cover.
10 Disconnect the wiring connectors from the following components, labelling each connector to avoid confusion when refitting:
  a) *Fuel injectors.*
  b) *Air conditioning compressor.*
  c) *Coolant temperature sensor.*
  d) *Air conditioning pressure switch.*
  e) *Throttle housing.*
  f) *Fuel injection ECU.*
  g) *Knock sensor.*
  h) *EGR valve.*
  i) *Ignition module.*
  j) *Oxygen sensor.*
  k) *Wiring harness block connector.*
11 Detach the knock sensor wiring harness plug bracket and the earth lead.
12 Release the wiring harness cable-ties and unscrew the bolt securing the plastic wiring trough to the engine lifting eye. Lift up the disconnected harness and place it to one side.
13 Disconnect the fuel feed hose quick-release connector at the fuel rail. Be prepared for some loss of fuel. A Vauxhall/Opel special tool is available to release the connector, but provided care is taken, it can be released using a pair of long-nosed pliers, or a similar tool, to depress the retaining tangs. Suitably cover or plug the open unions, to prevent dirt ingress and further fuel spillage.
14 Unscrew the two mounting bolts, then lift the fuel rail, complete with the injectors, off of the inlet manifold.

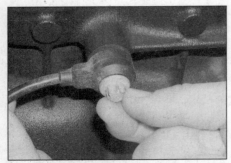

12.35 Undo the retaining bolt and release the knock sensor from the cylinder block

15 To remove an injector from the fuel rail, prise out the metal securing clip using a screwdriver or a pair of pliers, and pull the injector from the fuel rail. Remove and discard the injector sealing rings; new ones must be fitted on refitting.
16 Overhaul of the fuel injectors is not possible, as no spares are available. If faulty, an injector must be renewed.
17 Commence refitting by fitting new O-ring seals to both ends of the fuel injectors. Coat the seals with a thin layer of petroleum jelly before fitting.
18 Refitting is a reversal of removal, bearing in mind the following points:
  a) *When refitting the injectors to the fuel rail, note that the groove in the metal securing clip must engage with the lug on the injector body.*
  b) *Make sure that the quick-release connector audibly engages on the fuel rail.*
  c) *Ensure that all wiring connectors are securely reconnected, and that the wiring is secured in the relevant clips and brackets.*

Coolant temperature sensor

19 Refer to Chapter 3 for removal and refitting details.

Airflow meter

20 Slacken the retaining clip securing the air intake duct to the airflow meter and disconnect the duct.
21 Disconnect the airflow meter wiring connector.
22 Slacken the retaining clip and remove the airflow meter from the air cleaner housing lid.
23 Refitting is a reversal of removal, but ensure that the arrow on the airflow meter points toward the throttle body/housing when fitted.

Crankshaft sensor

24 The crankshaft sensor is mounted on the front of the cylinder block below the oil filter.
25 Firmly apply the handbrake, then jack up the front of the car and support it securely on axle stands (see *Jacking and vehicle support*).
26 Disconnect the wiring connector, then unscrew the retaining bolt and remove the sensor from the front of the cylinder block. Discard the sealing ring, a new one should be used on refitting.
27 Refitting is the reverse of removal using a new sealing ring and tightening the sensor bolt to the specified torque.

Camshaft sensor

28 Remove the plastic cover over the top of the engine.
29 Undo the three retaining screws, then unclip the timing belt upper cover from the rear cover and remove it from the engine compartment.
30 Unscrew the nut from the fuel line bracket, then unscrew the stud bolt. Disconnect the

camshaft sensor wiring connector, then unclip the wiring harness.
31 Undo the two retaining bolts and remove the sensor from the cylinder head (see illustration).
32 Refitting is the reverse of removal, tightening the sensor retaining bolts to the specified torque.

Knock sensor

33 Firmly apply the handbrake, then jack up the front of the car and support it securely on axle stands (see *Jacking and vehicle support*).
34 Unscrew the two retaining bolts and remove the inlet manifold support bracket.
35 Undo the retaining bolt securing the knock sensor to the cylinder block and release the sensor from its location (see illustration).
36 Trace the wiring back to the knock sensor wiring connector. Disconnect the connector, release the wiring harness and remove the sensor.
37 On refitting, ensure the mating surfaces are clean and dry then fit the sensor and tighten its retaining bolt to the specified torque. Ensure the wiring is correctly routed and securely reconnected.

Electronic control unit (ECU)

Note: *If a new ECU is to be fitted, this work must be entrusted to a Vauxhall/Opel dealer or suitably-equipped specialist as it is necessary to program the new ECU after installation. This work requires the use of dedicated Vauxhall/Opel diagnostic equipment or a compatible alternative.*

38 Remove the plastic cover over the top of the engine.
39 Lift up the locking bars and disconnect the two ECU wiring connectors.
40 Disconnect the knock sensor wiring connector.
41 Undo the retaining bolt and detach the earth lead from the ECU.
42 Undo the two retaining bolts and remove the ECU from the engine.
43 Refitting is a reversal of removal.

Oxygen sensors

44 Refer to Chapter 4C for removal and refitting details.

---

13 Simtec 75.1 injection system components – removal and refitting

Airflow meter

1 Disconnect the wiring connector from the airflow meter at the right-hand rear corner of the engine compartment.
2 Slacken the retaining clamps and remove the airflow meter from the air intake ducts.
3 Refitting is a reversal of removal, but ensure that the arrow on the airflow meter body points toward the throttle housing when fitted.

Fuel rail and injectors

Note: *Refer to the precautions given in Section 1*

before proceeding. The seals at both ends of the fuel injectors must be renewed on refitting.

4 Disconnect the battery negative terminal (refer to *Disconnecting the battery* in the Reference Chapter).

5 Depressurise the fuel system as described in Section 5.

6 Remove the air cleaner assembly and intake duct as described in Section 2.

7 Unclip the wiring harness trough from the rear of the camshaft cover **(see illustration)**.

8 Pull out the retaining wire clip and disconnect the breather hose from the camshaft cover **(see illustration)**.

9 Disconnect the wiring connectors from the following components, labelling each connector to avoid confusion when refitting:

a) *Engine management ECU.*
b) *Evaporative emission control system purge valve.*
c) *Throttle housing.*
d) *Inlet camshaft VVT oil control valve.*
e) *Fuel injectors.*

10 Unclip the wiring harness from the support brackets and move the harness to one side.

11 Disconnect the fuel feed hose quick-release connector at the fuel rail **(see illustration)**. Be prepared for some loss of fuel. A Vauxhall/Opel special tool is available to release the connector, but provided care is taken, it can be released using a pair of long-nosed pliers, or a similar tool, to depress the retaining tangs. Clamp or plug the open end of the hose, to prevent dirt ingress and further fuel spillage.

12 Unscrew the two mounting bolts, then lift the fuel rail complete with the injectors off of the inlet manifold.

13 To remove an injector from the fuel rail, prise out the metal securing clip using a screwdriver or a pair of pliers, and pull the injector from the fuel rail. Remove and discard the injector sealing rings; new ones must be fitted on refitting.

14 Overhaul of the fuel injectors is not possible, as no spares are available. If faulty, an injector must be renewed.

15 Commence refitting by fitting new O-ring seals to both ends of the fuel injectors. Coat the seals with a thin layer of petroleum jelly before fitting.

16 Refitting is a reversal of removal, bearing in mind the following points:

a) *When refitting the injectors to the fuel rail, note that the groove in the metal securing clip must engage with the lug on the injector body.*
b) *Make sure that the quick-release connector audibly engages on the fuel rail.*
c) *Ensure that all wiring connectors are securely reconnected, and that the wiring is secured in the relevant clips and brackets.*

Crankshaft position sensor

Note: *A new O-ring seal must be used on refitting.*

13.7 Unclip the wiring harness trough from the rear of the camshaft cover

17 The crankshaft sensor is located at the rear left-hand end of the cylinder block, below the starter motor.

18 Apply the handbrake, then jack up the front of the vehicle and support it on axle stands (see *Jacking and vehicle support*).

19 Remove the starter motor as described in Chapter 5A.

20 Disconnect the sensor wiring connector, then undo the retaining bolt and withdraw the sensor from the cylinder block.

21 Refitting is a reversal of removal, but ensure that the mating surfaces of the sensor and baseplate are clean and fit a new O-ring seal to the sensor before refitting. Tighten the bolt to the specified torque.

Camshaft sensor

22 Two sensors are fitted, one for each camshaft. Both sensors are located at the left-hand end of the cylinder head.

23 Disconnect the wiring connector from the relevant sensor **(see illustration)**. If removing the exhaust camshaft sensor, unclip the oxygen sensor wiring harness from the support bracket.

24 Undo the retaining bolt and remove the sensor from the cylinder head.

25 Refitting is a reversal of removal, tightening the sensor retaining bolt to the specified torque.

Coolant temperature sensor

26 Refer to Chapter 3 for removal and refitting details.

13.11 Disconnect the fuel feed hose quick-release connector (arrowed) at the fuel rail

13.8 Pull out the retaining wire clip and disconnect the breather hose from the camshaft cover

Knock sensor

27 The knock sensor is located on the rear of the cylinder block, just above the starter motor.

28 Apply the handbrake, then jack up the front of the vehicle and support it on axle stands (see *Jacking and vehicle support*).

29 Disconnect the oxygen sensor wiring connector, then unclip the connector from the support bracket.

30 Unscrew the two retaining bolts and remove the inlet manifold support bracket.

31 Disconnect the knock sensor wiring connector, then unscrew the retaining bolt and remove the sensor from the cylinder block.

32 Clean the contact surfaces of the sensor and block. Also clean the threads of the sensor mounting bolt.

33 Locate the sensor on the block and insert the mounting bolt. Tighten the bolt to the specified torque. Note that the torque setting is critical for the sensor to function correctly.

34 Refit the inlet manifold support bracket and oxygen sensor wiring connector, then lower the vehicle to the ground.

Electronic control unit (ECU)

Note: *If a new ECU is to be fitted, this work must be entrusted to a Vauxhall/Opel dealer or suitably-equipped specialist as it is necessary to program the new ECU after installation. This work requires the use of dedicated Vauxhall/Opel diagnostic equipment or a compatible alternative.*

35 The ECU is located on the left-hand side of the inlet manifold.

13.23 Disconnect the wiring connector (arrowed) from the camshaft sensor (exhaust sensor shown)

13.37 Lift up the locking bars and disconnect the two ECU wiring connectors

36 Disconnect the battery negative terminal (refer to *Disconnecting the battery* in the Reference Chapter).
37 Lift up the locking bars and disconnect the two ECU wiring connectors **(see illustration)**.

14.5a Release the clips (arrowed) securing the crankcase ventilation valve hoses to the camshaft cover . . .

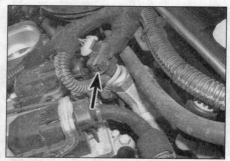

14.7a Disconnect the wiring connectors at the fuel pressure sensor (arrowed) . . .

14.8 Disconnect the fuel feed hose quick-release connector at the fuel pressure regulator (arrowed)

38 Undo the retaining bolt and detach the earth lead from the ECU.
39 Undo the four retaining bolts and remove the ECU from the engine.
40 Refitting is a reversal of removal.

Oxygen sensors

41 Refer to Chapter 4C for removal and refitting details.

14 Simtec 81.1 injection system components – removal and refitting

Fuel rail and injectors

Note 1: *Numerous special tools are required to remove and refit the injectors and fuel rail. Read through the entire procedure to familiarise yourself with the work involved,*

14.5b . . . and cylinder head

14.7b . . . and fuel pressure regulator (arrowed)

14.9a Disconnect the fuel return hose quick-release connectors at the fuel pressure regulator (arrowed) . . .

and ensure the special tools (or suitable alternatives) are available before proceeding.
Note 2: *New sealing rings and retaining clips will be required for each injector for refitting.*
1 Disconnect the battery negative terminal (refer to *Disconnecting the battery* in the Reference Chapter).
2 Remove the plastic cover over the top of the engine.
3 Depressurise the fuel system as described in Section 5.
4 Slacken the retaining clips securing the air intake duct to the airflow meter and throttle housing. Detach the intake duct from the airflow meter and throttle housing, and remove the duct from the engine.
5 Release the clips securing the crankcase ventilation valve hoses to the camshaft cover and cylinder head **(see illustrations)**. Unclip the ventilation valve and remove it from the engine.
6 Remove the engine management electronic control unit as described later in this Section.
7 Disconnect the wiring connectors at the fuel pressure sensor and fuel pressure regulator **(see illustrations)**.
8 Disconnect the fuel feed hose quick-release connector at the fuel pressure regulator **(see illustration)**. Be prepared for some loss of fuel. A Vauxhall/Opel special tool is available to release the connector, but provided care is taken, it can be released using a pair of long-nosed pliers, or a similar tool, to depress the retaining tangs. Suitably cover or plug the open unions, to prevent dirt ingress and further fuel spillage. Release the disconnected hose from its retaining clips and move it to one side.
9 Disconnect the fuel return hose quick-release connectors at the fuel pressure regulator and high-pressure fuel pump **(see illustrations)**. Be prepared for some loss of fuel. Suitably cover or plug the open unions, to prevent dirt ingress and further fuel spillage. Release the retaining clips and remove the hose from the engine.
10 Thoroughly clean the fuel pipe unions on the high-pressure fuel pump and fuel rail. Using an open-ended spanner, unscrew the union nuts securing the fuel pipe to the fuel pump and fuel rail **(see illustration)**. Be prepared for some loss of fuel. Withdraw the

14.9b . . . and high-pressure fuel pump (arrowed)

high-pressure fuel pipe and plug or cover the open unions to prevent dirt entry.

11 Disconnect the wiring harness connectors at the evaporative emission control purge valve, manifold absolute pressure sensor and the inlet manifold switchover solenoid valve. Undo the two nuts and detach the wiring harness bracket. Unclip the wiring harness and move it to one side.

12 Unscrew the two stud bolts and the four mounting bolts securing the fuel rail and injectors to the cylinder head.

13 Screw the Vauxhall/Opel special tool KM-6359 into the stud bolt holes at each end of the fuel rail. Tighten both tools to draw the fuel rail and injectors out from the cylinder head. Take care not to tilt the fuel rail as it is being removed.

14 Detach the injector wiring harness, then remove the spring clip and plastic clip and withdraw each injector from the fuel rail. Note that new clips and new injector seals will be required for each injector for refitting.

15 If the injectors remained in place in the cylinder head when the fuel rail was removed, it will be necessary to use Vauxhall/Opel special tools KM-6360 and KM-328-B to remove them. Detach the sealing ring and support ring from the top of each injector. Attach KM-6360 to the injector and turn the tool back and forth to release the injector from its seat. Once the injector is free, use tool KM-328-B to pull the injector from the cylinder head. Remove the remaining injectors in the same way.

16 Clean the body of each injector with a soft brass brush taking great care not to touch the injector nozzle.

17 Remove the combustion chamber sealing ring on each injector then fit a new sealing ring using the various components of Vauxhall/ Opel special tool KM-6364. Place the new sealing ring on the fitting sleeve, then locate the fitting sleeve on the injector. Push the sealing ring into position on the injector using the cylindrical side of the fitting tool, until the seal reaches the groove in the injector. Smooth the sealing ring by turning it slightly with the conical side of the fitting tool, then leave the tool in position until the injectors are ready for refitting. Repeat this procedure for the remaining injectors.

18 Remove the old sealing ring and support ring from the top of each injector and clean the ring locations. Using the fitting sleeve of tool KM-6364, fit a new support ring, then fit a new sealing ring. Repeat this procedure for the remaining injectors.

19 Using a circular movement, fit the four injectors into the fuel rail and secure each one with a new spring clip and plastic clip.

20 Refit the injector wiring harness and reconnect the injectors, fuel pressure regulator and fuel pressure sensor.

21 Clean the injector locations in the cylinder head and remove the fitting tools from the injectors. Refit the injector and fuel rail assembly to the cylinder head.

22 Insert the four retaining bolts and tighten

them in a spiral sequence, in two stages to the specified torque.

23 Refit the two stud bolts to the fuel rail and tighten to the specified torque.

24 The remainder of refitting is a reversal of removal, bearing in mind the following points:
 a) *Ensure that all wiring connectors are securely reconnected, and that the wiring is secured in the relevant clips and brackets.*
 b) *Tighten the high-pressure fuel pipe unions to the specified torque.*
 c) *On completion, reconnect the battery, start the engine and check for fuel leaks. If satisfactory, refit the engine cover.*

High-pressure fuel pump

25 Disconnect the battery negative terminal (refer to *Disconnecting the battery* in the Reference Chapter).

26 Remove the plastic cover over the top of the engine.

27 Depressurise the fuel system as described in Section 5.

28 Disconnect the fuel return hose quick-release connector at the high-pressure fuel pump **(see illustration 14.9b)**. Be prepared for some loss of fuel. A Vauxhall/ Opel special tool is available to release the connector, but provided care is taken, it can be released using a pair of long-nosed pliers, or a similar tool, to depress the retaining tangs. Suitably cover or plug the open unions, to prevent dirt ingress and further fuel spillage.

29 Thoroughly clean the fuel pipe unions on the high-pressure fuel pump and fuel rail. Using an open-ended spanner, unscrew the union nuts securing the fuel pipe to the fuel pump and fuel rail **(see illustration 14.10)**. Be prepared for some loss of fuel. Withdraw the high-pressure fuel pipe and plug or cover the open unions to prevent dirt entry.

30 Undo the three retaining bolts and remove the high-pressure pump from the cylinder head. Collect the gasket.

31 Thoroughly clean the mating faces of the cylinder head and fuel pump and locate a new gasket on the pump.

32 Place the pump in position on the cylinder head and refit the three retaining bolts. Tighten the bolts to the specified torque.

33 Reconnect the fuel pipe to the pump and fuel rail and tighten the union nuts to the specified torque.

34 Reconnect the fuel return hose to the pump.

35 Reconnect the battery, then start the engine and check for fuel leaks.

36 Refit the engine cover on completion.

Fuel pressure regulator

37 Disconnect the battery negative terminal (refer to *Disconnecting the battery* in the Reference Chapter).

38 Remove the plastic cover over the top of the engine.

39 Depressurise the fuel system as described in Section 5.

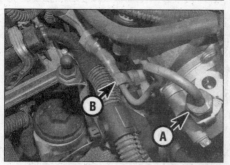

14.10 Unscrew the union nuts securing the fuel pipe to the fuel pump (A) and fuel rail (B)

40 Slacken the retaining clips securing the air intake duct to the airflow meter and throttle housing. Detach the intake duct from the airflow meter and throttle housing, and remove the duct from the engine.

41 Disconnect the wiring connector at the fuel pressure regulator, then undo the two retaining bolts and remove the regulator from the fuel rail **(see illustration)**. Be prepared for some loss of fuel. Remove the two sealing rings from the regulator.

42 Fit two new sealing rings to the regulator, then place the unit in position on the fuel rail. Refit and tighten the retaining bolts to the specified torque and reconnect the wiring connector.

43 Refit the air intake duct and securely tighten its retaining clips.

44 Refit the engine cover and reconnect the battery.

Fuel pressure sensor

45 Disconnect the battery negative terminal (refer to *Disconnecting the battery* in the Reference Chapter).

46 Remove the plastic cover over the top of the engine.

47 Depressurise the fuel system as described in Section 5.

48 Remove the cable-tie, then disconnect the wiring connector at the fuel pressure sensor **(see illustration 14.7a)**. Unscrew the sensor and remove it from the fuel rail. Collect the sealing ring.

49 Refit the sensor to the fuel rail using a

14.41 Undo the two retaining bolts (arrowed) and remove the fuel pressure regulator from the fuel rail

14.60 Disconnect the manifold absolute pressure sensor wiring connector (arrowed)

new sealing ring, and tighten the sensor to the specified torque.

50 Reconnect the wiring connector and secure with a new cable-tie.

51 Reconnect the battery, then start the engine and check for fuel leaks.

52 Refit the engine cover on completion.

Coolant temperature sensor

53 Refer to Chapter 3 for removal and refitting details.

Airflow meter

54 Slacken the retaining clip securing the air intake duct to the airflow meter and disconnect the duct.

55 Disconnect the airflow meter wiring connector.

56 Slacken the retaining clip and remove the airflow meter from the air cleaner housing lid.

57 Refitting is a reversal of removal, but ensure that the arrow on the airflow meter points toward the throttle body/housing when fitted.

Manifold absolute pressure sensor

58 Remove the plastic cover over the top of the engine.

59 Unclip the wiring harness connector located above the manifold absolute pressure sensor.

60 Disconnect the pressure sensor wiring connector, undo the retaining bolt and remove the sensor from the inlet manifold **(see illustration)**.

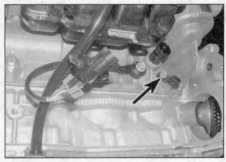

14.65 Crankshaft sensor retaining bolt (arrowed)

61 Refit the sensor to the manifold, refit the retaining bolt and tighten to the specified torque.

62 Reconnect the sensor wiring connector, secure the wiring harness connector, and refit the engine cover.

Crankshaft sensor

63 Remove the starter motor as described in Chapter 5A.

64 Trace the wiring back from the sensor, releasing it from all the relevant clips and ties whilst noting its correct routing. Disconnect the wiring connector from the sensor.

65 Unscrew the retaining bolt and remove the sensor from the cylinder block **(see illustration)**.

66 Refitting is the reverse of removal, tightening the retaining bolt to the specified torque. Ensure the wiring is correctly routed and retained by all the necessary clips and ties.

Camshaft sensor

67 Remove the plastic cover over the top of the engine.

68 Remove the air cleaner assembly and air intake duct as described in Section 2.

69 Disconnect the wiring connector, undo the retaining bolt and remove the sensor from the cylinder head.

70 Refitting is a reversal of removal.

Knock sensor

71 Remove the starter motor as described in Chapter 5A.

72 Disconnect the wiring block connector, so the wiring is free to be removed with the sensor.

73 Unscrew the retaining bolt and remove the sensor from the cylinder block **(see illustration)**.

74 On refitting ensure the mating surfaces are clean and dry then fit the sensor and tighten its retaining bolt to the specified torque. Ensure the wiring is correctly routed and retained by all the necessary clips and ties.

Electronic control unit (ECU)

Note: *If a new ECU is to be fitted, this work must be entrusted to a Vauxhall/Opel dealer or suitably-equipped specialist as it is necessary to program the new ECU after installation. This work requires the use of dedicated Vauxhall/*

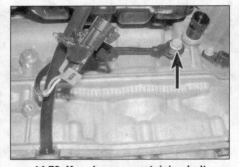

14.73 Knock sensor retaining bolt (arrowed)

Opel diagnostic equipment or a compatible alternative.

75 Disconnect the battery negative terminal (refer to *Disconnecting the battery* in the Reference Chapter).

76 Remove the plastic cover over the top of the engine.

77 Lift up the locking bars and disconnect the two ECU wiring connectors **(see illustration)**.

78 Undo the retaining bolt and disconnect the earth lead from the centre of the ECU.

79 Disconnect the wiring connector at the throttle body/housing and move the wiring harness clear of the ECU.

80 Undo the three retaining bolts and remove the ECU from the inlet manifold.

81 Refitting is a reversal of removal.

Oxygen sensors

82 Refer to Chapter 4C for removal and refitting details.

15 Inlet manifold – removal and refitting

1.8 litre Z18XE engines

Removal

1 Disconnect the battery negative terminal (refer to *Disconnecting the battery* in the Reference Chapter).

2 Remove the plastic cover over the top of the engine.

3 Drain the cooling system as described in Chapter 1A.

4 Remove the air cleaner assembly and air intake duct as described in Section 2.

5 Depressurise the fuel system as described in Section 5.

6 Remove the auxiliary drivebelt as described in Chapter 1A.

7 Remove the alternator as described in Chapter 5A.

8 Remove the fuel rail and injectors as described in Section 12.

9 Undo the two bolts and remove the inlet manifold support bracket.

10 Disconnect the remaining vacuum hoses, wiring connectors and auxiliary fittings to enable removal of the inlet manifold.

14.77 Lift up the locking bars and disconnect the two ECU wiring connectors

11 Slacken and remove the retaining nuts and manoeuvre the manifold assembly away from the engine. Remove the gasket and discard it. **Note:** *The manifold assembly must be treated as a sealed unit; do not attempt to dismantle it as no components, other than the switchover diaphragm and solenoid, are available separately.*

Refitting

12 Refitting is the reverse of removal noting the following.
  a) *Prior to refitting, check the manifold studs and renew any that are worn or damaged.*
  b) *Ensure the manifold and cylinder mating surfaces are clean and dry and fit the new gasket. Refit the manifold and tighten the retaining nuts evenly and progressively to the specified torque.*
  c) *Ensure that all relevant hoses are reconnected to their original positions, and are securely held (where necessary) by their retaining clips.*
  d) *On completion, refill the cooling system as described in Chapter 1A.*

1.8 litre Z18XER engines

Removal

13 Disconnect the battery negative terminal (refer to *Disconnecting the battery* in the Reference Chapter).
14 Firmly apply the handbrake, then jack up the front of the car and support it securely on axle stands (see *Jacking and vehicle support*).
15 Drain the cooling system as described in Chapter 1A.
16 Remove the air cleaner assembly and air intake duct as described in Section 2.
17 Depressurise the fuel system as described in Section 5.
18 Remove the throttle housing as described in Section 9.
19 From under the car, disconnect the oxygen sensor wiring connector, then unclip the connector from the support bracket.
20 Unscrew the two retaining bolts and remove the inlet manifold support bracket.
21 Unclip the wiring harness from the base of the inlet manifold.
22 Disconnect the wiring connector from the evaporative emission control system purge valve **(see illustration)**.
23 Slide the purge valve rubber mounting off the mounting bracket, then disconnect the vapour hose from the inlet manifold. Place the valve to one side.
24 Unclip the wiring harness trough from the rear of the camshaft cover **(see illustration 13.7)**.
25 Pull out the retaining wire clip and disconnect the breather hose from the camshaft cover **(see illustration 13.8)**.
26 Remove the engine management ECU as described in Section 15.
27 Disconnect the wiring connectors from the inlet camshaft VVT oil control valve and the four fuel injectors. Release the wiring harness from the support brackets and place it to one side.

15.22 Disconnect the wiring connector (arrowed) from the evaporative emission control system purge valve

28 Disconnect the wiring harness block connector on the left-hand side of the inlet manifold **(see illustration)**.
29 Release the throttle housing coolant hoses from their clips and supports on the inlet manifold and disconnect the hoses from the coolant expansion tank and thermostat housing. Move the hoses to one side.
30 Disconnect the wiring connectors at the manifold switchover valve diaphragm and solenoid.
31 Undo the retaining bolt and detach the wiring harness support bracket from the engine lifting bracket.
32 Disconnect the quick-release fitting and detach the brake servo vacuum hose from the inlet manifold.
33 Slacken and remove the seven retaining bolts and manoeuvre the manifold assembly away from the cylinder head. Remove the gasket and discard it. **Note:** *The manifold assembly must be treated as a sealed unit; do not attempt to dismantle it as no components, other than the switchover diaphragm and solenoid, are available separately.*

Refitting

34 Refitting is the reverse of removal noting the following.
  a) *Ensure the manifold and cylinder head mating surfaces are clean and dry and fit the new gasket. Refit the manifold and tighten the retaining bolts evenly and progressively to the specified torque.*
  b) *Ensure that all relevant hoses are reconnected to their original positions, and are securely held (where necessary) by their retaining clips.*
  c) *On completion, refill the cooling system as described in Chapter 1A.*

2.2 litre engines

Removal

35 Disconnect the battery negative terminal (refer to *Disconnecting the battery* in the Reference Chapter).
36 Remove the plastic cover over the top of the engine.
37 Depressurise the fuel system as described in Section 5.
38 Slacken the retaining clips securing the air intake duct to the airflow meter and throttle

15.28 Disconnect the wiring harness block connector on the left-hand side of the inlet manifold

housing. Detach the intake duct from the airflow meter and throttle housing, and remove the duct from the engine.
39 Remove the throttle housing as described in Section 9.
40 Remove the engine management electronic control unit as described in Section 14.
41 Unscrew the bolt securing the engine oil dipstick guide tube to the inlet manifold.
42 Remove the exhaust gas recirculation pipe by undoing the two nuts and detaching the engine cover bracket. Unscrew the two stud bolts, and undo the pipe support bracket bolt. Undo the two bolts securing the pipe to the inlet manifold, and remove the pipe. Recover the gasket.
43 Release the clips securing the crankcase ventilation valve hoses to the camshaft cover and cylinder head **(see illustration 14.5a and 14.5b)**. Unclip the ventilation valve and remove it from the engine.
44 Disconnect the wiring harness connectors at the evaporative emission control purge valve, manifold absolute pressure sensor, inlet manifold switchover solenoid valve and the fuel pressure regulator. Unclip the wiring harness and move it to one side.
45 Firmly apply the handbrake, then jack up the front of the car and support it securely on axle stands (see *Jacking and vehicle support*).
46 Unclip the knock sensor wiring connector then remove the oil dipstick guide tube.
47 Undo the bolt securing the inlet manifold support bracket to the cylinder block.
48 Remove the auxiliary drivebelt as described in Chapter 1A.
49 Remove the alternator as described in Chapter 5A.
50 Disconnect the brake servo vacuum pipe at the quick-release fitting.
51 Undo the two retaining bolts and remove the fuel pressure regulator from the fuel rail **(see illustration 14.41)**. Be prepared for some loss of fuel. Remove the two sealing rings from the regulator.
52 Undo the seven bolts and two nuts securing the inlet manifold to the cylinder head. Remove the manifold from the cylinder head.
53 Remove the four switchover valves from the manifold ports, then remove the manifold gasket. Clean the mating surface and fit a new gasket, then refit the switchover valves.

Refitting

54 Refitting is the reverse of removal noting the following.

  a) *Ensure the cylinder head mating surface is clean and dry, refit the manifold and tighten the retaining bolts and nuts evenly and progressively to the specified torque.*

  b) *Renew the fuel pressure regulator sealing rings and the exhaust gas recirculation pipe gasket.*

  c) *Ensure that all relevant hoses are reconnected to their original positions, and are securely held (where necessary) by their retaining clips.*

16 Exhaust manifold – removal and refitting

1.8 litre Z18XE engines

Note: *New manifold and exhaust front pipe retaining nuts, a new manifold gasket and exhaust front pipe gasket must be used on refitting.*

Removal

1 Disconnect the battery negative terminal (refer to *Disconnecting the battery* in the Reference Chapter).

2 Remove the plastic cover over the top of the engine.

3 Apply the handbrake, then jack up the front of the vehicle and support it on axle stands (see *Jacking and vehicle support*).

4 Undo the three retaining nuts and separate the exhaust front pipe from the exhaust manifold, taking care to support the flexible section. **Note:** *Angular movement in excess of 10° can cause permanent damage to the flexible section.* Recover the gasket.

5 Release the mounting rubbers and support the front of the exhaust pipe to one side.

6 Trace the wiring back from the oxygen sensor (mixture regulation) and disconnect its wiring connector. Free the wiring from all the necessary clips and ties so the sensor is free to be removed with the manifold.

7 Drain the cooling system as described in Chapter 1A, or alternatively place a suitable container beneath the radiator top hose to collect escaping coolant. Release the retaining clip and disconnect the top hose from the thermostat housing.

8 Undo the three retaining bolts and remove the heat shield from the manifold.

9 Slacken and remove the ten retaining nuts, and manoeuvre the manifold out of the engine compartment. Recover the gasket.

Refitting

10 Examine all the exhaust manifold studs for signs of damage and corrosion; remove all traces of corrosion, and repair or renew any damaged studs.

11 Ensure that the manifold and cylinder head sealing faces are clean and flat, and fit the new gasket.

12 Refit the manifold then fit the new retaining nuts and tighten them progressively, in a diagonal sequence, to the specified torque. Wait thirty seconds and tighten the nuts to the specified torque again.

13 Align the heat shield with the manifold, and tighten the screws to the specified torque.

14 Reconnect the exhaust front pipe, using a new gasket. Tighten the new nuts to the specified torque.

15 Reconnect the oxygen sensor wiring connector making sure the wiring is correctly routed and retained by all the necessary clips.

16 Refit the engine cover.

17 Reconnect the battery, then refill or top-up the cooling system as described in Chapter 1A, or *Weekly checks*, as applicable.

1.8 litre Z18XER engines

Note: *New manifold and exhaust front pipe retaining nuts, a new manifold gasket, exhaust front pipe gasket and oil dipstick guide tube O-rings must be used on refitting.*

Removal

18 Disconnect the battery negative terminal (refer to *Disconnecting the battery* in the Reference Chapter).

19 Remove the air cleaner assembly and air intake ducts as described in Section 2.

20 Unbolt and remove the oil dipstick guide tube, and withdraw it from the cylinder block. Remove and discard the O-ring seals.

21 Trace the wiring back from the manifold oxygen sensor and disconnect its wiring connector. Free the wiring from the support bracket so the sensor is free to be removed with the manifold.

22 Apply the handbrake, then jack up the front of the vehicle and support it on axle stands (see *Jacking and vehicle support*).

23 Disconnect the wiring from the oxygen sensor, then unbolt the exhaust front pipe from the exhaust manifold, taking care to support the flexible section. **Note:** *Angular movement in excess of 10° can cause permanent damage to the flexible section.* Recover the gasket.

24 Release the mounting rubbers and support the front of the exhaust pipe to one side.

25 Undo the two lower bolts securing the heat shield to the exhaust manifold.

26 Undo the two bolts securing the manifold to the lower support bracket, and the two bolts securing the support bracket to the cylinder block. Remove the bracket.

27 On models with air conditioning, unbolt the compressor from the front of the engine with reference to Chapter 3, and support it to one side. **Do not** disconnect the refrigerant lines from the compressor.

28 Unbolt the two engine lifting brackets from the exhaust manifold.

29 Undo the bolt securing the wiring harness support bracket, then remove the bracket and the exhaust manifold heat shield.

30 Slacken and remove the nine retaining nuts, and manoeuvre the manifold out of the engine compartment. Recover the gasket.

Refitting

31 Examine all the exhaust manifold studs for signs of damage and corrosion; remove all traces of corrosion, and repair or renew any damaged studs.

32 Ensure that the manifold and cylinder head sealing faces are clean and flat, and fit the new gasket.

33 Refit the manifold then fit the new retaining nuts and tighten them progressively, in a diagonal sequence, to the specified torque.

34 Align the heat shield with the manifold, then refit the wiring harness support bracket and tighten the retaining bolt securely.

35 On air conditioning models, refit the compressor with reference to Chapter 3.

36 Refit the lower support bracket to the cylinder block and manifold and tighten the retaining bolts securely.

37 Refit and tighten the two lower bolts securing the heat shield to the exhaust manifold.

38 Reconnect the exhaust front pipe, using a new gasket. Tighten the new nuts to the specified torque. Reconnect the oxygen sensor wiring connector.

39 Reconnect the exhaust manifold oxygen sensor wiring connector making sure the wiring is correctly routed and retained by the support bracket.

40 Fit the new O-ring seals to the oil dipstick guide tube, then insert the tube in the cylinder block. Insert and tighten the retaining bolt.

41 Refit the air cleaner assembly and air intake ducts as described in Section 2.

42 Lower the vehicle to the ground, then reconnect the battery negative lead.

2.2 litre engines

Note: *New manifold and exhaust front pipe retaining nuts, a new manifold gasket and exhaust front pipe gasket must be used on refitting.*

Removal

43 Disconnect the battery negative terminal (refer to *Disconnecting the battery* in the Reference Chapter).

44 Remove the plastic cover over the top of the engine.

45 Apply the handbrake, then jack up the front of the vehicle and support it on axle stands (see *Jacking and vehicle support*).

46 Undo the three retaining nuts and separate the exhaust front pipe from the exhaust manifold, taking care to support the flexible section. **Note:** *Angular movement in excess of 10° can cause permanent damage to the flexible section.* Recover the gasket.

47 Release the mounting rubbers and support the front of the exhaust pipe to one side.

48 Disconnect the two oxygen sensor wiring connectors at the right-hand end of the cylinder head. Unclip the wiring harness from the support bracket.

49 Undo the nut and bolt and remove the right-hand engine lifting eye from the cylinder head.

50 Unbolt the heat shield from the exhaust manifold.

51 Slacken and remove the ten retaining nuts, and manoeuvre the manifold out of the engine compartment. Recover the gasket.

Refitting

52 Examine all the exhaust manifold studs for signs of damage and corrosion; remove all traces of corrosion, and repair or renew any damaged studs.

53 Ensure that the manifold and cylinder head sealing faces are clean and flat, and fit the new gasket.

54 Refit the manifold then fit the new retaining nuts and tighten them progressively, in a diagonal sequence, to the specified torque. Wait thirty seconds and tighten the nuts to the specified torque again.

55 Refit the heat shield and lifting eye, then reconnect the oxygen sensor wiring connectors.

56 Reconnect the exhaust front pipe, using a new gasket. Tighten the new nuts to the specified torque.

57 Refit the engine cover.

58 Lower the car to the ground and reconnect the battery.

---

17 Exhaust system –
general information,
removal and refitting

General information

1 The exhaust system consists of three sections: the front pipe which incorporates the oxygen sensor (catalytic converter control), the intermediate pipe and front silencer, and the tailpipe and rear silencer.

2 The front pipe is attached to the exhaust manifold (catalytic converter) by a flange joint secured by nuts. All other exhaust sections are joined by overlap joints which are secured by clamps. The system is suspended throughout its entire length by rubber mountings.

3 To remove an individual exhaust section, the complete system is first removed as a unit. The sections are then separated with the system off the car.

4 The manufacturers specify that if any of the exhaust sections are separated, the clamps must be renewed. As the clamps are attached to the exhaust sections by means of a spot weld at manufacture, it will be necessary to use a suitable grinder to remove the spot weld.

Complete system removal

5 To remove the system, first jack up the front and rear of the car and support it securely on axle stands. Alternatively, position the car over an inspection pit or on car ramps. The help of an assistant will be needed.

6 Trace the wiring back from the oxygen sensor, noting its correct routing, and disconnect its wiring connector. Free the wiring from any clips so the sensor is free to be removed with the system.

7 Spray some penetrating oil over the exhaust rubber mounting blocks so that the mounting blocks will slide easily on the exhaust and underbody hangers **(see illustration)**.

8 Undo the three retaining nuts and separate the exhaust front pipe from the exhaust manifold, taking care to support the flexible section. **Note:** *Angular movement in excess of 10° can cause permanent damage to the flexible section.* Recover the gasket.

9 Slide the front pipe rubber mounting blocks as far forward as possible. Move the exhaust system to the rear and disengage the front pipe hangers from the mounting blocks.

10 Move the exhaust system forward and disengage the intermediate pipe and tailpipe hangers from the rubber mounting blocks. Lower the system to the ground and slide it out from under the car.

Individual section removal

11 Remove the complete system as described previously.

12 Slacken and remove the nut from the relevant exhaust clamp retaining bolt. Apply liberal amounts of penetrating oil to the joint and tap around the joint and clamp with a hammer to free it. Twist the pipe to be removed in both directions while holding the adjacent pipe. Once the joint is free, pull the pipes apart.

13 Mark the position of the clamp on the pipe, so the new clamp can be fitted in the same position, then grind off the clamp retaining spot weld. Remove the clamp.

14 If the front pipe has been removed for renewal, refer to the procedures contained in Chapter 4C and transfer the oxygen sensor to the new pipe.

Catalytic converter removal

15 The catalytic converter is an integral part of the exhaust manifold and cannot be separated. Refer to Section 16 for exhaust manifold removal and refitting procedures.

Heat shield(s) removal

16 The heat shields are secured to the underside of the body by various nuts and threaded caps. Each shield can be removed once the relevant exhaust section has been removed. If a shield is being removed to gain access to a component located behind it, it may prove sufficient in some cases to remove the retaining nuts/caps, and simply lower the shield, without disturbing the exhaust system. If any of the threaded caps are damaged during removal, a suitable nut and washer can be used when refitting.

Refitting

17 Refitting is a reversal of the removal sequence, noting the following points:

a) *Ensure that all traces of corrosion have been removed from the system joints and renew all disturbed clamps.*

b) *Inspect the rubber mountings for signs of damage or deterioration, and renew as necessary.*

c) *When refitting the front pipe to the manifold (catalytic converter), use a new gasket and new retaining nuts, and tighten the nuts to the specified torque.*

d) *Prior to tightening the exhaust system clamps, ensure that all rubber mountings are correctly located, and that there is adequate clearance between the exhaust system and vehicle underbody. Tighten the clamp bolt retaining nuts securely.*

Notes

Chapter 4 Part B:
Fuel and exhaust systems – diesel engines

Contents

Degrees of difficulty

Easy, suitable for novice with little experience	**Fairly easy,** suitable for beginner with some experience	**Fairly difficult,** suitable for competent DIY mechanic	**Difficult,** suitable for experienced DIY mechanic	**Very difficult,** suitable for expert DIY or professional

Specifications

Fuel system data

System type	Bosch EDC 16C9 or EDC 16C39 high-pressure direct injection 'common-rail' system, electronically-controlled
Firing order	1–3–4–2 (No 1 at timing belt end of engine)
Fuel system operating pressure	1400 bar at 2200 rpm
Idle speed.	Controlled by ECU
Maximum speed.	Controlled by ECU
High-pressure fuel pump	Bosch CP1H
Fuel supply pump:	
Type	Electric, mounted in fuel tank
Delivery pressure	3.3 bar (maximum)
Injectors	Bosch CRIP 2-MI

Torque wrench settings

	Nm	lbf ft
Alternator and high-pressure fuel pump bracket bolts	25	18
Camshaft sensor retaining bolt(s).	9	7
Catalytic converter clamp bolt.	20	15
Charge (boost) pressure sensor retaining bolts	9	7
Crankshaft sensor retaining bolt	9	7
ECU bracket lower mounting bolt:*		
Stage 1	80	59
Stage 2	Angle-tighten a further 120°	
Stage 3	Angle-tighten a further 15°	
EGR valve pipe to exhaust manifold	25	18
Exhaust manifold nuts*.	25	18
Exhaust front pipe-to-catalytic converter nuts*	20	15
Exhaust front pipe-to-diesel particulate filter nuts*	20	15
Exhaust system clamp nuts	45	33
Fuel injector clamp bracket nuts:		
Z19DT engines.	32	24
Z19DTH engines.	25	18
Fuel pressure regulator to fuel rail	60	44
Fuel pressure sensor to fuel rail	70	52
Fuel rail retaining nuts/bolts	25	18
High-pressure fuel pipe unions:		
M12 union nuts.	22	16
M14 union nuts.	30	22
High-pressure fuel pump mounting bolts.	25	18
Inlet manifold bolts.	25	18
Temperature sensor to diesel particulate filter	45	33
Throttle housing bolts:		
Z19DT engines	25	18
Z19DTH engines.	9	7
Turbocharger oil return pipe bolts:		
M6 bolts	9	7
M8 bolts	25	18
Turbocharger oil supply pipe banjo union bolt.	15	11

* Use new fasteners

1 General information and precautions

1 The engines are equipped with a high-pressure direct injection system which incorporates the very latest in diesel injection technology. On this system, a high-pressure fuel pump is used purely to provide the pressure required for the injection system and has no control over the injection timing (unlike conventional diesel injection systems). The injection timing is controlled by the electronic control unit (ECU) via the electrically-operated injectors. The system operates as follows.

2 The fuel system consists of a fuel tank (which is mounted under the rear of the car, with an electric fuel supply pump immersed in it), a fuel filter with integral water separator, a high-pressure fuel pump, injectors and associated components.

3 Fuel is supplied to the fuel filter housing which is located in the engine compartment. The fuel filter removes all foreign matter and water and ensures that the fuel supplied to the pump is clean. Excess fuel is returned from the outlet on the filter housing lid to the tank via the fuel cooler. The fuel cooler is fitted to the underside of the vehicle and is cooled by the passing airflow to ensure the fuel is cool before it enters the fuel tank.

4 The fuel is heated to ensure no problems occur when the ambient temperature is very low. This is achieved by an electrically-operated fuel heater incorporated in the filter housing, the heater is controlled by the ECU.

5 The high-pressure fuel pump is driven at half-crankshaft speed by the timing belt. The high pressure required in the system (up to 1350 bar) is produced by the three pistons in the pump. The high-pressure pump supplies high pressure fuel to the fuel rail which acts as a reservoir for the four injectors. Since the pump has no control over the injection timing, there is no need to time the pump when installing the timing belt.

6 The electrical control system consists of the ECU, along with the following sensors:

a) *Accelerator pedal position sensor – informs the ECU of the accelerator pedal position, and the rate of throttle opening/ closing.*

b) *Coolant temperature sensor – informs the ECU of engine temperature.*

c) *Airflow meter – informs the ECU of the amount of air passing through the intake duct.*

d) *Crankshaft sensor – informs the ECU of the crankshaft position and speed of rotation.*

e) *Camshaft sensor – informs the ECU of the positions of the pistons.*

f) *Charge (boost) pressure sensor – informs ECU of the pressure in the inlet manifold.*

g) *Fuel pressure sensor – informs the ECU of the fuel pressure present in the fuel rail.*

h) *ABS control unit – informs the ECU of the vehicle speed.*

7 All the above signals are analysed by the ECU which selects the fuelling response appropriate to those values. The ECU controls the fuel injectors (varying the pulse width – the length of time the injectors are held open – to provide a richer or weaker mixture, as appropriate). The mixture is constantly varied by the ECU, to provide the best setting for cranking, starting (with either a hot or cold engine), warm-up, idle, cruising and acceleration.

8 The ECU also has full control over the fuel pressure present in the fuel rail via the high-pressure fuel regulator and third piston deactivator solenoid valve which are fitted to the high-pressure pump. To reduce the pressure, the ECU opens the high-pressure fuel regulator which allows the excess fuel to return direct to the tank from the pump. The third piston deactivator is used mainly to reduce the load on the engine, but can also be used to lower the fuel pressure. The deactivator solenoid valve relieves the fuel pressure from the third piston of the pump which results in only two of the pistons pressurising the fuel system.

9 The ECU also controls the exhaust gas recirculation (EGR) system, described in detail in Part C of this Chapter, the pre/post-heating system (see Chapter 5A), and the engine cooling fan.

10 The inlet manifold is fitted with a butterfly valve arrangement to improve efficiency at low engine speeds. Each cylinder has two intake tracts in the manifold, one of which is fitted with a valve; the operation of the valve is controlled by the ECU via an electric motor actuator drive arrangement. At low engine speeds (below approximately 1500 rpm) the valves remain closed, meaning that air entering each cylinder is passing through only one of the two manifold tracts. At higher engine speeds, the ECU opens up each of the four valves allowing the air passing through the manifold to pass through both inlet tracts.

11 A variable-vane turbocharger is fitted to increases engine efficiency. It does this by raising the pressure in the inlet manifold above atmospheric pressure. Instead of the air simply being sucked into the cylinders, it is forced in.

12 Between the turbocharger and the inlet manifold, the compressed air passes through an intercooler. This is an air-to-air heat exchanger is mounted next to the radiator, and supplied with cooling air from the front of the vehicle. The purpose of the intercooler is to remove some of the heat gained in being compressed from the inlet air. Because cooler air is denser, removal of this heat further increases engine efficiency.

13 Energy for the operation of the turbocharger comes from the exhaust gas. The gas flows through a specially-shaped housing (the turbine housing) and in so doing, spins the turbine wheel. The turbine wheel is attached to a shaft, at the end of which is another vaned wheel known as the compressor wheel. The compressor wheel spins in its own housing, and compresses the inlet air on the way to the inlet manifold. The turbo shaft is pressure-lubricated by an oil feed pipe from the main oil gallery. The shaft 'floats' on a cushion of oil. A drain pipe returns the oil to the sump. Boost pressure (the pressure in the inlet manifold) is limited by a wastegate, which diverts the exhaust gas away from the turbine wheel in response to a pressure-sensitive actuator.

14 If certain sensors fail, and send abnormal signals to the ECU, the ECU has a back-up programme. In this event, the abnormal signals are ignored, and a pre-programmed value is substituted for the sensor signal, allowing the engine to continue running, albeit at reduced efficiency. If the ECU enters its back-up mode, a warning light on the instrument panel will illuminate, and a fault code will be stored in the ECU memory. This fault code can be read using suitable specialist test equipment plugged into the system's diagnostic socket. The diagnostic socket is located in the centre

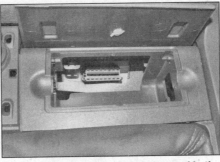

1.14 The diagnostic socket is located in the centre console, beneath the ashtray insert

console, beneath the ashtray insert **(see illustration)**.

⚠️ *Warning: It is necessary to take certain precautions when working on the fuel system components, particularly the high-pressure side of the system. Before carrying out any operations on the fuel system, refer to the precautions given in 'Safety first!' at the beginning of this manual, and to any additional warning notes at the start of the relevant Sections. Also refer to the additional information contained in Section 2.*

Caution: Do not operate the engine if any of air intake ducts are disconnected or the filter element is removed. Any debris entering the engine will cause severe damage to the turbocharger.

Caution: To prevent damage to the turbocharger, do not race the engine immediately after start-up, especially if it is cold. Allow it to idle smoothly to give the oil a few seconds to circulate around the turbocharger bearings. Always allow the engine to return to idle speed before switching it off – do not blip the throttle and switch off, as this will leave the turbo spinning without lubrication.

Caution: Observe the recommended intervals for oil and filter changing, and use a reputable oil of the specified quality. Neglect of oil changing, or use of inferior oil, can cause carbon formation on the turbo shaft, leading to subsequent failure.

2.4 Typical plastic plug and cap set for sealing disconnected fuel pipes and components

2 High-pressure diesel injection system – special information

Warnings and precautions

1 It is essential to observe strict precautions when working on the fuel system components, particularly the high-pressure side of the system. Before carrying out any operations on the fuel system, refer to the precautions given in *Safety first!* at the beginning of this manual, and to the following additional information.

• Do not carry out any repair work on the high-pressure fuel system unless you are competent to do so, have all the necessary tools and equipment required, and are aware of the safety implications involved.

• Before starting any repair work on the fuel system, wait at least 30 seconds after switching off the engine to allow the fuel circuit to return to atmospheric pressure.

• Never work on the high-pressure fuel system with the engine running.

• Keep well clear of any possible source of fuel leakage, particularly when starting the engine after carrying out repair work. A leak in the system could cause an extremely high pressure jet of fuel to escape, which could result in severe personal injury.

• Never place your hands or any part of your body near to a leak in the high-pressure fuel system.

• Do not use steam cleaning equipment or compressed air to clean the engine or any of the fuel system components.

General information

2 Strict cleanliness must be observed at all times when working on any part of the fuel system. This applies to the working area in general, the person doing the work, and the components being worked on.

3 Before working on the fuel system components, they must be thoroughly cleaned with a suitable degreasing fluid. Cleanliness is particularly important when working on the fuel system connections at the following components:

a) *Fuel filter.*
b) *High-pressure fuel pump.*
c) *Fuel rail.*
d) *Fuel injectors.*
e) *High-pressure fuel pipes.*

4 After disconnecting any fuel pipes or components, the open union or orifice must be immediately sealed to prevent the entry of dirt or foreign material. Plastic plugs and caps in various sizes are available in packs from motor factors and accessory outlets, and are particularly suitable for this application **(see illustration)**. Fingers cut from disposable rubber gloves should be used to protect components such as fuel pipes, fuel injectors and wiring connectors, and can be secured in place using elastic bands. Suitable gloves of this type are available at no cost from most petrol station forecourts.

5 Whenever any of the high-pressure fuel pipes are disconnected or removed, a new pipe(s) must be obtained for refitting.

6 The torque wrench settings given in the Specifications must be strictly observed when tightening component mountings and connections. This is particularly important when tightening the high-pressure fuel pipe unions. To enable a torque wrench to be used on the fuel pipe unions, two crow-foot adaptors are required. Suitable types are available from motor factors and accessory outlets **(see illustration)**.

3 Air cleaner assembly and intake ducts – removal and refitting

Removal

1 Slacken the retaining clips securing the air intake duct to the airflow meter and turbocharger intake duct **(see illustration)**. Where applicable, release the clip and disconnect the crankcase ventilation hose from the camshaft cover. Detach the intake duct from the airflow meter and turbocharger intake duct and remove the duct from the engine.

2 Disconnect the wiring connector from the side of the airflow meter **(see illustration)**.

3 Unclip the wiring harness from the side of the air cleaner housing **(see illustration)**.

4 Lift up the inner rear corner of the filter housing to release the mounting grommet.

2.6 Two crow-foot adaptors will be necessary for tightening the fuel pipe unions

Move the filter housing toward the engine to disengage the front and rear mounting rubbers, then release the air intake duct at the front **(see illustrations)**. Lift the filter housing out from the engine compartment.

5 The various air intake pipes/ducts linking the intercooler to the manifold and turbocharger can be disconnected and removed once the retaining clips have been slackened. In some cases it will be necessary to disconnect breather hoses, vacuum pipes and wiring connectors to allow the pipe/duct to be removed; the pipe/duct may also be bolted to a support bracket.

Refitting

6 Refitting is the reverse of removal, making sure all the air intake ducts/hoses are securely reconnected.

4 Accelerator pedal/ position sensor – removal and refitting

Refer to Chapter 4A, Section 3.

5 Fuel system – priming and bleeding

1 After disconnecting part of the fuel supply system or running out of fuel, it is necessary to prime the fuel system and bleed off any air which may have entered the system components, as follows.

2 Prime the system by switching on the ignition three times for approximately 15 seconds each time. Operate the starter for a maximum of 30 seconds. If the engine does not start within this time, wait 5 seconds and repeat the procedure.

3 When the engine starts, run it at a fast idle speed for a minute or so to purge any trapped air from the fuel lines. After this time the engine should idle smoothly at a constant speed.

4 If the engine idles roughly, then there is still some air trapped in the fuel system. Increase the engine speed again for another minute or so then allow it to idle. Repeat this procedure as necessary until the engine is idling smoothly.

6 Fuel gauge sender unit – removal and refitting

1 The fuel gauge sender unit can be removed as described in Chapter 4A, Section 6.

2 On completion, bleed the fuel system as described in Section 5.

7 Fuel supply pump – removal and refitting

1 The diesel fuel supply pump is located in the same position as the fuel supply pump on petrol engine models, and the removal and refitting procedures are virtually identical. Refer to Chapter 4A, Section 7.

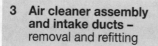

3.1 Slacken the clips (arrowed) securing the air intake duct to the airflow meter and turbocharger intake

3.2 Disconnect the wiring connector from the airflow meter

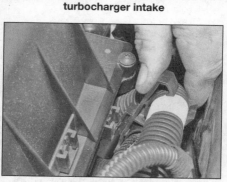

3.3 Unclip the wiring harness from the side of the air cleaner housing

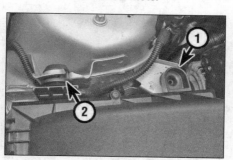

3.4a Lift up the filter housing to release the mounting grommet (1) then move the housing to disengage the rear mounting rubber (2) . . .

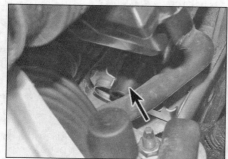

3.4b . . . and front mounting rubber (arrowed)

9.2a Disconnect the heater element wiring connector from the fuel filter cover . . .

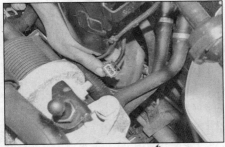

9.2b . . . and the water level sensor wiring connector from the base of the filter housing

9.3 Lift the fuel filter from the crash box

9.5 Pull up the weatherseal from the flange at the rear of the engine compartment . . .

9.6 . . . then open the access cover in the water deflector

9.8 Remove the crash box from the bulkhead

2 On completion, bleed the fuel system as described in Section 5.

8 Fuel tank – removal and refitting

1 Refer to Chapter 4A, Section 8, noting that there is no fuel filter clipped to the tank, and no charcoal canister.
2 On completion, bleed the fuel system as described in Section 5.

9 Fuel filter crash box – removal and refitting

Removal

1 The fuel filter and crash box are located at the rear of the engine compartment, in the centre of the bulkhead.
2 Disconnect the heater element wiring connector from the fuel filter cover, and the water level sensor wiring connector from the base of the filter housing **(see illustrations)**.
3 Using a screwdriver inserted from the right-hand side, depress the retaining clip and lift the filter from the crash box **(see illustration)**.
4 Unclip the wiring harness from the side of the crash box.
5 Pull up the rubber weatherseal from the flange at the rear of the engine compartment **(see illustration)**.

6 Open the pollen filter access cover in the water deflector **(see illustration)**.
7 Reach in through the pollen filter access cover and undo the three nuts securing the crash box to the bulkhead.
8 Remove the reinforcement plate and remove the crash box from the bulkhead **(see illustration)**.

Refitting

9 Refitting is the reverse of the removal procedure.

10 Injection system electrical components – removal and refitting

Airflow meter

1 Slacken the retaining clip securing the air

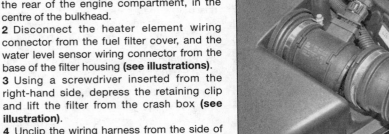

10.1 Disconnect the air intake duct from the airflow meter

intake duct to the airflow meter and disconnect the duct **(see illustration)**.
2 Disconnect the airflow meter wiring connector **(see illustration 3.2)**.
3 Slacken the retaining clip and remove the airflow meter from the air cleaner housing lid.
4 Refitting is a reversal of removal, but ensure that the arrow on the airflow meter points toward the throttle housing when fitted.

Throttle housing

Z19DT engines

5 Remove the plastic cover from the top of the engine.
6 Release the retaining clip and disconnect the charge air hose from the throttle body/housing.
7 Undo the four bolts and disconnect the metal EGR pipe from the EGR valve and throttle housing, noting its correct fitted position **(see illustration)**. Recover the two gaskets.

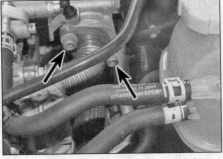

10.7 EGR pipe-to-EGR valve retaining bolts (arrowed)

10.11 Disconnect the charge air hose from the throttle housing, and intercooler charge air pipe

8 Undo the three retaining bolts and remove the throttle housing from the inlet manifold. Not the location of any wiring harness support brackets also secured by the retaining bolts.
9 Refitting is a reversal of removal, but thoroughly clean the mating faces and use a new gasket/seal and new EGR pipe gaskets. Tighten the retaining bolts to the specified torque.

Z19DTH engines

10 Remove the plastic cover from the top of the engine.
11 Release the two retaining clips and disconnect the charge air hose from the throttle housing, and intercooler charge air pipe **(see illustration)**.
12 Slacken the retaining clip and disconnect the crankcase ventilation hose from the oil filler housing.
13 Disconnect the wiring connector from the throttle housing.

10.16 The crankshaft sensor (arrowed) is located below the starter motor

10.32 Disconnect the wiring connector (arrowed) from the charge pressure sensor

14 Undo the three retaining bolts and remove the throttle housing from the inlet manifold. Not the location of any wiring harness support brackets also secured by the retaining bolts.
15 Refitting is a reversal of removal, but thoroughly clean the mating faces and use a new gasket/seal. Tighten the retaining bolts to the specified torque.

Crankshaft sensor

16 The sensor is located at the rear of the cylinder block, below the starter motor **(see illustration)**. To gain access, firmly apply the handbrake, then jack up the front of the car and support it securely on axle stands (see *Jacking and vehicle support*).
17 Undo the retaining bolts and remove the undertray from beneath the engine/transmission unit.
18 Wipe clean the area around the crankshaft sensor then disconnect the wiring connector.
19 Slacken and remove the retaining bolt and remove the sensor from the cylinder block. Recover the sealing ring.
20 Refitting is the reverse of removal, using a new sealing ring. Tighten the sensor retaining bolt to the specified torque.

Camshaft sensor

Z19DT engines

21 The camshaft sensor is located at the right-hand end of the cylinder head, behind the camshaft sprocket.
22 Remove the timing belt and camshaft sprocket as described in Chapter 2C.

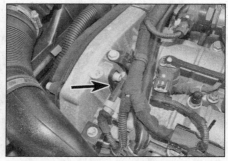

10.26 Camshaft sensor location (arrowed) – Z19DTH engines

10.38 Disconnect the wiring connector from the fuel pressure regulator – Z19DTH engines

23 Undo the two bolts securing the camshaft sensor bracket to the cylinder head.
24 Disconnect the sensor wiring connector, undo the two bolts and remove the sensor.
25 Refit the sensor using the reverse of removal, tightening the retaining bolts to the specified torque. Refit the camshaft sprocket and timing belt as described in Chapter 2C.

Z19DTH engines

26 The camshaft sensor is located at the right-hand end of the camshaft housing **(see illustration)**. To gain access, remove the plastic cover from the top of the engine.
27 Wipe clean the area around the camshaft sensor then disconnect the wiring connector.
28 Slacken and remove the retaining bolt and remove the sensor from the camshaft cover. Recover the sealing ring.
29 Refitting is the reverse of removal, using a new sealing ring. Tighten the sensor retaining bolt to the specified torque.

Coolant temperature sensor

30 The coolant temperature sensor is located on the thermostat housing on the left-hand end of the cylinder head. Refer to Chapter 3 for removal and refitting details.

Charge (boost) pressure sensor

31 Remove the plastic cover from the top of the engine.
32 Disconnect the wiring connector from the charge pressure sensor located in the centre of the inlet manifold **(see illustration)**.
33 Slacken and remove the retaining bolt and remove the sensor from the manifold. Recover the sealing ring.
34 Refitting is the reverse of removal, using a new sealing ring. Tighten the sensor retaining bolt to the specified torque.

Fuel pressure regulator

35 Disconnect the battery negative terminal (refer to *Disconnecting the battery* in the Reference Chapter).
36 Remove the plastic cover over the top of the engine.
37 On Z19DT engines, remove the fuel rail as described in Section 12.
38 On Z19DTH engines, disconnect the wiring connector from the fuel pressure regulator **(see illustration)**.
39 Remove the regulator from the fuel rail by unscrewing the inner nut (nearest the fuel rail) while counterholding the regulator body with a second spanner. Be prepared for some loss of fuel.
40 Refitting is the reverse of removal, tightening the regulator to the specified torque.

Fuel pressure sensor

Note: *On later models, the fuel pressure sensor is incorporated in the high-pressure fuel pump and a separate sensor on the fuel rail is not fitted.*

41 Disconnect the battery negative terminal (refer to *Disconnecting the battery* in the Reference Chapter).

10.43 Disconnect the fuel pressure sensor wiring connector

10.49a Undo the ECU mounting bracket lower retaining bolt . . .

10.49b . . . and upper retaining bolt (arrowed)

10.50a Release the locking clip . . .

10.50b . . . open the locking bar . . .

10.50c . . . and disconnect the ECU wiring connectors

42 Remove the plastic cover over the top of the engine.

43 Disconnect the wiring connector at the fuel pressure sensor **(see illustration)**.

44 Unscrew the sensor and remove it from the fuel rail. Be prepared for some loss of fuel.

45 Refitting is the reverse of removal, tightening the sensor to the specified torque.

Electronic control unit (ECU)

Note: *If a new ECU is to be fitted, this work must be entrusted to a Vauxhall/Opel dealer or suitably-equipped specialist as it is necessary to program the new ECU after installation. This work requires the use of dedicated Vauxhall/Opel diagnostic equipment or a compatible alternative.*

46 Disconnect the battery negative terminal (refer to *Disconnecting the battery* in the Reference Chapter).

47 Firmly apply the handbrake, then jack up the front of the car and support it securely on axle stands (see *Jacking and vehicle support*).

48 Undo the three bolts and remove the access cover from under the front bumper on the right-hand side.

49 Undo the two ECU mounting bracket retaining bolts, noting that the larger bolt also secures the front subframe and must be renewed when refitting **(see illustrations)**.

50 Release the locking clip, then open the locking bar and disconnect both wiring connectors from the ECU **(see illustrations)**. Release the wiring harness from its cable-ties and withdraw the ECU and mounting bracket from under the front wing.

51 Release the retaining catch and remove the ECU from the mounting bracket.

52 Refit the ECU to the mounting bracket, then locate the bracket in position under the front wing.

53 Refit the upper mounting bolt and the new lower mounting bolt. Tighten the upper mounting bolt securely, then tighten the lower mounting bolt to the specified torque, then through the specified angles.

54 Refit the access cover, then lower the car to the ground and reconnect the battery.

Turbocharger wastegate solenoid

55 The wastegate (charge pressure) solenoid valve is located at the front of the engine compartment above the radiator **(see illustration)**.

56 Disconnect the wiring connector and the two vacuum hoses from the valve then undo

10.55 Turbocharger wastegate solenoid valve (arrowed)

the retaining nuts and remove the valve from its mounting bracket.

57 Refitting is the reverse of removal.

11 High-pressure fuel pump – removal and refitting

Warning: Refer to the information contained in Section 2 before proceeding.

Z19DT engines

Note: *A complete new set of high-pressure fuel pipes will be required for refitting.*

Removal

1 Disconnect the battery negative terminal (refer to *Disconnecting the battery* in the Reference Chapter).

2 Remove the plastic cover over the top of the engine.

3 Remove the timing belt and the high-pressure fuel pump sprocket as described in Chapter 2C.

4 Remove the fuel rail as described in Section 12.

5 Disconnect the fuel return hose quick-release fitting on the top of the high-pressure fuel pump. Suitably plug or cover the open unions to prevent dirt entry.

6 Disconnect the wiring connector from the high-pressure fuel pump.

7 Unscrew the three retaining nuts and remove the pump from the engine bracket **(see illustrations)**.

11.7a Unscrew the three retaining nuts (arrowed) . . .

11.7b . . . and remove the high-pressure fuel pump from the engine bracket

11.18a Release the clips and disconnect the upper (arrowed) . . .

11.18b . . . and lower (arrowed) fuel return hoses at the damping chamber

Caution: The high-pressure fuel pump is manufactured to extremely close tolerances and must not be dismantled in any way. No parts for the pump are available separately and if the unit is in any way suspect, it must be renewed.

Refitting

8 Refit the pump to the engine bracket and tighten the retaining bolts to the specified torque.

9 Reconnect the pump wiring connector and the fuel return hose quick-release fitting.

10 Refit the fuel rail as described in Section 12.

11 Refit the high-pressure fuel pump sprocket and the timing belt as described in Chapter 2C.

12 Reconnect the battery negative terminal.

13 Observing the precautions listed in Section 2, prime the fuel system as described in Section 5, then start the engine and allow it to idle. Check for leaks at the high-pressure

11.22 Counterhold the fuel pipe union on the pump with a second spanner, while unscrewing the union nut

fuel pipe unions with the engine idling. If satisfactory, increase the engine speed to 4000 rpm and check again for leaks. If any leaks are detected, obtain and fit a new high-pressure fuel pipe.

14 Refit the engine cover on completion.

Z19DTH engines

Note: *A new fuel pump-to-fuel rail high-pressure fuel pipe will be required for refitting.*

Removal

15 Disconnect the battery negative terminal (refer to *Disconnecting the battery* in the Reference Chapter).

16 Remove the plastic cover over the top of the engine.

17 Remove the timing belt and the high-pressure fuel pump sprocket as described in Chapter 2D.

18 Release the retaining clips and disconnect the two fuel return hoses at the fuel return damping chamber **(see illustrations)**. Suitably plug or cover the open unions to prevent dirt entry.

19 Disconnect the injector leak-off pipe and the fuel return quick-release fitting, then undo the two bolts and remove the damping chamber. Suitably plug or cover the open unions to prevent dirt entry.

20 Disconnect the fuel return hose quick-release fitting on the top of the high-pressure fuel pump. Suitably plug or cover the open unions to prevent dirt entry.

21 Disconnect the wiring connector from the high-pressure fuel pump.

22 Thoroughly clean the fuel pipe unions

on the fuel pump and fuel rail. Using an open-ended spanner, unscrew the union nuts securing the high-pressure fuel pipe to the fuel pump and fuel rail. Counterhold the union on the pump with a second spanner, while unscrewing the union nut **(see illustration)**. Withdraw the high-pressure fuel pipe and plug or cover the open unions to prevent dirt entry.

23 Unscrew the three retaining nuts and remove the pump from the engine bracket **(see illustrations 11.7a and 11.7b)**.

Caution: The high-pressure fuel pump is manufactured to extremely close tolerances and must not be dismantled in any way. No parts for the pump are available separately and if the unit is in any way suspect, it must be renewed.

Refitting

24 Refit the pump to the engine bracket and tighten the retaining bolts to the specified torque.

25 Remove the blanking plugs from the fuel pipe unions on the pump and fuel rail. Locate a new high-pressure fuel pipe over the unions and screw on the union nuts finger tight at this stage.

26 Using a torque wrench and crow-foot adaptor, tighten the fuel pipe union nuts to the specified torque. Counterhold the unions on the pump with an open-ended spanner, while tightening the union nuts.

27 Reconnect the pump wiring connector and the fuel return hose quick-release fitting.

28 Refit the damping chamber and tighten the retaining bolts securely. Reconnect the injector leak-off pipe, and the two remaining fuel return hoses.

29 Refit the high-pressure fuel pump sprocket and the timing belt as described in Chapter 2D.

30 Reconnect the battery negative terminal.

31 Observing the precautions listed in Section 2, prime the fuel system as described in Section 5, then start the engine and allow it to idle. Check for leaks at the high-pressure fuel pipe unions with the engine idling. If satisfactory, increase the engine speed to 4000 rpm and check again for leaks. If any leaks are detected, obtain and fit a new high-pressure fuel pipe.

32 Refit the engine cover on completion.

12 Fuel rail –
removal and refitting

 Warning: Refer to the information contained in Section 2 before proceeding.

Note: *A complete new set of high-pressure fuel pipes will be required for refitting.*

Z19DT engines

Removal

1 Disconnect the battery negative terminal (refer to *Disconnecting the battery* in the Reference Chapter).

2 Remove the plastic cover over the top of the engine.

3 Release the locking catches securing the wiring connectors to the four injectors, then disconnect the injector wiring.

4 Undo the two bolts at the top and the two bolts at the front, securing the plastic wiring trough to the inlet manifold **(see illustrations)**. Move the wiring trough and injector wiring harness to one side.

5 Release the retaining clips and disconnect the two fuel return hoses at the fuel return damping chamber. Suitably plug or cover the open unions to prevent dirt entry.

6 Disconnect the injector leak-off pipe and the fuel return quick-release fitting, then undo the two bolts and remove the damping chamber. Suitably plug or cover the open unions to prevent dirt entry.

7 Thoroughly clean the fuel pipe unions on the fuel pump and fuel rail. Using an open-ended spanner, unscrew the union nuts securing the high-pressure fuel pipe to the fuel pump and fuel rail. Counterhold the unions on the pump with a second spanner, while unscrewing the union nuts. Withdraw the high-pressure fuel pipe and plug or cover the open unions to prevent dirt entry.

8 Using two spanners, hold the unions and unscrew the union nuts securing the high-pressure fuel pipes to the fuel injectors. Unscrew the union nuts securing the high-pressure fuel pipes to the fuel rail, withdraw the pipes and plug or cover the open unions to prevent dirt entry.

9 Disconnect the wiring connectors at the fuel pressure regulator and fuel pressure sensor, then undo the two nuts and remove the fuel rail.

Refitting

10 Refit the fuel rail and tighten the retaining nuts to the specified torque. Reconnect the fuel pressure regulator and fuel pressure sensor wiring connectors.

11 Working on one fuel injector at a time, remove the blanking plugs from the fuel pipe unions on the fuel rail and the relevant injector. Locate the new high-pressure fuel pipe over the unions and screw on the union nuts finger-tight. Tighten the union nuts to the specified torque using a torque wrench and crow-foot adaptor. Counterhold the union on the injector with an open-ended spanner, while tightening the union nut. Repeat this operation for the remaining three injectors.

12 Similarly, fit the new high-pressure fuel pipe to the fuel pump and fuel rail, and tighten the union nuts to the specified torque. Counterhold the union on the pump with an open-ended spanner, while tightening the union nut.

13 Refit the damping chamber and tighten the retaining bolts securely. Reconnect the injector leak-off pipe, and the fuel return hoses.

14 Refit the wiring trough, and secure with the four retaining bolts. Reconnect the wiring

12.4a Undo the two bolts at the top (arrowed) . . .

12.19 Unscrew the union nuts securing the high-pressure fuel pipes to the fuel rail and injectors

connectors to the fuel injectors. Reconnect the battery negative terminal.

15 Observing the precautions listed in Section 2, prime the fuel system as described in Section 5, then start the engine and allow it to idle. Check for leaks at the high-pressure fuel pipe unions with the engine idling. If satisfactory, increase the engine speed to 4000 rpm and check again for leaks. If any leaks are detected, obtain and fit a new high-pressure fuel pipe.

16 Refit the engine cover on completion.

Z19DTH engines

Removal

17 Disconnect the battery negative terminal (refer to *Disconnecting the battery* in the Reference Chapter).

18 Remove the plastic cover over the top of the engine.

19 Thoroughly clean all the high-pressure

12.21a Disconnect the fuel return hose . . .

12.4b . . . and the two bolts at the front (arrowed) and move the wiring trough and harness to one side

12.20 Unscrew the union nuts securing the high-pressure fuel pipe to the fuel pump and fuel rail

fuel pipe unions on the fuel rail, fuel pump and injectors. Using two spanners, hold the unions and unscrew the union nuts securing the high-pressure fuel pipes to the fuel injectors. Unscrew the union nuts securing the high-pressure fuel pipes to the fuel rail, withdraw the pipes and plug or cover the open unions to prevent dirt entry **(see illustration)**.

20 Using an open-ended spanner, unscrew the union nuts securing the high-pressure fuel pipe to the fuel pump and fuel rail **(see illustration)**. Counterhold the unions on the pump with a second spanner, while unscrewing the union nuts. Withdraw the high-pressure fuel pipe and plug or cover the open unions to prevent dirt entry.

21 Disconnect the wiring connectors at the fuel pressure regulator and fuel pressure sensor, then release the clip and disconnect the fuel return hose. Undo the two bolts and remove the fuel rail **(see illustrations)**.

12.21b . . . then undo the two bolts (arrowed) and remove the fuel rail

Refitting

22 Refit the fuel rail and tighten the retaining bolts to the specified torque. Reconnect the fuel pressure regulator and fuel pressure sensor wiring connectors, and reconnect the fuel return hose.

23 Working on one fuel injector at a time, remove the blanking plugs from the fuel pipe unions on the fuel rail and the relevant injector. Locate the new high-pressure fuel pipe over the unions and screw on the union nuts finger tight. Tighten the union nuts to the specified torque using a torque wrench and crow-foot adaptor. Counterhold the union on the injector with an open-ended spanner, while tightening the union nut. Repeat this operation for the remaining three injectors.

24 Similarly, fit the new high-pressure fuel pipe to the fuel pump and fuel rail, and tighten the union nuts to the specified torque. Counterhold the union on the pump with an open-ended spanner, while tightening the union nut.

25 Reconnect the battery negative terminal.

26 Observing the precautions listed in Section 2, prime the fuel system as described in Section 5, then start the engine and allow it to idle. Check for leaks at the high-pressure fuel pipe unions with the engine idling. If satisfactory, increase the engine speed to 4000 rpm and check again for leaks. If any leaks are detected, obtain and fit a new high-pressure fuel pipe.

27 Refit the engine cover on completion.

---

13 Fuel injectors – removal and refitting

⚠️ **Warning: Refer to the information contained in Section 2 before proceeding.**

Note 1: *A new copper washer, retaining nut and high-pressure fuel pipe will be required for each removed injector when refitting.*

Note 2: *The injector is an extremely tight fit in the cylinder head, and it is likely that the special Vauxhall/Opel puller (KM-328-B) and adapter (EN-46786) or suitable alternatives, will be needed.*

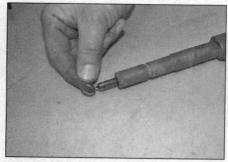

13.9 Remove the copper washer from the injector base

Z19DT engines
Removal

1 Disconnect the battery negative terminal (refer to *Disconnecting the battery* in the Reference Chapter).

2 Remove the plastic cover over the top of the engine.

3 Release the locking catches securing the wiring connectors to the four injectors, then disconnect the injector wiring.

4 Undo the two bolts at the top and the two bolts at the front, securing the plastic wiring trough to the inlet manifold **(see illustrations 12.4a and 12.4b)**. Move the wiring trough and injector wiring harness to one side.

5 Thoroughly clean the fuel pipe unions on the fuel rail and injector. Using two spanners, hold the unions and unscrew the union nut securing the high-pressure fuel pipe to the fuel injector. Unscrew the union nut securing the high-pressure fuel pipe to the fuel rail, withdraw the pipe and plug or cover the open unions to prevent dirt entry.

6 Disconnect the fuel leak-off hose connection at each injector by pushing in the locking clip and lifting out the hose fitting. Suitably plug or cap the leak-off hose union on each injector, and slip a plastic bag over the disconnected leak-off hose to prevent dirt entry.

7 Unscrew the retaining nut then remove the washer from the injector clamp bracket.

8 Withdraw the injector, together with the clamp bracket, from the cylinder head. If difficulty is experienced removing the injector, liberally apply penetrating oil to the base of the injector and allow time for the oil to penetrate. If the injector is still reluctant to free, it will be necessary to use a small slide hammer engaged under the flange of the injector body casting, and gently tap free. If available, use Vauxhall/Opel special tools EN-46786 and KM-328-B for this purpose. Note that it is not possible to twist the injector from side-to-side to free them due to the design of the clamp bracket.

9 Once the injector has been removed, separate it from the clamp bracket and remove the copper washer from the injector base **(see illustration)**. The copper washer may have remained in place at the base of the injector orifice in the cylinder head. If so, hook it out with a length of wire.

10 Remove the remaining injectors in the same way.

11 Examine the injector visually for any signs of obvious damage or deterioration. If any defects are apparent, renew the injector.

Caution: The injectors are manufactured to extremely close tolerances and must not be dismantled in any way. Do not unscrew the fuel pipe union on the side of the injector, or separate any parts of the injector body. Do not attempt to clean carbon deposits from the injector nozzle or carry out any form of ultrasonic or pressure testing.

12 If the injectors are in a satisfactory condition, plug the fuel pipe union (if not already done) and suitably cover the electrical element and the injector nozzle.

13 Prior to refitting, obtain a new copper washer a new retaining nut and new high-pressure fuel pipe for each injector.

Refitting

14 Thoroughly clean the injector seat in the cylinder head, ensuring all traces of carbon and other deposits are removed.

15 Locate a new copper washer on the base of the injector.

16 Place the injector clamp bracket in the slot on the injector body and refit the injector to the cylinder head.

17 Fit the washer and the new injector clamp bracket retaining nut and tighten the nut to the specified torque.

18 Remove the blanking plug from the fuel pipe union on the fuel rail and the injector. Locate the new high-pressure fuel pipe over the unions and screw on the union nuts. Take care not to cross-thread the nuts or strain the fuel pipe as it is fitted.

19 Tighten the fuel pipe union nuts to the specified torque using a torque wrench and crow-foot adaptor **(see illustration 13.44)**. Counterhold the union on the injector with an open-ended spanner, while tightening the union nut.

20 Repeat this procedure for the remaining injectors.

21 Refit the wiring trough, and secure with the four retaining bolts. Reconnect the wiring connectors to the fuel injectors.

22 Reconnect the leak-off hose fittings to the injectors by pushing in the locking clip, attaching the fitting, then releasing the locking clip. Ensure that each fitting is securely connected and retained by the clip.

23 Reconnect the battery negative terminal.

24 Observing the precautions listed in Section 2, prime the fuel system as described in Section 5, then start the engine and allow it to idle. Check for leaks at the high-pressure fuel pipe unions with the engine idling. If satisfactory, increase the engine speed to 4000 rpm and check again for leaks. If any leaks are detected, obtain and fit a new high-pressure fuel pipe.

25 Refit the engine cover on completion.

Z19DTH engines
Removal

26 Disconnect the battery negative terminal (refer to *Disconnecting the battery* in the Reference Chapter).

27 Remove the plastic cover over the top of the engine.

28 Release the retaining clip securing the engine breather hose to the breather pipe adjacent to the engine oil dipstick. Undo the two bolts securing the breather pipe to the cylinder head, and disconnect the pipe from the hose **(see illustration)**.

29 Release the locking catches securing

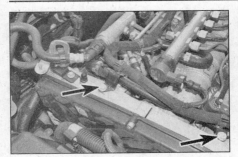

13.28 Undo the two bolts (arrowed) and remove the breather pipe from the cylinder head

13.29a Release the locking catches . . .

13.29b . . . and disconnect the injector wiring connectors

the wiring connectors to the four injectors, then disconnect the injector wiring **(see illustrations)**.

30 Disconnect the fuel leak-off hose connection at each injector by pushing in the locking clip and lifting out the hose fitting. Suitably plug or cap the leak-off hose union on each injector, and slip a plastic bag over the disconnected leak-off hose to prevent dirt entry **(see illustrations)**.

31 Thoroughly clean the fuel pipe unions on the fuel rail and injector. Using two spanners, hold the unions and unscrew the union nut securing the high-pressure fuel pipe to the fuel injector **(see illustration)**. Unscrew the union nut securing the high-pressure fuel pipe to the fuel rail, withdraw the pipe and plug or cover the open unions to prevent dirt entry.

32 Starting with injector No 1, unscrew the retaining nut then remove the washer from the injector clamp bracket **(see illustration)**.

33 Withdraw the injector together with the clamp bracket from the cylinder head. If difficulty is experienced removing the injector, liberally apply penetrating oil to the base of the injector and allow time for the oil to penetrate. If the injector is still reluctant to free, it will be necessary to use a small slide hammer engaged under the flange of the injector body casting, and gently tap it free **(see illustration)**. If available, use Vauxhall/Opel special tools EN-46786 and KM-328-B for this purpose. Note that it is not possible to twist the injector from side-to-side to free them due to the design of the clamp bracket.

34 Once the injector has been removed, separate it from the clamp bracket and remove the copper washer from the injector base **(see illustration)**. The copper washer may have remained in place at the base of the injector orifice in the cylinder head. If so, hook it out with a length of wire.

35 Remove the remaining injectors in the same way.

36 Examine the injector visually for any signs of obvious damage or deterioration. If any defects are apparent, renew the injector.
Caution: The injectors are manufactured to extremely close tolerances and must not be dismantled in any way. Do not unscrew the fuel pipe union on the side of the injector, or separate any parts of the injector body. Do not attempt to clean carbon deposits from the injector nozzle or carry out any form of ultrasonic or pressure testing.

37 If the injectors are in a satisfactory condition, plug the fuel pipe union (if not already done) and suitably cover the electrical element and the injector nozzle.

38 Prior to refitting, obtain a new set of copper washers, retaining nuts and high-pressure fuel pipes.

13.30a Disconnect the fuel leak-off hose connection at each injector . . .

13.30b . . . then plug or cap the leak-off hose union on each injector

13.31 Counterhold the injector union when unscrewing the high-pressure fuel pipe unions

13.32 Unscrew the injector clamp bracket retaining nut then remove the washer

13.33 Using a small slide hammer to free the injector body from the cylinder head

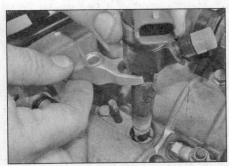

13.34 Once the injector has been removed, separate it from the clamp bracket

13.42a Fit the washer . . .

13.42b . . . and the injector clamp bracket retaining nut

Refitting

39 Thoroughly clean the injector seat in the cylinder head, ensuring all traces of carbon and other deposits are removed.

40 Starting with injector No 4, locate a new copper washer on the base of the injector.

41 Place the injector clamp bracket in the slot on the injector body and refit the injector to the cylinder head.

42 Fit the washer and the injector clamp bracket retaining nut and tighten the nut to the specified torque **(see illustrations)**.

43 Remove the blanking plug from the fuel pipe union on the fuel rail and the injector. Locate the new high-pressure fuel pipe over the unions and screw on the union nuts. Take care not to cross-thread the nuts or strain the fuel pipe as it is fitted.

44 Tighten the fuel pipe union nuts to the specified torque using a torque wrench and crow-foot adaptor **(see illustration)**. Counterhold the union on the injector with an open-ended spanner, while tightening the union nut.

45 Repeat this procedure for the remaining injectors.

46 Reconnect the leak-off hose fittings to the injectors by pushing in the locking clip, attaching the fitting, then releasing the locking clip. Ensure that each fitting is securely connected and retained by the clip.

47 Reconnect the wiring connectors to the fuel injectors.

48 Attach the engine breather hose to the breather pipe and secure with the retaining clip. Secure the breather pipe to the cylinder head with the two bolts securely tightened.

13.44 Tighten the fuel pipe union nuts to the specified torque using a torque wrench and crow-foot adaptor

49 Reconnect the battery negative terminal.

50 Observing the precautions listed in Section 2, prime the fuel system as described in Section 5, then start the engine and allow it to idle. Check for leaks at the high-pressure fuel pipe unions with the engine idling. If satisfactory, increase the engine speed to 4000 rpm and check again for leaks. If any leaks are detected, obtain and fit a new high-pressure fuel pipe.

51 Refit the engine cover on completion.

14 Inlet manifold – removal and refitting

Z19DT engines

Removal

1 Disconnect the battery negative terminal (refer to *Disconnecting the battery* in the Reference Chapter).

2 Remove the plastic cover over the top of the engine.

3 Drain the cooling system as described in Chapter 1B.

4 Remove the exhaust gas recirculation (EGR) valve as described in Chapter 4C.

5 Remove the high-pressure fuel pump as described in Section 11.

6 Undo the retaining bolt(s) to release the vacuum lines running over the top of the camshaft cover **(see illustration)**.

7 Remove the throttle housing as described in Section 10.

14.6 Undo the retaining bolt(s) to release the vacuum lines from the camshaft cover

8 Disconnect the wiring connectors at the four glow plugs.

9 Undo the three retaining bolts and detach the vacuum reservoir from the rear of the cylinder block.

10 Release the retaining clips and disconnect the two coolant hoses at the EGR heat exchanger, and the adjacent hose at the thermostat housing.

11 Unscrew the nut and two bolts securing the coolant pipes to the starter motor bracket.

12 Release the clamp and disconnect the metal pipe from the EGR heat exchanger. Undo the retaining nut and bolt and remove the heat exchanger.

13 Remove the alternator as described in Chapter 5A.

14 Undo the six bolts securing the alternator and high-pressure fuel pump mounting bracket to the cylinder block and cylinder head. There are five bolts securing the bracket to the block at the rear, and one securing the bracket to the head at the front.

15 Undo the nine retaining nuts and remove the inlet manifold from the cylinder head studs. Recover the gasket.

Refitting

16 Thoroughly clean the inlet manifold and cylinder head mating faces, then locate a new gasket on the inlet manifold flange.

17 Locate the manifold in position and refit the retaining nuts. Diagonally and progressively, tighten the nuts to the specified torque.

18 Refit the alternator and high-pressure fuel pump bracket and tighten the retaining bolts to the specified torque.

19 Refit the alternator as described in Chapter 5A.

20 Refit the EGR heat exchanger and securely tighten the retaining nut and bolt. Reconnect the metal EGR pipe and secure with the retaining clamp.

21 Locate the coolant pipe on the starter motor bracket. Refit and securely tighten the retaining nut and bolts.

22 Reconnect the coolant hoses to the EGR heat exchanger and thermostat housing and secure with the retaining clips.

23 Attach the vacuum reservoir to the cylinder block, refit the three retaining bolts and tighten securely.

24 Reconnect the wiring connectors to the glow plugs.

25 Refit the throttle housing as described in Section 10.

26 Refit the vacuum lines running over the top of the camshaft cover and reconnect the vacuum hoses.

27 Refit the high-pressure fuel pump as described in Section 11.

28 Refit the exhaust gas recirculation (EGR) valve as described in Chapter 4C.

29 Refill the cooling system as described in Chapter 1B.

30 Reconnect the battery negative terminal.

31 Observing the precautions listed in Section 2, prime the fuel system as described

14.39 Unscrew the two nuts and free the wiring harness and coolant pipes from the starter motor bracket

14.41a Undo the two nuts (arrowed) above the vacuum reservoir . . .

14.41b . . . the bolt at the base of the vacuum reservoir . . .

14.41c . . . and the bolt at the right-hand side of the oil separator . . .

14.41d . . . then remove the mounting bracket complete with oil separator and vacuum reservoir

in Section 5, then start the engine and allow it to idle. Check for leaks at the high-pressure fuel pipe unions with the engine idling. If satisfactory, increase the engine speed to 4000 rpm and check again for leaks. If any leaks are detected, obtain and fit a new high-pressure fuel pipe.

32 Refit the engine cover on completion.

Z19DTH engines

Removal

33 Disconnect the battery negative terminal (refer to *Disconnecting the battery* in the Reference Chapter).

34 Remove the plastic cover over the top of the engine.

35 Remove the fuel filter crash box as described in Section 9.

36 Remove the high-pressure fuel pump as described in Section 11.

37 Remove the exhaust gas recirculation (EGR) valve as described in Chapter 4C.

38 Disconnect the four vacuum hoses then undo the bolt(s) and remove the two vacuum pipes over the top of the inlet manifold.

39 Unscrew the two nuts securing the wiring harness and coolant pipes to the starter motor bracket. Free the harness and pipes from the bracket (see illustration).

40 Release the clips and disconnect the crankcase breather hoses from the top and bottom of the oil separator.

41 Remove the oil separator and vacuum reservoir mounting bracket by undoing the two nuts above the vacuum reservoir, the bolt at the base of the vacuum reservoir, and the bolt at the right-hand side of the oil separator. Remove the mounting bracket complete with oil separator and vacuum reservoir (see illustrations).

42 Undo the three bolts, release the hose clip, free the wiring harness and detach the coolant pipe from the inlet manifold.

43 Screw two nuts onto the inner high-pressure fuel pump mounting stud. Lock the two nuts together and unscrew the stud from the engine bracket (see illustration).

44 Disconnect the wiring connectors at the throttle housing and charge (boost) pressure sensor.

45 Undo the nine retaining nuts and remove

the inlet manifold from the cylinder head studs (see illustration). Recover the gasket.

46 With the manifold removed, if required, remove the throttle housing with reference to Section 10.

47 The changeover flap actuator drive can be removed by disconnecting the drive motor actuating rod ball socket, and undoing the two stud bolts.

Refitting

48 If removed, refit the throttle housing with reference to Section 10, then refit the changeover flap actuator drive.

49 Thoroughly clean the inlet manifold and cylinder head mating faces, then locate a new gasket on the inlet manifold flange.

50 Locate the manifold in position and refit the retaining nuts. Diagonally and progressively, tighten the nuts to the specified torque.

51 Reconnect the wiring connectors at the

throttle body/housing and charge (boost) pressure sensor.

52 Refit the high-pressure fuel pump mounting stud, then remove the two nuts used to remove/refit the stud.

53 Refit the coolant pipe to the manifold, and secure with the three bolts tightened securely. Reconnect the coolant pipe and attach the wiring harness.

54 Refit the oil separator and vacuum reservoir mounting bracket. Refit and tighten the two bolts and two nuts, then reconnect the crankcase breather hoses.

55 Refit the coolant pipe and wiring harness to the starter motor bracket, then refit and tighten the two nuts.

56 Refit the vacuum pipes over the manifold and reconnect the four vacuum pipes.

57 Refit the exhaust gas recirculation (EGR) valve as described in Chapter 4C.

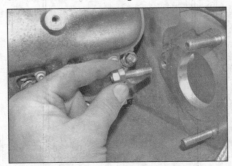

14.43 Lock two nuts together and unscrew the fuel pump stud from the engine bracket

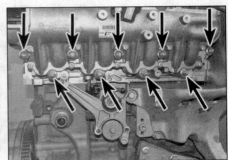

14.45 Inlet manifold retaining nuts (arrowed)

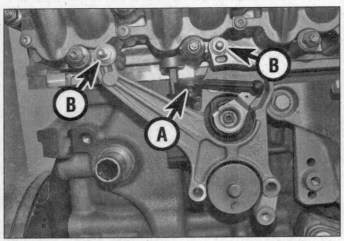

15.8 Disconnect the actuating rod ball socket (A), undo the two stud bolts (B) and remove the actuator drive

16.5a Slacken the bolt (arrowed) securing the radiator left-hand . . .

58 Refit the high-pressure fuel pump as described in Section 11.

59 Refit the fuel filter crash box as described in Section 9.

60 Reconnect the battery negative terminal.

61 Observing the precautions listed in Section 2, prime the fuel system as described in Section 5, then start the engine and allow it to idle. Check for leaks at the high-pressure fuel pipe unions with the engine idling. If satisfactory, increase the engine speed to 4000 rpm and check again for leaks. If any leaks are detected, obtain and fit a new high-pressure fuel pipe.

62 Refit the engine cover on completion.

15 Inlet manifold changeover flap actuator drive (Z19DTH engines) – removal and refitting

Removal

1 Disconnect the battery negative terminal (refer to *Disconnecting the battery* in the Reference Chapter).

2 Remove the plastic cover over the top of the engine.

3 Remove the fuel filter crash box as described in Section 9.

4 Disconnect the four vacuum hoses then undo the bolt(s) and remove the two vacuum pipes over the top of the inlet manifold.

5 Unscrew the two nuts securing the wiring harness and coolant pipes to the starter motor bracket. Free the harness and pipes from the bracket (**see illustration 14.39**).

6 Release the clips and disconnect the crankcase breather hoses from the top and bottom of the oil separator.

7 Remove the oil separator and vacuum reservoir mounting bracket by undoing the two nuts above the vacuum reservoir, the bolt at the base of the vacuum reservoir, and the bolt at the right-hand side of the oil separator. Remove the mounting bracket complete

with oil separator and vacuum reservoir (**see illustrations 14.41a to 14.41d**).

8 Disconnect the drive motor actuating rod ball socket, and undoing the two stud bolts (**see illustration**).

9 Withdraw the assembly from the inlet manifold and disconnect the wiring connector.

Refitting

10 Refitting is the reverse of removal.

16 Intercooler – removal and refitting

Removal

1 Disconnect the battery negative terminal (refer to *Disconnecting the battery* in the Reference Chapter).

2 Remove the plastic cover from the top of the engine.

3 Apply the handbrake, then jack up the front of the vehicle and support it on axle stands (see *Jacking and vehicle support*).

4 Remove the front bumper as described in Chapter 11.

5 Slacken (but do not remove) the two bolts securing the radiator left-hand and right-hand mounting brackets to the subframe (**see illustrations**).

6 Release the radiator upper rubber mounting bushes on each side from their guides, and carefully move the top of the radiator forward.

7 On models with air conditioning, undo the bolt each side securing the condenser upper mounting brackets to the intercooler (**see illustration**). Carefully lift up or remove the plastic panels on each side of the radiator for improved access, if necessary.

8 Carefully lift the condenser upwards, disengage the lower mounting lugs from the intercooler and secure the condenser to the upper body panel using cable-ties or similar (**see illustration**).

16.5b . . . and right-hand mounting brackets to the subframe

16.7 Undo the bolt (arrowed) each side securing the condenser upper mounting brackets to the intercooler

16.8 Lift the condenser upwards and disengage the lower mounting lug (arrowed) on each side

9 Slacken the retaining clips and remove the left-hand and right-hand lower charge air hoses from the intercooler and charge air pipes **(see illustrations)**.

10 Undo the bolt each side securing the intercooler upper mounting brackets to the radiator **(see illustration)**.

11 Carefully lift the intercooler upwards, disengage the lower mounting lugs from the radiator, then lower the intercooler down and remove it from under the car **(see illustration)**.

Refitting

12 Refitting is the reverse of removal.

---

17 Turbocharger – description and precautions

1 The turbocharger increases engine efficiency by raising the pressure in the inlet manifold above atmospheric pressure. Instead of the air simply being sucked into the cylinders, it is forced in.

2 Energy for the operation of the turbocharger comes from the exhaust gas. The gas flows through a specially-shaped housing (the turbine housing) and, in so doing, spins the turbine wheel. The turbine wheel is attached to a shaft, at the end of which is another vaned wheel known as the compressor wheel. The compressor wheel spins in its own housing, and compresses the inlet air on the way to the inlet manifold.

3 The turbocharger operates on the principle of variable vane geometry. At low engine speeds the vanes close to give less flow cross-section, then as the speed increases the vanes open to give an increased flow cross-section. This helps improve the efficiency of the turbocharger.

4 Boost pressure (the pressure in the inlet manifold) is limited by a wastegate, which diverts the exhaust gas away from the turbine wheel in response to a pressure-sensitive actuator.

5 The turbo shaft is pressure-lubricated by an oil feed pipe from the main oil gallery. The shaft 'floats' on a cushion of oil. A drain pipe returns the oil to the sump.

Precautions

6 The turbocharger operates at extremely high speeds and temperatures. Certain precautions must be observed, to avoid premature failure of the turbo, or injury to the operator.

• Do not operate the turbo with any of its parts exposed, or with any of its hoses removed. Foreign objects falling onto the rotating vanes could cause excessive damage, and (if ejected) personal injury.

• Do not race the engine immediately after start-up, especially if it is cold. Give the oil a few seconds to circulate.

• Always allow the engine to return to idle speed before switching it off – do not blip the throttle and switch off, as this will leave the turbo spinning without lubrication.

16.9a Slacken the retaining clips and remove the left-hand (arrowed) . . .

16.10 Undo the bolt (arrowed) each side securing the intercooler upper mounting brackets to the radiator

• Allow the engine to idle for several minutes before switching off after a high-speed run.

• Observe the recommended intervals for oil and filter changing, and use a reputable oil of the specified quality. Neglect of oil changing, or use of inferior oil, can cause carbon formation on the turbo shaft, leading to subsequent failure.

---

18 Exhaust manifold and turbocharger – removal and refitting

Note: *New manifold retaining nuts, new gaskets for all disturbed joints, and new copper washers for the turbocharger oil supply pipe banjo union will be required for refitting.*

Removal

1 Disconnect the battery negative terminal (refer to *Disconnecting the battery* in the Reference Chapter).

2 Remove the plastic cover from the top of the engine

3 Firmly apply the handbrake, then jack up the front of the car and support it securely on axle stands (see *Jacking and vehicle support*). Undo the retaining bolts and screws and remove the engine undertray.

4 Drain the cooling system as described in Chapter 1B.

5 Remove the complete exhaust system as described in Section 19.

6 Remove the air cleaner assembly and air intake duct as described in Section 3.

16.9b . . . and right-hand (arrowed) lower charge air hoses from the intercooler and charge air pipes

16.11 Lower the intercooler down and remove it from under the car

7 On Z19DT engines, undo the retaining bolt(s) to release the vacuum lines running over the top of the camshaft cover **(see illustration 14.6)**.

8 Release the retaining clips and remove the charge air pipe above the right-hand side of the radiator. Suitably cover the turbocharger air inlet to prevent the entry of dirt and foreign material.

9 On Z19DTH engines, release the retaining clip securing the engine breather hose to the breather pipe adjacent to the engine oil dipstick. Undo the two bolts securing the breather pipe to the cylinder head, and disconnect the pipe from the hose **(see illustration 13.28)**.

10 On Z19DT engines, release the retaining clip and disconnect the breather hose from the front of the camshaft cover **(see illustration)**.

18.10 Release the retaining clip and disconnect the breather hose from the front of the camshaft cover

18.13a Undo the turbocharger charge air pipe upper retaining bolt (arrowed) . . .

18.13b . . . then slacken the clip (arrowed) and move the pipe to one side

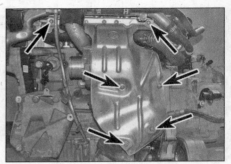

18.18 Heat shield retaining nuts and bolts (arrowed)

11 Release the two retaining clips and disconnect the charge air hose from the throttle housing, and intercooler charge air pipe **(see illustration 10.11)**.

12 Release the clip and disconnect the radiator top hose from the thermostat housing.

13 Undo the bolt securing the turbocharger charge air pipe to the right-hand end of the camshaft housing (Z19DTH engines) or support bracket (Z19DT engines). Slacken the retaining clip securing the charge air pipe to the turbocharger and move the pipe to one side **(see illustrations)**.

14 Undo the bolt and detach the engine oil dipstick guide tube upper mounting.

15 Release the retaining clip and disconnect the radiator hose from the coolant pipe, then undo the two bolts securing the coolant pipe flange to the right-hand end of the cylinder head.

16 Release the retaining clips securing the heater hose and EGR valve heat exchanger hose at the left-hand end of the pipe assembly. Undo the bolt securing the heater pipe to the left-hand end of the cylinder head, and the nut securing the pipe to the thermostat housing stud. Remove the pipe assembly from the engine and recover the flange gasket.

17 Undo the nut and bolt and remove the engine lifting eye from the cylinder head.

18 Undo the three nuts and three bolts securing the heat shield to the exhaust manifold and catalytic converter **(see illustration)**. Manipulate the heat shield off the studs and remove it from the engine.

19 Disconnect the vacuum hose from the turbocharger wastegate actuator.

20 Undo the retaining nut and bolt and release the metal EGR pipe clamp from the EGR valve heat exchanger. Separate the pipe from the

heat exchanger and recover the gasket from the pipe fitting **(see illustration)**.

21 Undo the two bolts securing the other end of the pipe to the exhaust manifold. Remove the pipe and recover the gasket **(see illustration)**.

22 Unscrew the two bolts and one nut, and remove the catalytic converter lower support bracket.

23 Disconnect the temperature/oxygen sensor wiring connector, unscrew the clamp bolt nut and remove the catalytic converter **(see illustrations)**.

24 Unscrew the four bolts securing the oil return pipe to the turbocharger and cylinder block **(see illustration)**. Remove the pipe and recover the gaskets.

25 Unscrew the turbocharger oil supply pipe banjo union from the cylinder block and collect the two copper washers **(see illustration)**.

18.20 Release the EGR pipe clamp from the heat exchanger, separate the pipe and recover the gasket

18.21 Disconnect the other end of the pipe from the exhaust manifold, then remove the pipe and recover the gasket

18.23a Unscrew the clamp bolt nut (arrowed) . . .

18.23b . . . and remove the catalytic converter

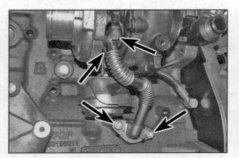

18.24 Unscrew the bolts (arrowed) securing the oil return pipe to the turbocharger and cylinder block

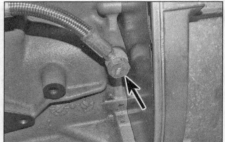

18.25 Unscrew the turbocharger oil supply pipe banjo union (arrowed) and collect the two copper washers

26 Unscrew the eight nuts securing the exhaust manifold to the cylinder head **(see illustration)**. Note that new nuts will be required for refitting. Withdraw the manifold and turbocharger assembly from the mounting studs, manipulate it sideways, and remove from under the car. Recover the gasket.

Refitting

27 Refitting is the reverse of removal, noting the following points.
a) *Ensure all mating surfaces are clean and dry and renew all gaskets, seals and copper washers.*
b) *Fit the new manifold nuts and tighten them evenly and progressively to the specified torque, working in a diagonal sequence.*
c) *Tighten all other retaining nuts and bolts to the specified torque (where given).*
d) *Refit the exhaust system as described in Section 19.*
e) *On completion refill the cooling system as described in Chapter 1B and, if necessary, top-up the oil level as described in 'Weekly checks'.*
f) *On starting the engine for the first time, allow the engine to idle for a few minutes before increasing the engine speed; this will allow oil to be circulated around the turbocharger bearings.*

19 Exhaust system – general information, removal and refitting

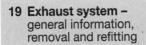

General information
Models without a particulate filter

1 The exhaust system consists of four sections comprising a primary catalytic converter, a front pipe incorporating a secondary catalytic converter, an intermediate pipe, and a tailpipe and silencer.
2 The front pipe is attached to the primary catalytic converter by a flange joint secured by nuts. All other exhaust sections are joined by overlap joints which are secured by clamps. The system is suspended throughout its entire length by rubber mountings.

Models with a particulate filter

3 The exhaust system consists of five sections comprising a primary catalytic converter, a front pipe, a diesel particulate filter, an intermediate pipe, and a tailpipe and silencer.
4 The front pipe is attached to the primary catalytic converter and diesel particulate filter by flange joints secured by nuts. All other exhaust sections are joined by overlap joints which are secured by clamps. The system is suspended throughout its entire length by rubber mountings.

All models

5 To remove an individual exhaust section, the complete system is first removed as a

18.26 Exhaust manifold retaining nuts (arrowed)

unit. The sections are then separated with the system off the car.
6 The manufacturers specify that if any of the exhaust sections are separated, the clamps must be renewed. As the clamps are attached to the exhaust sections by means of a spot weld at manufacture, it will be necessary to use a suitable grinder to remove the spot weld.

Complete system removal

7 To remove the system, first jack up the front and rear of the car and support it securely on axle stands. Alternatively, position the car over an inspection pit or on car ramps. The help of an assistant will be needed.
8 Undo the retaining bolts and screws and remove the engine undertray.
9 On models equipped with a diesel particulate filter, release the retaining clips and disconnect the two differential pressure sensor vacuum hoses from the two pipes adjacent to the particulate filter. Unscrew the retaining nut and remove the temperature sensor from the diesel particulate filter.
10 Spray some penetrating oil over the exhaust rubber mounting blocks so that the mounting blocks will slide easily on the exhaust and underbody hangers **(see illustration)**.
11 Undo the two bolts securing the front pipe support bracket to the transmission bracket.
12 Undo the three retaining nuts and separate the exhaust front pipe from the primary catalytic converter, taking care to support the flexible section. **Note:** *Angular movement in excess of 10° can cause permanent damage*

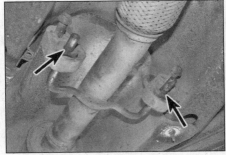
19.10 Spray penetrating oil over the exhaust rubber mounting blocks in the area arrowed

to the flexible section. Recover the gasket **(see illustration)**. Note that new nuts will be required for refitting.
13 On models equipped with a diesel particulate filter, undo the two bolts securing the particulate filter rear mounting bracket to the underbody.
14 Slide the front pipe rubber mounting blocks as far forward as possible. Move the exhaust system to the rear and disengage the front pipe hangers from the mounting blocks.
15 Move the exhaust system forward and disengage the intermediate pipe and tailpipe hangers from the rubber mounting blocks. Lower the system to the ground and slide it out from under the car.

Individual section removal

16 Remove the complete system as described previously.
17 If removing the front pipe on models equipped with a diesel particulate filter, undo the three nuts and separate the flange joint. Recover the gasket.
18 To remove any other individual section, slacken and remove the nut from the relevant exhaust clamp retaining bolt. Apply liberal amounts of penetrating oil to the joint and tap around the joint and clamp with a hammer to free it. Twist the pipe to be removed in both directions while holding the adjacent pipe. Once the joint is free, pull the pipes apart.
19 Mark the position of the clamp on the pipe, so the new clamp can be fitted in the same position, then grind off the clamp retaining spot weld. Remove the clamp.

Primary catalytic converter removal

20 Refer to Section 18, paragraphs 1 to 23 for removal and refitting details for the primary catalytic converter fitted between the exhaust front pipe and manifold.

Heat shield(s) removal

21 The heat shields are secured to the underside of the body by various nuts and threaded caps. Each shield can be removed once the relevant exhaust section has been removed. If a shield is being removed to gain access to a component located behind it, it may prove sufficient in some cases to remove

19.12 Separate the exhaust front pipe from the catalytic converter and recover the gasket

the retaining nuts/caps, and simply lower the shield, without disturbing the exhaust system. If any of the threaded caps are damaged during removal, a suitable nut and washer can be used when refitting.

Refitting

22 Refitting is a reversal of the removal sequence, noting the following points:

a) Ensure that all traces of corrosion have been removed from the system joints and renew all disturbed clamps.

b) When refitting the primary catalytic converter, refer to Section 18, paragraph 27.

c) Inspect the rubber mountings for signs of damage or deterioration, and renew as necessary.

d) When reconnecting a flange joint, use a new gasket and new retaining nuts, and tighten the nuts to the specified torque.

e) Prior to tightening the exhaust system clamps, ensure that all rubber mountings are correctly located, and that there is adequate clearance between the exhaust system and vehicle underbody. Tighten the clamp bolt retaining nuts to the specified torque.

Chapter 4 Part C:
Emission control systems

Contents

Degrees of difficulty

Easy, suitable for novice with little experience	**Fairly easy,** suitable for beginner with some experience	**Fairly difficult,** suitable for competent DIY mechanic	**Difficult,** suitable for experienced DIY mechanic	**Very difficult,** suitable for expert DIY or professional

Specifications

Torque wrench settings	Nm	lbf ft
Petrol engines		
EGR valve bolts:		
1.8 litre engines	20	15
2.2 litre engines	23	17
Oxygen sensor for catalytic converter (in exhaust front pipe):		
1.8 litre engines	30	22
2.2 litre engines	40	30
Oxygen sensor for mixture regulation (in exhaust manifold):		
1.8 litre engines	30	22
2.2 litre engines	40	30
Diesel engines		
EGR valve heat exchanger mounting bolt	25	18
EGR valve heat exchanger mounting nut	9	7
EGR valve heat exchanger pipe flange bolts	25	18
EGR valve mounting bolts/nuts	25	18
Oxygen sensor	55	41
Particulate filter temperature sensor	45	33
Pre-catalytic converter temperature sensor	45	33
Vacuum reservoir mounting bracket bolts	25	18

1 General information

1 All petrol engine models use unleaded petrol and also have various other features built into the fuel system to help minimise harmful emissions. These include a crankcase emission control system, a catalytic converter, an evaporative emission control system and, on certain models, an exhaust gas recirculation (EGR) system to keep fuel vapour/exhaust gas emissions down to a minimum.

2 All diesel engine models are also designed to meet strict emission requirements. The engines are fitted with a crankcase emission control system, a catalytic converter and, on certain models, a diesel particulate filter to keep exhaust emissions down to a minimum. An exhaust gas recirculation (EGR) system is also fitted to further decrease exhaust emissions.

3 The emission control systems function as follows.

Petrol engines

Crankcase emission control

4 To reduce the emission of unburned hydrocarbons from the crankcase into the atmosphere, the engine is sealed and the blow-by gases and oil vapour are drawn from inside the crankcase, through an oil separator, into the inlet tract to be burned by the engine during normal combustion.

5 Under all conditions the gases are forced out of the crankcase by the (relatively) higher crankcase pressure; if the engine is worn, the raised crankcase pressure (due to increased blow-by) will cause some of the flow to return under all manifold conditions.

Exhaust emission control

6 To minimise the amount of pollutants which escape into the atmosphere, all models are fitted with a catalytic converter in the exhaust system. The system is of the closed-loop type, in which the oxygen sensors in the exhaust system provides the fuel injection/ignition system ECU with constant feedback, enabling the ECU to adjust the mixture to provide the best possible conditions for the converter to operate.

7 Two heated oxygen sensors are fitted to the exhaust system. The sensor nearest the engine (before the catalytic converter) determines the residual oxygen content of the exhaust gases for mixture correction. The sensor in the exhaust front pipe (after the catalytic converter) monitors the function of the catalytic converter to give the driver a warning signal if there is a fault.

8 The oxygen sensor's tip is sensitive to oxygen and sends the ECU a varying voltage signal depending on the amount of oxygen in the exhaust gases. Peak conversion efficiency of all major pollutants occurs if the intake air/fuel mixture is maintained at the chemically-correct ratio for the complete combustion of petrol of 14.7 parts (by weight) of air to 1 part of fuel (the 'stoichiometric' ratio). The sensor output voltage alters in a large step at this point, the ECU using the signal change as a reference point and correcting the intake air/fuel mixture accordingly by altering the fuel injector pulse width.

Evaporative emission control

9 To minimise the escape into the atmosphere of unburned hydrocarbons, an evaporative emissions control system is also fitted to all models. The fuel tank filler cap is sealed and a charcoal canister is mounted on the fuel tank. The canister collects the petrol vapours generated in the tank when the car is parked and stores them until they can be cleared from the canister (under the control of the fuel injection/ignition system ECU) via the purge valve into the inlet tract to be burned by the engine during normal combustion.

10 To ensure that the engine runs correctly when it is cold and/or idling and to protect the catalytic converter from the effects of an over-rich mixture, the purge control valve is not opened by the ECU until the engine has warmed-up, and the engine is under load; the valve solenoid is then modulated on and off to allow the stored vapour to pass into the inlet tract.

Exhaust gas recirculation system

11 This system is designed to recirculate small quantities of exhaust gas into the inlet tract, and therefore into the combustion process. This process reduces the level of unburnt hydrocarbons present in the exhaust gas before it reaches the catalytic converter. The system is controlled by the fuel injection/ignition ECU, using the information from its various sensors, via the electrically-operated EGR valve mounted on a housing bolted to the left-hand end of the cylinder head.

Diesel engines

Crankcase emission control

12 Refer to paragraphs 4 and 5.

Exhaust emission control

13 To minimise the level of exhaust pollutants released into the atmosphere, two catalytic converters, or one catalytic converter and a diesel particulate filter are fitted in the exhaust system, according to model.

14 The catalytic converter consists of a canister containing a fine mesh impregnated with a catalyst material, over which the hot exhaust gases pass. The catalyst speeds up the oxidation of harmful carbon monoxide and unburned hydrocarbons, effectively reducing the quantity of harmful products released into the atmosphere via the exhaust gases.

15 On certain models, a diesel particulate filter is incorporated in the exhaust system and contains a silicon carbide honeycomb block containing microscopic channels in which the exhaust gases flow. As the gases flow through the honeycomb channels, soot particles are deposited on the channel walls. To prevent clogging of the honeycomb channels, the soot particles are burned off at regular intervals during what is known as a 'regeneration phase'. Under the control of the injection system ECU, the injection characteristics are altered to raise the temperature of the exhaust gases to approximately 600°C. At this temperature, the soot particles are effectively burned off the honeycomb walls as the exhaust gases pass through. A differential pressure sensor and two temperature sensors are used to inform the ECU of the condition of the particulate filter, and the temperature of the exhaust gases during the regeneration phase. When the ECU detects that soot build-up is reducing the efficiency of the particulate filter, it will instigate the regeneration process. This occurs at regular intervals under certain driving conditions and will normally not be detected by the driver.

Exhaust gas recirculation system

16 This system is designed to recirculate small quantities of exhaust gas into the inlet tract, and therefore into the combustion process. This process reduces the level of unburnt hydrocarbons present in the exhaust gas before it reaches the catalytic converter. The system is controlled by the injection system ECU, using the information from its various sensors, via the electrically-operated EGR valve.

2 Petrol engine emission control systems – testing and component renewal

Crankcase emission control

1 The components of this system require no attention other than to check that the hose(s) are clear and undamaged at regular intervals.

Evaporative emission control

Testing

2 If the system is thought to be faulty, disconnect the hoses from the charcoal canister and purge control valve and check that they are clear by blowing through them. Full testing of the system can only be carried out using specialist electronic equipment which is connected to the engine management system diagnostic connector. If the purge control valve or charcoal canister are thought to be faulty, they must be renewed.

Charcoal canister renewal

3 The charcoal canister is located on the fuel tank. To gain access to the canister, remove the fuel tank as described in Chapter 4A.

4 With the fuel tank removed, disconnect the vapour hose quick-release fittings at the charcoal canister.

5 Detach the locking clamp and release the canister from its mounting bracket on the fuel tank. Remove the canister from the tank.

6 Refitting is a reverse of the removal procedure, ensuring the hoses are correctly and securely reconnected.

Purge valve renewal

7 The purge valve is mounted on the inlet manifold **(see illustration)**. For improved access, where necessary, remove the air cleaner intake duct as described in Chapter 4A.

8 To renew the valve, ensure the ignition is switched off then depress the retaining clip and disconnect the wiring connector from the valve.

9 Disconnect the hoses from the valve, noting their correct fitted locations then unclip and remove the valve from the engine.

10 Refitting is a reversal of the removal procedure, ensuring the valve is fitted the correct way around and the hoses are securely connected.

Exhaust emission control

Testing

11 The performance of the catalytic converter can be checked only by measuring the exhaust gases using a good-quality, carefully-calibrated exhaust gas analyser.

12 If the CO level at the tailpipe is too high, the vehicle should be taken to a Vauxhall/Opel dealer or engine diagnostic specialist so that the complete fuel injection and ignition systems, including the oxygen sensors, can be thoroughly checked using diagnostic equipment. This equipment will give an indication as to where the fault lies and the necessary components can then be renewed.

Catalytic converter renewal

13 The catalytic converter is an integral part of the exhaust manifold. Exhaust manifold removal and refitting procedures are contained in Chapter 4A.

Oxygen sensor renewal

Note 1: *There are two heated oxygen sensors fitted to the exhaust system. The sensor in the exhaust manifold is for mixture regulation and the sensor in the exhaust front pipe is to check the operation of the catalytic converter (see Section 1).*

Note 2: *The oxygen sensor is delicate and will not work if it is dropped or knocked, if its power supply is disrupted, or if any cleaning materials are used on it.*

14 Warm the engine up to normal operating temperature then stop the engine and disconnect the battery negative terminal (refer to *Disconnecting the battery* in the Reference Chapter). Remove the plastic cover from the top of the engine.

15 For the sensor fitted in the exhaust front pipe, firmly apply the handbrake, then jack up the front of the car and support it securely on axle stands (see *Jacking and vehicle support*).

16 Trace the wiring back from the oxygen sensor which is to be renewed, and disconnect its wiring connector, freeing the wiring from any relevant retaining clips or ties and noting its correct routing.

Caution: Take great care not burn yourself on the hot manifold/sensor.

2.7 Typical purge valve location (arrowed)

17 Unscrew the sensor and remove it from the exhaust system front pipe/manifold **(see illustration)**. Where applicable recover the sealing washer and discard it; a new one should be used on refitting.

18 Refitting is a reverse of the removal procedure, using a new sealing washer (where applicable). Prior to installing the sensor, apply a smear of high-temperature grease to the sensor threads (Vauxhall/Opel recommend the use of special grease available from your dealer). Tighten the sensor to the specified torque and ensure that the wiring is correctly routed and in no danger of contacting either the exhaust system or engine.

Exhaust gas recirculation

Testing

19 Comprehensive testing of the system can only be carried out using specialist electronic equipment which is connected to the engine management system diagnostic connector.

EGR valve renewal

20 Ensure the ignition is switched off then disconnect the wiring connector from the EGR valve which mounted at the left-hand end of the cylinder head **(see illustration)**.

21 Undo the mounting bolts and remove the valve from its location. Recover the gasket.

22 Refitting is the reverse of removal using a new gasket and tightening the valve bolts to the specified torque.

---

3 Diesel engine emission control systems – testing and component renewal

Crankcase emission control

1 The components of this system require no attention other than to check that the hose(s) are clear and undamaged at regular intervals.

Exhaust emission control

Testing

2 The performance of the catalytic converter(s) and diesel particulate filter can only be checked using special diagnostic equipment. If a system fault is suspected, the vehicle

2.17 Oxygen sensor (arrowed) located in the exhaust manifold

should be taken to a Vauxhall/Opel dealer so that the complete fuel injection system can be thoroughly checked.

Catalytic converter/ particulate filter renewal

3 Refer to Chapter 4B, for removal and refitting details.

Oxygen sensor/pre-catalytic converter temperature sensor renewal

Note: *An oxygen sensor is fitted to vehicles without a diesel particulate filter, and a pre-catalytic converter temperature sensor is fitted to vehicles with a diesel particulate filter. Both sensors are screwed into the exhaust manifold and the removal and refitting details are identical.*

4 Warm the engine up to normal operating temperature then stop the engine and disconnect the battery negative terminal (refer to *Disconnecting the battery* in the Reference Chapter). Remove the plastic cover from the top of the engine.

5 Firmly apply the handbrake, then jack up the front of the car and support it securely on axle stands (see *Jacking and vehicle support*). Undo the retaining bolts and screws and remove the engine undertray.

6 Disconnect the sensor wiring connector, then unclip the wiring plug from the bracket on the front of the transmission.

Caution: Take great care not burn yourself on the hot manifold/sensor.

7 Unscrew the sensor and remove it from the exhaust manifold **(see illustration)**.

8 Refitting is a reverse of the removal

2.20 Disconnect the wiring connector (arrowed) from the EGR valve

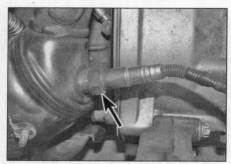

3.7 Unscrew the oxygen sensor (arrowed) and remove it from the exhaust manifold

procedure. Prior to installing the sensor, apply a smear of high-temperature grease to the sensor threads (Vauxhall/Opel recommend the use of a special grease available from your dealer). Tighten the sensor to the specified torque and ensure that the wiring is correctly routed and in no danger of contacting either the exhaust system or engine.

Particulate filter temperature sensor renewal

9 Firmly apply the handbrake, then jack up the front of the car and support it securely on axle stands (see *Jacking and vehicle support*). Undo the retaining bolts and screws and remove the engine undertray.
10 Trace the wiring from the sensor back to the connector in the engine compartment. Disconnect the wiring connector, then release the wiring from the clips on the underbody.
11 Unscrew the retaining nut and remove the temperature sensor from the diesel particulate filter.
12 Refitting is the reverse of removal tightening the sensor retaining nut to the specified torque.

Differential pressure sensor renewal

13 The differential pressure sensor is located on the side of the fuel filter crash box in the engine compartment.
14 Disconnect the pressure sensor wiring connector.
15 Undo the retaining nut and withdraw the sensor from the fuel filter crash box.
16 Noting their correct fitted positions, release the retaining clips and disconnect the

3.27 Unscrew the two bolts, detach the metal EGR pipe flange and recover the gasket

3.23 EGR valve retaining bolts (arrowed)

two vacuum hoses from the sensor. Remove the sensor from the engine compartment.
17 Refitting is the reverse of removal.

Exhaust gas recirculation system

Testing

18 Comprehensive testing of the system can only be carried out using specialist electronic equipment which is connected to the injection system diagnostic wiring connector.

EGR valve renewal – Z19DT engines

19 Disconnect the battery negative terminal (refer to *Disconnecting the battery* in the Reference Chapter). Remove the plastic cover over the top of the engine.
20 Disconnect the EGR valve wiring connector.
21 Undo the two bolts and disconnect the metal EGR pipe from the throttle housing. Recover the gasket.
22 Undo the two bolts securing the EGR heat exchanger metal pipe to the base of the valve.
23 Undo the three bolts securing the EGR valve to the inlet manifold **(see illustration)**. Remove the valve together with the engine lifting eye bracket and recover the gasket fitted on each side of the lifting eye bracket.
24 Refitting is the reverse of removal using new gaskets and tightening the retaining bolts to the specified torque.

EGR valve renewal – Z19DTH engines

25 Disconnect the battery negative terminal

3.28 Unscrew the two nuts and two bolts (arrowed) securing the EGR valve to the inlet manifold

(refer to *Disconnecting the battery* in the Reference Chapter). Remove the plastic cover over the top of the engine.
26 Disconnect the EGR valve wiring connector.
27 Unscrew the two bolts on the top of the valve and detach the metal EGR pipe flange from the base of the valve. Recover the gasket **(see illustration)**.
28 Unscrew the two nuts and two bolts securing the EGR valve to the inlet manifold and lift off the engine cover bracket **(see illustration)**.
29 To provide sufficient clearance to remove the valve, it will be necessary to unscrew the two mounting studs from the manifold. To do this, lock two nuts together on each stud and remove the studs by unscrewing the inner nut.
30 With the studs removed, lift off the valve and recover the gasket **(see illustration)**.
31 Refitting is the reverse of removal using new gaskets and tightening the retaining nuts and bolts to the specified torque.

EGR valve heat exchanger renewal – Z19DT engines

32 Drain the cooling system as described in Chapter 1B.
33 Remove the plastic cover over the top of the engine.
34 Remove the battery and battery box as described in Chapter 5A.
35 Slacken the retaining clips and remove the charge air pipe from the throttle housing and intercooler.
36 Slacken the retaining clips and disconnect the two coolant hoses from the metal coolant pipe assembly at the rear of the engine.
37 Unscrew the two nuts securing the wiring harness and coolant pipe assembly to the starter motor bracket and the nut securing the pipes to the thermostat housing stud. Free the harness and pipes from the bracket.
38 Slacken the retaining clips securing the remaining coolant hoses to the coolant pipe assembly and manoeuvre the pipe assembly from the engine.
39 Undo the two bolts securing the rear metal EGR pipe to the EGR valve. Undo the retaining nut and bolt and release the metal EGR pipe clamp from the EGR valve heat exchanger.

3.30 Lift off the valve and recover the gasket

Separate the pipe from the heat exchanger and recover the gasket from the pipe fitting.

40 Similarly, undo the retaining nut and bolt and release the front metal EGR pipe clamp from the EGR valve heat exchanger.

41 Free the vacuum reservoir mounting bracket from the rear of the cylinder block by undoing the three mounting bracket retaining bolts.

42 Slacken the retaining clips and disconnect the two coolant hoses from the EGR valve heat exchanger. Undo the retaining nut and bolt securing the heat exchanger to the cylinder head and remove the heat exchanger from the engine.

43 Refitting is the reverse of removal, bearing in mind the following points:

a) *Renew all disturbed gaskets and seals.*
b) *Tighten the retaining bolts/nuts to the specified torque.*
c) *Refit the battery box and battery as described in Chapter 5A.*
d) *Refill the cooling system as described in Chapter 1B.*

EGR valve heat exchanger renewal – Z19DTH engines

44 Drain the cooling system as described in Chapter 1B.

45 Remove the plastic cover over the top of the engine.

46 Remove the battery and battery box as described in Chapter 5A.

47 Slacken the retaining clips and disconnect the two coolant hoses from the metal coolant pipe assembly at the rear of the engine.

48 Unscrew the two nuts securing the wiring harness and coolant pipe assembly to the starter motor bracket and the nut securing the pipes to the thermostat housing stud. Free the harness and pipes from the bracket.

49 Slacken the retaining clips securing the remaining coolant hoses to the coolant pipe assembly and manoeuvre the pipe assembly from the engine.

50 Remove the thermostat housing as described in Chapter 3.

51 Slacken the retaining clips and remove the charge air hose from the turbocharger and intercooler.

52 Release the retaining clip and disconnect the coolant hose from the metal coolant pipe at the front of the engine.

53 Release the retaining clips and disconnect the coolant hoses from the EGR valve heat exchanger.

54 Undo the two bolts securing the rear metal EGR pipe to the EGR valve. Undo the retaining nut and bolt and release the metal EGR pipe clamp from the EGR valve heat exchanger. Separate the pipe from the heat exchanger and recover the gasket from the pipe fitting.

55 Similarly, undo the two bolts securing the front metal EGR pipe to the exhaust manifold. Undo the retaining nut and bolt and release the metal EGR pipe clamp from the EGR valve heat exchanger. Separate the pipe from the heat exchanger and recover the gasket from the pipe fitting.

56 Undo the two bolts and remove the heat exchanger from the engine.

57 Refitting is the reverse of removal, bearing in mind the following points:

a) *Renew all disturbed gaskets and seals.*
b) *Tighten the retaining bolts to the specified torque.*
c) *Refit the thermostat housing as described in Chapter 3.*
d) *Refit the battery tray and battery as described in Chapter 5A.*
e) *Refill the cooling system as described in Chapter 1B.*

**4 Catalytic converter –
general information
and precautions**

1 The catalytic converter is a reliable and simple device which needs no maintenance in itself, but there are some facts of which an owner should be aware if the converter is to function properly for its full service life.

Petrol engines

a) *DO NOT use leaded petrol (or LRP) in a car equipped with a catalytic converter – the lead will coat the precious metals, reducing their converting efficiency and will eventually destroy the converter.*
b) *Always keep the ignition and fuel systems well-maintained in accordance with the manufacturer's schedule.*
c) *If the engine develops a misfire, do not drive the car at all (or at least as little as possible) until the fault is cured.*
d) *DO NOT push- or tow-start the car – this will soak the catalytic converter in unburned fuel, causing it to overheat when the engine does start.*
e) *DO NOT switch off the ignition at high engine speeds.*
f) *DO NOT use fuel or engine oil additives – these may contain substances harmful to the catalytic converter.*
g) *DO NOT continue to use the car if the engine burns oil to the extent of leaving a visible trail of blue smoke.*
h) *Remember that the catalytic converter operates at very high temperatures. DO NOT, therefore, park the car in dry undergrowth, over long grass or piles of dead leaves after a long run.*
i) *Remember that the catalytic converter is FRAGILE – do not strike it with tools during servicing work.*
j) *In some cases a sulphurous smell (like that of rotten eggs) may be noticed from the exhaust. This is common to many catalytic converter-equipped cars and once the car has covered a few thousand miles the problem should disappear. It may also be caused by the brand of petrol used.*
k) *The catalytic converter, used on a well-maintained and well-driven car, should last for between 50 000 and 100 000 miles – if the converter is no longer effective it must be renewed.*

Diesel engines

2 Refer to the information given in parts f, g, h, i and k of the petrol engines information given above.

Chapter 5 Part A:
Starting and charging systems

Contents

Degrees of difficulty

Easy, suitable for novice with little experience	**Fairly easy,** suitable for beginner with some experience	**Fairly difficult,** suitable for competent DIY mechanic	**Difficult,** suitable for experienced DIY mechanic	**Very difficult,** suitable for expert DIY or professional

Specifications

General
Electrical system type . . . .   12 volt negative earth

Battery
Type . . . .   Lead-acid, 'maintenance-free' (sealed for life)
Charge condition:
   Poor . . . .   12.5 volts
   Normal . . . .   12.6 volts
   Good. . . . .   12.7 volts

Torque wrench settings

	Nm	lbf ft
Alternator:		
Petrol engine models:		
1.8 litre Z18XE engines:		
Alternator mounting bracket to cylinder block	35	26
Alternator-to-mounting bracket lower bolt	35	26
Alternator-to-mounting bracket upper bolt	20	15
1.8 litre Z18XER engines:		
Alternator mounting bolts	35	26
2.2 litre engines:		
Alternator mounting bolts	20	15
Diesel engine models:		
Alternator mounting bolts	60	44
Auxiliary drivebelt tensioner:		
Petrol engine models:		
1.8 litre engines:		
Z18XE	35	26
Z18XER	50	37
2.2 litre engines	43	32
Diesel engine models	50	37
Engine mountings (2.2 litre petrol engines):		
Front mounting/torque link bracket to transmission	80	59
Front mounting/torque link to subframe	80	59
Rear mounting/torque link bracket to transmission	80	59
Rear mounting/torque link to transmission bracket	80	59
Right-hand engine bracket-to-cylinder head bolts	55	41
Right-hand mounting-to-body bolts/nut	55	41
Right-hand mounting-to-engine bracket bolts	55	41
Exhaust system front pipe to catalytic converter (2.2 litre petrol engines)	20	15
Glow plugs	10	7
Oil pressure warning light switch:		
Petrol engine models:		
1.8 litre engines:		
Z18XE	30	22
Z18XER	20	15
2.2 litre engines	18	13
Diesel engine models	22	16
Roadwheel bolts	110	81
Starter motor:		
Petrol engine models:		
1.8 litre Z18XE engines:		
Inlet manifold support bracket to cylinder block	35	26
Inlet manifold support bracket to manifold	20	15
Starter motor mounting bolts	25	18
1.8 litre Z18XER engines:		
Inlet manifold support bracket bolts	8	6
Starter motor mounting bolts	25	18
2.2 litre engines:		
Starter motor mounting bolts	40	30
Diesel engine models	25	18

1 General information, precautions and battery disconnection

The engine electrical system consists mainly of the charging and starting systems, and the diesel engine pre/post-heating system. Because of their engine-related functions, these components are covered separately from the body electrical devices such as the lights, instruments, etc (which are covered in Chapter 12). On petrol engine models refer to Part B for information on the ignition system.

The electrical system is of 12-volt negative earth type.

The battery is of the maintenance-free (sealed for life) type, and is charged by the alternator, which is belt-driven from the crankshaft pulley.

The starter motor is of pre-engaged type incorporating an integral solenoid. On starting, the solenoid moves the drive pinion into engagement with the flywheel/driveplate ring gear before the starter motor is energised. Once the engine has started, a one-way clutch prevents the motor armature being driven by the engine until the pinion disengages.

Further details of the various systems are given in the relevant Sections of this Chapter. While some repair procedures are given, the usual course of action is to renew the component concerned.

Precautions

It is necessary to take extra care when

working on the electrical system to avoid damage to semi-conductor devices (diodes and transistors), and to avoid the risk of personal injury. In addition to the precautions given in *Safety first!* at the beginning of this manual, observe the following when working on the system:

• Always remove rings, watches, etc, before working on the electrical system. Even with the battery disconnected, capacitive discharge could occur if a component's live terminal is earthed through a metal object. This could cause a shock or nasty burn.

• Do not reverse the battery connections. Components such as the alternator, electronic control units, or any other components having semi-conductor circuitry could be irreparably damaged.

• If the engine is being started using jump leads and a slave battery, connect the batteries positive-to-positive and negative-to-negative (see *Jump starting*). This also applies when connecting a battery charger but in this case both of the battery terminals should first be disconnected.

• Never disconnect the battery terminals, the alternator, any electrical wiring or any test instruments when the engine is running.

• Do not allow the engine to turn the alternator when the alternator is not connected.

• Never test for alternator output by flashing the output lead to earth.

• Never use an ohmmeter of the type incorporating a hand-cranked generator for circuit or continuity testing.

• Always ensure that the battery negative lead is disconnected when working on the electrical system.

• Before using electric-arc welding equipment on the car, disconnect the battery, alternator and components such as the fuel injection/ignition electronic control unit to protect them from the risk of damage.

Battery disconnection

Refer to the precautions listed in *Disconnecting the battery* in the Reference Chapter.

2 Electrical fault finding – general information

Refer to Chapter 12.

3 Battery – testing and charging

Testing

Traditional and low maintenance battery

1 If the vehicle covers a small annual mileage, it is worthwhile checking the specific gravity of the electrolyte every three months to determine the state of charge of the battery.

Use a hydrometer to make the check and compare the results with the following table. Note that the specific gravity readings assume an electrolyte temperature of 15°C; for every 10°C below 15°C subtract 0.007. For every 10°C above 15°C add 0.007.

	Ambient temperature	
	Above 25°C	Below 25°C
Fully-charged	1.210 to 1.230	1.270 to 1.290
70% charged	1.170 to 1.190	1.230 to 1.250
Discharged	1.050 to 1.070	1.110 to 1.130

2 If the battery condition is suspect, first check the specific gravity of electrolyte in each cell. A variation of 0.040 or more between any cells indicates loss of electrolyte or deterioration of the internal plates.

3 If the specific gravity variation is 0.040 or more, the battery should be renewed. If the cell variation is satisfactory but the battery is discharged, it should be charged as described later in this Section.

Maintenance-free battery

4 Where a 'sealed for life' maintenance-free battery is fitted, topping-up and testing of the electrolyte in each cell is not possible. The condition of the battery can therefore only be tested using a battery condition indicator or a voltmeter.

5 Some models are fitted with a maintenance-free battery with a built-in 'magic-eye' charge condition indicator. The indicator is located in the top of the battery casing, and indicates the condition of the battery from its colour **(see illustration)**. If the indicator shows green, then the battery is in a good state of charge. If the indicator turns darker, eventually to black, then the battery requires charging, as described later in this Section. If the indicator shows clear/yellow, then the electrolyte level in the battery is too low to allow further use, and the battery should be renewed. Do not attempt to charge, load or jump start a battery when the indicator shows clear/yellow.

All battery types

6 If testing the battery using a voltmeter, connect the voltmeter across the battery and compare the result with those given in the Specifications under 'charge condition'. The test is only accurate if the battery has not been subjected to any kind of charge for the previous six hours. If this is not the case, switch on the headlights for 30 seconds, then wait four to five minutes before testing the battery after switching off the headlights. All other electrical circuits must be switched off, so check that the doors and tailgate are fully shut when making the test.

7 If the voltage reading is less than 12.2 volts, then the battery is discharged, whilst a reading of 12.2 to 12.4 volts indicates a partially-discharged condition.

8 If the battery is to be charged, remove it from the vehicle (Section 4) and charge it as described later in this Section.

3.5 Battery charge condition indicator – 'Delco' type battery

Charging

Note: *The following is intended as a guide only. Always refer to the manufacturer's recommendations (often printed on a label attached to the battery) before charging a battery.*

Traditional and low maintenance battery

9 Charge the battery at a rate of 3.5 to 4 amps and continue to charge the battery at this rate until no further rise in specific gravity is noted over a four hour period.

10 Alternatively, a trickle charger charging at the rate of 1.5 amps can safely be used overnight.

11 Specially rapid 'boost' charges which are claimed to restore the power of the battery in 1 to 2 hours are not recommended, as they can cause serious damage to the battery plates through overheating.

12 While charging the battery, note that the temperature of the electrolyte should never exceed 38°C.

Maintenance-free battery

13 This battery type takes considerably longer to fully recharge than the standard type, the time taken being dependent on the extent of discharge, but it will take anything up to three days.

14 A constant voltage type charger is required, to be set, when connected, to 13.9 to 14.9 volts with a charger current below 25 amps. Using this method, the battery should be usable within three hours, giving a voltage reading of 12.5 volts, but this is for a partially-discharged battery and, as mentioned, full charging can take considerably longer.

15 If the battery is to be charged from a fully-discharged state (condition reading less than 12.2 volts), have it recharged by your Vauxhall/Opel dealer or local automotive electrician, as the charge rate is higher and constant supervision during charging is necessary.

4 Battery and battery box – removal and refitting

Note: *Refer to 'Disconnecting the battery' in the Reference Chapter before proceeding.*

4.2 Lift open the battery box lid . . .

4.3 . . . then unclip the insulation jacket and lift open the jacket cover

4.4a Unscrew the battery negative (–) terminal retaining nut . . .

4.4b . . . then lift the terminal clamp off the battery post

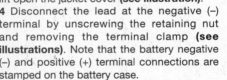

4.10 Release the coolant hose from the clips on the side of the battery box

4.11 Depress the tab and release the positive cable terminal box from the side of the battery box

Battery

Removal

1 The battery is located at the front, left-hand side of the engine compartment, housed in a protective plastic box.

2 Open the battery box by releasing the lid at the front and pivoting it upwards (see illustration). If necessary, the lid can be removed completely by disengaging its hinges from the rear of the battery box.

3 Where fitted, unclip the insulation jacket and lift open the jacket cover (see illustration).

4 Disconnect the lead at the negative (–) terminal by unscrewing the retaining nut and removing the terminal clamp (see illustrations). Note that the battery negative (–) and positive (+) terminal connections are stamped on the battery case.

5 Disconnect the lead at the positive (+) terminal by unscrewing the retaining nut and

removing the terminal clamp. If necessary, the auxiliary lead may also be unbolted from the terminal.

6 On the inner side of the battery, unscrew the bolt and remove the retaining clamp.

7 Carefully lift the battery from its location and remove it from the car. Make sure the battery is kept upright at all times.

Refitting

Note: *As a precaution, before refitting the battery check that all doors are unlocked.*

8 Refitting is a reversal of removal, but smear petroleum jelly on the terminals after reconnecting the leads to reduce corrosion, and always reconnect the positive lead first, followed by the negative lead.

Battery box

Removal

9 Remove the battery as described previously.

10 Release the coolant expansion tank hose from the clips on the side of the battery box (see illustration).

11 Depress the plastic tab and release the positive cable terminal box from the side of the battery box (see illustration).

12 On diesel engine models, unclip the pre/post-heating system control unit from the side of the battery box (see illustration).

13 On 2.2 litre automatic transmission models, unclip the transmission electronic control unit mounting bracket and lift the control unit and bracket upwards and out of the battery box.

14 Depress the retaining tab and lift out the battery box corner panel (see illustrations).

15 Release the battery cable guides from the base of the battery box, by depressing the retaining tabs with a small screwdriver, and pulling outwards (see illustration).

16 Undo the three retaining bolts and lift

4.12 On diesel engine models, unclip the pre/post-heating system control unit from the side of the battery box

4.14a Depress the retaining tab . . .

4.14b . . . and lift out the battery box corner panel

the battery box up and out of the engine compartment **(see illustration)**.

Refitting

17 Refitting is a reversal of removal.

5 Charging system – testing

Note: *Refer to the precautions given in 'Safety first!' and in Section 1 of this Chapter before starting work.*

1 If the ignition no-charge warning light fails to illuminate when the ignition is switched on, first check the alternator wiring connections for security. If satisfactory, check the condition of all related fuses, fusible links, wiring connections and earthing points. If this fails to reveal the fault, the vehicle should be taken to a Vauxhall/Opel dealer or auto-electrician, as further testing entails the use of specialist diagnostic equipment.

2 If the ignition warning light illuminates when the engine is running, stop the engine and check the condition of the auxiliary drivebelt (see Chapter 1A or 1B) and the security of the alternator wiring connections. If satisfactory, have the alternator checked by a Vauxhall/Opel dealer or auto-electrician.

3 If the alternator output is suspect even though the warning light functions correctly, the regulated voltage may be checked as follows.

4 Connect a voltmeter across the battery terminals, and start the engine.

5 Increase the engine speed until the voltmeter reading remains steady; the reading should be approximately 12 to 13 volts, and no more than 14 volts.

6 Switch on as many electrical accessories (eg, the headlights, heated rear window and heater blower) as possible, and check that the

4.15 Depress the retaining tabs and release the battery cable guides by pulling outwards

alternator maintains the regulated voltage at around 13.5 to 14.5 volts.

7 If the regulated voltage is not as stated, the fault may be due to worn brushes, weak brush springs, a faulty voltage regulator, a faulty diode, a severed phase winding, or worn or damaged slip-rings. The alternator should be renewed or taken to a Vauxhall/Opel dealer or auto-electrician for testing and repair.

6 Auxiliary drivebelt – removal and refitting

Refer to Chapter 1A or 1B.

7 Auxiliary drivebelt tensioner – removal and refitting

Removal

1.8 litre petrol engines

1 Firmly apply the handbrake, then jack up the front of the car and support it securely on axle stands (see *Jacking and vehicle support*). Remove the right-hand front roadwheel.

2 Remove the auxiliary drivebelt as described in Chapter 1A.

3 Undo the central mounting bolt, and remove the tensioner assembly from the engine **(see illustrations)**.

2.2 litre petrol engines

4 Disconnect the battery negative terminal (refer to *Disconnecting the battery* in the Reference Chapter).

5 Remove the air cleaner assembly and air intake duct as described in Chapter 4A.

6 Firmly apply the handbrake, then jack up the front of the car and support it securely on axle stands (see *Jacking and vehicle support*).

7 Remove the right-hand front roadwheel.

8 Remove the auxiliary drivebelt as described in Chapter 1A.

9 Undo the three nuts securing the exhaust system front pipe to the catalytic converter, taking care to support the flexible section.

Note: *Angular movement in excess of 10°*

4.16 Undo the three bolts (arrowed) and lift out the battery box

can cause permanent damage to the flexible section. Separate the flange joint and recover the gasket.

10 Undo the through-bolt securing the rear engine mounting/torque link to the mounting bracket, and the three bolts securing the mounting bracket to the transmission. Remove the mounting bracket from under the car.

11 Unscrew the nut and remove the through-bolt securing the front engine mounting/torque link to the subframe.

12 Connect a suitable hoist and lifting tackle to the right-hand end of the engine and support its weight. If available, the type of support bar which locates in the engine compartment side channels is to be preferred.

13 Mark the bolt positions for correct refitting, then undo the three bolts securing the right-hand engine mounting to the engine bracket, and the two bolts and one nut securing the mounting to the body. Remove the mounting.

14 Using the hoist, carefully raise the right-hand end of the engine until the bolts securing the engine mounting bracket to the cylinder head are accessible. Undo the three bolts and remove the engine bracket.

15 Reposition the hoist as necessary, then undo the drivebelt tensioner central mounting bolt. Remove the tensioner assembly from the engine **(see illustration)**.

Diesel engines

16 Firmly apply the handbrake, then jack up the front of the car and support it securely on axle stands (see *Jacking and vehicle support*).

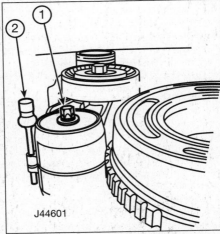

7.3a Auxiliary drivebelt tensioner – 1.8 litre Z18XE petrol engines

1 *Central mounting bolt*
2 *Locking tool*

7.3b Auxiliary drivebelt tensioner mounting bolt (arrowed) – 1.8 litre Z18XER petrol engines

**7.15 Removing the auxiliary drivebelt tensioner –
2.2 litre petrol engines**

**7.19 Undo the central mounting bolt (arrowed) and remove the
tensioner assembly – diesel engines**

17 Remove the right-hand front roadwheel.
18 Remove the auxiliary drivebelt as described in Chapter 1B.
19 Undo the central mounting bolt, and remove the tensioner assembly from the engine **(see illustration)**.

Refitting

1.8 litre petrol engines

20 Place the tensioner assembly in position ensuring that the locating pegs on the tensioner mounting surface engage correctly with the corresponding holes in the mounting bracket. Tighten the tensioner central mounting bolt to the specified torque.
21 Refit the auxiliary drivebelt as described in Chapter 1A.
22 Refit the roadwheel then lower the car to the ground. Tighten the roadwheel bolts to the specified torque.

2.2 litre petrol engines

23 Place the tensioner assembly in position ensuring that the locating peg on the tensioner mounting surface engages correctly with the corresponding hole in the timing chain cover. Tighten the tensioner central mounting bolt to the specified torque.
24 Refit the engine mounting bracket to the cylinder head and tighten the three retaining bolts to the specified torque.
25 Locate the right-hand engine mounting in position, then refit the three bolts securing the mounting to the engine bracket and the two bolts and one nut securing the mounting to the body. Align the mounting in its original position, then tighten the bolts and nut to the specified torque.
26 Remove the hoist and lifting tackle from the engine.
27 Refit the through-bolt and nut securing the front engine mounting/torque link to the subframe. Tighten the nut to the specified torque.
28 Place the rear engine mounting/torque link mounting bracket in position and refit the three

bolts securing the bracket to the transmission. Tighten the bolts to the specified torque.
29 Refit the rear engine mounting/torque link through-bolt and tighten the bolt to the specified torque.
30 Using a new gasket, refit the exhaust front pipe flange joint to the catalytic converter and tighten the three retaining nuts to the specified torque.
31 Refit the auxiliary drivebelt as described in Chapter 1A.
32 Refit the roadwheel then lower the car to the ground. Tighten the roadwheel bolts to the specified torque.
33 Refer to Chapter 4A if necessary and refit the air cleaner assembly and air intake duct.
34 On completion, reconnect the battery negative terminal.

Diesel engines

35 Place the tensioner assembly in position ensuring that the locating peg on the tensioner mounting surface engages correctly with the corresponding hole in the mounting bracket, Tighten the tensioner central mounting bolt to the specified torque.
36 Refit the auxiliary drivebelt as described in Chapter 1B.
37 Refit the roadwheel then lower the car to the ground. Tighten the roadwheel bolts to the specified torque.

**8.11 Alternator mounting bracket bolts
(arrowed) – 1.8 litre Z18XE petrol engines**

8 Alternator –
removal and refitting

Removal

1.8 litre Z18XE petrol engines

1 Disconnect the battery negative terminal (refer to *Disconnecting the battery* in the Reference Chapter).
2 Firmly apply the handbrake, then jack up the front of the car and support it securely on axle stands (see *Jacking and vehicle support*). Remove the right-hand front roadwheel.
3 Remove the air cleaner assembly and air intake duct as described in Chapter 4A.
4 Release the quick-release fittings and disconnect the two evaporative emission control purge valve vacuum hoses. Disconnect the wiring connector, undo the retaining bolt and remove the purge valve.
5 Remove the auxiliary drivebelt as described in Chapter 1A.
6 Undo the central mounting bolt, and remove the auxiliary drivebelt tensioner assembly from the engine **(see illustration 7.3a)**.
7 Remove the upper alternator mounting bolt.
8 Slacken the lower alternator bolt, and swing the alternator to the rear.
9 Disconnect the oil pressure switch wiring connector and move the cable to one side.
10 Remove the rubber covers (where fitted) from the alternator terminals, then unscrew the retaining nuts and disconnect the wiring from the rear of the alternator.
11 Slacken and remove the bolts securing the alternator mounting bracket to the cylinder block, then manoeuvre the alternator and bracket assembly upwards and out of position **(see illustration)**.
12 Undo the bolt securing the alternator to its mounting bracket and separate the two components **(see illustration)**.

8.12 Undo the bolt securing the alternator to its mounting bracket and separate the two components – 1.8 litre Z18XE petrol engines

8.29a Undo the retaining nut . . .

8.29b . . . and disconnect the wiring terminal – 2.2 litre petrol engines

1.8 litre Z18XER petrol engines

13 Disconnect the battery negative terminal (refer to *Disconnecting the battery* in the Reference Chapter).
14 Firmly apply the handbrake, then jack up the front of the car and support it securely on axle stands (see *Jacking and vehicle support*). Remove the right-hand front roadwheel.
15 Remove the auxiliary drivebelt as described in Chapter 1A.
16 Remove the rubber covers (where fitted) from the alternator terminals, then unscrew the two retaining nuts and disconnect the wiring from the rear of the alternator.
17 Unscrew the upper and lower mounting bolts and withdraw the alternator upwards from the block.

2.2 litre petrol engines

18 Disconnect the battery negative terminal (refer to *Disconnecting the battery* in the Reference Chapter).
19 Firmly apply the handbrake, then jack up the front of the car and support it securely on axle stands (see *Jacking and vehicle support*). Remove the right-hand front roadwheel.
20 Remove the air cleaner assembly and air intake duct as described in Chapter 4A.
21 Remove the auxiliary drivebelt as described in Chapter 1A.
22 Drain the cooling system as described in Chapter 1A.
23 Release the retaining clip and disconnect the radiator top hose from the cylinder head.
24 Release the quick-release fittings and

disconnect the two evaporative emission control purge valve vacuum hoses. Disconnect the wiring connector, then unclip and remove the purge valve.
25 Unscrew the nut and remove the through-bolt securing the front engine mounting/torque link to the subframe.
26 Connect a suitable hoist and lifting tackle to the right-hand end of the engine. If available, the type of support bar which locates in the engine compartment side channels is to be preferred.
27 Mark the bolt positions for correct refitting, then undo the two bolts and one nut securing the right-hand engine mounting to the body.
28 Using the hoist, carefully raise the right-hand end of the engine approximately 3.5 cm.
29 Unscrew the retaining nut and disconnect the wiring terminal **(see illustrations)**, then unplug the wiring block connector from the rear of the alternator.
30 Slacken and remove the four alternator mounting bolts, and manoeuvre the alternator out of position **(see illustration)**.

Diesel engines

31 Disconnect the battery negative terminal (refer to *Disconnecting the battery* in the Reference Chapter).
32 Firmly apply the handbrake, then jack up the front of the car and support it securely on axle stands (see *Jacking and vehicle support*). Remove the right-hand front roadwheel.
33 Remove the auxiliary drivebelt as described in Chapter 1B.

34 Undo the alternator lower front mounting bolt **(see illustration)**.
35 Remove the fuel filter crash box as described in Chapter 4B.
36 On Z19DTH engines, undo the two bolts securing the wiring harness support bracket to the high-pressure fuel pump mounting bracket. Unclip the wiring harness as necessary and move it clear of the alternator.
37 Unscrew the two retaining nuts and disconnect the wiring connectors from the alternator terminals.
38 Undo the alternator upper rear mounting bolts and manoeuvre the alternator upwards and out of position **(see illustration)**.

Refitting

1.8 litre Z18XE petrol engines

39 Refit the mounting bracket to the alternator and secure with the mounting bolt, tightened finger-tight only at this stage.
40 Manoeuvre the alternator and mounting bracket assembly into position and refit the mounting bracket retaining bolts. Tighten the bolts to the specified torque.
41 Reconnect the wiring to the alternator terminals and tighten the retaining nuts securely. Where applicable, refit the rubber covers to the alternator terminals.
42 Reconnect the wiring to the oil pressure switch.
43 Refit the alternator upper mounting bolt, then tighten the upper and lower mounting bolts to the specified torque.
44 Place the auxiliary drivebelt tensioner

8.30 Alternator mounting bracket bolts arrowed – 2.2 litre petrol engines

8.34 Alternator lower front mounting bolt (arrowed) – diesel engines

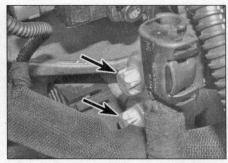

8.38 Alternator upper rear mounting bolts (arrowed) – diesel engines

assembly in position ensuring that the locating pegs on the tensioner mounting surface engage correctly with the corresponding holes in the mounting bracket. Tighten the tensioner central mounting bolt to the specified torque.

45 Refit the auxiliary drivebelt as described in Chapter 1A.

46 Refit the evaporative emission control purge valve and secure with the mounting bolt. Reconnect the two vacuum hose quick-release fittings.

47 Refit the air cleaner assembly and air intake duct as described in Chapter 4A.

48 Refit the roadwheel then lower the car to the ground. Tighten the roadwheel bolts to the specified torque.

49 On completion, reconnect the battery negative terminal.

1.8 litre Z18XER petrol engines

50 Manoeuvre the alternator into position and refit the upper and lower mounting bolts. Tighten the bolts to the specified torque.

51 Reconnect the wiring to the alternator terminals and tighten the retaining nuts securely. Where applicable, refit the rubber covers to the alternator terminals.

52 Refit the auxiliary drivebelt as described in Chapter 1A.

53 Refit the roadwheel then lower the car to the ground. Tighten the roadwheel bolts to the specified torque.

54 On completion, reconnect the battery negative terminal.

2.2 litre petrol engines

55 Manoeuvre the alternator into position and refit the four retaining bolts. Tighten the bolts to the specified torque.

56 Reconnect the alternator wiring block connector and the terminal wiring, tightening the retaining nut securely.

57 Lower the engine until the right-hand engine mounting contacts the body.

58 Refit the two bolts and one nut securing the mounting to the body. Align the mounting in its original position, then tighten the bolts and nut to the specified torque.

59 Remove the hoist and lifting tackle from the engine.

60 Refit the through-bolt and nut securing the front engine mounting/torque link to the subframe. Tighten the nut to the specified torque.

61 Refit the emission control purge valve, then reconnect the vacuum hoses and wiring connector.

62 Reconnect the radiator top hose to the cylinder head.

63 Refit the auxiliary drivebelt as described in Chapter 1A.

64 Refit the air cleaner assembly and air intake duct as described in Chapter 4A.

65 Refit the roadwheel then lower the car to the ground. Tighten the roadwheel bolts to the specified torque.

66 Reconnect the battery negative terminal, then refill the cooling system as described in Chapter 1A.

Diesel engines

67 Manoeuvre the alternator into position and refit the upper rear retaining bolt(s). Tighten the bolt(s) finger-tight only at this stage.

68 Reconnect the wiring to the alternator terminals and tighten the retaining nuts securely.

69 On Z19DTH engines, refit the wiring harness support bracket to the fuel pump mounting bracket and secure with the two bolts. Clip the wiring harness back into position in the bracket.

70 Refit the alternator lower front mounting bolt, then tighten the upper and lower mounting bolts to the specified torque.

71 Refit the auxiliary drivebelt as described in Chapter 1B.

72 Refit the fuel filter crash box as described in Chapter 4B.

73 Refit the roadwheel then lower the car to the ground. Tighten the roadwheel bolts to the specified torque.

74 On completion, reconnect the battery negative terminal.

9 Alternator – testing and overhaul

If the alternator is thought to be suspect, it should be removed from the vehicle and taken to an auto-electrician for testing. Most auto-electricians will be able to supply and fit brushes at a reasonable cost. However, check on the cost of repairs before proceeding as it may prove more economical to obtain a new or exchange alternator.

10 Starting system – testing

Note: *Refer to the precautions given in 'Safety first!' and in Section 1 of this Chapter before starting work.*

1 If the starter motor fails to operate when the ignition key is turned to the appropriate position, the possible causes are as follows:
  a) *The engine immobiliser is faulty.*
  b) *The battery is faulty.*
  c) *The electrical connections between the switch, solenoid, battery and starter motor are somewhere failing to pass the necessary current from the battery through the starter to earth.*
  d) *The solenoid is faulty.*
  e) *The starter motor is mechanically or electrically defective.*

2 To check the battery, switch on the headlights. If they dim after a few seconds, this indicates that the battery is discharged – recharge (see Section 3) or renew the battery. If the headlights glow brightly, operate the starter switch while watching the headlights. If they dim, then this indicates that current is reaching the starter motor, therefore the fault must lie in the starter motor. If the lights

continue to glow brightly (and no clicking sound can be heard from the starter motor solenoid), this indicates that there is a fault in the circuit or solenoid – see the following paragraphs. If the starter motor turns slowly when operated, but the battery is in good condition, then this indicates either that the starter motor is faulty, or there is considerable resistance somewhere in the circuit.

3 If a fault in the circuit is suspected, disconnect the battery leads (including the earth connection to the body), the starter/solenoid wiring and the engine/transmission earth strap. Thoroughly clean the connections, and reconnect the leads and wiring. Use a voltmeter or test light to check that full battery voltage is available at the battery positive lead connection to the solenoid. Smear petroleum jelly around the battery terminals to prevent corrosion – corroded connections are among the most frequent causes of electrical system faults.

4 If the battery and all connections are in good condition, check the circuit by disconnecting the ignition switch supply wire from the solenoid terminal. Connect a voltmeter or test lamp between the wire end and a good earth (such as the battery negative terminal), and check that the wire is live when the ignition switch is turned to the 'start' position. If it is, then the circuit is sound – if not the circuit wiring can be checked as described in Chapter 12.

5 The solenoid contacts can be checked by connecting a voltmeter or test light between the battery positive feed connection on the starter side of the solenoid and earth. When the ignition switch is turned to the 'start' position, there should be a reading or lighted bulb, as applicable. If there is no reading or lighted bulb, the solenoid is faulty and should be renewed.

6 If the circuit and solenoid are proved sound, the fault must lie in the starter motor. In this event, it may be possible to have the starter motor overhauled by a specialist, but check on the cost of spares before proceeding, as it may prove more economical to obtain a new or exchange motor.

11 Starter motor – removal and refitting

Removal

1.8 litre petrol engines

1 Disconnect the battery negative terminal (refer to *Disconnecting the battery* in the Reference Chapter).

2 Firmly apply the handbrake, then jack up the front of the car and support it securely on axle stands (see *Jacking and vehicle support*).

3 Disconnect the oxygen sensor wiring at the cable connector below the inlet manifold.

4 Undo the two retaining bolts and remove the support bracket from the underside of the inlet manifold.

5 Slacken and remove the two retaining nuts and disconnect the wiring from the starter motor solenoid. Recover the washers under the nuts.

6 Where applicable, unscrew the retaining nut and disconnect the earth lead from the starter motor upper bolt.

7 Slacken and remove the retaining bolts then manoeuvre the starter motor out from underneath the engine.

2.2 litre petrol engines

8 Disconnect the battery negative terminal (refer to *Disconnecting the battery* in the Reference Chapter).

9 Firmly apply the handbrake, then jack up the front of the car and support it securely on axle stands (see *Jacking and vehicle support*).

10 Disconnect the wiring connector at the oil level sensor located on the front face of the sump.

11 Slacken and remove the two retaining nuts, release the cable tie and disconnect the wiring from the starter motor solenoid. Recover the washers under the nuts.

12 Disconnect the crankshaft sensor wiring connector.

13 Slacken and remove the two retaining bolts then manoeuvre the starter motor out from underneath the engine.

Diesel engines

14 Disconnect the battery negative terminal (refer to *Disconnecting the battery* in the Reference Chapter).

15 Firmly apply the handbrake, then jack up the front of the car and support it securely on axle stands (see *Jacking and vehicle support*).

16 On Z19DT engines, remove the oil filler cap and unscrew the two bolts securing the plastic cover over the top of the engine. Release the engine breather hose, then lift off the cover and refit the oil filler cap **(see illustrations)**. On Z19DTH engines, remove the plastic cover by pulling it upwards off the mounting studs.

17 Undo the retaining bolts and screws and remove the undertray from beneath the engine.

18 Slacken and remove the two retaining nuts and disconnect the wiring from the starter motor solenoid **(see illustration)**. Recover the washers under the nuts.

19 Unscrew the retaining nut and disconnect the earth lead from the starter motor lower stud bolt **(see illustration)**.

20 Open the retaining clips and release the two heater hoses from the coolant pipe support bracket.

21 Undo the two nuts and release the wiring harness from the support bracket above the starter motor **(see illustration)**.

22 Carefully lift the cooling system expansion tank out of its mounting bracket and place the tank to one side.

23 Unscrew the starter motor lower stud bolt and the two upper mounting bolts **(see illustration)**. Collect the wiring harness support bracket then manoeuvre the starter motor upwards and out of position.

11.16a Remove the oil filler cap . . .

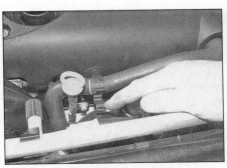

11.16c . . . release the engine breather hose . . .

Refitting

24 Refitting is a reversal of removal tightening the retaining bolts to the specified

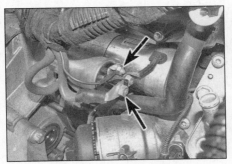

11.18 Undo the nuts (arrowed) and disconnect the starter solenoid wiring connectors – diesel engines

11.21 Undo the nuts and release the wiring harness from the support bracket – diesel engines

11.16b . . . unscrew the two bolts (arrowed) . . .

11.16d . . . and lift off the plastic engine cover – Z19DT diesel engines

torque. Ensure all wiring is correctly routed and its retaining nuts are securely tightened.

11.19 Unscrew the nut (arrowed) and disconnect the earth lead from the starter motor stud bolt – diesel engines

11.23 Unscrew the bolts (arrowed), collect the wiring harness bracket and remove the starter from above – diesel engines

14.3 Oil pressure warning light switch (arrowed) – 1.8 litre Z18XE petrol engines

14.8 Oil pressure warning light switch (arrowed) – 2.2 litre petrol engines

14.10 Oil pressure warning light switch (arrowed) – diesel engines

12 Starter motor – testing and overhaul

If the starter motor is thought to be suspect, it should be removed from the vehicle and taken to an auto-electrician for testing. Most auto-electricians will be able to supply and fit brushes at a reasonable cost. However, check on the cost of repairs before proceeding as it may prove more economical to obtain a new or exchange motor.

13 Ignition switch – removal and refitting

The switch is integral with the steering column lock, and removal and refitting is described in Chapter 10.

14 Oil pressure warning light switch – removal and refitting

Removal

1.8 litre Z18XE petrol engines

1 The switch is screwed into the rear of the oil pump housing which is located on the right-hand end of the engine, on the end of the crankshaft.
2 Firmly apply the handbrake, then jack up the front of the car and support it securely on axle stands (see *Jacking and vehicle support*).
3 Disconnect the wiring connector then unscrew the switch and recover the sealing washer. Be prepared for oil spillage, and if the switch is to be left removed from the engine for any length of time, plug the switch aperture **(see illustration)**.

1.8 litre Z18XER petrol engines

4 The oil pressure warning light switch is screwed into the front of the cylinder block.
5 Firmly apply the handbrake, then jack up the front of the car and support it securely on axle stands (see *Jacking and vehicle support*).
6 On models equipped with air conditioning,

refer to Chapter 3 and unbolt the air conditioning compressor from the cylinder block **without disconnecting the refrigerant lines**. Support the compressor to one side for access to the oil pressure warning light switch.
7 Disconnect the wiring connector then unscrew the switch and recover the sealing washer. Be prepared for oil spillage, and if the switch is to be left removed from the engine for any length of time, plug the switch aperture.

2.2 litre petrol engines

8 The switch is screwed into the front of the cylinder block, behind the starter motor **(see illustration)**. To gain access to the switch, it will be necessary to remove the starter motor as described in Section 11.
9 Disconnect the wiring connector then unscrew the switch and recover the sealing washer. Be prepared for oil spillage, and if the switch is to be left removed from the engine for any length of time, plug the switch aperture.

Diesel engines

10 The switch is screwed into the oil filter housing at the rear of the engine **(see illustration)**.
11 Firmly apply the handbrake, then jack up the front of the car and support it securely on axle stands (see *Jacking and vehicle support*).
12 Undo the retaining bolts and screws and remove the undertray from beneath the engine.
13 Disconnect the wiring connector then unscrew the switch and recover the sealing

15.5 Remove the oil level sensor and renew the seal – 1.8 litre Z18XE petrol engines

washer. Be prepared for oil spillage, and if the switch is to be left removed from the engine for any length of time, plug the switch aperture.

Refitting

14 Examine the sealing washer for signs of damage or deterioration and if necessary renew.
15 Refit the switch and washer, tightening it to the specified torque, and reconnect the wiring connector.
16 On 2.2 litre petrol engines, refit the starter motor as described in Section 11.
17 On diesel engine models, refit the engine undertray.
18 Lower the vehicle to the ground then check and, if necessary, top-up the engine oil as described in *Weekly checks*.

15 Oil level sensor – removal and refitting

Removal

1.8 litre Z18XE petrol engines

1 The oil level sensor is located on the front face of the engine sump.
2 Firmly apply the handbrake, then jack up the front of the car and support it securely on axle stands (see *Jacking and vehicle support*).
3 Drain the engine oil into a clean container then refit the drain plug and tighten it to the specified torque (see Chapter 1A).
4 Disconnect the wiring connector from the sensor.
5 Unscrew the retaining bolts then ease the sensor out from the sump and remove it along with its sealing ring/washer. Discard the sealing ring/washer, a new one should be used on refitting **(see illustration)**.

All other engines

6 The oil level sensor is located inside the sump which must first be removed (see the appropriate Part of Chapter 2).
7 With the sump removed, slide off the retaining clip and free the sensor wiring connector from the sump **(see illustration)**.
8 Where fitted, undo the retaining bolts and

15.7 Slide off the retaining clip (arrowed) and free the oil level sensor wiring connector from the sump

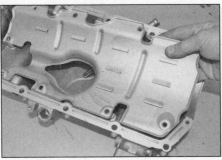

15.8 Where fitted, undo the retaining bolts and remove the oil baffle plate

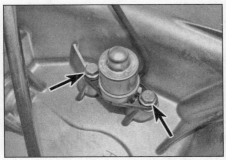

15.9 Undo the two bolts (arrowed) and remove the oil level sensor from the sump

remove the oil baffle plate from inside the sump (see illustration).

9 Note the correct routing of the wiring then undo the retaining bolts and remove the sensor assembly from the sump (see illustration). Check the wiring connector seal for signs or damage and renew if necessary.

Refitting

1.8 litre Z18XE petrol engines

10 Refitting is the reverse of removal ensuring the wiring is correctly routed and securely reconnected. On completion refill the engine with oil (see Chapter 1A).

All other engines

11 Prior to refitting remove all traces of locking compound from the sensor retaining bolt and sump threads. Apply a drop of fresh locking compound to the bolt threads and lubricate the wiring connector seal with a smear of engine oil.

12 Fit the sensor, making sure the wiring is correctly routed, and securely tighten its retaining bolts. Ease the wiring connector through the sump, taking care not to damage its seal, and secure it in position with the retaining clip.

13 Ensure the sensor is correctly refitted then, where applicable, refit the oil baffle plate.

14 Refit the sump as described in the appropriate Part of Chapter 2.

16 Pre/post-heating system (diesel engine models) – description and testing

Description

1 Each cylinder of the engine is fitted with a heater plug (commonly called a glow plug) screwed into it. The plugs are electrically-operated before and during start-up when the engine is cold. Electrical feed to the glow plugs is controlled via the pre/post-heating system control unit.

2 A warning light in the instrument panel tells the driver that pre/post-heating is taking place. When the light goes out, the engine is ready to be started. The voltage supply to the glow plugs continues for several seconds after the light goes out. If no attempt is made to start,

the timer then cuts off the supply, in order to avoid draining the battery and overheating the glow plugs.

3 The glow plugs also provide a 'post-heating' function, whereby the glow plugs remain switched on after the engine has started. The length of time 'post-heating' takes place is also determined by the control unit, and is dependent on engine temperature.

4 The fuel filter is fitted with a heating element to prevent the fuel 'waxing' in extreme cold temperature conditions and to improve combustion. The heating element is an integral part of the fuel filter housing and is controlled by the pre/post-heating system control unit.

Testing

5 If the system malfunctions, testing is ultimately by substitution of known good units, but some preliminary checks may be made as follows.

6 Connect a voltmeter or 12 volt test lamp between the glow plug supply cable and earth (engine or vehicle metal). Make sure that the live connection is kept clear of the engine and bodywork.

7 Have an assistant switch on the ignition, and check that voltage is applied to the glow plugs. Note the time for which the warning light is lit, and the total time for which voltage is applied before the system cuts out. Switch off the ignition.

8 At an underbonnet temperature of 20°C, typical times noted should be approximately 3 seconds for warning light operation. Warning light time will increase with lower temperatures and decrease with higher temperatures.

9 If there is no supply at all, the control unit or associated wiring is at fault.

10 To locate a defective glow plug, disconnect the wiring connector from each plug.

11 Use a continuity tester, or a 12 volt test lamp connected to the battery positive terminal, to check for continuity between each glow plug terminal and earth. The resistance of a glow plug in good condition is very low (less than 1 ohm), so if the test lamp does not light or the continuity tester shows a high resistance, the glow plug is certainly defective.

12 If an ammeter is available, the current draw of each glow plug can be checked. After an initial surge of 15 to 20 amps, each

plug should draw 12 amps. Any plug which draws much more or less than this is probably defective.

13 As a final check, the glow plugs can be removed and inspected as described in the following Section.

17 Glow plugs (diesel engine models) – removal, inspection and refitting

Caution: If the pre/post-heating system has just been energised, or if the engine has been running, the glow plugs will be very hot.

Removal

1 The glow plugs are located at the rear of the cylinder head above the inlet manifold.

2 On Z19DT engines, remove the oil filler cap and unscrew the two bolts securing the plastic cover over the top of the engine. Release the engine breather hose, then lift off the cover and refit the oil filler cap (see illustrations 11.16a to 11.16d). On Z19DTH engines, remove the plastic cover by pulling it upwards off the mounting studs.

3 On Z19DT engines, undo the two retaining bolts, disconnect the four vacuum hoses and remove the vacuum pipe assembly from the top of the camshaft cover.

4 Disconnect the wiring from the glow plugs by squeezing the connectors with thumb and forefinger, and pulling them from the plugs.

5 Unscrew the glow plugs and remove them from the cylinder head (see illustration).

17.5 Unscrew the glow plugs and remove them from the cylinder head – Z19DTH diesel engines

Inspection

6 Inspect each glow plug for physical damage. Burnt or eroded glow plug tips can be caused by a bad injector spray pattern. Have the injectors checked if this type of damage is found.

7 If the glow plugs are in good physical condition, check them electrically using a 12 volt test lamp or continuity tester as described in the previous Section.

8 The glow plugs can be energised by applying 12 volts to them to verify that they heat up evenly and in the required time. Observe the following precautions.

a) *Support the glow plug by clamping it carefully in a vice or self-locking pliers. Remember it will become red-hot.*

b) *Make sure that the power supply or test lead incorporates a fuse or overload trip to protect against damage from a short-circuit.*

c) *After testing, allow the glow plug to cool for several minutes before attempting to handle it.*

9 A glow plug in good condition will start to glow red at the tip after drawing current for 5 seconds or so. Any plug which takes much longer to start glowing, or which starts glowing in the middle instead of at the tip, is defective.

Refitting

10 Carefully refit the plugs and tighten to the specified torque. Do not overtighten, as this can damage the glow plug element. Push the electrical connectors firmly onto the glow plugs.

11 The remainder of refitting is a reversal of removal, checking the operation of the glow plugs on completion.

18 Pre/post-heating system control unit (diesel engine models) – removal and refitting

Removal

1 The pre/post-heating system control unit is located on the left-hand side of the engine compartment where it is mounted onto the side of the battery box.

18.3 Unclip the control unit and slide it up and off the battery box

2 Disconnect the battery negative terminal (refer to *Disconnecting the battery* in the Reference Chapter).

3 Unclip the control unit and slide it up and off the battery box **(see illustration)**.

4 Disconnect the wiring connector from the base of the control unit and remove the unit from the engine compartment.

Refitting

5 Refitting is a reversal of removal.

Chapter 5 Part B:
Ignition system – petrol engines

Contents

Degrees of difficulty

Easy, suitable for novice with little experience	**Fairly easy,** suitable for beginner with some experience	**Fairly difficult,** suitable for competent DIY mechanic	**Difficult,** suitable for experienced DIY mechanic	**Very difficult,** suitable for expert DIY or professional

Specifications

General
System type . . . . Distributorless ignition system
System application:
  1.8 litre engines:
    Z18XE . . . . Simtec 71.5
    Z18XER . . . . Simtec 75.1
  2.2 litre engines . . . . Simtec 81.1
Location of No 1 cylinder . . . . Timing chain/timing belt end of engine
Firing order 1-3-4-2

Torque wrench setting
	Nm	lbf ft
Ignition module retaining bolts.	8	6

1 Ignition system – general information

The ignition system is integrated with the fuel injection system to form a combined engine management system under the control of one electronic control unit (ECU) – see Chapter 4A for further information. The ignition side of the system is of the distributorless type, and consists of the ignition module and the knock sensor.

The ignition module consists of four ignition coils, one per cylinder, in one casing mounted directly above the spark plugs. This module eliminates the need for any HT leads as the coils locate directly onto the relevant spark plug. The ECU uses its inputs from the various sensors to calculate the required ignition advance setting and coil charging time.

The knock sensor is mounted onto the cylinder block and informs the ECU when the engine is 'pinking' under load. The sensor is sensitive to vibration and detects the knocking which occurs when the engine starts to 'pink' (pre-ignite). The knock sensor sends an electrical signal to the ECU which in turn retards the ignition advance setting until the 'pinking' ceases.

The ignition systems fitted to the engines covered by this manual all operate in a similar fashion under the overall control of the engine management ECU. The systems comprise various sensors (whose inputs also provide data to control the fuel injection system) and the ECU, in addition to the ignition module and spark plugs. Further details of the system sensors and the ECU are given in Chapter 4A.

The ECU selects the optimum ignition advance setting based on the information received from the various sensors, and fires the relevant ignition coil accordingly. The degree of advance can thus be constantly varied to suit the prevailing engine operating conditions.

Warning: Due to the high voltages produced by the electronic ignition system, extreme care must be taken when working on the system with the ignition switched on. Persons with surgically-implanted cardiac pacemaker devices should keep well clear of the ignition circuits, components and test equipment.

2 Ignition system – testing

1 If a fault appears in the engine management system, first ensure that all the system wiring connectors are securely connected and free of corrosion. Ensure that the fault is not due to poor maintenance; ie, check that the air cleaner filter element is clean, the spark plugs are in good condition and correctly gapped, the cylinder compression pressures are correct and that the engine breather hoses are clear and undamaged, referring to Chapters 1A, 2A and 2B for further information.
2 If these checks fail to reveal the cause of the problem, the vehicle should be taken to a suitably-equipped Vauxhall/Opel dealer or engine management diagnostic specialist for testing. A diagnostic socket is located at the base of the facia, behind the ashtray, to which a fault code reader or other suitable test equipment can be connected **(see illustration)**. By using the code reader or test equipment, the engine management ECU can be interrogated, and any stored fault codes

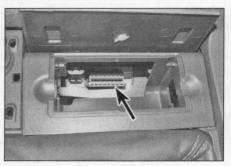

2.2 The vehicle diagnostic socket (arrowed) is located at the base of the facia, behind the ashtray

3.2 On 1.8 litre Z18XER engines, remove the ignition module cover by sliding it towards the transmission and lifting off

3.3 On 2.2 litre engines, remove the engine cover, then unclip and lift off the ignition module cover

can be retrieved. This will allow the fault to be quickly and simply traced, alleviating the need to test all the system components individually, which is a time-consuming operation that carries a risk of damaging the ECU.

3 The only ignition system checks which can be carried out by the home mechanic are those described in Chapter 1A relating to the spark plugs. If necessary, the system wiring and wiring connectors can be checked as described in Chapter 12, ensuring that the ECU wiring connector(s) have first been disconnected.

3 Ignition module – removal and refitting

Removal

1 On 1.8 litre Z18XE engines, remove the oil filler cap and unscrew the two bolts securing the plastic cover over the top of the engine. Lift off the cover and refit the oil filler cap.

2 On 1.8 litre Z18XER engines, unclip the wiring trough from the left-hand end of the cylinder head, then remove the cover from the ignition module by sliding it towards the transmission and lifting off **(see illustration)**.
3 On 2.2 litre engines unclip and lift off the plastic engine cover, then lift off the cover over the ignition module **(see illustration)**.
4 Disconnect the wiring connector at the left-hand end of the ignition module **(see illustration)**.
5 Undo the retaining bolts, and lift the module up and out of position **(see illustration)**. If the module proves reluctant to separate from the spark plugs, insert two long 8 mm bolts into the threaded holes in the top of the module, and pull up on the bolts to free the module from the plugs.
6 With the module removed, check the condition of the sealing grommets and renew if necessary **(see illustration)**.

Refitting

7 Refitting is the reversal of removal, tightening the retaining bolts to the specified torque.

4 Ignition timing – checking and adjustment

Due to the nature of the ignition system, the ignition timing is constantly being monitored and adjusted by the engine management ECU.
The only way in which the ignition timing can be checked is by using specialist diagnostic test equipment, connected to the engine management system diagnostic socket. No adjustment of the ignition timing is possible. Should the ignition timing be incorrect, then a fault is likely to be present in the engine management system.

5 Knock sensor – removal and refitting

Refer to the procedures contained in Chapter 4A.

3.4 Disconnect the ignition module wiring connector

3.5 Undo the retaining bolts and pull the ignition module up and off the spark plugs

3.6 Check the condition of the sealing grommets and renew if necessary

Chapter 6
Clutch

Contents

Degrees of difficulty

Easy, suitable for novice with little experience	**Fairly easy,** suitable for beginner with some experience	**Fairly difficult,** suitable for competent DIY mechanic	**Difficult,** suitable for experienced DIY mechanic	**Very difficult,** suitable for expert DIY or professional

Specifications

Type . . . . Single dry plate with diaphragm spring, hydraulically-operated

Friction disc
Diameter:
  Petrol engine models:
    1.8 litre engines. . . . . 205 mm
    2.2 litre engines. . . . . 228 mm
  Diesel engine models . . . . 239 mm
New lining thickness:
  Petrol engine models:
    1.8 litre engines. . . . . 7.65 mm
    2.2 litre engines. . . . . 8.4 mm
  Diesel engine models . . . . 7.8 mm

Torque wrench settings

	Nm	lbf ft
ABS hydraulic modulator mounting bracket bolts	20	15
Brake master cylinder retaining nuts*	50	37
Clutch master cylinder retaining nuts*	20	15
Pedal mounting bracket nuts*	20	15
Pressure plate retaining bolts:		
M7 bolts	15	11
M8 bolts	28	21
Release cylinder mounting bolts	5	4
Vacuum servo unit stud bolts*	20	15

* Use new nuts/bolts

2.8 Clutch bleed screw (arrowed)

1 General information

The clutch consists of a friction disc, a pressure plate assembly, and the hydraulic release cylinder (which incorporates the release bearing); all of these components are contained in the large cast-aluminium alloy bellhousing, sandwiched between the engine and the transmission.

The friction disc is fitted between the engine flywheel and the clutch pressure plate, and is allowed to slide on the transmission input shaft splines.

The pressure plate assembly is bolted to the engine flywheel. When the engine is running, drive is transmitted from the crankshaft, via the flywheel, to the friction disc (these components being clamped securely together by the pressure plate assembly) and from the friction disc to the transmission input shaft.

To interrupt the drive, the spring pressure must be relaxed. This is achieved using a hydraulic release mechanism which consists of the master cylinder, the release cylinder and the pipe/hose linking the two components. Depressing the pedal pushes on the master cylinder pushrod which hydraulically forces the release cylinder piston against the pressure plate spring fingers. This causes the springs to deform and releases the clamping force on the friction disc.

The clutch is self-adjusting and requires no manual adjustment.

The clutch pedal support and clutch pedal are one assembly and must be renewed as a complete unit. In the event of a frontal collision, the clutch pedal is released from its bearing in the support bracket to prevent injury to the driver's feet and legs (this also applies to the brake pedal). If an airbag has been deployed, inspect the clutch pedal assembly and if necessary renew the complete unit.

Semi-automatic clutch

Models equipped with the Easytronic MTA (Manual Transmission with Automatic shift), are fitted with a semi-automatic clutch. The clutch may be operated either fully-automatically or semi-automatically by means of the gear selector lever. There is no conventional clutch pedal fitted.

The Easytronic system essentially consists of a conventional manual gearbox and clutch fitted with electrical and hydraulic controls, the clutch being operated by a clutch module attached to the side of the transmission casing. Refer to Chapter 7C for more information. The clutch component removal and refitting procedures are included in this Chapter as they are very similar to those for the standard manual transmission.

2 Clutch hydraulic system – bleeding

Note: *On models equipped with the Easytronic transmission, the following manual method of bleeding the clutch is not possible since the hydraulic control unit is integral with the transmission. On these models, bleeding is carried out using the Vauxhall/Opel TECH2 diagnostic instrument, therefore this work should be entrusted to a Vauxhall/Opel dealer.*

⚠️ *Warning: Hydraulic fluid is poisonous; wash off immediately and thoroughly in the case of skin contact, and seek immediate medical advice if any fluid is swallowed or gets into the eyes. Certain types of hydraulic fluid are flammable, and may ignite when allowed into contact with hot components; when servicing any hydraulic system, it is safest to assume that the fluid is flammable, and to take precautions against the risk of fire as though it is petrol that is being handled. Hydraulic fluid is also an effective paint stripper, and will attack plastics; if any is spilt, it should be washed off immediately, using copious quantities of fresh water. Finally, it is hygroscopic (it absorbs moisture from the air) – old fluid may be contaminated and unfit for further use. When topping-up or renewing the fluid, always use the recommended type, and ensure that it comes from a freshly-opened sealed container.*

1 The correct operation of any hydraulic system is only possible after removing all air from the components and circuit; this is achieved by bleeding the system.

2 The manufacturer stipulates that the system must be initially bled by the 'back-bleeding' method using Vauxhall/Opel special bleeding equipment. This entails connecting a pressure bleeding unit containing fresh brake fluid to the release cylinder bleed screw, with a collecting vessel connected to the brake fluid master cylinder reservoir. The pressure bleeding unit is then switched on, the bleed screw is opened and hydraulic fluid is delivered under pressure, backwards, to be expelled from the reservoir into the collecting vessel. Final bleeding is then carried out in the conventional way.

3 In practice, this method would normally only be required if new hydraulic components

have been fitted, or if the system has been completely drained of hydraulic fluid. If the system has only been disconnected to allow component removal and refitting procedures to be carried out, such as removal and refitting of the transmission (for example for clutch renewal) or engine removal and refitting, then it is quite likely that normal bleeding will be sufficient.

4 Our advice would therefore be as follows:
a) *If the hydraulic system has only been partially disconnected, try bleeding by the conventional methods described in paragraphs 10 to 15, or 16 to 19.*
b) *If the hydraulic system has been completely drained and new components have been fitted, try bleeding by using the pressure bleeding method described in paragraphs 20 to 22.*
c) *If the above methods fail to produce a firm pedal on completion, it will be necessary to 'back-bleed' the system using Vauxhall/Opel bleeding equipment, or suitable alternative equipment as described in paragraphs 23 to 28.*

5 During the bleeding procedure, add only clean, unused hydraulic fluid of the recommended type; never re-use fluid that has already been bled from the system. Ensure that sufficient fluid is available before starting work.

6 If there is any possibility of incorrect fluid being already in the system, the hydraulic circuit must be flushed completely with uncontaminated, correct fluid.

7 If hydraulic fluid has been lost from the system, or air has entered because of a leak, ensure that the fault is cured before continuing further.

8 The bleed screw is located in the hose end fitting which is situated on the top of the transmission housing **(see illustration)**. On some models access to the bleed screw is limited and it may be necessary to jack up the front of the vehicle and support it on axle stands so that the screw can be reached from below, or remove the battery and battery box as described in Chapter 5A, so that the screw can be reached from above.

9 Check that all pipes and hoses are secure, unions tight and the bleed screw is closed. Clean any dirt from around the bleed screw.

Bleeding

Basic (two-man) method

10 Collect a clean glass jar, a suitable length of plastic or rubber tubing which is a tight fit over the bleed screw, and a ring spanner to fit the screw. The help of an assistant will also be required.

11 Unscrew the master cylinder fluid reservoir cap (the clutch shares the same fluid reservoir as the braking system), and top the master cylinder reservoir up to the upper (MAX) level line. Ensure that the fluid level is maintained at least above the lower level line in the reservoir throughout the procedure.

12 Remove the dust cap from the bleed screw. Fit the spanner and tube to the screw, place the other end of the tube in the jar, and pour in sufficient fluid to cover the end of the tube.

13 Have the assistant fully depress the clutch pedal several times to build-up pressure, then maintain it on the final down stroke.

14 While pedal pressure is maintained, unscrew the bleed screw (approximately one turn) and allow the compressed fluid and air to flow into the jar. The assistant should maintain pedal pressure and should not release it until instructed to do so. When the flow stops, tighten the bleed screw again, have the assistant release the pedal slowly, and recheck the reservoir fluid level.

15 Repeat the steps given in paragraphs 13 and 14 until the fluid emerging from the bleed screw is free from air bubbles. If the master cylinder has been drained and refilled allow approximately five seconds between cycles for the master cylinder passages to refill.

Using a one-way valve kit

16 As their name implies, these kits consist of a length of tubing with a one-way valve fitted, to prevent expelled air and fluid being drawn back into the system; some kits include a translucent container, which can be positioned so that the air bubbles can be more easily seen flowing from the end of the tube.

17 The kit is connected to the bleed screw, which is then opened.

18 The user returns to the driver's seat, depresses the clutch pedal with a smooth, steady stroke, and slowly releases it; this is repeated until the expelled fluid is clear of air bubbles.

19 Note that these kits simplify work so much that it is easy to forget the clutch fluid reservoir level; ensure that this is maintained at least above the lower level line at all times.

Pressure-bleeding method

20 These kits are usually operated by the reservoir of pressurised air contained in the spare tyre. However, note that it will probably be necessary to reduce the pressure to a lower level than normal; refer to the instructions supplied with the kit.

21 By connecting a pressurised, fluid-filled container to the clutch fluid reservoir, bleeding can be carried out simply by opening the bleed screw and allowing the fluid to flow out until no more air bubbles can be seen in the expelled fluid.

22 This method has the advantage that the large reservoir of fluid provides an additional safeguard against air being drawn into the system during bleeding.

'Back-bleeding' method

23 The following procedure describes the bleeding method using Vauxhall/Opel equipment. Alternative equipment is available and should be used in accordance with the maker's instructions.

24 Connect the pressure hose (MKM-6174-1)

to the bleed screw located in the hose end fitting situated on the top of the transmission housing **(see illustration 2.8)**. Connect the other end of the hose to a suitable pressure bleeding device set to operate at approximately 2.0 bar.

25 Attach the cap (MKM-6174-2) to the master cylinder reservoir, and place the hose in a collecting vessel.

26 Switch on the pressure bleeding equipment, open the bleed screw, and allow fresh hydraulic fluid to flow from the pressure bleeding unit, through the system and out through the top of the reservoir and into the collecting vessel. When fluid, free from air bubbles appears in the reservoir, close the bleed screw and switch off the bleeding equipment.

27 Disconnect the bleeding equipment from the bleed screw and reservoir.

28 Carry out a final conventional bleeding procedure as described in paragraphs 10 to 15, or 16 to 19.

All methods

29 When bleeding is complete, no more bubbles appear and correct pedal feel is restored, tighten the bleed screw securely (do not overtighten). Remove the tube and spanner, and wash off any spilt fluid. Refit the dust cap to the bleed screw.

30 Check the hydraulic fluid level in the master cylinder reservoir, and top-up if necessary (see *Weekly checks*).

31 Discard any hydraulic fluid that has been bled from the system; it will not be fit for re-use.

32 Check the operation of the clutch pedal. If the clutch is still not operating correctly, air must still be present in the system, and further bleeding is required. Failure to bleed satisfactorily after a reasonable repetition of the bleeding procedure may be due to worn master cylinder/release cylinder seals.

3 Master cylinder – removal and refitting

Note 1: *New master cylinder retaining nuts will be required for refitting.*
Note 2: *This procedure does not apply to models fitted with the Easytronic transmission.*

Removal

Right-hand drive models

1 Where fitted, remove the plastic cover over the top of the engine.

2 Release the clutch hydraulic pipe from the support clip(s) on the bulkhead.

3 Unscrew the brake/clutch hydraulic fluid reservoir filler cap, and top-up the reservoir to the MAX mark (see *Weekly checks*). Place a piece of polythene over the filler neck, and secure the polythene with the filler cap. This will minimise brake fluid loss during subsequent operations.

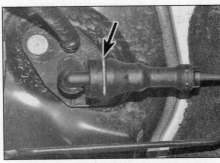

3.5 Extract the retaining clip (arrowed) and disconnect the hydraulic pipe from the master cylinder connector

4 Remove all traces of dirt from the outside of the master cylinder and the brake/clutch hydraulic fluid reservoir, then position some cloth beneath the cylinder to catch any spilt fluid.

5 Extract the retaining clip and disconnect the hydraulic pipe from the connector on the end of the master cylinder **(see illustration)**. Plug the pipe end and master cylinder port to minimise fluid loss and prevent the entry of dirt.

6 Release the retaining clip (where fitted) and disconnect the fluid supply hose from the brake/clutch hydraulic fluid reservoir **(see illustration)**.

7 From inside the car, remove the lower facia panel on the driver's side as described in Chapter 11.

8 Where fitted, remove the clutch switch from the pedal mounting bracket.

9 Separate the clutch pedal from the master cylinder piston rod by releasing the retaining clip at the pedal. Vauxhall technicians use a special tool to do this, however, the clip may be released by pressing the retaining tabs together using screwdrivers, while at the same time pulling the clutch pedal rearwards. **Note:** *Do not remove the clip from the master cylinder piston rod, just release it from the pedal.*

10 On diesel engine models, move the bulkhead insulation to one side for access to the master cylinder retaining nuts. Use a plastic wedge or similar tool to retain the insulation clear of the nuts.

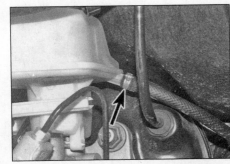

3.6 Release the retaining clip (arrowed) and disconnect the fluid supply hose from the reservoir

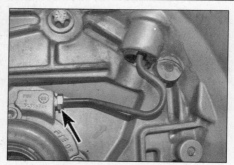

4.2 Clutch release cylinder hydraulic pipe union nut (arrowed)

11 Unscrew the two nuts securing the master cylinder to the bulkhead, then return to the engine compartment and remove the master cylinder from the vehicle. If the master cylinder is faulty it must be renewed; overhaul of the unit is not possible.

Left-hand drive models

12 Remove the battery and battery box as described in Chapter 5A.
13 Pull up the locking bar and disconnect the ABS wiring harness multiplug connector from the electronic control unit located on the hydraulic modulator.
14 Undo the two bolts securing the ABS hydraulic modulator mounting bracket to the bulkhead. Taking great care not to strain the hydraulic brake pipes, carefully lift the modulator and mounting bracket upward to disengage the mounting bracket lower guide. Move the assembly to one side as far as the brake pipes will allow and support it in this position.
15 Release the clutch hydraulic pipe from the two support clips beneath the battery box location.
16 Continue with the removal procedure as described in paragraphs 3 to 11.

Refitting

Right-hand drive models

17 Manoeuvre the master cylinder into position whilst ensuring that the piston rod and its retaining clip align correctly with the pedal. Fit two new master cylinder retaining nuts and tighten them to the specified torque.

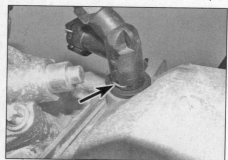

4.5 Extract the retaining clip (arrowed) and remove the hydraulic hose end fitting from the fastening sleeve

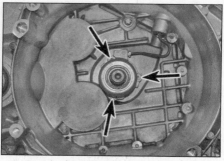

4.3 Clutch release cylinder retaining bolts (arrowed)

18 On diesel engine models, locate the bulkhead insulation back into position.
19 Push the master cylinder piston rod retaining clip into the clutch pedal, ensuring that the two lugs on the clip fully engage.
20 Where applicable, refit the clutch switch to the pedal mounting bracket.
21 Refit the lower facia panel on the driver's side as described in Chapter 11.
22 Connect the fluid supply hose to the brake/clutch hydraulic fluid reservoir and, where applicable, secure with the retaining clip.
23 Press the hydraulic pipe back into the connector on the end of the master cylinder and refit the retaining clip. Ensure that the retaining clip engages fully and the pipe is securely retained. Secure the pipe with the support clip(s).
24 Bleed the clutch hydraulic system as described in Section 2, then refit the engine cover (where applicable).

Left-hand drive models

25 Carry out the operations described in paragraphs 17 to 24.
26 Carefully locate the ABS hydraulic modulator and mounting bracket back into position and secure with the two bolts, tightened to the specified torque.
27 Connect the ABS wiring harness multiplug connector to the electronic control unit and secure with the locking bar.
28 Refit the battery box and battery described in Chapter 5A.

---

4   Release cylinder – removal and refitting

Note 1: *Due to the amount of work necessary to remove and refit clutch components, it is usually considered good practice to renew the clutch friction disc, pressure plate assembly and release cylinder as a matched set, even if only one of these is actually worn enough to require renewal. It is also worth considering the renewal of the clutch components on a preventative basis if the engine and/or transmission have been removed for some other reason.*
Note 2: *Refer to the warning concerning the*

dangers of asbestos dust at the beginning of Section 6.
Note 3: *On models equipped with the Easytronic transmission, Vauxhall/Opel TECH2 diagnostic equipment will be required to bleed the clutch hydraulic system and carry out a clutch Contact Point Determination program. If this equipment is not available, the following procedure should be entrusted to a Vauxhall/ Opel dealer.*

Removal

1 Unless the complete engine/transmission unit is to be removed from the car and separated for major overhaul (see the relevant Part of Chapter 2), the clutch release cylinder can be reached by removing the transmission only, as described in Chapter 7A or 7C.
2 Wipe clean the outside of the release cylinder then slacken the union nut and disconnect the hydraulic pipe **(see illustration)**. Wipe up any spilt fluid with a clean cloth.
3 Unscrew the three retaining bolts and slide the release cylinder off from the transmission input shaft **(see illustration)**. Remove the sealing ring which is fitted between the cylinder and transmission housing and discard it; a new one must be used on refitting. Whilst the cylinder is removed, take care not to allow any debris to enter the transmission unit.
4 The release cylinder is a sealed unit and cannot be overhauled. If the cylinder seals are leaking or the release bearing is noisy or rough in operation, then the complete unit must be renewed.
5 To remove the hydraulic pipe, extract the retaining clip and remove the hydraulic hose end fitting from the fastening sleeve on top of the transmission housing **(see illustration)**. Gently squeeze the legs of the retaining clip together and re-insert the clip back into position in the end fitting.
6 Using a small screwdriver, carefully spread the retaining lugs of the fastening sleeve to release the hydraulic pipe connection, and remove the pipe from inside the transmission housing. Check the condition of the sealing ring on the hydraulic pipe and renew if necessary.
7 If required, the fastening sleeve can be removed by squeezing the lower retaining lugs together with pointed-nose pliers, then withdrawing the sleeve upwards and out of the transmission. Note that if the fastening sleeve is removed, a new one must be obtained for refitting.

Refitting

8 Ensure the release cylinder and transmission mating surfaces are clean and dry and fit the new sealing ring to the transmission recess.
9 Lubricate the release cylinder seal with a smear of transmission oil then carefully ease the cylinder along the input shaft and into position. **Note:** *Vauxhall/Opel technicians use a special tapered sleeve on the input shaft to prevent damage to the seal. If necessary, wrap suitable tape around the end of the*

shaft. Ensure the sealing ring is still correctly seated in its groove then refit the release cylinder retaining bolts and tighten them to the specified torque.

10 If removed, fit the new fastening sleeve, engaging the lug on the sleeve with the cut-out in the housing **(see illustration)**. Ensure that the sleeve can be felt to positively lock in position.

11 Insert the hydraulic pipe into the fastening sleeve until the end fitting can be felt to positively lock in position.

12 Reconnect the hydraulic pipe to the release cylinder, tightening its union nut securely.

13 Refit the hydraulic hose end fitting to the fastening sleeve ensuring that it is positively retained by its clip.

14 Refit the transmission unit as described in Chapter 7A or 7C.

15 Bleed the clutch hydraulic system as described in Section 2.

16 On models equipped with a conventional transmission, bleed the clutch hydraulic system as described in Section 2.

17 On models equipped with the Easytronic transmission, bleed the clutch hydraulic system and carry out a clutch Contact Point Determination program using Vauxhall/Opel TECH2 diagnostic equipment.

---

5 Clutch pedal – removal and refitting

Note 1: *The clutch pedal mounting bracket, the clutch pedal and the brake pedal are one assembly and must be renewed as a complete unit. In the event of a frontal collision, the clutch pedal is released from its bearing in the mounting bracket to prevent injury to the driver's feet and legs (this also applies to the brake pedal). If an airbag has been deployed, inspect the pedal and mounting bracket assembly and if necessary renew the complete unit.*

Note 2: *New pedal mounting bracket retaining nuts, vacuum servo unit stud bolts and brake master cylinder retaining nuts will be required for refitting.*

Removal

1 Disconnect the battery negative terminal (refer to *Disconnecting the battery* in the Reference Chapter).

2 Remove the steering column as described in Chapter 10.

3 Remove the complete facia assembly and the facia crossmember as described in Chapter 11.

4 Remove the stop-light switch from the pedal mounting bracket as described in Chapter 9.

5 Refer to Chapter 4A or 4B as applicable and remove the air cleaner assembly, the accelerator pedal/position sensor and, where fitted, the clutch switch from the pedal mounting bracket.

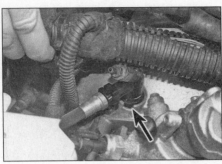

4.10 Make sure the lug (arrowed) on the fastening sleeve is located correctly in the transmission housing

6 Working in the engine compartment, unscrew the two nuts securing the brake master cylinder to the vacuum servo unit. Now unscrew the two stud bolts securing the vacuum servo unit to the bulkhead **(see illustration)**.

7 Separate the clutch pedal from the clutch master cylinder piston rod by releasing the retaining clip at the pedal. Vauxhall/Opel technicians use a special tool to do this, however, the clip may be released by pressing the retaining tabs together using screwdrivers, while at the same time pulling the clutch pedal rearwards. **Note:** *Do not remove the clip from the master cylinder piston rod, just release it from the pedal.*

8 Unhook the return spring from behind the brake pedal to release all tension in the spring.

9 Carefully prise open and remove the retaining clip, and withdraw the clevis pin securing the brake pedal to the vacuum servo unit pushrod.

10 From inside the car, slacken and remove the three nuts securing the pedal mounting bracket to the bulkhead. Note that two of the three nuts also secure the clutch master cylinder. On diesel engine models, move the bulkhead insulation to one side for access to the nuts, and use a plastic wedge or similar tool to retain the insulation clear.

11 Withdraw the mounting bracket and pedal assembly from the bulkhead, while at the same time guiding the clutch master cylinder piston rod and retaining clip out of the clutch pedal.

5.6 Vacuum servo unit retaining stud bolts (arrowed)

Refitting

12 Manoeuvre the mounting bracket and pedal assembly into position, whilst ensuring that the clutch master cylinder piston rod and its retaining clip align correctly with the clutch pedal. Also ensure that the vacuum servo unit pushrod locates around the brake pedal. Fit three new pedal mounting bracket retaining nuts and tighten them to the specified torque.

13 On diesel engine models, locate the bulkhead insulation back into position.

14 Push the clutch master cylinder piston rod retaining clip into the clutch pedal, ensuring that the two lugs on the clip fully engage.

15 Apply a smear of multipurpose grease to the clevis pin then align the vacuum servo unit pushrod with the brake pedal hole and insert the pin. Secure the pin in position with the retaining clip, making sure it is correctly located in the groove.

16 Hook the return spring into position behind the brake pedal.

17 Working in the engine compartment, fit the two new stud bolts securing the vacuum servo unit to the bulkhead and tighten the bolts to the specified torque. Fit the two new brake master cylinder retaining nuts and tighten the nuts to the specified torque.

18 Refer to Chapter 4A or 4B as applicable and refit the air cleaner assembly and the accelerator pedal/position sensor. Where fitted, refit the clutch switch to the pedal mounting bracket.

19 Refit the stop-light switch to the pedal mounting bracket as described in Chapter 9.

20 Refit the facia crossmember and facia assembly as described in Chapter 11.

21 Refit the steering column as described in Chapter 10.

22 Reconnect the battery negative terminal on completion.

---

6 Clutch assembly – removal, inspection and refitting

 Warning: Dust created by clutch wear and deposited on the clutch components may contain asbestos, which is a health hazard. DO NOT blow it out with compressed air, or inhale any of it. DO NOT use petrol or petroleum-based solvents to clean off the dust. Brake system cleaner or methylated spirit should be used to flush the dust into a suitable receptacle. After the clutch components are wiped clean with rags, dispose of the contaminated rags and cleaner in a sealed, marked container.

Note 1: *To prevent possible damage to the ends of the pressure plate diaphragm spring fingers, Vauxhall/Opel recommend the use of a special jig (KM-6263) to remove the clutch assembly, however, with care it is possible to carry out the work without the jig.*

Note 2: *On models equipped with the Easytronic transmission, Vauxhall/Opel TECH2*

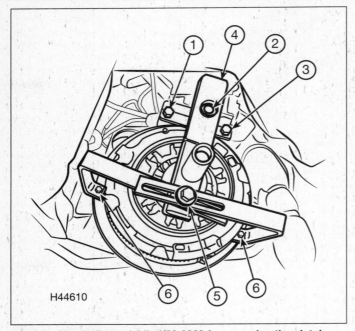

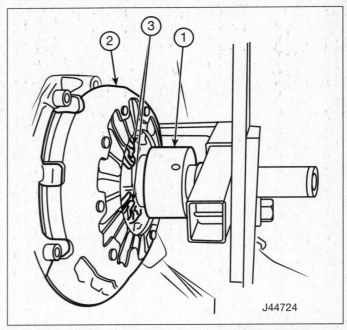

6.3a Vauxhall special jig KM-6263 for removing the clutch pressure plate and friction disc

6.3b Thrust piece (1) in contact with the diaphragm spring fingers (3) of the pressure plate (2)

1, 3 and 6 Bolts securing the jig to the engine
2 and 5   Bolts for adjusting the jig to the centre of the crankshaft

diagnostic equipment will be required to carry out a clutch Contact Point Determination program after the transmission has been refitted. If this equipment is not available, the following procedure should be entrusted to a Vauxhall/Opel dealer.

Removal

1 Unless the complete engine/transmission unit is to be removed from the car and separated for major overhaul (see Chapter 2E), the clutch can be reached by removing the transmission as described in Chapter 7A or 7C.
2 Before disturbing the clutch, use chalk or a marker pen to mark the relationship of the pressure plate assembly to the flywheel.
3 At this stage, Vauxhall technicians fit the special jig KM-6263 to the rear of the engine and compress the diaphragm spring fingers until the friction disc is released **(see illustrations)**. The pressure plate mounting bolts are then unscrewed, and the jig spindle backed off.
4 If the jig is not available, progressively unscrew the pressure plate retaining bolts in diagonal sequence by half a turn at a time, until spring pressure is released and the bolts can be unscrewed by hand.
5 Remove the pressure plate assembly and collect the friction disc, noting which way round the disc is fitted. It is recommended that new pressure plate retaining bolts are obtained.

Inspection

Note: *Due to the amount of work necessary to remove and refit clutch components, it is*

usually considered good practice to renew the clutch friction disc, pressure plate assembly and release bearing as a matched set, even if only one of these is actually worn enough to require renewal. It is also worth considering the renewal of the clutch components on a preventative basis if the engine and/or transmission have been removed for some other reason.
6 When cleaning clutch components, read first the warning at the beginning of this Section; remove dust using a clean, dry cloth, and working in a well-ventilated atmosphere.
7 Check the friction disc facings for signs of wear, damage or oil contamination. If the friction material is cracked, burnt, scored or damaged, or if it is contaminated with oil or grease (shown by shiny black patches), the friction disc must be renewed.
8 If the friction material is still serviceable, check that the centre boss splines are unworn, that the torsion springs are in good condition and securely fastened, and that all the rivets are tight. If any wear or damage is found, the friction disc must be renewed.
9 If the friction material is fouled with oil, this must be due to an oil leak from the crankshaft oil seal, from the sump-to-cylinder block joint, or from the release cylinder assembly (either the main seal or the sealing ring). Renew the crankshaft oil seal or repair the sump joint as described in the appropriate Part of Chapter 2, before installing the new friction disc. The clutch release cylinder is covered in Section 4.
10 Check the pressure plate assembly for obvious signs of wear or damage; shake it to check for loose rivets, or worn or damaged

fulcrum rings, and check that the drive straps securing the pressure plate to the cover do not show signs of overheating (such as a deep yellow or blue discoloration). If the diaphragm spring is worn or damaged, or if its pressure is in any way suspect, the pressure plate assembly should be renewed.
11 Examine the machined bearing surfaces of the pressure plate and of the flywheel; they should be clean, completely flat, and free from scratches or scoring. If either is discoloured from excessive heat, or shows signs of cracks, it should be renewed – although minor damage of this nature can sometimes be polished away using emery paper.
12 Check that the release cylinder bearing rotates smoothly and easily, with no sign of noise or roughness. Also check that the surface itself is smooth and unworn, with no signs of cracks, pitting or scoring. If there is any doubt about its condition, the clutch release cylinder should be renewed (it is not possible to renew the bearing separately).

Refitting

13 On diesel engine models and certain petrol engine models, the clutch pressure plate is unusual, as there is a pre-adjustment mechanism to compensate for wear in the friction disc (this is termed by Vauxhall/Opel as a self-adjusting clutch (SAC), which is slightly ambiguous as all clutches fitted to these models are essentially self-adjusting). However, this mechanism must be reset before refitting the pressure plate. A new plate may be supplied preset, in which case this procedure can be ignored.

6.15 Mount a large bolt and washer into a vice, then fit the pressure plate over it

6.16 Fit large washers and a nut to the bolt and hand-tighten

6.17a Tighten the nut until the spring adjuster is free to turn . . .

14 A large diameter bolt (M14 at least) long enough to pass through the pressure plate, a matching nut, and several large diameter washers, will be needed for this procedure. Mount the bolt head in the jaws of a sturdy bench vice, with one large washer fitted.

15 Offer the plate over the bolt, friction disc surface facing down, and locate it centrally over the bolt and washer – the washer should bear on the centre hub **(see illustration)**.

16 Fit several further large washers over the bolt, so that they bear on the ends of the spring fingers, then add the nut and tighten by hand to locate the washers **(see illustration)**.

17 The purpose of the procedure is to turn the plate's internal adjuster disc so that the three small coil springs visible on the plate's outer surface are fully compressed. Tighten the nut just fitted until the adjuster disc is free to turn. Using a pair of thin-nosed, or circlip pliers, in one of the three windows in the top surface, open the jaws of the pliers to turn the adjuster disc anti-clockwise, so that the springs are fully compressed **(see illustrations)**.

18 Hold the pliers in this position, then unscrew the centre nut. Once the nut is released, the adjuster disc will be gripped in position, and the pliers can be removed. Take the pressure plate from the vice, and it is ready to fit.

19 On reassembly, ensure that the friction surfaces of the flywheel and pressure plate are completely clean, smooth, and free from oil or grease. Use solvent to remove any protective grease from new components.

20 Lightly grease the teeth of the friction disc hub with high melting-point grease. Do not apply too much, otherwise it may eventually contaminate the friction disc linings.

Using the Vauxhall jig

21 Fit the special Vauxhall guide bush to the centre of the crankshaft, and locate the friction disc on it, making sure that the lettering 'transmission side' or 'Getriebeseite' points towards the transmission **(see illustration)**.

22 Locate the pressure plate on the special centring pins on the flywheel, then compress the diaphragm spring fingers with the jig, until the friction disc is in full contact with the flywheel.

23 Insert new pressure plate retaining

6.17b . . . then open up the jaws of suitable pliers to compress the springs

bolts, and progressively tighten them to the specified torque. If necessary, hold the flywheel stationary while tightening the bolts, using a screwdriver engaged with the teeth of the starter ring gear.

24 Back off the jig spindle so that the diaphragm spring forces the pressure plate against the friction disc and flywheel, then remove the jig and guide bush from the engine.

25 Refit the transmission as described in Chapter 7A or 7C.

Without using the Vauxhall jig

26 Locate the friction disc on the flywheel, making sure that the lettering 'transmission side' or 'Getriebeseite' points towards the transmission **(see illustration 6.21)**.

27 Refit the pressure plate assembly, aligning the marks made on dismantling (if the original pressure plate is re-used). Fit new pressure

6.27 Fit the pressure plate assembly over the friction disc

6.21 The lettering 'transmission side' or 'Getriebeseite' on the friction disc must point towards the transmission

plate bolts, but tighten them only finger-tight so that the friction disc can still be moved **(see illustration)**.

28 The friction disc must now be centralised so that, when the transmission is refitted, its input shaft will pass through the splines at the centre of the friction disc.

29 Centralisation can be achieved by passing a screwdriver or other long bar through the friction disc and into the hole in the crankshaft. The friction disc can then be moved around until it is centred on the crankshaft hole. Alternatively, a clutch-aligning tool can be used to eliminate the guesswork; these can be obtained from most accessory shops **(see illustration)**.

30 When the friction disc is centralised, tighten the pressure plate bolts evenly and in a diagonal sequence to the specified torque setting.

31 Refit the transmission as described in Chapter 7A or 7C.

6.29 Centralise the friction disc using a clutch aligning tool or similar

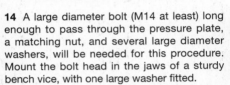

Chapter 7 Part A:
Manual transmission

Contents

Degrees of difficulty

Easy, suitable for novice with little experience	Fairly easy, suitable for beginner with some experience	Fairly difficult, suitable for competent DIY mechanic	Difficult, suitable for experienced DIY mechanic	Very difficult, suitable for expert DIY or professional

Specifications

General

Type:
1.8 litre petrol engine models.............................. Five forward speeds and reverse. Synchromesh on all forward speeds
2.2 litre petrol engine models.............................. Five or six forward speeds and reverse. Synchromesh on all forward speeds

Diesel engine models.................................... Six forward speeds and reverse. Synchromesh on all forward speeds
Manufacturer's designation:*
1.8 litre petrol engine models.............................. F17+ WR or CR
2.2 litre petrol engine models.............................. F23 SR or M32 WR
1.9 litre diesel engine models............................. F40 WR or M32 WR
* WR = Wide Ratio (wide ratio gear set)
  SR = Standard Ratio (standard ratio gear set)
  CR = Close Ratio (close ratio gear set)

Final drive ratios

F17+ transmissions 3.94:1
F23 transmissions 3.95:1
F40 transmissions 3.55:1
M32 transmissions:
Petrol engine models 3.65:1
Diesel engine models 3.35:1

Lubrication

Lubricant type	See *Lubricants and fluids*
Lubricant capacity	See Chapter 1A or 1B

Gear ratios

F17+ WR transmissions:
1st...	3.73:1
2nd..	1.96:1
3rd...	1.32:1
4th...	0.95:1
5th...	0.76:1
Reverse.......................................	3.31:1

F17+ CR transmissions:
1st...	3.73:1
2nd..	2.14:1
3rd...	1.14:1
4th...	1.12:1
5th...	0.89:1
Reverse.......................................	3.31:1

F23 SR transmissions:
1st...	3.58:1
2nd..	2.02:1
3rd...	1.35:1
4th...	0.98:1
5th...	0.81:1
Reverse.......................................	3.31:1

F40 WR transmissions:
1st...	3.92:1
2nd..	2.04:1
3rd...	1.32:1
4th...	0.95:1
5th...	0.76:1
6th...	0.62:1
Reverse.......................................	3.75:1

M32 WR transmissions:	**Petrol engine**	**Diesel engine**
1st...	3.82:1	3.82:1
2nd..	2.16:1	2.05:1
3rd...	1.47:1	1.30:1
4th...	1.07:1	0.96:1
5th...	0.88:1	0.74:1
6th...	0.74:1	0.61:1
Reverse.......................................	3.54:1	3.54:1

Torque wrench settings

	Nm	lbf ft
Differential lower cover plate bolts (F17+ transmissions)............	18	13
Engine/transmission mountings................................	See the relevant Part of Chapter 2	
Engine-to-transmission bolts	See the relevant Part of Chapter 2	
Gearchange lever assembly mounting bolts	10	7
Oil drain plug:		
F23 transmissions	35	26
F40 transmissions	50	37
M32 transmissions	20	15
Oil filler plug:		
F23 transmissions	35	26
F40 transmissions	50	37
M32 transmissions	30	22
Oil level plug:		
F17+ transmissions:		
Stage 1	4	3
Stage 2	Angle-tighten a further 45°	
Stage 3	Angle-tighten a further 135°	
F23 transmissions	35	26
Oil seal carrier to differential (M32 transmissions):		
Stage 1	20	15
Stage 2	Angle-tighten a further 45°	
Reversing light switch	20	15
Roadwheel bolts..	110	81

1 General information

The transmission is contained in a cast-aluminium alloy casing bolted to the engine's left-hand end, and consists of the gearbox and final drive differential – often called a transaxle.

Drive is transmitted from the crankshaft via the clutch to the input shaft, which has a splined extension to accept the clutch friction disc, and rotates in sealed ball-bearings. From the input shaft, drive is transmitted to the output shaft, which rotates in a roller bearing at its right-hand end, and a sealed ball-bearing at its left-hand end. From the output shaft, the drive is transmitted to the differential crownwheel, which rotates with the differential case and planetary gears, thus driving the sun gears and driveshafts. The rotation of the planetary gears on their shaft allows the inner roadwheel to rotate at a slower speed than the outer roadwheel when the car is cornering.

The input and output shafts are arranged side-by-side, parallel to the crankshaft and driveshafts, so that their gear pinion teeth are in constant mesh. In the neutral position, the output shaft gear pinions rotate freely, so that drive cannot be transmitted to the crownwheel.

Gear selection is via a floor-mounted lever and cable-operated selector linkage mechanism. The selector linkage causes the appropriate selector fork to move its respective synchro-sleeve along the shaft, to lock the gear pinion to the synchro-hub. Since the synchro-hubs are splined to the output shaft, this locks the pinion to the shaft, so that drive can be transmitted. To ensure that gearchanging can be made quickly and quietly, a synchromesh system is fitted to all forward gears, consisting of baulk rings and spring-loaded fingers, as well as the gear pinions and synchro-hubs. The synchromesh cones are formed on the mating faces of the baulk rings and gear pinions.

2 Transmission oil – level check, draining and refilling

1 The oil level must be checked before the car is driven, or at least 5 minutes after the engine has been switched off. If the oil is checked immediately after driving the car, some of the oil will remain distributed around the transmission components, resulting in an inaccurate level reading.
2 Draining the oil is much more efficient if the car is first taken on a journey of sufficient length to warm the engine/transmission up to normal operating temperature.
Caution: If the procedure is to be carried out on a hot transmission unit, take care not to burn yourself on the hot exhaust or the transmission/engine unit.

2.4 Transmission oil level plug (arrowed) – F17+ transmissions

3 Position the vehicle over an inspection pit, on vehicle ramps, or jack it up and support it securely on axle stands (see *Jacking and vehicle support*), but make sure that it is level. To drain the oil on diesel engine models, undo the retaining bolts and screws and remove the undertray from beneath the engine.

F17+ transmissions

Level check

4 Wipe clean the area around the level plug. The level plug is located behind the driveshaft inner joint on the left-hand side of the transmission **(see illustration)**. Unscrew the plug and clean it.
5 The oil level should reach the lower edge of the level plug aperture.
6 The transmission is topped-up via the reversing light switch aperture **(see illustration)**. Wipe clean the area around the reversing light switch, and remove the switch as described in Section 6. Refill the transmission with the specified grade of oil given in *Lubricants and fluids* until it reaches the bottom of the level plug aperture. Allow any excess oil to drain, then refit and tighten the level plug to the specified torque.
7 Refit the reversing light switch with reference to Section 6.

Draining

Note: *A new differential lower cover plate gasket will be required for this operation.*
8 Since the transmission oil is not renewed as part of the manufacturer's maintenance schedule, no drain plug is fitted to the

2.10 Undo the bolts (arrowed) and remove the cover plate – F17+ transmissions

2.6 Using a funnel to fill the transmission via the reversing light switch aperture – F17+ transmissions

transmission. If for any reason the transmission needs to be drained, the only way of doing so is to remove the differential lower cover plate.
9 Wipe clean the area around the differential cover plate and position a suitable container underneath the cover.
10 Evenly and progressively slacken and remove the retaining bolts then withdraw the cover plate and allow the transmission oil to drain into the container **(see illustration)**. Remove the gasket and discard it; a new one should be used on refitting.
11 Allow the oil to drain completely into the container. If the oil is hot, take precautions against scalding. Remove all traces of dirt and oil from the cover and transmission mating surfaces and wipe clean the inside of the cover plate.
12 Once the oil has finished draining, ensure the mating surfaces are clean and dry then refit the cover plate to the transmission unit, complete with a new gasket. Refit the retaining bolts and evenly and progressively tighten them to the specified torque.

Refilling

13 Refer to paragraphs 4 to 7.

F23 transmissions

Level check

14 Wipe clean the area around the level plug located on the rear of the differential housing **(see illustration)**. Unscrew the plug and clean it.
15 The oil level should reach the lower edge of the level plug aperture. If topping-up is

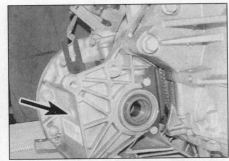

2.14 Transmission oil level plug (arrowed) – F23 transmissions

**2.15 Transmission oil filler plug (arrowed) –
F23 transmissions**

**2.26 Transmission oil filler plug (arrowed) –
F40 and M32 transmissions**

**2.23 Transmission oil drain plug (arrowed)
– F40 transmissions**

**2.27 Use a graduated container to fill the
transmission with the specified quantity of
oil – F40 and M32 transmissions**

necessary, wipe clean the area around the filler
plug on the top of the casing and unscrew the
plug **(see illustration)**.
16 Add the specified grade of oil given in
Lubricants and fluids through the filler plug
aperture, until it reaches the bottom of the
level plug aperture. Allow any excess oil to
drain, then refit and tighten the level plug to
the specified torque.
17 Refit the oil filler plug and tighten it to the
specified torque, then lower the vehicle to the
ground.

Draining

18 Wipe clean the area around the drain plug,
located below the left-hand driveshaft, and
position a suitable container under the plug.
19 Undo the drain plug and allow the oil to
drain.
20 Once the oil has finished draining, refit
the drain plug with a new sealing washer

where applicable, and tighten the plug to the
specified torque.

Refilling

21 Refer to paragraphs 14 to 17.

F40 and M32 transmissions

Note: *A new transmission oil drain plug will be
required.*

Level check

22 On the F40 and M32 transmissions, there
is no provision for oil level checking once the
transmission has been initially filled. If for any
reason it is thought that the oil level may be
low, the transmission oil must be completely
drained, then refilled with an exact specified
quantity of oil as described below.

Draining

23 Wipe clean the area around the drain
plug, located at the base of the differential

housing (F40 transmissions), or on the lower
left-hand side of the differential housing
(M32 transmissions), and position a suitable
container under the plug **(see illustration)**.
24 Undo the drain plug and allow the oil to
drain.
25 Once the oil has finished draining, fit the
new drain plug and tighten the plug to the
specified torque.

Refilling

26 The transmission is refilled via the oil filler
plug on the top of the casing **(see illustration)**.
To gain access to the plug, remove the battery
and battery box as described in Chapter 5A.
27 Wipe clean the area around the plug and
unscrew it. Refill the transmission with *exactly*
2.2 litres of the specified grade of oil given in
Lubricants and fluids, then refit and tighten
the oil filler plug to the specified torque **(see
illustration)**.
28 Refit the engine undertray, then lower the
vehicle to the ground.
29 Refit the battery box and battery as
described in Chapter 5A.

3 Gearchange mechanism –
adjustment

F17+, F40 and
M32 transmissions

Note: *A 5 mm drill bit or dowel rod will be
required to carry out this procedure.*

1 From inside the car, unclip the gearchange
lever gaiter retaining frame from the centre
console and lift it off the gearchange lever
(see illustration).
2 Remove the ashtray from the centre console
by opening the lid, depressing the internal tabs
each side and lifting out **(see illustration)**.
3 Release the retaining lugs around the
sides and rear of the gearchange lever gaiter.
Disengage the locating pegs at the front and
fold the gaiter up over the gearchange lever
knob **(see illustrations)**.
4 Using a small screwdriver, open the
clamping piece on the end of each selector
cable as far as the notch. Opening them any
further may damage the clamping pieces **(see
illustrations)**.

**3.1 Unclip and remove the gearchange
lever gaiter retaining frame from the centre
console**

**3.2 Remove the ashtray by depressing the
internal tabs each side and lifting out**

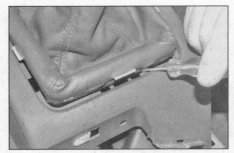

**3.3a Release the retaining lugs around
the sides and rear of the gearchange lever
gaiter . . .**

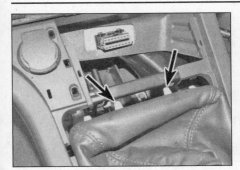

3.3b . . . then disengage the pegs (arrowed) and fold the gaiter up the lever

3.4a Using a small screwdriver, open the clamping piece on the end of each selector cable . . .

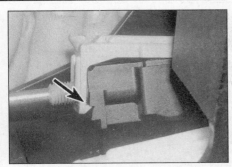

3.4b . . . until the lug (arrowed) rests on the notch

3.5 Pull up the reverse gear detent ring on the gearchange lever to expose the two tabs (arrowed) on the locking block

3.6 Engage the lug (arrowed) at the base of the locking block with the slot on the side of the gearchange lever base

5 Pull up the reverse gear detent ring on the gearchange lever to expose the two tabs on the locking block. Depress the two tabs until the locking block releases and moves down the lever (see illustration).

6 Move the gearchange lever to the left and engage the lug at the base of the locking block with the slot on the side of the gearchange lever base (see illustration). The lever is now locked in the adjustment position.

7 In the engine compartment, set the gearchange selector on the transmission to the 'neutral' position. Press the selector down (F17+ transmissions) or pull it up (F40 and M32 transmissions) and lock it in the adjustment position by inserting a 5 mm drill bit or dowel rod through the hole in the side of the housing (see illustration). Ensure that the drill bit or dowel rod fully engages with the selector.

8 Working back inside the car, lock both gearshift cable clamping pieces by pushing them down.

9 Remove the drill bit or dowel rod used to lock the gearchange selector on the transmission.

10 Lift the locking block on the gearchange lever out of the slot on the lever base, and slide it fully up the lever until it locks back in its original position.

11 Refit the gearchange lever gaiter and retaining frame to the centre console, then refit the ashtray. Check the gear selector mechanism for correct operation.

F23 transmissions

12 Carry out the operations described in paragraphs 1 to 4 above.

13 In the engine compartment, set the gearchange selector on the transmission to the 'neutral' position.

14 Working back inside the car, position the gearchange lever in the 'neutral' position, and lock it there by pushing in the clamp (see illustration).

15 Lock both gearshift cable clamping pieces by pushing them down.

16 Pull out the clamp locking the gearchange lever, then refit the lever gaiter and retaining frame to the centre console. Refit the ashtray and check the gear selector mechanism for correct operation.

3.7 Using a 5 mm drill bit (arrowed) to lock the selector mechanism in the adjustment position – F40 transmission shown

3.14 Lock the gearchange lever in 'neutral' by pushing in the clamp with a screwdriver – F23 transmissions

4.2a Extract the retaining clip . . .

4.2b . . . and remove the rear passenger air duct

4.5 Depress the lugs on the sides of the outer cable ends and lift the cables from the gearchange lever base

4.7a Gearchange lever assembly front retaining bolts (arrowed) . . .

4.7b . . . and rear retaining bolts (arrowed)

4 Gearchange mechanism – removal and refitting

Gearchange lever

Removal

1 Remove the centre console as described in Chapter 11.

2 Extract the retaining clip and remove the rear passenger air duct (see illustrations).

3 Undo the retaining bolt each side and release the diagnostic socket mounting bracket from the base of the facia. Disconnect the wiring connector and remove the bracket and diagnostic socket.

4 Using a small screwdriver, open the clamping piece on the end of each selector cable as far as the notch. Opening them any

further may damage the clamping pieces (see illustrations 3.4a and 3.4b).

5 Note the fitted locations of the two cables, then depress the lugs on the sides of the outer cable ends and lift the outer cables from the gearchange lever base (see illustration).

6 Move the two selector cables forward to disengage the inner cables from the gearchange lever clamping pieces.

7 Undo the four retaining bolts and lift the gearchange lever assembly from the floor (see illustrations).

8 If required, the cable clamping pieces attached to the gearchange lever can be carefully prised from their position using a forked tool. No further dismantling of the assembly is recommended.

Refitting

9 If previously removed, attached the cable clamping pieces to the base of the lever using a pair of pliers.

10 Position the gearchange lever assembly on the floor, insert the securing bolts and tighten to the specified torque.

11 Engage the selector inner cables with the clamping pieces, then refit the outer cables to the gearchange lever base. Do not lock the clamping pieces at this stage.

12 Carry out the gearchange mechanism adjustment procedure, as described in the previous Section.

13 Refit the rear passenger air duct and secure with the retaining clip.

14 Reconnect the wiring connector to the diagnostic socket then refit the mounting bracket and secure with the two bolts.

15 Refit the centre console as described in Chapter 11.

Selector cables

Removal

16 Carry out the operations described in paragraphs 1 to 6 above.

17 Working in the engine compartment, note the fitted locations of the cables at their transmission attachments.

18 Using a suitable forked tool, release the inner cable end fittings from the transmission selector levers (see illustration).

19 Pull back the retaining sleeves and detach the outer cables from the mounting bracket on the transmission (see illustration).

20 Release the rubber grommet at the cable entry point on the engine compartment bulkhead, then pull the cables (complete with grommet) out of the bulkhead and into the engine compartment (see illustration).

4.18 Release the inner cable end fittings from the transmission selector levers

4.19 Pull back the retaining sleeves and detach the outer cables from the transmission mounting bracket

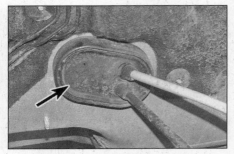

4.20 Release the bulkhead rubber grommet (arrowed), then pull the cables into the engine compartment

Refitting

21 Push the selector cables through the bulkhead passage from the engine compartment and locate the rubber grommet back into position in the bulkhead.

22 Refit the outer cables to the mounting bracket on the transmission.

23 Engage the inner cable end fittings with the transmission selector levers, squeezing them together with pliers if necessary.

24 Carry out the operations described in paragraphs 11 to 15 above.

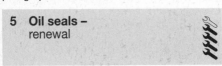

5 Oil seals – renewal

Driveshaft oil seals

F17+, F23 and F40 transmissions

1 Firmly apply the handbrake, then jack up the front of the car and support it securely on axle stands (see *Jacking and vehicle support*).

2 Drain the transmission oil as described in Section 2.

3 Remove the driveshaft/intermediate shaft as described in Chapter 8.

4 Note the correct fitted depth of the seal in its housing then carefully prise it out of position using a large flat-bladed screwdriver **(see illustration)**.

5 Remove all traces of dirt from the area around the oil seal aperture, then lubricate the outer lip of the new oil seal with transmission oil. Ensure the seal is correctly positioned, with its sealing lip facing inwards, and tap it squarely into position, using a suitable tubular drift (such as a socket) which bears only on the hard outer edge of the seal **(see illustration)**. Ensure the seal is fitted at the same depth in its housing that the original was.

6 Refit the driveshaft/intermediate shaft as described in Chapter 8.

7 Refill the transmission with the specified type and amount of oil, as described in Section 2.

M32 transmissions – right-hand oil seal

8 Proceed as described above in paragraphs 1 to 7.

M32 transmissions – left-hand oil seal

Note: *A hydraulic press, together with tubes and mandrels of suitable diameters will be needed for this operation.*

9 Firmly apply the handbrake, then jack up the front of the car and support it securely on axle stands (see *Jacking and vehicle support*).

10 Drain the transmission oil as described in Section 2.

11 Remove the driveshaft as described in Chapter 8.

12 Undo the four bolts and remove the oil seal carrier from the side of the differential housing.

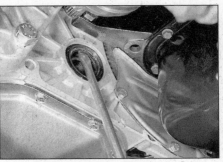

5.4 Prising out a driveshaft oil seal

13 Place the oil seal carrier on the press bed with its outer surface facing down. Using a suitable mandrel, press the oil seal out of the carrier.

14 Using a small screwdriver, remove the sealing O-ring from the oil seal carrier.

15 Support the inner surface of the oil seal carrier on the press bed. Lubricate the new oil seal with transmission oil, then press it fully into position in the carrier using a suitable tube which bears only on the hard outer edge of the seal.

16 Fit a new O-ring to the oil seal carrier, then refit the carrier to the differential housing, tightening the retaining bolts to the specified torque.

17 Refit the driveshaft as described in Chapter 8.

18 Refill the transmission with the specified type and amount of oil, as described in Section 2.

Input shaft oil seal

19 The input shaft oil seal is an integral part of the clutch release cylinder; if the seal is leaking the complete release cylinder assembly must be renewed. Before condemning the release cylinder, check that the leak is not coming from the sealing ring which is fitted between the cylinder and the transmission housing; the sealing ring can be renewed once the release cylinder assembly has been removed. Refer to Chapter 6 for removal and refitting details.

6 Reversing light switch – testing, removal and refitting

F17+ transmissions

1 The reversing light circuit is controlled by a plunger-type switch screwed into the top of the transmission towards the front of the housing.

Testing

2 If a fault develops in the circuit, first ensure that the circuit fuse has not blown and that the reversing light bulbs are sound.

3 To test the switch, disconnect the wiring connector. Use a multimeter (set to the resistance function) or a battery-and-bulb

5.5 Fitting a new driveshaft oil seal using a socket as a tubular drift

test circuit to check that there is continuity between the switch terminals only when reverse gear is selected. If this is not the case, and there are no obvious breaks or other damage to the wires, the switch is faulty, and must be renewed.

Removal

4 Disconnect the wiring connector, then unscrew the switch and remove it from the transmission casing along with its sealing washer **(see illustration)**.

Refitting

5 Fit a new sealing washer to the switch, then screw it back into position in the top of the transmission housing and tighten it to the specified torque. Reconnect the wiring connector, then test the operation of the circuit.

F23 transmissions

6 The reversing light circuit is controlled by a plunger-type switch screwed into the rear of the transmission above the left-hand driveshaft.

7 To gain access to the switch, firmly apply the handbrake, then jack up the front of the car and support it securely on axle stands (see *Jacking and vehicle support*).

Testing

8 Proceed as described in paragraphs 2 and 3 above.

Removal

9 Disconnect the wiring connector, then

6.4 Unscrew and remove the reversing light switch together with its sealing washer – F17+ transmissions

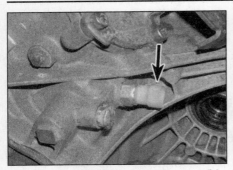

6.9 The reversing light switch (arrowed) is positioned above the left-hand driveshaft – F23 transmissions

unscrew the switch and remove it from the transmission casing along with its sealing washer **(see illustration)**.

Refitting

10 Fit a new sealing washer to the switch, then screw it back into position in the rear of the transmission housing and tighten it to the specified torque. Reconnect the wiring connector, then test the operation of the circuit.
11 On completion, lower the vehicle to the ground.

F40 transmissions

12 The reversing light circuit is controlled by a plunger-type switch screwed into the selector lever housing on top of the transmission.

Testing

13 Proceed as described in paragraphs 2 and 3 above.

Removal

14 Disconnect the wiring connector, then unscrew the switch and remove it from the selector lever housing along with its sealing washer **(see illustration)**.

Refitting

15 Fit a new sealing washer to the switch, then screw it back into position in the selector lever housing and tighten it to the specified torque. Reconnect the wiring connector, then test the operation of the circuit.

M32 transmissions

16 The reversing light circuit is controlled by

7.7a Using a small screwdriver, prise out the retaining clip . . .

6.14 The reversing light switch (arrowed) is screwed into the transmission selector lever housing – F40 transmissions

a plunger-type switch screwed into the front of the transmission casing.
17 To gain access to the switch, firmly apply the handbrake, then jack up the front of the car and support it securely on axle stands (see *Jacking and vehicle support*). Undo the retaining bolts and screws and remove the undertray from beneath the engine.

Testing

18 Proceed as described in paragraphs 2 and 3 above.

Removal

19 Disconnect the wiring connector, then unscrew the switch and remove it from the transmission casing along with its sealing washer.

Refitting

20 Fit a new sealing washer to the switch, then screw it back into position in the transmission casing and tighten it to the specified torque. Reconnect the wiring connector, then test the operation of the circuit.
21 On completion, refit the engine undertray and lower the vehicle to the ground.

---

7 Transmission – removal and refitting

Removal

1 Apply the handbrake, then jack up the front of the vehicle and support it on axle

7.7b . . . and disconnect the clutch hydraulic hose from the end fitting on the transmission bellhousing

stands (see *Jacking and vehicle support*). Allow sufficient working room to remove the transmission from under the left-hand side of the engine compartment. Remove both front roadwheels then, on diesel engine models, undo the retaining bolts and screws bolts and remove the undertray from beneath the engine. Also remove the engine top cover where fitted.
2 Remove the battery, battery box, and the starter motor as described in Chapter 5A.
3 Remove the air cleaner housing and intake ducts as described in the relevant Part of Chapter 4.
4 Remove the front bumper as described in Chapter 11.
5 Drain the transmission oil as described in Section 2.
6 Remove the filler cap from the brake/clutch fluid reservoir on the bulkhead, then tighten it onto a piece of polythene. This will reduce the loss of fluid when the clutch hydraulic hose is disconnected. Alternatively, fit a hose clamp to the flexible hose next to the clutch hydraulic connection on the transmission housing.
7 Place some cloth rags beneath the hose, then prise out the retaining clip securing the clutch hydraulic hose to the end fitting on top of the transmission bellhousing. Detach the hose from the end fitting **(see illustrations)**. Gently squeeze the two legs of the retaining clip together and re-insert the retaining clip back into position in the end fitting. Discard the sealing ring from the hose end; a new sealing ring must be used on refitting. Plug/cover both the end fitting and hose end to minimise fluid loss and prevent the entry of dirt into the hydraulic system. **Note:** *Whilst the hose is disconnected, do not depress the clutch pedal.*
8 Note the fitted locations of the gearchange selector cables at their transmission attachments. Using a suitable forked tool, release the inner cable end fittings from the transmission selector levers. Pull back the retaining sleeves and release the outer cables from the mounting bracket on the transmission **(see illustrations 4.18 and 4.19)**. Undo the retaining bolts and remove the cable mounting bracket(s) from the transmission.
9 Disconnect the wiring connector from the reversing light switch and free the wiring from the transmission unit and retaining brackets.
10 On diesel engine models with the M32 transmission, remove the EGR valve heat exchanger as described in Chapter 4C.
11 Working as described in Chapter 8, disconnect the inner ends of both driveshafts from the differential and intermediate shaft, then remove the intermediate shaft. There is no need to disconnect the driveshafts from the swivel hub. Support the driveshafts by suspending them with wire or string – do not allow the driveshafts to hang down under their own weight, or the joints may be damaged.
12 Unscrew and remove the upper bolts securing the transmission to the rear of the

engine. Where necessary, pull up the coolant hoses and secure them away from the transmission using plastic cable ties.

13 Remove the front subframe assembly as described in Chapter 10, ensuring that the engine unit is securely supported by connecting a hoist to the engine assembly. If available, the type of support bar which locates in the engine compartment side channels is to be preferred.

14 Unbolt and remove the front and rear engine/transmission mounting torque link brackets with reference to the relevant Part of Chapter 2.

15 Place a jack with a block of wood beneath the transmission, and raise the jack to take the weight of the transmission.

16 Unbolt and remove the left-hand engine/transmission mounting bracket from the transmission with reference to the relevant Part of Chapter 2.

17 Lower the engine and transmission by approximately 5 cm making sure that the coolant hoses and wiring harnesses are not stretched.

18 Slacken and remove the remaining bolts securing the transmission to the engine and sump flange. Note the correct fitted positions of each bolt and the relevant brackets as they are removed to use as a reference on refitting. Make a final check that all components have been disconnected, and are positioned clear of the transmission so that they will not hinder the removal procedure.

19 With the bolts removed, move the trolley jack and transmission, to free it from its locating dowels. Once the transmission is free, lower the jack and manoeuvre the unit out from under the car. Remove the locating dowels from the transmission or engine if they are loose, and keep them in a safe place.

Refitting

20 The transmission is refitted by a reversal of the removal procedure, bearing in mind the following points.
 a) Ensure the locating dowels are correctly positioned prior to installation.
 b) Tighten all nuts and bolts to the specified torque (where given).
 c) Renew the driveshaft oil seals (see Section 5) before refitting the driveshafts/intermediate shaft.
 d) Refit the front subframe assembly as described in Chapter 10.
 e) Fit a new sealing ring to the clutch hydraulic hose before clipping the hose into the end fitting. Ensure the hose is securely retained by its clip then bleed the hydraulic system as described in Chapter 6.
 f) On M32 transmissions, refit the EGR valve heat exchanger as described in Chapter 4C.
 g) Refill the transmission with the specified type and quantity of oil, as described in Section 2.
 h) On completion, adjust the gearchange mechanism as described in Section 3.

8 Transmission overhaul – general information

1 Overhauling a manual transmission unit is a difficult and involved job for the DIY home mechanic. In addition to dismantling and reassembling many small parts, clearances must be precisely measured and, if necessary, changed by selecting shims and spacers. Internal transmission components are also often difficult to obtain, and in many instances, extremely expensive. Because of this, if the transmission develops a fault or becomes noisy, the best course of action is to have the unit overhauled by a specialist repairer, or to obtain an exchange reconditioned unit.

2 Nevertheless, it is not impossible for the more experienced mechanic to overhaul the transmission, provided the special tools are available, and the job is done in a deliberate step-by-step manner, so that nothing is overlooked.

3 The tools necessary for an overhaul include internal and external circlip pliers, bearing pullers, a slide hammer, a set of pin punches, a dial test indicator, and possibly a hydraulic press. In addition, a large, sturdy workbench and a vice will be required.

4 During dismantling of the transmission, make careful notes of how each component is fitted, to make reassembly easier and more accurate.

5 Before dismantling the transmission, it will help if you have some idea what area is malfunctioning. Certain problems can be closely related to specific areas in the transmission, which can make component examination and renewal easier. Refer to the *Fault finding* Section of this manual for more information.

Notes

Chapter 7 Part B:
Automatic transmission

Contents

Degrees of difficulty

Easy, suitable for novice with little experience | **Fairly easy,** suitable for beginner with some experience | **Fairly difficult,** suitable for competent DIY mechanic | **Difficult,** suitable for experienced DIY mechanic | **Very difficult,** suitable for expert DIY or professional

Specifications

General
Type:
- Petrol engine models: Electronically-controlled adaptive automatic, five forward speeds and reverse, with sequential manual gear selection capability
- Diesel engine models: Electronically-controlled adaptive automatic, six forward speeds and reverse, with sequential manual gear selection capability

Manufacturer's designation:
- Petrol engine models: AF23
- Diesel engine models: AF40

Lubrication
Lubricant type: See *Lubricants and fluids*
Lubricant capacity: See Chapter 1A or 1B

Torque wrench settings

	Nm	lbf ft
Automatic transmission fluid drain/filler plugs:		
AF23 transmissions:		
Dipstick retaining bolt	20	15
Drain plug	40	30
Filler plug	30	22
AF40 transmissions:		
Drain plug	50	37
Filler plug	40	30
Level checking plug	8	6
Electronic control unit mounting bolts (AF40 transmissions)	25	18
Engine/transmission mountings	See the relevant Part of Chapter 2	
Engine-to-transmission bolts	See the relevant Part of Chapter 2	
Fluid cooler pipes to transmission	7	5
Input shaft speed sensor bolt	6	4
Output shaft speed sensor bolt	6	4
Roadwheel bolts	110	81
Selector lever assembly mounting bolts	8	6
Selector lever position switch:		
Lever-to-selector shaft	15	11
Selector shaft main nut	7	5
Switch retaining bolts	25	18
Torque converter-to-driveplate bolts:*		
AF23 transmissions	60	44
AF40 Transmissions	30	22

* Use new bolts

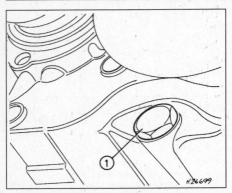

2.2 Transmission fluid drain plug (1) – AF23 transmissions

1 General information

A five- or six-speed, electronically-controlled automatic transmission was optionally available on certain models covered by this manual. The transmission consists of a torque converter, an epicyclic geartrain, and hydraulically-operated clutches and brakes. The unit is controlled by the electronic control unit (ECU) via electrically-operated solenoid valves. In addition to the fully-automatic operation, the transmission can also be operated manually with five-speed or six-speed sequential gear selection.

The torque converter provides a fluid coupling between engine and transmission, which acts as an automatic clutch, and also provides a degree of torque multiplication when accelerating. The torque converter incorporates a lock-up function whereby the engine and transmission can be directly coupled by means of a clutch unit inside the torque converter. The lock-up function is controlled by the ECU according to operating conditions.

The epicyclic geartrain provides five or six forward and one reverse gear ratio, according to which of its component parts are held stationary or allowed to turn. The components of the geartrain are held or released by hydraulically actuated brakes and clutches. A fluid pump within the transmission provides the necessary hydraulic pressure to operate the brakes and clutches.

In automatic mode, the transmission is fully-adaptive, whereby the shift points are dependent on driver input, roadspeed, engine speed and vehicle operating conditions. The ECU receives inputs from various engine and drivetrain related sensors, and determines the appropriate shift point for each gear. Additionally, the transmission can be placed into winter mode using the button on the selector lever indicator panel. The transmission will select fourth gear as the vehicle pulls away from a standing start; this helps to maintain traction on very slippery surfaces.

Driver control of the transmission is by a four-position selector lever. The drive D position, allows automatic changing throughout the range of forward gear ratios. An automatic kickdown facility shifts the transmission down a gear if the accelerator pedal is fully depressed. If the selector lever is moved to the left from the D position, the transmission enters manual mode. In manual mode the gear selector lever can be used to shift the transmission up or down each gear sequentially.

Due to the complexity of the automatic transmission, any repair or overhaul work must be left to a Vauxhall/Opel dealer or transmission specialist with the necessary special equipment for fault diagnosis and repair. The contents of the following Sections are therefore confined to supplying general information, and any service information and instructions that can be used by the owner.

2 Automatic transmission fluid – draining and refilling

AF23 transmissions

Draining

1 Firmly apply the handbrake, then jack up the front of the car and support it securely on axle stands (see *Jacking and vehicle support*).

2 Position a container under the drain plug at the rear right-hand side of the transmission, below the driveshaft. Unscrew the plug and remove it along with its sealing washer **(see illustration)**.

3 Allow the fluid to drain completely into the container.

4 When the fluid has finished draining, clean the drain plug threads and those of the transmission casing, fit a new sealing washer and refit the drain plug, tightening it to the specified torque. Refit the engine undertray (where applicable) and lower the vehicle to the ground.

Refilling

5 Where applicable, lift off the plastic cover over the top of the engine.

6 Using a suitable forked tool, release the selector cable end fitting from the selector lever position switch on the top of the transmission **(see illustration)**.

7 Move the selector cable to one side and wipe clean the area around the transmission fluid filler plug, located just to the rear of the selector lever position switch. Unscrew and remove the filler plug along with its sealing washer.

8 Refill the transmission using approximately 3.0 litres of the specified type of fluid, via the filler plug aperture. Use a funnel with a fine mesh gauze, to avoid spillage, and to ensure that no foreign matter enters the transmission.

9 Refit and securely tighten the filler plug, then

2.6 Transmission fluid dipstick and related components – AF23 transmissions

1 Dipstick retaining bolt	*4 Selector cable end fitting*
2 Dipstick	*5 Selector lever position switch*
3 Transmission fluid filler plug	*6 HOT mark grooves on dipstick*

reconnect the selector cable to the selector lever position switch.

10 Start the engine, and allow it to idle for a few minutes whilst moving the selector lever through its various positions. Take the car on a moderate run to fully distribute the new fluid around the transmission, and to bring the transmission up to normal operating temperature (70° to 80°C). On returning, park the car on level ground and leave the engine idling.

11 Slowly move the selector lever from position P to position D and back to position P.

12 Unscrew the retaining bolt and withdraw the transmission fluid dipstick, located at the front left-hand side of the transmission. Where necessary, unclip the transmission wiring harness and move it to one side for improved access to the dipstick.

13 Wipe the dipstick with a clean cloth and insert it fully into the transmission. Withdraw the dipstick and check the fluid level which must be between the grooves of the HOT mark. Note that 0.3 litres of fluid is required to raise the level from the COLD mark to the HOT mark on the dipstick.

14 If topping-up is necessary, stop the engine, and remove the fluid filler plug as described previously. Add additional fluid, as required, then refit the filler plug, using a new sealing washer. Tighten the filler plug to the specified torque, then reconnect the selector cable to the selector lever position switch.

15 Refit the dipstick and secure with the retaining bolt, tightened to the specified torque. If disturbed, clip the transmission wiring harness back into position.

16 Where applicable, refit the plastic cover over the top of the engine.

AF40 transmissions

Draining

17 Position the vehicle over an inspection pit, on vehicle ramps, or jack it up and support it securely on axle stands (see *Jacking and vehicle support*), but make sure that it is level. Undo the retaining bolts and screws and remove the undertray from beneath the engine.

18 Position a container under the combined drain plug/level checking plug at the base of the transmission. Note that the drain plug and level checking plug are incorporated into one unit – the drain plug is the larger of the two plugs, with the level checking plug screwed into the centre of it **(see illustration)**.

19 Unscrew the level checking plug and remove it, along with its sealing washer, from the centre of the drain plug. Now unscrew the drain plug and remove it, along with its sealing washer, from the transmission. Allow the fluid to drain completely into the container.

20 When the fluid has finished draining, clean the drain plug threads and those of the transmission casing, fit a new sealing washer and refit the drain plug, tightening it to the specified torque.

Refilling

21 Wipe clean the area around the transmission fluid filler plug, located on the top of the transmission housing, adjacent to the selector cable **(see illustration)**. Unscrew and remove the filler plug along with its sealing washer.

22 Slowly refill the transmission with the specified type of fluid, via the filler plug aperture until fluid just starts to drip out of the level checking plug aperture. Use a funnel

with a fine mesh gauze, to avoid spillage, and to ensure that no foreign matter enters the transmission.

23 Refit the level checking plug and tighten it securely.

24 Add a further 0.5 litre of fluid via the filler plug aperture.

25 Start the engine and allow it to idle. With the footbrake firmly applied, slowly move the selector lever from position P to position D and back to position P, stopping at each position for at least two seconds. Repeat this procedure twice.

26 With the engine still idling, unscrew the fluid level checking plug once more. Allow the excess fluid to run from the level checking plug aperture until it is only dripping out. Refit the level checking plug with a new sealing washer, and tighten the plug to the specified torque.

27 If no fluid runs from the level checking plug aperture, switch the engine off and repeat paragraphs 24 to 26.

28 Once the fluid level is correct, refit the filler plug with a new sealing washer, and tighten the plug to the specified torque.

29 On completion, refit the engine undertray and lower the vehicle to the ground.

3 Selector cable – adjustment

Note: *If the battery is disconnected with the selector lever in the P (park) position, the lever will be locked in position. To manually release the lever, remove the ashtray from the centre console by opening the lid, depressing the internal tabs each side and lifting out. Using a flat-bladed screwdriver, depress*

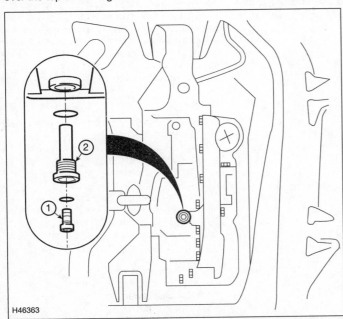

2.18 Transmission fluid level checking plug (1) and drain plug (2) – AF40 transmissions

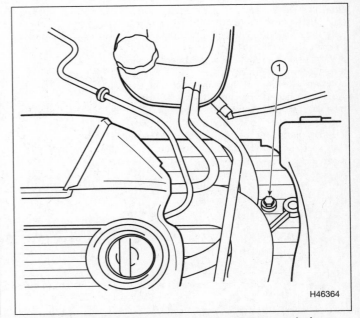

2.21 Transmission fluid filler plug (1) – AF40 transmissions

H46363

H46364

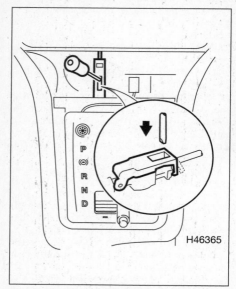

3.4a Use a small screwdriver to open the clamping piece on the selector cable . . .

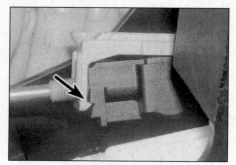

3.4b . . . until the lug (arrowed) rests on the notch

6 Check the operation of the selector lever and, if necessary, repeat the adjustment procedure. On completion, refit the ashtray to the centre console.

4 Selector cable – removal and refitting

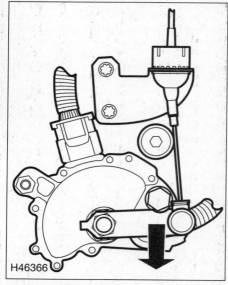

3.5 Move the lever on the selector lever position switch fully forwards so the transmission is in the P position

the emergency release lever in the ashtray aperture, whilst moving the selector lever to the N (neutral) position.

1 Operate the selector lever throughout its entire range and check that the transmission engages the correct gear indicated on the selector lever position indicator. If adjustment is necessary, continue as follows.

2 Position the selector lever in the P (park) position.

3 Remove the ashtray from the centre console by opening the lid, depressing the internal tabs each side and lifting out.

4 Working in the ashtray aperture, use a small screwdriver to open the clamping piece on the selector cable as far as the notch (see illustrations). Opening any further may damage the clamping piece.

5 Working in the engine compartment, move the lever on the transmission selector lever position switch fully forwards so that the transmission is also positioned in the P position (see illustration). With both the selector lever and transmission correctly positioned, lock the clamping piece on the selector cable by pushing it down until it clicks in position.

Removal

1 Remove the centre console as described in Chapter 11 then position the selector lever in the P (park) position.

2 Undo the retaining bolt and remove the rear passenger air duct (see illustration).

3 Undo the retaining bolt each side and release the diagnostic socket mounting bracket from the base of the facia. Disconnect the wiring connector and remove the bracket and diagnostic socket.

4 Using a small screwdriver, open the clamping piece on the end of the selector cable as far as the notch. Opening any further may damage the clamping piece (see illustration 3.4b).

5 Again using a small screwdriver, lift up the locking clip securing the outer cable to the selector lever housing (see illustration).

6 Move the selector cable forward to disengage the inner cable from the selector lever clamping piece.

7 Working in the engine compartment, use a forked tool or flat-bladed screwdriver, and carefully lever the selector inner cable end fitting off the balljoint on the selector lever position switch. Pull back the retaining sleeve and detach the outer cable from the mounting bracket on the transmission (see illustration).

8 Release the rubber grommet at the cable entry point on the engine compartment bulkhead, then pull the cable (complete with

4.2 Undo the retaining bolt and remove the rear passenger air duct

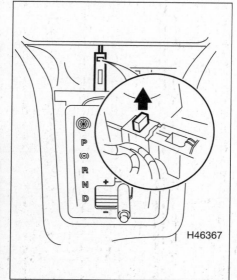

4.5 Lift up the locking clip securing the outer cable to the selector lever housing

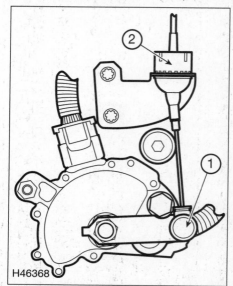

4.7 Selector inner cable end fitting (1) and outer cable retaining sleeve (2)

grommet) out of the bulkhead and into the engine compartment.

Refitting

9 Push the selector cable through the bulkhead passage from the engine compartment and locate the rubber grommet back into position in the bulkhead.

10 Refit the outer cable to the mounting bracket on the transmission.

11 Engage the inner cable end fitting with the balljoint on the selector lever position switch, squeezing them together with pliers if necessary.

12 Move the lever on the selector lever position switch fully forwards so that the transmission is positioned in the P position.

13 From inside the car, position the selector lever in the P position and guide the cable back into its location in the selector lever housing, engaging the inner cable with the clamping piece. Push down the outer cable locking clip and the inner cable clamping piece ensuring they both lock fully into position.

14 Refit the rear passenger air duct and securely tighten the retaining bolt.

15 Reconnect the wiring connector to the diagnostic socket then refit the mounting bracket and secure with the two bolts.

16 Refit the centre console as described in Chapter 11.

5 Selector lever assembly – removal and refitting

Removal

1 Carry out the operations described in Section 4, paragraphs 1 to 6.

2 Disconnect the selector lever assembly wiring connector and release the wiring harness from the retaining clips and ties.

3 Undo the four mounting bolts and lift the selector lever assembly from the floor.

Refitting

4 Working in the engine compartment, check that the transmission is in the P (park) position by moving the lever on the selector lever position switch fully forwards (see illustration 3.5).

5 From inside the car, position the selector lever in the P position, then manoeuvre the selector lever assembly into place, engaging it with the selector cable. Refit the mounting bolts and tighten them to the specified torque.

6 Reconnect the selector lever assembly wiring connector and secure the wiring harness with the retaining clips and ties.

7 Push down the selector outer cable locking clip and the inner cable clamping piece ensuring they both lock fully into position.

8 Refit the rear passenger air duct and securely tighten the retaining bolt.

9 Reconnect the wiring connector to the diagnostic socket then refit the mounting bracket and secure with the two bolts.

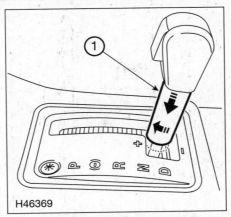

6.2 Rotate the locking sleeve (1) clockwise, and push it down, away from the knob

10 Refit the centre console as described in Chapter 11.

6 Selector lever assembly components – removal and refitting

Selector lever knob

Removal

1 Move the selector lever to the D (drive) position.

2 Rotate the locking sleeve, located directly beneath the lever knob, clockwise, and push it down, away from the knob, using a screwdriver (see illustration).

3 Using a small screwdriver, open the lug at the base of the lever knob, and pull the knob up and off the selector lever (see illustration).

4 Slide the locking sleeve up and off the lever.

Refitting

5 Make sure the selector lever is still in the D position, then refit the locking sleeve and slide it down the lever.

6 Place the knob on the selector lever, press the button on the front of the knob, and push the knob fully into position.

7 Slide the locking sleeve up the lever and turn it anti-clockwise to secure.

Selector lever position indicator

Removal

8 Remove the selector lever knob as described previously.

9 Remove the ashtray from the centre console by opening the lid, depressing the internal tabs each side and lifting out.

10 Carefully unclip and remove the upper trim panel around the edge of the position indicator panel.

11 Release the wiring harness at the front of the selector lever housing from its retaining clips and ties, and disconnect the wiring harness connector (see illustration).

12 Lift the position indicator assembly and

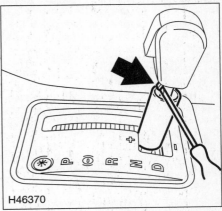

6.3 Open the lug (arrowed) with a small screwdriver, and pull the knob up and off the selector lever

remove the intermediate mounting frame. Withdraw the unit up and off the selector lever.

13 Release the two clips each side securing the position indicator panel, then remove the panel and slide from the indicator body.

Refitting

14 Insert the slide into the indicator body, then clip the indicator panel into position.

15 Refit the position indicator assembly and intermediate mounting frame to the selector lever housing.

16 Reconnect the wiring harness and secure the harness with the clips and ties.

17 Refit the upper trim panel and ashtray, then refit the selector lever knob as described previously.

Selector lever control unit

Removal

18 Remove the centre console as described in Chapter 11.

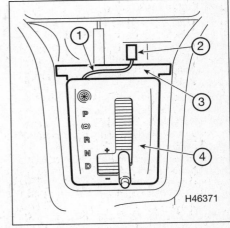

6.11 Selector lever position indicator components

1 Wiring harness
2 Wiring harness connector
3 Position indicator assembly
4 Intermediate mounting frame

19 Undo the retaining bolt and remove the rear passenger air duct **(see illustration 4.2)**.
20 Undo the retaining bolt each side and release the diagnostic socket mounting bracket from the base of the facia. Disconnect the wiring connector and remove the bracket and diagnostic socket.
21 Carefully unclip the selector emergency release lever from its guides on the side of the selector lever housing.
22 Disconnect the three wiring harness connectors then unclip and remove the control unit from the side of the selector lever housing.

Refitting

23 Refitting is a reversal of removal.

Selector lever lock switch

Removal

24 Carry out the operations described in paragraphs 18 to 21.
25 Disconnect the wiring harness connector then withdraw the switch from its guide on the side of the selector lever housing.

Refitting

26 Refitting is a reversal of removal.

7 Oil seals –
renewal

Driveshaft oil seals

1 Firmly apply the handbrake, then jack up the front of the car and support it securely on axle stands (see *Jacking and vehicle support*).
2 Drain the transmission fluid as described in Section 2.
3 Remove the driveshaft/intermediate shaft as described in Chapter 8.
4 Note the correct fitted depth of the seal in its housing then carefully prise it out of position using a large flat-bladed screwdriver.
5 Remove all traces of dirt from the area around the oil seal aperture, then lubricate the new oil seal with automatic transmission fluid. Ensure the seal is correctly positioned, with its sealing lip facing inwards, and tap it squarely into position, using a suitable tubular drift (such as a socket) which bears only on the hard outer edge of the seal. Ensure the seal is fitted at the same depth in its housing that the original was.
6 Refit the driveshaft/intermediate shaft as described in Chapter 8.
7 Refill the transmission with fresh fluid as described in Section 2.

Torque converter oil seal

8 Remove the transmission as described in Section 12.
9 Carefully slide the torque converter off of the transmission shaft whilst being prepared for fluid spillage.
10 Note the correct fitted position of the seal in the oil pump housing then carefully lever the

seal out of position taking care not to mark the housing or input shaft.
11 Remove all traces of dirt from the area around the oil seal aperture then press the new seal into position, ensuring its sealing lip is facing inwards.
12 Lubricate the seal with clean transmission fluid then carefully ease the torque converter into position. On the AF40 transmissions, slide the torque converter onto the transmission shaft by turning it until it fully engages with the oil pump.
13 Refit the transmission as described in Section 12.

8 Fluid cooler –
general information

The transmission fluid cooler is an integral part of the radiator assembly. Refer to Chapter 3 for removal and refitting details, if the cooler is damaged the complete radiator assembly must be renewed.

9 Selector lever
position switch –
removal and refitting

AF23 transmissions

1 The switch is a dual-function switch, performing the reversing light and starter inhibitor switch functions. The switch operates the reversing lights when reverse gear is selected and prevents the engine being started when the transmission is in gear. If at any time the reversing light operation becomes faulty, or it is noted that the engine can be started with the selector lever in any position other than P (park) or N (neutral), then it is likely that the switch is faulty. If adjustment fails to correct the fault then the complete switch must be renewed as a unit.

Removal

2 Ensure the handbrake is fully applied, then move the gear selector lever to the N (neutral) position.
3 Where applicable, lift off the plastic cover over the top of the engine.
4 Unscrew the retaining bolt and nut and release the wiring harness support bracket (where fitted) from the selector lever position switch.
5 Using a forked tool or flat-bladed screwdriver, carefully lever the selector inner cable end fitting off the balljoint on the selector lever position switch. Pull back the retaining sleeve and detach the outer cable from the mounting bracket on the transmission **(see illustration 4.7)**.
6 Unscrew the retaining nut and remove the lever from the transmission selector shaft.
7 Disconnect the selector lever position switch wiring connector.
8 Bend back the lockwasher then unscrew

and remove the main nut and the lockwasher from the transmission selector shaft.
9 Unscrew and remove the two switch retaining bolts, and manoeuvre the switch assembly upwards and off the transmission selector shaft.

Refitting

10 Prior to refitting, first make sure that the transmission selector shaft is still in the N (neutral) position. If there is any doubt, temporarily engage the selector shaft lever with the transmission selector shaft and move the lever fully forwards (to the P position) then move it two notches backwards.
11 Locate the switch on the transmission selector shaft then refit the two retaining bolts, tightening them by hand only at this stage.
12 Refit the lockwasher and main nut to the selector shaft. Tighten the nut to the specified torque setting and secure it in position by bending up the locking washer against one of its flats.
13 Adjust the switch as described in paragraph 20.
14 Once the switch is correctly adjusted, reconnect the wiring connector, ensuring that the wiring is correctly routed.
15 Refit the selector lever to the shaft and tighten its retaining nut to the specified torque.
16 Refit the selector outer cable to the mounting bracket on the transmission. Engage the selector inner cable end fitting with the balljoint on the selector lever, squeezing them together with pliers if necessary.
17 Where applicable, refit the plastic engine cover.
18 If necessary, adjust the selector cable as described in Section 4.

Adjustment

19 Carry out the operations described in paragraphs 2 to 6.
20 With the transmission in neutral, the flats on the selector shaft should be parallel to the marking on the switch assembly **(see illustration)**. Place a straight-edge against the flats on the shaft to check this. If adjustment is necessary, slacken the switch retaining bolts and rotate the switch assembly as necessary before retightening the bolts to the specified torque.
21 Refit the selector lever to the shaft and tighten its retaining nut to the specified torque.
22 Refit the selector outer cable to the mounting bracket on the transmission. Engage the selector inner cable end fitting with the balljoint on the selector lever, squeezing them together with pliers if necessary.
23 Where applicable, refit the plastic engine cover.
24 If necessary, adjust the selector cable as described in Section 3.

AF40 transmissions

25 On the AF40 transmissions, the selector lever position switch is an integral part of the transmission electronic control unit and cannot be separated. Removal and refitting procedures for the electronic control unit are contained in Section 11.

10 Transmission input/ output speed sensors – removal and refitting

AF23 transmissions

Removal

1 The speed sensors are fitted to the top of the transmission unit. The input shaft speed sensor is the front of the two sensors and is situated beneath the selector cable. The output shaft sensor is the rear of the two.

2 Where applicable, lift off the plastic cover over the top of the engine.

3 If removing the input shaft speed sensor, use a forked tool or flat-bladed screwdriver, and carefully lever the selector inner cable end fitting off the balljoint on the selector lever position switch. Pull back the retaining sleeve and detach the outer cable from the mounting bracket on the transmission.

4 Wipe clean the area around the relevant sensor, then undo the retaining bolt and withdraw the sensor from the transmission.

5 Disconnect the wiring connector and remove the sensor. Remove the sealing ring from the sensor and discard it, a new one should be used on refitting.

Refitting

6 Fit the new sealing ring to the sensor groove and lubricate it with a smear of transmission fluid.

7 Reconnect the wiring connector, then ease the sensor into position and refit the retaining bolt. Tighten the bolt to the specified torque.

8 If working on the input shaft speed sensor, refit the selector outer cable to the mounting bracket on the transmission. Engage the selector inner cable end fitting with the balljoint on the selector lever, squeezing them together with pliers if necessary.

9 Where applicable, refit the plastic engine cover.

AF40 transmissions

10 On the AF40 transmissions, the input and output shaft speed sensors are located internally within the transmission and are not individually available. If one or both speed sensors are diagnosed as faulty, it will be necessary to obtain a complete new transmission.

11 Electronic control unit – removal and refitting

Note: If a new ECU is to be fitted, this work must be entrusted to a Vauxhall/Opel dealer or suitably-equipped specialist. It is necessary

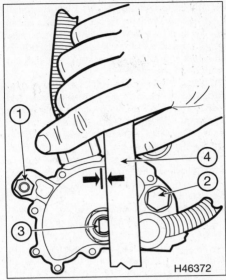

9.20 Selector lever position switch adjustment – AF23 transmissions

1 Switch retaining bolts
2 Switch retaining bolts
3 Selector shaft
4 Straight-edge parallel with mark on switch assembly (arrows)

to reset the transmission electronic control system prior to removal, and to programme the new ECU after installation. This work requires the use of dedicated Vauxhall/Opel diagnostic equipment or a compatible alternative.

AF23 transmissions

Removal

1 The ECU is located at the front, left-hand side of the engine compartment, inside the battery box.

2 Open the battery box by releasing the lid at the front and pivoting it upwards.

3 Release the ECU wiring harness from its retaining clips, then disconnect the upper wiring harness connector from the ECU.

4 Unclip the ECU mounting bracket from the

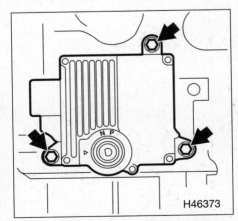

11.14 Electronic control unit mounting bolts (arrowed) – AF40 transmissions

battery box, then lift the ECU and mounting bracket upwards.

5 Release the ECU wiring harness from its retaining clips, then disconnect the lower wiring harness connector from the ECU. Remove the ECU and mounting bracket from the car.

Refitting

6 Refitting is a reversal of removal.

AF40 transmissions

Removal

7 The combined ECU and selector lever position switch are located on the top of the transmission housing.

8 Ensure the handbrake is fully applied, then move the gear selector lever to the N (neutral) position.

9 Remove the battery and battery box as described in Chapter 5A.

10 Unclip the pre/post-heating system control unit wiring harness from the battery box support.

11 Release the ECU wiring harness from its retaining clips, then disconnect the wiring harness connector from the ECU.

12 Using a forked tool or flat-bladed screwdriver, carefully lever the selector inner cable end fitting off the balljoint on the selector lever position switch. Pull back the retaining sleeve and detach the outer cable from the mounting bracket on the transmission (see illustration 4.7).

13 Unscrew the retaining nut and remove the lever from the transmission selector shaft.

14 Unscrew and remove the three mounting bolts, then carefully lift the ECU upwards and remove it from the transmission (see illustration). Take great care not to damage the wiring connector pins on the underside of the ECU as it is lifted off.

Refitting

15 Prior to refitting, first make sure that the transmission selector shaft is still in the N (neutral) position. If there is any doubt, temporarily engage the selector shaft lever with the transmission selector shaft and move the lever fully forwards (to the P position) then move it two notches backwards.

16 Set the selector lever position switch on the ECU to the N position by turning the switch until the two arrows are aligned.

17 Check that the transmission wiring harness is correctly located, then carefully place the ECU in position. Take great care not to damage the wiring connector pins as the ECU is fitted.

18 Refit the three bolts and tighten to the specified torque.

19 Refit the selector lever to the shaft and tighten its retaining nut to the specified torque.

20 Refit the selector outer cable to the mounting bracket on the transmission. Engage the selector inner cable end fitting with the balljoint on the selector lever, squeezing them together with pliers if necessary.

21 Reconnect the ECU wiring harness connector, then secure the harness in its retaining clips.

22 Clip the pre/post-heating system control unit wiring harness to the battery box support.

23 Refit the battery box and battery as described in Chapter 5A.

12 Automatic transmission – removal and refitting

Note: *New torque converter-to-driveplate bolts will be required for refitting.*

Removal

1 Apply the handbrake, then jack up the front of the vehicle and support it on axle stands (see *Jacking and vehicle support*). Allow sufficient working room to remove the transmission from under the left-hand side of the engine compartment. Remove both front roadwheels then, on diesel engine models, undo the retaining bolts and screws and remove the undertray from beneath the engine. Also remove the engine top cover where fitted.

2 Remove the battery, battery box, and starter motor as described in Chapter 5A.

3 Remove the air cleaner housing and intake ducts as described in the relevant Part of Chapter 4.

4 Remove the front bumper as described in Chapter 11.

5 Drain the transmission fluid as described in Section 2.

6 Using a forked tool or flat-bladed screwdriver, carefully lever the selector inner cable end fitting off the balljoint on the selector lever position switch. Pull back the retaining sleeve and detach the outer cable from the mounting bracket on the transmission.

7 On the AF23 transmissions, disconnect the transmission main wiring harness connector, then release the harness from the clips or ties securing it to the engine/transmission unit.

8 On the AF40 transmissions, unclip the pre/post-heating system control unit wiring harness from the battery box support. Release the ECU wiring harness from its retaining clips, then disconnect the wiring harness connector from the ECU.

9 Disconnect the breather hose (where fitted) from the top of the transmission unit.

10 Unscrew the central retaining bolt (or nut) and detach the fluid cooler pipes from the transmission. Suitably cover the pipe ends and plug the transmission orifices to prevent dirt entry.

11 Disconnect the inner ends of both driveshafts/intermediate shaft from the differential as described in Chapter 8. There is no need to disconnect the driveshafts from the swivel hub. Support the driveshafts by suspending them with wire or string – do not allow the driveshafts to hang down under their own weight, or the joints may be damaged.

12 Unscrew and remove the upper bolts securing the transmission to the rear of the engine. Where necessary, pull up the coolant hoses and secure them away from the transmission using plastic cable ties.

13 Remove the front subframe assembly as described in Chapter 10, ensuring that the engine unit is securely supported by connecting a hoist to the engine assembly. If available, the type of support bar which locates in the engine compartment side channels is to be preferred.

14 Unbolt and remove the front and rear engine/transmission mounting torque link brackets with reference to the relevant Part of Chapter 2.

15 Using a socket and extension bar, turn the crankshaft pulley until one of the bolts securing the torque converter to the driveplate becomes accessible through the starter motor aperture. Slacken and remove the bolt, then turn the crankshaft pulley as necessary and undo the remaining bolts as they become accessible. On the AF23 transmissions there are three securing bolts and on the AF40 transmissions there are six. Discard the bolts, new ones must be used on refitting.

16 Place a jack with a block of wood beneath the transmission, and raise the jack to take the weight of the transmission.

17 Unbolt and remove the left-hand engine/transmission mounting bracket from the transmission with reference to the relevant Part of Chapter 2.

18 Lower the engine and transmission by approximately 5 cm making sure that the coolant hoses and wiring harnesses are not stretched.

19 Slacken and remove the remaining bolts securing the transmission to the engine and sump flange. Note the correct fitted positions of each bolt, and the relevant brackets, as they are removed to use as a reference on refitting. Make a final check that all components have been disconnected, and are positioned clear of the transmission so that they will not hinder the removal procedure.

20 With all the bolts removed, move the trolley jack and transmission, to free it from its locating dowels. Once the transmission is free, lower the jack and manoeuvre the unit out from under the car, taking care to ensure that the torque converter does not fall off. Remove the locating dowels from the transmission or engine if they are loose, and keep them in a safe place. Retain the torque converter while the transmission is removed by bolting a strip of metal across the transmission bellhousing end face.

Refitting

21 The transmission is refitted by a reversal of the removal procedure, bearing in mind the following points.

a) Prior to refitting, remove all traces of old locking compound from the torque converter threads by running a tap of the correct thread diameter and pitch down the holes. In the absence of a suitable tap, use one of the old bolts with slots cut in its threads.

b) Ensure the engine/transmission locating

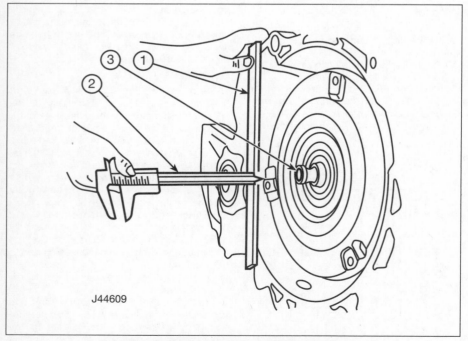

12.21 Check that the torque converter is fully entered

1 Straight-edge	*3 Torque converter centre stub*
2 Vernier calipers on bolt hole	

dowels are correctly positioned and apply a smear of molybdenum disulphide grease to the torque converter locating pin and its centering bush in the crankshaft end.

c) Check that the torque converter is fully entered inside the transmission bellhousing by measuring the distance from the flange to the bolt holes in the torque converter, using a straight-edge and vernier calipers **(see illustration)**. The distance must measure approximately 16.0 mm (AF23 transmissions) or 20.0 mm (AF40 transmissions).

d) Once the transmission and engine are correctly joined, refit the securing bolts, tightening them to the specified torque setting.

e) Fit the new torque converter-to-driveplate bolts and tighten them lightly only to start then go around and tighten them to the specified torque setting in a diagonal sequence.

f) Tighten all nuts and bolts to the specified torque (where given).

g) Renew the driveshaft oil seals (see Section 7) and refit the driveshafts/ intermediate shaft to the transmission as described in Chapter 8.

h) Refit the front subframe assembly as described in Chapter 10.

i) On completion, refill the transmission with the specified type and quantity of fluid as described in Section 2 and adjust the selector cable as described in Section 3.

13 Automatic transmission overhaul – general information

1 In the event of a fault occurring with the transmission, it is first necessary to determine whether it is of a mechanical, electrical or hydraulic nature, and to do this, special test equipment is required. It is therefore essential to have the work carried out by a Vauxhall/ Opel dealer or suitably-equipped specialist if a transmission fault is suspected.

2 Do not remove the transmission from the car for possible repair before professional fault diagnosis has been carried out, since most tests require the transmission to be in the vehicle.

Notes

Chapter 7 Part C:
Easytronic transmission

Contents

Degrees of difficulty

Easy, suitable for novice with little experience	Fairly easy, suitable for beginner with some experience	Fairly difficult, suitable for competent DIY mechanic	Difficult, suitable for experienced DIY mechanic	Very difficult, suitable for expert DIY or professional

Specifications

General

Type . . . . Five forward speeds and one reverse, automatic or manual selection. Integral differential

Manufacturer's designation . . . . F17+ MTA

Gear ratios

1st. 3.73:1
2nd 2.14:1
3rd 1.32:1
4th 0.89:1
5th 0.67:1
Reverse 3.31:1

Final drive ratio 4.19:1

Lubrication

Lubricant type . . . . See Lubricants and fluids
Lubricant capacity . . . . See Chapter 1A

Torque wrench settings

	Nm	lbf ft
Differential lower cover plate bolts.	18	13
Clutch module with MTA control unit	11	8
Engine/transmission mountings.	See Chapter 2A	
Reversing light switch	20	15
Transmission oil filler/level plug:		
Stage 1.	4	3
Stage 2.	Angle-tighten a further 45°	
Stage 3.	Angle-tighten a further 135°	
Transmission shift module	11	8
Transmission-to-engine bolts.	See Chapter 2A	

1 General information

1 The Easytronic MTA transmission (Manual Transmission Automatic-shift) is essentially a conventional manual transmission with the addition of a clutch module and shift module, used in conjunction with a self-adjusting clutch plate **(see illustration)**.

2 The description of the MTA transmission is basically as for the manual transmission given in Chapter 7A, but with an electronically-operated hydraulic clutch control module and gear selection module. The transmission can be switched between fully-automatic and manual mode, even while driving.

3 The clutch control module incorporates its own master cylinder and pushrod, which is operated electrically by a worm gear.

4 The gear selection module is fitted with a shifting motor and a selector motor, which together position the selector lever to move the selector forks in the transmission. It is located in exactly the same position as the gear selection cover fitted to the conventional manual transmission.

5 Since the transmission is electronically-controlled, in the event of a problem, in the first instance the vehicle should be taken to a Vauxhall/Opel dealer or diagnostic specialist who will have the TECH2 diagnostic

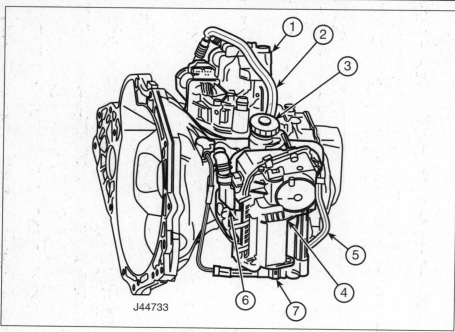

1.1 Easytronic (MTA) transmission

1 Transmission shift module
2 Wiring harness
3 Hydraulic fluid reservoir
4 Clutch control module
5 Hydraulic supply line to clutch control module
6 Wiring harness for clutch control module
7 Hydraulic pressure line to clutch release cylinder

equipment (or equivalent) necessary to pin-point the faulty area. Note also that if the transmission assembly, shift module or clutch module are renewed, the vehicle must be taken to a Vauxhall/Opel dealer or diagnostic specialist in order to have the fault memory erased and new parameters programmed into the ECU.

2 Transmission oil – draining and refilling

1 This operation is much more efficient if the car is first taken on a journey of sufficient length to warm the engine/transmission up to normal operating temperature.

Caution: If the procedure is to be carried out on a hot transmission unit, take care not to burn yourself on the hot exhaust or the transmission/engine unit.

2 Position the vehicle over an inspection pit, on vehicle ramps, or jack it up and support it securely on axle stands (see *Jacking and vehicle support*), but make sure that it is level.

Draining

Note: *A new differential lower cover plate gasket will be required for this operation.*

3 Since the transmission oil is not renewed as part of the manufacturer's maintenance schedule, no drain plug is fitted to the transmission. If for any reason the transmission needs to be drained, the only way of doing so is to remove the differential lower cover plate.

4 Wipe clean the area around the differential lower cover plate and position a suitable container underneath the cover plate.

5 Evenly and progressively slacken and remove the retaining bolts then withdraw the cover plate and allow the transmission oil to drain into the container (see illustration). Remove the gasket and discard it; a new one should be used on refitting.

6 Allow the oil to drain completely into the container. If the oil is hot, take precautions against scalding. Remove all traces of dirt and oil from the cover plate and transmission mating surfaces and wipe clean the inside of the cover plate.

7 Once the oil has finished draining, ensure the mating surfaces are clean and dry then refit the cover plate to the transmission unit, complete with a new gasket. Refit the retaining bolts and evenly and progressively tighten them to the specified torque.

Refilling

8 Wipe clean the area around the filler/level plug. The filler/level plug is located behind the driveshaft inner joint on the left-hand side of the transmission **(see illustration)**. Unscrew the plug and clean it.

9 Refill the transmission via the filler/level plug orifice with the specified type of oil until it begins to trickle out of the orifice. Once the oil level is correct, refit the filler/level plug and tighten to the specified torque.

10 On completion, lower the vehicle to the ground.

3 Selector lever assembly – removal and refitting

Removal

1 Remove the centre console as described in Chapter 11.

2 Disconnect the wiring from the selector lever.

3 Unscrew the mounting bolts and withdraw the selector lever assembly from the floor.

Refitting

4 Refitting is a reversal of removal.

4 Transmission shift module – removal and refitting

Removal

1 Switch on the ignition, then depress the footbrake pedal and move the selector lever to position N. Switch off the ignition.

2 Remove the battery and battery box as described in Chapter 5A.

3 Disconnect the two wiring plugs and release the harness from the support cable ties on the top of the transmission.

4 Unbolt and remove the transmission shift

2.5 Differential cover plate securing bolts (arrowed)

2.8 Transmission oil filler/level plug (arrowed)

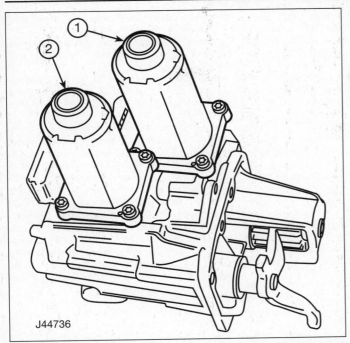

4.5 Shift motor (1) and selector motor (2) on the transmission shift module

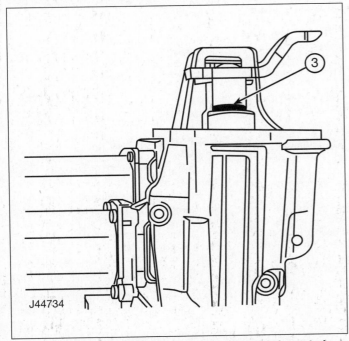

4.7b Groove (3) visible when the shift module is in neutral

4.7a Neutral mark (1) and shift lever shaft (2) on the transmission shift module

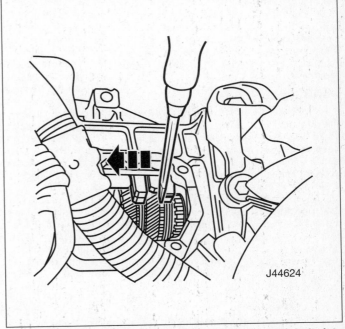

4.7c Using a screwdriver to move the transmission shift forks into neutral

module from the top of the transmission. To do this, lift it and tilt it slightly forwards before removing. Recover the gasket.

5 If the module cannot be removed because of internal jamming, unbolt the selector motor followed by the shifting motor **(see illustration)**, and use a screwdriver to move the selector lever to its neutral position first.

The selector motor is the uppermost unit.
Note: *The manufacturers recommend that the shift module assembly is never re-used if dismantled.*

Refitting

6 Clean the gasket faces of the module and transmission, and obtain a new gasket.

7 Make sure that the selector lever is in neutral, by checking that the mark on the segment is aligned with the pinion tooth. Check also that the lever is fully extended so that the annular groove is visible. The shift forks in the transmission must also be in neutral – use a screwdriver to move them if necessary **(see illustrations)**.

8 Refit the shift module together with a new gasket, then insert the bolts and tighten to the specified torque.

9 Reconnect the wiring and secure with new cable ties.

10 Refit the battery box and battery as described in Chapter 5A.

11 Finally, it may be necessary to have a Vauxhall/Opel dealer or diagnostic specialist reprogramme all volatile control unit memories. If a new control unit has been fitted, a Vauxhall/Opel dealer or diagnostic specialist must program the unit specifically for the model to which it is fitted.

5 Clutch module with MTA control unit – removal and refitting

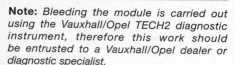

Note: *Bleeding the module is carried out using the Vauxhall/Opel TECH2 diagnostic instrument, therefore this work should be entrusted to a Vauxhall/Opel dealer or diagnostic specialist.*

Removal

1 Apply the handbrake, then jack up the front of the vehicle and support it on axle stands (see *Jacking and vehicle support*).

2 Remove the battery and battery box as described in Chapter 5A.

3 Disconnect the wiring from the Easytronic transmission and release it from the cable tie supports.

4 Place a suitable container beneath the front of the transmission to catch spilt hydraulic fluid.

5 Fit a hose clamp to the hydraulic hose leading from the hydraulic fluid reservoir to the clutch control unit, then disconnect the hose.

6 Disconnect the hydraulic quick-release pressure hose from the clutch control unit.

7 Unscrew the mounting bolts and remove the clutch module with MTA control unit from the transmission.

Refitting

8 Refitting is a reversal of removal, but tighten the mounting bolts to the specified torque. Make sure that the quick-release pressure hose is fully engaged – it must make an audible sound. Bleed the hydraulic circuit. Finally, it may be necessary to reprogramme all volatile control unit memories. If a new control unit has been fitted, a Vauxhall/Opel dealer or diagnostic specialist must program the unit specifically for the model to which it is fitted.

6 Driveshaft oil seals – renewal

1 Apply the handbrake, then jack up the front of the vehicle and support it on axle stands (see *Jacking and vehicle support*). Remove the relevant front roadwheel.

2 Drain the transmission oil as described in Section 2 or be prepared for oil loss as the seal is changed.

3 Disconnect the inner end of the relevant driveshaft from the differential as described in Chapter 8. There is no need to disconnect the driveshaft from the swivel hub. Support the driveshaft by suspending it with wire or string – do not allow the driveshaft to hang down under its own weight, or the joints may be damaged.

4 Prise the now-exposed oil seal from the differential housing, using a screwdriver or similar instrument.

5 Smear the sealing lip of the new oil seal with a little transmission oil, then using a metal tube or socket of suitable diameter, drive the new seal into the differential casing until the outer surface of the seal is flush with the outer surface of the differential casing.

6 Reconnect the driveshaft to the differential as described in Chapter 8.

7 Refill or top-up the transmission oil level with reference to Section 2.

8 Refit the roadwheel, then lower the vehicle to the ground.

7 Easytronic transmission – removal and refitting

Removal

1 Apply the handbrake, then jack up the front of the vehicle and support it on axle stands (see *Jacking and vehicle support*). Allow sufficient working room to remove the transmission from under the left-hand side of the engine compartment. Remove both front roadwheels and also the engine top cover where fitted.

2 Remove the battery and battery box as described in Chapter 5A.

3 Drain the transmission oil as described in Section 2 or be prepared for oil loss as the transmission is removed.

4 Attach a suitable hoist and lifting tackle to the lifting bracket(s) located on the left-hand side of the cylinder head, and support the weight of the engine/transmission.

5 Refer to Chapter 10 and remove the front subframe.

6 Disconnect the inner ends of both driveshafts from the differential as described in Chapter 8. There is no need to disconnect the driveshafts from the swivel hub. Support the driveshafts by suspending them with wire or string – do not allow the driveshafts to hang down under their own weight, or the joints may be damaged.

7 Disconnect the wiring from the transmission clutch and shift modules, and release the wiring from the support cables.

8 Place a jack with a block of wood beneath the transmission, and raise the jack to take the weight of the transmission.

9 Unbolt the left-hand engine/transmission mounting bracket from the transmission with reference to Chapter 2A.

10 Lower the engine and transmission by approximately 5 cm making sure that the coolant hoses and wiring harnesses are not stretched.

11 Unscrew and remove the upper bolts securing the transmission to the rear of the engine. Where necessary, pull up the coolant hoses and secure them away from the transmission using plastic cable ties.

12 Slacken and remove the remaining bolts securing the transmission to the engine and sump flange. Note the correct fitted positions of each bolt, and the relevant brackets, as they are removed to use as a reference on refitting. Make a final check that all components have been disconnected, and are positioned clear of the transmission so that they will not hinder the removal procedure.

13 With the bolts removed, move the trolley jack and transmission to free it from its locating dowels. Once the transmission is free, lower the jack and manoeuvre the unit out from under the car. Remove the locating dowels from the transmission or engine if they are loose, and keep them in a safe place.

Refitting

14 The transmission is refitted by a reversal of the removal procedure, bearing in mind the following points.

a) Tighten all nuts and bolts to the specified torque (where given).
b) Renew the driveshaft oil seals (see Section 6) before refitting the driveshafts.
c) Refit the front subframe assembly with reference to Chapter 10.
d) Refill or top-up the transmission with the specified type and quantity of oil, as described in Section 2.
e) Finally, it may be necessary to have a dealer or diagnostic specialist reprogramme all volatile control unit memories.

8 Easytronic transmission overhaul – general information

In the event of a fault occurring on the transmission, it is first necessary to determine whether it is of an electrical, mechanical or hydraulic nature, and to achieve this, special test equipment is required. It is therefore essential to have the work carried out by a Vauxhall/Opel dealer if a transmission fault is suspected.

Do not remove the transmission from the car for possible repair before professional fault diagnosis has been carried out, since most tests require the transmission to be in the vehicle.

Chapter 8
Driveshafts

Contents

Degrees of difficulty

Easy, suitable for novice with little experience	**Fairly easy,** suitable for beginner with some experience	**Fairly difficult,** suitable for competent DIY mechanic	**Difficult,** suitable for experienced DIY mechanic	**Very difficult,** suitable for expert DIY or professional

Specifications

General
Driveshaft type . . . . Solid steel shafts with inner and outer constant velocity (CV) joints. Right-hand driveshaft incorporating intermediate shaft (except on 1.8 litre petrol engine models)

Lubrication (overhaul only – see text)
Lubricant type/specification . . . . Use only special grease supplied in sachets with gaiter kits – joints are otherwise pre-packed with grease and sealed

Torque wrench settings

	Nm	lbf ft
Anti-roll bar connecting link retaining nut*	65	48
Driveshaft retaining nut:*		
Stage 1	150	111
Stage 2	Slacken the nut by 45°	
Stage 3	250	185
Intermediate shaft bearing housing to support bracket	18	13
Lower arm balljoint clamp bolt nut:*		
Stage 1	30	22
Stage 2	Angle-tighten a further 60°	
Stage 3	Angle-tighten a further 15°	
Roadwheels	110	81
Track rod end to swivel hub*	35	26

* Use new nuts/bolts.

2.3 Where fitted, tap off the driveshaft retaining nut dust cap

1 General information

Drive is transmitted from the differential to the front wheels by means of two, unequal-length driveshafts.

Both driveshafts are splined at their outer ends to accept the wheel hubs, and are threaded so that each hub can be fastened by a large nut. The inner end of each driveshaft is splined to accept the intermediate shaft or differential sun gear and is held in place by an internal circlip.

Constant velocity (CV) joints are fitted to each end of the driveshafts, to ensure the smooth and efficient transmission of drive at all the angles possible as the roadwheels move up-and-down with the suspension, and as they turn from side-to-side under steering.

2.6 Unscrew the retaining nut, then use a balljoint separator tool to remove the track rod end from the swivel hub

2.8a Unscrew the retaining nut (arrowed) . . .

A tool to hold the wheel hub stationary whilst the driveshaft retaining nut is slackened can be fabricated from two lengths of steel strip (one long, one short) and a nut and bolt; the nut and bolt forming the pivot of a forked tool.

Both inner and outer constant velocity joints are of the ball-and-cage type.

The right-hand driveshaft has an intermediate shaft attached to the rear of the cylinder block on all except 1.8 litre petrol engine models.

2 Driveshaft – removal and refitting

Note: *A new driveshaft retaining nut, inner joint circlip, lower arm balljoint clamp bolt and nut, anti-roll bar connecting link retaining nut*

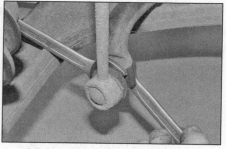

2.7 Unscrew the nut securing the connecting link to the anti-roll bar, while holding the link stub with a further spanner

2.8b . . . and withdraw the clamp bolt from the swivel hub

and a new track rod end retaining nut will be needed for refitting. The driveshaft outer joint splines may be a tight fit in the hub and it is possible that a puller/extractor will be required to draw the hub assembly off the driveshaft during removal.

Removal

1 Firmly apply the handbrake, then jack up the front of the car and support it securely on axle stands (see *Jacking and vehicle support*). Remove the relevant front roadwheel.

2 On diesel engine models, undo the retaining bolts and screws and remove the undertray from beneath the engine.

3 Where fitted, tap off the driveshaft retaining nut dust cap using a cold chisel or large screwdriver **(see illustration)**.

4 To prevent rotation of the wheel hub as the driveshaft retaining nut is slackened, make up a holding tool and bolt the tool to the wheel hub using two wheel bolts **(see Tool Tip)**.

5 With the holding tool in place, slacken and remove the driveshaft retaining nut using a socket and long bar. Where necessary, support the socket on an axle stand to prevent it slipping off the nut. This nut is very tight; make sure that there is no risk of pulling the car off the axle stands as the nut is slackened.

6 Unscrew the nut securing the track rod end to the steering arm on the swivel hub, then use a balljoint separator tool to remove the track rod end **(see illustration)**.

7 Unscrew and remove the nut securing the connecting link to the anti-roll bar, while holding the link stub on the flats provided with a further spanner **(see illustration)**. Release the link from the anti-roll bar and move it to one side.

8 Unscrew the nut and remove the clamp bolt securing the front suspension lower arm to the swivel hub. Note that the bolt head faces the front of the vehicle **(see illustrations)**.

9 Using a lever, push down on the suspension lower arm to free the balljoint from the swivel hub, then move the swivel hub to one side and release the arm, taking care not to damage the balljoint rubber boot **(see illustration)**. It is advisable to place a protective cover over the rubber boot such as the plastic cap from an aerosol can, suitably cut to fit.

10 The hub must now be freed from the end

2.9 Push down the lower suspension arm to free the balljoint from the swivel hub

of the driveshaft (see illustration). It may be possible to pull the hub off the driveshaft, but if the end of the driveshaft is tight in the hub, temporarily refit the driveshaft retaining nut to protect the driveshaft threads, then tap the end of the driveshaft with a soft-faced hammer while pulling outwards on the swivel hub. Alternatively, use a suitable puller to press the driveshaft through the hub.

11 With the driveshaft detached from the swivel hub, tie the suspension strut to one side and support the driveshaft on an axle stand.

12 If working on the left-hand driveshaft (or the right-hand driveshaft on 1.8 litre petrol models), place a suitable container beneath the differential, to collect escaping transmission oil/fluid when the driveshaft is withdrawn.

13 Using a stout bar, release the inner end of the driveshaft from the differential or intermediate shaft. Lever between the constant velocity joint and differential housing, or between the constant velocity joint and intermediate shaft bearing housing, to release the driveshaft retaining circlip (see illustration).

14 Withdraw the driveshaft, ensuring that the constant velocity joints are not placed under excessive strain, and remove the driveshaft from beneath the vehicle. Whilst the driveshaft is removed, plug or tape over the differential aperture to prevent dirt entry.

Caution: Do not allow the vehicle to rest on its wheels with one or both driveshafts removed, as damage to the wheel bearings(s) may result. If the vehicle must be moved on its wheels, clamp the wheel bearings using spacers and a long threaded rod to take the place of the driveshaft.

Refitting

15 Before refitting the driveshaft, examine the oil seal in the transmission housing and renew it if necessary as described in the relevant Part of Chapter 7.

16 Remove the circlip from the end of the driveshaft inner joint splines, or from the end of the intermediate shaft (as applicable) and discard it. Fit a new circlip, making sure it is correctly located in the groove.

17 Thoroughly clean the driveshaft splines, intermediate shaft splines (where applicable), and the apertures in the transmission and hub assembly. Apply a thin film of grease to the oil seal lips, and to the driveshaft splines and shoulders. Check that all gaiter clips are securely fastened.

18 Offer up the driveshaft, and engage the inner joint splines with those of the differential sun gear or intermediate shaft, taking care not to damage the oil seal. Push the joint fully into position, then check that the circlip is correctly located and securely holds the joint in position. If necessary, use a soft-faced mallet or drift to drive the driveshaft inner joint fully into position.

19 Align the outer constant velocity joint

2.10 Pull the swivel hub outwards then withdraw the driveshaft from the hub splines

splines with those of the hub, and slide the joint back into position in the hub.

20 Using a lever, push down on the lower suspension arm, then relocate the balljoint and release the arm. Make sure that the balljoint stub is fully entered in the swivel hub.

21 Insert a new lower arm balljoint clamp bolt with its head facing the front of the vehicle, fit a new retaining nut and tighten the nut to the specified torque in the stages given in the Specifications.

22 Refit the track rod end to the steering arm on the swivel hub and tighten the new nut to the specified torque.

23 Locate the connecting link on the anti-roll bar, fit a new retaining nut and tighten the nut to the specified torque.

24 Lubricate the inner face and threads of the new driveshaft retaining nut with clean engine oil, and refit it to the end of the driveshaft. Use the method employed on removal to prevent the hub from rotating, and tighten the driveshaft retaining nut to the specified torque in the stages given in the Specifications. Check that the hub rotates freely.

25 Where fitted, tap a new driveshaft retaining nut dust cap into position.

26 On diesel engine models, refit the engine undertray and secure with the retaining bolts and screws.

27 Refit the roadwheel, lower the vehicle to the ground and tighten the roadwheel bolts to the specified torque.

28 Check and if necessary top-up the transmission oil/fluid level, using the information given in the relevant Part of Chapter 7.

3.6 Intermediate shaft bearing housing retaining bolts (arrowed)

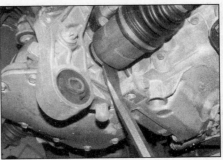

2.13 Using a stout bar, release the inner end of the driveshaft from the differential or intermediate shaft

3 Intermediate shaft – removal and refitting

Note 1: *An intermediate shaft is not fitted to 1.8 litre petrol engine models.*

Note 2: *A new driveshaft inner joint circlip, lower arm balljoint clamp bolt and nut, anti-roll bar connecting link retaining nut and a new track rod end retaining nut will be needed for refitting.*

Removal

1 Firmly apply the handbrake, then jack up the front of the car and support it securely on axle stands (see *Jacking and vehicle support*). Remove the right-hand front roadwheel.

2 On diesel engine models, undo the retaining bolts and screws and remove the undertray from beneath the engine.

3 Carry out the operations described in paragraphs 6 to 9 of Section 2.

4 Using a stout bar, release the inner end of the driveshaft from the intermediate shaft. Lever between the constant velocity joint and intermediate shaft bearing housing, to release the driveshaft retaining circlip. Support the driveshaft to one side.

5 Place a suitable container beneath the differential, to collect escaping transmission oil/fluid when the intermediate shaft is withdrawn.

6 Undo the three bolts securing the intermediate shaft bearing housing to the support bracket on the cylinder block (see illustration). Pull the intermediate shaft out of the transmission, slide it through the support bracket and remove the shaft from under the car.

Refitting

7 Before refitting the intermediate shaft, examine the oil seal in the transmission housing and renew it if necessary as described in the relevant Part of Chapter 7.

8 Remove the circlip from the end of the driveshaft inner joint splines, or from the end of the intermediate shaft (as applicable) and discard it. Fit a new circlip, making sure it is correctly located in the groove.

9 Thoroughly clean the driveshaft splines,

4.3 Extract the circlip (arrowed) securing the intermediate shaft in the bearing

intermediate shaft splines, and the aperture in the transmission. Apply a thin film of grease to the oil seal lips, and to the driveshaft and intermediate shaft splines and shoulders.

10 Insert the intermediate shaft into the transmission, engaging the splines with the differential sun gear, taking care not to damage the oil seal.

11 Refit the three bolts securing the intermediate shaft bearing housing to the support bracket on the cylinder block. Tighten the bolts to the specified torque.

12 Locate the driveshaft inner joint on the intermediate shaft splines, then use a soft-metal drift to drive the joint onto the intermediate shaft until it is retained by the circlip.

13 Using a lever, push down on the lower suspension arm, then relocate the balljoint and release the arm. Make sure that the balljoint stub is fully entered in the swivel hub.

14 Insert a new lower arm balljoint clamp bolt with its head facing the front of the vehicle, fit a new retaining nut and tighten the nut to the specified torque in the stages given in the Specifications.

15 Refit the track rod end to the steering arm on the swivel hub and tighten the new nut to the specified torque.

16 Locate the connecting link on the anti-roll bar, fit a new retaining nut and tighten the nut to the specified torque.

17 On diesel engine models, refit the engine undertray and secure with the retaining bolts and screws.

18 Refit the roadwheel, lower the vehicle to the ground and tighten the roadwheel bolts to the specified torque.

19 Check and if necessary top-up the transmission oil/fluid level, using the information given in the relevant Part of Chapter 7.

4 Intermediate shaft bearing – renewal

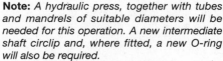

Note: *A hydraulic press, together with tubes and mandrels of suitable diameters will be needed for this operation. A new intermediate shaft circlip and, where fitted, a new O-ring will also be required.*

1 Remove the intermediate shaft as described in Section 3.

2 Where fitted, remove the O-ring from the end of the intermediate shaft.

3 Using circlip pliers, or a small screwdriver,

extract the circlip securing the intermediate shaft in the bearing **(see illustration)**.

4 Support the underside of the bearing housing on the press bed and press the intermediate shaft downwards out of the bearing.

5 With the intermediate shaft removed, press the bearing out of the housing using a suitable mandrel.

6 Locate the new bearing in the housing and press it fully into position using a suitable tube in contact with the bearing outer race.

7 With the bearing supported on its inner race, press the intermediate shaft back into the bearing until it is fully engaged.

8 Secure the intermediate shaft with a new circlip then, where applicable, fit a new O-ring to the end of the shaft.

9 On completion, refit the intermediate shaft as described in Section 3.

5 Driveshaft joint gaiters – renewal

Outer CV joint

1 Remove the driveshaft from the car as described in Section 2, then secure the shaft in a vice equipped with soft jaws.

2 Release the rubber gaiter inner and outer retaining clips by cutting through them using a junior hacksaw **(see illustration)**. Spread the clips and remove them from the gaiter.

3 Slide the rubber gaiter down the shaft to expose the CV joint or, alternatively, cut the gaiter open using a suitable knife and remove it from the driveshaft **(see illustration)**.

4 Using old rags, clean away as much of the old grease as possible from the CV joint. It is advisable to wear disposable rubber gloves during this operation.

5 The outer CV joint will be retained on the driveshaft either by an external snap-ring, or by an internal circlip **(see illustration)**. If an external snap-ring is fitted, use circlip pliers to expand the snap-ring as the CV joint is removed.

6 Using a mallet, sharply strike the edge of the outer joint to drive it off the end of the shaft **(see illustrations)**.

7 Once the joint has been removed, extract

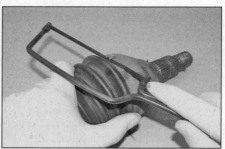

5.2 Release the rubber gaiter retaining clips by cutting through them using a hacksaw

5.3 Cut the gaiter open using a suitable knife and remove it from the driveshaft

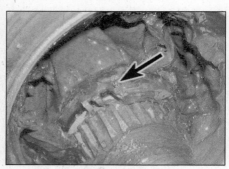

5.5 Outer CV joint snap-ring (B) and driveshaft groove (A)

5.6a Sharply strike the edge of the outer joint to drive it off the end of the shaft

5.6b If an external snap-ring is fitted, use circlip pliers to expand the snap-ring as the joint is removed

5.7 Removing the circlip from the groove in the driveshaft splines

5.12 Components required for driveshaft gaiter renewal

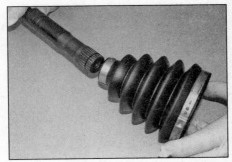

5.13 Slide the new rubber gaiter and retaining clips onto the driveshaft

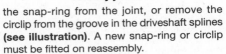

5.14a Fit a new snap-ring to the constant velocity joint . . .

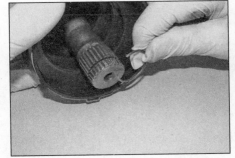

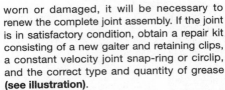

5.14b . . . or a new circlip to the groove in the driveshaft

5.15 Pack the joint with the grease supplied in the repair kit

the snap-ring from the joint, or remove the circlip from the groove in the driveshaft splines **(see illustration)**. A new snap-ring or circlip must be fitted on reassembly.

8 If still in place, withdraw the rubber gaiter from the driveshaft.

9 With the CV joint removed from the driveshaft, wipe away the remaining grease (do not use any solvent) to allow the joint components to be inspected.

10 Move the inner splined driving member from side-to-side, to expose each ball in turn at the top of its track. Examine the balls for cracks, flat spots, or signs of surface pitting.

11 Inspect the ball tracks on the inner and outer members. If the tracks have widened, the balls will no longer be a tight fit. At the same time, check the ball cage windows for wear or cracking between the windows.

12 If on inspection any of the constant velocity joint components are found to be

worn or damaged, it will be necessary to renew the complete joint assembly. If the joint is in satisfactory condition, obtain a repair kit consisting of a new gaiter and retaining clips, a constant velocity joint snap-ring or circlip, and the correct type and quantity of grease **(see illustration)**.

13 Slide the new rubber gaiter and retaining clips onto the driveshaft **(see illustration)**.

14 Fit a new snap-ring to the constant velocity joint, or a new circlip to the groove in the driveshaft, as applicable **(see illustrations)**.

15 Pack the joint with the grease supplied in the repair kit **(see illustration)**. Work the grease well into the bearing tracks whilst twisting the joint, and fill the rubber gaiter with any excess.

16 Screw on the driveshaft retaining nut two or three turns to protect the threads, then engage the joint with the driveshaft splines. Tap the joint onto the driveshaft until the

snap-ring or circlip engages in its groove **(see illustration)**. Make sure that the joint is securely retained, by pulling on the joint, not the shaft.

17 Ease the gaiter over the joint, and ensure that the gaiter lips are correctly located in the grooves on both the driveshaft and constant velocity joint. Lift the outer sealing lip of the gaiter, to equalise air pressure within the gaiter.

18 Pull the large gaiter retaining clip as tight as possible, and locate the hooks on the clip in their slots. Remove any slack in the gaiter retaining clip by carefully compressing the raised section of the clip. In the absence of the special tool, a pair of side-cutters may be used. Secure the small retaining clip using the same procedure **(see illustrations)**.

19 Check that the constant velocity joint moves freely in all directions, then refit the driveshaft to the car as described in Section 2.

5.16 Tap the joint onto the driveshaft until the snap-ring or circlip engages in its groove

5.18a Secure the large gaiter retaining clip in position by compressing the raised section of the clip

5.18b The small inner retaining clip is secured in the same way

5.21a Remove the circlip from the groove in the inner CV joint splines . . .

5.21b . . . then, where fitted, slide off the rubber dust cover

5.22 Cut off the rubber gaiter retaining clips, then slide the gaiter down the shaft

5.24 Clean away as much of the old grease as possible from the CV joint

5.25a Expand the joint retaining snap-ring using circlip pliers . . .

5.25b . . . then remove the joint by tapping it off the driveshaft with a hammer and punch

Inner CV joint

20 Remove the driveshaft from the car as described in Section 2, then secure the shaft in a vice equipped with soft jaws.

21 Remove the circlip from the groove in the CV joint splines then, where fitted, slide off the rubber dust cover **(see illustrations)**. Note that a new circlip must be fitted on reassembly.

22 Release the rubber gaiter inner and outer retaining clips by cutting through them using a junior hacksaw **(see illustration)**. Spread the clips and remove them from the gaiter.

23 Slide the rubber gaiter down the shaft to expose the CV joint.

24 Using old rags, clean away as much of the old grease as possible from the CV joint **(see illustration)**. It is advisable to wear disposable rubber gloves during this operation.

25 Expand the CV joint retaining snap-ring using circlip pliers, then remove the joint by tapping it off the driveshaft with a hammer and

punch in contact with the joint inner member **(see illustrations)**.

26 Once the joint has been removed, extract the snap-ring noting that a new snap-ring must be fitted on reassembly.

27 Withdraw the rubber gaiter from the driveshaft.

28 With the CV joint removed from the driveshaft, wipe away the remaining grease (do not use any solvent) and inspect the joint components as described previously in paragraphs 10 and 11.

29 If on inspection any of the constant velocity joint components are found to be worn or damaged, it will be necessary to renew the complete joint assembly. If the joint is in satisfactory condition, obtain a repair kit consisting of a new gaiter and retaining clips, a constant velocity joint snap-ring and circlip, and the correct type and quantity of grease.

30 Slide the new rubber gaiter and retaining clips onto the driveshaft **(see illustration)**.

31 Fit a new snap-ring to the constant velocity joint, then engage the joint with the driveshaft splines. Tap the joint onto the driveshaft until the snap-ring engages in its groove **(see illustration)**. Make sure that the joint is securely retained, by pulling on the joint, not the shaft.

32 Pack the joint with the grease supplied in the repair kit **(see illustration)**. Work the grease well into the bearing tracks whilst twisting the joint, and fill the rubber gaiter with any excess.

33 Ease the gaiter over the joint, and ensure that the gaiter lips are correctly located in the grooves on both the driveshaft and constant velocity joint. Lift the outer sealing lip of the gaiter, to equalise air pressure within the gaiter.

34 Pull the large gaiter retaining clip as tight as possible, and locate the hooks on the clip in their slots. Remove any slack in the gaiter retaining clip by carefully compressing the raised section of the clip. In the absence of

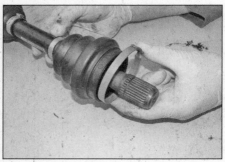

5.30 Slide the new rubber gaiter and retaining clips onto the driveshaft

5.31 Tap the joint onto the driveshaft until the snap-ring engages in its groove

5.32 Pack the joint with the grease supplied in the repair kit

the special tool, a pair of side-cutters may be used. Secure the small retaining clip using the same procedure **(see illustrations)**.

35 Where applicable, slide the rubber dust cover onto the CV joint, then fit a new circlip to the groove in the joint splines.

36 Check that the constant velocity joint moves freely in all directions, then refit the driveshaft to the car as described in Section 2.

6 Driveshaft overhaul – general information

1 If any of the checks described in Chapter 1A or 1B reveal possible wear in any driveshaft joint, carry out the following procedures to identify the source of the problem.

2 Firmly apply the handbrake, then jack up the front of the vehicle and support it securely on axle stands (see *Jacking and vehicle support*).

3 Referring to the information contained in Section 2, make up a tool to hold the wheel hub, and bolt the tool to the hub. Use a torque

5.34a Secure the large gaiter retaining clip in position by compressing the raised section of the clip

5.34b The small inner retaining clip is secured in the same way

wrench to check that the driveshaft retaining nut is securely fastened, then repeat this check on the remaining driveshaft nut.

4 Road test the vehicle, and listen for a metallic clicking from the front as the vehicle is driven slowly in a circle on full-lock. If a clicking noise is heard, this indicates wear in the outer constant velocity joint.

5 If vibration, consistent with roadspeed, is felt through the car when accelerating, there is a possibility of wear in the inner constant velocity joints.

6 To check the joints for wear, remove the driveshafts, then dismantle them as described in Section 3; if any wear or free play is found, the affected joint must be renewed.

Chapter 9
Braking system

Contents

Degrees of difficulty

Easy, suitable for novice with little experience	**Fairly easy,** suitable for beginner with some experience	**Fairly difficult,** suitable for competent DIY mechanic	**Difficult,** suitable for experienced DIY mechanic	**Very difficult,** suitable for expert DIY or professional

Specifications

Front brakes

Type	Ventilated disc, with single-piston sliding caliper
Disc diameter...	285.0 mm
Disc thickness:	
New	25.0 mm
Minimum...	22.0 mm
Maximum disc run-out..................................	0.12 mm
Brake pad thickness:	
New (including backing plate)	20.0 mm
Minimum thickness (including backing plate).........	9.0 mm
Brake caliper piston diameter	57.0 mm

Rear Brakes

Type	Solid disc, with single-piston sliding caliper
Disc diameter...	278.0 mm
Disc thickness:	
New	12.0 mm
Minimum...	10.0 mm
Maximum disc run-out..................................	0.03 mm
Brake pad thickness:	
New (including backing plate)	17.0 mm
Minimum thickness (including backing plate).........	8.0 mm
Brake caliper piston diameter	38.0 mm

Handbrake

Type	Cable-operated, acting on rear brake calipers. Self-adjusting

ABS system type

Standard ABS system	EBC 430 EV
ABS with traction control...............................	EBC 430 EV/TC
ABS with electronic stability program	EBC 430 EV/ESP

Torque wrench settings

	Nm	lbf ft
ABS hydraulic modulator mounting bracket bolts	20	15
ABS hydraulic modulator to mounting bracket	10	7
Brake caliper bleed screws	6	4
Brake caliper guide bolts	30	22
Brake caliper mounting bracket bolts:*		
Front caliper mounting bracket bolts	230	170
Rear caliper mounting bracket bolts	130	96
Brake fluid pipe unions.	16	12
Brake hydraulic hose banjo union bolts	40	30
Brake pedal mounting bracket nuts*	20	15
Handbrake lever retaining nuts	10	7
Master cylinder retaining nuts*.	50	37
Roadwheel bolts.	110	81
Vacuum pump mounting bolts (diesel engines)	20	15
Vacuum servo unit stud bolts*	20	15

* Use new fasteners

1 General information

The braking system is of servo-assisted, dual-circuit hydraulic type split diagonally. The arrangement of the hydraulic system is such that each circuit operates one front and one rear brake from a tandem master cylinder. Under normal circumstances, both circuits operate in unison. However, in the event of hydraulic failure in one circuit, full braking force will still be available at two wheels.

All models are fitted with front and rear disc brakes. The disc brakes are actuated by single-piston sliding type calipers, which ensure that equal pressure is applied to each disc pad.

An Anti-lock Braking System (ABS) is fitted as standard equipment to all vehicles covered in this manual. On higher specification models, the ABS may also incorporate traction control or an electronic stability program. Refer to Section 17 for further information on ABS operation.

The self-adjusting, cable-operated handbrake provides an independent mechanical means of rear brake application.

On diesel engine models, since there is no throttling as such of the inlet manifold, the manifold is not a suitable source of vacuum to operate the vacuum servo unit. The servo unit is therefore connected to a separate vacuum pump bolted to the left-hand end of the cylinder head and driven by the camshaft.

Warning: When servicing any part of the system, work carefully and methodically; also observe scrupulous cleanliness when overhauling any part of the hydraulic system. Always renew components (in axle sets, where applicable) if in doubt about their condition, and use only genuine Vauxhall/Opel parts, or at least those of known good quality. Note the warnings given in 'Safety first!' and at relevant points in this Chapter concerning the dangers of asbestos dust and hydraulic fluid.

2 Hydraulic system – bleeding

Warning: Hydraulic fluid is poisonous; wash off immediately and thoroughly in the case of skin contact, and seek immediate medical advice if any fluid is swallowed or gets into the eyes. Certain types of hydraulic fluid are inflammable, and may ignite when allowed into contact with hot components; when servicing any hydraulic system, it is safest to assume that the fluid is inflammable, and to take precautions against the risk of fire as though it is petrol that is being handled. Hydraulic fluid is also an effective paint stripper, and will attack plastics; if any is spilt, it should be washed off immediately, using copious quantities of fresh water. Finally, it is hygroscopic (it absorbs moisture from the air) – old fluid may be contaminated and unfit for further use. When topping-up or renewing the fluid, always use the recommended type, and ensure that it comes from a freshly-opened sealed container.

General

1 The correct operation of any hydraulic system is only possible after removing all air from the components and circuit; this is achieved by bleeding the system.

2 During the bleeding procedure, add only clean, unused hydraulic fluid of the recommended type; never re-use fluid that has already been bled from the system. Ensure that sufficient fluid is available before starting work.

3 If there is any possibility of incorrect fluid being already in the system, the brake components and circuit must be flushed completely with uncontaminated, correct fluid, and new seals should be fitted to the various components.

4 If hydraulic fluid has been lost from the system, or air has entered because of a leak, ensure that the fault is cured before proceeding further.

5 Park the vehicle over an inspection pit or on car ramps. Alternatively, apply the handbrake then jack up the front and rear of the vehicle and support it on axle stands (see *Jacking and vehicle support*). For improved access with the vehicle jacked up, remove the roadwheels.

6 Check that all pipes and hoses are secure, unions tight and bleed screws closed. Clean any dirt from around the bleed screws.

7 Unscrew the master cylinder reservoir cap, and top the master cylinder reservoir up to the MAX level line; refit the cap loosely, and remember to maintain the fluid level at least above the MIN level line throughout the procedure, otherwise there is a risk of further air entering the system.

8 There are a number of one-man, do-it-yourself brake bleeding kits currently available from motor accessory shops. It is recommended that one of these kits is used whenever possible, as they greatly simplify the bleeding operation, and also reduce the risk of expelled air and fluid being drawn back into the system. If such a kit is not available, the basic (two-man) method must be used, which is described in detail below.

Caution: Vauxhall recommend using a pressure bleeding kit for this operation (see paragraphs 24 to 27).

9 If a kit is to be used, prepare the vehicle as described previously, and follow the kit manufacturer's instructions, as the procedure may vary slightly according to the type being used; generally, they are as outlined below in the relevant sub-section.

10 Whichever method is used, the same sequence should be followed (paragraphs 11 and 12) to ensure the removal of all air from the system.

Bleeding sequence

11 If the system has been only partially disconnected, and suitable precautions were taken to minimise fluid loss, it should only be necessary to bleed that part of the system (ie, the primary or secondary circuit). If the master cylinder or main brake lines have been disconnected, then the complete system must be bled.

12 The manufacturer does not give any sequence for bleeding the brake circuit, however, we recommend the following for right-hand drive models; for left-hand drive models, bleed the opposite sides:

 a) *Left-hand rear brake.*
 b) *Right-hand front brake.*
 c) *Right-hand rear brake.*
 d) *Left-hand front brake.*

Bleeding

Basic (two-man) method

13 Collect together a clean glass jar, a suitable length of plastic or rubber tubing which is a tight fit over the bleed screw, and a ring spanner to fit the screw. The help of an assistant will also be required.

14 Remove the dust cap from the first bleed screw in the sequence **(see illustrations)**. Fit the spanner and tube to the screw, place the other end of the tube in the jar, and pour in sufficient fluid to cover the end of the tube.

15 Ensure that the master cylinder reservoir fluid level is maintained at least above the MIN level line throughout the procedure.

16 Have the assistant fully depress the brake pedal several times to build-up pressure, then maintain it on the final downstroke.

17 While pedal pressure is maintained, unscrew the bleed screw (approximately one turn) and allow the compressed fluid and air to flow into the jar. The assistant should maintain pedal pressure, following it down to the floor if necessary, and should not release it until instructed to do so. When the flow stops, tighten the bleed screw again, have the assistant release the pedal slowly, and recheck the reservoir fluid level.

18 Repeat the steps given in paragraphs 16 and 17 until the fluid emerging from the bleed screw is free from air bubbles. If the master cylinder has been drained and refilled, and air is being bled from the first screw in the sequence, allow approximately five seconds between cycles for the master cylinder passages to refill.

19 When no more air bubbles appear, securely tighten the bleed screw, remove the tube and spanner, and refit the dust cap. Do not overtighten the bleed screw.

20 Repeat the procedure on the remaining screws in the sequence, until all air is removed from the system and the brake pedal feels firm again.

Using a one-way valve kit

21 As the name implies, these kits consist of a length of tubing with a one-way valve fitted, to prevent expelled air and fluid being drawn back into the system; some kits include a translucent container, which can be positioned so that the air bubbles can be more easily seen flowing from the end of the tube.

22 The kit is connected to the bleed screw, which is then opened. The user returns to the driver's seat, depresses the brake pedal with a smooth, steady stroke, and slowly releases it; this is repeated until the expelled fluid is clear of air bubbles.

2.14a Remove the dust caps from the front . . .

23 Note that these kits simplify work so much that it is easy to forget the master cylinder reservoir fluid level; ensure that this is maintained at least above the MIN level line at all times.

Using a pressure-bleeding kit

24 These kits are usually operated by a reservoir of pressurised air contained in the spare tyre. However, note that it will probably be necessary to reduce the pressure to a lower level than normal; refer to the instructions supplied with the kit.

25 By connecting a pressurised, fluid-filled container to the master cylinder reservoir, bleeding can be carried out simply by opening each screw in turn (in the specified sequence), and allowing the fluid to flow out until no more air bubbles can be seen in the expelled fluid.

26 This method has the advantage that the large reservoir of fluid provides an additional safeguard against air being drawn into the system during bleeding.

27 Pressure-bleeding is particularly effective when bleeding 'difficult' systems, or when bleeding the complete system at the time of routine fluid renewal.

All methods

28 When bleeding is complete, and firm pedal feel is restored, wash off any spilt fluid, securely tighten the bleed screws, and refit the dust caps.

29 Check the hydraulic fluid level in the master cylinder reservoir, and top-up if necessary (see *Weekly checks*).

30 Discard any hydraulic fluid that has been

3.2a Pull out the spring clip . . .

2.14b . . . and rear bleed screws

bled from the system; it will not be fit for re-use.

31 Check the feel of the brake pedal. If it feels at all spongy, air must still be present in the system, and further bleeding is required. Failure to bleed satisfactorily after a reasonable repetition of the bleeding procedure may be due to worn master cylinder seals.

---

3 Hydraulic pipes and hoses – renewal

Note: *Before starting work, refer to the note at the beginning of Section 2 concerning the dangers of hydraulic fluid.*

1 If any pipe or hose is to be renewed, minimise fluid loss by first removing the master cylinder reservoir cap and screwing it down onto a piece of polythene. Alternatively, flexible hoses can be sealed, if required, using a proprietary brake hose clamp. Metal brake pipe unions can be plugged (if care is taken not to allow dirt into the system) or capped immediately they are disconnected. Place a wad of rag under any union that is to be disconnected, to catch any spilt fluid.

2 If a flexible hose is to be disconnected, unscrew the brake pipe union nut before removing the spring clip which secures the hose to its mounting bracket. Where applicable, unscrew the banjo union bolt securing the hose to the caliper and recover the copper washers. When removing the front flexible hose, pull out the spring clip and disconnect it from the strut **(see illustrations)**.

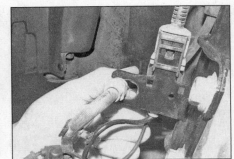

3.2b . . . and disconnect the hydraulic hose from the strut bracket

3 To unscrew union nuts, it is preferable to obtain a brake pipe spanner of the correct size; these are available from most motor accessory shops. Failing this, a close-fitting open-ended spanner will be required, though if the nuts are tight or corroded, their flats may be rounded-off if the spanner slips. In such a case, a self-locking wrench is often the only way to unscrew a stubborn union, but it follows that the pipe and the damaged nuts must be renewed on reassembly. Always clean a union and surrounding area before disconnecting it. If disconnecting a component with more than one union, make a careful note of the connections before disturbing any of them.

4 If a brake pipe is to be renewed, it can be obtained, cut to length and with the union nuts and end flares in place, from Vauxhall/Opel dealers. All that is then necessary is to bend it to shape, following the line of the original, before fitting it to the car. Alternatively, most motor accessory shops can make up brake pipes from kits, but this requires very careful measurement of the original, to ensure that the new one is of the correct length. The safest answer is usually to take the original to the shop as a pattern.

5 On refitting, do not overtighten the union nuts.

6 When refitting hoses to the calipers, always use new copper washers and tighten the banjo union bolts to the specified torque. Make sure that the hoses are positioned so that they will not touch surrounding bodywork or the roadwheels.

7 Ensure that the pipes and hoses are correctly routed, with no kinks, and that they are secured in the clips or brackets provided. After fitting, remove the polythene from the reservoir, and bleed the hydraulic system as described in Section 2. Wash off any spilt fluid, and check carefully for fluid leaks.

4 Front brake pads – renewal

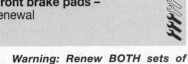

⚠️ **Warning: Renew BOTH sets of front brake pads at the same time – NEVER renew the pads on only one wheel, as uneven braking may result. Note that the dust created by wear of the pads may contain asbestos, which is a health hazard. Never blow it out with compressed air, and do not inhale any of it. An approved filtering mask should be worn when working on the brakes. DO NOT use petroleum-based solvents to clean brake parts – use brake cleaner or methylated spirit only.**

1 Apply the handbrake, then jack up the front of the vehicle and support it on axle stands (see *Jacking and vehicle support*). Remove the front roadwheels.

2 Push in the caliper piston by sliding the caliper body towards the outside of the vehicle by hand.

3 Follow the accompanying photos **(illustrations 4.3a to 4.3ab)** for the actual pad renewal procedure, bearing in mind the additional points listed below. Be sure to stay in order and read the caption under each illustration. Note that if the old pads are to be refitted, ensure that they are identified so that they can be returned to their original positions.

4 After removing the caliper from the mounting bracket, tie it to the suspension strut using a cable tie or suitable piece of wire. Do not

4.3a Extract the retaining clip and release the hydraulic hose from the suspension strut

4.3b If working on the left-hand caliper, lift up the bleed screw cap to release the wire for the pad wear warning indicator

4.3c Unclip the wiring guide from the brake hose

4.3d Depress the locking tab and release the wiring connector from the suspension strut

4.3e Slide the locking bar on the wiring connector downward . . .

4.3f . . . then hold the upper part of the connector and twist the lower part in the direction of the arrow

4.3g Disconnect the pad wear warning indicator wire from the connector

4.3h Release the legs of the retaining spring from the caliper body . . .

4.3i . . . then remove the spring from the caliper mounting bracket

4.3j Remove the dust caps from the upper and lower guide bolts

4.3k Unscrew the upper . . .

4.3l . . . and lower guide bolts and remove them from the caliper

4.3m Lift the caliper and inner pad off the mounting bracket

4.3n Remove the inner pad from the caliper piston, noting that it is retained by a spring clip attached to the pad backing plate

4.3o Remove the outer pad from the mounting bracket

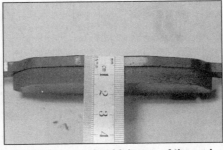

4.3p Measure the thickness of the pad friction material and backing plate. If any are worn down to the specified minimum, or fouled with oil or grease, all four pads must be renewed

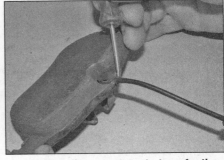

4.3q It may be necessary to transfer the pad wear warning indicator wire to the new pad, if so extract the retaining clip and the wire from the old pad

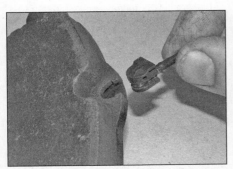

4.3r With the retaining clip in place on the end of the wire, push the wire back into position on the new pad

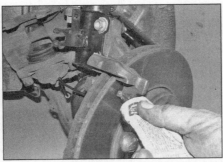

4.3s Apply a little high melting-point copper brake grease to the pad backing plate contact areas on the mounting bracket

4.3t If new pads are to be fitted, before refitting the caliper, push back the caliper piston whilst opening the bleed screw. This is to prevent any dirt/debris being forced back up the hydraulic circuit in the ABS modulator

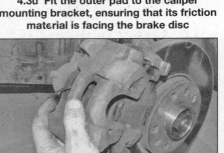

4.3u Fit the outer pad to the caliper mounting bracket, ensuring that its friction material is facing the brake disc

4.3v Where applicable, feed the pad wear warning indicator wire through the hole in the caliper . . .

4.3w . . . then fit the inner pad to the caliper, ensuring that its clip is correctly located in the caliper piston

4.3x Slide the caliper into position in the mounting bracket and refit the guide bolts

4.3y Tighten the guide bolts to the specified torque, then refit the dust caps . . .

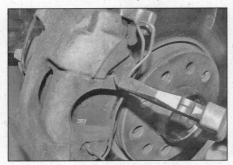

4.3z Locate the retaining spring legs into the holes in the caliper . . .

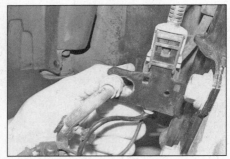

4.3aa . . . then hold the legs in place and locate the upper part of the spring behind the lugs on the mounting bracket

4.3ab Refit the hydraulic hose to the suspension strut and secure with the retaining clip. Where applicable, reconnect and secure the pad wear warning indicator to complete

allow the caliper to hang unsupported on the flexible brake hose.

5 If the original brake pads are still serviceable, carefully clean them using a clean, fine wire brush or similar, paying particular attention to the sides and back of the metal backing plate. Clean out the grooves in the friction material, and pick out any large embedded particles of dirt or debris. Carefully clean the pad locations in the caliper body/mounting bracket.

6 Prior to fitting the pads, check that the guide bolts are a snug fit in the caliper mounting bracket. Brush the dust and dirt from the caliper and piston, but do not inhale it, as it is injurious to health. Inspect the dust seal around the piston for damage, and the piston for evidence of fluid leaks, corrosion or damage. If attention to any of these

components is necessary, refer to Section 7.

7 If new brake pads are to be fitted, the caliper piston must be pushed back into the cylinder to allow for the extra pad thickness. Either use a G-clamp or similar tool, or use suitable pieces of wood as levers. Clamp off the flexible brake hose leading to the caliper then connect a brake bleeding kit to the caliper bleed screw. Open the bleed screw as the piston is retracted, the surplus brake fluid will then be collected in the bleed kit vessel (see illustration 4.3t). Close the bleed screw just before the caliper piston is pushed fully into the caliper. This should ensure no air enters the hydraulic system.

Caution: The ABS unit contains hydraulic components that are very sensitive to impurities in the brake fluid. Even the

smallest particles can cause the system to fail through blockage. The pad retraction method described here prevents any debris in the brake fluid expelled from the caliper from being passed back to the ABS hydraulic unit, as well as preventing any chance of damage to the master cylinder seals.

8 On later models, the brake pads may be fitted with mechanical rather than electrical brake pad wear warning indicators. The mechanical warning indicators consist of a metal strip riveted to the backing plate. When the pad friction material reaches the minimum thickness, the metal strip contacts the disc causing a squeaking noise audible to the driver. When fitting brake pads of this type, the metal strip must point downwards, and the arrow on the pad backing plate must point in the direction of forward rotation of the disc.

9 With the brake pads installed, depress the brake pedal repeatedly, until normal (non-assisted) pedal pressure is restored, and the pads are pressed into firm contact with the brake disc.

10 Repeat the above procedure on the remaining front brake caliper.

11 Refit the roadwheels, then lower the vehicle to the ground and tighten the roadwheel bolts to the specified torque setting.

12 Check the hydraulic fluid level as described in *Weekly checks.*

Caution: New pads will not give full braking efficiency until they have bedded-in. Be prepared for this, and avoid hard braking as far as possible for the first hundred miles or so after pad renewal.

5 Rear brake pads – renewal

Warning: *Renew BOTH sets of rear brake pads at the same time – NEVER renew the pads on only one wheel, as uneven braking may result. Note that the dust created by wear of the pads may contain asbestos, which is a health hazard. Never blow it out with compressed air, and do not inhale any of it. An approved filtering mask should be worn when working on the brakes. DO NOT use petroleum-based solvents to clean brake parts – use brake cleaner or methylated spirit only.*

1 Chock the front wheels then jack up the rear of the car and securely support it on axle stands (see *Jacking and vehicle support*). Remove the rear roadwheels.

2 Follow the accompanying photos (**illustrations 5.2a to 5.2o**) for the actual pad renewal procedure, bearing in mind the additional points listed below. Be sure to stay in order and read the caption under each illustration. Note that if the old pads are to be refitted, ensure that they are identified so that they can be returned to their original positions.

3 If the original brake pads are still serviceable, carefully clean them using a clean, fine wire brush or similar, paying particular attention to the sides and back of the metal backing plate. Clean out the grooves in the friction material, and pick out any large embedded particles of dirt or debris. Carefully clean the pad locations in the caliper body/mounting bracket.

4 Prior to fitting the pads, check that the guide bolts are a snug fit in the caliper mounting bracket. Brush the dust and dirt from the caliper and piston, but do not inhale it, as it is injurious to health. Inspect the dust seal around the piston for damage, and the piston for evidence of fluid leaks, corrosion or damage. If attention to any of these components is necessary, refer to Section 8.

5 If new brake pads are to be fitted, it will be necessary to retract the piston fully into the caliper bore by rotating it in a clockwise direction. This can be achieved by using sturdy circlip pliers, noting that as well as being turned, the piston has to be pressed in very firmly. Special tools are readily available to achieve this with less effort. While the caliper is being retracted, clamp off the flexible brake hose leading to the caliper then connect a brake bleeding kit to the caliper bleed screw. Open the bleed screw as the piston is retracted, the surplus brake fluid will then be collected in the bleed kit vessel **(see

illustrations 5.2h and 5.2i)**. Close the bleed screw just before the caliper piston is pushed fully into the caliper. This should ensure no air enters the hydraulic system.

Caution: The ABS unit contains hydraulic components that are very sensitive to impurities in the brake fluid. Even the smallest particles can cause the system to fail through blockage. The pad retraction method described here prevents any debris in the brake fluid expelled from the caliper from being passed back to the ABS hydraulic unit, as well as preventing any chance of damage to the master cylinder seals.

6 With the brake pads installed, depress the brake pedal repeatedly, until normal (non-assisted) pedal pressure is restored, and the pads are pressed into firm contact with the brake disc.

7 Repeat the above procedure on the remaining rear brake caliper.

8 Refit the roadwheels, then lower the vehicle to the ground and tighten the roadwheel bolts to the specified torque setting.

9 Check the hydraulic fluid level as described in *Weekly checks*.

Caution: New pads will not give full braking efficiency until they have bedded-in. Be prepared for this, and avoid hard braking as far as possible for the first hundred miles or so after pad renewal.

5.2a Release the legs of the retaining spring from the caliper body and remove the spring

5.2b Remove the dust caps from the upper and lower caliper guide bolts . . .

5.2c . . . then unscrew both guide bolts and remove them from the caliper

5.2d Lift the caliper off the mounting bracket and suspend it from a suitable place under the wheel arch using a cable tie or similar

5.2e Remove the outer pad . . .

5.2f . . . and inner pad from the caliper mounting bracket

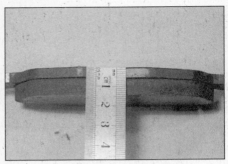

5.2g Measure the thickness of the pad friction material and backing plate. If any are worn down to the specified minimum, or fouled with oil or grease, all four pads must be renewed

5.2h Turn and press the caliper piston firmly clockwise using suitable pliers . . .

5.2i . . . or alternatively use a caliper retracting tool to retract the piston

5.2j Apply a little high melting-point copper brake grease to the pad backing plate contact areas on the mounting bracket

5.2k Fit the inner pad to the caliper mounting bracket . . .

5.2l . . . followed by the outer pad

5.2m Slide the caliper into position in the mounting bracket and refit the guide bolts

5.2n Tighten the guide bolts to the specified torque, then refit the dust caps

5.2o Locate the retaining spring legs into the holes in the caliper, then hold the legs in place and locate the upper part of the spring behind the lugs on the mounting bracket

6 Brake disc – inspection, removal and refitting

Note: *Before starting work, refer to the warning at the beginning of Section 4 or 5 concerning the dangers of asbestos dust. If either disc requires renewal, both should be renewed at the same time together with new pads, to ensure even and consistent braking.*

Inspection

1 Remove the wheel trim, then loosen the roadwheel bolts. If checking a front disc,

apply the handbrake, and if checking a rear disc, chock the front wheels and release the handbrake, then jack up the relevant end of the vehicle and support on axle stands (see *Jacking and vehicle support*). Remove the roadwheel.

2 Check that the brake disc securing screw is tight, then fit a spacer approximately 10.0 mm thick to one of the roadwheel bolts, and refit and tighten the bolt in the hole opposite the disc securing screw.

3 Rotate the brake disc, and examine it for deep scoring or grooving. Light scoring is normal, but if excessive, the disc should be removed and either renewed or machined

(within the specified limits) by an engineering works. The minimum thickness is given in the Specifications at the start of this Chapter.

4 Using a dial gauge, or a flat metal block and feeler blades, check that the disc run-out does not exceed the figure given in the Specifications. Measure the run-out 10.0 mm in from the outer edge of the disc.

5 If the disc run-out is excessive, remove the disc as described later, and check that the disc-to-hub surfaces are perfectly clean. Refit the disc and check the run-out again.

6 If the run-out is still excessive, the disc should be renewed.

7 To remove a disc, proceed as follows.

Front disc

Removal

8 Remove the roadwheel bolt and spacer used when checking the disc.
9 Remove the front brake pads as described in Section 4.
10 Undo the two bolts securing the caliper mounting bracket to the swivel hub and remove the mounting bracket **(see illustrations)**.
11 Remove the securing screw and withdraw the disc from the hub **(see illustrations)**.

Refitting

12 Refit the disc, making sure that the mating faces of the disc and hub are perfectly clean, and apply a little locking fluid to the threads of the securing screw.
13 Refit the caliper mounting bracket and tighten the bolts to the specified torque.
14 Refit the brake pads as described in Section 4.

Rear disc

Removal

15 Where applicable, remove the roadwheel bolt and spacer used when checking the disc.
16 Remove the rear brake pads as described in Section 5.
17 Undo the two bolts securing the caliper mounting bracket to the hub carrier and remove the mounting bracket **(see illustration)**.
18 Remove the securing screw and withdraw the disc from the hub **(see illustrations)**.

Refitting

19 Refit the disc, making sure that the mating faces of the disc and hub are perfectly clean, and apply a little locking fluid to the threads of the securing screw.
20 Refit the caliper mounting bracket and tighten the bolts to the specified torque.
21 Refit the brake pads as described in Section 5.

7 Front brake caliper – removal, overhaul and refitting

Note: *New brake hose copper washers will be required when refitting. Before starting work,*

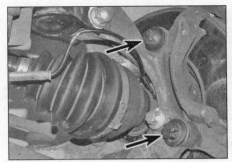
6.10a Undo the two bolts (arrowed) . . .

6.11a Remove the securing screw . . .

6.10b . . . and remove the caliper mounting bracket from the swivel hub

6.11b . . . and withdraw the disc from the hub

refer to the note at the beginning of Section 2 concerning the dangers of hydraulic fluid, and to the warning at the beginning of Section 4 concerning the dangers of asbestos dust.

Removal

1 Apply the handbrake, then jack up the front of the vehicle and support it on axle stands (see *Jacking and vehicle support*). Remove the roadwheel.
2 Minimise fluid loss by first removing the master cylinder reservoir cap and screwing it down onto a piece of polythene. Alternatively, use a brake hose clamp to clamp the flexible hose leading to the brake caliper.
3 Clean the area around the caliper brake hose union. Unscrew and remove the union bolt, and recover the copper sealing washer from each side of the hose union. Discard the washers; new ones must be used on

refitting. Plug the hose end and caliper hole, to minimise fluid loss and prevent the ingress of dust and dirt into the hydraulic system.
4 Remove the brake pads as described in Section 4, then remove the caliper from the vehicle.

Overhaul

Note: *Vauxhall/Opel special tool KM-6629-5 or a suitable alternative will be required to fit the piston dust seal to the caliper body.*
5 With the caliper on the bench, wipe it clean with a cloth rag.
6 Withdraw the partially-ejected piston from the caliper body, and remove the dust seal. The piston can be withdrawn by hand, or if necessary pushed out by applying compressed air to the brake hose union hole. Only low pressure should be required, such as is generated by a foot pump.

6.17 Undo the two bolts and remove the brake caliper mounting bracket from the hub carrier

6.18a Remove the securing screw (arrowed) . . .

6.18b . . . and withdraw the disc from the hub

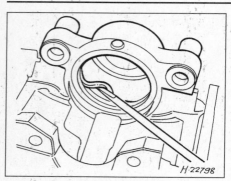

7.7 Removing the piston seal from the caliper body

7 Using a small screwdriver, carefully remove the piston seal from the groove in the caliper, taking care not to mark the bore **(see illustration).**

8 Carefully press the guide bushes out of the caliper body.

9 Thoroughly clean all components, using only methylated spirit or clean hydraulic fluid. Never use mineral-based solvents such as petrol or paraffin, which will attack the rubber components of the hydraulic system. Dry the components using compressed air or a clean, lint-free cloth. If available, use compressed air to blow clear the fluid passages.

 Warning: Wear eye protection when using compressed air.

10 Check all components, and renew any that are worn or damaged. If the piston and/or cylinder bore are scratched excessively, renew the complete caliper body. Similarly check the condition of the guide bushes and bolts; both bushes and bolts should be undamaged and (when cleaned) a reasonably tight sliding fit. If there is any doubt about the condition of any component, renew it.

11 If the caliper is fit for further use, obtain the necessary components from your Vauxhall/Opel dealer. Renew the caliper seals and dust covers as a matter of course; these should never be re-used.

12 On reassembly, ensure that all components are absolutely clean and dry.

13 Dip the piston and the new piston seal in clean hydraulic fluid, and smear clean fluid on the cylinder bore surface.

14 Locate the new seal in the cylinder bore groove, using only the fingers to manipulate it into position.

15 Fit the new dust seal to the piston, then insert the piston into the cylinder bore using a twisting motion to ensure it enters the seal correctly.

16 Ensure that the piston dust seal sits squarely and evenly on the caliper body then place the Vauxhall/Opel special tool, or suitable alternative, over the dust seal. Using a piston retracting tool or G-clamp push the tool outwards to seat the dust seal onto the edge of the caliper body. With the seal correctly located, remove the tool.

17 Insert the guide bushes into position in the caliper body.

Refitting

18 Refit the brake pads as described in Section 4, together with the caliper which at this stage will not have the hose attached.

19 Position a new copper sealing washer on each side of the hose union, and connect the brake hose to the caliper. Ensure that the hose is correctly positioned against the caliper body lug, then install the union bolt and tighten it to the specified torque setting.

20 Remove the brake hose clamp or polythene, and bleed the hydraulic system as described in Section 2. Note that, providing the precautions described were taken to minimise brake fluid loss, it should only be necessary to bleed the relevant front brake circuit.

21 Refit the roadwheel, then lower the vehicle to the ground and tighten the roadwheel bolts to the specified torque.

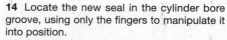

8 Rear brake caliper –
removal, overhaul and refitting

Note 1: *Before starting work, refer to the note at the beginning of Section 2 concerning the dangers of hydraulic fluid, and to the warning at the beginning of Section 5 concerning the dangers of asbestos dust.*

Note 2: *Due to the integral handbrake operating mechanism incorporated in the caliper piston, it is not possible to fully dismantle the caliper.*

Only the guide bushes and dust seal can be individually renewed.

Removal

1 Chock the front wheels, then jack up the rear of the vehicle and support on axle stands (see *Jacking and vehicle support*). Remove the roadwheel.

2 Minimise fluid loss by first removing the master cylinder reservoir cap and screwing it down onto a piece of polythene. Alternatively, use a brake hose clamp to clamp the flexible hose leading to the brake caliper.

3 Clean the area around the caliper brake hose union. Unscrew and remove the union bolt, and recover the copper sealing washer from each side of the hose union **(see illustration)**. Discard the washers; new ones must be used on refitting. Plug the hose end and caliper hole, to minimise fluid loss and prevent the ingress of dust and dirt into the hydraulic system.

4 Disengage the handbrake inner cable from the caliper lever, then pull the outer cable grommet out of the caliper bracket **(see illustrations)**.

5 Remove the brake pads as described in Section 5, then remove the caliper from the vehicle.

Overhaul

Note: *Vauxhall/Opel special tool KM-6629-4 or a suitable alternative will be required to fit the piston dust seal to the caliper body.*

6 With the caliper on the bench, wipe it clean with a cloth rag.

7 Using a small screwdriver, carefully prise out the dust seal from the caliper, taking care not to damage the piston.

8 Carefully press the guide bushes out of the caliper body.

9 Further dismantling of the caliper is not possible as individual parts are not available separately.

10 Thoroughly clean all components, using only methylated spirit or clean hydraulic fluid. Dry the components using a clean, lint-free cloth.

11 Check the condition of the exposed portion of the caliper piston. If the piston and/or cylinder bore are scratched excessively or corroded, renew the complete caliper body.

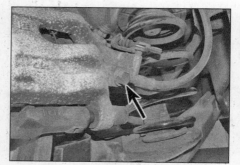

8.3 Rear caliper brake hose union bolt (arrowed)

8.4a Disengage the handbrake inner cable from the caliper lever . . .

8.4b . . . then pull the outer cable grommet out of the caliper bracket

Similarly check the condition of the guide bushes and bolts; both bushes and bolts should be undamaged and (when cleaned) a reasonably tight sliding fit. If there is any doubt about the condition of any component, renew it.

12 If the caliper is fit for further use, obtain the necessary components from your Vauxhall/Opel dealer. Renew the caliper dust seal as a matter of course; it should never be re-used.

13 Locate the new dust seal in the groove in the piston. Ensure that the piston dust seal sits squarely and evenly on the caliper body then place the Vauxhall/Opel special tool, or suitable alternative, over the dust seal. Using a piston retracting tool or G-clamp push the tool outwards to seat the dust seal onto the edge of the caliper body. With the seal correctly located, remove the tool.

14 Insert the guide bushes into position in the caliper body.

Refitting

15 Refit the brake pads as described in Section 5, together with the caliper which at this stage will not have the hose attached.

16 Position a new copper sealing washer on each side of the hose union, and connect the brake hose to the caliper. Ensure that the hose is correctly positioned against the caliper body lug, then install the union bolt and tighten it to the specified torque setting.

17 Engage the handbrake outer cable grommet with the caliper bracket, then pull back the operating lever and reconnect the handbrake inner cable.

18 Remove the brake hose clamp or polythene, and bleed the hydraulic system as described in Section 2. Note that, providing the precautions described were taken to minimise brake fluid loss, it should only be necessary to bleed the relevant front brake circuit.

19 Refit the roadwheel, then lower the vehicle to the ground and tighten the roadwheel bolts to the specified torque.

9 Master cylinder – removal, overhaul and refitting

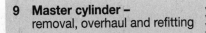

Note 1: *Before starting work, refer to the warning at the beginning of Section 2 concerning the dangers of hydraulic fluid.*
Note 2: *New master cylinder retaining nuts will be required for refitting.*

Removal

1 Remove the master cylinder reservoir cap, and siphon the hydraulic fluid from the reservoir. **Note:** *Do not siphon the fluid by mouth, as it is poisonous; use a syringe or an old hydrometer.* Alternatively, open any convenient bleed screw in the system, and gently pump the brake pedal to expel the fluid through a plastic tube connected to the screw (see Section 2).

9.3 Disconnect the wiring connector (arrowed) from the brake fluid level sensor

2 On left-hand drive models, lift up the cooling system expansion tank and remove it from the mounting bracket. Place the tank to one side.

3 Disconnect the wiring connector from the brake fluid level sensor at the base of the reservoir **(see illustration)**.

4 On models with manual transmission, release the clip and disconnect the clutch hydraulic pipe from the fluid reservoir **(see illustration)**. Tape over or plug the outlet.

5 Place cloth rags beneath the fluid reservoir then carefully prise it from the top of the master cylinder and withdraw from the engine compartment. If necessary, prise the reservoir seals from the top of the cylinder.

6 Place cloth rags beneath the master cylinder to collect escaping brake fluid. Identify the brake lines for position, then unscrew the union nuts and move the lines to one side. Tape over or plug the line outlets.

7 Unscrew the mounting nuts and withdraw the master cylinder from the vacuum servo unit **(see illustration)**. Recover the seal. Take care not to spill fluid on the vehicle paintwork. Note that new retaining nuts will be required for refitting.

Overhaul

8 At the time of writing, master cylinder overhaul is not possible as no spares are available.

9 The only parts available individually are the fluid reservoir, its mounting seals, the filler cap and the master cylinder mounting seal.

10 If the master cylinder is worn excessively, it must be renewed.

11 To remove the fluid reservoir, undo the retaining bolt and pull the reservoir out of the rubber seals in the master cylinder body. Place absorbent rags under the master cylinder as you do this to catch the escaping hydraulic fluid.

12 Remove the reservoir seals from the master cylinder body and obtain new seals for reassembly.

13 Lubricate the new seals with clean brake hydraulic fluid and push the new seals into position.

14 Refit the reservoir and secure with the retaining bolt.

Refitting

15 Ensure that the mating surfaces are clean

9.4 Release the clip (arrowed) and disconnect the clutch hydraulic pipe from the fluid reservoir

and dry then fit the new seal to the rear of the master cylinder.

16 Fit the master cylinder to the servo unit, ensuring that the servo unit pushrod enters the master cylinder piston centrally. Fit the new retaining nuts and tighten them to the specified torque setting.

17 Refit the brake lines and tighten the union nuts securely.

18 On manual transmission models, reconnect the clutch hydraulic pipe and secure with the clip.

19 Reconnect the wiring connector to the brake fluid level sensor.

20 On left-hand drive models, refit the cooling system expansion tank to its mounting bracket.

21 Remove the reservoir filler cap and polythene, then top-up the reservoir with fresh hydraulic fluid to the MAX mark (see *Weekly checks*).

22 Bleed the hydraulic systems as described in Section 2 and Chapter 6 then refit the filler cap. Thoroughly check the operation of the brakes and clutch before using the vehicle on the road.

10 Brake pedal – removal and refitting

Note 1: *The brake pedal mounting bracket, the brake pedal and the clutch pedal are one assembly and must be renewed as a complete unit. In the event of a frontal collision, the*

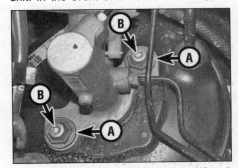
9.7 Master cylinder mounting nuts (A) and vacuum servo unit stud bolts (B)

brake pedal is released from its bearing in the mounting bracket to prevent injury to the driver's feet and legs (this also applies to the clutch pedal). If an airbag has been deployed, inspect the pedal and mounting bracket assembly and if necessary renew the complete unit.

Note 2: *New pedal mounting bracket retaining nuts, vacuum servo unit stud bolts and brake master cylinder retaining nuts will be required for refitting.*

Removal

1 Disconnect the battery negative terminal (refer to *Disconnecting the battery* in the Reference Chapter).
2 Remove the steering column as described in Chapter 10.
3 Remove the complete facia assembly and the facia crossmember as described in Chapter 11.
4 Remove the stop-light switch from the pedal mounting bracket as described in Section 15.
5 Refer to Chapter 4A or 4B as applicable and remove the air cleaner assembly and the accelerator pedal/position sensor. Where fitted, remove the clutch switch from the pedal mounting bracket.
6 Working in the engine compartment, unscrew the two nuts securing the brake master cylinder to the vacuum servo unit. Now unscrew the two stud bolts securing the vacuum servo unit to the bulkhead **(see illustration 9.7)**.
7 Separate the clutch pedal from the clutch master cylinder piston rod by releasing the retaining clip at the pedal. Vauxhall/Opel technicians use a special tool to do this, however, the clip may be released by pressing the retaining tabs together using screwdrivers, while at the same time pulling the clutch pedal rearwards. **Note:** *Do not remove the clip from the master cylinder piston rod, just release it from the pedal.*
8 Unhook the return spring from behind the brake pedal to release all tension in the spring.
9 Carefully prise open and remove the retaining clip, and withdraw the clevis pin securing the brake pedal to the vacuum servo unit pushrod.
10 From inside the car, slacken and remove the three nuts securing the pedal mounting bracket to the bulkhead. Note that two of the three nuts also secure the clutch master cylinder. On diesel engine models, move the bulkhead insulation to one side for access to the nuts, and use a plastic wedge or similar tool to retain the insulation clear.
11 Withdraw the mounting bracket and pedal assembly from the bulkhead, while at the same time guiding the clutch master cylinder piston rod and retaining clip out of the clutch pedal.

Refitting

12 Manoeuvre the mounting bracket and pedal assembly into position, whilst ensuring

that the clutch master cylinder piston rod and its retaining clip align correctly with the clutch pedal. Also ensure that the vacuum servo unit pushrod locates around the brake pedal. Fit three new pedal mounting bracket retaining nuts and tighten them to the specified torque.
13 On diesel engine models, locate the bulkhead insulation back into position.
14 Push the clutch master cylinder piston rod retaining clip into the clutch pedal, ensuring that the two lugs on the clip fully engage.
15 Apply a smear of multipurpose grease to the clevis pin then align the vacuum servo unit pushrod with the brake pedal hole and insert the pin. Secure the pin in position with the retaining clip, making sure it is correctly located in the groove.
16 Hook the return spring into position behind the brake pedal.
17 Working in the engine compartment, fit the two new stud bolts securing the vacuum servo unit to the bulkhead and tighten the bolts to the specified torque. Fit the two new brake master cylinder retaining nuts and tighten the nuts to the specified torque.
18 Refer to Chapter 4A or 4B as applicable and refit the air cleaner assembly and the accelerator pedal/position sensor. Where fitted, refit the clutch switch to the pedal mounting bracket.
19 Refit the stop-light switch to the pedal mounting bracket as described in Section 15.
20 Refit the facia crossmember and facia assembly as described in Chapter 11.
21 Refit the steering column as described in Chapter 10.
22 Reconnect the battery negative terminal on completion.

---

11 Vacuum servo unit – testing, removal and refitting

Testing

1 To test the operation of the servo unit, with the engine off, depress the footbrake several times to exhaust the vacuum. Now start the engine, keeping the pedal firmly depressed. As the engine starts, there should be a noticeable 'give' in the brake pedal as the

11.10 Pull out the vacuum hose (arrowed) from the rubber grommet in the vacuum servo

vacuum builds-up. Allow the engine to run for at least two minutes, then switch it off. The brake pedal should now feel normal, but further applications should result in the pedal feeling firmer, the pedal stroke decreasing with each application.
2 If the servo does not operate as described, first inspect the servo unit check valve as described in Section 12.
3 If the servo unit still fails to operate satisfactorily, the fault lies within the unit itself. Repairs to the unit are not possible; if faulty, the servo unit must be renewed.

Removal

Right-hand drive models

4 On diesel engine models, it will first be necessary to remove the engine and transmission assembly as described in Chapter 2C or 2D to obtain the necessary clearance for removal of the servo unit.
5 Disconnect the battery negative terminal (refer to *Disconnecting the battery* in the Reference Chapter).
6 Remove the master cylinder as described in Section 9.
7 Remove the facia footwell trim panel on the driver's side as described in Chapter 11.
8 Unhook the return spring from behind the brake pedal to release all tension in the spring.
9 Carefully prise open and remove the retaining clip, and withdraw the clevis pin securing the brake pedal to the vacuum servo unit pushrod.
10 Pull out the vacuum hose from the rubber grommet in the vacuum servo **(see illustration)**.
11 Unscrew the two stud bolts securing the vacuum servo unit to the bulkhead, and remove the servo unit from the engine compartment **(see illustration 9.7)**. Note that new bolts will be required for refitting.

Left-hand drive models

12 Remove the battery and battery box as described in Chapter 5A.
13 Lift up the cooling system expansion tank and remove it from the mounting bracket. Place the tank to one side.
14 Remove the ABS hydraulic modulator together with its mounting bracket as described in Section 18.
15 Remove the master cylinder as described in Section 9.
16 Remove the facia footwell trim panel on the driver's side as described in Chapter 11.
17 Unhook the return spring from behind the brake pedal to release all tension in the spring.
18 Carefully prise open and remove the retaining clip, and withdraw the clevis pin securing the brake pedal to the vacuum servo unit pushrod.
19 Pull out the vacuum hose from the rubber grommet in the vacuum servo **(see illustration 11.10)**.
20 Unscrew the two stud bolts securing

the vacuum servo unit to the bulkhead, and remove the servo unit from the engine compartment (see illustration 9.7). Note that new bolts will be required for refitting.

Refitting

Right-hand drive models

21 Locate the vacuum servo unit in position on the bulkhead ensuring that the servo unit pushrod locates correctly around the brake pedal. Refit the two new retaining stud bolts and tighten them to the specified torque.
22 Refit the vacuum hose to the servo grommet, ensuring that the hose is correctly seated.
23 Apply a smear of multipurpose grease to the clevis pin then align the servo unit pushrod with the brake pedal hole and insert the pin. Secure the pin in position with the retaining clip, making sure it is correctly located in the groove.
24 Hook the return spring into position behind the brake pedal, then refit the facia footwell trim panel as described in Chapter 11.
25 Refit the brake master cylinder as described in Section 9.
26 On diesel engine models, refit the engine and transmission assembly as described in Chapter 2C or 2D.
27 On completion, reconnect the battery negative terminal.

Left-hand drive models

28 Locate the vacuum servo unit in position on the bulkhead ensuring that the servo unit pushrod locates correctly around the brake pedal. Refit the two new retaining stud bolts and tighten them to the specified torque.
29 Refit the vacuum hose to the servo grommet, ensuring that the hose is correctly seated.
30 Apply a smear of multipurpose grease to the clevis pin then align the servo unit pushrod with the brake pedal hole and insert the pin. Secure the pin in position with the retaining clip, making sure it is correctly located in the groove.
31 Hook the return spring into position behind the brake pedal, then refit the facia footwell trim panel as described in Chapter 11.
32 Refit the brake master cylinder as

12.3 Disconnect the vacuum hose quick-release fitting at the vacuum pump on diesel engines

described in Section 9, but don't bleed the hydraulic circuits at this stage.
33 Refit the ABS hydraulic modulator and mounting bracket as described in Section 18.
34 Refit the cooling system expansion tank to the mounting bracket.
35 Refit the battery box and battery as described in Chapter 5A.
36 Remove the master cylinder reservoir filler cap and polythene, then top-up the reservoir with fresh hydraulic fluid to the MAX mark (see *Weekly checks*).
37 Bleed the hydraulic systems as described in Section 2 and Chapter 6 then refit the filler cap. Thoroughly check the operation of the brakes and clutch before using the vehicle on the road.

12 Vacuum servo unit check valve and hose – removal, testing and refitting

Removal

1 Pull out the vacuum hose from the rubber grommet in the vacuum servo unit (see illustration 11.10).
2 Remove the plastic cover over the top of the engine.
3 Disconnect the hose quick-release fitting from the inlet manifold (petrol engines) or vacuum pump (diesel engines) (see illustration).
4 Unclip the vacuum hose from its supports

on the bulkhead and engine, then remove the hose and check valve from the car.

Testing

5 Examine the check valve and hose for signs of damage, and renew if necessary. The valve may be tested by blowing through it in both directions. Air should flow through the valve in one direction only – when blown through from the servo unit end. If air flows in both directions, or not at all, renew the valve and hose as an assembly.
6 Examine the servo unit rubber sealing grommet for signs of damage or deterioration, and renew as necessary.

Refitting

7 Refitting is a reversal of removal ensuring that the quick-release connector audibly locks in position, and that the hose is correctly seated in the servo grommet.
8 On completion, start the engine and check that there are no air leaks.

13 Handbrake lever – removal and refitting

Removal

1 Remove the rear centre console as described in Chapter 11.
2 Ensure that the handbrake lever is released (off).
3 Set the handbrake cable self-adjusting mechanism to the fully released position as follows. Push the piston rod and spring rearward with a suitable tool. Hold them in this position and press down the transport fixing to lock the mechanism in the released position (see illustration).
4 Remove the complete exhaust system and centre heat shield as described in Chapter 4A or 4B as applicable.
5 From under the car, use a suitable socket to depress the lugs of the clevis pin retaining collar (see illustrations). Pull the clevis pin upwards and out of the handbrake cable equaliser to release the handbrake lever connecting rod. Note that a new retaining collar will be required for refitting.

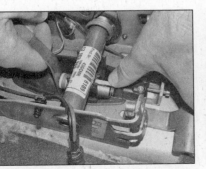

13.3 Push the piston rod and spring rearward with a suitable tool, then press down the transport fixing to lock the mechanism

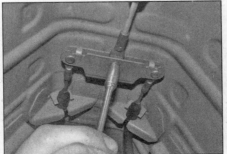

13.5a Push a suitable socket over the clevis pin . . .

13.5b . . . to depress the lugs (arrowed) of the clevis pin retaining collar

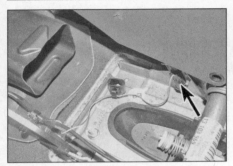

13.6 Disconnect the wiring connector (arrowed) from the handbrake lever warning light switch

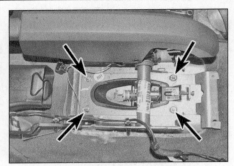

13.7 Handbrake lever retaining nuts (arrowed)

6 From inside the car, disconnect the wiring connector from the handbrake lever warning light switch **(see illustration)**. Release the plastic cable guide from the handbrake lever mounting stud and move the cable to one side.

7 Undo the four retaining nuts and remove the handbrake lever assembly from inside the car **(see illustration)**. Recover the seal between the handbrake lever and vehicle floor.

Refitting

8 Ensure that the seal is correctly seated on the vehicle floor then locate the handbrake lever assembly in position over the mounting studs. Refit the four retaining nuts and tighten to the specified torque.

9 Reconnect the handbrake lever warning light switch wiring connector and clip the plastic guide onto the mounting stud.

10 Fit a new retaining collar to the handbrake lever connecting rod clevis pin. Align the connecting rod with the hole in the equaliser and fit the retaining collar from above. Ensure that the clevis pin is pushed fully home so that the lugs on the retaining collar lock the clevis pin in position.

11 Refit the heat shield and the exhaust system as described in Chapter 4A or 4B, as applicable.

12 Pull the handbrake lever up to release the transport fixing and automatically adjust the handbrake cable.

13 Refit the centre console as described in Chapter 11.

14 Handbrake cable – removal and refitting

Removal

1 The handbrake cable consists of two parts, a short front connecting rod which connects the lever to the equaliser plate, and the main cable which links the equaliser plate to the left-hand and right-hand rear brakes. The connecting rod is an integral part of the handbrake lever assembly and cannot be separated. The main cable is supplied as one part, together with the equaliser plate.

2 Carry out the operations described in Section 13, paragraphs 1 to 5.

3 Disengage the handbrake inner cable from the rear brake caliper levers, then pull the outer cable grommets out of the caliper brackets **(see illustrations 8.4a and 8.4b)**.

4 Undo the bolt securing the handbrake cable support bracket to the underbody on each side **(see illustration)**.

5 Release the cable from the remaining support brackets and clips on the underbody and suspension arms, and remove the cable from under the car **(see illustrations)**.

Refitting

6 Locate the cable in position in the underbody support clips and brackets, and tighten the support bracket bolt on each side securely.

7 Engage the handbrake outer cable grommet with the caliper bracket on each side, then pull back the caliper operating levers and reconnect the handbrake inner cable.

8 Carry out the operations described in Section 13, paragraphs 10 to 13.

15 Stop-light switch – removal, refitting and adjustment

Removal

1 The stop-light switch is located on the pedal bracket in the driver's footwell, behind the facia **(see illustration)**.

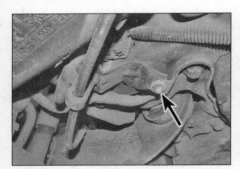

14.4 Undo the bolt (arrowed) securing the handbrake cable support bracket to the underbody on each side

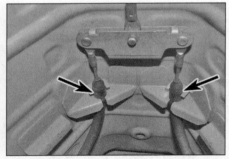

14.5a Release the handbrake cable from the mounting bracket (arrowed) ...

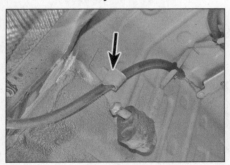

14.5b ... from the cable guides (arrowed) ...

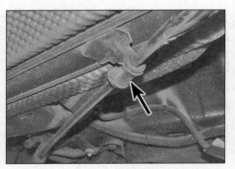

14.5c ... and support clips (arrowed)

15.1 Stop-light switch location (arrowed) on the brake pedal bracket

2 Remove the facia footwell trim panel on the driver's side as described in Chapter 11.

3 Disconnect the wiring plug from the stop-light switch.

4 Push the brake pedal down, pull out the brake switch actuating pin, then unclip the locking sleeve from around the actuating pin **(see illustrations)**.

5 Release the securing clips and pull the switch to disengage it from the pedal mounting bracket.

Refitting and adjustment

6 With the actuating pin pulled out, and the locking sleeve unclipped, refit the switch to the pedal bracket.

7 Secure the switch with the locking sleeve.

8 Release the brake pedal and the pedal will automatically adjust the position of the actuating pin.

9 Reconnect the wiring connector, then refit the facia footwell trim panel as described in Chapter 11.

16 Handbrake warning light switch – removal and refitting

Removal

1 Remove the rear centre console as described in Chapter 11.

2 Disconnect the wiring connector from the warning light switch on the side of the handbrake lever.

3 Unclip the trim on the side of the handbrake lever, then unscrew the mounting bolt and remove the switch from the handbrake lever bracket **(see illustration)**.

Refitting

4 Refitting is a reversal of removal.

17 Anti-lock Braking and Traction Control systems – general information

ABS is fitted as standard to all models. On higher specification models, the ABS may also incorporate traction control or an electronic stability program as additional safety features.

The ABS system comprises a hydraulic modulator and electronic control unit together with four wheel speed sensors. The hydraulic modulator contains the electronic control unit (ECU), the hydraulic solenoid valves (one set for each brake) and the electrically-driven pump. The purpose of the system is to prevent the wheel(s) locking during heavy braking. This is achieved by automatic release of the brake on the relevant wheel, followed by re-application of the brake.

The solenoid valves are controlled by the ECU, which itself receives signals from the four wheel speed sensors which monitor the speed of rotation of each wheel. By comparing these signals, the ECU can determine the speed

15.4a Pull out the centre actuating pin arrowed (switch removed for clarity) . . .

at which the vehicle is travelling. It can then use this speed to determine when a wheel is decelerating at an abnormal rate, compared to the speed of the vehicle, and therefore predicts when a wheel is about to lock. During normal operation, the system functions in the same way as a conventional braking system.

If the ECU senses that a wheel is about to lock, it operates the relevant solenoid valve(s) in the hydraulic unit, which then isolates from the master cylinder the relevant brake(s) on the wheel(s) which is/are about to lock, effectively sealing-in the hydraulic pressure.

If the speed of rotation of the wheel continues to decrease at an abnormal rate, the ECU operates the electrically-driven pump which pumps the hydraulic fluid back into the master cylinder, releasing the brake. Once the speed of rotation of the wheel returns to an acceptable rate, the pump stops, and the solenoid valves switch again, allowing the hydraulic master cylinder pressure to return to the caliper, which then re-applies the brake. This cycle can be carried out many times a second.

The action of the solenoid valves and return pump creates pulses in the hydraulic circuit. When the ABS system is functioning, these pulses can be felt through the brake pedal.

On early models with traction control, the ABS hydraulic modulator incorporates an additional set of solenoid valves which operate the traction control system. The system operates at speeds up to approximately 30 mph using the signals supplied by the wheel speed sensors. If the ECU senses that a driving wheel is about to lose traction, it prevents this by momentarily applying the relevant front brake. The ABS ECU also communicates with the engine management ECU during traction control operation. In severe cases of traction loss the engine management ECU will reduce engine power to assist with traction recovery. On later models with traction control, the additional solenoids in the modulator are not used, and the traction control function is provided solely by a reduction in engine power.

The electronic stability program (ESP) is a further development of ABS and traction control. Using additional sensors to monitor steering wheel position, vehicle yaw rate, acceleration and deceleration, in conjunction

15.4b . . . and unclip the locking sleeve

with the ABS sensors, the ECU can intervene under conditions of vehicle instability. Using the signals from the various sensors, the ECU can determine driver intent (steering wheel position, throttle position, vehicle speed and engine speed). From the sensor inputs from the wheel speed sensors, yaw rate sensors and acceleration sensors the ECU can calculate whether the vehicle is responding to driver input, or whether an unstable driving situation is occurring. If instability is detected, the ECU will intervene by applying or releasing the relevant front or rear brake, in conjunction with a power reduction, until vehicle stability returns.

The operation of the ABS, traction control and stability programs is entirely dependent on electrical signals. To prevent the system responding to any inaccurate signals, a built-in safety circuit monitors all signals received by the ECU. If an inaccurate signal or low battery voltage is detected, the system is automatically shut down, and the relevant warning light on the instrument panel is illuminated, to inform the driver that the system is not operational. Normal braking is still available, however.

If a fault develops in the ABS/traction control/ESP system, the vehicle must be taken to a Vauxhall/Opel dealer for fault diagnosis and repair.

18 Anti-lock Braking and Traction Control system components – removal and refitting

Note 1: *Faults on the ABS system can only*

16.3 Handbrake warning light switch mounting bolt (arrowed)

18.3 Pull out the locking bar (arrowed) to disconnect the wiring harness plug from the ECU

be diagnosed using Vauxhall/Opel diagnostic equipment or compatible alternative equipment.

Note 2: *Before starting work, refer to the note at the beginning of Section 2 concerning the dangers of hydraulic fluid.*

Hydraulic modulator and ECU

1 Remove the battery and battery box as described in Chapter 5A.

2 Minimise fluid loss by first removing the master cylinder reservoir cap and screwing it down onto a piece of polythene.

3 Pull out the locking bar and disconnect the wiring harness plug from the ECU **(see illustration)**.

4 Note and record the fitted position of the brake pipes at the modulator, then unscrew the union nuts and release the pipes. As a precaution, place absorbent rags beneath the brake pipe unions when unscrewing them. Suitably plug or cap the disconnected unions to prevent dirt entry and fluid loss.

5 Unscrew the retaining bolts and remove the hydraulic modulator from the mounting bracket.

6 Refitting is the reverse of the removal procedure, noting the following points:
   a) *Tighten the modulator retaining bolts to the specified torque.*
   b) *Refit the brake pipes to their respective locations, and tighten the union nuts to the specified torque.*
   c) *Ensure that the wiring is correctly routed, and that the ECU wiring harness plug is firmly pressed into position and secured with the locking bar.*
   d) *Refit the battery box and battery as described in Chapter 5A.*
   e) *On completion, bleed the complete hydraulic system as described in Section 2. Ensure that the system is bled in the correct order, to prevent air entering the modulator return pump.*

Electronic control unit (ECU)

7 Remove the hydraulic modulator from the car as described previously in this Section.

8 Undo the two retaining bolts and carefully withdraw the ECU upwards and off the hydraulic modulator.

9 Prior to refitting, clean and then carefully inspect, the condition of the gasket sealing surfaces on the ECU and hydraulic modulator. If the surfaces are in any way deformed, damaged, or rough to the extent that a perfect gasket seal cannot be maintained, the complete modulator and ECU assembly must be renewed.

10 Holding the ECU by the outer edges, carefully lower it over the solenoid valves on the modulator, keeping it square and level.

Ensure that the wiring connectors correctly engage.

11 Fit the two retaining bolts and tighten securely.

12 On completion, refit the hydraulic modulator as described previously in this Section.

Wheel speed sensors

13 The front and rear wheel speed sensors are an integral part of the hub bearings and cannot be separated.

14 Refer to Chapter 10 for front and rear hub bearing removal and refitting procedures.

19 Vacuum pump (diesel engine models) – removal and refitting

Removal

1 Remove the plastic cover over the top of the engine.

2 Disconnect the quick-release fitting and detach the vacuum servo unit vacuum hose from the pump **(see illustration)**. Disconnect the smaller vacuum hose from the outlet on the side of the pump.

3 Undo the three mounting bolts and remove the pump from the cylinder head/camshaft housing **(see illustrations)**. Recover the gasket.

Refitting

4 Refitting is a reversal of removal, but clean the mating faces of the pump and cylinder head/camshaft housing, and fit a new gasket or O-ring as applicable. Tighten the mounting bolts to the specified torque.

19.2 Disconnect the quick-release fitting and detach the servo unit vacuum hose

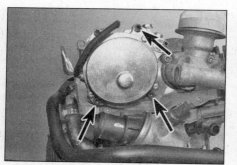

19.3a Undo the three mounting bolts (arrowed) . . .

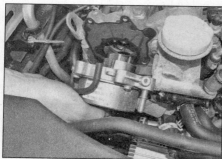

19.3b . . . and remove the vacuum pump from the cylinder head/camshaft housing

Chapter 10
Suspension and steering

Contents

Degrees of difficulty

Easy, suitable for novice with little experience	**Fairly easy,** suitable for beginner with some experience	**Fairly difficult,** suitable for competent DIY mechanic	**Difficult,** suitable for experienced DIY mechanic	**Very difficult,** suitable for expert DIY or professional

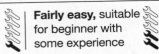

Specifications

Front suspension

Type .... Independent, with MacPherson struts and anti-roll bar

Rear suspension

Type .... Independent multilink with coil springs, gas-filled shock absorbers and anti-roll bar

Steering

Type .... Rack and pinion with electro-hydraulic power steering (EHPS)

Front and rear hub bearings

Bearing play (maximum) .... 0.1 mm
Bearing radial run-out .... 0.04 mm
Bearing lateral run-out .... 0.05 mm

Torque wrench settings

	Nm	lbf ft
Front suspension		
Anti-roll bar link:*		
To strut	65	48
To anti-roll bar	65	48
Anti-roll bar to subframe*	20	15
Driveshaft retaining nut:*		
Stage 1	150	111
Stage 2	Slacken the nut by 45°	
Stage 3	250	185
Hub bearing assembly to swivel hub:*		
Stage 1	100	74
Stage 2	Angle-tighten a further 60°	
Stage 3	Angle-tighten a further 15°	
Lower arm balljoint clamp bolt nut:*		
Stage 1	30	22
Stage 2	Angle-tighten through a further 60°	
Stage 3	Angle-tighten through a further 15°	
Lower arm front pivot bolt:*		
Stage 1	90	66
Stage 2	Angle-tighten a further 75°	
Stage 3	Angle-tighten a further 15°	
Lower arm rear mounting bush to lower arm:*		
Stage 1	40	30
Stage 2	Angle-tighten a further 40°	
Lower arm rear mounting bush to subframe:*		
Stage 1	90	66
Stage 2	Angle-tighten a further 75°	
Stage 3	Angle-tighten a further 15°	
Subframe:		
Front engine mounting/torque link to subframe*	80	59
Rear engine mounting/torque link to subframe*	60	44
Front mounting bolts:*		
Stage 1	80	59
Stage 2	Angle-tighten a further 120°	
Stage 3	Angle-tighten a further 15°	
Rear mounting reinforcement plates to underbody:*		
Stage 1	90	66
Stage 2	Angle-tighten a further 45°	
Stage 3	Angle-tighten a further 15°	
Rear mounting reinforcement plates to subframe:*		
Stage 1	100	74
Stage 2	Angle-tighten a further 90°	
Stage 3	Angle-tighten a further 15°	
Suspension strut piston rod nut*	100	74
Suspension strut to swivel hub:*		
Stage 1	50	37
Stage 2	85	63
Stage 3	Angle-tighten a further 75°	
Stage 4	Angle-tighten a further 15°	
Suspension strut upper mounting bolts:*		
Stage 1	20	15
Stage 2	Angle-tighten a further 45°	
Stage 3	Angle-tighten a further 15°	
Rear suspension		
Anti-roll bar clamp bolts:*		
Stage 1	25	18
Stage 2	Angle-tighten a further 30°	
Stage 3	Angle-tighten a further 15°	
Anti-roll bar link rod to hub carrier:*		
Stage 1	45	33
Stage 2	Angle-tighten a further 60°	
Stage 3	Angle-tighten a further 15°	

Torque wrench settings (continued)

	Nm	lbf ft
Rear suspension (continued)		
Auxiliary control arm to hub carrier:*		
Stage 1	150	111
Stage 2	Angle-tighten a further 45°	
Stage 3	Angle-tighten a further 15°	
Auxiliary control arm to rear axle body:*		
Stage 1	90	66
Stage 2	Angle-tighten a further 60°	
Stage 3	Angle-tighten a further 15°	
Hub bearing assembly to hub carrier:*		
Stage 1	60	44
Stage 2	Angle-tighten a further 60°	
Stage 3	Angle-tighten a further 15°	
Lower control arm to hub carrier and rear axle body:*		
Stage 1	90	66
Stage 2	Angle-tighten a further 60°	
Stage 3	Angle-tighten a further 15°	
Rear axle body mounting bolts:*		
Stage 1	90	66
Stage 2	Slacken bolts	
Stage 3	90	66
Stage 4	Angle-tighten a further 90°	
Stage 5	Angle-tighten a further 15°	
Shock absorber lower mounting bolt*	150	111
Shock absorber upper mounting bolt*	90	66
Trailing arm front mounting bracket bolts:*		
Stage 1	90	66
Stage 2	Slacken bolts	
Stage 3	90	66
Stage 4	Angle-tighten a further 90°	
Stage 5	Angle-tighten a further 15°	
Trailing arm to hub carrier*	150	111
Upper control arm to hub carrier:*		
Stage 1	150	111
Stage 2	Angle-tighten a further 45°	
Stage 3	Angle-tighten a further 15°	
Upper control arm to rear axle body:*		
Stage 1	90	66
Stage 2	Angle-tighten a further 60°	
Stage 3	Angle-tighten a further 15°	
Steering		
EHPS supply unit:		
Fluid supply pipe union	30	22
Mounting bracket to subframe	20	15
Mounting bracket to underbody:		
Upper bolts	22	16
Lower bolt (subframe mounting bolt):*		
Stage 1	80	59
Stage 2	Angle-tighten a further 120°	
Stage 3	Angle-tighten a further 15°	
Supply unit to mounting bracket	7	5
Hydraulic fluid pipes to steering gear	11	8
Intermediate shaft to steering column*	25	18
Intermediate shaft to steering gear pinion*	25	18
Steering column mounting bolts*	25	18
Steering gear to subframe:*		
Stage 1	45	33
Stage 2	Angle-tighten through a further 45°	
Stage 3	Angle-tighten through a further 15°	
Steering wheel bolt	30	22
Track rod end to swivel hub*	35	26
Track rod inner balljoint to steering rack	90	66
Roadwheels		
All models	110	81

* Use new nuts/bolts.

2.3 On early models, remove the ABS wheel speed sensor wiring plug (arrowed) from the suspension strut and disconnect the wiring connector

1 General information

The independent front suspension is of the MacPherson strut type, incorporating coil springs and integral telescopic shock absorbers. The MacPherson struts are located by transverse lower suspension arms, which utilise rubber inner mounting bushes, and incorporate a balljoint at the outer ends. The front swivel hubs, which carry the hub bearings, brake calipers and disc assemblies, are bolted to the MacPherson struts, and connected to the lower arms via the balljoints. A front anti-roll bar is fitted, which has link rods with balljoints at each end to connect it to the strut.

The rear suspension is of fully independent multilink type, with a central axle body (crossmember), gas-filled shock absorbers, coil springs, trailing arms, upper and lower transverse control arms, auxiliary transverse control arms and an anti-roll bar. The shock absorbers are attached at their upper ends to the vehicle underbody and at their lower ends to the hub carriers. The rear hub carriers are attached to the trailing arms, upper and lower control arms and auxiliary control arms by means of flexible rubber bushes. The anti-roll bar is mounted on the axle body and is connected to the hub carriers by drop links.

The steering system is of the electro-hydraulic power steering (EHPS) type. This system utilises a conventional rack-and-pinion type steering gear mounted on the front subframe, with variable power assistance generated by a hydraulic pump, driven by an electric motor. The degree of power assistance available is governed by the speed of the electric motor which is controlled by the steering system electronic control unit. The ECU receives input signals on steering wheel position (from a steering angle sensor) and roadspeed (from the ABS wheel speed sensors) and calculates the amount of power assistance required.

Two versions of the EHPS system are used on the Vectra: a standard EHPS system and a compact EHPS system. The standard EHPS system has the hydraulic pump, electric motor and hydraulic fluid reservoir assembly remotely sited under the front wheel arch and connected to the rack-and-pinion steering gear by hydraulic supply and return pipes. On the compact EHPS system, the hydraulic pump, electric motor and hydraulic fluid reservoir are mounted above the rack-and-pinion steering gear on the front subframe.

There is no definitive list of which models have which type of steering. The only way to tell is by the location of the fluid reservoir. If it's visible in the engine compartment, then it's compact EHPS. If it's not visible in the engine compartment then it's under the wheel arch, and it's standard EHPS.

The steering column is linked to the steering gear by an intermediate shaft. The intermediate shaft has a universal joint fitted to its upper end, and is secured to the column by a clamp bolt. The lower end of the intermediate shaft is attached to the steering gear pinion by means of a clamp bolt.

2 Front swivel hub – removal and refitting

Note: *A new driveshaft retaining nut, lower arm balljoint clamp bolt and nut, anti-roll bar connecting link retaining nut, brake caliper mounting bracket bolts and a new track rod end retaining nut will be needed for refitting. The driveshaft outer joint splines may be a tight fit in the hub and it is possible that a puller/extractor will be required to draw the hub assembly off the driveshaft during removal.*
Caution: The front wheel camber setting is controlled by the bolts securing the hub carrier to the front suspension strut. Before removing the bolts, mark the hub carrier in relation to the strut accurately. On completion, the camber setting must be checked and adjusted by a suitably-equipped garage.

Removal

1 Firmly apply the handbrake, then jack up the front of the car and support it securely on axle stands (see *Jacking and vehicle support*). Remove the relevant front roadwheel.
2 On diesel engine models, undo the retaining bolts and screws and remove the undertray from beneath the engine.
3 On early models, remove the ABS wheel speed sensor wiring plug from the suspension strut bracket and disconnect the wiring connector **(see illustration)**.
4 On later models, depress the locking tab and release the wiring connector from the suspension strut. Slide the locking bar on the connector downward, then hold the upper part of the connector and twist the lower part to open the connector. Disconnect the ABS wheel speed sensor wire from the connector and, if working on the left-hand swivel hub, also disconnect the brake pad wear warning indicator wire **(see illustrations)**.
5 Where fitted, tap off the driveshaft retaining nut dust cap using a cold chisel or large screwdriver **(see illustration)**.

2.4a Depress the locking tab and release the wiring connector from the suspension strut

2.4b Slide the locking bar on the wiring connector downward . . .

2.4c . . . then hold the upper part of the connector and twist the lower part in the direction of the arrow

2.4d Disconnect the wires from the connector

2.5 Where fitted, tap off the driveshaft retaining nut dust cap

A tool to hold the wheel hub stationary whilst the driveshaft retaining nut is slackened can be fabricated from two lengths of steel strip (one long, one short) and a nut and bolt; the nut and bolt forming the pivot of a forked tool.

2.8 Extract the retaining clip and release the hydraulic hose from the suspension strut

6 To prevent rotation of the wheel hub as the driveshaft retaining nut is slackened, make up a holding tool and bolt the tool to the wheel hub using two wheel bolts **(see Tool Tip)**.

7 With the holding tool in place, slacken and remove the driveshaft retaining nut using a socket and long bar. Where necessary, support the socket on an axle stand to prevent it slipping off the nut. This nut is very tight; make sure that there is no risk of pulling the car off the axle stands as the nut is slackened.

8 Extract the retaining clip and release the hydraulic hose from the suspension strut **(see illustration)**. If working on the left-hand swivel hub on early models, also release the brake pad wear warning indicator wire from the strut bracket.

9 Undo the two bolts securing the brake caliper mounting bracket to the swivel hub.

Slide the mounting bracket, complete with brake caliper and pads off, the brake disc, and tie it to the coil spring using wire or a cable-tie. Note that new caliper mounting bracket bolts will be required for refitting.

10 Undo the securing screw and remove the brake disc from the wheel hub **(see illustrations)**.

11 Unscrew the nut securing the track rod end to the steering arm on the swivel hub, then use a balljoint separator tool to remove the track rod end **(see illustration)**.

12 Unscrew the nut and remove the clamp bolt securing the front suspension lower arm balljoint to the swivel hub **(see illustrations)**.

Note that a new clamp bolt and nut will be required for refitting.

13 Using a lever, push down on the suspension lower arm to free the balljoint from the swivel hub, then move the swivel hub to one side and release the arm, taking care not to damage the balljoint rubber boot **(see illustration)**. It is advisable to place a protective cover over the rubber boot, such as the plastic cap from an aerosol can, suitably cut to fit.

14 The hub must now be freed from the end of the driveshaft **(see illustration)**. It may be possible to pull the hub off the driveshaft, but if the end of the driveshaft is tight in the hub, temporarily refit the driveshaft retaining nut to protect the driveshaft threads, then tap the end of the driveshaft with a soft-faced hammer while pulling outwards on the swivel

2.10a Undo the securing screw . . .

2.10b . . . and remove the brake disc from the wheel hub

2.11 Unscrew the retaining nut, then use a balljoint separator tool to remove the track rod end from the swivel hub

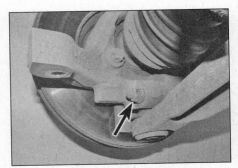

2.12a Unscrew the retaining nut (arrowed) . . .

2.12b . . . and withdraw the clamp bolt from the swivel hub

2.13 Push down the lower suspension arm to free the balljoint from the swivel hub

2.14 Pull the swivel hub outwards then withdraw the driveshaft from the hub splines

hub. Alternatively, use a suitable puller to press the driveshaft through the hub.

15 Mark the position of the suspension strut on the swivel hub by drawing a circle around the heads of the two retaining bolts. **Note:** *This is important to maintain the camber setting.*

16 Slacken and remove the two nuts and bolts securing the suspension strut to the swivel hub, noting that new nuts and bolts will be required for refitting **(see illustration)**. Disengage the swivel hub from the strut and remove it from the car.

Refitting

17 Ensure that the driveshaft outer constant velocity joint and hub splines are clean, then slide the hub onto the driveshaft splines. Fit the new driveshaft retaining nut, tightening it by hand only at this stage.

18 Engage the swivel hub with the suspension strut, and insert the new bolts from the front of the strut so that their threads are facing to the rear. Fit the new nuts, tightening them by hand only at this stage.

19 Locate the lower arm balljoint in the swivel hub. Insert the clamp bolt from the front of the swivel hub, so that its threads are facing to the rear. Fit the new nut to the clamp bolt, and tighten it to the specified torque and through the specified angles given in the Specifications, using a torque wrench and angle-tightening gauge.

20 With the hub correctly located, align the strut-to-swivel hub bolt heads with the marks made on the strut during removal. Tighten the bolts to the specified torque and through the specified angles given in the Specifications, using a torque wrench and angle-tightening gauge.

21 Engage the track rod end in the swivel hub, then fit the new retaining nut and tighten it to the specified torque setting.

22 Refit the brake disc and tighten its retaining screw securely.

23 Slide the brake pads, caliper and mounting bracket over the disc and into position on the swivel hub. Fit the two new caliper mounting bracket retaining bolts and tighten them to the specified torque (see Chapter 9).

24 Reconnect the ABS wheel speed sensor wiring connector and, where applicable, the break pad wear warning indicator wire. Secure the wiring in the relevant support brackets and clips.

25 Refit the brake hydraulic hose to the suspension strut and secure with the retaining clip.

26 Using the method employed on removal to prevent rotation, tighten the driveshaft retaining nut through the stages given in the Specifications. Where fitted, tap a new driveshaft retaining nut dust cap into position.

27 Refit the roadwheel, then lower the vehicle to the ground and tighten the roadwheel bolts to the specified torque.

3 Front hub bearings – checking and renewal

Note: *The front hub bearing and integral ABS wheel speed sensor is a sealed unit and no repairs are possible. If the bearing is worn or the speed sensor is faulty, a new bearing assembly must be obtained.*

Checking

1 Firmly apply the handbrake, then jack up the front of the car and support it securely on axle stands (see *Jacking and vehicle support*). Remove the roadwheel.

2 A dial test indicator (DTI) will be required to measure the amount of play in the bearing. Locate the DTI on the suspension strut and zero the probe on the brake disc.

3 Lever the hub in and out and measure the amount of play in the bearing.

4 To measure the bearing lateral and radial run-out, undo the two bolts securing the brake caliper mounting bracket to the swivel hub. Slide the mounting bracket, complete with brake caliper and pads off the brake disc, and tie it to the coil spring using wire or a cable-tie. Note that new caliper mounting bracket bolts will be required for refitting.

5 Undo the securing screw and remove the brake disc from the wheel hub.

6 To check the lateral run-out, locate the DTI on the suspension strut and zero the probe on the front face of the hub flange. Rotate the hub and measure the run-out.

7 To check the radial run-out, zero the DTI probe on the upper face of the extended portion at the centre of the hub. Rotate the hub and measure the run-out.

8 If the play or run-out exceeds the specified amounts, renew the hub bearing as described below.

9 If the bearing is satisfactory, refit the brake disc and tighten its retaining screw securely.

10 Slide the brake pads, caliper and mounting bracket over the disc and into position on the swivel hub. Fit the two new caliper mounting bracket retaining bolts and tighten them to the specified torque (see Chapter 9).

11 Refit the roadwheel, then lower the vehicle to the ground and tighten the roadwheel bolts to the specified torque.

Renewal

Note: *New hub bearing retaining bolts will be required for refitting.*

12 Remove the swivel hub as described in Section 2.

13 Undo the three bolts securing the bearing assembly to the swivel hub **(see illustration)**.

2.16 Slacken and remove the two nuts and bolts securing the suspension strut to the swivel hub

3.13 Undo the three bolts (arrowed) securing the bearing assembly to the swivel hub

14 Remove the bearing and the brake shield from the swivel hub **(see illustrations)**.
15 Thoroughly clean the swivel hub and brake shield, then place the shield in position on the swivel hub.
16 Locate the wheel bearing over the brake shield and into the swivel hub. Position the bearing so that the wheel speed sensor wiring connector is toward the brake caliper side of the swivel hub (ie, towards the front of the vehicle). Align the retaining bolt holes and fit the three new bolts.
17 Tighten the retaining bolts progressively to the specified Stage 1 torque setting using a torque wrench, and then through the specified Stage 2 and Stage 3 angles, using an angle tightening gauge.
18 Refit the swivel hub as described in Section 2.

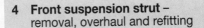

4 Front suspension strut – removal, overhaul and refitting

Note: New strut-to-swivel hub bolts and nuts, strut upper mounting bolts and strut link rod nut, will be required for refitting. Ideally, both front suspension struts should be renewed at the same time in order to maintain good steering and suspension characteristics.

Removal

1 Apply the handbrake, then jack up the front of the vehicle and support it on axle stands (see *Jacking and vehicle support*). Remove the front roadwheel.
2 Extract the retaining clip and release the hydraulic hose from the suspension strut **(see illustration 2.8)**. If working on the left-hand suspension strut on early models, also release the brake pad wear warning indicator wire from the strut bracket.
3 On early models, unscrew the retaining bolt and release the ABS wheel speed sensor wiring plug support plate from the suspension strut bracket **(see illustration)**.
4 On later models, depress the locking tab and release the wiring connector from the suspension strut bracket **(see illustration 2.4a)**.
5 Unscrew the nut and disconnect the anti-roll bar link rod from the strut. Use a spanner on the special flats to hold the link

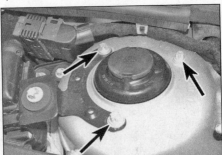

4.8 Unscrew the three suspension strut upper mounting bolts (arrowed)

3.14a Remove the bearing . . .

while the nut is being loosened **(see illustration)**.
6 Mark the position of the suspension strut on the swivel hub by drawing a circle around the heads of the two retaining bolts. **Note:** *This is important to maintain the camber setting.*
7 Slacken and remove the two nuts and bolts securing the suspension strut to the swivel hub, noting that new nuts and bolts will be required for refitting **(see illustration 2.16)**. Disengage the top of the swivel hub from the strut.
8 Support the strut beneath the front wing then, from within the engine compartment, unscrew the three strut upper mounting bolts **(see illustration)**.
9 Lower the strut and withdraw it from under the front wing.

Overhaul

Note 1: *A spring compressor tool will be*

4.3 On early models, unscrew the retaining bolt (arrowed) and release the wiring plug support plate from the strut bracket

4.10 Prise out the plastic cap from the strut upper mounting

3.14b . . . and the brake shield from the swivel hub

required for this operation. Before overhaul, mark the position of each component in relationship with each other for reassembly.
Note 2: *A new piston rod nut will be required for reassembly.*
10 Using a screwdriver, prise out the plastic cap from the upper mounting **(see illustration)**.
11 With the suspension strut resting on a bench, or clamped in a vice, fit a spring compressor tool, and compress the coil spring to relieve the pressure on the spring seats. Ensure that the compressor tool is securely located on the spring, in accordance with the tool manufacturer's instructions.
12 Mark the position of the spring relevant to the top and bottom mountings, then counter-hold the strut piston rod with an Allen key or suitable bit, and unscrew the piston rod nut **(see illustration)**.

4.5 Use a spanner on the flats to hold the link while the nut is being loosened

4.12 Counter-hold the strut piston rod with an Allen key or suitable bit, and unscrew the piston rod nut

4.13a Remove the strut upper mounting . . .

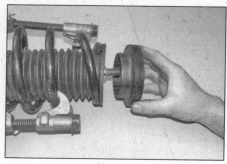

4.13b . . . upper spring seat . . .

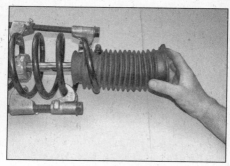

4.13c . . . rubber gaiter . . .

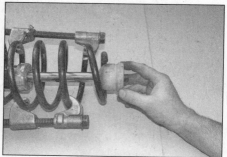

4.13d . . . buffer . . .

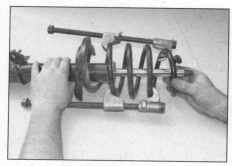

4.13e . . . and spring from the strut

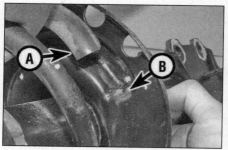

4.18 Locate the spring on the strut making sure that its lower end (A) is against the raised stop (B)

13 Remove the strut upper mounting, upper spring seat, rubber gaiter, buffer and spring from the strut (see illustrations).

14 With the strut assembly now completely dismantled, examine all the components for wear, damage or deformation. Renew any of the components as necessary.

15 Examine the strut for signs of fluid leakage. Check the strut piston for signs of pitting along its entire length, and check the strut body for signs of damage. While holding it in an upright position, test the operation of the strut by moving the piston through a full stroke, and then through short strokes of 50 to 100 mm. In both cases, the resistance felt should be smooth and continuous. If the resistance is jerky or uneven or if there is any visible sign of wear or damage to the strut, renewal is necessary.

16 If any doubt exists as to the condition of the coil spring, carefully remove the spring compressors and check the spring for distortion and signs of cracking. Renew the spring if it is damaged or distorted, or if there is any doubt as to its condition.

17 Inspect all other components for damage or deterioration, and renew any that are suspect.

18 With the spring compressed with the compressor tool, locate the spring on the strut making sure that it is correctly seated with its lower end against the raised stop (see illustration).

19 Refit the buffer, rubber gaiter, upper spring seat and the upper mounting.

20 Refit the new piston rod nut and tighten it to the specified torque while counter-holding

the piston rod. Refit the plastic cap to the upper mounting.

21 Slowly slacken the spring compressor tool to relieve the tension in the spring. Check that the ends of the spring locate correctly against the stops on the spring seats. If necessary, turn the spring and the upper seat so that the components locate correctly before the compressor tool is removed. Remove the compressor tool when the spring is fully seated.

Refitting

22 Locate the strut in position under the front wing and refit the three new retaining bolts. Tighten the retaining bolts progressively to the specified Stage 1 torque setting using a torque wrench, and then through the specified Stage 2 and Stage 3 angles, using an angle tightening gauge.

23 Engage the swivel hub with the suspension strut, and insert the new bolts from the front of the strut so that their threads are facing to the rear. Fit the new nuts, tightening them by hand only at this stage.

24 Align the strut-to-swivel hub bolt heads with the marks made on the strut during removal. Tighten the bolts to the specified torque and through the specified angles given in the Specifications, using a torque wrench and angle-tightening gauge.

25 Locate the hydraulic hose in the strut bracket and secure with the retaining clip. Where applicable, also refit the brake pad wear warning indicator wire to the strut bracket.

26 On early models, refit the ABS wheel speed sensor wiring plug support plate to

the suspension strut bracket and tighten the retaining bolt securely.

27 On later models, refit the wiring connector to the suspension strut bracket.

28 Connect the anti-roll bar link rod to the strut and use a spanner on the flats to hold the link while tightening the nut to the specified torque.

29 Refit the roadwheel, then lower the vehicle to the ground and tighten the roadwheel bolts to the specified torque.

5 Front lower arm – removal, overhaul and refitting

Note: *New lower arm pivot bolts, and new lower arm-to-balljoint nut/bolt, will be required.*

Removal

1 Firmly apply the handbrake, then jack up the front of the car and support it securely on axle stands (see *Jacking and vehicle support*). Remove the appropriate front roadwheel.

2 On models with xenon headlights, if working on the left-hand lower arm, undo the bolt securing the range control sensor to the lower arm, and the two bolts securing the sensor to the subframe. Move the sensor to one side.

3 Unscrew the nut and remove the clamp bolt securing the lower arm balljoint to the swivel hub (see illustrations 2.12a and 2.12b). Note that a new bolt and nut will be required for refitting.

4 Using a lever, push down on the lower arm to free the balljoint from the swivel hub, then move the swivel hub to one side and release the arm, taking care not to damage the balljoint rubber boot (see illustration 2.13). It is advisable to place a protective cover over the rubber boot, such as the plastic cap from an aerosol can, suitably cut to fit.
5 Unscrew the pivot bolt securing the lower arm front mounting to the subframe. Note that a new bolt will be required for refitting.
6 Undo the two bolts securing the lower arm rear mounting bush to the subframe. Note that new bolts will be required for refitting.
7 Disengage the front mounting from the subframe and remove the lower arm from under the car.

Overhaul

8 Thoroughly clean the lower arm and the area around the arm mountings, removing all traces of dirt and underseal if necessary. Check carefully for cracks, distortion, or any other signs of wear or damage, paying particular attention to the mounting bushes and lower arm balljoint. If the front mounting bush or the balljoint are worn, the lower arm must be renewed as these components are not available separately.
9 To renew the rear mounting bush, undo the retaining bolt and remove the bush from the arm. Fit the new bush together with a new retaining bolt. Tighten the bolt just sufficiently to retain the bush. Final tightening is carried out with the car on its roadwheels.

Refitting

10 Offer up the lower arm, aligning the front end of the arm with its subframe bracket. Insert the new front pivot bolt, and secure the rear mounting with two new retaining bolts. Tighten the rear mounting bush retaining bolts to the specified torque and through the specified angles given in the Specifications. Only tighten the pivot bolts hand-tight at this stage.
11 Locate the lower arm balljoint in the swivel hub. Insert the clamp bolt from the front of the swivel hub, so that its threads are facing to the rear. Fit the new nut to the clamp bolt, and tighten it to the specified torque and through the specified angles given in the Specifications, using a torque wrench and angle-tightening gauge.
12 On models with xenon headlights, if working on the left-hand lower arm, refit and tighten the bolt securing the range control sensor to the lower arm, and the two bolts securing the sensor to the subframe.
13 Refit the roadwheel, lower the car to the ground, and tighten the roadwheel bolts to the specified torque setting.
14 Push the car forwards and backwards slightly to settle the suspension and allow the car to adopt its normal ride height. Now tighten the lower arm front pivot bolt to the specified torque and through the specified angles given in the Specifications. If the rear

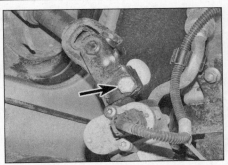
6.5 Unscrew the bolt (arrowed) securing the steering column intermediate shaft to the steering gear pinion

mounting bush has been renewed, tighten its mounting bolt to the specified torque and through the specified angles also.

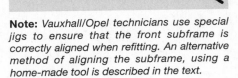

6 Front subframe – removal and refitting

Note: *Vauxhall/Opel technicians use special jigs to ensure that the front subframe is correctly aligned when refitting. An alternative method of aligning the subframe, using a home-made tool is described in the text.*

Removal

1 Jack up the front and rear of the car and support it securely on axle stands (see *Jacking and vehicle support*). Preferably position the car over an inspection pit, or on a lift. The help of an assistant will be needed for this procedure.
2 On diesel engine models, undo the retaining bolts and screws and remove the engine undertray.
3 Set the front wheels in the straight-ahead position, then remove the ignition key and lock the column by turning the steering wheel as required. Remove both front roadwheels.
4 Remove the complete exhaust system as described in Chapter 4A or 4B, as applicable.
5 Working in the engine compartment, unscrew the bolt securing the bottom of the steering column intermediate shaft to the steering gear pinion (see illustration). Use paint or a suitable marker pen to make

6.7 Undo the nut securing the front engine mounting/torque link to the subframe and withdraw the through-bolt (arrowed)

6.6 Undo the through-bolt (arrowed) securing the rear engine mounting/torque link to the subframe

alignment marks between the intermediate shaft and the steering gear pinion, then pull the shaft from the pinion and position to one side.
6 Undo the through-bolt securing the rear engine mounting/torque link to the subframe (see illustration).
7 Similarly, slacken and remove the nut securing the front engine mounting/torque link to the subframe bracket and withdraw the through-bolt (see illustration).
8 Disconnect the steering track rod ends from the swivel hubs by unscrewing the nuts and using a balljoint separator tool (see illustration 2.11).
9 Unscrew the nut and remove the clamp bolt each side securing the lower arm balljoint to the swivel hub (see illustrations 2.12a and 2.12b). Note that new bolts and nuts will be required for refitting.
10 Working on one side at a time, use a lever to push down on the lower arm to free the balljoint from the swivel hub, then move the swivel hub to one side and release the arm, taking care not to damage the balljoint rubber boot (see illustration 2.13). It is advisable to place a protective cover over the rubber boot, such as the plastic cap from an aerosol can, suitably cut to fit.
11 Unscrew the nuts and disconnect the anti-roll bar link rods from the anti-roll bar on both sides. Use a further spanner to hold the studs while the nuts are being loosened (see illustration).
12 Undo the retaining screws, release the

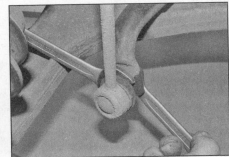
6.11 Unscrew the nuts and disconnect the anti-roll bar link rods from the anti-roll bar on both sides

6.12 Undo the retaining screws, release the clips and remove the wheel arch liner from the wheel arch and subframe

clips and remove the wheel arch liner from the wheel arch and subframe on the right-hand side **(see illustration)**.

13 Remove the front bumper as described in Chapter 11.

6.17a Attach a nut and bolt to one end of the steel strip . . .

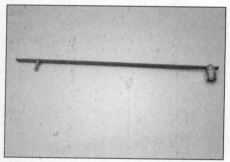

6.17c . . . to make the subframe aligning tool

6.17e . . . and engage the socket at the other end of the tool with the hole in the underbody

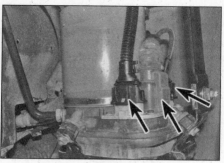

6.14 Disconnect the wiring connectors (arrowed) at the EHPS supply unit – standard EHPS unit shown

14 Disconnect the wiring connectors at the EHPS supply unit. On models with standard EHPS, the supply unit is located under the wheel arch on the right-hand side. On models with compact EHPS, the supply unit

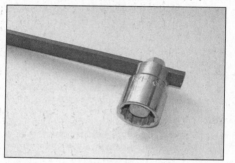

6.17b . . . and attach a 40 mm socket to the other end . . .

6.17d Engage the bolt on the tool with the hole in the subframe . . .

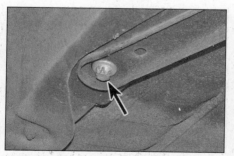

6.20a Undo the bolts (arrowed) each side securing the subframe reinforcement plates to the underbody . . .

is mounted on the subframe, above the rack-and-pinion steering gear **(see illustration)**.
15 On models with standard EHPS, release the wiring harness from the clips on the subframe and hydraulic pipes.
16 On models with xenon headlights, disconnect the wiring connector from the range control sensor, and release the wiring harness from the clips on the subframe.
17 If the Vauxhall/Opel alignment jigs are not being used, it will be necessary to make up an alignment tool to ensure the subframe is correctly positioned when refitting. Obtain a length of steel strip long enough to reach from the 12 mm hole in the side of the subframe just in front of the lower arm front mounting, to the 40 mm hole in the underbody, outboard and to the rear of the subframe. Mark the position of these two holes as accurately as possible on the steel strip, then drill a 12 mm hole at each marked position. Attach a nut and bolt to one hole, and secure a 40 mm socket, using a nut and bolt, to the other hole. Engage the bolt on the tool with the hole in the subframe and engage the socket at the other end of the tool with the hole in the underbody. Reposition the bolt and socket as necessary until the tool is an accurate fit. It may be necessary to elongate the holes in the strip to achieve perfect alignment. Once the tool fits accurately on one side of the car, try it on the other side; the fit should be the same **(see illustrations)**.
18 Use cable-ties to secure the top of the radiator on each side to prevent the radiator dropping when the subframe is removed.
19 Support the subframe with a cradle across a trolley jack. Alternatively, two trolley jacks and the help of an assistant will be required.
20 Undo the two bolts each side securing the subframe rear mountings and the reinforcement plates to the underbody **(see illustration)**. Remove the reinforcement plates.
21 Undo the subframe front mounting bolt on the right-hand side, noting that, on models with standard EHPS, this bolt also secures the EHPS supply unit mounting bracket **(see illustration)**.
22 On diesel engine models, remove the engine management system ECU as described in Chapter 4B.

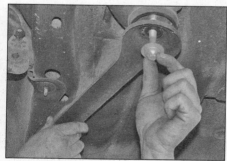

6.20b . . . and to the subframe

23 On models with standard EHPS, undo the two upper mounting bolts securing the EHPS supply unit mounting bracket to the underbody.

24 Undo the subframe front mounting bolt on the left-hand side **(see illustration)**.

25 Slowly and carefully lower the subframe to the ground. As the subframe is lowered, make sure there are no cables or wiring still attached.

26 Remove the lower suspension arms from the subframe with reference to Section 5, the anti-roll bar with reference to Section 7, the rear engine mounting/torque link with reference to the relevant part of Chapter 2, and the steering gear with reference to Section 22.

Refitting

27 Refitting is a reversal of removal, bearing in mind the following points:

a) *Ensure that the radiator lower mounting pegs engage correctly in the subframe brackets as the subframe is refitted.*

b) *Tighten all nuts and bolts to the specified torque and, where necessary, in the stages given. Note that new nuts/bolts should be used on all disturbed fittings.*

c) *Make sure that the subframe is correctly aligned with the underbody before fully-tightening the mounting bolts.*

7 Front anti-roll bar – removal and refitting

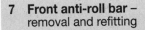

Note: *It is recommended that all mounting nuts and bolts are renewed when refitting.*

Removal

1 Remove the front subframe assembly as described in Section 6.

2 Unscrew the retaining nut and disconnect the link rod from the ends of the anti-roll bar, discard the retaining nut; a new one should be used on refitting **(see illustration 6.11)**. Use a spanner on the flats to hold the link while the nut is being loosened.

3 Unscrew the two bolts from each anti-roll bar mounting clamp, and remove the anti-roll bar from the subframe **(see illustration)**.

4 If any damage or deterioration of the mounting clamp rubber bushes is detected, the complete anti-roll bar must be renewed; the rubber bushes are not available separately and must not be disturbed.

Refitting

5 Refit the anti-roll bar to the subframe, and fit the mounting clamp retaining bolts. Tighten the retaining bolts to the specified torque.

6 Refit the link rods to the ends of the anti-roll bar using new retaining nuts, tightened to the specified torque.

7 Refit the front subframe assembly as described in Section 6.

8 Refit the roadwheels if not already done,

6.21 Undo the subframe front mounting bolt on the right-hand side

then lower the vehicle to the ground and tighten the roadwheel bolts to the specified torque.

8 Rear hub bearings – checking and renewal

Note: *The rear hub bearing and integral ABS wheel speed sensor is a sealed unit and no repairs are possible. If the bearing is worn or the speed sensor is faulty, a new bearing assembly must be obtained.*

Checking

1 Chock the front wheels then jack up the rear of the car and securely support it on axle stands (see *Jacking and vehicle support*). Remove the roadwheel.

2 A dial test indicator (DTI) will be required to measure the amount of play in the bearing. Locate the DTI on the trailing arm and zero the probe on the brake disc.

3 Lever the hub in and out and measure the amount of play in the bearing.

4 To measure the bearing lateral and radial run-out, undo the two bolts securing the brake caliper mounting bracket to the hub carrier. Slide the mounting bracket, complete with brake caliper and pads off the brake disc, and tie it to the shock absorber upper mounting using wire or cable-ties. Note that new caliper mounting bracket bolts will be required for refitting.

5 Undo the securing screw and remove the brake disc from the wheel hub.

7.3 Anti-roll bar clamp mounting bolts (arrowed)

6.24 Subframe left-hand side front mounting bolt (arrowed)

6 To check the lateral run-out, locate the DTI on the trailing arm and zero the probe on the front face of the hub flange. Rotate the hub and measure the run-out.

7 To check the radial run-out, zero the DTI probe on the upper face of the extended portion at the centre of the hub. Rotate the hub and measure the run-out.

8 If the play or run-out exceeds the specified amounts, renew the hub bearing as described below.

9 If the bearing is satisfactory, refit the brake disc and tighten its retaining screw securely.

10 Slide the brake pads, caliper and mounting bracket over the disc and into position on the hub carrier. Fit the two new caliper mounting bracket retaining bolts and tighten them to the specified torque (see Chapter 9).

11 Refit the roadwheel, then lower the vehicle to the ground and tighten the roadwheel bolts to the specified torque.

Renewal

Note: *New hub bearing retaining nuts will be required for refitting.*

12 Chock the front wheels then jack up the rear of the car and securely support it on axle stands (see *Jacking and vehicle support*). Remove the roadwheel.

13 Undo the two bolts securing the brake caliper mounting bracket to the hub carrier. Slide the mounting bracket, complete with brake caliper and pads off the brake disc, and tie it to the shock absorber upper mounting using wire or cable-ties. Note that new caliper mounting bracket bolts will be required for refitting.

14 Undo the securing screw and remove the brake disc from the wheel hub.

15 Disconnect the ABS wheel speed sensor wiring connector from the rear of the bearing assembly **(see illustration)**.

16 Undo the four retaining nuts and remove the bearing unit and brake disc shield from the hub carrier **(see illustration)**.

17 Thoroughly clean the hub carrier, bearing unit and brake shield mating faces, then place the shield in position on the bearing unit.

18 Refit the bearing unit and brake shield to the hub carrier, and screw on four new retaining nuts.

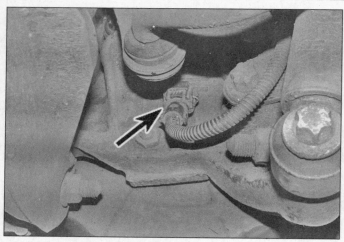

8.15 Disconnect the ABS wheel speed sensor wiring connector (arrowed) from the rear of the bearing assembly

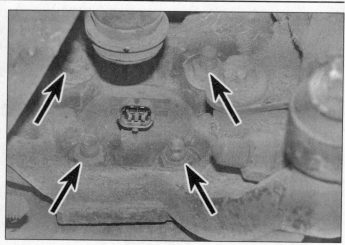

8.16 Undo the four retaining nuts (arrowed) and remove the bearing unit and brake disc shield from the hub carrier

19 Tighten the retaining nuts progressively to the specified Stage 1 torque setting using a torque wrench, and then through the specified Stage 2 and Stage 3 angles, using an angle tightening gauge.

20 Reconnect the ABS wheel speed sensor wiring connector.

21 Refit the brake disc and tighten its retaining screw securely.

22 Slide the brake pads, caliper and mounting bracket over the disc and into position on the hub carrier. Fit the two new caliper mounting bracket retaining bolts and tighten them to the specified torque (see Chapter 9).

23 Refit the roadwheel, then lower the vehicle to the ground and tighten the roadwheel bolts to the specified torque.

---

9 Rear hub carrier –
   removal and refitting

Note: *It is recommended that all mounting nuts and bolts are renewed when refitting.*

Removal

1 Chock the front wheels then jack up the rear of the car and securely support it on axle stands (see *Jacking and vehicle support*). Remove the roadwheel.

2 Disengage the handbrake inner cable from the rear brake caliper lever, then pull the outer cable grommet out of the caliper bracket **(see illustrations)**.

3 Release the handbrake cable from the clip on the trailing arm, then undo the bolt securing the handbrake cable support bracket to the trailing arm front mounting **(see illustration)**. Move the handbrake cable to one side.

4 Remove the rear hub bearing as described in Section 8.

5 Remove the rear coil spring as described in Section 10.

6 Unscrew the shock absorber lower mounting bolt and detach the shock absorber from the hub carrier.

7 Unclip the ABS wheel speed sensor wiring harness from the trailing arm, then undo the four bolts securing the trailing arm front mounting bracket to the underbody **(see illustration)**.

8 Undo the bolt and detach the anti-roll bar link rod from the hub carrier **(see illustration)**.

9 Undo the three bolts securing the trailing arm to the hub carrier and remove the trailing arm from the car.

9.2a Disengage the handbrake inner cable from the caliper lever . . .

9.2b . . . then pull the outer cable grommet out of the caliper bracket

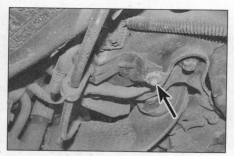

9.3 Undo the bolt (arrowed) securing the handbrake cable support bracket to the trailing arm front mounting

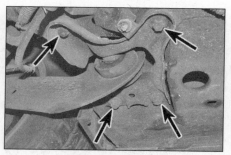

9.7 Undo the four bolts (arrowed) securing the trailing arm front mounting bracket to the underbody

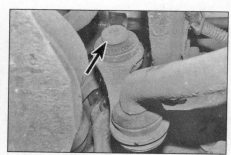

9.8 Undo the bolt (arrowed) and detach the anti-roll bar link rod from the hub carrier

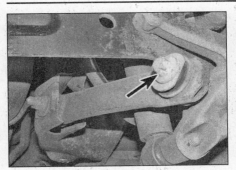

9.10a Undo the bolts securing the auxiliary control arm (arrowed) . . .

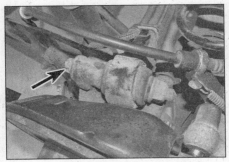

9.10b . . . upper control arm (arrowed) . . .

9.10c . . . and lower control arm (arrowed) to the hub carrier

10 Undo the bolts securing the auxiliary control arm, upper control arm and lower control arm to the hub carrier, and remove the hub carrier from the car (see illustrations).

Refitting

11 Refitting is a reversal of removal, bearing in mind the following points:
a) Tighten all nuts and bolts to the specified torque and, where necessary, in the stages given. Note that new nuts/bolts should be used on all disturbed fittings.
b) Refit the rear coil spring as described in Section 10.
c) Refit the rear hub bearing as described in Section 8.
d) Have the rear wheel toe-in setting and camber angle checked and if necessary adjusted at the earliest opportunity.

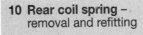 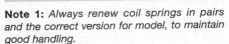

10 Rear coil spring – removal and refitting

Note 1: Always renew coil springs in pairs and the correct version for model, to maintain good handling.
Note 2: Suitable coil spring compressors will be required for this operation.

Removal

1 Chock the front wheels then jack up the rear of the car and securely support it on axle stands (see Jacking and vehicle support). Remove the roadwheel.
2 Undo the two bolts securing the brake caliper mounting bracket to the hub carrier. Slide the mounting bracket, complete with brake caliper and pads off the brake disc, and tie it to the shock absorber upper mounting using wire or cable-ties. Note that new caliper mounting bracket bolts will be required for refitting.
3 Fit a spring compressor tool to the coil spring, and compress the spring to relieve the pressure on the spring seats. Ensure that the compressor tool is securely located on the spring in accordance with the tool manufacturer's instructions. Remove the spring together with the upper damper ring and lower spring stop.

Refitting

4 Locate the compressed spring in position ensuring that the upper damper ring and lower spring stop are correctly seated. Release the tension on the spring compressor and remove the compressor from the spring.
5 Slide the brake pads, caliper and mounting bracket over the disc and into position on the hub carrier. Fit the two new caliper mounting bracket retaining bolts and tighten them to the specified torque (see Chapter 9).
6 Refit the roadwheel, then lower the vehicle to the ground and tighten the roadwheel bolts to the specified torque.

11 Rear suspension upper control arm – removal and refitting

Note: It is recommended that all mounting nuts and bolts are renewed when refitting.

Removal

1 Chock the front wheels then jack up the rear of the car and securely support it on axle stands (see Jacking and vehicle support). Remove the roadwheel.
2 Remove the rear coil spring as described in Section 10.
3 Release the clips securing the ABS wheel speed sensor wiring harness to the upper control arm.
4 Place a jack under the hub carrier and just take the weight of the rear suspension assembly.

11.6 Undo the bolt (arrowed) securing the upper control arm to the rear axle body

5 Undo the bolt securing the upper control arm to the hub carrier (see illustration 9.10b).
6 Undo the bolt securing the upper control arm to the rear axle body and remove the control arm from the car (see illustration).

Refitting

7 Refitting is a reversal of removal, bearing in mind the following points:
a) Tighten all nuts and bolts to the specified torque and, where necessary, in the Stages given. Note that new nuts/bolts should be used on all disturbed fittings.
b) Refit the rear coil spring as described in Section 10.
c) Have the rear wheel toe-in setting and camber angle checked and if necessary adjusted at the earliest opportunity.

12 Rear suspension lower control arm – removal and refitting

Note: It is recommended that all mounting nuts and bolts are renewed when refitting.

Removal

1 Chock the front wheels then jack up the rear of the car and securely support it on axle stands (see Jacking and vehicle support). Remove the roadwheel.
2 If working on the left-hand lower control arm, suitably support the exhaust system and release the rubber mounting blocks at the rear. Lower the system slightly for access to the control arm.
3 If working on the left-hand lower control arm on models with xenon headlights, undo the retaining bolt and detach the headlight range control linkage from the lower control arm.
4 Remove the rear coil spring as described in Section 10.
5 Undo the bolt securing the lower control arm to the hub carrier (see illustration 9.10c).
6 Accurately mark the position of the camber adjustment eccentric disc on the lower control arm inner mounting (see illustration). Undo the bolt securing the lower control arm to the rear axle body and remove the control arm from the car.

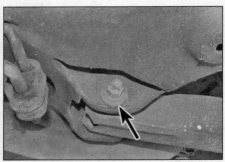

12.6 Camber adjustment eccentric disc (arrowed) on the lower control arm inner mounting

Refitting

7 Refitting is a reversal of removal, bearing in mind the following points:
a) *Tighten all nuts and bolts to the specified torque and, where necessary, in the stages given. Note that new nuts/bolts should be used on all disturbed fittings.*
b) *Align the camber adjustment eccentric disc with the marks made on removal when tightening the control arm inner mounting bolt.*
c) *Refit the rear coil spring as described in Section 10.*
d) *Have the rear wheel toe-in setting and camber angle checked and if necessary adjusted at the earliest opportunity.*

13 Rear suspension auxiliary control arm – removal and refitting

Note: *It is recommended that all mounting nuts and bolts are renewed when refitting.*

Removal

1 Chock the front wheels then jack up the rear of the car and securely support it on axle stands (see *Jacking and vehicle support*). Remove the roadwheel.
2 Remove the rear coil spring as described in Section 10.
3 Place a jack under the hub carrier and just take the weight of the rear suspension assembly.
4 Undo the bolt securing the auxiliary control arm to the hub carrier **(see illustration 9.10a)**.
5 Accurately mark the position of the toe-in adjustment eccentric disc on the auxiliary control arm inner mounting **(see illustration)**. Undo the bolt securing the auxiliary control arm to the rear axle body and remove the control arm from the car.

Refitting

6 Refitting is a reversal of removal, bearing in mind the following points:
a) *Tighten all nuts and bolts to the specified torque and, where necessary, in the stages given. Note that new nuts/bolts should be used on all disturbed fittings.*

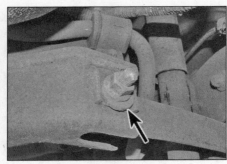

13.5 Toe-in adjustment eccentric disc (arrowed) on the auxiliary control arm inner mounting

b) *Align the toe-in adjustment eccentric disc with the marks made on removal when tightening the control arm inner mounting bolt.*
c) *Refit the rear coil spring as described in Section 10.*
d) *Have the rear wheel toe-in setting and camber angle checked and if necessary adjusted at the earliest opportunity.*

14 Rear suspension trailing arm – removal and refitting

Note: *It is recommended that all mounting nuts and bolts are renewed when refitting.*

Removal

1 Chock the front wheels then jack up the rear of the car and securely support it on axle stands (see *Jacking and vehicle support*). Remove the roadwheel.
2 Release the handbrake cable from the clip on the trailing arm, then undo the bolt securing the handbrake cable support bracket to the trailing arm front mounting **(see illustration 9.3)**. Move the handbrake cable to one side.
3 Unclip the ABS wheel speed sensor wiring harness from the trailing arm.
4 Place a jack under the hub carrier and just take the weight of the rear suspension assembly.
5 Unscrew the shock absorber lower mounting bolt and detach the shock absorber from the hub carrier.

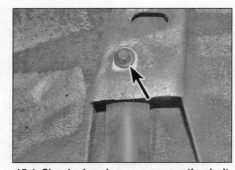

15.4 Shock absorber upper mounting bolt (arrowed)

6 Undo the four bolts securing the trailing arm front mounting bracket to the underbody **(see illustration 9.7)**.
7 Undo the three bolts securing the trailing arm to the hub carrier and remove the trailing arm from the car.

Refitting

8 Refitting is a reversal of removal, bearing in mind the following points:
a) *Tighten all nuts and bolts to the specified torque and, where necessary, in the stages given. Note that new nuts/bolts should be used on all disturbed fittings.*
b) *Have the rear wheel toe-in setting and camber angle checked and if necessary adjusted at the earliest opportunity.*

15 Rear shock absorber – removal, testing and refitting

Note 1: *Always renew shock absorbers in pairs and the correct version for the model to maintain good handling.*
Note 2: *It is recommended that the shock absorber mounting bolts are renewed when refitting.*

Removal

1 Chock the front wheels then jack up the rear of the car and securely support it on axle stands (see *Jacking and vehicle support*). Remove the roadwheel.
2 Place a jack under the hub carrier and just take the weight of the rear suspension assembly.
3 Unscrew the shock absorber lower mounting bolt and detach the shock absorber from the hub carrier.
4 Unscrew the shock absorber upper mounting bolt and remove the shock absorber from the car **(see illustration)**.

Testing

5 Examine the shock absorber for signs of fluid leakage or damage. Test the operation of the strut, while holding it in an upright position, by moving the piston through a full stroke, and then through short strokes of 50 to 100 mm. In both cases, the resistance felt should be smooth and continuous. If the resistance is jerky, or uneven, or if there is any visible sign of wear or damage to the strut, renewal is necessary. Also check the rubber mounting bush(es) for damage and deterioration. If the bushes are damaged or worn, the complete shock absorber will have to be renewed, as the mounting bushes are not available separately. Inspect the shanks of the mounting bolts for signs of wear or damage, and renew as necessary.

Refitting

6 Refitting is a reversal of removal, tightening the new mounting bolts to the specified torque.

16 Rear axle body –
removal and refitting

Note 1: *Vauxhall technicians use special jigs to ensure that the rear axle body is correctly aligned. Without the use of these tools it is important to note and suitably mark the position of the axle body accurately before removal. If necessary, refer to the information contained in Section 6 regarding the fabrication of a home-made aligning tool, and adapt the principle for the rear axle body.*

Note 2: *It is recommended that all mounting nuts and bolts are renewed when refitting.*

Removal

1 Chock the front wheels then jack up the rear of the car and securely support it on axle stands (see *Jacking and vehicle support*). Remove both rear the roadwheels.

2 Remove the complete exhaust system as described in Chapter 4A or 4B as applicable.

3 Disengage the handbrake inner cable from the rear brake caliper levers, then pull the outer cable grommet out of the caliper brackets **(see illustrations 9.2a and 9.2b)**.

4 Undo the two bolts securing the brake caliper mounting bracket to the hub carrier on each side. Slide the mounting bracket, complete with brake caliper and pads off the brake disc, and tie it to the shock absorber upper mounting using wire or cable-ties. Note that new caliper mounting bracket bolts will be required for refitting.

5 Release the handbrake cable from the clip on each trailing arm, then undo the bolt securing the handbrake cable support bracket to the trailing arm front mounting, on each side **(see illustration 9.3)**. Move the handbrake cables to one side.

6 Trace the ABS wheel speed sensor wiring harness back to the wiring connector on the underbody and disconnect the connector. Release the harness from the underbody clips so that its free to be removed with the rear axle body.

7 On models with a tyre pressure monitoring system, undo the screws and clips and remove the wheel arch liners on both sides. Trace the wiring harness back to the connectors, and disconnect the wiring connectors on each side. Release the harness from the clips on the underbody.

8 On models with xenon headlights, undo the retaining bolt and detach the headlight range control linkage from the lower control arm on the left-hand side.

9 Remove the rear coil spring on each side as described in Section 10.

10 Unscrew the shock absorber lower mounting bolt and detach the shock absorber from the hub carrier.

11 Undo the four bolts securing the trailing arm front mounting bracket to the underbody **(see illustration 9.7)**.

16.13a Rear axle body front mounting bolt (arrowed) . . .

12 Support the rear axle body with a cradle across a trolley jack. Alternatively, two trolley jacks and the help of an assistant will be required.

13 Undo the four bolts securing the rear axle body to the vehicle underbody **(see illustrations)**.

14 Slowly and carefully lower the rear axle body to the ground. As the assembly is lowered, make sure there are no cables or wiring still attached.

15 With the rear axle body removed from the car, if required, carry out further dismantling to remove the attached components, with reference to the applicable Sections of this Chapter.

Refitting

16 Refitting is a reversal of removal, bearing in mind the following points:

a) *Tighten all nuts and bolts to the specified torque and, where necessary, in the stages given. Note that new nuts/bolts should be used on all disturbed fittings.*

b) *Make sure that the rear axle body is correctly aligned with the vehicle underbody before fully-tightening the mounting bolts.*

17 Rear anti-roll bar –
removal and refitting

Note: *It is recommended that all mounting nuts and bolts are renewed when refitting.*

Removal

1 Remove the rear axle body as described in Section 16.

2 Undo the bolt and detach the anti-roll bar link rod from the hub carrier on each side **(see illustration 9.8)**.

3 Prior to removal of the anti-roll bar, mark the position of each anti-roll bar mounting clamp rubber.

4 Unscrew the two bolts from each mounting clamp, and remove the clamp. As the last clamp is removed, support the anti-roll bar and remove it from the rear axle body.

5 Inspect the mounting clamp rubbers for signs of damage and deterioration, and renew if necessary.

16.13b . . . and rear mounting bolt (arrowed)

Refitting

6 Align the mounting rubbers with the marks made on the anti-roll bar prior to removal.

7 Refit the anti-roll bar to the rear axle body, and fit the mounting clamps. Ensure that the clamp half is correctly engaged with the anti-roll bar rubbers, then tighten each clamp retaining bolt, by hand only at this stage.

8 With the two clamps loosely installed, check the position of the anti-roll bar to the marks made on removal, then tighten the clamp bolts to the specified torque setting.

9 Refit the link rods to the hub carriers using new bolts, and tighten the bolts to the specified torque setting.

10 Refit the rear axle body as described in Section 16.

18 Steering wheel –
removal and refitting

⚠️ **Warning: Make sure that the airbag safety recommendations given in Chapter 12 are followed, to prevent personal injury.**

Removal

1 Remove the airbag as described in Chapter 12.

2 Set the front wheels in the straight-ahead position, then lock the column in position after removing the ignition key.

3 Disconnect the wiring harness connector for the steering wheel switches **(see illustration)**.

18.3 Disconnect the wiring harness connector (arrowed) for the steering wheel switches

18.4 Steering wheel retaining bolt (arrowed)

18.5 Alignment marks (arrowed) between the steering column shaft and steering wheel

18.6 Guide the wiring for the airbag through the aperture in the wheel, taking care not to damage the wiring connectors

4 Unscrew the Torx retaining bolt securing the steering wheel to the column **(see illustration)**.

5 Check that there are alignment marks between the steering column shaft and steering wheel **(see illustration)**. If no marks are visible, centre punch the wheel and column shaft to ensure correct alignment when refitting.

6 Grip the steering wheel with both hands and carefully rock it from side-to-side to release it from the splines on the steering column. As the steering wheel is being removed, guide the wiring for the airbag through the aperture in the wheel, taking care not to damage the wiring connectors **(see illustration)**.

Refitting

7 Refit the steering wheel, aligning the marks made prior to removal. Route the airbag wiring connectors through the steering wheel aperture. **Note:** *Make sure the steering wheel centre hub locates correctly with the contact unit on the steering column.*

8 Clean the threads on the retaining bolt and the threads in the steering column. Coat the retaining bolt with locking compound, then fit the retaining bolt and tighten to the specified torque.

9 Reconnect the wiring connector for the steering wheel switches.

10 Release the steering lock, and refit the airbag as described in Chapter 12.

19 Ignition switch/ steering column lock – removal and refitting

Removal

1 Disconnect the battery negative terminal (refer to *Disconnecting the battery* in the Reference Chapter).

2 Remove the steering column shrouds as described in Chapter 11.

3 Insert the ignition key into the ignition switch/lock, and turn it to position I.

4 Insert a thin rod into the hole in the lock housing, press the rod to release the detent spring, and pull out the lock cylinder using the key **(see illustration)**.

Refitting

5 Insert the ignition switch/lock into the lock housing, while the key is in position I. Remove the rod from the lock housing.

6 Refit steering column shrouds as described in Chapter 11, then reconnect the battery.

20 Steering column – removal and refitting

Note: *It is recommended that all mounting nuts and bolts are renewed when refitting.*

Removal

1 Remove the steering wheel as described in Section 18.

2 Remove the facia footwell trim panel on the driver's side as described in Chapter 11.

3 Remove the steering column shrouds as described in Chapter 11.

4 Remove the steering column electronics module as described in Chapter 12.

5 If applicable, make sure the steering column adjustment handle is in the locked position.

6 Using paint or similar, make alignment marks between the steering column and intermediate shaft, then slacken and remove the clamp bolt securing the intermediate shaft to the steering column **(see illustration)**. Separate the intermediate shaft from the steering column shaft.

7 Undo the retaining bolt and disconnect the earth cable from the column. Unscrew the plastic retainer and release the wiring harness from the side of the column **(see illustration)**.

8 Where fitted, remove the clutch switch from the pedal bracket assembly.

9 Unscrew the steering column lower fastening clamp bolt, and the two upper mounting bolts **(see illustrations)**. Withdraw the steering column from the facia crossmember, and remove the column from inside the vehicle.

Refitting

10 Refitting is a reversal of removal, bearing in mind the following points:
a) Tighten all nuts and bolts to the specified

19.4 Insert a thin rod into the lock housing hole, press the rod to release the detent spring, and pull out the lock cylinder

20.6 Slacken and remove the clamp bolt (arrowed) securing the intermediate shaft to the steering column

20.7 Unscrew the plastic retainer (arrowed) and release the wiring harness from the side of the column

torque and, where necessary, in the stages given. Note that new nuts/bolts should be used on all disturbed fittings.

b) Ensure that the marks made on the steering column and intermediate shaft are correctly aligned.

c) Refit the steering column electronics module as described in Chapter 12.

d) Refit the steering column shrouds and facia footwell trim panel as described in Chapter 11.

e) Refit the steering wheel as described in Section 18.

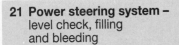

21 Power steering system – level check, filling and bleeding

Note: *There is no definitive list of which models have which type of steering. The only way to tell is by the location of the fluid reservoir. If it's visible in the engine compartment, then it's compact EHPS. If it's not visible in the engine compartment then it's under the wheel arch, and it's standard EHPS.*

Models with standard EHPS

1 Firmly apply the handbrake, then jack up the front of the car and support it securely on axle stands (see *Jacking and vehicle support*). Remove the right-hand front roadwheel.

2 Undo the retaining screws, release the clips and remove the wheel arch liner from the wheel arch and subframe on the right-hand side **(see illustration 6.12)**.

3 Check that the fluid level is between the upper MAX line and lower MIN line on the side of the EHPS supply unit reservoir **(see illustration)**.

4 If topping-up is necessary, remove the filler cap from the top of the reservoir. Obtain a clean funnel and a long length of flexible pipe to fit the end of the funnel. From within the engine compartment, insert the pipe through the gap between the air cleaner housing and the headlight and insert the pipe into the top of the reservoir **(see illustration)**.

5 Using power steering fluid of the specified type (see *Lubricants and fluids*), fill the reservoir up to the MAX line, by means of the funnel and tube.

6 If the system has been completely drained and is being refilled after a repair operation, carry out the following bleeding procedure. If the system was only being topped-up, remove the funnel and tube and refit the reservoir filler cap. Refit the wheel arch liner and roadwheel, then lower the car to the ground.

7 To bleed the system, make sure the fluid level in the reservoir is up to the MAX mark and check the level constantly during the bleeding procedure.

8 Start the engine, then switch it off again after approximately five seconds. Repeat this procedure two more times, pausing briefly between each stop/start and maintaining the fluid level in the reservoir.

20.9a Unscrew the steering column lower fastening clamp bolt (arrowed) . . .

9 Now start the engine again and allow it to idle. Turn the steering to full left lock, then full right lock five times. Switch the engine off.

10 Recheck the fluid level in the reservoir and top-up if necessary. Remove the funnel and tube and refit the reservoir filler cap.

11 Refit the wheel arch liner and roadwheel, then lower the car to the ground.

12 It is possible that some air may still remain in the system after bleeding but this will be expelled when the car is driven on the road.

Models with compact EHPS

13 Reach down behind the engine and unscrew the filler cap from the EHPS supply unit reservoir **(see illustration)**.

14 Wipe clean the dipstick which is integral with the cap. Refit the cap, then remove it

21.3 Fluid level MAX and MIN lines on the side of the standard EHPS supply unit reservoir

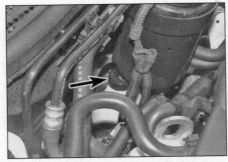

21.13 Reach down behind the engine and unscrew the filler cap from the compact EHPS supply unit reservoir

20.9b . . . and the two upper mounting bolts (one side arrowed

once more and observe the fluid level on the dipstick. The level should be up to the MAX mark **(see illustration)**.

15 If topping-up is necessary, obtain a clean funnel and a long length of flexible pipe to fit the end of the funnel. Insert the pipe down behind the engine and into the top of the reservoir. Using power steering fluid of the specified type (see *Lubricants and fluids*), fill the reservoir by means of the funnel and tube until the level is up to the MAX line on the dipstick.

16 If the system has been completely drained and is being refilled after a repair operation, carry out the bleeding procedure described previously in paragraphs 7 to 10. If the system was only being topped-up, remove the funnel and tube and refit the reservoir filler cap.

21.4 Insert a pipe through the gap between the air cleaner housing and the headlight and into the top of the reservoir

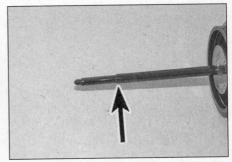

21.14 Maximum mark (arrowed) on the fluid level dipstick

22.5 Steering gear mounting bolt retaining nut (arrowed)

22 Steering gear assembly – removal, inspection and refitting

Note: *It is recommended that all mounting nuts and bolts are renewed when refitting.*

Removal

1 Remove the front subframe as described in Section 6.
2 On models with compact EHPS, remove the EHPS supply unit and mounting bracket as described in Section 23.
3 Disconnect the steering angle sensor wiring connector from the steering gear. Note the routing of the wiring harness, then release it from the clips on the hydraulic pipes and steering gear and move the harness to one side.
4 Place a suitable container beneath the hydraulic supply and return pipes on the steering gear and be prepared for escaping hydraulic fluid. Undo the bolt securing the hydraulic supply and return pipe retaining plate to the steering gear. Withdraw the pipes from the steering gear and collect the retaining plate. Collect the escaping fluid in the container. Note that new sealing O-rings will be required for the hydraulic pipes for refitting. Suitably cover or plug the disconnected unions to prevent dirt entry.
5 Undo the nuts from the two steering gear mounting bolts, while counter-holding the bolts from under the subframe **(see illustration)**.

Lift off the two washers then remove the bolts. Note that new nuts and bolts will be required for refitting.
6 Twist the anti-roll bar upwards, then lift the steering gear off the subframe.
7 If a new steering gear assembly is to be fitted, then the track rod ends will need to be removed from each end of the steering track rods (see Section 25).

Inspection

8 Examine the steering gear assembly for signs of wear or damage, and check that the rack moves freely throughout the full length of its travel, with no signs of roughness or excessive free play between the steering gear pinion and rack. If any problems of this nature are noted, renewal of the steering gear will be necessary. The only components which can be renewed separately are the steering gear gaiters, the track rod ends and the track rods. Steering gear gaiter, track rod end and track rod renewal procedures are covered in Sections 24, 25 and 26 respectively.

Refitting

9 Refitting is a reverse of the removal procedure, bearing in mind the following points:
  a) *Renew the sealing O-rings on the hydraulic supply and return pipes.*
  b) *Tighten the steering gear mounting bolt nuts to the specified torque in the stages given. Note that new nuts/bolts should be used.*
  c) *On models with compact EHPS, refit the supply unit and mounting bracket as described in Section 23.*
  d) *Set the steering gear in the straight-ahead position prior to refitting the front subframe.*
  e) *Refit the front subframe as described in Section 6.*
  f) *Where applicable, fit new track rod balljoints as described in Section 25.*
  g) *On completion, fill and bleed the power steering system as described in Section 21.*
  h) *Have the front wheel toe setting checked and if necessary adjusted at the earliest opportunity.*

23 Electro-hydraulic power steering (EHPS) supply unit – removal and refitting

Note 1: *The EHPS supply unit comprises the power steering pump, electric pump drive motor and the EHPS electronic control unit. The supply unit is a sealed component and the individual parts cannot be removed separately.*
Note 2: *If a new EHPS supply unit is to be fitted, it will be necessary to programme the new ECU after installation. This work requires the use of dedicated Vauxhall/Opel diagnostic equipment or a compatible alternative.*

Standard EHPS

Removal

1 The EHPS supply unit is located under the front wheel-arch on the right-hand side, behind the wheel arch liner.
2 Firmly apply the handbrake, then jack up the front of the car and support it securely on axle stands (see *Jacking and vehicle support*). Remove the right-hand front roadwheel.
3 On diesel engine models, undo the retaining bolts and screws and remove the engine undertray.
4 Undo the retaining screws, release the clips and remove the wheel arch liner from the wheel arch and subframe on the right-hand side **(see illustration 6.12)**.
5 Disconnect the wiring connectors at the EHPS supply unit, then release the wiring harness from the retaining clips on the mounting bracket **(see illustration)**.
6 Place a suitable container beneath the hydraulic supply and return pipes on the side of the EHPS supply unit and be prepared for escaping hydraulic fluid **(see illustration)**.
7 Wipe clean the area around the supply pipe and return hose connections. Undo the supply pipe union and withdraw the pipe from the EHPS supply unit. Collect the escaping fluid in the container.
8 Slacken the hose clip and disconnect the fluid return hose from the supply unit. Suitably cover or plug the disconnected unions to prevent dirt entry.

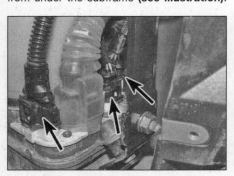

23.5 Disconnect the wiring connectors (arrowed) at the EHPS supply unit

23.6 Hydraulic supply and return pipe connections (arrowed) on the side of the EHPS supply unit

23.9 Undo the lower EHPS supply unit mounting bracket retaining bolt (arrowed)

9 Undo the lower EHPS supply unit mounting bracket retaining bolt, noting that this bolt also secures the front subframe (see illustration). Note that a new bolt will be required for refitting.

10 Undo the two upper supply unit mounting bracket retaining bolts and withdraw the supply unit and mounting bracket from under the wheel arch.

11 If required, undo the three nuts and remove the supply unit from the mounting bracket.

Refitting

12 Refitting is a reverse of the removal procedure, bearing in mind the following points:

a) *Renew the sealing O-ring on the hydraulic supply pipe if there is any sign of deterioration.*

b) *Tighten all nuts, bolts and unions to the specified torque and, where necessary, in the stages given. Note that a supply unit mounting bracket lower retaining bolt must be used.*

c) *On completion, fill and bleed the power steering system as described in Section 21.*

Compact EHPS

Removal

13 The EHPS supply unit is mounted on the front subframe, above the steering gear.

14 Firmly apply the handbrake, then jack up the front of the car and support it securely on axle stands (see *Jacking and vehicle support*). On diesel engine models, undo the retaining bolts and screws and remove the engine undertray.

15 On diesel engine models, remove the fuel filter crash box as described in Chapter 4B.

16 If necessary, for improved access below the car, remove the exhaust system as described in Chapter 4A or 4B, as applicable.

17 Disconnect the wiring connectors at the EHPS supply unit.

18 Place a suitable container beneath the hydraulic supply and return pipes on the steering gear and be prepared for escaping hydraulic fluid. Undo the bolt securing the hydraulic supply and return pipe retaining plate to the steering gear. Withdraw the pipes from the steering gear and collect the retaining plate. Collect the escaping fluid in the container. Note that new sealing O-rings will be required for the hydraulic pipes for refitting. Suitably cover or plug the disconnected unions to prevent dirt entry.

19 Undo the three nuts securing the EHPS supply unit to its mounting bracket. Lift the supply unit, complete with hydraulic pipes, and remove it from the car. On diesel engine models, the unit is removed from above; on petrol engine models, from below.

20 If required the supply unit mounting bracket can be removed from the subframe, after undoing the three retaining bolts.

Refitting

21 Refitting is a reverse of the removal

procedure, bearing in mind the following points:

a) *Renew the sealing O-rings on the hydraulic supply and return pipes.*

b) *Tighten all nuts, bolts and unions to the specified torque.*

c) *On diesel engine models, refit the fuel filter crash box as described in Chapter 4B.*

d) *If removed, refit the exhaust system as described in Chapter 4A or 4B as applicable.*

e) *On completion, fill and bleed the power steering system as described in Section 21.*

24 Steering gear rubber gaiters – renewal

1 Remove the track rod end as described in Section 25.

2 Mark the correct fitted position of the gaiter on the track rod, then release the retaining clips, and slide the gaiter off the steering gear housing and track rod.

3 Thoroughly clean the track rod and the steering gear housing, clean off any corrosion, burrs or sharp edges which might damage the new gaiter's sealing lips on installation.

4 Carefully slide the new gaiter onto the track rod end, and locate it on the steering gear housing. Align the outer edge of the gaiter with the mark made on the track rod prior to removal, then secure it in position with new retaining clips.

5 Refit the track rod end as described in Section 25.

25 Track rod end – removal and refitting

Note: *A new track rod end-to-swivel hub retaining nut will be required when refitting.*

Removal

1 Firmly apply the handbrake, then jack up the front of the car and support it securely on axle stands (see *Jacking and vehicle support*). Remove the appropriate front roadwheel.

2 If the track rod end is to be re-used, use a scriber, or similar, to mark its relationship to the track rod.

3 Hold the track rod arm, and unscrew the track rod end locknut by a quarter of a turn.

4 Slacken and remove the nut securing the track rod end to the swivel hub, and release the balljoint tapered shank using a universal balljoint separator (see illustration). Discard the nut; a new one must be used of refitting.

5 Counting the exact number of turns necessary to do so, unscrew the track rod end from the track rod.

6 Count the number of exposed threads between the end of the track rod and the

25.4 Release the balljoint tapered shank using a universal balljoint separator

locknut, and record this figure. If a new gaiter is to be fitted, unscrew the locknut from the track rod.

7 Carefully clean the track rod end and the track rod threads. Renew the track rod end if there is excessive free play of the balljoint shank, or if the shank is excessively stiff. If the balljoint gaiter is damaged, the complete track rod end assembly must be renewed; it is not possible to obtain the gaiter separately.

Refitting

8 If it was removed, screw the locknut onto the track rod threads, and position it so that the same number of exposed threads are visible as was noted prior to removal.

9 Screw the track rod end on to the track rod by the number of turns noted on removal. This should bring the track rod end to within approximately a quarter of a turn from the locknut, with the alignment marks that were noted on removal.

10 Refit the track rod end balljoint shank to the swivel hub, then fit a new retaining nut and tighten it to the specified torque setting. If the balljoint shank turns as the nut is being tightened, press down on the track rod end to force the tapered part of the shank into the arm on the swivel hub.

11 Tighten the track rod end securing locknut on the track rod while holding the track rod stationary with a second spanner on the flats provided.

12 Refit the roadwheel, then lower the vehicle to the ground and tighten the roadwheel bolts to the specified torque setting.

13 Have the front wheel toe setting checked and if necessary adjusted at the earliest opportunity.

26 Track rod – renewal

Note: *When refitting, a new track rod end-to-swivel hub nut and new gaiter retaining clips will be required. Vauxhall/Opel special tool KM-6321, or a suitable equivalent, will be required to unscrew the track rod inner balljoint from the end of the steering rack.*

1 Remove the track rod end as described in Section 25.

2 Release the retaining clips, and slide the steering gear gaiter off the end of the track rod as described in Section 24.

3 If the track rod on the passenger's side is being removed, it will be necessary to release the clip and fold back the gaiter on the driver's side also. A flat is provided on the rack, on the driver's side, to enable the rack to be held stationary while the track rod is unscrewed.

4 Turn the steering on full lock, so that the rack protrudes from the steering gear housing on the relevant side, slide the cover (where fitted) off the inner balljoint.

5 Engage the help of an assistant, if necessary, and prevent the rack from rotating using an open-ended spanner located on the rack flat on the driver's side. Unscrew and remove the track rod inner balljoint from the end of the steering rack using the special tool or suitable equivalent.

6 Remove the track rod assembly, and examine the track rod inner balljoint for signs of slackness or tight spots. Check that the track rod itself is straight and free from damage. If necessary, renew the track rod; it is also recommended that the steering gear gaiter/dust cover is renewed.

7 Screw the balljoint into the end of the steering rack. Tighten the track rod inner balljoint to the specified torque, whilst retaining the steering rack with an open-ended spanner.

8 Install the steering gaiter(s) and track rod end as described in Sections 24 and 25.

27 Wheel alignment and steering angles – general information

Definitions

1 A car's steering and suspension geometry is defined in four basic settings – all angles are expressed in degrees (toe settings are also expressed as a measurement); the steering axis is defined as an imaginary line drawn through the axis of the suspension strut, extended where necessary to contact the ground.

2 Camber is the angle between each roadwheel and a vertical line drawn through its centre and tyre contact patch, when viewed from the front or rear of the car. Positive camber is when the roadwheels are tilted outwards from the vertical at the top; negative camber is when they are tilted inwards. Slight adjustment of the front camber angle is possible, by altering the position of the swivel hub at its attachment to the front suspension strut. The rear camber angle can be adjusted by altering the position of the eccentric disc on the lower control arm inner mounting.

3 Castor is the angle between the steering axis and a vertical line drawn through each roadwheel's centre and tyre contact patch, when viewed from the side of the car. Positive castor is when the steering axis is tilted so that it contacts the ground ahead of the vertical; negative castor is when it contacts the ground behind the vertical. The castor angle is not adjustable.

4 Toe is the difference, viewed from above, between lines drawn through the roadwheel centres and the car's centre-line. 'Toe-in' is when the roadwheels point inwards, towards each other at the front, while 'toe-out' is when they splay outwards from each other at the front.

5 The front wheel toe setting is adjusted by screwing the track rod in or out of its balljoints, to alter the effective length of the track rod assembly. The rear wheel toe setting can be adjusted by altering the position of the eccentric disc on the auxiliary control arm inner mounting.

Checking and adjustment

6 Due to the special measuring equipment necessary to check the wheel alignment and steering angles, and the skill required to use it properly, the checking and adjustment of these settings is best left to a Vauxhall/Opel dealer or similar expert. Note that most tyre-fitting shops now possess sophisticated checking equipment.

Chapter 11
Bodywork and fittings

Contents

Degrees of difficulty

| **Easy,** suitable for novice with little experience | | **Fairly easy,** suitable for beginner with some experience | | **Fairly difficult,** suitable for competent DIY mechanic | | **Difficult,** suitable for experienced DIY mechanic | | **Very difficult,** suitable for expert DIY or professional | 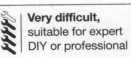 |

Specifications

Torque wrench settings	Nm	lbf ft
Front seat belt anchorage bolts	25	18
Front seat belt inertia reel bolt	20	15
Front seat mounting bolts	25	18
Rear seat belt anchorage bolts	35	26
Rear seat belt inertia reel bolt.	35	26
Rear seat belt stalk retaining bolts.	35	26
Rear seat belt tensioner mounting bolts	35	26
Seat belt-to-height adjuster mounting bolts	35	26

1 General information

The bodyshell is made of pressed-steel sections, and is available in three- and five-door Saloon, Hatchback and Estate versions. Most components are welded together, but some use is made of structural adhesives; the front wings are bolted on.

The bonnet is made of aluminium, whereas the doors, and some other vulnerable panels, are made of zinc-coated metal. These are further protected by being coated with an anti-chip primer, prior to being sprayed.

Extensive use is made of plastic materials, mainly on the interior, but also in exterior components. The front and rear bumpers are injection-moulded from a synthetic material which is very strong and yet light. Plastic components such as wheel arch liners are fitted to the underside of the vehicle, to improve the body's resistance to corrosion.

2 Maintenance – bodywork and underframe

The general condition of a vehicle's body-work is the one thing that significantly affects its value. Maintenance is easy, but needs to be regular. Neglect, particularly after minor damage, can lead quickly to further deterioration and costly repair bills. It is important also to keep watch on those parts of the vehicle not immediately visible, for instance the underside, inside all the wheel arches, and the lower part of the engine compartment.

The basic maintenance routine for the bodywork is washing – preferably with a lot of water, from a hose. This will remove all the loose solids which may have stuck to the vehicle. It is important to flush these off in such a way as to prevent grit from scratching the finish. The wheel arches and underframe need washing in the same way, to remove any accumulated mud, which will retain moisture and tend to encourage rust. Paradoxically enough, the best time to clean the underframe and wheel arches is in wet weather, when the mud is thoroughly wet and soft. In very wet weather, the underframe is usually cleaned of large accumulations automatically, and this is a good time for inspection.

Periodically, except on vehicles with a wax-based underbody protective coating, it is a good idea to have the whole of the underframe of the vehicle steam-cleaned, engine compartment included, so that a thorough inspection can be carried out to see what minor repairs and renovations are necessary. Steam-cleaning is available at many garages, and is necessary for the removal of the accumulation of oily grime, which sometimes is allowed to become thick in certain areas. If steam-cleaning facilities are not available, there are some excellent grease solvents available which can be brush-applied; the dirt can then be simply hosed off. Note that these methods should not be used on vehicles with wax-based underbody protective coating, or the coating will be removed. Such vehicles should be inspected annually, preferably just prior to Winter, when the underbody should be washed down, and any damage to the wax coating repaired. Ideally, a completely fresh coat should be applied. It would also be worth considering the use of such wax-based protection for injection into door panels, sills, box sections, etc, as an additional safeguard against rust damage, where such protection is not provided by the vehicle manufacturer.

After washing paintwork, wipe off with a chamois leather to give an unspotted clear finish. A coat of clear protective wax polish will give added protection against chemical pollutants in the air. If the paintwork sheen has dulled or oxidised, use a cleaner/polisher combination to restore the brilliance of the shine. This requires a little effort, but such dulling is usually caused because regular washing has been neglected. Care needs to be taken with metallic paintwork, as special non-abrasive cleaner/polisher is required to avoid damage to the finish. Always check that the door and ventilator opening drain holes and pipes are completely clear, so that water can be drained out. Brightwork should be treated in the same way as paintwork. Windscreens and windows can be kept clear of the smeary film which often appears, by the use of proprietary glass cleaner. Never use any form of wax or other body or chromium polish on glass.

3 Maintenance of upholstery and carpets – general

Mats and carpets should be brushed or vacuum-cleaned regularly, to keep them free of grit. If they are badly stained, remove them from the vehicle for scrubbing or sponging, and make quite sure they are dry before refitting. Seats and interior trim panels can be kept clean by wiping with a damp cloth. If they do become stained (which can be more apparent on light-coloured upholstery), use a little liquid detergent and a soft nail brush to scour the grime out of the grain of the material. Do not forget to keep the headlining clean in the same way as the upholstery. When using liquid cleaners inside the vehicle, do not over-wet the surfaces being cleaned. Excessive damp could get into the seams and padded interior, causing stains, offensive odours or even rot.

If the inside of the vehicle gets wet accidentally, it is worthwhile taking some trouble to dry it out properly, particularly where carpets are involved. Do not leave oil or electric heaters inside the vehicle for this purpose.

4 Minor body damage – repair

Minor scratches

If the scratch is very superficial, and does not penetrate to the metal of the bodywork, repair is very simple. Lightly rub the area of the scratch with a paintwork renovator, or a very fine cutting paste, to remove loose paint from the scratch, and to clear the surrounding bodywork of wax polish. Rinse the area with clean water.

Apply touch-up paint to the scratch using a fine paint brush; continue to apply fine layers of paint until the surface of the paint in the scratch is level with the surrounding paintwork. Allow the new paint at least two weeks to harden, then blend it into the surrounding paintwork by rubbing the scratch area with a paintwork renovator or a very fine cutting paste. Finally, apply wax polish.

Where the scratch has penetrated right through to the metal of the bodywork, causing the metal to rust, a different repair technique is required. Remove any loose rust from the bottom of the scratch with a penknife, then apply rust-inhibiting paint to prevent the formation of rust in the future. Using a rubber or nylon applicator, fill the scratch with bodystopper paste. If required, this paste can be mixed with cellulose thinners to provide a very thin paste which is ideal for filling narrow scratches. Before the stopper-paste in the scratch hardens, wrap a piece of smooth cotton rag around the top of a finger. Dip the finger in cellulose thinners, and quickly sweep it across the surface of the stopper-paste in the scratch; this will ensure that the surface of the stopper-paste is slightly hollowed. The scratch can now be painted over as described earlier in this Section.

Dents

When deep denting of the vehicle's bodywork has taken place, the first task is to pull the dent out, until the affected bodywork almost attains its original shape. There is little point in trying to restore the original shape completely, as the metal in the damaged area will have stretched on impact, and cannot be reshaped fully to its original contour. It is better to bring the level of the dent up to a point which is about 3 mm below the level of the surrounding bodywork. In cases where the dent is very shallow anyway, it is not worth trying to pull it out at all. If the underside of the dent is accessible, it can be hammered out gently from behind, using a mallet with a wooden or plastic head. Whilst doing this, hold a suitable block of wood firmly against the outside of the panel, to absorb the impact from the hammer blows and thus prevent a large area of the bodywork from being 'belled-out'.

Should the dent be in a section of the

bodywork which has a double skin, or some other factor making it inaccessible from behind, a different technique is called for. Drill several small holes through the metal inside the area – particularly in the deeper section. Then screw long self-tapping screws into the holes, just sufficiently for them to gain a good purchase in the metal. Now the dent can be pulled out by pulling on the protruding heads of the screws with a pair of pliers.

The next stage of the repair is the removal of the paint from the damaged area, and from an inch or so of the surrounding 'sound' bodywork. This is accomplished most easily by using a wire brush or abrasive pad on a power drill, although it can be done just as effectively by hand, using sheets of abrasive paper. To complete the preparation for filling, score the surface of the bare metal with a screwdriver or the tang of a file, or alternatively, drill small holes in the affected area. This will provide a really good 'key' for the filler paste.

To complete the repair, see the Section on filling and respraying.

Rust holes or gashes

Remove all paint from the affected area, and from an inch or so of the surrounding 'sound' bodywork, using an abrasive pad or a wire brush on a power drill. If these are not available, a few sheets of abrasive paper will do the job most effectively. With the paint removed, you will be able to judge the severity of the corrosion, and therefore decide whether to renew the whole panel (if this is possible) or to repair the affected area. New body panels are not as expensive as most people think, and it is often quicker and more satisfactory to fit a new panel than to attempt to repair large areas of corrosion.

Remove all fittings from the affected area, except those which will act as a guide to the original shape of the damaged bodywork (eg headlight shells etc). Then, using tin snips or a hacksaw blade, remove all loose metal and any other metal badly affected by corrosion. Hammer the edges of the hole inwards, in order to create a slight depression for the filler paste.

Wire-brush the affected area to remove the powdery rust from the surface of the remaining metal. Paint the affected area with rust-inhibiting paint, if the back of the rusted area is accessible, treat this also.

Before filling can take place, it will be necessary to block the hole in some way. This can be achieved by the use of aluminium or plastic mesh, or aluminium tape.

Aluminium or plastic mesh, or glass-fibre matting, is probably the best material to use for a large hole. Cut a piece to the approximate size and shape of the hole to be filled, then position it in the hole so that its edges are below the level of the surrounding bodywork. It can be retained in position by several blobs of filler paste around its periphery.

Aluminium tape should be used for small or very narrow holes. Pull a piece off the roll, trim it to the approximate size and shape required, then pull off the backing paper (if used) and stick the tape over the hole; it can be overlapped if the thickness of one piece is insufficient. Burnish down the edges of the tape with the handle of a screwdriver or similar, to ensure that the tape is securely attached to the metal underneath.

Filling and respraying

Before using this Section, see the Sections on dent, deep scratch, rust holes and gash repairs.

Many types of bodyfiller are available, but generally speaking, those proprietary kits which contain a tin of filler paste and a tube of resin hardener are best for this type of repair. A wide, flexible plastic or nylon applicator will be found invaluable for imparting a smooth and well-contoured finish to the surface of the filler.

Mix up a little filler on a clean piece of card or board – measure the hardener carefully (follow the maker's instructions on the pack), otherwise the filler will set too rapidly or too slowly. Using the applicator, apply the filler paste to the prepared area; draw the applicator across the surface of the filler to achieve the correct contour and to level the surface. As soon as a contour that approximates to the correct one is achieved, stop working the paste – if you carry on too long, the paste will become sticky and begin to 'pick-up' on the applicator. Continue to add thin layers of filler paste at 20-minute intervals, until the level of the filler is just proud of the surrounding bodywork.

Once the filler has hardened, the excess can be removed using a metal plane or file. From then on, progressively-finer grades of abrasive paper should be used, starting with a 40-grade production paper, and finishing with a 400-grade wet-and-dry paper. Always wrap the abrasive paper around a flat rubber, cork, or wooden block – otherwise the surface of the filler will not be completely flat. During the smoothing of the filler surface, the wet-and-dry paper should be periodically rinsed in water. This will ensure that a very smooth finish is imparted to the filler at the final stage.

At this stage, the 'dent' should be surrounded by a ring of bare metal, which in turn should be encircled by the finely 'feathered' edge of the good paintwork. Rinse the repair area with clean water, until all of the dust produced by the rubbing-down operation has gone.

Spray the whole area with a light coat of primer – this will show up any imperfections in the surface of the filler. Repair these imperfections with fresh filler paste or bodystopper, and once more smooth the surface with abrasive paper. Repeat this spray-and-repair procedure until you are satisfied that the surface of the filler, and the feathered edge of the paintwork, are perfect. Clean the repair area with clean water, and allow to dry fully.

The repair area is now ready for final spraying. Paint spraying must be carried out in a warm, dry, windless and dust-free atmosphere. This condition can be created artificially if you have access to a large indoor working area, but if you are forced to work in the open, you will have to pick your day very carefully. If you are working indoors, dousing the floor in the work area with water will help to settle the dust which would otherwise be in the atmosphere. If the repair area is confined to one body panel, mask off the surrounding panels; this will help to minimise the effects of a slight mis-match in paint colours. Bodywork fittings (eg chrome strips, door handles etc) will also need to be masked off. Use genuine masking tape, and several thicknesses of newspaper, for the masking operations.

Before commencing to spray, agitate the aerosol can thoroughly, then spray a test area (an old tin, or similar) until the technique is mastered. Cover the repair area with a thick coat of primer; the thickness should be built up using several thin layers of paint, rather than one thick one. Using 400-grade wet-and-dry paper, rub down the surface of the primer until it is really smooth. While doing this, the work area should be thoroughly doused with water, and the wet-and-dry paper periodically rinsed in water. Allow to dry before spraying on more paint.

Spray on the top coat, again building up the thickness by using several thin layers of paint. Start spraying at one edge of the repair area, and then, using a side-to-side motion, work until the whole repair area and about 2 inches of the surrounding original paintwork is covered. Remove all masking material 10 to 15 minutes after spraying on the final coat of paint.

Allow the new paint at least two weeks to harden, then, using a paintwork renovator, or a very fine cutting paste, blend the edges of the paint into the existing paintwork. Finally, apply wax polish.

Plastic components

With the use of more and more plastic body components by the vehicle manufacturers (eg bumpers, spoilers, and in some cases major body panels), rectification of more serious damage to such items has become a matter of either entrusting repair work to a specialist in this field, or renewing complete components. Repair of such damage by the DIY owner is not really feasible, owing to the cost of the equipment and materials required for effecting such repairs. The basic technique involves making a groove along the line of the crack in the plastic, using a rotary burr in a power drill. The damaged part is then welded back together, using a hot-air gun to heat up and fuse a plastic filler rod into the groove. Any excess plastic is then removed, and the area rubbed down to a smooth finish. It is important that a filler rod of the correct plastic is used, as body components can be made of a variety of different types (eg polycarbonate, ABS, polypropylene).

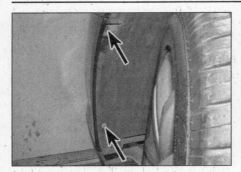

6.1 Undo the screws (arrowed) securing the wheel arch liner to the front bumper on each side

6.2a Insert a screwdriver or similar tool into the wheel arch liner-to-bumper upper retaining screw hole . . .

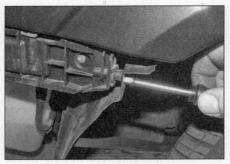

6.2b . . . and push the sliding bumper guide rail fully forward to its stop (shown with bumper removed for clarity)

6.3a Pull out the centre pins . . .

6.3b . . . and remove the four plastic rivets securing the lower centre of the bumper to the front subframe

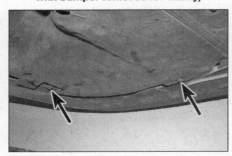

6.4 On diesel engine models, unscrew the two screws each side (arrowed) securing the engine undertray to the bumper

Damage of a less serious nature (abrasions, minor cracks etc) can be repaired by the DIY owner using a two-part epoxy filler repair material. Once mixed in equal proportions, this is used in similar fashion to the bodywork filler used on metal panels. The filler is usually cured in twenty to thirty minutes, ready for sanding and painting.

If the owner is renewing a complete component himself, or if he has repaired it with epoxy filler, he will be left with the problem of finding a suitable paint for finishing which is compatible with the type of plastic used. At one time, the use of a universal paint was not possible, owing to the complex range of plastics encountered in body component applications. Standard paints, generally speaking, will not bond to plastic or rubber satisfactorily. However, it is now possible to obtain a plastic body parts finishing kit which consists of a pre-primer treatment, a primer and coloured top coat. Full

instructions are normally supplied with a kit, but basically, the method of use is to first apply the pre-primer to the component concerned, and allow it to dry for up to 30 minutes. Then the primer is applied, and left to dry for about an hour before finally applying the special-coloured top coat. The result is a correctly-coloured component, where the paint will flex with the plastic or rubber, a property that standard paint does not normally possess.

5 Major body damage repair – general

Where serious damage has occurred, or large areas need renewal due to neglect, it means that complete new panels will need welding-in, and this is best left to professionals. If the damage is due to impact, it will also be necessary to check

completely the alignment of the bodyshell, and this can only be carried out accurately by a Vauxhall/Opel dealer, or accident repair specialist, using special jigs. If the body is left misaligned, it is primarily dangerous as the car will not handle properly, and secondly, uneven stresses will be imposed on the steering, suspension and possibly transmission, causing abnormal wear, or complete failure, particularly to such items as the tyres.

6 Front bumper – removal and refitting

Removal

1 Working under the wheel arch, undo the four retaining screws (two on each side) securing the wheel arch liner to the bumper **(see illustration)**.
2 Using a screwdriver or similar tool inserted into the wheel arch liner-to-bumper upper retaining screw hole each side, push the sliding bumper guide rail fully forward to its stop **(see illustrations)**.
3 Release the four plastic rivets securing the lower centre of the bumper to the front subframe **(see illustrations)**.
4 On diesel engine models, unscrew the two screws each side securing the engine undertray to the lower sides of the bumper **(see illustration)**.
5 Undo the four screws securing the upper section of the bumper to the crossmember **(see illustration)**.

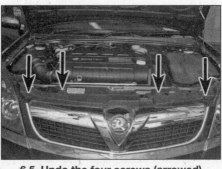

6.5 Undo the four screws (arrowed) securing the bumper to the crossmember

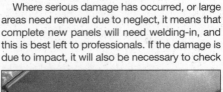
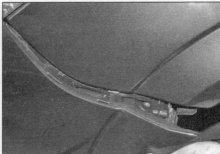

6.6 Pull the bumper out at the sides to disengage it from the sliding guide rails

6 With the aid of an assistant, pull the bumper out at the sides to disengage the bumper from the sliding guide rails then pull the bumper forward **(see illustration)**.

7 Where applicable, disconnect the foglight, exterior temperature sensor and parking distance sensor wiring connectors, and the headlight washer hose **(see illustrations)**. Carefully remove the bumper from the car.

Refitting

8 Refitting is a reversal of the removal procedure, ensuring that all bumper fasteners are securely tightened.

7 Rear bumper – removal and refitting

Removal

Saloon and Hatchback models

1 Remove the rear light cluster each side and the rear number plate lights as described in Chapter 12.

2 Working under the wheel arch, undo the six retaining screws (three on each side) securing the wheel arch liner to the bumper **(see illustration)**.

3 Undo the retaining screw above the number plate on each side **(see illustration)**.

4 Open the two locking catches securing the underside of the bumper to the support bracket **(see illustration)**.

5 With the aid of an assistant, pull the bumper out at the sides to disengage the support bracket. Disengage the bumper from the peg and guides on each side and withdraw it from the support bracket **(see illustrations)**.

6 Detach the wiring harness clip from the bumper, then remove the bumper from the car **(see illustration)**.

Estate models

7 Remove the rear light cluster each side and the rear number plate lights as described in Chapter 12.

8 Working under the wheel arch, undo the six retaining screws (three on each side) securing the wheel arch liner to the bumper **(see illustration 7.2)**.

6.7a Where applicable, disconnect the foglight . . .

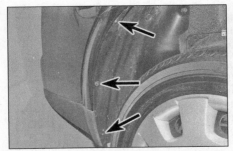

7.2 Undo the screws (arrowed) securing the wheel arch liner to the rear bumper on each side

9 Remove the trim panel from the top of the bumper by pulling it sharply rearward **(see illustration)**.

10 Undo the two upper screws on each side of the bumper, and the four screws in the tailgate aperture **(see illustrations)**.

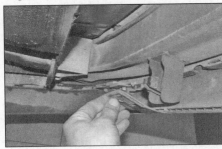

7.4 Open the two locking catches securing the underside of the bumper to the support bracket

7.5b . . . disengage the bumper from the peg (arrowed) . . .

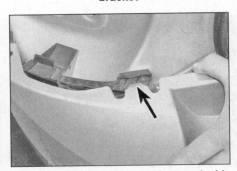

7.5c . . . and guides (arrowed) on each side

6.7b . . . and exterior temperature sensor wiring connectors

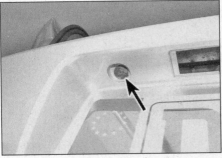

7.3 Undo the retaining screw (arrowed) above the number plate on each side

11 Open the two locking catches securing the underside of the bumper to the support bracket **(see illustration 7.4)**.

12 Where fitted, unclip the four parking sensors.

13 With the aid of an assistant, pull the

7.5a Pull the bumper out at the sides to disengage the support bracket . . .

7.6 Detach the wiring harness clip from the bumper

7.9 Remove the trim panel from the top of the bumper by pulling it sharply rearward

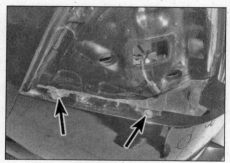

7.10a Undo the two upper screws (arrowed) on each side of the bumper . . .

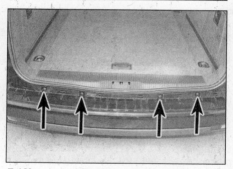

7.10b . . . and the four screws (arrowed) in the tailgate aperture

bumper out at the sides to disengage the support bracket, and remove the bumper from the car.

Refitting

14 Refitting is a reversal of the removal procedure, ensuring that all bumper fasteners are securely tightened.

8 Bonnet – removal, refitting and adjustment

Removal

1 Open the bonnet, and have an assistant support it.
2 Using a marker pen or paint, mark around the hinge positions on the bonnet.
3 With the aid of the assistant, unscrew the bolts securing the bonnet to the hinges on both sides.
4 Lift off the bonnet taking care not to damage the vehicle paintwork.

Refitting

5 Align the marks made on the bonnet before removal with the hinges, then refit and tighten the bonnet securing bolts.
6 Check the bonnet adjustment as follows.

Adjustment

7 Close the bonnet, and check that there is an equal gap (approximately 4.0 mm) at each side, between the bonnet and the wing panels. Check also that the bonnet sits flush in relation to the surrounding body panels.

8 The bonnet should close smoothly and positively without excessive pressure. If this is not the case, adjustment will be required.
9 To adjust the bonnet alignment, loosen the bonnet-to-hinge mounting bolts, and move the bonnet on the bolts as required (the bolt holes in the hinges are enlarged). If necessary, the scissor-type hinge mounting bolts may be loosened as well. Access to the hinge retaining bolts can be gained after removing the water deflector (see Section 23). To adjust the bonnet front height in relation to the front wings, adjustable rubber bump stops are fitted to the front corners of the bonnet. These may be screwed in or out as necessary. After making an adjustment, the bonnet striker must be adjusted so that the lock spring holds the bonnet firmly against the rubber bump stops. Loosen the locknut and screw the striker in or out as necessary.

9 Bonnet release cable – removal and refitting

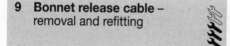

Removal

1 Remove the facia footwell trim panel and the front footwell side trim panel on the driver's side as described in Section 27.
2 Remove the water deflector as described in Section 23.
3 Remove the bonnet lock spring as described in Section 10.
4 Insert a small screwdriver through the opening at the top of the release handle, and

move the handle rearward slightly to free the detent lugs. Lift the release handle off the mounting bracket (**see illustrations**).
5 Release the cable from the support clips and brackets in the engine compartment, then withdraw the cable through the rubber grommet and into the passenger compartment. As an aid to refitting, tie a length of string to the cable before removing it and leave the string in position ready for refitting.

Refitting

6 Refitting is a reversal of removal, but tie the string to the end of the cable, and use the string to pull the cable into position. Ensure that the cable is routed as noted before removal, and make sure that the grommet is correctly seated. On completion, refit the water deflector and the interior trim panels as described in Sections 23 and 27.

10 Bonnet lock spring – removal and refitting

Removal

1 The bonnet is held in its locked position with a strong spring which engages with the striker on the front edge of the bonnet. The release cable is connected to the end of the spring.
2 The striker may be removed from the bonnet by unscrewing the locknut, however measure its fitted length first as a guide to refitting it.
3 To remove the lock spring, disengage the

9.4a Move the bonnet release handle rearward slightly to free the detent lugs . . .

9.4b . . . then lift the release handle off the mounting bracket

10.3a Disengage the bonnet lock spring leg from the front crossmember . . .

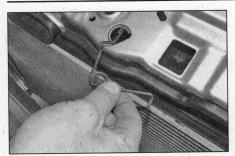

10.3b ... slide the other end off the release cable and remove the spring from the crossmember

spring leg from the front crossmember, slide the other end of the spring off the release cable and remove the spring from the crossmember (**see illustrations**).

Refitting

4 Refitting is a reversal of removal.

11 Door – removal, refitting and adjustment

Removal

1 Open the door and disconnect the wiring connector which is fitted to the front edge of the door (**see illustration**).
2 Undo the bolt securing the door check strap to the vehicle body (**see illustration**).
3 Undo the grub screw from the upper and lower hinge (**see illustration**).
4 With the aid of an assistant, lift the door upward and off the hinge pins.

Refitting and adjustment

5 Refit the door using the reverse of the removal procedure, then close the door and check that it fits correctly in its aperture, with equal gaps at all points between it and the surrounding bodywork.
6 If adjustment is required, slacken the bolts securing the hinges to the door and reposition the door as required. Securely tighten the bolts after completing the adjustment.
7 The striker alignment should be checked after either the door or the lock has been disturbed. To adjust a striker, slacken its screws, reposition it and securely tighten the screws (**see illustration**).

12 Door inner trim panel – removal and refitting

Front door

Removal

1 Open the door window.
2 If working on the driver's door, carefully prise out the control switch assembly

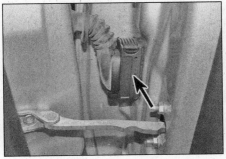

11.1 Disconnect the door wiring connector (arrowed) – front door shown

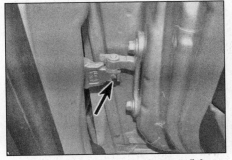

11.3 Undo the grub screw (arrowed) from the upper and lower hinge

and disconnect the wiring connector (**see illustrations**).
3 Using a plastic wedge or similar tool, carefully prise the door grab handle plastic

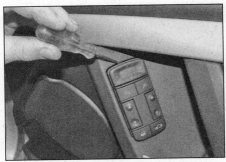

12.2a Prise out the control switch assembly ...

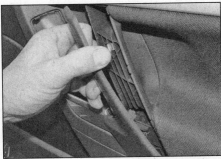

12.3a Prise the door grab handle plastic cover away from the handle at the top ...

11.2 Undo the bolt (arrowed) securing the door check strap to the body

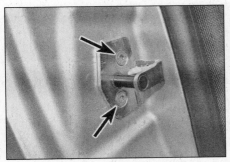

11.7 Door striker retaining screws (arrowed)

cover away from the handle at the top. Disengage the lower retaining lug from the door panel and remove the cover (**see illustrations**).

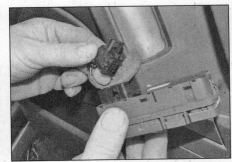

12.2b ... and disconnect the wiring connector

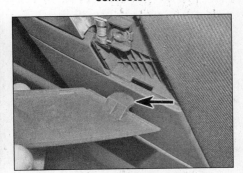

12.3b ... then disengage the lower retaining lug (arrowed)

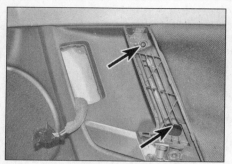

12.4 Undo the two screws (now exposed) now exposed

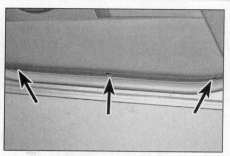

12.5 Undo the three screws (arrowed) securing the lower edge of the trim panel to the door

lock operating cable retainer. Slide the outer cable to the rear and disengage the inner cable end from the interior handle (see illustrations).

8 If working on the passenger's door, disconnect the wiring connector from the window control switch.

Refitting

9 Refitting is a reversal of removal. If working on the driver's door, make sure the control switch wiring is pulled through the aperture in the trim panel as the panel is fitted.

Rear door

Removal

10 Open the door window.

11 On Hatchback and Estate models, using a plastic wedge or similar tool, carefully prise the triangular panel away from the door to release the three retaining clips (see illustration).

12 Where a manual window regulator is fitted, locate a cloth rag between the handle and the trim panel and pull it to one side to release the spring clip. Remove the handle from the splined shaft and refit the spring clip to the handle (see illustrations).

13 Using a plastic wedge or similar tool, carefully prise the door grab handle plastic cover away from the handle at the top. Disengage the lower retaining lug from the door panel and remove the cover (see illustrations 12.3a and 12.3b).

14 Undo the two screws now exposed after removal of the grab handle plastic cover (see illustration 12.4).

15 Undo the two screws securing the lower edge of the trim panel to the door (see illustration).

12.6 Prise the bottom and sides of the panel away from the door to release the internal clips

4 Undo the two screws now exposed after removal of the grab handle plastic cover (see illustration).

5 Undo the three screws securing the lower edge of the trim panel to the door (see illustration).

6 Using a wide-bladed screwdriver or removal

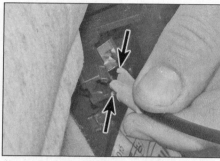

12.7a Lift the front edge (arrowed) of the lock operating cable retainer . . .

tool, carefully prise the bottom and sides of the panel away from the door to release the internal clips (see illustration). Lift the panel upward to release it from the window aperture.

7 Once the panel is free, reach behind and, using a small screwdriver, lift the front edge of the door

12.7b . . . slide the outer cable to the rear and disengage the inner cable end from the interior handle

12.11 Prise the triangular panel away from the door to release the retaining clips – Hatchback and Estate models

12.12a Where a manual regulator is fitted, use a cloth rag to release the handle spring clip . . .

12.12b . . . remove the handle from the splined shaft . . .

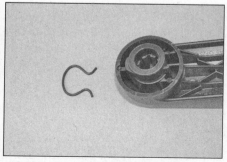

12.12c . . . and refit the spring clip to the handle

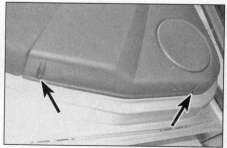

12.15 Undo the two screws (arrowed) securing the lower edge of the trim panel to the door

16 Using a wide-bladed screwdriver or removal tool, carefully prise the bottom and sides of the panel away from door to release the internal clips. Lift the panel upward to release it from the window aperture **(see illustration)**.

17 Once the panel is free, reach behind, and using a small screwdriver, lift the front edge of the door lock operating cable retainer. Slide the outer cable to the rear and disengage the inner cable end from the interior handle **(see illustrations 12.7a and 12.7b)**.

18 Disconnect the wiring connector from the window control switch and tweeter speaker, where applicable.

19 Disconnect the interior lock button operating rod from the bellcrank, and remove the panel from the door.

Refitting

20 Refitting is a reversal of removal.

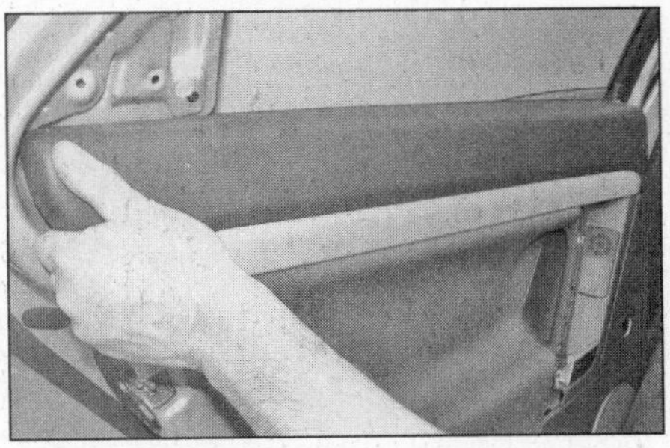

12.16 Prise the bottom and sides of the panel away from door to release the internal clips

13 Door handles and lock components – removal and refitting

Door interior handle

1 The door interior handle is an integral part of the door inner trim panel and cannot be individually removed. If there are any problems with the interior handle, a new inner trim panel will be required.

Front door exterior handle

Removal

2 Open the door and carefully prise out the blanking cap from the rear edge of the door to gain access to the handle locking screw **(see illustrations)**.

3 Pull the exterior door handle outwards and hold it in that position. With the exterior door handle held in the open position, turn the handle locking screw anti-clockwise until it reaches its stop. The exterior door handle should now be fixed in the open position.

4 Withdraw the fixed part of the handle, containing the lock cylinder, from the door **(see illustration)**.

5 Slide the exterior door handle to the rear, disengage the front pivot from the handle frame and remove the handle from the door **(see illustration)**.

Refitting

6 Engage the handle front pivot with the frame and move the handle back into position.

7 Refit the fixed part of the handle with the lock cylinder to the door.

8 Hold the exterior handle and turn the handle locking screw clockwise to retain the handle.

9 Check the operation of the handle then refit the blanking cap to the edge of the door.

Rear door exterior handle

Removal

10 Open the door and carefully prise out the blanking cap from the rear edge of the door to gain access to the handle locking screw **(see illustrations)**.

11 Pull the exterior door handle outwards and hold it in that position. With the exterior door handle held in the open position, turn the handle locking screw anti-clockwise until it reaches its stop **(see illustration)**. The exterior door handle should now be fixed in the open position.

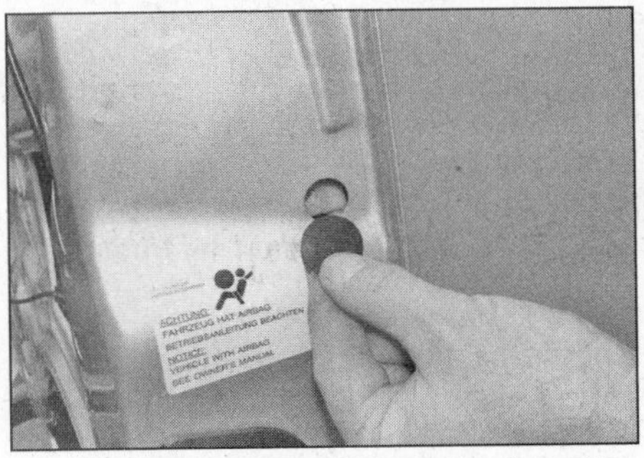

13.2a Prise out the blanking cap from the rear edge of the door . . .

13.2b . . . to gain access to the handle locking screw (arrowed)

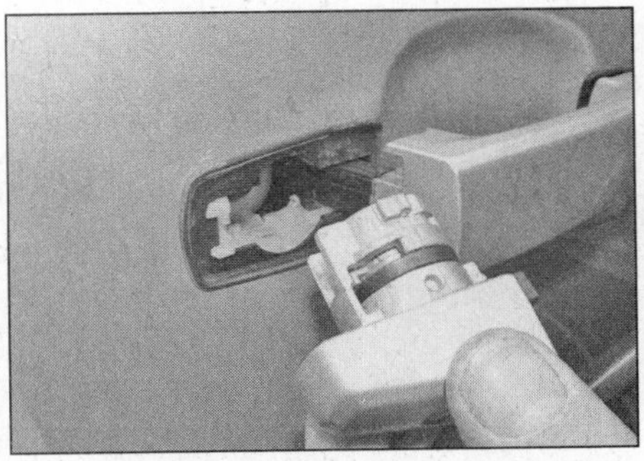

13.4 Withdraw the fixed part of the handle, containing the lock cylinder, from the door

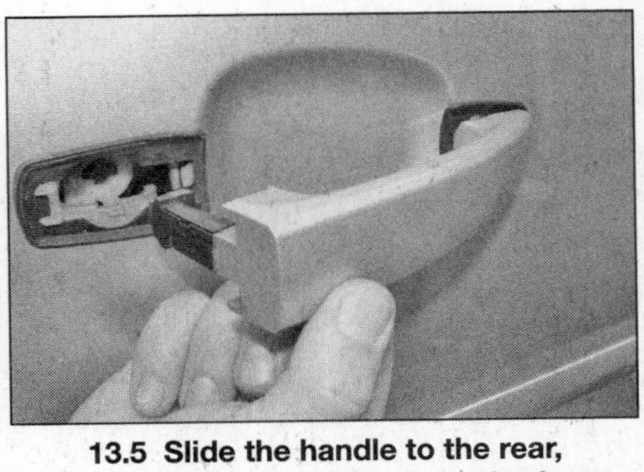

13.5 Slide the handle to the rear, disengage the front pivot from the frame and remove the handle

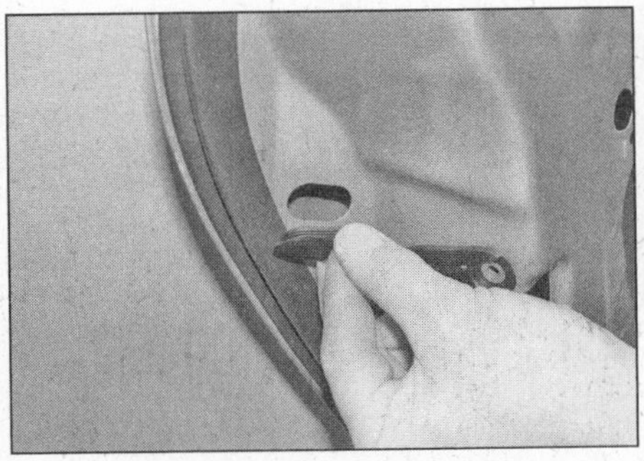

13.10a Prise out the blanking cap from the rear edge of the door . . .

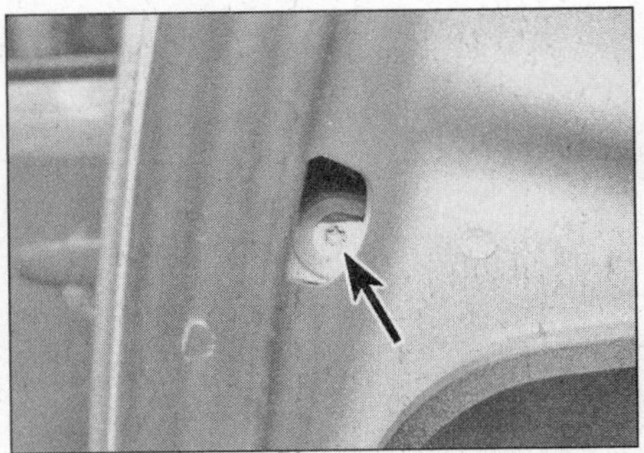

13.10b . . . to gain access to the handle locking screw (arrowed)

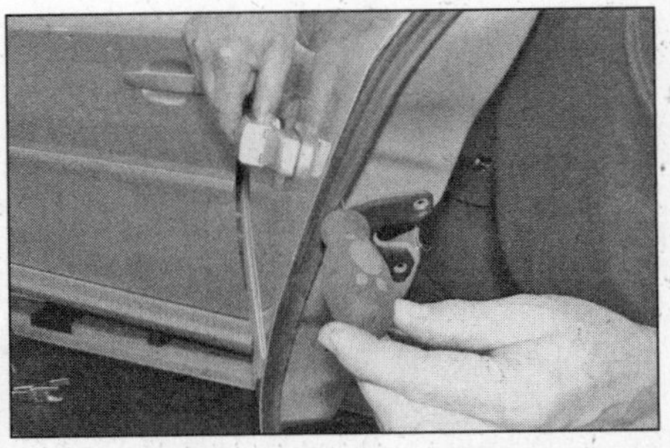

13.11 With the exterior handle held open, turn the locking screw anti-clockwise until it reaches its stop

13.12 Withdraw the fixed part of the handle from the door

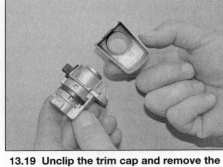

13.19 Unclip the trim cap and remove the cap from the lock cylinder housing

16 Hold the exterior handle and turn the handle locking screw clockwise to retain the handle.
17 Check the operation of the handle then refit the blanking cap to the edge of the door.

Front door lock cylinder

Removal

18 Remove the exterior handle as described previously in this Section.
19 Unclip the trim cap and remove the cap from the lock cylinder housing (see illustration).
20 The lock cylinder body is an integral part of the housing and no further dismantling is possible.

Refitting

21 Refitting is a reversal of removal.

Front door exterior handle frame

Note: A pop-rivet gun and suitable rivets will be required when refitting. The rivets should be approximately 4.8 mm in diameter and 11 mm in length.

Removal

22 Disconnect the battery negative terminal (refer to Disconnecting the battery in the Reference Chapter).
23 Remove the exterior handle as described previously in this Section.
24 Remove the door inner trim panel as described in Section 12.
25 Undo the three screws securing the loudspeaker to the door. Withdraw the speaker and disconnect the wiring connector. Unclip the wiring from the guide and remove the speaker (see illustrations).
26 Undo the three screws securing the door electronics module to the door. Pull out the locking bar, disconnect the wiring connector and remove the module (see illustrations).
27 Reach in through the loudspeaker aperture and push out the clips securing the wiring harness to the door (see illustration).
28 Carefully peel back the protective plastic sheet and remove the sheet from the door (see illustration).
29 Using an 8.5 mm drill bit, carefully drill off the heads and remove the two rivets securing the window rear guide rail to the door, taking great care not to damage the door panel (see illustrations).
30 Disengage the top of the guide rail from

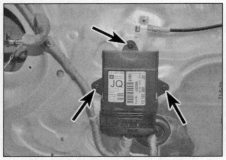

13.25a Undo the screws (arrowed) and withdraw the loudspeaker . . .

13.25b . . . disconnect the wiring connector and unclip the wiring from the guide (arrowed)

12 Withdraw the fixed part of the handle from the door (see illustration).
13 Slide the exterior door handle to the rear, disengage the front pivot from the handle frame and remove the handle from the door (see illustration 13.5).

Refitting

14 Engage the handle front pivot with the frame and move the handle back into position.
15 Refit the fixed part of the handle to the door.

13.26a Undo the screws (arrowed) and withdraw the door electronics module . . .

13.26b . . . pull out the locking bar and disconnect the wiring connector

13.27 Push out the clips securing the wiring harness to the door

13.28 Carefully peel back the protective plastic sheet and remove the sheet from the door

13.29a Drill out the upper rivet . . .

13.29b . . . and lower rivet, securing the window rear guide rail to the door

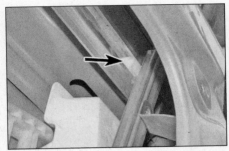

13.30a Disengage the top of the guide rail (arrowed) from the window lifting channel . . .

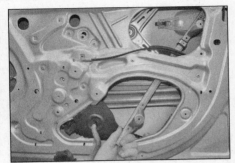

13.30b . . . then remove the guide rail through the door aperture

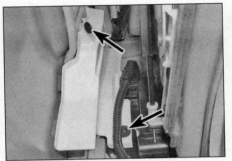

13.31a Undo the two screws (arrowed) . . .

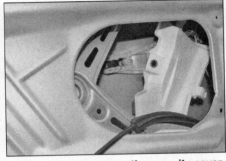

13.31b . . . and remove the security cover through the door aperture

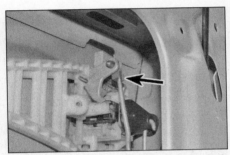

13.32 Release the retaining clip (arrowed) and disconnect the lock operating rod from the lever

the window lifting channel by moving it rearward, and remove the guide rail through the door aperture (see illustrations).

31 Undo the two screws securing the security cover to the exterior handle frame and door lock, and remove the cover through the door aperture (see illustrations).

32 Release the retaining clip and disconnect the lock operating rod from the lever on the exterior handle frame (see illustration).

33 Slacken the exterior handle frame front retaining screw approximately five turns. Slide the handle frame forward to release the rear locating lugs, disengage the lock cylinder operating rod and remove the frame through the door aperture (see illustrations).

34 Clean out the remains of the old rivets from inside the door.

Refitting

35 Connect the lock cylinder operating rod, then place the exterior handle frame in

position in the door. Tighten the front retaining screw securely.

36 Engage the lock operating rod with the lever on the exterior handle frame and push the retaining clip back into position on the rod.

37 Refit the security cover and secure with the two screws.

38 Engage the top of the window guide rail with the lifting channel and position the guide rail in the door. Secure the guide rail with new pop rivets (see illustration).

39 Refit the protective plastic sheet to the door ensuring it is firmly stuck with no air bubbles. If the sheet was damaged during removal it should be renewed. This entails cutting a new sheet to the correct size and shape using the old sheet as a template. The new sheet can then be attached to the door with fresh adhesive.

40 Refit the wiring harness clips to the door ensuring they are firmly attached.

41 Refit the door electronics module, securely tighten the three retaining screws and reconnect the wiring connector.

42 Reconnect the wiring to the loudspeaker, position the speaker in the door and secure with the three screws.

43 Refit the door inner trim panel as described in Section 12.

44 Refit the exterior handle as described previously in this Section, then reconnect the battery negative terminal.

Rear door exterior handle frame

Removal

45 Disconnect the battery negative terminal (refer to *Disconnecting the battery* in the Reference Chapter).

46 Remove the exterior handle as described previously in this Section.

47 Remove the door inner trim panel as described in Section 12.

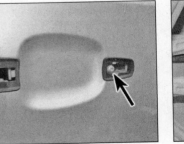

13.33a Slacken the exterior handle frame front retaining screw (arrowed) approximately five turns . . .

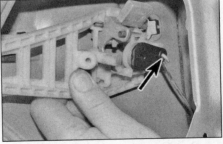

13.33b . . . slide the frame forward to release the rear lugs, disengage the lock cylinder operating rod (arrowed)

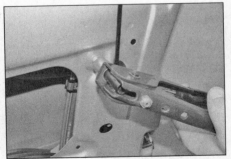

13.38 Secure the window guide rail with new pop rivets

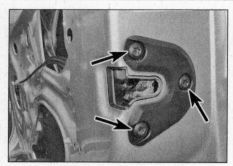

13.55 Undo the three screws (arrowed) securing the lock to the door

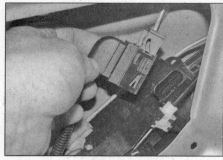

13.56 Lift the locking bar and disconnect the wiring connector

13.57a Lower the lock and bring the interior lock button and rod in through the hole provided . . .

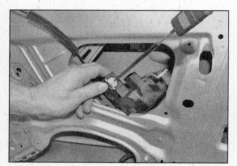

13.57b . . . then remove the lock assembly through the upper door aperture

48 Remove the rear door lock as described later in this Section.
49 Slacken the exterior handle frame front retaining screw approximately five turns. Slide the handle frame forward to release the rear

13.58 If required, disconnect the operating cables from the lock linkage and bracket

locating lugs and remove the frame through the door aperture **(see illustrations 13.33a and 13.33b)**.

Refitting

50 Place the exterior handle frame in position

in the door and tighten the front retaining screw securely.
51 Refit the rear door lock as described later in this Section.
52 Refit the door inner trim panel as described in Section 12.
53 Refit the exterior handle as described previously in this Section, then reconnect the battery negative terminal.

Front door lock

Removal

54 Remove the front door exterior handle frame as described earlier in this Section.
55 Undo the three screws securing the lock to the door **(see illustration)**.
56 Withdraw the lock from its location, then lift the locking bar and disconnect the wiring connector **(see illustration)**.
57 Lower the lock assembly down into the door, bringing the interior lock button and rod in through the hole provided. Now remove the lock assembly through the upper door aperture **(see illustrations)**.
58 If required, disconnect the operating cables from the lock linkage and bracket **(see illustration)**.

Refitting

59 Refitting is a reversal of removal.

Rear door lock

Removal – Hatchback models

60 Remove the door inner trim panel as described in Section 12.
61 Carefully peel back the protective plastic sheet and remove the sheet from the door **(see illustration)**.
62 Undo the upper and lower screws securing the window rear guide rail to the door **(see illustrations)**.
63 Pull the rubber window channel out of the guide rail, then remove the guide rail through the door aperture **(see illustrations)**.
64 Undo the screw securing the door lock operating cable guide to the door, then disconnect the inner cable from the bellcrank **(see illustration)**.
65 Release the retaining clip and disconnect the lock operating rod from the lever on the exterior handle frame **(see illustration 13.32)**.

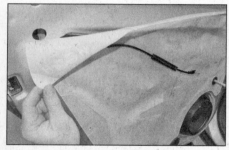

13.61 Carefully peel back the protective plastic sheet and remove the sheet from the door

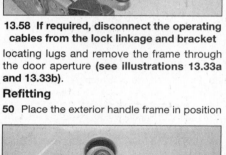

13.62a Undo the upper screw (arrowed) . . .

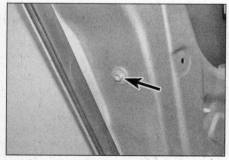

13.62b . . . and lower screw securing the window rear guide rail to the door

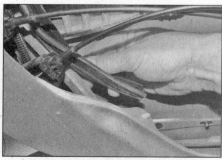

13.63a Pull the rubber window channel out of the guide rail . . .

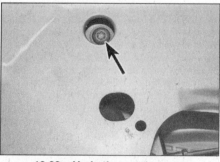

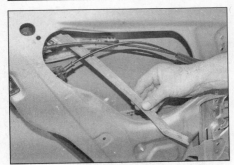

13.63b ... then remove the guide rail through the door aperture

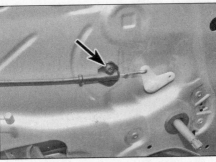

13.64 Undo the screw (arrowed) securing the lock operating cable guide to the door

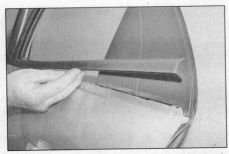

13.80 Tap up the window outer waist seal from the door aperture, then lift the seal up and remove it from the door

66 Undo the three screws securing the lock to the door **(see illustration 13.55)**.

67 Withdraw the lock from its location, then lift the locking bar and disconnect the wiring connector **(see illustration13.56)**. Unclip the wiring harness from the lock body.

68 Remove the lock assembly through the upper door aperture.

69 If required, disconnect the operating cables from the lock linkage and bracket **(see illustration 13.58)**.

Refitting – Hatchback models

70 If removed, reconnect the operating cables to the lock linkage and bracket.

71 Insert the lock assembly into the door and reconnect the wiring connector. Secure the wiring harness to the lock body.

72 Position the lock assembly in its location, refit the three retaining screws and tighten securely.

73 Engage the lock operating rod with the lever on the exterior handle frame, and push the retaining clip back into position on the rod.

74 Connect the lock operating cable to the bellcrank, then secure the cable guide with the retaining screw.

75 Locate the guide rail in position in the door and refit the rubber window channel to the guide rail. Secure the guide rail with the upper and lower retaining screws.

76 Refit the protective plastic sheet to the door ensuring it is firmly stuck with no air bubbles. If the sheet was damaged during removal it should be renewed. This entails cutting a new sheet to the correct size and shape using the old sheet as a template. The new sheet can then be attached to the door with fresh adhesive.

77 Refit the door inner trim panel as described in Section 12.

Removal – Saloon and Estate models

78 Remove the door inner trim panel as described in Section 12.

79 Carefully peel back the protective plastic sheet and remove the sheet from the door **(see illustration 13.61)**.

80 Using a plastic wedge or similar tool, tap up the window outer waist seal from the door aperture. Lift the seal up and remove it from the door **(see illustration)**.

81 Remove the door sealing weatherstrip from the top and rear side of the door.

82 Lift the fixed window glass upward and remove it rearwards from the door.

83 Undo the screw securing the window rear guide rail to the door **(see illustration 13.62a)**. Slide the guide rail down to release it from its upper location, then remove it upwards and out from the outside of the door.

84 Undo the screw securing the door lock operating cable guide to the door, then disconnect the inner cable from the bellcrank **(see illustration 13.64)**.

85 Release the retaining clip and disconnect the lock operating rod from the lever on the exterior handle frame **(see illustration 13.32)**.

86 Undo the three screws securing the lock to the door **(see illustration 13.55)**.

87 Withdraw the lock from its location, then lift the locking bar and disconnect the wiring connector **(see illustration 13.56)**. Unclip the wiring harness from the lock body.

88 Remove the lock assembly through the upper door aperture.

89 If required, disconnect the operating cables from the lock linkage and bracket **(see illustration 13.58)**.

Refitting – Saloon and Estate models

90 If removed, reconnect the operating cables to the lock linkage and bracket.

91 Insert the lock assembly into the door and reconnect the wiring connector. Secure the wiring harness to the lock body.

92 Position the lock assembly in its location, refit the three retaining screws and tighten securely.

93 Engage the lock operating rod with the lever on the exterior handle frame, and push the retaining clip back into position on the rod.

94 Connect the lock operating cable to the bellcrank, then secure the cable guide with the retaining screw.

95 Locate the window rear guide rail in position in the door and engage its upper mounting location. Secure the guide rail with the retaining screw.

96 Place the fixed window glass in position in the door.

97 Refit the door sealing weatherstrip to the top and rear side of the door.

98 Refit the window outer waist seal to the door aperture, ensuring that the retaining clips securely engage.

99 Refit the protective plastic sheet to the door ensuring it is firmly stuck with no air bubbles. If the sheet was damaged during removal it should be renewed. This entails cutting a new sheet to the correct size and shape using the old sheet as a template. The new sheet can then be attached to the door with fresh adhesive.

100 Refit the door inner trim panel as described in Section 12.

14 Door window regulator and glass – removal and refitting

Front door window regulator

Note: *A pop-rivet gun and suitable rivets will be required when refitting. The rivets should be approximately 4.8 mm in diameter and 11 mm in length.*

Removal

1 Remove the door inner trim panel as described in Section 12.

2 Open the window so that it is approximately 50 mm downward from the closed position. Using adhesive tape over the top of the door frame, retain the window in this position.

3 Undo the three screws securing the loudspeaker to the door. Withdraw the speaker and disconnect the wiring connector. Unclip the wiring from the guide and remove the speaker **(see illustrations 13.25a and 13.25b)**.

4 Undo the three screws securing the door electronics module to the door. Pull out the locking bar, disconnect the wiring connector and remove the module **(see illustrations 13.26a and 13.26b)**.

5 Reach in through the loudspeaker aperture and push out the clips securing the wiring harness to the door **(see illustration 13.27)**.

6 Carefully peel back the protective plastic sheet and remove the sheet from the door **(see illustration 13.28)**.

7 Using an 8.5 mm drill bit, carefully drill off the heads and remove the two rivets securing the window rear guide rail to the door, taking great care not to damage the door panel **(see illustrations 13.29a and 13.29b)**.

8 Disengage the top of the guide rail from the

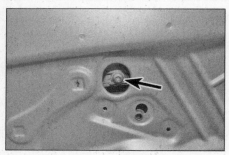

14.9 Undo the screw (arrowed) securing the regulator front lifting arm to the window lift channel

14.11 Pull out the locking bar and disconnect the window regulator wiring connector

window lifting channel by moving it rearward, and remove the guide rail through the door aperture (see illustrations 13.30a and 13.30b).
9 Undo the screw securing the regulator front lifting arm to the window lift channel (see illustration).

14.13a Lift the regulator up to disengage the front locating dowel (arrowed) . . .

14.13c . . . then remove the regulator through the door aperture

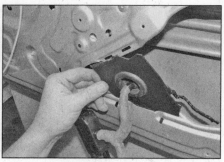

14.10 Unclip the wiring harness support panel from the base of the door

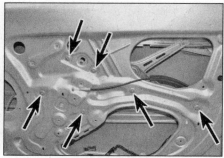

14.12 Drill out the rivets (arrowed) securing the window regulator to the door

10 Unclip the wiring harness support panel from the base of the door (see illustration).
11 Pull out the locking bar and disconnect the window regulator wiring connector (see illustration).
12 Using an 8.5 mm drill bit, carefully drill off

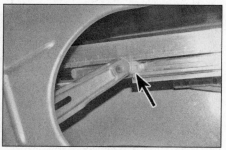

14.13b . . . slide it sideways to disengage the regulator arm (arrowed) from the window guide channel . . .

14.27 Position the window so that the window fixing clip is accessible through the small opening (arrowed) in the door

the heads and remove the six rivets securing the window regulator to the door, taking great care not to damage the door panel (see illustration).
13 Lift the regulator up to disengage the front locating dowel, slide it sideways to disengage the regulator arm from the window guide channel, then remove the regulator through the door aperture (see illustrations).
14 Clean out the remains of the old rivets from inside the door.

Refitting

15 Engage the regulator arm with the window guide channel, then locate the regulator dowel in the slot in the door panel. Secure the regulator with new pop rivets.
16 Reconnect the regulator wiring connector, then clip the wiring harness support panel back into position.
17 Refit and tighten the screw securing the regulator front lifting arm to the window lift channel.
18 Engage the top of the window guide rail with the lifting channel and position the guide rail in the door. Secure the guide rail with new pop rivets (see illustration 13.38).
19 Refit the protective plastic sheet to the door ensuring it is firmly stuck with no air bubbles. If the sheet was damaged during removal it should be renewed. This entails cutting a new sheet to the correct size and shape using the old sheet as a template. The new sheet can then be attached to the door with fresh adhesive.
20 Refit the wiring harness clips to the door ensuring they are firmly attached.
21 Refit the door electronics module, securely tighten the three retaining screws and reconnect the wiring connector.
22 Reconnect the wiring to the loudspeaker, position the speaker in the door and secure with the three screws.
23 Remove the adhesive tape used to retain the window, then refit the door inner trim panel as described in Section 12.

Rear door window regulator

Note: A pop-rivet gun and suitable rivets will be required when refitting. The rivets should be approximately 4.8 mm in diameter and 11 mm in length.

Removal

24 Remove the door inner trim panel as described in Section 12.
25 Carefully peel back the protective plastic sheet and remove the sheet from the door (see illustration 13.61).
26 Undo the screw securing the door lock operating cable guide to the door, then disconnect the inner cable from the bellcrank (see illustration 13.64).
27 Position the window in the assembly position so that the window fixing clip is accessible through the small opening in the door (see illustration). On models with manually-operated windows, temporarily refit the regulator handle to reposition the window. On models with electric windows,

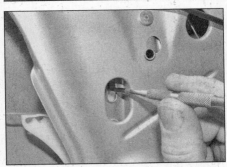

14.28a Push the tool through the centre of the two-part window fixing clip . . .

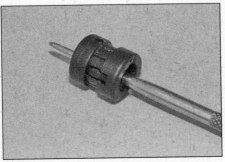

14.28b . . . to expand the internal locking lugs (shown with clip removed) . . .

14.28c . . . and separate the clip

it will be necessary to remove the window control switch from the door trim panel and temporarily reconnect the switch wiring.

28 Obtain a scribe or similar pointed tool with a 4.0 mm shaft diameter. Push the tool through the centre of the two-part window fixing clip to expand the internal locking lugs and separate the clip **(see illustrations)**. Disengage the window from the regulator lifting block and recover the two parts of the fixing clip.

29 Slide the window to the fully closed position. Using adhesive tape over the top of the door frame, retain the window in this position.

30 On models with electric windows, pull out the locking bar and disconnect the window regulator wiring connector.

31 Using an 8.5 mm drill bit, carefully drill off the heads and remove the two rivets (electric windows) or five rivets (manual windows) securing the window regulator to the door, taking great care not to damage the door panel **(see illustration)**. On models with electric windows, also undo the retaining bolt located just in front of the regulator motor.

32 Push the regulator into the door, turn it clockwise and manipulate it out through the door aperture **(see illustration)**.

33 Clean out the remains of the old rivets from inside the door.

Refitting

34 Manipulate the regulator back into position in the door, then secure the regulator with new pop rivets **(see illustration)**.

35 On models with electric windows, refit the additional motor retaining bolt and reconnect the wiring connector.

36 Reposition the regulator in the assembly position to provide access for the window fixing clip.

37 Refit the two parts of the fixing clip to the window, remove the tape retaining the window in position and slide the window down and into engagement with the regulator lifting block.

38 Connect the lock operating cable to the bellcrank, then secure the cable guide with the retaining screw.

39 Refit the protective plastic sheet to the door ensuring it is firmly stuck with no air bubbles. If the sheet was damaged during removal it should be renewed. This entails cutting a new sheet to the correct size and shape using the old sheet as a template. The

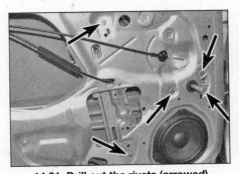

14.31 Drill out the rivets (arrowed) securing the window regulator to the door

new sheet can then be attached to the door with fresh adhesive.

40 Refit the door inner trim panel as described in Section 12.

Front door window glass

Removal

41 Remove the regulator as previously described in this Section.

42 Using a plastic wedge or similar tool, tap up the window outer waist seal from the door aperture. Lift the seal up and remove it from the door **(see illustration)**.

43 Tilt the window glass down at the front, then carefully lift it upwards and remove it from the outside of the door.

Refitting

44 Refitting is a reversal of removal. Position the window glass so that it is approximately 50 mm downward from the closed position. Using adhesive tape over the top of the door

14.34 Secure the regulator with new pop rivets

14.32 Manipulate the regulator out through the door aperture

frame, retain the window in this position during the remainder of refitting.

Rear door window glass

Removal – Hatchback models

45 Remove the door inner trim panel as described in Section 12.

46 Carefully peel back the protective plastic sheet and remove the sheet from the door **(see illustration 13.61)**.

47 Using a plastic wedge or similar tool, tap up the window outer waist seal from the door aperture. Lift the seal up and remove it from the door **(see illustration 13.80)**.

48 Undo the upper and lower screws securing the window rear guide rail to the door **(see illustrations 13.62a and 13.62b)**.

49 Pull the rubber window channel out of the guide rail, then remove the guide rail through the door aperture **(see illustrations 13.63a and 13.63b)**.

14.42 Tap up the front door window outer waist seal and remove it from the door

50 Release the window glass from the regulator as described previously in paragraphs 27 and 28.
51 Move the window and regulator to the fully open position.
52 Pull the rubber window channel out of the triangular panel at the rear of the door, then carefully lift the window glass upwards and remove it from the outside of the door.

Refitting – Hatchback models

53 Position the window regulator in the assembly position as described previously in paragraph 27.
54 Refit the two parts of the fixing clip to the window, place the window in the door and slide it down and into engagement with the regulator lifting block.
55 Refit the rubber window channel to the triangular panel at the rear of the door.
56 Locate the guide rail in position in the door and refit the rubber window channel to the guide rail. Secure the guide rail with the upper and lower retaining screws.
57 Refit the window outer waist seal to the door aperture, ensuring that the retaining clips securely engage.
58 Refit the protective plastic sheet to the door ensuring it is firmly stuck with no air bubbles. If the sheet was damaged during removal it should be renewed. This entails cutting a new sheet to the correct size and shape using the old sheet as a template. The new sheet can then be attached to the door with fresh adhesive.
59 Refit the door inner trim panel as described in Section 12.

Removal – Saloon and Estate models

60 Remove the door inner trim panel as described in Section 12.
61 Carefully peel back the protective plastic sheet and remove the sheet from the door (see illustration 13.61).
62 Using a plastic wedge or similar tool, tap up the window outer waist seal from the door aperture. Lift the seal up and remove it from the door (see illustration 13.80).
63 Remove the door sealing weatherstrip from the top and rear side of the door.
64 Lift the fixed window glass upward and remove it rearwards from the door.
65 Undo the screw securing the window rear guide rail to the door (see illustration 13.62b).

Slide the guide rail down to release it from its upper location, then remove it upwards and out from the outside of the door.
66 Release the window glass from the regulator as described previously in paragraphs 27 and 28.
67 Move the window and regulator to the fully open position.
68 Carefully lift the window glass upwards and remove it from the outside of the door.

Refitting – Saloon and Estate models

69 Position the window regulator in the assembly position as described previously in paragraph 27.
70 Refit the two parts of the fixing clip to the window, place the window in the door and slide it down and into engagement with the regulator lifting block.
71 Locate the window rear guide rail in position in the door and engage its upper mounting location. Secure the guide rail with the retaining screw.
72 Place the fixed window glass in position in the door.
73 Refit the door sealing weatherstrip to the top and rear side of the door.
74 Refit the window outer waist seal to the door aperture, ensuring that the retaining clips securely engage.
75 Refit the protective plastic sheet to the door ensuring it is firmly stuck with no air bubbles. If the sheet was damaged during removal it should be renewed. This entails cutting a new sheet to the correct size and shape using the old sheet as a template. The new sheet can then be attached to the door with fresh adhesive.
76 Refit the door inner trim panel as described in Section 12.

15 Rear quarter window glass – removal and refitting

Removal

1 Remove the relevant inner trim panels for access to the rear quarter window glass with reference to Section 27.
2 Unscrew the plastic retaining nuts and remove the window glass from the body. On

Estate models there are 10 nuts; on Hatchback models there are 6 nuts.

Refitting

3 Refitting is a reversal of removal, using new plastic retaining nuts.

16 Boot lid and support struts – removal, refitting and adjustment

Boot lid

Removal

1 Open the boot lid, and have an assistant support it.
2 Disconnect the wiring at the connector.
3 Using a pencil or marker pen, mark around the hinges on the boot lid as a guide for refitting.
4 Using a screwdriver prise out the retaining spring clips and disconnect the upper ends of the support struts from the boot lid.
5 Unscrew the mounting bolts then lift the boot lid from the hinges.
6 The hinges can be removed if required by unbolting the hinges from the body.

Refitting and adjustment

7 Refitting is a reversal of removal, but make sure that the hinges are positioned as noted on removal and tighten the mounting bolts securely. With the boot lid closed, check that it is positioned centrally within the body aperture. If adjustment is necessary, loosen the boot lid mounting bolts and/or hinge mounting bolts and reposition the boot lid, then retighten the bolts. Check that the striker enters the lock centrally, and if necessary adjust the striker position by loosening the mounting bolts. Tighten the bolts on completion.

Support struts

Removal

8 Open the boot lid, and have an assistant support it.
9 Using a screwdriver prise out the retaining spring clips and disconnect the struts from the boot lid and body. Note which way round the strut is fitted.

Refitting

10 Refitting is a reversal of removal.

17 Boot lid lock components – removal and refitting

Lock assembly

Removal

1 Open the boot lid and remove the trim panel. Use a forked tool or removal tool to prise out the thirteen retaining clips, and the centre pins of the four plastic rivets.
2 Spread the retaining legs of the lock trim

17.2a Spread the retaining legs of the lock trim panel . . .

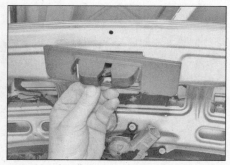
17.2b . . . and remove the panel from the lock

17.3 Disconnect the lock wiring connector

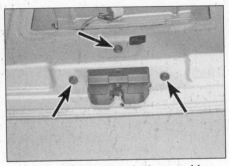

17.4 Undo the three lock assembly retaining screws (arrowed)

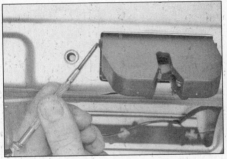

17.5 Depress the retaining lugs on each side of the lock extension

17.6 Lift the lock assembly up and withdraw it from the inside

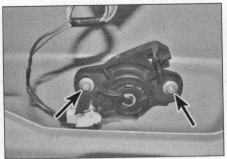

17.10a Undo the two retaining screws (arrowed) . . .

17.10b . . . free the lock cylinder from its location and disconnect the wiring connector

panel and remove the panel from the lock **(see illustrations)**.

3 Disconnect the lock wiring connector **(see illustration)**.

4 Undo the three lock assembly retaining screws **(see illustration)**.

5 Using a small screwdriver, depress the retaining lugs on each side of the lock extension **(see illustration)**.

6 Lift the lock assembly up and withdraw it from the inside **(see illustration)**.

Refitting

7 Refitting is a reversal of removal. Check that when closed the boot lid lock engages the lock striker centrally. If necessary loosen the bolts and adjust the position of the striker, then tighten the bolts.

Lock cylinder

Removal

8 Open the boot lid and remove the trim panel as previously described.

9 Remove the lock assembly as previously described.

10 Undo the two retaining screws, free the lock cylinder from its location and disconnect the wiring connector **(see illustrations)**.

11 Where applicable, depress the retaining catch and release the operating cable from the lock cylinder. Disconnect the operating cable inner end fitting from the lock cylinder and remove the cylinder.

Refitting

12 Refitting is a reversal of removal.

---

18 Tailgate and support struts – removal, refitting and adjustment

Tailgate

Removal

1 Open the tailgate, release the wiring harness grommet, then depress the locking catch and disconnect the tailgate wiring connector on each side **(see illustration)**.

2 Have an assistant support the tailgate, then disconnect the tops of the support struts by prising out the spring clips with a small screwdriver. Lower the struts to the body.

3 Drive out the tailgate hinge pins from outside to inside with a suitable drift, while the assistant supports the tailgate **(see illustration)**. Withdraw the tailgate from the body.

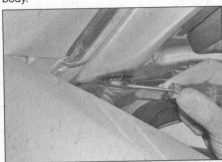

18.1 Disconnect the tailgate wiring connector on each side

Refitting

4 Refitting is a reversal of removal, but apply a little grease to the pivot pins, and check that when closed the tailgate is positioned centrally within the body aperture and flush with the surrounding bodywork. If necessary, adjust the position of the rubber supports so that the tailgate is flush with the surrounding bodywork. After making adjustments, check that the striker enters the lock centrally and if necessary loosen the striker bolts to reposition it. Tighten the bolts on completion.

Support struts

Removal

5 Open the tailgate and note which way round the struts are fitted. Have an assistant support the tailgate in its open position.

6 Using a small screwdriver, prise the spring clip from the top of the strut and disconnect it from the ball on the tailgate **(see illustrations)**.

18.3 Drive out the tailgate hinge pins (arrowed) from outside to inside

7 Similarly prise the spring clip from the bottom of the strut and disconnect it from the ball on the body. Withdraw the strut.

Refitting

8 Refitting is a reversal of removal.

19 Tailgate lock components – removal and refitting

Removal

Hatchback models

1 Open the tailgate and remove the trim caps over the upper side trim panel retaining screws. Undo the screw each side **(see illustrations)**.

2 Unscrew the parcel shelf lifting pins on each side.

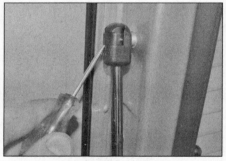

18.6a Prise the spring clip from the top of the strut . . .

18.6b . . . and disconnect it from the ball on the tailgate

3 Carefully prise free the side trim panel on each side to release the three retaining clips **(see illustration)**.

4 Using a forked tool, or removal tool, extract the four stud retaining clips at the lower edge of the lower trim panel **(see illustration)**.

5 Undo the retaining screws in the centre of the panel and pull out the centre pins of the four plastic rivets.

6 Pull the panel away from the tailgate to release the remaining internal clips and remove the panel from the tailgate **(see illustration)**.

7 With the trim panel removed, proceed as described in Section 17 for the lock assembly and lock cylinder removal and refitting procedures.

Estate models

8 Undo the retaining screw located in the tailgate release handle aperture, and remove the release handle **(see illustration)**.

9 Using a small screwdriver, extract the centre pins and remove the plastic securing rivets **(see illustration)**.

10 Pull the lower trim panel away from the tailgate to release the remaining internal clips and remove the panel from the tailgate **(see illustration)**.

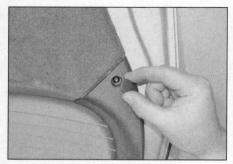

19.1a Remove the trim caps over the upper side trim panel retaining screws . . .

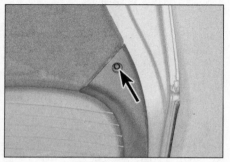

19.1b . . . then undo the screw (arrowed) each side

19.3 Prise free the side trim panel on each side to release the three retaining clips

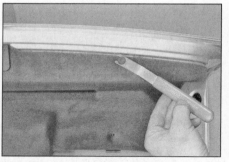

19.4 Extract the four stud retaining clips at the lower edge of the lower trim panel

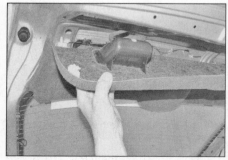

19.6 Pull the panel away from the tailgate to release the remaining internal clips

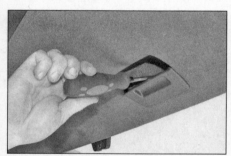

19.8 Undo the retaining screw located in the release handle aperture, and remove the release handle

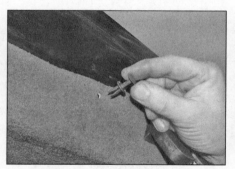

19.9 Extract the centre pins and remove the plastic securing rivets

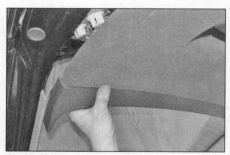

19.10 Pull the lower trim panel away from the tailgate to release the remaining internal clips

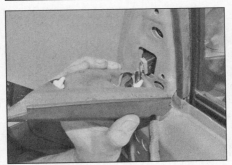

20.3 Prise off the mirror interior trim panel to release the two retaining clips

20.4 Disconnect the wiring connector from the mirror

20.5a Release the tweeter speaker wiring harness retaining clip . . .

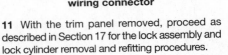

20.5b . . . and disconnect the tweeter wiring connector

11 With the trim panel removed, proceed as described in Section 17 for the lock assembly and lock cylinder removal and refitting procedures.

Refitting

12 Refitting is a reversal of removal.

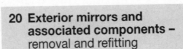

20 Exterior mirrors and associated components –
removal and refitting

Exterior mirror

Removal

1 Fully open the door window.
2 Remove the door inner trim panel as described in Section 12.
3 Carefully prise off the mirror interior trim panel to release the two retaining clips **(see illustration)**.

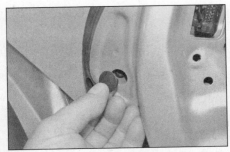

20.6 Extract the blanking plug from the front edge of the door and undo the mirror lower retaining bolt now exposed

4 Disconnect the wiring connector from the mirror **(see illustration)**.
5 Release the tweeter speaker wiring harness retaining clip from the interior trim panel, and disconnect the tweeter wiring connector **(see illustrations)**. Remove the trim panel.
6 Extract the blanking plug from the front edge of the door and undo the mirror lower retaining bolt now exposed **(see illustration)**.
7 Undo the two upper retaining bolts and remove the mirror assembly from the door **(see illustration)**.

Refitting

8 Refitting is a reversal of removal.

Mirror glass

Removal

9 Press the inner edge of the glass inwards so that the glass is forced out from the centre.
10 Using a plastic wedge, prise the outer

20.7 Undo the two upper retaining bolts (arrowed) and remove the mirror assembly from the door

edge of the glass outwards to release the internal retaining clips **(see illustration)**.
11 Withdraw the mirror glass and disconnect the wiring connectors **(see illustration)**.

Refitting

12 Refitting is a reversal of removal. Carefully press the mirror glass into the housing until the centre retainer clips are engaged.

Outer cover

Removal

13 Remove the mirror glass as described previously in this Section.
14 Using a small screwdriver, carefully prise the outer cover away from the mirror body to release the inner locating pin from its hole **(see illustration)**.
15 Compress the four clips securing the cover to the mirror body, starting with the two inner clips, then the two outer clips **(see**

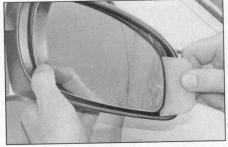

20.10 Prise the outer edge of the glass outwards to release the internal retaining clips

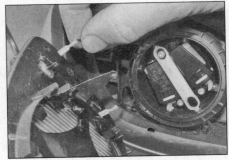

20.11 Withdraw the mirror glass and disconnect the wiring connectors

20.14 Prise the outer cover away from the mirror body to release the inner locating pin (arrowed) from its hole

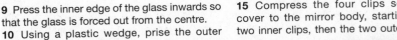
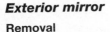

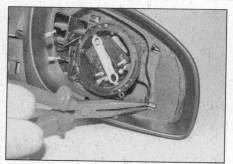

20.15 Compress the four clips securing the cover to the mirror body

20.18 Remove the rubber seal from the mirror frame

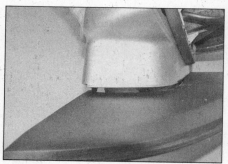

20.19a Carefully release the base cover from the mirror frame . . .

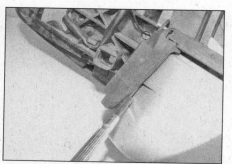

20.19b . . . and mirror body . . .

20.19c . . . and withdraw the cover

illustration). Withdraw the cover from the mirror body.

Refitting

16 Refitting is a reversal of removal.

Base cover

Removal

17 Remove the mirror from the car as described previously in this Section.
18 Remove the rubber seal from the mirror frame **(see illustration)**.
19 Using a small screwdriver, carefully release the base cover from the mirror frame and mirror body, and withdraw the cover **(see illustrations)**.

Refitting

20 Refitting is a reversal of removal.

23.1 Carefully release the twenty tabs and remove the grille from the bumper

21 Windscreen and fixed window glass – general information

The windscreen and rear window glass are cemented in position with a special adhesive and require the use of specialist equipment for their removal and refitting. Renewal of such fixed glass is considered beyond the scope of the home mechanic. Owners are strongly advised to have the work carried out by one of the many specialist windscreen fitting specialists.

22 Sunroof – general information

A manual or electric sunroof was offered as an optional extra on most models, and is fitted as standard equipment on some models.

Due to the complexity of the sunroof mechanism, considerable expertise is needed to repair, renew or adjust the sunroof components successfully. Removal of the roof first requires the headlining to be removed, which is a complex and tedious operation in itself, and not a task to be undertaken lightly. Therefore, any problems with the sunroof should be referred to a Vauxhall/Opel dealer.

On models with an electric sunroof, if the sunroof motor fails to operate, first check the relevant fuse. If the fault cannot be traced and rectified, the sunroof can be opened and closed manually using an Allen key to turn the

motor spindle. To gain access to the motor spindle, carefully prise out the trim cover situated at the rear of the sunroof. Insert the Allen key in the motor spindle, and turn to move the sunroof to the required position. A suitable Allen key is supplied with the vehicle, and is attached to the inside of the trim cover.

23 Body exterior fittings – removal and refitting

Radiator grille

1 Remove the front bumper as described in Section 6. Carefully release the twenty tabs and remove the grille from the bumper **(see illustration)**.
2 Refit the grille to the bumper ensuring it is securely held by the retaining tabs, then refit the front bumper as described in Section 6.

Wheel arch liners and body under-panels

3 The various plastic covers fitted to the underside of the vehicle are secured in position by a mixture of screws, nuts and retaining clips, and removal will be fairly obvious on inspection. Work methodically around the liner/panel, removing its retaining screws and releasing its retaining clips until it is free to be removed from the underside of the vehicle. Most clips used on the vehicle, with the exception of the fasteners which are used to secure the wheel arch liners, are simply prised out of position. The wheel arch liner clips are released by tapping their centre pins through the clip, and then removing the outer section of the clip; new clips will be required on refitting if the centre pins are not recovered.
4 When refitting, renew any retaining clips that may have been broken on removal, and ensure that the panel is securely retained by all the relevant clips, nuts and screws. Vauxhall/Opel also recommend that plastic nuts (where used) are renewed, regardless of their apparent condition, whenever they are disturbed.

Undertray

5 On diesel engine models an undertray is fitted beneath the engine/transmission

assembly. The undertray is secured to the front subframe and underbody with a selection of bolts and screws.

Water deflector

6 Remove the windscreen wiper arms as described in Chapter 12.

7 Open the bonnet, and pull up the rubber weatherseal from the flange at the rear of the engine compartment **(see illustration)**.

8 Carefully prise free the water deflector from the base of the windscreen to release the retaining clips, and remove the water deflector from the car **(see illustration)**.

9 Refit the water deflector using a reversal of the removal procedure. Refit the wiper arms as described in Chapter 12.

Body trim strips and badges

10 The various body trim strips and badges are held in position with a special adhesive tape. Removal requires the trim/badge to be heated, to soften the adhesive, and then cut away from the surface. Due to the high risk of damage to the vehicle's paintwork during this operation, it is recommended that this task should be entrusted to a Vauxhall/Opel dealer.

24 Seats –
removal and refitting

⚠ *Warning: The front seats are equipped with seat belt tensioners, and side airbags may be built into the outer sides of the seats. The seat belt tensioners and side airbags may cause injury if triggered accidentally. If the tensioner has been triggered due to a sudden impact or accident, the unit must be renewed, as it cannot be reset. If a seat is to be disposed of, the tensioner must be triggered before the seat is removed from the vehicle. Due to safety considerations, tensioner renewal or seat disposal must be entrusted to a Vauxhall/Opel dealer. Where side airbags are fitted, refer to Chapter 12 for the precautions which should be observed when dealing with an airbag system.*

1 Disconnect the battery negative terminal (refer to *Disconnecting the battery* in the Reference Chapter). Wait 2 minutes for the

23.7 Pull up the rubber weatherseal from the flange at the rear of the engine compartment

capacitors to discharge, before working on the seat electrics.

Front seat removal

2 Depress the two tabs and remove the front seat headrest.

3 Slide the seat adjustment fully forward.

4 Unclip the cover over the seat belt mounting, then undo the seat belt retaining bolt **(see illustration)**.

5 Pull out the locking bar and disconnect the wiring connector from the underside of the seat, at the rear **(see illustration)**.

6 Slacken and remove the seat retaining bolts from the rear of the guide rails **(see illustration)**.

7 Pull the seat backwards to disengage the guide rail front mounting lugs from the floor. The seat can now be lifted out of the vehicle.

Front seat refitting

8 Refitting is a reverse of the removal procedure, noting the following points:

a) *Remove all traces of old thread-locking compound from the threads of the seat retaining bolts, and clean the threaded holes in the vehicle floor, ideally by running a tap of the correct size and pitch down them.*

b) *Apply a suitable thread-locking compound to the threads of the seat bolts. Refit the bolts, and tighten them to the specified torque setting.*

c) *Reconnect the seat wiring connector making sure it has locked securely, then reconnect the battery negative terminal.*

23.8 Prise free the water deflector from the base of the windscreen to release the retaining clips

Rear seat removal

Cushion

9 Pull the front of the rear seat cushion upwards to disengage the front mountings. Where applicable, disconnect the wiring for the seat heater.

10 On Saloon and Hatchback models, lift the cushion out of the rear mountings and remove it from the car.

11 On Estate models, push the cushion and move it to the left to disengage the left-hand rear mounting, then move it to the right to disengage the right-hand rear mounting. Remove the cushion from the car.

Backrest

12 Remove the rear seat cushion as described previously in this Section.

13 Pull the upper portion of the backrest side padding forward to disengage the upper mounting, then lift it up to disengage the lower hook **(see illustrations)**. Remove the side padding from the car.

14 Unscrew the retaining nut and remove the centre seat belt buckle.

15 Fold the backrest forward then, using a screwdriver, press the outer hinge pin locking collar in, to free the hinge pin, while at the same time pulling upward to release the backrest **(see illustration)**.

16 Fold the backrest upward, then pull the hinge pin out of the centre support (left-hand side), or pull the backrest off the hinge pin (right-hand side) **(see illustration)**. Remove the backrest from the vehicle.

24.4 Undo the seat belt retaining bolt from the front seat

24.5 Pull out the locking bar and disconnect the wiring connector from the underside of the seat

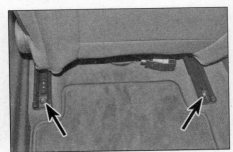

24.6 Slacken and remove the seat retaining bolts (arrowed) from the rear of the guide rails

24.13a Pull the upper portion of the backrest side padding forward to disengage the upper mounting . . .

24.13b . . . then lift it up to disengage the lower hook

26 Seat belt components – removal and refitting

24.15 Press the outer hinge pin locking collar in, while at the same time pulling upward to release the backrest

24.16 Pull the backrest off the hinge pin (arrowed) – right-hand backrest shown

⚠ **Warning:** *The front seats (and on certain models, the outer rear seats) are fitted with pyrotechnic seat belt tensioners which are triggered by the airbag control system. Before removing a seat belt, disconnect the battery and wait at least 2 minutes to allow the system capacitors to discharge.*

Front belt and reel

Removal

1 Unclip the cover over the seat belt mounting on the front seat, then undo the seat belt retaining bolt **(see illustration 24.4)**.
2 Remove the B-pillar inner trim panel and sill trim panel as described in Section 27.
3 Undo the seat belt upper mounting bolt **(see illustration)**.
4 Prise the cover from the lower outside of the B-pillar for access to the front seat belt reel mounting nut **(see illustrations)**. Using a 13 mm socket, 65 mm deep on the inside, unscrew the nut taking care not to drop it inside the B-pillar. Note that an extension pin is provided to enable the nut to be removed safely.
5 With the nut removed, remove the reel from the inside of the pillar.

Refitting

6 Refitting is a reversal of removal, but tighten the mounting bolts to the specified torque.

Front belt stalk and tensioner

Removal

7 Remove the front seat as described in Section 24.
8 From underneath the seat, slide out the wiring connector locking bar and disconnect the wiring connector **(see illustrations)**. Unclip the wiring harness from the seat.
9 Undo the retaining bolt and withdraw the tensioner from the seat **(see illustration)**.
10 Release the cable retaining clip and remove the tensioner **(see illustration)**.

Rear seat refitting

17 Refitting is a reverse of the removal procedure.

25 Seat belt tensioning mechanism – general information

All models covered in this manual are fitted with a front seat belt pyrotechnic tensioner system. On certain models, this system is also fitted to the outer rear seat belts. The system is designed to instantaneously take up any slack in the seat belt in the case of a sudden frontal impact, therefore reducing the possibility of injury to the front seat occupants. Each front seat is fitted with its own system, the components of which are mounted on the seat frame.

The seat belt tensioner is triggered by a frontal impact causing a deceleration of six times the force of gravity or greater. Lesser impacts, including impacts from behind, will not trigger the system.

When the system is triggered, a pretensioned spring draws back the seat belt via a cable which acts on the seat belt stalk. The cable can move by up to 80.0 mm, which therefore reduces the slack in the seat belt around the shoulders and waist of the occupant by a similar amount.

There is a risk of injury if the system is triggered inadvertently when working on the vehicle, and it is therefore strongly recommended that any work involving the seat belt tensioner system is entrusted to a Vauxhall/Opel dealer. Refer to the warning given at the beginning of Section 24 before contemplating any work on the front seats.

26.3 Undo the front seat belt upper mounting bolt

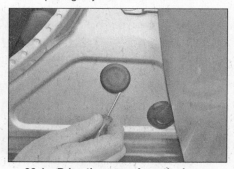

26.4a Prise the cover from the lower outside of the B-pillar . . .

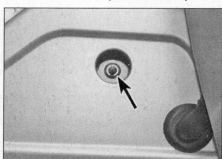

26.4b . . . for access to the front seat belt reel mounting nut (arrowed)

26.8a Slide out the wiring connector locking bar . . .

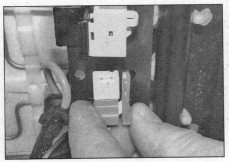

26.8b . . . and disconnect the seat belt tensioner wiring connector

26.9 Undo the retaining bolt (arrowed) and withdraw the tensioner from the seat

26.10 Release the cable retaining clip (arrowed) and remove the tensioner

26.14 Undo the rear seat belt lower mounting bolt (arrowed)

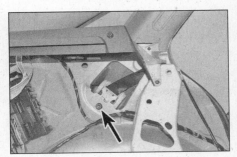

26.15 Undo the rear seat belt reel mounting bolt (arrowed) and remove the reel and belt from the car

Refitting

11 Refitting is a reverse of the removal procedure, noting the following points:

a) *Remove all traces of old thread-locking compound from the thread of the tensioner retaining bolt, and clean the threaded hole in the seat, ideally by running a tap of the correct size and pitch down it.*

b) *Apply a suitable thread-locking compound to the thread of the tensioner retaining bolt. Refit the bolt, and tighten it to the specified torque setting.*

Rear outer belt and reel

Removal

12 Remove the rear seat cushion as described in Section 24.

13 Remove the luggage compartment upper side trim and sill rear trim panel as described in Section 27.

14 Undo the seat belt lower mounting bolt **(see illustration)**.

15 Undo the seat belt reel mounting bolt and remove the reel and belt from the car **(see illustration)**.

Refitting

16 Refitting is a reversal of removal, but tighten the mounting bolts to the specified torque.

Rear centre belt and reel

17 The inertia reel for the centre rear seat belt is located internally within the rear seat backrest. To gain access, the backrest must be removed and completely dismantled. This is a complex operation and considerable expertise is needed to remove and refit the seat upholstery and internal components without damage. Therefore, any problems with the centre seat belt and reel should be referred to a Vauxhall/Opel dealer.

Rear belt stalk and tensioner

Removal

18 Remove the rear seat cushion as described in Section 24.

19 On models without seat belt tensioners, undo the retaining nut and remove the relevant stalk from the floor **(see illustration)**.

20 On models with seat belt tensioners, slide out the wiring connector locking bar and disconnect the wiring connector.

21 Undo the retaining nut and remove the relevant tensioner from the floor. Note that a new retaining nut will be required for refitting.

Refitting

22 Refitting is a reversal of removal, but tighten the mounting bolts to the specified torque.

27 Interior trim – removal and refitting

1 The interior trim panels are secured by a combination of clips and screws. Removal and refitting is generally self-explanatory, noting that it may be necessary to remove or loosen surrounding panels to allow a particular panel to be removed. The following paragraphs describe the general removal and refitting details of the major panels.

A-pillar trim panel

2 Pull off the front door weather strip in the vicinity of the A-pillar trim panel **(see illustration)**.

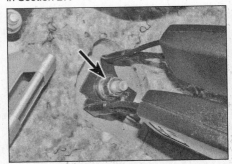

26.19 Undo the retaining nut (arrowed) and remove the relevant stalk from the floor

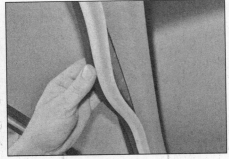

27.2 Pull off the front door weather strip in the vicinity of the A-pillar trim panel

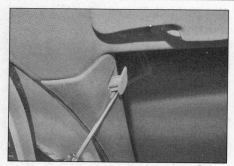

27.3 Pull out the airbag positioning clip from the trim panel

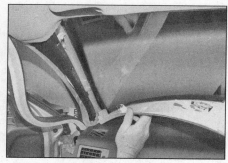

27.4 Pull the trim panel away from the A-pillar and remove it from the car

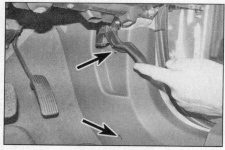

27.7 Undo the two screws (arrowed) securing the footwell side trim panel to the body

27.8 Pull the overlapping side sill panel from its location, then disengage and remove the footwell panel

3 On models equipped with curtain airbags, pull out the airbag positioning clip from the trim panel (see illustration).
4 Pull the trim panel away from the A-pillar and remove it from the car (see illustration).
5 Refitting is a reversal of removal.

Front footwell side trim panel

6 Open the front door and pull the weatherstrip away from the side trim panel and side sill panel.
7 Undo the two screws securing the footwell side trim panel to the body (see illustration).
8 Pull the overlapping side sill panel from its location at the front, then disengage and remove the footwell panel (see illustration).
9 Refitting is a reversal of removal.

B-pillar upper trim panel

10 Open the front and rear doors and pull the weatherstrip away from the B-pillar.

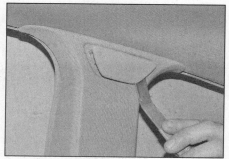

27.12 Prise out the plastic cover at the top of the B-pillar upper trim panel

11 Unclip the cover over the seat belt mounting on the front seat, then undo the seat belt retaining bolt (see illustration 24.4).
12 Prise out the plastic cover at the top of the panel (see illustration).
13 Prise the trim panel away from the B-pillar at the top (see illustration).
14 Disengage the lower end of the panel from the B-pillar lower trim panel, feed the seat belt through the opening and remove the panel from the car (see illustration).
15 Refitting is a reversal of removal.

B-pillar lower trim panel

16 Open the front and rear doors and pull the weatherstrip away from the B-pillar.
17 Pull the overlapping side sill panel from its location to allow the B-pillar lower trim to be removed.
18 Unclip the B-pillar lower trim panel from the upper panel at the top (see illustration).

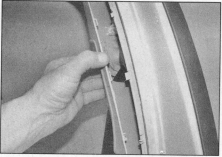

27.13 Prise the trim panel away from the B-pillar at the top

19 Unclip the bottom of the panel from the B-pillar and remove the panel from the car.
20 Refitting is a reversal of removal.

Side sill inner trim panel

21 Open the front and rear doors and pull the weatherstrip away from the B-pillar and the lower part of the door apertures.
22 Remove the rear seat cushion as described in Section 24.
23 Pull the upper portion of the seat backrest side padding forward to disengage the upper mounting, then lift it up to disengage the lower hook (see illustrations 24.13a and 24.13b). Remove the side padding from the car.
24 Spread the sides of the side sill inner trim panel outward and release it from the B-pillar lower trim panel (see illustration).
25 Starting at the front and working rearwards, unclip the panel from the sill and remove the panel from the car.

27.14 Disengage the lower end of the panel from the B-pillar lower trim panel and feed the seat belt through the opening

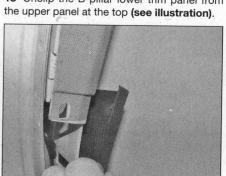

27.18 Unclip the B-pillar lower trim panel from the upper panel at the top

27.24 Spread the sides of the side sill inner trim panel outward and release it from the B-pillar lower trim panel

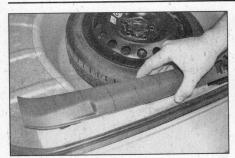

27.30 Pull the tailgate aperture trim panel away to release the internal retaining clips and remove the panel from the car

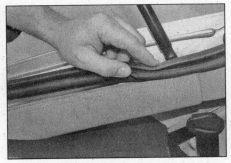

27.31 Pull the weatherstrip away from the boot lid/tailgate aperture

27.32 Prise out the retaining clips at the rear of the panel

27.39 Carefully unclip the upper and lower cover strips from the side trim panel

27.40 Unscrew the six panel retaining screws

27.41 Unclip and remove the covers over the luggage retaining lugs

26 Refitting is a reversal of removal.

Luggage compartment lower side trim panel

Saloon and Hatchback models

27 Fold the rear seat backrests forward.
28 Open the boot lid or tailgate.
29 Remove the luggage compartment floor covering.
30 Pull the tailgate aperture trim panel away to release the internal retaining clips and remove the panel from the car (see illustration).
31 Pull the weatherstrip away from the boot lid/tailgate aperture (see illustration).
32 Using a forked tool, or removal tool, prise out the retaining clips at the rear of the panel (see illustration).
33 Pull the panel away to release the internal clips, disconnect the wiring for the luggage compartment light (where applicable) and remove the panel.
34 Refitting is a reversal of removal.

Estate models

35 Open the tailgate.
36 Remove the luggage compartment floor covering.
37 Pull the weatherstrip away from the rear door aperture.
38 Remove the tailgate aperture lower centre trim panel, as described later in this Section.
39 Carefully unclip the upper and lower cover strips from the side trim panel (see illustration).
40 Unscrew the six panel retaining screws (see illustration).

41 Unclip and remove the covers over the luggage retaining lugs (see illustration).
42 Undo the retaining bolts and remove the luggage retaining lugs (see illustration).
43 Pull the panel away to release the internal clips, and remove the panel from the car (see illustration).
44 Refitting is a reversal of removal.

C-pillar trim panel

Saloon models

45 Pull the weatherstrip away from the rear door aperture.
46 Pull the upper portion of the seat backrest side padding forward to disengage the upper mounting, then lift it up to disengage the lower hook (see illustrations 24.13a and 24.13b). Remove the side padding from the car.
47 Prise off the cover and undo the rear seat belt upper mounting bolt.
48 On models equipped with curtain airbags,

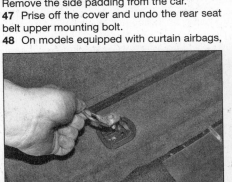

27.42 Undo the retaining bolts and remove the luggage retaining lugs

pull out the airbag positioning clip from the trim panel.
49 Pull the panel away to release the internal clips, and remove the panel from the car.
50 Refitting is a reversal of removal, but tighten the seat belt retaining bolt to the specified torque.

C/D-pillar trim panel

Hatchback and Estate models

51 Remove the luggage compartment lower side trim panel as described previously in this Section.
52 Pull the upper portion of the seat backrest side padding forward to disengage the upper mounting, then lift it up to disengage the lower hook (see illustrations 24.13a and 24.13b). Remove the side padding from the car.
53 Prise off the cover and undo the rear seat belt upper mounting bolt (see illustrations).

27.43 Pull the panel away to release the internal clips, and remove the panel from the car

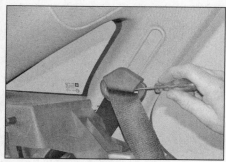

27.53a Prise off the cover . . .

27.53b . . . and undo the rear seat belt upper mounting bolt

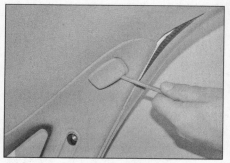

27.55 Pull out the airbag positioning clip from the trim panel

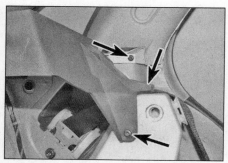

27.56a Undo the three screws at the front (arrowed) . . .

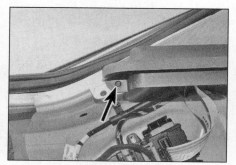

27.56b . . . and the screw at the rear (arrowed) securing the panel to the body

27.57 Pull the panel away to release the internal clips, and remove the panel from the car

54 Pull the weatherstrip away from the rear door aperture.
55 On models equipped with curtain airbags, pull out the airbag positioning clip from the trim panel (see illustration).
56 Undo the three screws at the front and

the screw at the rear securing the panel to the body (see illustrations).
57 Pull the panel away to release the internal clips, and remove the panel from the car (see illustration).
58 Refitting is a reversal of removal, but

tighten the seat belt retaining bolt to the specified torque.

Boot lid/tailgate aperture centre trim panel

Upper panel
59 Open the boot lid or tailgate.
60 Pull the panel away to release the internal clips, and remove the panel from the car (see illustration).
61 Refitting is a reversal of removal.

Lower panel
62 Open the boot lid or tailgate.
63 Remove the luggage compartment floor covering.
64 On Estate models, prise up the trim caps and undo the panel retaining screws (see illustrations).
65 Pull the panel away to release the internal clips, and remove the panel from the car (see illustration).
66 Refitting is a reversal of removal.

Interior mirror
67 On models fitted with a rain sensor, unclip and remove the sensor trim panel and release the retaining clip(s) and disconnect the wiring connectors from the mirror assembly.
68 Press the retaining clip at the top of the interior mirror mounting bracket, then carefully release the interior mirror in the downwards direction to remove it from the windscreen.
69 Refitting is the reverse of removal.

27.60 Pull the panel away to release the internal clips, and remove the panel from the car

27.64a On Estate models, prise up the trim caps . . .

27.64b . . . and undo the panel retaining screws

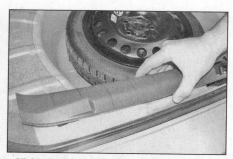

27.65 Pull the panel away to release the internal clips, and remove the panel from the car

28.3 Remove the centre console storage compartment

28.4a Carefully release the facia decorative strip using a plastic spatula or similar tool . . .

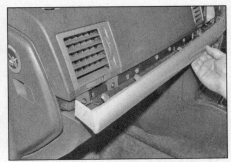

28.4b . . . and remove the strip from the facia

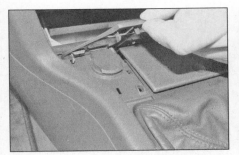

28.5 Prise up and remove the trim panel around the cigarette lighter/accessory socket

28.6 Remove the ashtray by opening the lid, depressing the internal tabs each side and lifting out

28.8 Unclip the gearchange/selector lever gaiter retaining frame from the centre console

28 Centre console – removal and refitting

Front console

Removal

1 Disconnect the battery negative terminal (refer to *Disconnecting the battery* in the Reference Chapter).
2 Remove the rear centre console as described later in this Section.
3 Unclip and remove the centre console storage compartment below the heater/ventilation control panel **(see illustration)**.
4 Carefully release the facia decorative strip using a plastic spatula or similar tool **(see illustrations)**.
5 Carefully prise up and remove the trim panel around the cigarette lighter/accessory socket **(see illustration)**.
6 Remove the ashtray from the centre console by opening the lid, depressing the internal tabs each side and lifting out **(see illustration)**.
7 Disconnect the wiring connector at the rear of the cigarette lighter/accessory socket.
8 Unclip the gearchange/selector lever gaiter retaining frame from the centre console and lift it off the gearchange lever **(see illustration)**.
9 On manual transmission models, release the retaining lugs around the sides and rear of the gearchange lever gaiter. Disengage the locating pegs at the front and fold the gaiter up over the gearchange lever knob **(see illustrations)**.

10 Undo the two upper screws securing the centre console to the facia **(see illustration)**.
11 Undo the retaining screw at the rear left-hand side of the centre console **(see illustration)**.
12 Prise out the two trim caps on each side of the centre console at the front, and undo the screw and nut each side **(see illustrations)**.
13 Lift the console up and slide it to the rear,

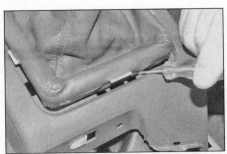

28.9a Release the retaining lugs around the sides and rear of the gearchange lever gaiter . . .

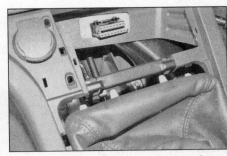

28.9b . . . then disengage the locating pegs at the front and fold the gaiter up over the gearchange lever knob

28.10 Undo the two upper screws (arrowed) securing the centre console to the facia

28.11 Undo the retaining screw (arrowed) at the rear left-hand side of the centre console

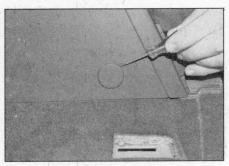

28.12a Prise out the two trim caps on each side of the centre console at the front . . .

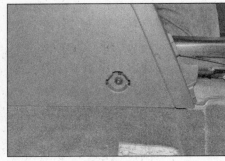

28.12b . . . and undo the screw and nut each side

28.13 Lift the console up and slide it to the rear, then remove the console from the car

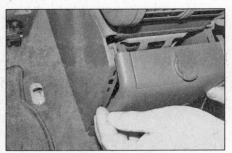

28.16 Prise free the cigarette lighter/ accessory socket panel at the rear of the centre console

then remove the console from the car **(see illustration)**.

Refitting

14 Refitting is a reversal of removal.

28.19a Carefully prise free the storage compartment at the front of the centre console . . .

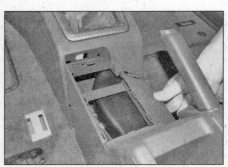

28.20 Pull the console to the rear to disengage the front locating pegs

28.17 Undo the two screws (arrowed) securing the rear of the centre console to the floor

Rear console

Removal

15 Disconnect the battery negative terminal (refer to *Disconnecting the battery* in the Reference Chapter).

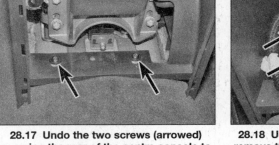

28.19b . . . then undo the screw (arrowed) in the storage compartment aperture

29.2 Prise out the glovebox interior light and disconnect the wiring connector

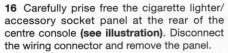

28.18 Undo the four bolts (arrowed) and remove the armrest and rear vent housing from the console

16 Carefully prise free the cigarette lighter/ accessory socket panel at the rear of the centre console **(see illustration)**. Disconnect the wiring connector and remove the panel.

17 Undo the two screws now exposed securing the rear of the centre console to the floor **(see illustration)**.

18 Undo the four bolts and remove the armrest and rear vent housing from the console **(see illustration)**.

19 Carefully prise free the storage compartment at the front of the centre console, then undo the screw in the storage compartment aperture **(see illustrations)**.

20 Pull the console to the rear to disengage the front locating pegs, lift it over the handbrake lever and remove the console from the car **(see illustration)**.

Refitting

21 Refitting is a reversal of removal.

29 Facia panel components –
removal and refitting

Glovebox

Removal

1 Carefully release the facia decorative strip using a plastic spatula or similar tool **(see illustrations 28.4a and 28.4b)**.

2 Prise out the glovebox interior light and disconnect the wiring connector **(see illustration)**.

3 Undo the screw each side securing the base of the glovebox to the facia **(see illustrations)**.

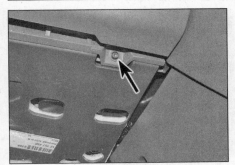

29.3a Undo the right-hand screw (arrowed) . . .

29.3b . . . and left-hand screw (arrowed) securing the base of the glovebox to the facia

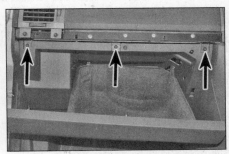

29.4 Undo the three screws (arrowed) securing the top of the glovebox to the facia

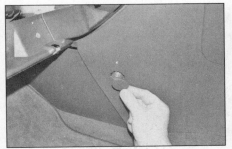

29.7 Prise out the trim cap on the side of the centre console at the front, and undo the retaining nut

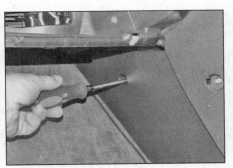

29.8 Undo the screw securing the footwell trim panel at the front

29.9 Ease the front of the centre console outwards to expose the recessed hidden bolt (arrowed)

4 Open the glovebox and undo the three screws securing the top of the glovebox to the facia **(see illustration)**.
5 Withdraw the glovebox from the facia and remove it from the car.

Refitting

6 Refitting is a reversal of removal.

Facia footwell trim panel

Removal

7 Prise out the trim cap on the side of the centre console at the front, and undo the retaining nut **(see illustration)**.
8 Undo the screw securing the footwell trim panel at the front **(see illustration)**.
9 Ease the front of the centre console outwards to expose the recessed hidden bolt **(see illustration)**. Unscrew and remove the bolt.
10 While still holding the front of the centre console outwards, remove the footwell trim panel from the side of the facia **(see illustration)**.

Refitting

11 Refitting is a reversal of removal.

Centre air vents

Removal

12 Carefully release the facia decorative strip using a plastic spatula or similar tool **(see illustrations 28.4a and 28.4b)**.
13 Undo the four bolts securing the centre vent housing to the facia and withdraw the housing from its location **(see illustrations)**. Lift the locking bar(s) and disconnect the

wiring connector(s) from the rear of the information display unit, then remove the vent housing from the facia.

Refitting

14 Refitting is a reversal of removal.

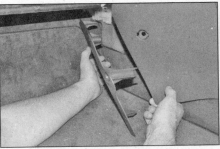

29.10 While still holding the front of the centre console outwards, remove the footwell trim panel from the side of the facia

29.13b . . . and withdraw the housing from its location

Side air vents

Removal

15 To remove the vent from the driver's side of the facia, carefully release the facia decorative

29.13a Undo the four bolts (arrowed) securing the centre vent housing to the facia (arrowed) . . .

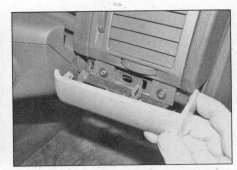

29.15 Release the facia decorative strip using a plastic spatula or similar

29.16a Undo the two screws (arrowed) securing the base of the vent to the facia . . .

29.16b . . . pull the vent out at the bottom and disengage the two upper retaining lugs (arrowed)

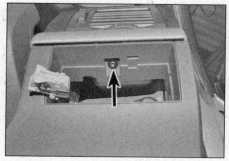

29.19 Undo the screw (arrowed) at the top of the headlight switch aperture

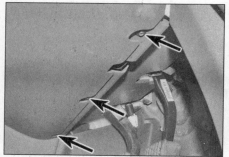

29.20a Undo the two upper screws, and three lower screws (arrowed) . . .

29.20b . . . and remove the lower trim panel from under the facia

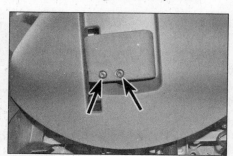

29.25 Undo the two screws (arrowed) and remove the steering column height adjuster handle

strip using a plastic spatula or similar tool (see illustration).

16 Undo the two screws securing the base of the vent to the facia. Pull the vent out at the bottom, disengage the two upper retaining

lugs, and remove the vent from the facia (see illustrations).

17 To remove the vent from the passenger's side of the facia, release the facia decorative strip as described in paragraph 12,

then remove the vent as described in paragraph 16.

Refitting

18 Refitting is a reversal of removal.

Driver's side lower trim panel

Removal

19 Remove the headlight switch as described in Chapter 12, then undo the screw at the top of the light switch aperture (see illustration).
20 Undo the two upper screws, and three lower screws and remove the lower trim panel from under the facia (see illustrations).

Refitting

21 Refitting is a reversal of removal.

Steering column shrouds

Removal

22 Carefully release the facia decorative strip below the side vent panel using a plastic spatula or similar tool (see illustration 29.15).
23 Remove the driver's side lower trim panel as described previously in this Section.
24 Move the steering column to its lowest position by means of the height adjuster.
25 Undo the two screws and remove the column height adjuster handle (see illustration).
26 Carefully prise off the circular trim panel around the ignition switch (see illustration).
27 Using a small screwdriver, hook out the trim caps and undo the shroud upper retaining screw on each side (see illustrations).
28 Undo the shroud lower retaining screw in the column height adjuster handle aperture (see illustration).

29.26 Prise off the circular trim panel around the ignition switch

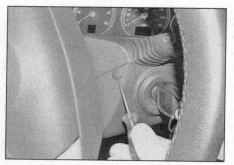

29.27a Hook out the trim caps . . .

29.27b . . . and undo the shroud upper retaining screw on each side

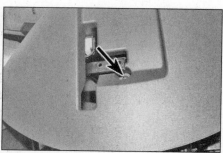

29.28 Undo the shroud lower retaining screw (arrowed) in the column height adjuster handle aperture

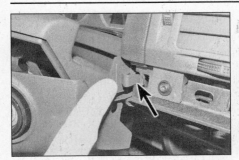

29.30 Unhook the shroud inner panel from the facia (arrowed) on both sides, then lift the upper shroud off the steering column

29.31 Undo the screw (arrowed) each side securing the lower shroud to the switch assembly

29.41 Remove the side cover panels at the left-hand and right-hand ends of the facia

29.42a Undo the bolt (arrowed) securing the radio/CD player mounting frame to the facia . . .

29.42b . . . prise free the upper and lower retaining tabs . . .

29.42c . . . and remove the frame from the facia

29 Carefully prise the upper shroud off the lower shroud.

30 Unhook the shroud inner panel from the facia on both sides, then lift the upper shroud up and off the steering column **(see illustration)**.

31 Undo the screw each side securing the lower shroud to the switch assembly **(see illustration)**.

32 Disengage the lower shroud from the steering column height adjuster and ignition switch and remove the shroud from the column.

Refitting

33 Refitting is a reversal of removal.

Complete facia assembly

Note: *This is an involved operation entailing the removal of numerous components and assemblies, and the disconnection of a multitude of wiring connectors. Make notes*

on the location of all disconnected wiring, or attach labels to the connectors, to avoid confusion when refitting.

Removal

34 Disconnect the battery negative terminal (refer to *Disconnecting the battery* in the Reference Chapter).

35 Remove the A-pillar trim panels on both sides as described in Section 27.

36 Remove the front centre console as described in Section 28.

37 Remove the following facia panels as described previously in this Section:
   a) *Glovebox.*
   b) *Facia footwell trim panels.*
   c) *Centre and side air vents.*
   d) *Driver's side lower trim panel.*
   e) *Steering column shrouds.*

38 Remove the steering wheel as described in Chapter 10.

39 Remove the steering column electronics

module, instrument panel, radio/CD player and all the facia switches as described in Chapter 12.

40 Remove the heater control assembly as described in Chapter 3.

41 Remove the side cover panels at the left-hand and right-hand ends of the facia **(see illustration)**.

42 Undo the bolt securing the radio/CD player mounting frame to the facia. Prise free the upper and lower retaining tabs and remove the frame from the facia **(see illustrations)**.

43 Release the locking catches with a small screwdriver, and detach the switch plug strips on the left-hand and right-hand side of the radio/CD player aperture **(see illustrations)**.

44 Carefully prise out the sun sensor panel from the top of the facia and disconnect the wiring connector **(see illustration)**. On models fitted with a loudspeaker in the sun sensor aperture, undo the two retaining bolts,

29.43a Release the locking catches with a small screwdriver . . .

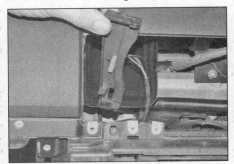

29.43b . . . and detach the switch plug strips

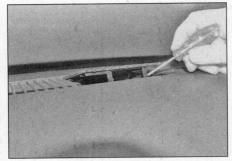

29.44 Carefully prise out the sun sensor panel from the top of the facia

29.46 Extract the plastic rivet and remove the footwell air duct on the driver's side

29.47a Undo the bolt (arrowed) at each end of the facia . . .

29.47b . . . the bolt at each lower corner (arrowed) . . .

29.47c . . . the lower centre bolt (arrowed) each side . . .

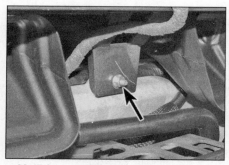

29.47d . . . and the nut (arrowed) in the centre vent aperture

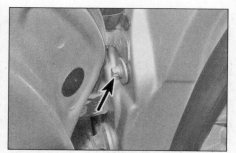

29.57 Undo the through-bolt (arrowed) securing the crossmember to the A-pillar on each side

29.58a Undo the upper outer bolt (arrowed) . . .

29.58b . . . and lower nut (arrowed) securing the crossmember to the body on each side

remove the speaker and disconnect the wiring connector.

45 Unclip and remove the glovebox cooling duct, then undo the bolt and remove the footwell air duct on the passenger's side.

46 Extract the plastic rivet and remove the footwell air duct on the driver's side **(see illustration)**.

47 Undo the following fasteners securing the facia to the mounting bracket **(see illustrations)**:

a) 1 bolt at the left-hand and right-hand end.
b) 1 bolt each side at the lower left-hand and right-hand corners of the facia.
c) 1 lower centre bolt each side.
d) 1 nut in the centre vent panel aperture.

48 With the help of an assistant, carefully lift the facia from its location. Check that all wiring has been disconnected, then remove the facia from the car.

Refitting

49 Refitting is a reversal of removal ensuring that all wiring is correctly reconnected and all mounting securely tightened.

Facia crossmember

Note: *This is an involved operation entailing the disconnection of a multitude of wiring connectors. Make notes on the location of all disconnected wiring, or attach labels to the connectors, to avoid confusion when refitting.*

Removal

50 Remove the facia as described previously in this Section.

51 Remove the steering column as described in Chapter 10.

52 Remove the passenger's airbag as described in Chapter 12.

53 Undo the retaining bolts and remove the electronics modules from the crossmember on each side.

54 Disconnect all remaining earth cables and wiring connections, making careful notes as to their locations.

55 Undo the upper and lower retaining bolts and remove the crossmember centre brace.

56 Undo the bolts securing the crossmember to the heater/air conditioning system air distribution housing.

57 From outside the car, undo the long through-bolt securing the crossmember to the A-pillar on each side **(see illustration)**.

58 Undo the upper and lower outer bolt and nut securing the crossmember to the body on each side **(see illustrations)**.

59 With the help of an assistant, check that all wiring has been disconnected, then remove the crossmember from the car.

Refitting

60 Refitting is a reversal of removal ensuring that all wiring is correctly reconnected and all mounting securely tightened.

Chapter 12
Body electrical systems

Contents

Degrees of difficulty

Easy, suitable for novice with little experience	**Fairly easy,** suitable for beginner with some experience	**Fairly difficult,** suitable for competent DIY mechanic	**Difficult,** suitable for experienced DIY mechanic	**Very difficult,** suitable for expert DIY or professional

Specifications

System type. . . . . 12 volt negative earth

Bulbs	**Wattage***
Direction indicator side repeater	5
Direction indicator	21
Foglight:	
Front	55
Rear	21
Headlight (halogen type).	55
Interior lights.	10
Number plate light	10
Reversing light	21
Sidelight	5
Stop/tail-light.	21/5

* Note: *The bulb wattage information given is for guidance only as no information is provided by Vauxhall/Opel. The wattage is stamped on the base or side of the bulb.*

1 General information and precautions

⚠️ *Warning: Before carrying out any work on the electrical system, read through the precautions given in 'Safety first!' at the beginning of this manual, and in Chapter 5A.*

1 The electrical system is of the 12 volt negative earth type. Power for the lights and all electrical accessories is supplied by a lead-acid type battery, which is charged by the engine-driven alternator.

2 This Chapter covers repair and service procedures for the various electrical components not associated with the engine. Information on the battery, alternator and starter motor can be found in Chapter 5A.

3 It should be noted that, prior to working on any component in the electrical system, the battery negative terminal should first be disconnected, to prevent the possibility of electrical short-circuits and/or fires.
Caution: Before proceeding, refer to 'Disconnecting the battery' in the Reference Chapter for further information.

2 Electrical fault finding – general information

Note: *Refer to the precautions given in 'Safety first!' and in Section 1 before starting work. The following tests relate to testing of the main electrical circuits, and should not be used to test delicate electronic circuits (such as the anti-lock braking system or fuel injection system), particularly where an electronic control unit is used.*

General

1 A typical electrical circuit consists of an electrical component, any switches, relays, motors, fuses, fusible links or circuit breakers related to that component, and the wiring and connectors which link the component to both the battery and the vehicle body. To help to pinpoint a problem in an electrical circuit, wiring diagrams are shown at the end of this Chapter.

2 Before attempting to diagnose an electrical fault, first study the appropriate wiring diagram to obtain a complete understanding of the components included in the particular circuit concerned. The possible sources of a fault can be narrowed down by noting if other components related to the circuit are operating properly. If several components or circuits fail at one time, the problem is likely to be related to a shared fuse or earth connection.

3 Electrical problems usually stem from simple causes, such as loose or corroded connections, a faulty earth connection, a blown fuse, a melted fusible link, or a faulty relay (refer to Section 3 for details of testing relays). Inspect the condition of all fuses, wires and connections in a problem circuit before testing the components. Use the wiring diagrams to determine which terminal connections will need to be checked in order to pinpoint the trouble-spot.

4 The basic tools required for electrical fault finding include a circuit tester or voltmeter (a 12 volt bulb with a set of test leads can also be used for certain tests); a self-powered test light (sometimes known as a continuity tester); an ohmmeter (to measure resistance); a battery and set of test leads; and a jumper wire, preferably with a circuit breaker or fuse incorporated, which can be used to bypass suspect wires or electrical components. Before attempting to locate a problem with test instruments, use the wiring diagram to determine where to make the connections.

5 To find the source of an intermittent wiring fault (usually due to a poor or dirty connection, or damaged wiring insulation), a 'wiggle' test can be performed on the wiring. This involves wiggling the wiring by hand to see if the fault occurs as the wiring is moved. It should be possible to narrow down the source of the fault to a particular section of wiring. This method of testing can be used in conjunction with any of the tests described in the following sub-Sections.

6 Apart from problems due to poor connections, two basic types of fault can occur in an electrical circuit – open-circuit, or short-circuit.

7 Open-circuit faults are caused by a break somewhere in the circuit, which prevents current from flowing. An open-circuit fault will prevent a component from working, but will not cause the relevant circuit fuse to blow.

8 Short-circuit faults are caused by a 'short' somewhere in the circuit, which allows the current flowing in the circuit to 'escape' along an alternative route, usually to earth. Short-circuit faults are normally caused by a breakdown in wiring insulation, which allows a feed wire to touch either another wire, or an earthed component such as the bodyshell. A short-circuit fault will normally cause the relevant circuit fuse to blow.

Finding an open-circuit

9 To check for an open-circuit, connect one lead of a circuit tester or voltmeter to either the negative battery terminal or a known good earth.

10 Connect the other lead to a connector in the circuit being tested, preferably nearest to the battery or fuse.

11 Switch on the circuit, bearing in mind that some circuits are live only when the ignition switch is turned to a particular position.

12 If voltage is present (indicated either by the tester bulb lighting or a voltmeter reading, as applicable), this means that the section of the circuit between the relevant connector and the battery is problem-free.

13 Continue to check the remainder of the circuit in the same fashion.

14 When a point is reached at which no voltage is present, the problem must lie between that point and the previous test point with voltage. Most problems can be traced to a broken, corroded or loose connection.

Finding a short-circuit

15 To check for a short-circuit, first disconnect the load(s) from the circuit (loads are the components which draw current from a circuit, such as bulbs, motors, heating elements, etc).

16 Remove the relevant fuse from the circuit, and connect a circuit tester or voltmeter to the fuse connections.

17 Switch on the circuit, bearing in mind that some circuits are live only when the ignition switch is turned to a particular position.

18 If voltage is present (indicated either by the tester bulb lighting or a voltmeter reading, as applicable), this means that there is a short-circuit.

19 If no voltage is present, but the fuse still blows with the load(s) connected, this indicates an internal fault in the load(s).

Finding an earth fault

20 The battery negative terminal is connected to 'earth' – the metal of the engine/transmission unit and the car body – and most systems are wired so that they only receive a positive feed, the current returning via the metal of the car body. This means that the component mounting and the body form part of that circuit. Loose or corroded mountings can therefore cause a range of electrical faults, ranging from total failure of a circuit, to a puzzling partial fault. In particular, lights may shine dimly (especially when another circuit sharing the same earth point is in operation), motors (eg, wiper motors or the radiator cooling fan motor) may run slowly, and the operation of one circuit may have an apparently-unrelated effect on another. Note that on many vehicles, earth straps are used between certain components, such as the engine/transmission and the body, usually where there is no metal-to-metal contact between components, due to flexible rubber mountings, etc.

21 To check whether a component is properly earthed, disconnect the battery, and connect one lead of an ohmmeter to a known good earth point. Connect the other lead to the wire or earth connection being tested. The resistance reading should be zero; if not, check the connection as follows.

22 If an earth connection is thought to be faulty, dismantle the connection, and clean back to bare metal both the bodyshell and the wire terminal or the component earth connection mating surface. Be careful to remove all traces of dirt and corrosion, then use a knife to trim away any paint, so that a clean metal-to-metal joint is made. On reassembly, tighten the joint fasteners securely; if a wire terminal is being refitted, use serrated washers between the terminal and the bodyshell, to ensure a clean and secure connection. When the connection is remade, prevent the onset of corrosion in the future by applying a coat of petroleum jelly or silicone-based grease. Alternatively, at regular intervals, spray on a proprietary ignition sealer or a water-dispersant lubricant.

3 Fuses and relays – general information

Fuses

1 The main fuses are located behind a cover on the left-hand edge of the facia, with additional fuses and relays located in the fuse/relay box on the left-hand side of the engine compartment, and in the left-hand side of the luggage compartment.
2 To gain access to the facia fuses, pull open and remove the cover (see illustration).
3 To gain access to the engine compartment fuses, open the battery box cover and lift the lid off the fusebox (see illustration).
4 Access to the fuses in the luggage compartment can be gained by opening the stowage compartment cover (see illustration).
5 To remove a fuse, first switch off the circuit concerned (or the ignition), then pull the fuse out of its terminals using the plastic removal tool provided (see illustration). The wire within the fuse is clearly visible; if the fuse is blown, it will be broken or melted.
6 Always renew a fuse with one of an identical rating; never use a fuse with a different rating from the original, nor substitute anything else. Never renew a fuse more than once without tracing the source of the trouble. The fuse rating is stamped on top of the fuse; note that the fuses are also colour-coded for easy recognition.
7 If a new fuse blows immediately, find the cause before renewing it again; a short to earth as a result of faulty insulation is most likely. Where a fuse protects more than one circuit, try to isolate the defect by switching on each circuit in turn (if possible) until the fuse blows again. Always carry a supply of spare fuses of each relevant rating on the vehicle, a spare of each rating should be clipped into the base of the fuse/relay box.

Relays

8 Most of the relays are located in the fuse/relay box in the engine compartment (see illustration 3.3).
9 If a circuit or system controlled by a relay develops a fault and the relay is suspect, operate the system; if the relay is functioning, it should be possible to hear it click as it is energised. If this is the case, the fault lies with the components or wiring of the system. If the relay is not being energised, then either the relay is not receiving a main supply or a switching voltage, or the relay itself is faulty.

3.2 Pull open and remove the cover for access to the fuses in the facia

3.4 Access to the fuses in the luggage compartment can be gained by opening the stowage compartment cover

Testing is by the substitution of a known good unit, but be careful; while some relays are identical in appearance and in operation, others look similar but perform different functions.
10 To renew a relay, first ensure that the ignition switch is off. The relay can then simply be pulled out from the socket and the new relay pressed in.

4 Switches – removal and refitting

Note: Disconnect the battery negative terminal (refer to 'Disconnecting the battery' in the Reference Chapter) before removing any switch, and reconnect the terminal after refitting.

Ignition switch/steering column lock

1 Refer to Chapter 10.

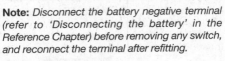
4.4a Press switch the knob in and turn it to the vertical position . . .

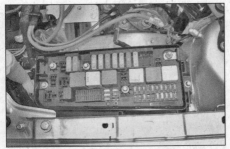
3.3 Open the battery box cover and lift off the fusebox lid for access to the engine compartment fuses

3.5 Pull the fuse out of its terminals using the plastic removal tool provided

Steering column switches

2 The direction indicator and windscreen wiper switches are an integral part of the steering column electronics module, and cannot be individually renewed.
3 To remove the steering column electronics module, which also contains the airbag rotary connector, proceed as described in Section 23.

Lighting switch assembly

4 With the light switch knob in the off position, press the knob in and turn it to the vertical position (sidelights 'on'). The switch assembly internal catch is now unlocked and the switch assembly can be withdrawn from the facia (see illustrations). Once the switch is released, turn the switch off.
5 Release the locking catch and disconnect the switch wiring connector.
6 Note that the switch assembly cannot be

4.4b . . . then withdraw the switch assembly from the facia

4.13a Carefully prise out the control switch assembly . . .

4.13b . . . and disconnect the wiring connector

4.21 Undo the retaining screw from the rear of the steering wheel to release the switches

4.22 Unclip the switch surround from the steering wheel, then disconnect the switch wiring connector

is an integral part of the heating/ventilation control unit, and cannot be removed. Should the switch become faulty, the complete control unit assembly must be renewed (see Chapter 3).

19 The air conditioning system control switch is an integral part of the heater control assembly. Removal and refitting procedures are contained in Chapter 3.

Steering wheel switches

20 Remove the driver's airbag as described in Section 23.

21 Turn the steering wheel so that the switch retaining screw opening is accessible, then undo the retaining screw from the rear of the steering wheel **(see illustration)**.

22 Unclip the switch surround from the steering wheel, then disconnect the wiring connector from the switch **(see illustration)**.

23 Refitting is the reverse of removal. On completion, refit the airbag as described in Section 23.

| 5 | Bulbs (exterior lights) – renewal | |

General

1 Whenever a bulb is renewed, note the following points:

a) *Make sure the switch is in the OFF position, for the bulb you are working on.*

b) *Remember that if the light has just been in use, the bulb may be extremely hot.*

c) *Always check the bulb contacts and holder, ensuring that there is clean metal-to-metal contact between the bulb and its live(s) and earth. Clean off any corrosion or dirt before fitting a new bulb.*

d) *Wherever bayonet-type bulbs are fitted, ensure that the live contact(s) bear firmly against the bulb contact.*

e) *Always ensure that the new bulb is of the correct rating, and that it is completely clean before fitting it; this applies particularly to headlight/foglight bulbs.*

Halogen type headlight unit

Note: *The outer bulb in the headlight unit is the dipped beam bulb and the inner bulb is the main beam bulb.*

Dipped beam

2 Remove the headlight unit as described in Section 7.

3 Rotate the plastic cover anti-clockwise and remove it from the rear of the headlight unit **(see illustration)**.

4 Push the bulb base sideways and withdraw the bulb from the headlight unit **(see illustration)**.

5 Hold the bulb by its base and disconnect the wiring connector **(see illustration)**. When handling the new bulb, use a tissue or clean cloth to avoid touching the glass with the fingers; moisture and grease from the skin can

dismantled; if any of its functions are faulty, the complete assembly must be renewed.

7 Reconnect the wiring connector and push the switch back into the facia.

Facia centre switches

8 Using a small screwdriver inserted at the top of the switch, carefully ease the relevant switch from its location.

9 To refit, push the switch back into position in the facia.

Heated rear window/ blower motor switches

10 The heated rear window and blower motor switches are an integral part of the heater control assembly. Removal and refitting procedures are contained in Chapter 3.

Handbrake warning light switch

11 Refer to Chapter 9.

5.3 Unscrew the plastic cover from the rear of the headlight

Stop-light switch

12 Refer to Chapter 9.

Electric window/mirror switches

Driver's door

13 Carefully prise out the control switch assembly and disconnect the wiring connector **(see illustrations)**.

14 Refitting is the reverse of removal.

Passenger's door

15 Remove the front/rear door inner trim panel as described in Chapter 11.

16 Carefully release the retaining clips at the rear of the trim panel and remove the switch from the panel.

17 Refitting is the reverse of removal.

Air conditioning system switch

18 The air conditioning system control switch

5.4 Push the dipped beam bulb base sideways and withdraw the bulb from the headlight unit

5.5 Hold the bulb by its base and disconnect the wiring connector

5.9 Unscrew the plastic cover from the rear of the headlight

5.10 Disconnect the main beam wiring connector from the rear of the bulb

5.11a Disengage the legs of the retaining spring clip from the lugs on the bulb . . .

5.11b . . . then lift the bulb out of the headlight unit

5.16a Withdraw the sidelight bulbholder from the rear of the headlight unit

cause blackening and rapid failure of this type of bulb. If the glass is accidentally touched, wipe it clean using methylated spirit.

6 Fit the new bulb to the headlight unit ensuring that the tab on the bulb base engages with the slot in the headlight unit. Reconnect the wiring connector.

7 Refit the plastic cover to the rear of the headlight unit, then refit the headlight unit as described in Section 7.

Main beam

8 Remove the headlight unit as described in Section 7.

9 Rotate the plastic cover anti-clockwise and remove it from the rear of the headlight unit **(see illustration)**.

10 Disconnect the wiring connector from the rear of the bulb **(see illustration)**.

11 Disengage the legs of the retaining spring clip from the lugs on the bulb by pushing

the clip down and swivelling it to the side. Lift the bulb out of the headlight unit **(see illustrations)**. When handling the new bulb, use a tissue or clean cloth to avoid touching the glass with the fingers; moisture and grease from the skin can cause blackening and rapid failure of this type of bulb. If the glass is accidentally touched, wipe it clean using methylated spirit.

12 Fit the new bulb to the headlight unit and secure with the spring clip. Reconnect the wiring connector.

13 Refit the plastic cover to the rear of the headlight unit, then refit the headlight unit as described in Section 7.

Sidelight

14 Remove the headlight unit as described in Section 7.

15 Remove the main beam plastic cover from the rear of the headlight unit **(see illustration 5.9)**.

16 Withdraw the sidelight bulbholder from the rear of the headlight unit. The bulb is of the capless (push-fit) type, and can be removed by simply pulling it out of the bulbholder **(see illustrations)**.

17 Refitting is the reverse of the removal procedure, ensuring that the bulbholder is fully engaged. On completion, refit the headlight unit as described in Section 7.

Front indicator

18 Remove the headlight unit as described in Section 7.

19 Twist the indicator bulbholder anti-clockwise, and remove it from the rear of the headlight unit **(see illustration)**.

20 The bulb is a bayonet fit in the holder, and can be removed by pressing it and twisting in an anti-clockwise direction **(see illustration)**.

21 Refitting is a reverse of the removal procedure. On completion, refit the headlight unit as described in Section 7.

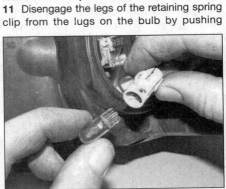

5.16b The bulb is a push-fit in the bulbholder

5.19 Twist the indicator bulbholder anti-clockwise, and remove it from the rear of the headlight unit

5.20 The bulb is a bayonet fit in the bulbholder

5.44 Twist the cover and free it from the foglight unit

Xenon type headlight unit

 Warning: Xenon headlights operate at very high voltage. Do not touch the associated wiring when the headlights are switched on.

Note: *The outer bulb in the headlight unit is the combined dipped/main beam xenon bulb and the inner bulb is the additional halogen main beam bulb.*

Dipped/main beam xenon bulb

22 Remove the headlight unit as described in Section 7.

23 Detach the rubber cover at the rear of the dipped/main beam bulb aperture and remove it from the headlight unit.

24 Compress the legs of the retaining spring clip and pivot the clip off the xenon starter unit and bulb assembly. Withdraw the starter unit and bulb assembly from the rear of the headlight unit.

25 Disconnect the wiring connector and remove the xenon starter unit and bulb assembly. Note that the starter unit and bulb are a single unit and cannot be separated.

26 Refitting is the reverse of the removal procedure. On completion, refit the headlight unit as described in Section 7.

Additional main beam halogen bulb

27 Renewal of the additional main beam bulb is as described previously in this Section for the halogen type headlight unit.

Sidelight

28 Renewal of the front sidelight bulb is as described previously in this Section for the halogen type headlight unit.

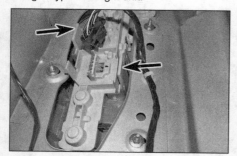

5.53 Depress the sides of the bulbholder in the area of the light unit retaining tabs (arrowed)

5.45 Release the spring clip and withdraw the foglight bulb from the light unit

Front indicator

29 Renewal of the front indicator bulb is as described previously in this Section for the halogen type headlight unit.

Adaptive forward lighting (AFL) headlight unit

 Warning: Xenon headlights operate at very high voltage. Do not touch the associated wiring when the headlights are switched on.

Cornering bulb and main beam bulb

30 Remove the headlight unit as described in Section 7.

31 Release the wire retaining clip and remove the cover from the rear of the headlight unit.

32 Compress the legs of the retaining spring clip and pivot the clip off the relevant bulb. Withdraw the bulb from the rear of the headlight unit.

33 Disconnect the wiring connector and remove the bulb.

34 Refitting is the reverse of the removal procedure. On completion, refit the headlight unit as described in Section 7.

Sidelight

35 Remove the headlight unit as described in Section 7.

36 Release the wire retaining clip and remove the cover from the rear of the headlight unit.

37 Withdraw the sidelight bulbholder from the rear of the headlight unit. The bulb is of the capless (push-fit) type, and can be removed by simply pulling it out of the bulbholder.

38 Refitting is the reverse of the removal procedure, ensuring that the bulbholder is fully

5.54 The relevant bulb can then be renewed

5.46 Disconnect the wiring connector and remove the bulb

engaged. On completion, refit the headlight unit as described in Section 7.

Front indicator

39 Renewal of the front indicator bulb is as described previously in this Section for the halogen type headlight unit.

Indicator side repeater

40 Push the light unit toward the front door, and release the front edge of the unit from the wing. If necessary, assist removal using a suitable plastic wedge, taking great care not damage the painted finish of the wing.

41 Withdraw the light unit from the wing, and pull the bulbholder out of the light unit. The bulb is of the capless (push-fit) type, and can be removed by simply pulling it out of the bulbholder.

42 Refitting is a reverse of the removal procedure.

Front foglight

43 Where applicable, remove the plastic panel at the base of the front bumper for access to the foglight unit.

44 Twist the cover and free it from the foglight unit **(see illustration)**.

45 Release the spring clip and withdraw the foglight bulb from the light unit **(see illustration)**.

46 Disconnect the wiring connector and remove the bulb **(see illustration)**.

47 When handling the new bulb, use a tissue or clean cloth to avoid touching the glass with the fingers; moisture and grease from the skin can cause blackening and rapid failure of this type of bulb. If the glass is accidentally touched, wipe it clean using methylated spirit.

48 Connect the wiring connector to the new bulb.

49 Insert the new bulb, making sure it is correctly located, and secure it in position with the spring clip.

50 Refit the cover to the rear of the unit then, where applicable, refit the plastic panel.

Rear light cluster

Saloon and Hatchback models

51 Press the catch and remove the access cover from the stowage compartment.

52 Reach in through the stowage compartment and disconnect the wiring connector from the bulbholder.

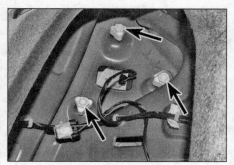

5.57 Slacken and remove the three light cluster plastic nuts (arrowed)

5.59a Withdraw the light cluster . . .

5.59b . . . and disconnect the wiring connector

53 Depress the sides of the bulbholder in the area of the light unit retaining tabs and withdraw the bulbholder from the light unit **(see illustration)**.

54 The relevant bulb can then be renewed; all bulbs have a bayonet fitting **(see illustration)**. Note that the stop/tail-light bulb has offset locating pins, to prevent it being installed incorrectly.

55 Refitting is the reverse of the removal sequence, ensuring that the bulbholder locates securely into position.

Estate models – rear wing light cluster

56 Press the catch and remove the access cover from the stowage compartment.

57 Reach in through the stowage compartment and use the wheel brace from the tool kit to slacken the three light cluster plastic nuts **(see illustration)**.

58 Hold the light cluster from the outside and unscrew the plastic nuts by hand the rest of the way.

59 Withdraw the light cluster and disconnect the wiring connector **(see illustrations)**.

60 Undo the three retaining screws and separate the bulbholder from the light cluster **(see illustrations)**.

61 The relevant bulb can then be renewed; both bulbs have a bayonet fitting.

62 Refitting is the reverse of the removal sequence.

Estate models – tailgate light cluster

63 Open the tailgate, undo the retaining screw located in the release handle aperture, and remove the release handle **(see illustration)**.

64 Using a small screwdriver, extract the centre pins and remove the plastic securing rivets **(see illustration)**.

65 Pull the lower trim panel away from the tailgate to release the remaining internal clips and remove the panel from the tailgate **(see illustration)**.

66 Release the bulbholder bayonet fitting, and remove the relevant bulbholder from the light cluster **(see illustration)**.

67 The relevant bulb can then be renewed; all bulbs have a bayonet fitting.

68 Refitting is the reverse of the removal sequence.

5.60a Undo the three retaining screws (arrowed) . . .

Number plate light

69 Using a small flat-bladed screwdriver, carefully prise the light unit out from its location **(see illustration)**.

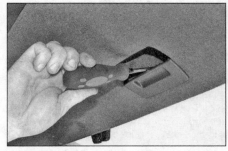

5.63 Undo the retaining screw located in the release handle aperture, and remove the release handle

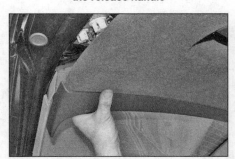

5.65 Pull the lower trim panel away from the tailgate to release the remaining internal clips

5.60b . . . and separate the bulbholder from the light cluster

70 Lift the tab and disconnect the wiring connector from the bulbholder **(see illustration)**.

71 Twist the bulbholder to remove it from the light unit, and remove the bulb **(see illustrations)**.

5.64 Extract the centre pins and remove the plastic securing rivets

5.66 Release the bayonet fitting, and remove the relevant bulbholder from the light cluster

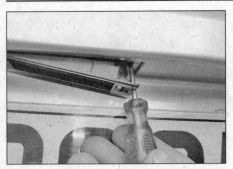

5.69 Carefully prise the number plate light unit out from its location

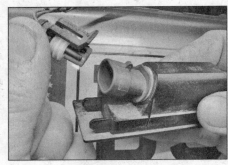

5.70 Lift the tab and disconnect the wiring connector

5.71a Twist the bulbholder to remove it from the light unit . . .

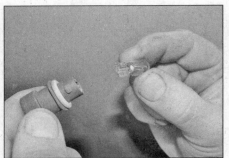

5.71b . . . and remove the push-fit bulb

6.2 Carefully prise the light unit lens from the overhead console

6.3 Pull the relevant bulb from its socket

72 Refitting is a reverse of the removal procedure.

High-level stop-light

73 The high-level stop-light bulbs are of the LED (light emitting diode) type and cannot be individually renewed. Remove the complete light unit as described in Section 7.

6 Bulbs (interior lights) – renewal

General

1 Refer to Section 5, paragraph 1.

Front courtesy light

2 Using a small screwdriver, carefully prise the light unit lens from the overhead console (see illustration).

3 Pull the relevant bulb from its socket (see illustration).
4 Install the new bulb, ensuring that it is securely held in position by the contacts, and clip the light unit lens back into position.

Rear courtesy light

5 Using a suitable screwdriver, carefully prise the right-hand side of the light unit out of position, and withdraw the light unit.
6 Release the locking plate and disconnect the wiring connector. Remove the relevant bulb from the light unit.
7 Install the new bulb, ensuring that it is securely held in position by the contacts. Refit the wiring connector and locking plate, then clip the light unit back into position.

Luggage compartment light

8 Using a suitable screwdriver, carefully prise the light unit out of position, and release

the bulb from the light unit contacts (see illustrations).
9 Install the new bulb, ensuring that it is securely held in position by the contacts, and clip the light unit back into position.

Cigarette lighter/ ashtray illumination

10 Carefully prise up and remove the trim panel around the cigarette lighter (see illustration).
11 Remove the ashtray from the centre console by opening the lid, depressing the internal tabs each side and lifting out (see illustration).
12 Disconnect the wiring connector at the rear of the cigarette lighter socket.
13 Using a small screwdriver, carefully prise the cigarette lighter body out of the illumination ring, then remove the illumination ring from the console.
14 Pull the bulbholder out of the illumination ring and renew the bulb.

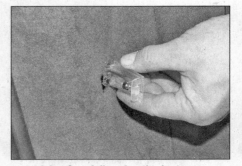

6.8a Carefully prise the luggage compartment light unit out of position . . .

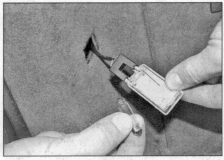

6.8b . . . and release the bulb from the light unit contacts

6.10 Prise up and remove the trim panel around the cigarette lighter

6.11 Remove the ashtray by opening the lid, depressing the internal tabs each side and lifting out

6.16a Carefully prise the glovebox light unit out of position . . .

6.16b . . . then release the bulb from its contacts

15 Refitting is a reverse of the removal procedure.

Glovebox light

16 Open the glovebox. Using a small flat-bladed screwdriver, carefully prise the light unit out of position, then release the bulb from its contacts **(see illustrations)**. Install the new bulb, ensuring it is securely held in position by the contacts, and clip the light unit back into position.

Switch illumination

17 All the switches are fitted with illumination bulbs; some are also fitted with a bulb to show when the circuit concerned is operating. These bulbs are an integral part of the switch assembly, and cannot be obtained separately.

7 Exterior light units – removal and refitting

Note: *Disconnect the battery negative terminal (refer to 'Disconnecting the battery' in the Reference Chapter) before removing any light unit, and reconnect the terminal after refitting.*

Headlight

⚠ *Warning: Xenon dipped beam headlights operate at very high voltage. Do not touch the associated wiring when the headlights are switched on.*

1 Remove the front bumper as described in Chapter 11.
2 Undo the three retaining bolts and withdraw

the headlight unit from the vehicle. Disconnect the wiring connectors from rear of the headlight unit as it is withdrawn **(see illustrations)**.
3 The headlight beam adjustment motor can be removed and refitted as follows. Remove the headlight unit rear cover and, on xenon and AFL headlight units, release the two retaining lugs and unlock the switch plate. Rotate the adjustment motor anti-clockwise to free the motor from the rear of the headlight unit. Unclip the balljoint from the rear of the light reflector and disconnect the wiring connector **(see illustrations)**.
4 On refitting, align the motor balljoint with the light unit socket, and clip it into position. Engage the motor assembly with the light, and twist it clockwise to secure it in position.
5 Refitting is a reverse of the removal procedure. On completion, check the headlight beam alignment using the information given in Section 8.

7.2a Undo the two upper retaining bolts (arrowed) . . .

Front indicator light

6 The front direction indicator lights are integral with the headlight units. Removal and refitting is as described above.

Indicator side repeater light

7 Push the light unit toward the front door, and release the front edge of the unit from the wing. If necessary, assist removal using a suitable plastic wedge, taking great care not damage the painted finish of the wing.
8 Withdraw the light unit from the wing, and disconnect its wiring connector. Tie a piece of string to the wiring, to prevent it falling back into the wing.
9 On refitting, connect the wiring connector, and clip the light unit back into position.

Front foglight

10 Remove the front bumper as described in Chapter 11.

7.2b . . . and the lower retaining bolt (arrowed) . . .

7.2c . . . then withdraw the headlight unit and disconnect the wiring connectors

7.3a Unclip the adjustment motor balljoint from the rear of the light reflector . . .

7.3b . . . then disconnect the wiring connector

7.11 Front foglight retaining bolts (arrowed)

11 Undo the three foglight retaining bolts and remove the light unit from the bumper (see illustration).
12 Refit the light unit to the bumper, and securely tighten its retaining bolts.
13 Refit the front bumper (see Chapter 11).

Rear light cluster

Saloon and Hatchback models

14 Press the catch and remove the access cover from the stowage compartment.
15 Reach in through the stowage compartment and disconnect the wiring connector from the bulbholder.
16 Undo the three retaining nuts and remove the light cluster from the rear wing (see illustrations).
17 Refitting is a reversal of removal.

Estate models – rear wing light cluster

18 Press the catch and remove the access cover from the stowage compartment.

7.26 Extract the two blanking caps from the tailgate . . .

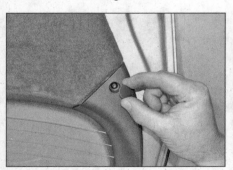

7.33a Remove the trim caps over the upper side trim panel retaining screws . . .

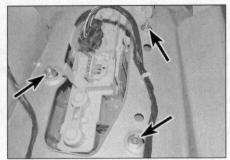

7.16a Undo the three retaining nuts (arrowed) . . .

19 Reach in through the stowage compartment and use the wheel brace from the tool kit to slacken the three light cluster plastic nuts (see illustration 5.57).
20 Hold the light cluster from the outside and unscrew the plastic nuts by hand the rest of the way.
21 Withdraw the light cluster and disconnect the wiring connector (see illustrations 5.59a and 5.59b)
22 Refitting is a reversal of removal.

Estate models – tailgate light cluster

23 Open the tailgate, undo the retaining screw located in the release handle aperture, and remove the release handle (see illustration 5.63).
24 Using a small screwdriver, extract the centre pins and remove the plastic securing rivets (see illustration 5.64).
25 Pull the lower trim panel away from the tailgate to release the remaining internal clips

7.27 . . . and undo the light cluster retaining nuts (arrowed)

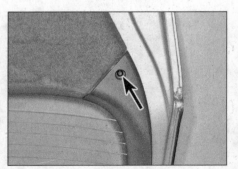

7.33b . . . then undo the screw (arrowed) each side

7.16b . . . and remove the light cluster from the rear wing

and remove the panel from the tailgate (see illustration 5.65).
26 Extract the blanking caps from the tailgate for access to the light cluster retaining nuts (see illustration).
27 Undo the three retaining nuts and remove the light unit from the tailgate (see illustration).
28 Refitting is a reversal of removal.

Number plate light

29 Using a small flat-bladed screwdriver, carefully prise the light unit out from its location (see illustration 5.69).
30 Lift the tab and disconnect the wiring connector from the bulbholder (see illustration 5.70).
31 Refitting is a reversal of removal.

High-level stop-light

Saloon models

32 To remove the high-level stop-light, it is necessary to drill holes in the inside of the boot lid panelling, for access to the stop-light retaining bolts. At the time of writing information on the position of these holes was not available. It is recommended that any problems with the high-level stop-light should be referred to a Vauxhall/Opel dealer.

Hatchback models

33 Open the tailgate and remove the trim caps over the upper side trim panel retaining screws. Undo the screw each side (see illustrations).
34 Unscrew the parcel shelf lifting pins on each side (see illustration).
35 Carefully prise free the side trim panel on

7.34 Unscrew the parcel shelf lifting pins on each side

7.35 Prise free the side trim panel on each side to release the three retaining clips

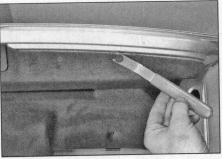

7.36 Extract the four stud retaining clips at the lower edge of the lower trim panel

7.38 Pull the panel away from the tailgate to release the remaining internal clips

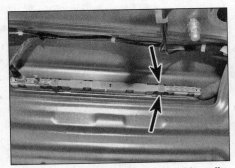

7.39a Compress the light unit locking clip (arrowed) with pliers, push in the lugs at the end . . .

7.39b . . . and release one side of the unit at a time from the tailgate

7.40 Withdraw the light unit from the tailgate and disconnect the wiring connector

each side to release the three retaining clips **(see illustration)**.

36 Using a forked tool, or removal tool, extract the four stud retaining clips at the lower edge of the lower trim panel **(see illustration)**.

37 Undo the retaining screws in the centre of the panel and pull out the centre pins of the four plastic rivets.

38 Pull the panel away from the tailgate to release the remaining internal clips and remove the panel from the tailgate **(see illustration)**.

39 Working on one side of the light unit at a time, compress the locking clip with pliers, push in the lugs at the end and release one side of the unit from the tailgate **(see illustrations)**. Repeat this procedure on the other side.

40 Once the light unit is free, withdraw it from the tailgate and disconnect the wiring connector **(see illustration)**.

41 Reconnect the wiring connector then push the light unit into the tailgate until it locks in position.

Estate models

42 Open the tailgate, undo the retaining screw located in the release handle aperture, and remove the release handle **(see illustration 5.63)**.

43 Using a small screwdriver, extract the centre pins and remove the plastic securing rivets **(see illustration 5.64)**.

44 Pull the lower trim panel away from the tailgate to release the remaining internal clips and remove the panel from the tailgate **(see illustration 5.65)**.

45 Pull the upper trim panel away from the

tailgate to release the internal retaining clips **(see illustration)**.

46 Disconnect the high-level stop-light wiring connector.

47 Release the three retaining catches and remove the high-level stop-light from the tailgate upper trim panel **(see illustration)**.

48 Refitting is a reversal of removal.

8 Headlight beam alignment – general information

1 Accurate adjustment of the headlight beam is only possible using optical beam-setting equipment, and this work should therefore be carried out by a Vauxhall/Opel dealer or suitably-equipped workshop.

2 For reference, the headlights can be adjusted using the adjuster assemblies fitted to the top of each light unit. The inner adjuster, alters the vertical position of the beam. The outer adjuster alters the horizontal aim of the beam.

3 Most models have an electrically-operated headlight beam adjustment system, controlled via a switch in the facia. The recommended settings are as follows.

0 Front seat(s) occupied
1 All seats occupied
2 All seats occupied, and load in luggage compartment
3 Driver's seat occupied and load in the luggage compartment

Note: *When adjusting the headlight aim, ensure that the switch is set to position 0.*

7.45 Pull the upper trim panel away from the tailgate to release the internal retaining clips

7.47 Release the retaining catches (arrowed) and remove the high-level stop-light from the trim panel

9.3a Undo the two lower retaining screws (arrowed) . . .

9.3b . . . then pull the instrument panel away from the facia at the bottom

9.4 Disengage the top of the panel from the facia and disconnect the wiring connector

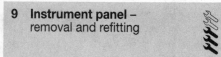

9 Instrument panel –
removal and refitting

Note: *The instrument panel is a complete sealed assembly, and no dismantling of the instrument panel is possible.*

Removal

1 Disconnect the battery negative terminal (refer to *Disconnecting the battery* in the Reference Chapter).
2 Remove the steering column shrouds as described in Chapter 11, Section 29.
3 Undo the two lower retaining screws, then pull the panel away from the facia at the bottom **(see illustrations)**.
4 Disengage the top of the panel from the facia, disconnect the wiring connector and remove the panel from the car **(see illustration)**.

Refitting

5 Refitting is a reversal of removal.

10 Information display unit –
removal and refitting

Removal

1 Disconnect the battery negative terminal (refer to *Disconnecting the battery* in the Reference Chapter).
2 Remove the centre vent housing as described in Chapter 3.
3 Undo the four screws and remove the information display unit from the centre vent housing **(see illustration)**.

Refitting

4 Refitting is a reversal of removal.

11 Cigarette lighter –
removal and refitting

Proceed as described in Section 6, paragraphs 10 to 15.

12 Horn –
removal and refitting

Removal

1 Firmly apply the handbrake, then jack up the front of the car and support it securely on axle stands (see *Jacking and vehicle support*).
2 Working under the bumper on the left-hand side, undo the retaining nut/bolt and remove the horn, disconnecting its wiring connector as they become accessible **(see illustration)**.

Refitting

3 Refitting is the reverse of removal.

13 Wiper arm –
removal and refitting

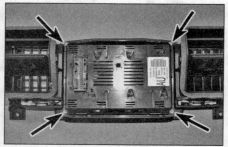

10.3 Undo the screws (arrowed) and remove the information display unit from the centre vent housing

12.2 Horn retaining nut and wiring connector

Removal

1 Operate the wiper motor, then switch it off so that the wiper arm returns to the at-rest (parked) position.

> **HAYNES HINT** *Stick a piece of masking tape along the edge of the wiper blade, to use as an alignment aid on refitting.*

2 Unclip the wiper arm spindle nut cover (windscreen wiper arm), or pivot the cover up (tailgate wiper arm), then slacken and remove the spindle nut and washer **(see illustrations)**.
3 Using a suitable puller, free the wiper arm from the spindle and remove the arm **(see**

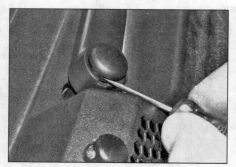

13.2a Unclip the windscreen wiper arm spindle nut cover . . .

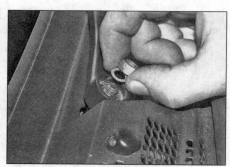

13.2b . . . then slacken and remove the spindle nut and washer

illustration). **Note:** *If both windscreen wiper arms are to be removed at the same time, mark them for identification. The arms are not interchangeable; the passenger-side wiper arm is longer than the driver's-side arm, and its shaft is also cranked slightly.*

Refitting

4 Ensure that the wiper arm and spindle splines are clean and dry, then refit the arm to the spindle, aligning the wiper blade with the tape fitted on removal. Refit the spindle nut, tightening it securely, and clip the nut cover back in position.

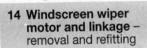

14 Windscreen wiper motor and linkage – removal and refitting

Removal

1 Disconnect the battery negative terminal (refer to *Disconnecting the battery* in the Reference Chapter).
2 Remove the wiper arms as described in the Section 13.
3 Remove the water deflector as described in Chapter 11, Section 23.
4 Pull out the locking bar and disconnect the wiring connector from the wiper motor (**see illustrations**).
5 Undo the three retaining bolts, and remove the wiper motor and linkage assembly out from the vehicle (**see illustrations**).
6 If necessary, mark the relative positions of the motor shaft and linkage arm, then unscrew the retaining nut from the motor spindle. Free the wiper linkage from the spindle, then remove the three motor retaining bolts, and separate the motor and linkage (**see illustration**).

Refitting

7 Where necessary, assemble the motor and linkage, and securely tighten the motor retaining bolts. Locate the linkage arm on the motor spindle, aligning the marks made prior to removal, and securely tighten its retaining nut.
8 Manoeuvre the motor assembly back into position in the vehicle. Refit the retaining bolts, and tighten them securely.

14.5a Undo the three retaining bolts (arrowed) . . .

13.3 Using a suitable puller, free the wiper arm from the spindle

9 Reconnect the wiper motor wiring connector.
10 Refit the water deflector as described in Chapter 11.
11 Install both the wiper arms as described in Section 13, and reconnect the battery negative terminal.

15 Tailgate wiper motor – removal and refitting

Removal

Hatchback models

1 Open the tailgate and remove the trim caps over the upper side trim panel retaining screws. Undo the screw each side (**see illustrations 7.33a and 7.33b**).

14.4a Pull out the locking bar . . .

14.5b . . . and remove the wiper motor and linkage assembly

2 Unscrew the parcel shelf lifting pins on each side (**see illustration 7.34**).
3 Carefully prise free the side trim panel on each side to release the three retaining clips (**see illustration 7.35**).
4 Using a forked tool, or removal tool, extract the four stud retaining clips at the lower edge of the lower trim panel (**see illustration 7.36**).
5 Undo the retaining screws in the centre of the panel and pull out the centre pins of the four plastic rivets.
6 Pull the panel away from the tailgate to release the remaining internal clips and remove the panel from the tailgate (**see illustration 7.38**).

Estate models

7 Open the tailgate, undo the retaining screw located in the release handle aperture, and remove the release handle (**see illustration 5.63**).
8 Using a small screwdriver, extract the centre pins and remove the plastic securing rivets (**see illustration 5.64**).
9 Pull the lower trim panel away from the tailgate to release the remaining internal clips and remove the panel from the tailgate (**see illustration 5.65**).

All models

10 Remove the wiper arm as described in Section 13.
11 Disconnect the wiring connector, then slacken and remove the wiper motor mounting bolts and remove the wiper motor (**see illustrations**).

14.4b . . . and disconnect the wiring connector from the wiper motor

14.6 Wiper motor retaining bolts (arrowed)

15.11a Disconnect the wiring connector . . .

Refitting

12 Refitting is the reverse of removal, ensuring the wiper motor retaining bolts are securely tightened.

16 Windscreen/tailgate washer system components – removal and refitting

Washer system reservoir

1 Remove the front bumper as described in Chapter 11.
2 If necessary, partially detach the wheel arch liner.
3 From within the engine compartment, unclip and remove the filler neck for the windscreen washer reservoir.
4 Disconnect the wiring connectors at the

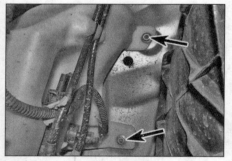

16.5a Washer reservoir upper retaining nuts (arrowed) . . .

16.11 Depress the retaining clip, then carefully prise the washer nozzle from the water deflector panel

15.11b . . . then slacken and remove the tailgate wiper motor mounting bolts (arrowed)

washer pump(s) and washer fluid level sensor, as applicable.
5 Undo the two upper nuts, and one lower nut, and remove the reservoir from under the car **(see illustrations)**.
6 Refitting is the reverse of removal, ensuring that the washer hose(s) are securely connected.

Washer pump

7 Remove the washer reservoir as described above.
8 Tip out the contents of the reservoir, then carefully ease the pump out from the reservoir and recover its sealing grommet.
9 Refitting is the reverse of removal, using a new sealing grommet if the original one shows signs of damage or deterioration.

Windscreen washer jets

10 Remove the water deflector as described in Chapter 11, Section 23.

16.5b . . . and lower retaining nut (arrowed)

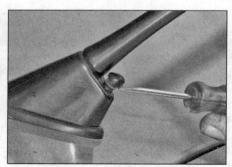

16.14 Carefully prise the washer jet out of the radio aerial base

11 Depress the retaining clip, then carefully prise the nozzle from the water deflector panel **(see illustration)**.
12 Disconnect the nozzle from its fluid hose, and remove it from the vehicle.
13 On refitting, securely connect the nozzle to the hose, and clip it into position in the water deflector panel. Refit the water deflector panel, then check the operation of the jet. If necessary, adjust the nozzle using a pin, aiming the spray to a point slightly above the centre of the swept area.

Tailgate washer jet

14 Carefully prise the washer jet out of the radio aerial base and disconnect it from its supply pipe **(see illustration)**. Whilst the jet is removed, tie a piece of string to the supply pipe, to ensure that it does not fall back into the tailgate.
15 When refitting, ensure that the jet is clipped securely in position. Check the operation of the jet. If necessary, adjust the nozzle using a pin, aiming the spray to a point slightly above the centre of the swept area.

17 Radio/CD player – removal and refitting

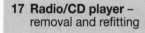

Note: *The following removal and refitting procedure is for the range of radio/CD units which Vauxhall/Opel fit as standard equipment. Removal and refitting procedures of non-standard units may differ slightly.*

Removal

1 All the radio/CD players fitted by Vauxhall have DIN standard fixings. Two special tools, obtainable from most car accessory shops, are required for removal. Alternatively, suitable tools can be fabricated from 3 mm diameter wire, such as welding rod.
2 Disconnect the battery negative terminal (refer to *Disconnecting the battery* in the Reference Chapter).
3 Insert the tools into the holes on the front of the unit, and push them until they snap into place. The radio/CD player can then be slid out of the facia **(see illustration)**.

17.3 Using welding rod to compress the clips (arrowed) on the radio/CD player

4 Disconnect the wiring and aerial connections at the rear of the unit, and remove the unit from the car.

Refitting

5 To refit the radio/CD player, reconnect the wiring and simply push the unit into the facia until the retaining lugs snap into place. On completion, reconnect the battery and enter the radio security code, where applicable.

---

18 Speakers – removal and refitting

Front door small speaker

1 Remove the front door inner trim panel as described in Chapter 11, Section 12.
2 Carefully prise off the door mirror interior trim panel to release the two retaining clips **(see illustration)**.
3 Disconnect the wiring connector from the mirror **(see illustration)**.
4 Release the speaker wiring harness retaining clip from the interior trim panel, and disconnect the wiring connector **(see illustrations)**. Remove the trim panel.
5 Remove the rubber pad from the panel base, then undo the three screws and remove the speaker from the panel **(see illustration)**.
6 Refitting is the reverse of removal.

Rear door small speaker

7 Remove the rear door inner trim panel as described in Chapter 11, Section 12.

8 Unclip the control switch panel from the door trim panel.
9 Unclip the speaker from the switch panel.
10 Refitting is the reverse of removal.

Door large speaker

11 Remove the door inner trim panel as described in Chapter 11, Section 12.
12 Undo the retaining screws, then free the speaker from the door **(see illustration)**. Disconnect the wiring connectors and remove the speaker.
13 Refitting is the reverse of removal.

---

19 Radio aerial – general information

1 Where required, the aerial mast can be unscrewed from the base unit.
2 Removal of the base unit entails removal of the headlining, which is a complicated operation, considered to be outside the scope of this manual. Therefore, any problems relating to the aerial base unit or wiring should be entrusted to a Vauxhall/Opel dealer.

---

20 Anti-theft alarm system – general information

Note: *This information is applicable only to the anti-theft alarm system fitted by Vauxhall/Opel as standard equipment.*
1 Most models in the range are fitted with an

anti-theft alarm system as standard equipment. The alarm is automatically armed and disarmed when the deadlocks are operated using the driver's door lock or remote control key. The alarm has switches on all the doors (including the tailgate), the bonnet, the radio/CD player and the ignition and starter circuits. If the tailgate, bonnet or any of the doors are opened whilst the alarm is set, the alarm horn will sound and the hazard warning lights will flash. The alarm also has an immobiliser function which makes the ignition and starter circuits inoperable whilst the alarm is triggered.
2 The alarm system performs a self-test every time it is switched on; this test takes approximately 10 seconds. During the self-test, the LED (light emitting diode) in the hazard warning light switch will come on. If the LED flashes, then either the tailgate, bonnet or one of the doors is open, or there is a fault in the circuit. After the initial 10 second period, the LED will flash to indicate that the alarm is switched on. On unlocking the driver's door lock, the LED will illuminate for approximately 1 second, then go out, indicating that the alarm has been switched off.
3 With the alarm set, if the tailgate is unlocked, the tailgate switch sensing will automatically be switched off, but the door and bonnet switches will still be active. Once the tailgate is shut and locked again, the tailgate switch sensing will be switched back on after approximately 10 seconds.
4 Should the alarm system develop a fault, the vehicle should be taken to a Vauxhall/Opel dealer for examination.

18.2 Carefully prise off the door mirror interior trim panel

18.3 Disconnect the wiring connector from the mirror

18.4a Release the wiring harness retaining clip from the interior trim panel . . .

18.4b . . . and disconnect the tweeter wiring connector

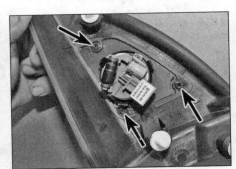

18.5 Undo the three screws (arrowed) and remove the speaker from the panel

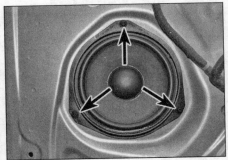

18.12 Door loudspeaker retaining screws (arrowed)

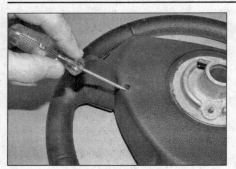

23.2a Insert screwdrivers into the holes at the rear of the steering wheel (shown with steering wheel removed) . . .

21 Heated seat components – general information

On models with heated seats, a heater mat is fitted to both the seat back and seat cushion. Renewal of either heater mat involves peeling back the upholstery, removing the old mat, sticking the new mat in position and then refitting the upholstery. Note that upholstery removal and refitting requires considerable skill and experience if it is to be carried out successfully, and is therefore best entrusted to your Vauxhall/Opel dealer. In practice, it will be very difficult for the home mechanic to carry out the job without ruining the upholstery.

22 Airbag system – general information and precautions

General information

A driver's airbag is fitted as standard equipment on all models. The airbag is fitted in the steering wheel centre pad. Additionally, a passenger's airbag located in the facia, side airbags located in the front seats, and curtain airbags located in the headlining are optionally available.

The system is armed only when the ignition is switched on, however, a reserve power source maintains a power supply to the system

23.2b . . . to depress the airbag internal spring retainers (arrowed – shown with airbag removed)

in the event of a break in the main electrical supply. The steering wheel and facia airbags are activated by a 'g' sensor (deceleration sensor), and controlled by an electronic control unit located under the centre console. The side airbags and curtain airbags are activated by severe side impact and operate independently of the main system. A separate electrical supply, control unit and sensor is provided for the side/curtain airbags on each side of the car.

The airbags are inflated by a gas generator, which forces the bag out from its location in the steering wheel, facia, seat back frame, or headlining.

Precautions

⚠️ *Warning: The following precautions must be observed when working on vehicles equipped with an airbag system, to prevent the possibility of personal injury.*

General precautions

The following precautions **must** be observed when carrying out work on a vehicle equipped with an airbag:

a) *Do not disconnect the battery with the engine running.*
b) *Before carrying out any work in the vicinity of the airbag, removal of any of the airbag components, or any welding work on the vehicle, de-activate the system as described in the following sub-Section.*
c) *Do not attempt to test any of the airbag system circuits using test meters or any other test equipment.*
d) *If the airbag warning light comes on, or any fault in the system is suspected, consult a Vauxhall/Opel dealer without delay.* **Do not** *attempt to carry out fault diagnosis, or any dismantling of the components.*

Precautions when handling an airbag

a) *Transport the airbag by itself, bag upward.*
b) *Do not put your arms around the airbag.*
c) *Carry the airbag close to the body, bag outward.*
d) *Do not drop the airbag or expose it to impacts.*
e) *Do not attempt to dismantle the airbag unit.*
f) *Do not connect any form of electrical equipment to any part of the airbag circuit.*

Precautions when storing an airbag

a) *Store the unit in a cupboard with the airbag upward.*
b) *Do not expose the airbag to temperatures above 80°C.*
c) *Do not expose the airbag to flames.*
d) *Do not attempt to dispose of the airbag – consult a Vauxhall/Opel dealer.*
e) *Never refit an airbag which is known to be faulty or damaged.*

De-activation of airbag system

The system must be de-activated

before carrying out any work on the airbag components or surrounding area:

a) *Switch on the ignition and check the operation of the airbag warning light on the instrument panel. The light should illuminate when the ignition is switched on, then extinguish.*
b) *Switch off the ignition.*
c) *Remove the ignition key.*
d) *Switch off all electrical equipment.*
e) *Disconnect the battery negative terminal (refer to 'Disconnecting the battery' in the Reference Chapter).*
f) *Insulate the battery negative terminal and the end of the battery negative lead to prevent any possibility of contact.*
g) *Wait for at least two minutes before carrying out any further work. Wait at least ten minutes if the airbag warning light did not operate correctly.*

Activation of airbag system

To activate the system on completion of any work, proceed as follows:

a) *Ensure that there are no occupants in the vehicle, and that there are no loose objects around the vicinity of the steering wheel. Close the vehicle doors and windows.*
b) *Ensure that the ignition is switched off then reconnect the battery negative terminal.*
c) *Open the driver's door and switch on the ignition, without reaching in front of the steering wheel. Check that the airbag warning light illuminates briefly then extinguishes.*
d) *Switch off the ignition.*
e) *If the airbag warning light does not operate as described in paragraph c), consult a Vauxhall/Opel dealer before driving the vehicle.*

23 Airbag system components – removal and refitting

⚠️ *Warning: Refer to the precautions given in Section 22 before attempting to carry out work on any of the airbag components.*

1 De-activate the airbag system as described in the previous Section, then proceed as described under the relevant heading.

Driver's airbag

2 Insert a screwdriver into the holes on both sides of the rear of the steering wheel to depress the internal spring retainers, and at the same time pull the airbag unit away from the steering wheel to release it **(see illustrations)**.
3 Release the locking clips, then disconnect the wiring connectors at the rear of the airbag unit **(see illustration)**. Remove the airbag unit. Note that the airbag must not be knocked or dropped, and should be stored with its padded surface uppermost.

23.3 Release the locking clips, then disconnect the wiring connectors

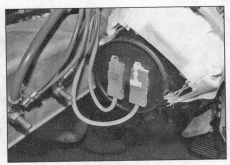

23.6 Passenger's airbag wiring connectors . . .

23.7 . . . and retaining bolts (arrowed)

23.18a Slacken the upper clamp nut (arrowed) . . .

23.18b . . . and the lower clamp bolt (arrowed)

23.19 Disconnect the wiring connector and remove the module

4 Refitting is a reversal of the removal procedure.

Passenger's airbag

5 Remove the glovebox as described in Chapter 11, Section 29.
6 Disconnect the airbag wiring connector(s) from the side of the unit **(see illustration)**.
7 Undo the two bolts securing the airbag to the facia crossmember and withdraw the airbag out through the glovebox aperture **(see illustration)**. Note that the airbag must not be knocked or dropped, and should be stored the correct way up (as mounted in the vehicle).
8 Refitting is a reversal of the removal procedure, tightening the retaining bolts securely.

Side airbags

9 The side airbags are located internally within the front seat back and no attempt should be made to remove them. Any suspected

problems with the side airbag system should be referred to a Vauxhall/Opel dealer.

Curtain airbags

10 The curtain airbags are located behind the headlining above the doors on each side and no attempt should be made to remove them. Any suspected problems with the curtain airbag system should be referred to a Vauxhall/Opel dealer.

Airbag control unit

11 The airbag control unit is located beneath the centre console and no attempt should be made to remove it. Any suspected problems with the control unit should be referred to a Vauxhall/Opel dealer.

Airbag rotary connector

12 The airbag rotary connector is an integral part of the steering column electronics

module. Removal and refitting procedures for the module are as follows:
13 Disconnect the battery negative terminal (refer to *Disconnecting the battery* in the Reference Chapter) and wait for 2 minutes.
14 Set the roadwheels in the straight-ahead position and ensure they remain in that position during the removal and refitting procedures.
15 Remove the steering wheel as described in Chapter 10.
16 Remove the steering column shrouds as described in Chapter 11, Section 29.
17 Mark the position of the electronics module in relation to the steering column.
18 Slacken the upper clamp nut, and the lower clamp bolt, and withdraw the module from the steering column **(see illustrations)**.
19 Disconnect the wiring connector and remove the module **(see illustration)**.
20 Refitting is a reversal of the removal procedure.

VAUXHALL VECTRA wiring diagrams

Diagram 1

Key to symbols

Bulb	—⊗—	Item no.	**2**
Flashing bulb	—⊗̸—	Single speed pump/motor	(M)
Switch contact	—•⁄ •—	Gauge/meter	(↗)
Fuse/fusible link and current rating	**F5** ⋈ **30A**	Earth point and location	⏚ **E4**
Wire splice, soldered joint or unspecified connection	⊥•	Diode	—▷|—
Connecting wires	—•—	Light emitting diode (LED)	↗↗ ▷|—
Variable resistor	▭	Heating element	⌐⌐⌐⌐
Resistor	—▭—	Solenoid actuator	▨

Wire colour (blue with white tracer) ▬▬▬ **Bu/Wh** ▬▬▬

Dashed outline denotes part of a larger item, containing in this case an electronic or solid state device. e.g. connector no. XC30, pin 2.

XC30/2

Engine fusebox 2

Fuse	Rating	Circuit protected
F1	20A	Engine management, automatic transmission
F2	25A	Starter
F3	15A	Horn
F4	10A	Air conditioning, climate control
F5	15A	Wash/wipe system
F6	-	-
F7	15A	Central control unit, ESP
F8	30A	Headlights, heated washer
F9	7.5A	Power steering
F10	10A	Adaptive lighting
F11	30A	Windscreen wiper
F12	30A	Windscreen wiper
F13	7.5A	Central control unit, ESP
F14	30A	Headlight wash system
F15	10A	Engine control unit
F16	7.5A	ABS
F17	-	-
F18	-	-
F19	10A	Adaptive lighting,
F19	5A	Headlight levelling,
F19	15A	Xenon headlights
F20	5A	Headlight levelling
F21	-	-
F22	30A	Wash/wipe
F23	20A	Auxiliary heating
F24	30A	Battery voltage, terminal 30
F25	30A	Battery voltage, terminal 30
F26	-	-
F27	-	-
F28	60A	Tailgate module control unit
F29	40A	ABS
F30	60A	Tailgate module control unit
F31	60A	Vehicle interior module control unit
F32	40A	ABS
F33	60A	Vehicle interior module control unit
F34	60A	Tailgate module control unit
F35	30A	Engine cooling fan
F36	20A	Engine cooling fan
F37	-	Adaptive lighting (slot for changing lighting for abroad)
F38	-	-

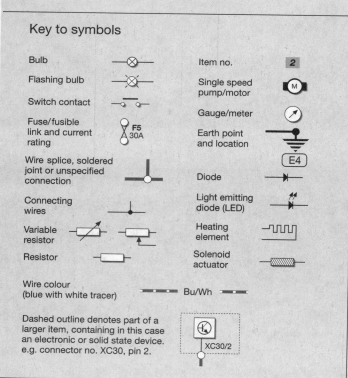

Passenger fusebox 12

Fuse	Rating	Circuit protected
F1	20A	Infotainment system, DVD
F2	7.5A	Heater blower, heating, air conditioning
F3	20A	Sunroof
F4	-	-
F5	7.5A	Door control units
F6	7.5A	Brake light
F7	30A	Body control unit
F8	30A	LH front door control unit
F9	7.5A	Central control unit
F10	7.5A	Steering column control unit
F11	7.5A	Diagnostic connector
F12	15A	Battery control unit
F13	-	-
F14	-	-
F15	30A	RH front door control unit
F16	-	-
F17	15A	Instrument, info display
F18	7.5A	Ignition terminal 15, air conditioning
F19	-	-
F20	7.5A	Yaw sensor (ESP)
F21	7.5A	Telematics
F22	30A	Cigar lighter, DVD
F23	40A	Heater blower, air conditioning, climate control
F24	-	-
F25	7.5A	Heating, air conditioning
F26	7.5A	Instruments, info display
F27	-	-

Rear fusebox 11

Fuse	Rating	Circuit protected
F1	-	-
F2	-	-
F3	40A	Electric seat adjustment
F4	40A	Heated rear window
F5	40A	Electric seat adjustment
F6	30A	RH rear electric window
F7	30A	LH rear electric window
F8	15A	RH rear seat heater
F9	15A	Horn, alarm
F10	20A	Fuel pump
F11	25A	Battery voltage
F12	15A	LH rear seat heater
F13	20A	Towing equipment
F14	15A	Rear wiper
F15	15A	LH front seat heater
F16	15A	RH front seat heater
F17	15A	Accessory socket
F18	30A	Tailgate lock
F19	10A	Terminal 30
F20	7.5A	Central locking
F21	5A	Alarm
F22	30A	Electrically operated tailgate
F23	7.5A	Alarm
F24	25A	Battery voltage
F25	10A	Electronic chassis
F26	25A	Terminal 15 (ignition lock)
F27	5A	Seat occupancy recognition, tyre pressure monitor, rain sensor, air conditioning
F28	7.5A	Parking distance sensor
F29	-	-

Earth locations

E1	Engine compartment strut tower RH side
E2	RH 'A' pillar
E3	Instrument panel cross member front passenger side
E4	LH engine compartment
E5	Instrument panel cross member front passenger side
E6	LH front frame side member
E7	Rear panel RH side
E8	Transmission tunnel
E9	LH 'A' pillar
E10	Engine starter/alternator
E11	RH 'C' pillar
E12	Rear panel LH side
E13	On engine
E14	Steering column bracket
E15	On tailgate
E16	Engine compartment strut tower LH side
E17	Rear panel RH side

H33648

Wire colours

Bg	Beige	**LBu**	Light blue
Bk	Black	**LGn**	Light green
Bn	Brown	**Og**	Orange
DBu	Dark blue	**Bn**	Brown
DGn	Dark green	**Pu**	Purple
Ye	Yellow	**Pk**	Pink
Gn	Green	**Rd**	Red
Gy	Grey	**Wh**	White
Vt	Violet	**Bu**	Blue

Key to items

1 Battery
2 Engine fusebox
  a = under bonnet control unit
  k1 = starter relay
  k3 = terminal 15 relay
  k4 = horn relay
3 Starter motor
4 Alternator
5 LH horn
6 RH horn
7 Horn switch
8 Steering column control unit
9 Engine cooling fan & control unit

Diagram 2

H33649/a

Starting & charging

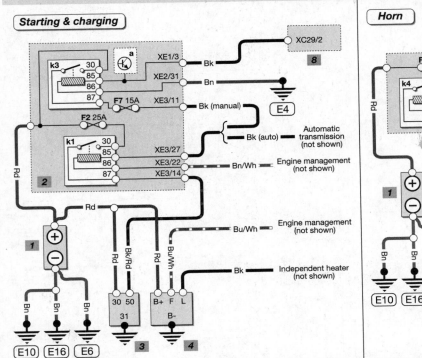

Horn

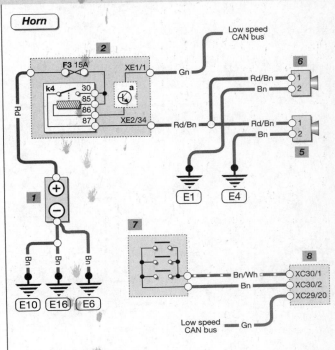

Single engine cooling fan

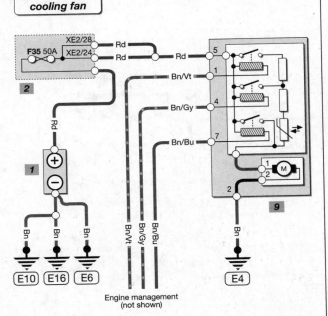

Dual engine cooling fan

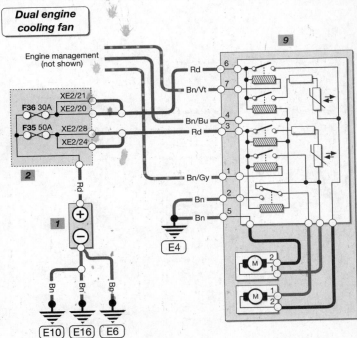

Wire colours

Bg	Beige	**LBu**	Light blue
Bk	Black	**LGn**	Light green
Bn	Brown	**Og**	Orange
DBu	Dark blue	**Bn**	Brown
DGn	Dark green	**Pu**	Purple
Ye	Yellow	**Pk**	Pink
Gn	Green	**Rd**	Red
Gy	Grey	**Wh**	White
Vt	Violet	**Bu**	Blue

Key to items

1 Battery
2 Engine fusebox
  a = under bonnet control unit
  k3 = terminal 15 relay
8 Steering column control unit
11 Rear fusebox
  a = rear electronic control unit
12 Passenger fusebox
13 Stop light switch
14 Reversing light switch
15 LH rear light unit (saloon/hatch)
  a = reversing light
  b = stop light
  c = tail light

16 RH rear light unit (saloon/hatch)
  a = reversing light
  b = stop light
  c = tail light
17 LH inner rear light unit (estate)
  a = reversing light
  b = tail light
18 RH inner rear light unit (estate)
  a = reversing light
  b = tail light
19 High level brake light
20 LH outer rear light unit (estate)
  a = stop light

21 RH outer rear light unit (estate)
  a = stop light
22 Number plate light
23 LH front light unit
  a = side light
24 RH front light unit
  a = side light
25 Light switch
  a = side/headlight switch
26 Body control unit

Diagram 3

H33650

Stop & reversing lights

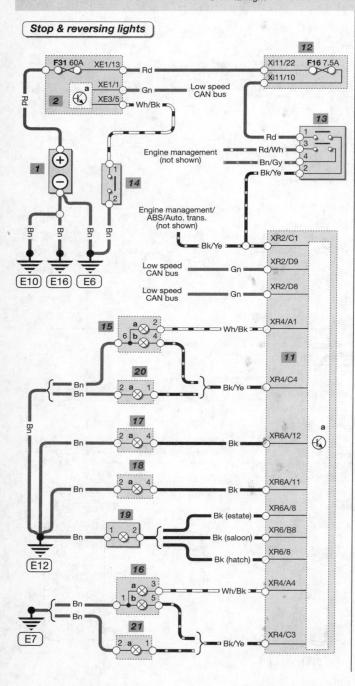

Side, tail & number plate lights

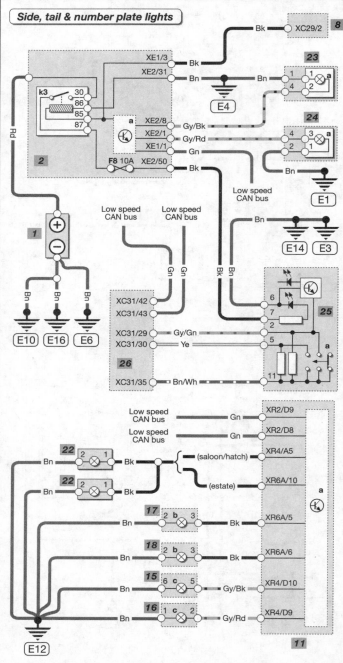

Wire colours

Bg	Beige	**LBu**	Light blue
Bk	Black	**LGn**	Light green
Bn	Brown	**Og**	Orange
DBu	Dark blue	**Bn**	Brown
DGn	Dark green	**Pu**	Purple
Ye	Yellow	**Pk**	Pink
Gn	Green	**Rd**	Red
Gy	Grey	**Wh**	White
Vt	Violet	**Bu**	Blue

Key to items

1 Battery
2 Engine fusebox
  a = under bonnet control unit
11 Rear fusebox
  a = rear electronic control unit
15 LH rear light unit (saloon/hatch)
  e = direction indicator
16 RH rear light unit (saloon/hatch)
  d = foglight
  e = direction indicator
18 RH inner rear light unit (estate)
  c = foglight
20 LH outer rear light unit (estate)
  b = direction indicator

21 RH outer rear light unit (estate)
  b = direction indicator
23 LH front light unit
  b = main beam
  c = dip beam
  d = ignition module
  e = controller
  f = direction indicator
24 RH front light unit
(as above)
25 Light switch
  a = side/headlight switch
  b = front foglight switch
  c = rear foglight switch

26 Body control unit
30 LH front fog light
31 RH front fog light
32 LH front indicator side repeater
33 RH front indicator side repeater
34 Hazard warning light switch
35 Trailer warning buzzer
36 Trailer hitch position switch
37 Trailer socket

Diagram 4

H33651

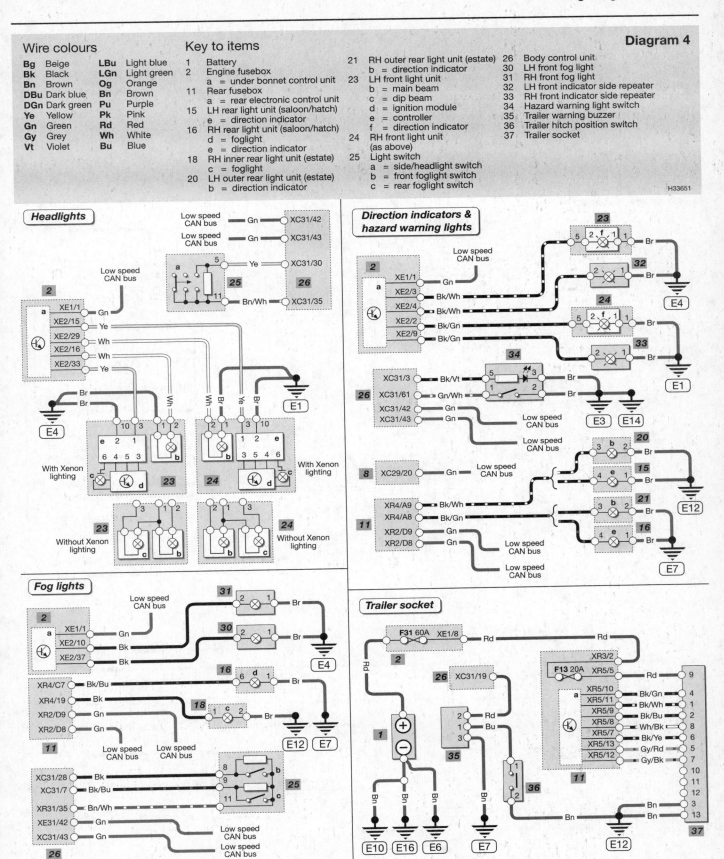

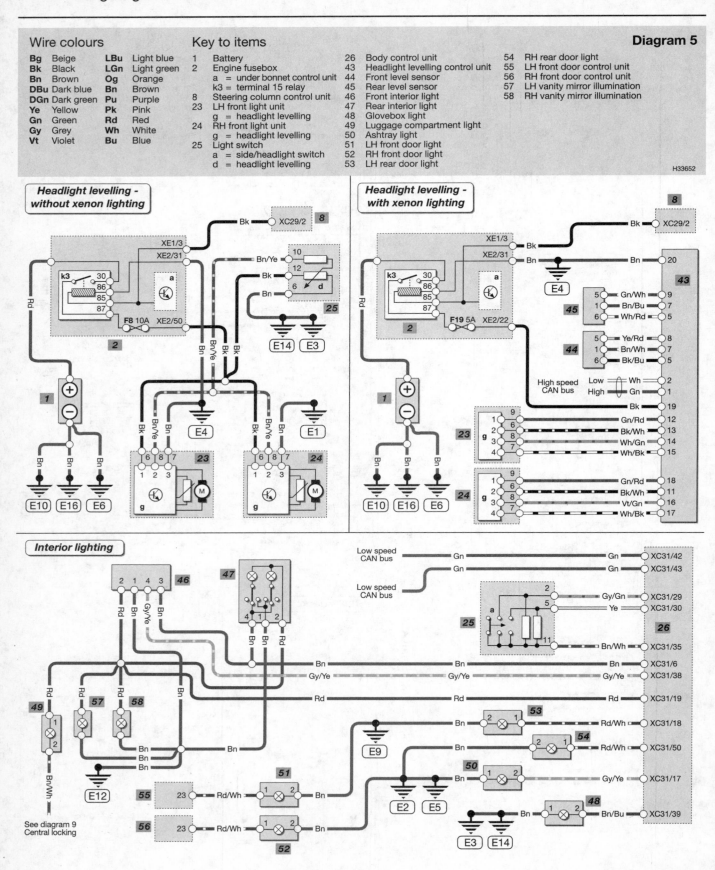

Wire colours

Bg	Beige	**LBu**	Light blue
Bk	Black	**LGn**	Light green
Bn	Brown	**Og**	Orange
DBu	Dark blue	**Bn**	Brown
DGn	Dark green	**Pu**	Purple
Ye	Yellow	**Pk**	Pink
Gn	Green	**Rd**	Red
Gy	Grey	**Wh**	White
Vt	Violet	**Bu**	Blue

Key to items

1	Battery	26	Body control unit	54	RH rear door light
2	Engine fusebox	43	Headlight levelling control unit	55	LH front door control unit
a = under bonnet control unit		44	Front level sensor	56	RH front door control unit
k3 = terminal 15 relay		45	Rear level sensor	57	LH vanity mirror illumination
8	Steering column control unit	46	Front interior light	58	RH vanity mirror illumination
23	LH front light unit	47	Rear interior light		
g = headlight levelling		48	Glovebox light		
24	RH front light unit	49	Luggage compartment light		
g = headlight levelling		50	Ashtray light		
25	Light switch	51	LH front door light		
a = side/headlight switch		52	RH front door light		
d = headlight levelling		53	LH rear door light		

Diagram 5

H33652

Wire colours

Bg	Beige	**LBu**	Light blue
Bk	Black	**LGn**	Light green
Bn	Brown	**Og**	Orange
DBu	Dark blue	**Bn**	Brown
DGn	Dark green	**Pu**	Purple
Ye	Yellow	**Pk**	Pink
Gn	Green	**Rd**	Red
Gy	Grey	**Wh**	White
Vt	Violet	**Bu**	Blue

Key to items

1   Battery
2   Engine fusebox
   a = under bonnet control unit
   k3 = terminal 15 relay
   k5 = front wiper slow/fast
   k6 = front wiper on/off
   k7 = headlight washer relay
   k9 = washer relay
8   Steering column control unit
11 Rear fusebox
   a = rear electronic control unit
   k1 = terminal 15 relay
   k2 = rear wiper relay

12 Passenger fusebox
   k3 = terminal 15 relay
26 Body control unit
60 Cigar lighter
61 Accessory socket
65 LH washer jet heater
66 RH washer jet heater
67 Front wiper motor
68 Rear wiper motor
69 Rain sensor
70 Screen washer pump
71 Headlight washer pump

Diagram 6

H33653

Cigar lighter & accessory socket

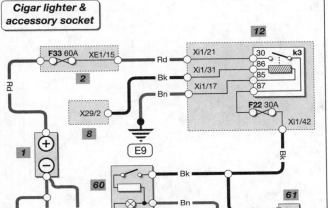

Heated washer jets

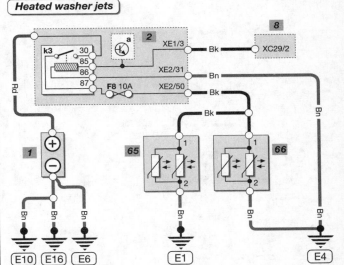

Wash/wipe & headlight washer

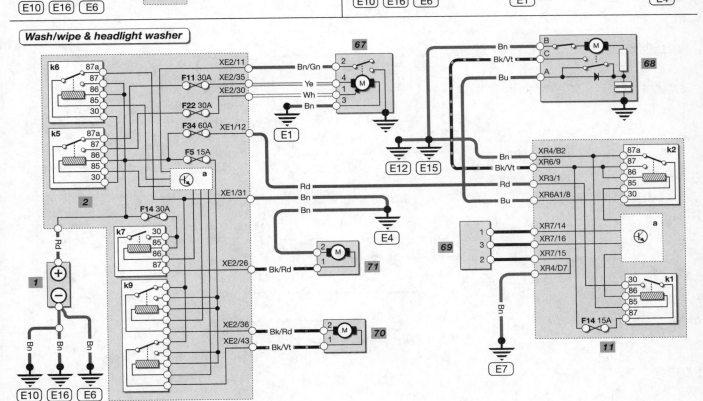

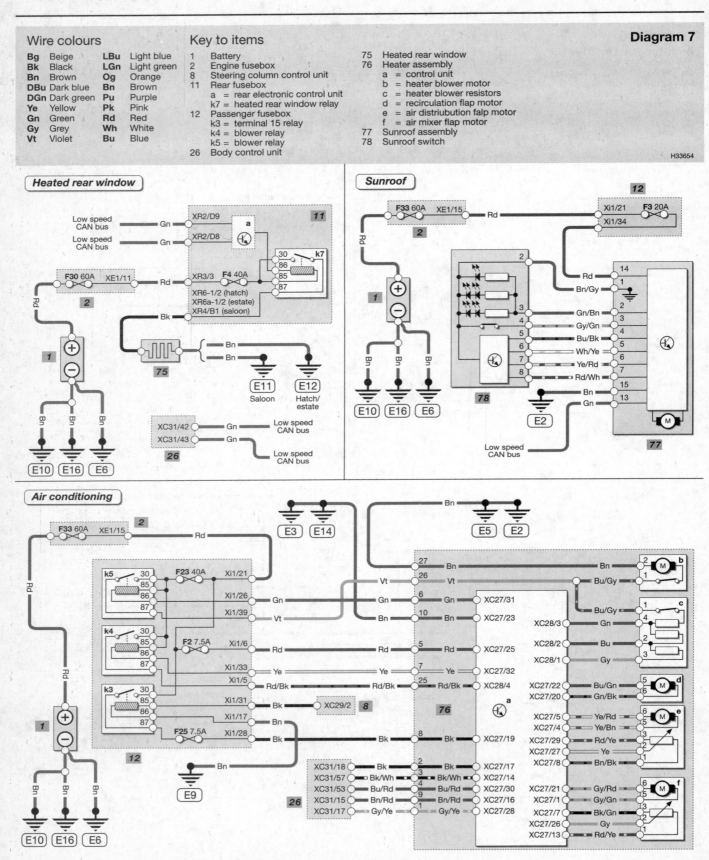

Diagram 7

Wire colours

Bg	Beige	LBu	Light blue
Bk	Black	LGn	Light green
Bn	Brown	Og	Orange
DBu	Dark blue	Bn	Brown
DGn	Dark green	Pu	Purple
Ye	Yellow	Pk	Pink
Gn	Green	Rd	Red
Gy	Grey	Wh	White
Vt	Violet	Bu	Blue

Key to items

1 Battery
2 Engine fusebox
8 Steering column control unit
11 Rear fusebox
   a = rear electronic control unit
   k7 = heated rear window relay
12 Passenger fusebox
   k3 = terminal 15 relay
   k4 = blower relay
   k5 = blower relay
26 Body control unit
75 Heated rear window
76 Heater assembly
   a = control unit
   b = heater blower motor
   c = heater blower resistors
   d = recirculation flap motor
   e = air distriubution falp motor
   f = air mixer flap motor
77 Sunroof assembly
78 Sunroof switch

H33654

Heated rear window

Sunroof

Air conditioning

Wire colours

Bg	Beige	**LBu**	Light blue
Bk	Black	**LGn**	Light green
Bn	Brown	**Og**	Orange
DBu	Dark blue	**Bn**	Brown
DGn	Dark green	**Pu**	Purple
Ye	Yellow	**Pk**	Pink
Gn	Green	**Rd**	Red
Gy	Grey	**Wh**	White
Vt	Violet	**Bu**	Blue

Key to items

1	Battery	80	Instrument cluster
2	Engine fusebox		a = illumination
8	Steering column control unit		b = engine management warning light
12	Passenger fusebox		c = warning lights/gauges/display
	k3 = terminal 15 relay	81	Low washer fluid switch
26	Body control unit	82	LH front brake pad wear sensor
55	LH front door control unit	83	Low ccolant level switch
56	RH front door control unit	84	Handbrake switch

Diagram 8

85	Low brake fluid level switch
86	LH mirror assembly
87	RH mirror assembly
88	RH front door switch unit
	a = mirror select switch
	b = mirror position switch

H33655

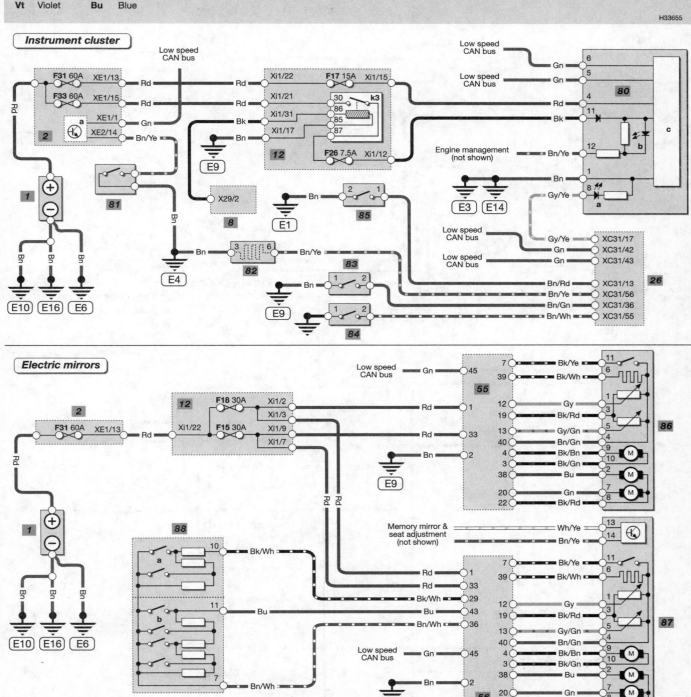

Instrument cluster

Electric mirrors

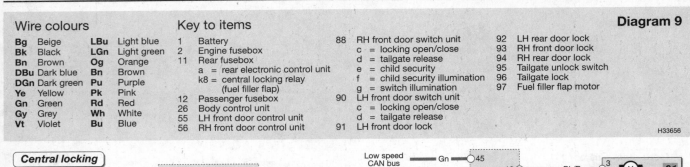

Diagram 9

Wire colours

Bg	Beige	**LBu**	Light blue
Bk	Black	**LGn**	Light green
Bn	Brown	**Og**	Orange
DBu	Dark blue	**Bn**	Brown
DGn	Dark green	**Pu**	Purple
Ye	Yellow	**Pk**	Pink
Gn	Green	**Rd**	Red
Gy	Grey	**Wh**	White
Vt	Violet	**Bu**	Blue

Key to items

1 = Battery
2 = Engine fusebox
11 = Rear fusebox
   a = rear electronic control unit
   k8 = central locking relay
        (fuel filler flap)
12 = Passenger fusebox
26 = Body control unit
55 = LH front door control unit
56 = RH front door control unit

88 = RH front door switch unit
   c = locking open/close
   d = tailgate release
   e = child security
   f = child security illumination
   g = switch illumination
90 = LH front door switch unit
   c = locking open/close
   d = tailgate release
91 = LH front door lock

92 = LH rear door lock
93 = RH front door lock
94 = RH rear door lock
95 = Tailgate unlock switch
96 = Tailgate lock
97 = Fuel filler flap motor

H33656

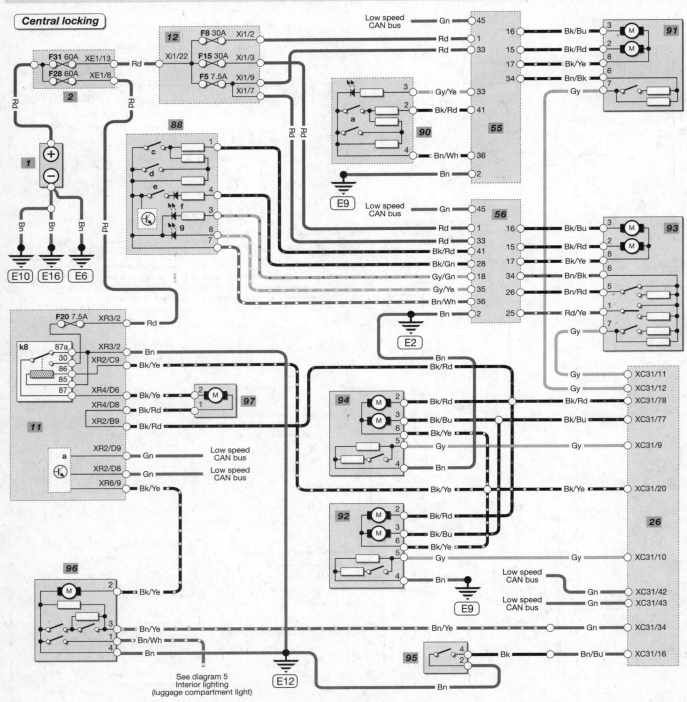

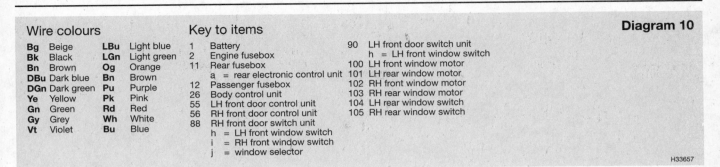

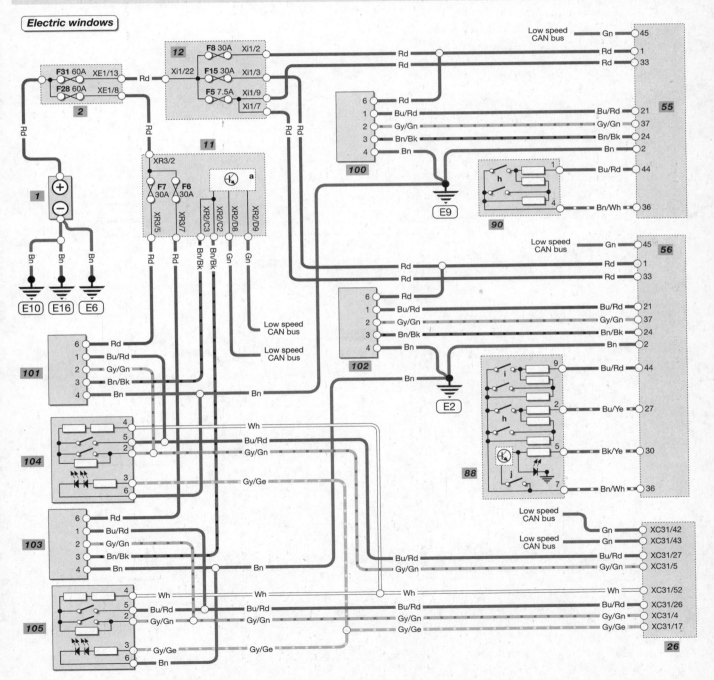

Dimensions and weights

Note: *All figures are approximate and may vary according to model. Refer to manufacturer's data for exact figures.*

Dimensions

Overall length:
  Saloon and Hatchback. . . . . 4611 mm
  Estate . . . . 4839 mm
Overall width (including door mirrors) . . . . 2036 mm
Overall height (unladen):
  Saloon and Hatchback. . . . . 1460 mm
  Estate . . . . 1500 mm
Wheelbase:
  Saloon and Hatchback. . . . . 2700 mm
  Estate . . . . 2830 mm
Turning circle diameter (wall to wall) . . . . 11.50 metres
Front track . . . . 1536 mm
Rear track. . . . . 1525 mm

Weights

Kerb weight:
  1.8 litre petrol engine models:
    Saloon. . . . . 1375 to 1395 kg
    Hatchback . . . . 1390 to 1410 kg
    Estate . . . . 1470 to 1490 kg
  2.2 litre petrol engine models:
    Saloon. . . . . 1435 to 1485 kg
    Hatchback . . . . 1450 to 1500 kg
    Estate . . . . 1530 to 1580 kg
  Diesel engine models:
    Saloon. . . . . 1503 to 1548 kg
    Hatchback . . . . 1503 to 1580 kg
    Estate . . . . 1585 to 1633 kg
Gross vehicle weight . . . . Refer to information contained on the vehicle identification plate
Maximum roof load (including weight of rack):
  Saloon and Hatchback. . . . . 90 kg
  Estate:
    Without roof railing. . . . . 75 kg
    With roof railing. . . . . 100 kg

Fuel economy

Although depreciation is still the biggest part of the cost of motoring for most car owners, the cost of fuel is more immediately noticeable. These pages give some tips on how to get the best fuel economy.

Working it out

Manufacturer's figures

Car manufacturers are required by law to provide fuel consumption information on all new vehicles sold. These 'official' figures are obtained by simulating various driving conditions on a rolling road or a test track. Real life conditions are different, so the fuel consumption actually achieved may not bear much resemblance to the quoted figures.

How to calculate it

Many cars now have trip computers which will

display fuel consumption, both instantaneous and average. Refer to the owner's handbook for details of how to use these.

To calculate consumption yourself (and maybe to check that the trip computer is accurate), proceed as follows.

1. Fill up with fuel and note the mileage, or zero the trip recorder.
2. Drive as usual until you need to fill up again.
3. Note the amount of fuel required to refill the tank, and the mileage covered since the previous fill-up.
4. Divide the mileage by the amount of fuel used to obtain the consumption figure.

For example:

Mileage at first fill-up (a) = 27,903
Mileage at second fill-up (b) = 28,346
Mileage covered (b - a) = 443
Fuel required at second fill-up = 48.6 litres

The half-completed changeover to metric units in the UK means that we buy our fuel in litres, measure distances in miles and talk about fuel consumption in miles per gallon. There are two ways round this: the first is to convert the litres to gallons before doing the calculation (by dividing by 4.546, or see Table 1). So in the example:

48.6 litres ÷ 4.546 = 10.69 gallons
443 miles ÷ 10.69 gallons = 41.4 mpg

The second way is to calculate the consumption in miles per litre, then multiply that figure by 4.546 (or see Table 2).

So in the example, fuel consumption is:

443 miles ÷ 48.6 litres = 9.1 mpl
9.1 mpl x 4.546 = 41.4 mpg

The rest of Europe expresses fuel consumption in litres of fuel required to travel 100 km (l/100 km). For interest, the conversions are given in Table 3. In practice it doesn't matter what units you use, provided you know what your normal consumption is and can spot if it's getting better or worse.

Table 1: conversion of litres to Imperial gallons

litres	1	2	3	4	5	10	20	30	40	50	60	70
gallons	0.22	0.44	0.66	0.88	1.10	2.24	4.49	6.73	8.98	11.22	13.47	15.71

Table 2: conversion of miles per litre to miles per gallon

miles per litre	5	6	7	8	9	10	11	12	13	14
miles per gallon	23	27	32	36	41	46	50	55	59	64

Table 3: conversion of litres per 100 km to miles per gallon

litres per 100 km	4	4.5	5	5.5	6	6.5	7	8	9	10
miles per gallon	71	63	56	51	47	43	40	35	31	28

Maintenance

A well-maintained car uses less fuel and creates less pollution. In particular:

Filters

Change air and fuel filters at the specified intervals.

Oil

Use a good quality oil of the lowest viscosity specified by the vehicle manufacturer (see *Lubricants and fluids*). Check the level often and be careful not to overfill.

Spark plugs

When applicable, renew at the specified intervals.

Tyres

Check tyre pressures regularly. Under-inflated tyres have an increased rolling resistance. It is generally safe to use the higher pressures specified for full load conditions even when not fully laden, but keep an eye on the centre band of tread for signs of wear due to over-inflation.

When buying new tyres, consider the 'fuel saving' models which most manufacturers include in their ranges.

Driving style

Acceleration

Acceleration uses more fuel than driving at a steady speed. The best technique with modern cars is to accelerate reasonably briskly to the desired speed, changing up through the gears as soon as possible without making the engine labour.

Air conditioning

Air conditioning absorbs quite a bit of energy from the engine – typically 3 kW (4 hp) or so. The effect on fuel consumption is at its worst in slow traffic. Switch it off when not required.

Anticipation

Drive smoothly and try to read the traffic flow so as to avoid unnecessary acceleration and braking.

Automatic transmission

When accelerating in an automatic, avoid depressing the throttle so far as to make the transmission hold onto lower gears at higher speeds. Don't use the 'Sport' setting, if applicable.

When stationary with the engine running, select 'N' or 'P'. When moving, keep your left foot away from the brake.

Braking

Braking converts the car's energy of motion into heat – essentially, it is wasted. Obviously some braking is always going to be necessary, but with good anticipation it is surprising how much can be avoided, especially on routes that you know well.

Carshare

Consider sharing lifts to work or to the shops. Even once a week will make a difference.

Electrical loads

Electricity is 'fuel' too; the alternator which charges the battery does so by converting some of the engine's energy of motion into electrical energy. The more electrical accessories are in use, the greater the load on the alternator. Switch off big consumers like the heated rear window when not required.

Freewheeling

Freewheeling (coasting) in neutral with the engine switched off is dangerous. The effort required to operate power-assisted brakes and steering increases when the engine is not running, with a potential lack of control in emergency situations.

In any case, modern fuel injection systems automatically cut off the engine's fuel supply on the overrun (moving and in gear, but with the accelerator pedal released).

Gadgets

Bolt-on devices claiming to save fuel have been around for nearly as long as the motor car itself. Those which worked were rapidly adopted as standard equipment by the vehicle manufacturers. Others worked only in certain situations, or saved fuel only at the expense of unacceptable effects on performance, driveability or the life of engine components.

The most effective fuel saving gadget is the driver's right foot.

Journey planning

Combine (eg) a trip to the supermarket with a visit to the recycling centre and the DIY store, rather than making separate journeys.

When possible choose a travelling time outside rush hours.

Load

The more heavily a car is laden, the greater the energy required to accelerate it to a given speed. Remove heavy items which you don't need to carry.

One load which is often overlooked is the contents of the fuel tank. A tankful of fuel (55 litres / 12 gallons) weighs 45 kg (100 lb) or so. Just half filling it may be worthwhile.

Lost?

At the risk of stating the obvious, if you're going somewhere new, have details of the route to hand. There's not much point in achieving record mpg if you also go miles out of your way.

Parking

If possible, carry out any reversing or turning manoeuvres when you arrive at a parking space so that you can drive straight out when you leave. Manoeuvering when the engine is cold uses a lot more fuel.

Driving around looking for free on-street parking may cost more in fuel than buying a car park ticket.

Premium fuel

Most major oil companies (and some supermarkets) have premium grades of fuel which are several pence a litre dearer than the standard grades. Reports vary, but the consensus seems to be that if these fuels improve economy at all, they do not do so by enough to justify their extra cost.

Roof rack

When loading a roof rack, try to produce a wedge shape with the narrow end at the front. Any cover should be securely fastened – if it flaps it's creating turbulence and absorbing energy.

Remove roof racks and boxes when not in use – they increase air resistance and can create a surprising amount of noise.

Short journeys

The engine is at its least efficient, and wear is highest, during the first few miles after a cold start. Consider walking, cycling or using public transport.

Speed

The engine is at its most efficient when running at a steady speed and load at the rpm where it develops maximum torque. (You can find this figure in the car's handbook.) For most cars this corresponds to between 55 and 65 mph in top gear.

Above the optimum cruising speed, fuel consumption starts to rise quite sharply. A car travelling at 80 mph will typically be using 30% more fuel than at 60 mph.

Supermarket fuel

It may be cheap but is it any good? In the UK all supermarket fuel must meet the relevant British Standard. The major oil companies will say that their branded fuels have better additive packages which may stop carbon and other deposits building up. A reasonable compromise might be to use one tank of branded fuel to three or four from the supermarket.

Switch off when stationary

Switch off the engine if you look like being stationary for more than 30 seconds or so. This is good for the environment as well as for your pocket. Be aware though that frequent restarts are hard on the battery and the starter motor.

Windows

Driving with the windows open increases air turbulence around the vehicle. Closing the windows promotes smooth airflow and

reduced resistance. The faster you go, the more significant this is.

And finally . . .

Driving techniques associated with good fuel economy tend to involve moderate acceleration and low top speeds. Be considerate to the needs of other road users who may need to make brisker progress; even if you do not agree with them this is not an excuse to be obstructive.

Safety must always take precedence over economy, whether it is a question of accelerating hard to complete an overtaking manoeuvre, killing your speed when confronted with a potential hazard or switching the lights on when it starts to get dark.

Conversion factors

Length (distance)

Inches (in)	x 25.4	=	Millimetres (mm)	x 0.0394 =	Inches (in)
Feet (ft)	x 0.305	=	Metres (m)	x 3.281 =	Feet (ft)
Miles	x 1.609	=	Kilometres (km)	x 0.621 =	Miles

Volume (capacity)

Cubic inches (cu in; in³)	x 16.387	=	Cubic centimetres (cc; cm³)	x 0.061 =	Cubic inches (cu in; in³)
Imperial pints (Imp pt)	x 0.568	=	Litres (l)	x 1.76 =	Imperial pints (Imp pt)
Imperial quarts (Imp qt)	x 1.137	=	Litres (l)	x 0.88 =	Imperial quarts (Imp qt)
Imperial quarts (Imp qt)	x 1.201	=	US quarts (US qt)	x 0.833 =	Imperial quarts (Imp qt)
US quarts (US qt)	x 0.946	=	Litres (l)	x 1.057 =	US quarts (US qt)
Imperial gallons (Imp gal)	x 4.546	=	Litres (l)	x 0.22 =	Imperial gallons (Imp gal)
Imperial gallons (Imp gal)	x 1.201	=	US gallons (US gal)	x 0.833 =	Imperial gallons (Imp gal)
US gallons (US gal)	x 3.785	=	Litres (l)	x 0.264 =	US gallons (US gal)

Mass (weight)

Ounces (oz)	x 28.35	=	Grams (g)	x 0.035 =	Ounces (oz)
Pounds (lb)	x 0.454	=	Kilograms (kg)	x 2.205 =	Pounds (lb)

Force

Ounces-force (ozf; oz)	x 0.278	=	Newtons (N)	x 3.6 =	Ounces-force (ozf; oz)
Pounds-force (lbf; lb)	x 4.448	=	Newtons (N)	x 0.225 =	Pounds-force (lbf; lb)
Newtons (N)	x 0.1	=	Kilograms-force (kgf; kg)	x 9.81 =	Newtons (N)

Pressure

Pounds-force per square inch (psi; lbf/in²; lb/in²)	x 0.070	=	Kilograms-force per square centimetre (kgf/cm²; kg/cm²)	x 14.223 =	Pounds-force per square inch (psi; lbf/in²; lb/in²)
Pounds-force per square inch (psi; lbf/in²; lb/in²)	x 0.068	=	Atmospheres (atm)	x 14.696 =	Pounds-force per square inch (psi; lbf/in²; lb/in²)
Pounds-force per square inch (psi; lbf/in²; lb/in²)	x 0.069	=	Bars	x 14.5 =	Pounds-force per square inch (psi; lbf/in²; lb/in²)
Pounds-force per square inch (psi; lbf/in²; lb/in²)	x 6.895	=	Kilopascals (kPa)	x 0.145 =	Pounds-force per square inch (psi; lbf/in²; lb/in²)
Kilopascals (kPa)	x 0.01	=	Kilograms-force per square centimetre (kgf/cm²; kg/cm²)	x 98.1 =	Kilopascals (kPa)
Millibar (mbar)	x 100	=	Pascals (Pa)	x 0.01 =	Millibar (mbar)
Millibar (mbar)	x 0.0145	=	Pounds-force per square inch (psi; lbf/in²; lb/in²)	x 68.947 =	Millibar (mbar)
Millibar (mbar)	x 0.75	=	Millimetres of mercury (mmHg)	x 1.333 =	Millibar (mbar)
Millibar (mbar)	x 0.401	=	Inches of water (inH₂O)	x 2.491 =	Millibar (mbar)
Millimetres of mercury (mmHg)	x 0.535	=	Inches of water (inH₂O)	x 1.868 =	Millimetres of mercury (mmHg)
Inches of water (inH₂O)	x 0.036	=	Pounds-force per square inch (psi; lbf/in²; lb/in²)	x 27.68 =	Inches of water (inH₂O)

Where superscripts appear: Kilograms-force per square centimetre (kgf/cm^2; kg/cm^2), pounds-force per square inch (psi; lbf/in^2; lb/in^2), inches of water (inH_2O).

Torque (moment of force)

Pounds-force inches (lbf in; lb in)	x 1.152	=	Kilograms-force centimetre (kgf cm; kg cm)	x 0.868 =	Pounds-force inches (lbf in; lb in)
Pounds-force inches (lbf in; lb in)	x 0.113	=	Newton metres (Nm)	x 8.85 =	Pounds-force inches (lbf in; lb in)
Pounds-force inches (lbf in; lb in)	x 0.083	=	Pounds-force feet (lbf ft; lb ft)	x 12 =	Pounds-force inches (lbf in; lb in)
Pounds-force feet (lbf ft; lb ft)	x 0.138	=	Kilograms-force metres (kgf m; kg m)	x 7.233 =	Pounds-force feet (lbf ft; lb ft)
Pounds-force feet (lbf ft; lb ft)	x 1.356	=	Newton metres (Nm)	x 0.738 =	Pounds-force feet (lbf ft; lb ft)
Newton metres (Nm)	x 0.102	=	Kilograms-force metres (kgf m; kg m)	x 9.804 =	Newton metres (Nm)

Power

Horsepower (hp)	x 745.7	=	Watts (W)	x 0.0013 =	Horsepower (hp)

Velocity (speed)

Miles per hour (miles/hr; mph)	x 1.609	=	Kilometres per hour (km/hr; kph)	x 0.621 =	Miles per hour (miles/hr; mph)

Fuel consumption*

Miles per gallon, Imperial (mpg)	x 0.354	=	Kilometres per litre (km/l)	x 2.825 =	Miles per gallon, Imperial (mpg)
Miles per gallon, US (mpg)	x 0.425	=	Kilometres per litre (km/l)	x 2.352 =	Miles per gallon, US (mpg)

Temperature

Degrees Fahrenheit = (°C x 1.8) + 32   Degrees Celsius (Degrees Centigrade; °C) = (°F - 32) x 0.56

It is common practice to convert from miles per gallon (mpg) to litres/100 kilometres (l/100km), where mpg x l/100 km = 282

Spare parts are available from many sources, including maker's appointed garages, accessory shops, and motor factors. To be sure of obtaining the correct parts, it will sometimes be necessary to quote the vehicle identification number. If possible, it can also be useful to take the old parts along for positive identification. Items such as starter motors and alternators may be available under a service exchange scheme – any parts returned should be clean.

Our advice regarding spare parts is as follows.

Officially appointed garages

This is the best source of parts which are peculiar to your car, and which are not otherwise generally available (eg, badges, interior trim, certain body panels, etc). It is also the only place at which you should buy parts if the car is still under warranty.

Accessory shops

These are very good places to buy materials and components needed for the maintenance of your car (oil, air and fuel filters, light bulbs, drivebelts, greases, brake pads, touch-up paint, etc). Components of this nature sold by a reputable shop are usually of the same standard as those used by the car manufacturer.

Besides components, these shops also sell tools and general accessories, usually have convenient opening hours, charge lower prices, and can often be found close to home. Some accessory shops have parts counters where components needed for almost any repair job can be purchased or ordered.

Motor factors

Good factors will stock all the more important components which wear out comparatively quickly, and can sometimes supply individual components needed for the overhaul of a larger assembly (eg, brake seals and hydraulic parts, bearing shells, pistons, valves). They may also handle work such as cylinder block reboring, crankshaft regrinding, etc.

Engine reconditioners

These specialise in engine overhaul and can also supply components. It is recommended that the establishment is a member of the Federation of Engine Re-Manufacturers, or a similar society.

Tyre and exhaust specialists

These outlets may be independent, or members of a local or national chain. They frequently offer competitive prices when compared with a main dealer or local garage, but it will pay to obtain several quotes before making a decision. When researching prices, also ask what extras may be added – for instance fitting a new valve, balancing the wheel and tyre disposal all both commonly charged on top of the price of a new tyre.

Other sources

Beware of parts or materials obtained from market stalls, car boot sales, on-line auctions or similar outlets. Such items are not invariably sub-standard, but there is little chance of compensation if they do prove unsatisfactory. In the case of safety-critical components such as brake pads, there is the risk not only of financial loss, but also of an accident causing injury or death.

Second-hand components or assemblies obtained from a car breaker can be a good buy in some circumstances, but this sort of purchase is best made by the experienced DIY mechanic.

Vehicle identification

Modifications are a continuing and unpublished process in vehicle manufacture, quite apart from major model changes. Spare parts manuals and lists are compiled upon a numerical basis, the individual vehicle numbers being essential to correct identification of the component required.

When ordering spare parts, always give as much information as possible. Quote the car model, year of manufacture and vehicle identification and/or engine numbers as appropriate.

The *vehicle identification plate* is attached to the front right-hand side door pillar **(see illustration)** and includes the Vehicle Identification Number (VIN), vehicle weight information and paint and trim colour codes.

The *Vehicle Identification Number (VIN)* is given on the vehicle identification plate and is also stamped into the body floor panel between the right-hand front seat and the door sill panel **(see illustration)**; lift the flap in the carpet to see it.

Vauxhall/Opel use a 'Car pass' scheme for vehicle identification. This is a card which is issued to the customer when the car is first purchased. It contains important information, eg, VIN number, key number and radio code. It also includes a special code for diagnostic equipment, therefore it must be kept in a secure place and not in the vehicle.

The engine number is stamped on a horizontal flat located on the front of the cylinder block, at the transmission end. The first part of the engine number gives the engine code – eg Z18XE.

Engine codes

1.8 litre (1796 cc) DOHC 16-valve
    petrol engine . . . . Z18XE and Z18XER

2.2 litre (2198 cc) DOHC 16-valve
    petrol engine Z22YH

1.9 litre (1910 cc) SOHC 8-valve
    diesel engine Z19DT

1.9 litre (1910 cc) DOHC 16-valve
    diesel engine Z19DTH

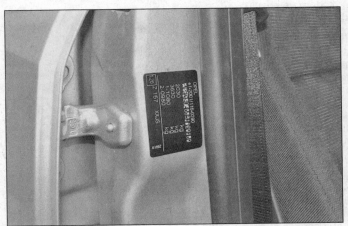

Vehicle Identification Number (VIN) plate attached to the front right-hand side door pillar

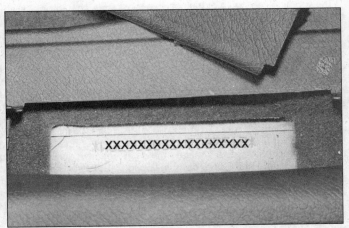

The VIN number is stamped into the body floor next to the right-hand front seat

Whenever servicing, repair or overhaul work is carried out on the car or its components, observe the following procedures and instructions. This will assist in carrying out the operation efficiently and to a professional standard of workmanship.

Joint mating faces and gaskets

When separating components at their mating faces, never insert screwdrivers or similar implements into the joint between the faces in order to prise them apart. This can cause severe damage which results in oil leaks, coolant leaks, etc upon reassembly. Separation is usually achieved by tapping along the joint with a soft-faced hammer in order to break the seal. However, note that this method may not be suitable where dowels are used for component location.

Where a gasket is used between the mating faces of two components, a new one must be fitted on reassembly; fit it dry unless otherwise stated in the repair procedure. Make sure that the mating faces are clean and dry, with all traces of old gasket removed. When cleaning a joint face, use a tool which is unlikely to score or damage the face, and remove any burrs or nicks with an oilstone or fine file.

Make sure that tapped holes are cleaned with a pipe cleaner, and keep them free of jointing compound, if this is being used, unless specifically instructed otherwise.

Ensure that all orifices, channels or pipes are clear, and blow through them, preferably using compressed air.

Oil seals

Oil seals can be removed by levering them out with a wide flat-bladed screwdriver or similar implement. Alternatively, a number of self-tapping screws may be screwed into the seal, and these used as a purchase for pliers or some similar device in order to pull the seal free.

Whenever an oil seal is removed from its working location, either individually or as part of an assembly, it should be renewed.

The very fine sealing lip of the seal is easily damaged, and will not seal if the surface it contacts is not completely clean and free from scratches, nicks or grooves. If the original sealing surface of the component cannot be restored, and the manufacturer has not made provision for slight relocation of the seal relative to the sealing surface, the component should be renewed.

Protect the lips of the seal from any surface which may damage them in the course of fitting. Use tape or a conical sleeve where possible. Where indicated, lubricate the seal lips with oil before fitting and, on dual-lipped seals, fill the space between the lips with grease.

Unless otherwise stated, oil seals must be fitted with their sealing lips toward the lubricant to be sealed.

Use a tubular drift or block of wood of the appropriate size to install the seal and, if the seal housing is shouldered, drive the seal down to the shoulder. If the seal housing is unshouldered, the seal should be fitted with its face flush with the housing top face (unless otherwise instructed).

Screw threads and fastenings

Seized nuts, bolts and screws are quite a common occurrence where corrosion has set in, and the use of penetrating oil or releasing fluid will often overcome this problem if the offending item is soaked for a while before attempting to release it. The use of an impact driver may also provide a means of releasing such stubborn fastening devices, when used in conjunction with the appropriate screwdriver bit or socket. If none of these methods works, it may be necessary to resort to the careful application of heat, or the use of a hacksaw or nut splitter device. Before resorting to extreme methods, check that you are not dealing with a left-hand thread!

Studs are usually removed by locking two nuts together on the threaded part, and then using a spanner on the lower nut to unscrew the stud. Studs or bolts which have broken off below the surface of the component in which they are mounted can sometimes be removed using a stud extractor.

Always ensure that a blind tapped hole is completely free from oil, grease, water or other fluid before installing the bolt or stud. Failure to do this could cause the housing to crack due to the hydraulic action of the bolt or stud as it is screwed in.

For some screw fastenings, notably cylinder head bolts or nuts, torque wrench settings are no longer specified for the latter stages of tightening, "angle-tightening" being called up instead. Typically, a fairly low torque wrench setting will be applied to the bolts/nuts in the correct sequence, followed by one or more stages of tightening through specified angles.

When checking or retightening a nut or bolt to a specified torque setting, slacken the nut or bolt by a quarter of a turn, and then retighten to the specified setting. However, this should not be attempted where angular tightening has been used.

Locknuts, locktabs and washers

Any fastening which will rotate against a component or housing during tightening should always have a washer between it and the relevant component or housing.

Spring or split washers should always be renewed when they are used to lock a critical component such as a big-end bearing retaining bolt or nut. Locktabs which are folded over to retain a nut or bolt should always be renewed.

Self-locking nuts can be re-used in non-critical areas, providing resistance can be felt when the locking portion passes over the bolt or stud thread. However, it should be noted that self-locking stiffnuts tend to lose their effectiveness after long periods of use, and should then be renewed as a matter of course.

Split pins must always be replaced with new ones of the correct size for the hole.

When thread-locking compound is found on the threads of a fastener which is to be re-used, it should be cleaned off with a wire brush and solvent, and fresh compound applied on reassembly.

Special tools

Some repair procedures in this manual entail the use of special tools such as a press, two or three-legged pullers, spring compressors, etc. Wherever possible, suitable readily-available alternatives to the manufacturer's special tools are described, and are shown in use. In some instances, where no alternative is possible, it has been necessary to resort to the use of a manufacturer's tool, and this has been done for reasons of safety as well as the efficient completion of the repair operation. Unless you are highly-skilled and have a thorough understanding of the procedures described, never attempt to bypass the use of any special tool when the procedure described specifies its use. Not only is there a very great risk of personal injury, but expensive damage could be caused to the components involved.

Environmental considerations

When disposing of used engine oil, brake fluid, antifreeze, etc, give due consideration to any detrimental environmental effects. Do not, for instance, pour any of the above liquids down drains into the general sewage system, or onto the ground to soak away. Many local council refuse tips provide a facility for waste oil disposal, as do some garages. You can find your nearest disposal point by calling the Environment Agency on 08708 506 506 or by visiting www.oilbankline.org.uk.

Note: It is illegal and anti-social to dump oil down the drain. To find the location of your local oil recycling bank, call 08708 506 506 or visit www.oilbankline.org.uk.

The jack supplied with the vehicle tool kit should only be used for changing roadwheels – see Wheel changing at the front of this manual. Ensure the jack head is correctly engaged before attempting to raise the vehicle. When carrying out any other kind of work, raise the vehicle using a hydraulic jack, and always supplement the jack with axle stands positioned under the vehicle jacking points.

When jacking up the vehicle with a trolley jack, position the jack head under one of the relevant jacking points. Use a block of wood between the jack or axle stand and the sill – the block of wood should have a groove cut into it , in which the welded flange of the sill will locate. **Do not** jack the vehicle under the sump or any of the steering or suspension components. Supplement the jack using axle stands **(see illustrations)**.

 Warning: Never work under, around, or near a raised vehicle, unless it is adequately supported in at least two places.

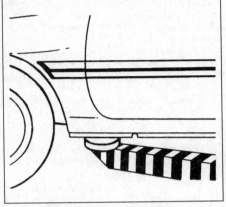

Front jacking point for hydraulic jack or axle stands

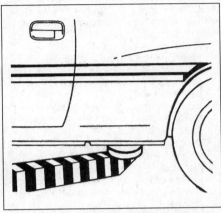

Rear jacking point for hydraulic jack or axle stands

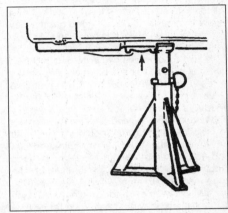

Axle stands should be placed under, or adjacent to the jacking point (arrowed)

Disconnecting the battery

Numerous systems fitted to the vehicle require battery power to be available at all times, either to ensure their continued operation (such as the clock) or to maintain control unit memories which would be erased if the battery were to be disconnected. Whenever the battery is to be disconnected therefore, first note the following, to ensure that there are no unforeseen consequences of this action:

a) *First, on any vehicle with central locking, it is a wise precaution to remove the key from the ignition, and to keep it with you, so that it does not get locked in, if the central locking should engage accidentally when the battery is reconnected.*

b) *Depending on model and specification, the Vauxhall anti-theft alarm system may be of the type which is automatically activated when the vehicle battery is disconnected and/or reconnected. To prevent the alarm sounding on models so equipped, switch the ignition on, then off, and disconnect the battery within15 seconds. If the alarm is activated when the battery is reconnected, switch the ignition on then off to deactivate the alarm.*

c) *If a security-coded audio unit is fitted, and the unit and/or the battery is disconnected, the unit will not function again on reconnection until the correct security code is entered. Details of this procedure, which varies according to the unit fitted, are given in the vehicle audio system operating instructions. Ensure you have the correct code before you disconnect the battery. If you do not have the code or details of the correct procedure, but can supply proof of ownership and a legitimate reason for wanting this information, a Vauxhall/Opel dealer may be able to help.*

d) *The engine management electronic control unit is of the 'self-learning' type, meaning that as it operates, it also monitors and stores the settings which give optimum engine performance under all operating conditions. When the battery is disconnected, these settings are lost and the ECU reverts to the base settings programmed into its memory at the factory. On restarting, this may lead to the engine running/idling roughly for a short while, until the ECU has relearned the optimum settings. This process is best accomplished by taking the vehicle on a road test (for approximately 15 minutes), covering all engine speeds and loads, concentrating mainly in the 2500 to 3500 rpm region.*

e) *On models equipped with automatic transmission, the transmission selector lever assembly incorporates an electrically-operated selector lever lock mechanism that prevents the lever being moved out of the P position unless the ignition is switched on and the brake pedal is depressed. If the selector lever is in the P position and the battery is disconnected, it will not be possible to move the selector lever out of position P by the normal means. Although it is possible to manually override the system (see Chapter 7B), it is sensible to move the selector lever to the N position before disconnecting the battery.*

f) *On models with electric windows, it will be necessary to reprogramme the motors to restore the one-touch function of the buttons, after reconnection of the battery. To do this, fully close both front windows. With the windows closed, depress the up button of the driver's side window for approximately 5 seconds, then release it and depress the passenger side window up button for approximately 5 seconds.*

g) *On models with an electric sliding sunroof, it will be necessary to fully open and fully close the sunroof after battery reconnection, to recalibrate the sensors.*

h) *On all models, when reconnecting the battery after disconnection, switch on the ignition and wait 10 seconds to allow the electronic vehicle systems to stabilise and re-initialise.*

Introduction

A selection of good tools is a fundamental requirement for anyone contemplating the maintenance and repair of a motor vehicle. For the owner who does not possess any, their purchase will prove a considerable expense, offsetting some of the savings made by doing-it-yourself. However, provided that the tools purchased meet the relevant national safety standards and are of good quality, they will last for many years and prove an extremely worthwhile investment.

To help the average owner to decide which tools are needed to carry out the various tasks detailed in this manual, we have compiled three lists of tools under the following headings: *Maintenance and minor repair*, *Repair and overhaul*, and *Special*. Newcomers to practical mechanics should start off with the *Maintenance and minor repair* tool kit, and confine themselves to the simpler jobs around the vehicle. Then, as confidence and experience grow, more difficult tasks can be undertaken, with extra tools being purchased as, and when, they are needed. In this way, a *Maintenance and minor repair* tool kit can be built up into a *Repair and overhaul* tool kit over a considerable period of time, without any major cash outlays. The experienced do-it-yourselfer will have a tool kit good enough for most repair and overhaul procedures, and will add tools from the *Special* category when it is felt that the expense is justified by the amount of use to which these tools will be put.

Maintenance and minor repair tool kit

The tools given in this list should be considered as a minimum requirement if routine maintenance, servicing and minor repair operations are to be undertaken. We recommend the purchase of combination spanners (ring one end, open-ended the other); although more expensive than open-ended ones, they do give the advantages of both types of spanner.

☐ *Combination spanners:*
Metric - 8 to 19 mm inclusive
☐ *Adjustable spanner - 35 mm jaw (approx.)*
☐ *Spark plug spanner (with rubber insert) - petrol models*
☐ *Spark plug gap adjustment tool - petrol models*
☐ *Set of feeler gauges*
☐ *Brake bleed nipple spanner*
☐ *Screwdrivers:*
Flat blade - 100 mm long x 6 mm dia
Cross blade - 100 mm long x 6 mm dia
Torx - various sizes (not all vehicles)
☐ *Combination pliers*
☐ *Hacksaw (junior)*
☐ *Tyre pump*
☐ *Tyre pressure gauge*
☐ *Oil can*
☐ *Oil filter removal tool (if applicable)*
☐ *Fine emery cloth*
☐ *Wire brush (small)*
☐ *Funnel (medium size)*
☐ *Sump drain plug key (not all vehicles)*

Repair and overhaul tool kit

These tools are virtually essential for anyone undertaking any major repairs to a motor vehicle, and are additional to those given in the *Maintenance and minor repair* list. Included in this list is a comprehensive set of sockets. Although these are expensive, they will be found invaluable as they are so versatile - particularly if various drives are included in the set. We recommend the half-inch square-drive type, as this can be used with most proprietary torque wrenches.

The tools in this list will sometimes need to be supplemented by tools from the *Special* list:

☐ *Sockets to cover range in previous list (including Torx sockets)*
☐ *Reversible ratchet drive (for use with sockets)*
☐ *Extension piece, 250 mm (for use with sockets)*
☐ *Universal joint (for use with sockets)*
☐ *Flexible handle or sliding T "breaker bar" (for use with sockets)*
☐ *Torque wrench (for use with sockets)*
☐ *Self-locking grips*
☐ *Ball pein hammer*
☐ *Soft-faced mallet (plastic or rubber)*
☐ *Screwdrivers:*
Flat blade - long & sturdy, short (chubby), and narrow (electrician's) types
Cross blade – long & sturdy, and short (chubby) types
☐ *Pliers:*
Long-nosed
Side cutters (electrician's)
Circlip (internal and external)
☐ *Cold chisel - 25 mm*
☐ *Scriber*
☐ *Scraper*
☐ *Centre-punch*
☐ *Pin punch*
☐ *Hacksaw*
☐ *Brake hose clamp*
☐ *Brake/clutch bleeding kit*
☐ *Selection of twist drills*
☐ *Steel rule/straight-edge*
☐ *Allen keys (inc. splined/Torx type)*
☐ *Selection of files*
☐ *Wire brush*
☐ *Axle stands*
☐ *Jack (strong trolley or hydraulic type)*
☐ *Light with extension lead*
☐ *Universal electrical multi-meter*

Sockets and reversible ratchet drive

Brake bleeding kit

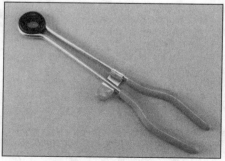
Torx key, socket and bit

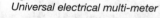
Hose clamp

Angular-tightening gauge

Special tools

The tools in this list are those which are not used regularly, are expensive to buy, or which need to be used in accordance with their manufacturers' instructions. Unless relatively difficult mechanical jobs are undertaken frequently, it will not be economic to buy many of these tools. Where this is the case, you could consider clubbing together with friends (or joining a motorists' club) to make a joint purchase, or borrowing the tools against a deposit from a local garage or tool hire specialist.

The following list contains only those tools and instruments freely available to the public, and not those special tools produced by the vehicle manufacturer specifically for its dealer network. You will find occasional references to these manufacturers' special tools in the text of this manual. Generally, an alternative method of doing the job without the vehicle manufacturers' special tool is given. However, sometimes there is no alternative to using them. Where this is the case and the relevant tool cannot be bought or borrowed, you will have to entrust the work to a dealer.

- ☐ *Angular-tightening gauge*
- ☐ *Valve spring compressor*
- ☐ *Valve grinding tool*
- ☐ *Piston ring compressor*
- ☐ *Piston ring removal/installation tool*
- ☐ *Cylinder bore hone*
- ☐ *Balljoint separator*
- ☐ *Coil spring compressors (where applicable)*
- ☐ *Two/three-legged hub and bearing puller*
- ☐ *Impact screwdriver*
- ☐ *Micrometer and/or vernier calipers*
- ☐ *Dial gauge*
- ☐ *Tachometer*
- ☐ *Fault code reader*
- ☐ *Cylinder compression gauge*
- ☐ *Hand-operated vacuum pump and gauge*
- ☐ *Clutch plate alignment set*
- ☐ *Brake shoe steady spring cup removal tool*
- ☐ *Bush and bearing removal/installation set*
- ☐ *Stud extractors*
- ☐ *Tap and die set*
- ☐ *Lifting tackle*

Buying tools

Reputable motor accessory shops and superstores often offer excellent quality tools at discount prices, so it pays to shop around.

Remember, you don't have to buy the most expensive items on the shelf, but it is always advisable to steer clear of the very cheap tools. Beware of 'bargains' offered on market stalls, on-line or at car boot sales. There are plenty of good tools around at reasonable prices, but always aim to purchase items which meet the relevant national safety standards. If in doubt, ask the proprietor or manager of the shop for advice before making a purchase.

Care and maintenance of tools

Having purchased a reasonable tool kit, it is necessary to keep the tools in a clean and serviceable condition. After use, always wipe off any dirt, grease and metal particles using a clean, dry cloth, before putting the tools away. Never leave them lying around after they have been used. A simple tool rack on the garage or workshop wall for items such as screwdrivers and pliers is a good idea. Store all normal spanners and sockets in a metal box. Any measuring instruments, gauges, meters, etc, must be carefully stored where they cannot be damaged or become rusty.

Take a little care when tools are used. Hammer heads inevitably become marked, and screwdrivers lose the keen edge on their blades from time to time. A little timely attention with emery cloth or a file will soon restore items like this to a good finish.

Working facilities

Not to be forgotten when discussing tools is the workshop itself. If anything more than routine maintenance is to be carried out, a suitable working area becomes essential.

It is appreciated that many an owner-mechanic is forced by circumstances to remove an engine or similar item without the benefit of a garage or workshop. Having done this, any repairs should always be done under the cover of a roof.

Wherever possible, any dismantling should be done on a clean, flat workbench or table at a suitable working height.

Any workbench needs a vice; one with a jaw opening of 100 mm is suitable for most jobs. As mentioned previously, some clean dry storage space is also required for tools, as well as for any lubricants, cleaning fluids, touch-up paints etc, which become necessary.

Another item which may be required, and which has a much more general usage, is an electric drill with a chuck capacity of at least 8 mm. This, together with a good range of twist drills, is virtually essential for fitting accessories.

Last, but not least, always keep a supply of old newspapers and clean, lint-free rags available, and try to keep any working area as clean as possible.

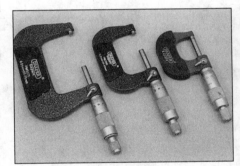
Micrometers

Dial test indicator ("dial gauge")

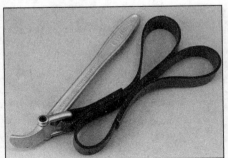
Oil filter removal tool (strap wrench type)

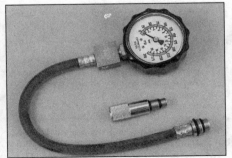
Compression tester

Fault code reader

This is a guide to getting your vehicle through the MOT test. Obviously it will not be possible to examine the vehicle to the same standard as the professional MOT tester. However, working through the following checks will enable you to identify any problem areas before submitting the vehicle for the test.

It has only been possible to summarise the test requirements here, based on the regulations in force at the time of printing. Test standards are becoming increasingly stringent, although there are some exemptions for older vehicles.

An assistant will be needed to help carry out some of these checks.

The checks have been sub-divided into four categories, as follows:

1 Checks carried out **FROM THE DRIVER'S SEAT**

2 Checks carried out **WITH THE VEHICLE ON THE GROUND**

3 Checks carried out **WITH THE VEHICLE RAISED AND THE WHEELS FREE TO TURN**

4 Checks carried out on **YOUR VEHICLE'S EXHAUST EMISSION SYSTEM**

---

1 Checks carried out **FROM THE DRIVER'S SEAT**

Handbrake

☐ Test the operation of the handbrake. Excessive travel (too many clicks) indicates incorrect brake or cable adjustment.
☐ Check that the handbrake cannot be released by tapping the lever sideways. Check the security of the lever mountings.

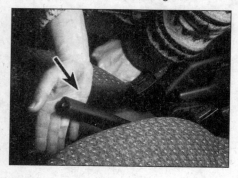

Footbrake

☐ Depress the brake pedal and check that it does not creep down to the floor, indicating a master cylinder fault. Release the pedal, wait a few seconds, then depress it again. If the pedal travels nearly to the floor before firm resistance is felt, brake adjustment or repair is necessary. If the pedal feels spongy, there is air in the hydraulic system which must be removed by bleeding.

☐ Check that the brake pedal is secure and in good condition. Check also for signs of fluid leaks on the pedal, floor or carpets, which would indicate failed seals in the brake master cylinder.
☐ Check the servo unit (when applicable) by operating the brake pedal several times, then keeping the pedal depressed and starting the engine. As the engine starts, the pedal will move down slightly. If not, the vacuum hose or the servo itself may be faulty.

Steering wheel and column

☐ Examine the steering wheel for fractures or looseness of the hub, spokes or rim.
☐ Move the steering wheel from side to side and then up and down. Check that the steering wheel is not loose on the column, indicating wear or a loose retaining nut. Continue moving the steering wheel as before, but also turn it slightly from left to right.
☐ Check that the steering wheel is not loose on the column, and that there is no abnormal

movement of the steering wheel, indicating wear in the column support bearings or couplings.

Windscreen, mirrors and sunvisor

☐ The windscreen must be free of cracks or other significant damage within the driver's field of view. (Small stone chips are acceptable.) Rear view mirrors must be secure, intact, and capable of being adjusted.

☐ The driver's sunvisor must be capable of being stored in the "up" position.

Seat belts and seats

Note: *The following checks are applicable to all seat belts, front and rear.*

☐ Examine the webbing of all the belts (including rear belts if fitted) for cuts, serious fraying or deterioration. Fasten and unfasten each belt to check the buckles. If applicable, check the retracting mechanism. Check the security of all seat belt mountings accessible from inside the vehicle.

☐ Seat belts with pre-tensioners, once activated, have a "flag" or similar showing on the seat belt stalk. This, in itself, is not a reason for test failure.

☐ The front seats themselves must be securely attached and the backrests must lock in the upright position.

Doors

☐ Both front doors must be able to be opened and closed from outside and inside, and must latch securely when closed.

2 Checks carried out WITH THE VEHICLE ON THE GROUND

Vehicle identification

☐ Number plates must be in good condition, secure and legible, with letters and numbers correctly spaced – spacing at (A) should be at least twice that at (B).

☐ The VIN plate and/or homologation plate must be legible.

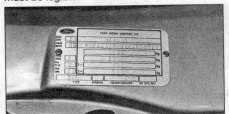

Electrical equipment

☐ Switch on the ignition and check the operation of the horn.

☐ Check the windscreen washers and wipers, examining the wiper blades; renew damaged or perished blades. Also check the operation of the stop-lights.

☐ Check the operation of the sidelights and number plate lights. The lenses and reflectors must be secure, clean and undamaged.

☐ Check the operation and alignment of the headlights. The headlight reflectors must not be tarnished and the lenses must be undamaged.

☐ Switch on the ignition and check the operation of the direction indicators (including the instrument panel tell-tale) and the hazard warning lights. Operation of the sidelights and stop-lights must not affect the indicators - if it does, the cause is usually a bad earth at the rear light cluster.

☐ Check the operation of the rear foglight(s), including the warning light on the instrument panel or in the switch.

☐ The ABS warning light must illuminate in accordance with the manufacturers' design. For most vehicles, the ABS warning light should illuminate when the ignition is switched on, and (if the system is operating properly) extinguish after a few seconds. Refer to the owner's handbook.

Footbrake

☐ Examine the master cylinder, brake pipes and servo unit for leaks, loose mountings, corrosion or other damage.

☐ The fluid reservoir must be secure and the fluid level must be between the upper (**A**) and lower (**B**) markings.

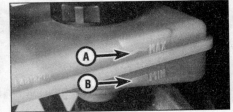

☐ Inspect both front brake flexible hoses for cracks or deterioration of the rubber. Turn the steering from lock to lock, and ensure that the hoses do not contact the wheel, tyre, or any part of the steering or suspension mechanism. With the brake pedal firmly depressed, check the hoses for bulges or leaks under pressure.

Steering and suspension

☐ Have your assistant turn the steering wheel from side to side slightly, up to the point where the steering gear just begins to transmit this movement to the roadwheels. Check for excessive free play between the steering wheel and the steering gear, indicating wear or insecurity of the steering column joints, the column-to-steering gear coupling, or the steering gear itself.

☐ Have your assistant turn the steering wheel more vigorously in each direction, so that the roadwheels just begin to turn. As this is done, examine all the steering joints, linkages, fittings and attachments. Renew any component that shows signs of wear or damage. On vehicles with power steering, check the security and condition of the steering pump, drivebelt and hoses.

☐ Check that the vehicle is standing level, and at approximately the correct ride height.

Shock absorbers

☐ Depress each corner of the vehicle in turn, then release it. The vehicle should rise and then settle in its normal position. If the vehicle continues to rise and fall, the shock absorber is defective. A shock absorber which has seized will also cause the vehicle to fail.

Exhaust system

☐ Start the engine. With your assistant holding a rag over the tailpipe, check the entire system for leaks. Repair or renew leaking sections.

3 Checks carried out **WITH THE VEHICLE RAISED AND THE WHEELS FREE TO TURN**

Jack up the front and rear of the vehicle, and securely support it on axle stands. Position the stands clear of the suspension assemblies. Ensure that the wheels are clear of the ground and that the steering can be turned from lock to lock.

Steering mechanism

☐ Have your assistant turn the steering from lock to lock. Check that the steering turns smoothly, and that no part of the steering mechanism, including a wheel or tyre, fouls any brake hose or pipe or any part of the body structure.
☐ Examine the steering rack rubber gaiters for damage or insecurity of the retaining clips. If power steering is fitted, check for signs of damage or leakage of the fluid hoses, pipes or connections. Also check for excessive stiffness or binding of the steering, a missing split pin or locking device, or severe corrosion of the body structure within 30 cm of any steering component attachment point.

Front and rear suspension and wheel bearings

☐ Starting at the front right-hand side, grasp the roadwheel at the 3 o'clock and 9 o'clock positions and rock gently but firmly. Check for free play or insecurity at the wheel bearings, suspension balljoints, or suspension mountings, pivots and attachments.
☐ Now grasp the wheel at the 12 o'clock and 6 o'clock positions and repeat the previous inspection. Spin the wheel, and check for roughness or tightness of the front wheel bearing.

☐ If excess free play is suspected at a component pivot point, this can be confirmed by using a large screwdriver or similar tool and levering between the mounting and the component attachment. This will confirm whether the wear is in the pivot bush, its retaining bolt, or in the mounting itself (the bolt holes can often become elongated).

☐ Carry out all the above checks at the other front wheel, and then at both rear wheels.

Springs and shock absorbers

☐ Examine the suspension struts (when applicable) for serious fluid leakage, corrosion, or damage to the casing. Also check the security of the mounting points.
☐ If coil springs are fitted, check that the spring ends locate in their seats, and that the spring is not corroded, cracked or broken.
☐ If leaf springs are fitted, check that all leaves are intact, that the axle is securely attached to each spring, and that there is no deterioration of the spring eye mountings, bushes, and shackles.

☐ The same general checks apply to vehicles fitted with other suspension types, such as torsion bars, hydraulic displacer units, etc. Ensure that all mountings and attachments are secure, that there are no signs of excessive wear, corrosion or damage, and (on hydraulic types) that there are no fluid leaks or damaged pipes.
☐ Inspect the shock absorbers for signs of serious fluid leakage. Check for wear of the mounting bushes or attachments, or damage to the body of the unit.

Driveshafts (fwd vehicles only)

☐ Rotate each front wheel in turn and inspect the constant velocity joint gaiters for splits or damage. Also check that each driveshaft is straight and undamaged.

Braking system

☐ If possible without dismantling, check brake pad wear and disc condition. Ensure that the friction lining material has not worn excessively, (A) and that the discs are not fractured, pitted, scored or badly worn (B).

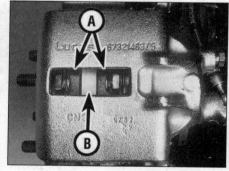

☐ Examine all the rigid brake pipes underneath the vehicle, and the flexible hose(s) at the rear. Look for corrosion, chafing or insecurity of the pipes, and for signs of bulging under pressure, chafing, splits or deterioration of the flexible hoses.
☐ Look for signs of fluid leaks at the brake calipers or on the brake backplates. Repair or renew leaking components.
☐ Slowly spin each wheel, while your assistant depresses and releases the footbrake. Ensure that each brake is operating and does not bind when the pedal is released.

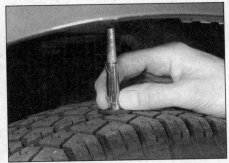

□ Examine the handbrake mechanism, checking for frayed or broken cables, excessive corrosion, or wear or insecurity of the linkage. Check that the mechanism works on each relevant wheel, and releases fully, without binding.

□ It is not possible to test brake efficiency without special equipment, but a road test can be carried out later to check that the vehicle pulls up in a straight line.

Fuel and exhaust systems

□ Inspect the fuel tank (including the filler cap), fuel pipes, hoses and unions. All components must be secure and free from leaks.

□ Examine the exhaust system over its entire length, checking for any damaged, broken or missing mountings, security of the retaining clamps and rust or corrosion.

Wheels and tyres

□ Examine the sidewalls and tread area of each tyre in turn. Check for cuts, tears, lumps, bulges, separation of the tread, and exposure of the ply or cord due to wear or damage. Check that the tyre bead is correctly seated on the wheel rim, that the valve is sound and properly seated, and that the wheel is not distorted or damaged.

□ Check that the tyres are of the correct size for the vehicle, that they are of the same size

and type on each axle, and that the pressures are correct.

□ Check the tyre tread depth. The legal minimum at the time of writing is 1.6 mm over at least three-quarters of the tread width. Abnormal tread wear may indicate incorrect front wheel alignment.

Body corrosion

□ Check the condition of the entire vehicle structure for signs of corrosion in load-bearing areas. (These include chassis box sections, side sills, cross-members, pillars, and all suspension, steering, braking system and seat belt mountings and anchorages.) Any corrosion which has seriously reduced the thickness of a load-bearing area is likely to cause the vehicle to fail. In this case professional repairs are likely to be needed.

□ Damage or corrosion which causes sharp or otherwise dangerous edges to be exposed will also cause the vehicle to fail.

4 Checks carried out on YOUR VEHICLE'S EXHAUST EMISSION SYSTEM

Petrol models

□ The engine should be warmed up, and running well (ignition system in good order, air filter element clean, etc).

□ Before testing, run the engine at around 2500 rpm for 20 seconds. Let the engine drop to idle, and watch for smoke from the exhaust. If the idle speed is too high, or if dense blue or black smoke emerges for more than 5 seconds, the vehicle will fail. Typically, blue smoke signifies oil burning (engine wear); black smoke means unburnt fuel (dirty air cleaner element, or other fuel system fault).

□ An exhaust gas analyser for measuring carbon monoxide (CO) and hydrocarbons (HC) is now needed. If one cannot be hired or borrowed, have a local garage perform the check.

CO emissions (mixture)

□ The MOT tester has access to the CO limits for all vehicles. The CO level is measured at idle speed, and at 'fast idle' (2500 to 3000 rpm). The following limits are given as a general guide:

At idle speed – Less than 0.5% CO
At 'fast idle' – Less than 0.3% CO
Lambda reading – 0.97 to 1.03

□ If the CO level is too high, this may point to poor maintenance, a fuel injection system problem, faulty lambda (oxygen) sensor or catalytic converter. Try an injector cleaning treatment, and check the vehicle's ECU for fault codes.

HC emissions

□ The MOT tester has access to HC limits for all vehicles. The HC level is measured at 'fast idle' (2500 to 3000 rpm). The following limits are given as a general guide:

At 'fast idle' – Less then 200 ppm

□ Excessive HC emissions are typically caused by oil being burnt (worn engine), or by a blocked crankcase ventilation system ('breather'). If the engine oil is old and thin, an oil change may help. If the engine is running badly, check the vehicle's ECU for fault codes.

Diesel models

□ The only emission test for diesel engines is measuring exhaust smoke density, using a calibrated smoke meter. The test involves accelerating the engine at least 3 times to its maximum unloaded speed.

Note: *On engines with a timing belt, it is VITAL that the belt is in good condition before the test is carried out.*

□ With the engine warmed up, it is first purged by running at around 2500 rpm for 20 seconds. A governor check is then carried out, by slowly accelerating the engine to its maximum speed. After this, the smoke meter is connected, and the engine is accelerated quickly to maximum speed three times. If the smoke density is less than the limits given below, the vehicle will pass:

Non-turbo vehicles: 2.5m-1
Turbocharged vehicles: 3.0m-1

□ If excess smoke is produced, try fitting a new air cleaner element, or using an injector cleaning treatment. If the engine is running badly, where applicable, check the vehicle's ECU for fault codes. Also check the vehicle's EGR system, where applicable. At high mileages, the injectors may require professional attention.

Engine

- ☐ Engine fails to rotate when attempting to start
- ☐ Engine rotates, but will not start
- ☐ Engine difficult to start when cold
- ☐ Engine difficult to start when hot
- ☐ Starter motor noisy or excessively-rough in engagement
- ☐ Engine starts, but stops immediately
- ☐ Engine idles erratically
- ☐ Engine misfires at idle speed
- ☐ Engine misfires throughout the driving speed range
- ☐ Engine hesitates on acceleration
- ☐ Engine stalls
- ☐ Engine lacks power
- ☐ Engine backfires
- ☐ Oil pressure warning light illuminated with engine running
- ☐ Engine runs-on after switching off
- ☐ Engine noises

Cooling system

- ☐ Overheating
- ☐ Overcooling
- ☐ External coolant leakage
- ☐ Internal coolant leakage
- ☐ Corrosion

Fuel and exhaust systems

- ☐ Excessive fuel consumption
- ☐ Fuel leakage and/or fuel odour
- ☐ Excessive noise or fumes from exhaust system

Clutch

- ☐ Pedal travels to floor – no pressure or very little resistance
- ☐ Clutch fails to disengage (unable to select gears)
- ☐ Clutch slips (engine speed increases, with no increase in vehicle speed)
- ☐ Judder as clutch is engaged
- ☐ Noise when depressing or releasing clutch pedal

Manual and Easytronic transmissions

- ☐ Noisy in neutral with engine running
- ☐ Noisy in one particular gear
- ☐ Difficulty engaging gears
- ☐ Jumps out of gear
- ☐ Vibration
- ☐ Lubricant leaks

Automatic transmission

- ☐ Fluid leakage
- ☐ Transmission fluid brown, or has burned smell
- ☐ General gear selection problems
- ☐ Transmission will not downshift (kickdown) with accelerator pedal fully depressed
- ☐ Engine will not start in any gear, or starts in gears other than Park or Neutral
- ☐ Transmission slips, shifts roughly, is noisy, or has no drive in forward or reverse gears

Driveshafts

- ☐ Vibration when accelerating or decelerating
- ☐ Clicking or knocking noise on turns (at slow speed on full-lock)

Braking system

- ☐ Vehicle pulls to one side under braking
- ☐ Noise (grinding or high-pitched squeal) when brakes applied
- ☐ Excessive brake pedal travel
- ☐ Brake pedal feels spongy when depressed
- ☐ Excessive brake pedal effort required to stop vehicle
- ☐ Judder felt through brake pedal or steering wheel when braking
- ☐ Brakes binding
- ☐ Rear wheels locking under normal braking

Suspension and steering

- ☐ Vehicle pulls to one side
- ☐ Wheel wobble and vibration
- ☐ Excessive pitching and/or rolling around corners, or during braking
- ☐ Wandering or general instability
- ☐ Excessively-stiff steering
- ☐ Excessive play in steering
- ☐ Lack of power assistance
- ☐ Tyre wear excessive

Electrical system

- ☐ Battery will not hold a charge for more than a few days
- ☐ Ignition/no-charge warning light remains illuminated with engine running
- ☐ Ignition/no-charge warning light fails to come on
- ☐ Lights inoperative
- ☐ Instrument readings inaccurate or erratic
- ☐ Horn inoperative, or unsatisfactory in operation
- ☐ Windscreen wipers inoperative, or unsatisfactory in operation
- ☐ Windscreen washers inoperative, or unsatisfactory in operation
- ☐ Electric windows inoperative, or unsatisfactory in operation
- ☐ Central locking system inoperative, or unsatisfactory in operation

Introduction

The vehicle owner who does his or her own maintenance according to the recommended service schedules should not have to use this section of the manual very often. Modern component reliability is such that, provided those items subject to wear or deterioration are inspected or renewed at the specified intervals, sudden failure is comparatively rare. Faults do not usually just happen as a result of sudden failure, but develop over a period of time. Major mechanical failures in particular are usually preceded by characteristic symptoms over hundreds or even thousands of miles. Those components which do occasionally fail without warning are often small and easily carried in the vehicle.

With any fault-finding, the first step is to decide where to begin investigations. Sometimes this is obvious, but on other occasions, a little detective work will be necessary. The owner who makes half a dozen haphazard adjustments or replacements may be successful in curing a fault (or its symptoms), but will be none the wiser if the fault recurs, and ultimately may have spent more time and money than was necessary. A calm and logical approach will be found to be more satisfactory in the long run. Always take into account any warning signs or abnormalities that may have been noticed in the period preceding the fault – power loss, high or low gauge readings, unusual smells,

etc – and remember that failure of components such as fuses or spark plugs may only be pointers to some underlying fault.

The pages which follow provide an easy-reference guide to the more common problems which may occur during the operation of the vehicle. These problems and their possible causes are grouped under headings denoting various components or systems, such as Engine, Cooling system, etc. The general Chapter which deals with the problem is also shown in brackets; refer to the relevant part of that Chapter for system-specific information. Whatever the fault, certain basic principles apply. These are as follows:

Verify the fault. This is simply a matter of

being sure that you know what the symptoms are before starting work. This is particularly important if you are investigating a fault for someone else, who may not have described it very accurately.

Don't overlook the obvious. For example, if the vehicle won't start, is there fuel in the tank? (Don't take anyone else's word on this particular point, and don't trust the fuel gauge either!) If an electrical fault is indicated, look for loose or broken wires before digging out the test gear.

Cure the disease, not the symptom. Substituting a flat battery with a fully-charged one will get you off the hard shoulder, but if the underlying cause is not attended to, the new battery will go the same way. Similarly, changing oil-fouled spark plugs for a new set will get you moving again, but remember that the reason for the fouling (if it wasn't simply an incorrect grade of plug) will have to be established and corrected.

Don't take anything for granted. Particularly, don't forget that a 'new' component may itself be defective (especially if it's been rattling around in the boot for months), and don't leave components out of a fault diagnosis sequence just because they are new or recently-fitted. When you do finally diagnose a difficult fault, you'll probably realise that all the evidence was there from the start.

Consider what work, if any, has recently been carried out. Many faults arise through careless or hurried work. For instance, if any work has been performed under the bonnet, could some of the wiring have been dislodged or incorrectly routed, or a hose trapped? Have all the fasteners been properly tightened? Were new, genuine parts and new gaskets used? There is often a certain amount of detective work to be done in this case, as an apparently-unrelated task can have far-reaching consequences.

Diesel fault diagnosis

The majority of starting problems on small diesel engines are electrical in origin. The mechanic who is familiar with petrol engines but less so with diesel may be inclined to view the diesel's injectors and pump in the same light as the spark plugs and distributor, but this is generally a mistake.

When investigating complaints of difficult starting for someone else, make sure that the correct starting procedure is understood and is being followed. Some drivers are unaware of the significance of the preheating warning light – many modern engines are sufficiently forgiving for this not to matter in mild weather, but with the onset of winter, problems begin.

As a rule of thumb, if the engine is difficult to start but runs well when it has finally got going, the problem is electrical (battery, starter motor or preheating system). If poor performance is combined with difficult starting, the problem is likely to be in the fuel system. The low-pressure (supply) side of the fuel system should be checked before suspecting the injectors and high-pressure pump. The most common fuel supply problem is air getting into the system, and any pipe from the fuel tank forwards must be scrutinised if air leakage is suspected. Normally the pump is the last item to suspect, since unless it has been tampered with, there is no reason for it to be at fault.

Engine

Engine fails to rotate when attempting to start

☐ Battery terminal connections loose or corroded (see *Weekly checks*)
☐ Battery discharged or faulty (Chapter 5A)
☐ Broken, loose or disconnected wiring in the starting circuit (Chapter 5A)
☐ Defective starter solenoid or ignition switch (Chapter 5A or 12)
☐ Defective starter motor (Chapter 5A)
☐ Starter pinion or flywheel ring gear teeth loose or broken (Chapter 2A, 2B, 2C, 2D or 5A)
☐ Engine earth strap broken or disconnected (Chapter 5A)
☐ Engine suffering 'hydraulic lock' (eg from water drawn into the engine after traversing flooded roads, or from a serious internal coolant leak) – consult a main dealer for advice
☐ Automatic transmission not in position P or N (Chapter 7B)

Engine rotates, but will not start

☐ Fuel tank empty
☐ Battery discharged (engine rotates slowly) (Chapter 5A)
☐ Battery terminal connections loose or corroded (see *Weekly checks*)
☐ Ignition components damp or damaged – petrol models (Chapter 1A or 5B)
☐ Immobiliser fault, or 'uncoded' ignition key being used (Chapter 12 or Roadside repairs)
☐ Broken, loose or disconnected wiring in the ignition circuit – petrol models (Chapter 1A or 5B)
☐ Worn, faulty or incorrectly-gapped spark plugs – petrol models (Chapter 1A)
☐ Preheating system faulty – diesel models (Chapter 5A)
☐ Fuel injection/engine management system fault (Chapter 4A, 4B or 4C)
☐ Air in fuel system – diesel models (Chapter 4B)
☐ Major mechanical failure (eg timing /beltchain snapped) (Chapter 2A, 2B, 2C or 2D)

Engine difficult to start when cold

☐ Battery discharged (Chapter 5A)
☐ Battery terminal connections loose or corroded (see *Weekly checks*)

☐ Worn, faulty or incorrectly-gapped spark plugs – petrol models (Chapter 1A)
☐ Other ignition system fault – petrol models (Chapter 1A or 5B)
☐ Preheating system faulty – diesel models (Chapter 5A)
☐ Fuel injection/engine management system fault (Chapter 4A, 4B or 4C)
☐ Wrong grade of engine oil used (*Weekly checks*, Chapter 1A or 1B)
☐ Low cylinder compression (Chapter 2A, 2B, 2C or 2D)

Engine difficult to start when hot

☐ Air filter element dirty or clogged (Chapter 1A or 1B)
☐ Fuel injection/engine management system fault (Chapter 4A, 4B or 4C)
☐ Low cylinder compression (Chapter 2A, 2B, 2C or 2D)

Starter motor noisy or excessively-rough in engagement

☐ Starter pinion or flywheel ring gear teeth loose or broken (Chapter 2A, 2B, 2C 2D or 5A)
☐ Starter motor mounting bolts loose or missing (Chapter 5A)
☐ Starter motor internal components worn or damaged (Chapter 5A)

Engine starts, but stops immediately

☐ Loose or faulty electrical connections in the ignition circuit – petrol models (Chapter 1A or 5B)
☐ Vacuum leak at the throttle housing or inlet manifold – petrol models (Chapter 4A)
☐ Blocked injectors/fuel injection system fault (Chapter 4A or 4B)

Engine idles erratically

☐ Air filter element clogged (Chapter 1A or 1B)
☐ Vacuum leak at the throttle housing, inlet manifold or associated hoses – petrol models (Chapter 4A)
☐ Worn, faulty or incorrectly-gapped spark plugs – petrol models (Chapter 1A)
☐ Uneven or low cylinder compression (Chapter 2A, 2B, 2C or 2D)
☐ Camshaft lobes worn (Chapter 2A, 2B, 2C or 2D)
☐ Blocked injectors/fuel injection system fault (Chapter 4A or 4B)

Engine (continued)

Engine misfires at idle speed

- [ ] Worn, faulty or incorrectly-gapped spark plugs – petrol models (Chapter 1A)
- [ ] Vacuum leak at the throttle housing, inlet manifold or associated hoses – petrol models (Chapter 4A)
- [ ] Blocked injectors/fuel injection system fault (Chapter 4A or 4B)
- [ ] Faulty injector(s) – diesel models (Chapter 4B)
- [ ] Uneven or low cylinder compression (Chapter 2A, 2B, 2C or 2D)
- [ ] Disconnected, leaking, or perished crankcase ventilation hoses (Chapter 4C)

Engine misfires throughout the driving speed range

- [ ] Fuel filter choked (Chapter 1A or 1B)
- [ ] Fuel pump faulty, or delivery pressure low – petrol models (Chapter 4A)
- [ ] Fuel tank vent blocked, or fuel pipes restricted (Chapter 4A, 4B or 4C)
- [ ] Vacuum leak at the throttle housing, inlet manifold or associated hoses – petrol models (Chapter 4A)
- [ ] Worn, faulty or incorrectly-gapped spark plugs – petrol models (Chapter 1A)
- [ ] Faulty injector(s) – diesel models (Chapter 4B)
- [ ] Faulty ignition module – petrol models (Chapter 5B)
- [ ] Uneven or low cylinder compression (Chapter 2A, 2B, 2C or 2D)
- [ ] Blocked injector/fuel injection system fault (Chapter 4A or 4B)
- [ ] Blocked catalytic converter (Chapter 4A or 4B)
- [ ] Engine overheating (Chapter 3)

Engine hesitates on acceleration

- [ ] Worn, faulty or incorrectly-gapped spark plugs – petrol models (Chapter 1A)
- [ ] Vacuum leak at the throttle housing, inlet manifold or associated hoses – petrol models (Chapter 4A)
- [ ] Blocked injectors/fuel injection system fault (Chapter 4A or 4B)
- [ ] Faulty injector(s) – diesel models (Chapter 4B)

Engine stalls

- [ ] Vacuum leak at the throttle housing, inlet manifold or associated hoses – petrol models (Chapter 4A)
- [ ] Fuel filter choked (Chapter 1A or 1B)
- [ ] Fuel pump faulty, or delivery pressure low – petrol models (Chapter 4A)
- [ ] Fuel tank vent blocked, or fuel pipes restricted (Chapter 4A, 4B or 4C)
- [ ] Blocked injectors/fuel injection system fault (Chapter 4A or 4B)
- [ ] Faulty injector(s) – diesel models (Chapter 4B)

Engine lacks power

- [ ] Air filter element blocked (Chapter 1A or 1B)
- [ ] Fuel filter choked (Chapter 1A or 1B)
- [ ] Fuel pipes blocked or restricted (Chapter 4A, 4B or 4C)
- [ ] Worn, faulty or incorrectly-gapped spark plugs – petrol models (Chapter 1A)
- [ ] Engine overheating (Chapter 3)
- [ ] Accelerator pedal position sensor faulty (Chapter 4A or 4B)
- [ ] Vacuum leak at the throttle housing, inlet manifold or associated hoses – petrol models (Chapter 4A)
- [ ] Blocked injectors/fuel injection system fault (Chapter 4A or 4B)
- [ ] Faulty injector(s) – diesel models (Chapter 4B)
- [ ] Fuel pump faulty, or delivery pressure low – petrol models (Chapter 4A)
- [ ] Uneven or low cylinder compression (Chapter 2A, 2B, 2C or 2D)
- [ ] Blocked catalytic converter (Chapter 4A or 4B)
- [ ] Brakes binding (Chapter 1A, 1B or 9)
- [ ] Clutch slipping (Chapter 6)

Engine backfires

- [ ] Vacuum leak at the throttle housing, inlet manifold or associated hoses – petrol models (Chapter 4A)
- [ ] Blocked injectors/fuel injection system fault (Chapter 4A or 4B)
- [ ] Blocked catalytic converter (Chapter 4A or 4B)
- [ ] Faulty ignition module – petrol models (Chapter 5B)

Oil pressure warning light illuminated with engine running

- [ ] Low oil level, or incorrect oil grade (see Weekly checks)
- [ ] Faulty oil pressure sensor, or wiring damaged (Chapter 2A, 2B, 2C or 2D)
- [ ] Worn engine bearings and/or oil pump (Chapter 2A, 2B, 2C, 2D or 2E)
- [ ] High engine operating temperature (Chapter 3)
- [ ] Oil pump pressure relief valve defective (Chapter 2A, 2B, 2C or 2D)
- [ ] Oil pump pick-up strainer clogged (Chapter 2A, 2B, 2C or 2D)

Engine runs-on after switching off

- [ ] Excessive carbon build-up in engine (Chapter 2A, 2B, 2C, 2D or 2E)
- [ ] High engine operating temperature (Chapter 3)
- [ ] Fuel injection/engine management system fault (Chapter 4A, 4B or 4C)

Engine noises

Pre-ignition (pinking) or knocking during acceleration or under load

- [ ] Ignition system/engine management system fault – petrol models (Chapter 1A, 4A or 5B)
- [ ] Incorrect grade of spark plug – petrol models (Chapter 1A)
- [ ] Incorrect grade of fuel (Chapter 4A or 4B)
- [ ] Knock sensor faulty – petrol models (Chapter 4A or 5B)
- [ ] Vacuum leak at the throttle housing, inlet manifold or associated hoses – petrol models (Chapter 4A)
- [ ] Excessive carbon build-up in engine (Chapter 2A, 2B, 2C, 2D or 2E)
- [ ] Fuel injection/engine management system fault (Chapter 4A, 4B or 4C)
- [ ] Faulty injector(s) – diesel models (Chapter 4B)

Whistling or wheezing noises

- [ ] Leaking inlet manifold or throttle housing gasket – petrol models (Chapter 4A)
- [ ] Leaking exhaust manifold gasket or pipe-to-manifold joint (Chapter 4A or 4B)
- [ ] Leaking vacuum hose (Chapter 4A, 4B, 4C or 9)
- [ ] Blowing cylinder head gasket (Chapter 2A, 2B, 2C or 2D)
- [ ] Partially blocked or leaking crankcase ventilation system (Chapter 4C)

Tapping or rattling noises

- [ ] Worn valve gear or camshaft (Chapter 2A, 2B, 2C or 2D)
- [ ] Ancillary component fault (coolant pump, alternator, etc) (Chapter 3, 5A, etc)

Knocking or thumping noises

- [ ] Worn big-end bearings (regular heavy knocking, perhaps less under load) (Chapter 2E)
- [ ] Worn main bearings (rumbling and knocking, perhaps worsening under load) (Chapter 2E)
- [ ] Piston slap – most noticeable when cold, caused by piston/bore wear (Chapter 2E)
- [ ] Ancillary component fault (coolant pump, alternator, etc) (Chapter 3, 5A, etc)
- [ ] Engine mountings worn or defective (Chapter 2A, 2B, 2C or 2D)
- [ ] Front suspension or steering components worn (Chapter 10)

Cooling system

Overheating

☐ Insufficient coolant in system (see *Weekly checks*)
☐ Thermostat faulty (Chapter 3)
☐ Radiator core blocked, or grille restricted (Chapter 3)
☐ Cooling fan or cooling module faulty (Chapter 3)
☐ Inaccurate coolant temperature sensor (Chapter 3)
☐ Airlock in cooling system (Chapter 1A, 1B or 3)
☐ Expansion tank pressure cap faulty (Chapter 3)
☐ Engine management system fault (Chapter 4A, 4B or 4C)

Overcooling

☐ Thermostat faulty (Chapter 3)
☐ Inaccurate coolant temperature sensor (Chapter 3)
☐ Cooling fan faulty (Chapter 3)
☐ Engine management system fault (Chapter 4A, 4B or 4C)

External coolant leakage

☐ Deteriorated or damaged hoses or hose clips (Chapter 1A or 1B)
☐ Radiator core or heater matrix leaking (Chapter 3)
☐ Expansion tank pressure cap faulty (Chapter 1A or 1B)
☐ Coolant pump internal seal leaking (Chapter 3)
☐ Coolant pump gasket leaking (Chapter 3)
☐ Boiling due to overheating (Chapter 3)
☐ Cylinder block core plug leaking (Chapter 2E)

Internal coolant leakage

☐ Leaking cylinder head gasket (Chapter 2A, 2B, 2C or 2D)
☐ Cracked cylinder head or cylinder block (Chapter 2A, 2B, 2C, 2D or 2E)

Corrosion

☐ Infrequent draining and flushing (Chapter 1A or 1B)
☐ Incorrect coolant mixture or inappropriate coolant type (see *Weekly checks*)

Fuel and exhaust systems

Excessive fuel consumption

☐ Air filter element dirty or clogged (Chapter 1A or 1B)
☐ Fuel injection system fault (Chapter 4A or 4B)
☐ Engine management system fault (Chapter 4A, 4B or 4C)
☐ Crankcase ventilation system blocked (Chapter 4C)
☐ Tyres under-inflated (see *Weekly checks*)
☐ Brakes binding (Chapter 1A, 1B or 9)
☐ Fuel leak, causing apparent high consumption (Chapter 1A, 1B, 4A, 4B or 4C)

Fuel leakage and/or fuel odour

☐ Damaged or corroded fuel tank, pipes or connections (Chapter 4A or 4B)
☐ Evaporative emissions system fault – petrol models (Chapter 4C)

Excessive noise or fumes from exhaust system

☐ Leaking exhaust system or manifold joints (Chapter 1A, 1B, 4A or 4B)
☐ Leaking, corroded or damaged silencers or pipe (Chapter 1A, 1B, 4A or 4B)
☐ Broken mountings causing body or suspension contact (Chapter 1A, 1B, 4A or 4B)

Clutch

Pedal travels to floor – no pressure or very little resistance

☐ Air in hydraulic system/faulty master or release cylinder (Chapter 6)
☐ Faulty hydraulic release system (Chapter 6)
☐ Clutch pedal return spring detached or broken (Chapter 6)
☐ Faulty clutch release cylinder (Chapter 6)
☐ Broken diaphragm spring in clutch pressure plate (Chapter 6)

Clutch fails to disengage (unable to select gears)

☐ Air in hydraulic system/faulty master or release cylinder (Chapter 6)
☐ Faulty hydraulic release system (Chapter 6)
☐ Clutch disc sticking on transmission input shaft splines (Chapter 6)
☐ Clutch disc sticking to flywheel or pressure plate (Chapter 6)
☐ Faulty pressure plate assembly (Chapter 6)
☐ Clutch release mechanism worn or incorrectly assembled (Chapter 6)

Clutch slips (engine speed increases, with no increase in vehicle speed)

☐ Faulty hydraulic release system (Chapter 6)
☐ Clutch disc linings excessively worn (Chapter 6)
☐ Clutch disc linings contaminated with oil or grease (Chapter 6)
☐ Faulty pressure plate or weak diaphragm spring (Chapter 6)

Judder as clutch is engaged

☐ Clutch disc linings contaminated with oil or grease (Chapter 6)
☐ Clutch disc linings excessively worn (Chapter 6)
☐ Faulty or distorted pressure plate or diaphragm spring (Chapter 6).
☐ Worn or loose engine or transmission mountings (Chapter 2A, 2B, 2C or 2D)
☐ Clutch disc hub or transmission input shaft splines worn (Chapter 6)

Noise when depressing or releasing clutch pedal

☐ Faulty clutch release cylinder (Chapter 6)
☐ Worn or dry clutch pedal bushes (Chapter 6)
☐ Faulty pressure plate assembly (Chapter 6)
☐ Pressure plate diaphragm spring broken (Chapter 6)
☐ Broken clutch disc cushioning springs (Chapter 6)

Manual and Easytronic transmissions

Note: *Fault finding for the Easytronic transmission should be entrusted to a Vauxhall/Opel dealer.*

Noisy in neutral with engine running

☐ Lack of oil (Chapter 7A)
☐ Input shaft bearings worn (noise apparent with clutch pedal released, but not when depressed) (Chapter 7A)*
☐ Clutch release cylinder faulty (noise apparent with clutch pedal depressed, possibly less when released) (Chapter 6)

Noisy in one particular gear

☐ Worn, damaged or chipped gear teeth (Chapter 7A)*

Difficulty engaging gears

☐ Clutch fault (Chapter 6)
☐ Worn, damaged, or poorly-adjusted gearchange (Chapter 7A)
☐ Lack of oil (Chapter 7A)
☐ Worn synchroniser units (Chapter 7A)*

Jumps out of gear

☐ Worn, damaged, or poorly-adjusted gearchange (Chapter 7A)
☐ Worn synchroniser units (Chapter 7A)*
☐ Worn selector forks (Chapter 7A)*

Vibration

☐ Lack of oil (Chapter 7A)
☐ Worn bearings (Chapter 7A)*

Lubricant leaks

☐ Leaking driveshaft or selector shaft oil seal (Chapter 7A)
☐ Leaking housing joint (Chapter 7A)*
☐ Leaking input shaft oil seal (Chapter 7A)*

Although the corrective action necessary to remedy the symptoms described is beyond the scope of the home mechanic, the above information should be helpful in isolating the cause of the condition, so that the owner can communicate clearly with a professional mechanic.

Automatic transmission

Note: *Due to the complexity of the automatic transmission, it is difficult for the home mechanic to properly diagnose and service this unit. For problems other than the following, the vehicle should be taken to a dealer service department or automatic transmission specialist. Do not be too hasty in removing the transmission if a fault is suspected, as most of the testing is carried out with the unit still fitted. Remember that, besides the sensors specific to the transmission, many of the engine management system sensors described in the relevant Part of Chapter 4 are essential to the correct operation of the transmission.*

Fluid leakage

☐ Automatic transmission fluid is usually dark red in colour. Fluid leaks should not be confused with engine oil, which can easily be blown onto the transmission by airflow.
☐ To determine the source of a leak, first remove all built-up dirt and grime from the transmission housing and surrounding areas using a degreasing agent, or by steam-cleaning. Drive the vehicle at low speed, so airflow will not blow the leak far from its source. Raise and support the vehicle, and determine where the leak is coming from. The following are common areas of leakage:
a) *Fluid pan*
b) *Dipstick tube (Chapter 7B)*
c) *Transmission-to-fluid cooler unions (Chapter 7B)*

Transmission fluid brown, or has burned smell

☐ Transmission fluid level low (Chapter 7B)

General gear selection problems

☐ Chapter 7B deals with checking the selector cable on automatic transmissions. The following are common problems which may be caused by a faulty cable or sensor:

a) *Engine starting in gears other than Park or Neutral.*
b) *Indicator panel indicating a gear other than the one actually being used.*
c) *Vehicle moves when in Park or Neutral.*
d) *Poor gear shift quality or erratic gear changes.*

Transmission will not downshift (kickdown) with accelerator pedal fully depressed

☐ Low transmission fluid level (Chapter 7B)
☐ Engine management system fault (Chapter 4A or 4B)
☐ Faulty transmission sensor or wiring (Chapter 7B)
☐ Incorrect selector cable adjustment (Chapter 7B)

Engine will not start in any gear, or starts in gears other than Park or Neutral

☐ Faulty transmission sensor or wiring (Chapter 7B)
☐ Engine management system fault (Chapter 4A or 4B)
☐ Incorrect selector cable adjustment (Chapter 7B)

Transmission slips, shifts roughly, is noisy, or has no drive in forward or reverse gears

☐ Transmission fluid level low (Chapter 7B)
☐ Faulty transmission sensor or wiring (Chapter 7B)
☐ Engine management system fault (Chapter 4A or 4B)

Note: *There are many probable causes for the above problems, but diagnosing and correcting them is considered beyond the scope of this manual. Having checked the fluid level and all the wiring as far as possible, a dealer or transmission specialist should be consulted if the problem persists.*

Driveshafts

Vibration when accelerating or decelerating

- [ ] Worn inner constant velocity joint (Chapter 8)
- [ ] Bent or distorted driveshaft (Chapter 8)
- [ ] Worn intermediate shaft bearing (Chapter 8)

Clicking or knocking noise on turns (at slow speed on full-lock)

- [ ] Worn outer constant velocity joint (Chapter 8)
- [ ] Lack of constant velocity joint lubricant, possibly due to damaged gaiter (Chapter 8)

Braking system

Note: *Before assuming that a brake problem exists, make sure that the tyres are in good condition and correctly inflated, that the front wheel alignment is correct, and that the vehicle is not loaded with weight in an unequal manner. Apart from checking the condition of all pipe and hose connections, any faults occurring on the anti-lock braking system should be referred to a Vauxhall/Opel dealer for diagnosis.*

Vehicle pulls to one side under braking

- [ ] Worn, defective, damaged or contaminated brake pads on one side (Chapter 1A, 1B or 9)
- [ ] Seized or partially-seized brake caliper piston (Chapter 1A, 1B or 9)
- [ ] A mixture of brake pad lining materials fitted between sides (Chapter 1A, 1B or 9)
- [ ] Brake caliper mounting bolts loose (Chapter 9)
- [ ] Worn or damaged steering or suspension components (Chapter 1A, 1B or 10)

Noise (grinding or high-pitched squeal) when brakes applied

- [ ] Brake pad wear sensor indicating worn brake pads (Chapter 1A, 1B or 9)
- [ ] Brake pad friction lining material worn down to metal backing (Chapter 1A, 1B or 9)
- [ ] Excessive corrosion of brake disc (may be apparent after the vehicle has been standing for some time (Chapter 1A, 1B or 9)
- [ ] Foreign object (stone chipping, etc) trapped between brake disc and shield (Chapter 1A, 1B or 9)

Excessive brake pedal travel

- [ ] Faulty master cylinder (Chapter 9)
- [ ] Air in hydraulic system (Chapter 1A, 1B, 6 or 9)
- [ ] Faulty vacuum servo unit (Chapter 9)

Brake pedal feels spongy when depressed

- [ ] Air in hydraulic system (Chapter 1A, 1B, 6 or 9)
- [ ] Deteriorated flexible rubber brake hoses (Chapter 1A, 1B or 9)
- [ ] Master cylinder mounting nuts loose (Chapter 9)
- [ ] Faulty master cylinder (Chapter 9)

Excessive brake pedal effort required to stop vehicle

- [ ] Faulty vacuum servo unit (Chapter 9)
- [ ] Faulty vacuum pump – diesel models (Chapter 9)
- [ ] Disconnected, damaged or insecure brake servo vacuum hose (Chapter 9)
- [ ] Primary or secondary hydraulic circuit failure (Chapter 9)
- [ ] Seized brake caliper piston (Chapter 9)
- [ ] Brake pads incorrectly fitted (Chapter 9)
- [ ] Incorrect grade of brake pads fitted (Chapter 9)
- [ ] Brake pad linings contaminated (Chapter 1A, 1B or 9)

Judder felt through brake pedal or steering wheel when braking

Note: *Under heavy braking on vehicles equipped with ABS, vibration may be felt through the brake pedal. This is a normal feature of ABS operation, and does not constitute a fault*

- [ ] Excessive run-out or distortion of discs (Chapter 1A, 1B or 9)
- [ ] Brake pad linings worn (Chapter 1A, 1B or 9)
- [ ] Brake caliper mounting bolts loose (Chapter 9)
- [ ] Wear in suspension or steering components or mountings (Chapter 1A, 1B or 10)
- [ ] Front wheels out of balance (see *Weekly checks*)

Brakes binding

- [ ] Seized brake caliper piston (Chapter 9)
- [ ] Faulty master cylinder (Chapter 9)

Rear wheels locking under normal braking

- [ ] Rear brake pad linings contaminated or damaged (Chapter 1 or 9)
- [ ] Rear brake discs warped (Chapter 1 or 9)

Suspension and steering

Note: *Before diagnosing suspension or steering faults, be sure that the trouble is not due to incorrect tyre pressures, mixtures of tyre types, or binding brakes.*

Vehicle pulls to one side

- ☐ Defective tyre (see *Weekly checks*)
- ☐ Excessive wear in suspension or steering components (Chapter 1A, 1B or 10)
- ☐ Incorrect front wheel alignment (Chapter 10)
- ☐ Accident damage to steering or suspension components (Chapter 1A or 1B)

Wheel wobble and vibration

- ☐ Front wheels out of balance (vibration felt mainly through the steering wheel) (see *Weekly checks*)
- ☐ Rear wheels out of balance (vibration felt throughout the vehicle) (see *Weekly checks*)
- ☐ Roadwheels damaged or distorted (see *Weekly checks*)
- ☐ Faulty or damaged tyre (see *Weekly checks*)
- ☐ Worn steering or suspension joints, bushes or components (Chapter 1A, 1B or 10)
- ☐ Wheel bolts loose (Chapter 1A or 1B)

Excessive pitching and/or rolling around corners, or during braking

- ☐ Defective shock absorbers (Chapter 1A, 1B or 10)
- ☐ Broken or weak spring and/or suspension component (Chapter 1A, 1B or 10)
- ☐ Worn or damaged anti-roll bar or mountings (Chapter 1A, 1B or 10)

Wandering or general instability

- ☐ Incorrect front wheel alignment (Chapter 10)
- ☐ Worn steering or suspension joints, bushes or components (Chapter 1A, 1B or 10)
- ☐ Roadwheels out of balance (see *Weekly checks*)
- ☐ Faulty or damaged tyre (see *Weekly checks*)
- ☐ Wheel bolts loose (Chapter 1A or 1B)
- ☐ Defective shock absorbers (Chapter 1A, 1B or 10)
- ☐ Power steering system fault (Chapter 10)

Excessively-stiff steering

- ☐ Seized steering linkage balljoint or suspension balljoint (Chapter 1A, 1B or 10)
- ☐ Incorrect front wheel alignment (Chapter 10)
- ☐ Steering rack damaged (Chapter 10)
- ☐ Power steering system fault (Chapter 10)

Excessive play in steering

- ☐ Worn steering column/intermediate shaft joints (Chapter 10)
- ☐ Worn track rod balljoints (Chapter 1A, 1B or 10)
- ☐ Worn steering rack (Chapter 10)
- ☐ Worn steering or suspension joints, bushes or components (Chapter 1A, 1B or 10)

Lack of power assistance

- ☐ Power steering system fault (Chapter 10)
- ☐ Faulty steering rack (Chapter 10)

Tyre wear excessive

Tyres worn on inside or outside edges

- ☐ Tyres under-inflated (wear on both edges) (see *Weekly checks*)
- ☐ Incorrect camber or castor angles (wear on one edge only) (Chapter 10)
- ☐ Worn steering or suspension joints, bushes or components (Chapter 1A, 1B or 10)
- ☐ Excessively-hard cornering or braking
- ☐ Accident damage

Tyre treads exhibit feathered edges

- ☐ Incorrect toe-setting (Chapter 10)

Tyres worn in centre of tread

- ☐ Tyres over-inflated (see *Weekly checks*)

Tyres worn on inside and outside edges

- ☐ Tyres under-inflated (see *Weekly checks*)

Tyres worn unevenly

- ☐ Tyres/wheels out of balance (see *Weekly checks*)
- ☐ Excessive wheel or tyre run-out
- ☐ Worn shock absorbers (Chapter 1A, 1B or 10)
- ☐ Faulty tyre (see *Weekly checks*)

Electrical system

Note: *For problems associated with the starting system, refer to the faults listed under 'Engine' earlier in this Section.*

Battery will not hold a charge for more than a few days

- ☐ Battery defective internally (Chapter 5A)
- ☐ Battery terminal connections loose or corroded (see *Weekly checks*)
- ☐ Auxiliary drivebelt worn or faulty automatic adjuster (Chapter 1A or 1B)
- ☐ Alternator not charging at correct output (Chapter 5A)
- ☐ Alternator or voltage regulator faulty (Chapter 5A)
- ☐ Short-circuit causing continual battery drain (Chapter 5A or 12)

Ignition/no-charge warning light remains illuminated with engine running

- ☐ Auxiliary drivebelt broken, worn, or or faulty automatic adjuster (Chapter 1A or 1B)
- ☐ Internal fault in alternator or voltage regulator (Chapter 5A)
- ☐ Broken, disconnected, or loose wiring in charging circuit (Chapter 5A or 12)

Ignition/no-charge warning light fails to come on

- ☐ Warning light bulb blown (Chapter 12)
- ☐ Broken, disconnected, or loose wiring in warning light circuit (Chapter 5A or 12)
- ☐ Alternator faulty (Chapter 5A)

Electrical system (continued)

Lights inoperative

☐ Bulb blown (Chapter 12)
☐ Corrosion of bulb or bulbholder contacts (Chapter 12)
☐ Blown fuse (Chapter 12)
☐ Faulty relay (Chapter 12)
☐ Broken, loose, or disconnected wiring (Chapter 12)
☐ Faulty switch (Chapter 12)

Instrument readings inaccurate or erratic

Fuel or temperature gauges give no reading

☐ Faulty gauge sender unit (Chapter 3 or 4)
☐ Wiring open-circuit (Chapter 12)
☐ Faulty gauge (Chapter 12)

Fuel or temperature gauges give continuous maximum reading

☐ Faulty gauge sender unit (Chapter 3 or 4)
☐ Wiring short-circuit (Chapter 12)
☐ Faulty gauge (Chapter 12)

Horn inoperative, or unsatisfactory in operation

Horn operates all the time

☐ Horn push either earthed or stuck down (Chapter 12)
☐ Horn cable-to-horn push earthed (Chapter 12)

Horn fails to operate

☐ Blown fuse (Chapter 12)
☐ Cable or connections loose, broken or disconnected (Chapter 12)
☐ Faulty horn (Chapter 12)

Horn emits intermittent or unsatisfactory sound

☐ Cable connections loose (Chapter 12)
☐ Horn mountings loose (Chapter 12)
☐ Faulty horn (Chapter 12)

Windscreen wipers inoperative, or unsatisfactory in operation

Wipers fail to operate, or operate very slowly

☐ Wiper blades stuck to screen, or linkage seized or binding (Chapter 12)
☐ Blown fuse (Chapter 12)
☐ Battery discharged (Chapter 5A)
☐ Cable or connections loose, broken or disconnected (Chapter 12)
☐ Faulty relay (Chapter 12)
☐ Faulty wiper motor (Chapter 12)

Wiper blades sweep over too large or too small an area of the glass

☐ Wiper blades incorrectly fitted, or wrong size used (see Weekly checks)
☐ Wiper arms incorrectly positioned on spindles (Chapter 12)
☐ Excessive wear of wiper linkage (Chapter 12)
☐ Wiper motor or linkage mountings loose or insecure (Chapter 12)

Wiper blades fail to clean the glass effectively

☐ Wiper blade rubbers dirty, worn or perished (see Weekly checks)
☐ Wiper blades incorrectly fitted, or wrong size used (see Weekly checks)
☐ Wiper arm tension springs broken, or arm pivots seized (Chapter 12)
☐ Insufficient windscreen washer additive to adequately remove road film (see Weekly checks)

Windscreen washers inoperative, or unsatisfactory in operation

One or more washer jets inoperative

☐ Blocked washer jet
☐ Disconnected, kinked or restricted fluid hose (Chapter 12)
☐ Insufficient fluid in washer reservoir (see Weekly checks)

Washer pump fails to operate

☐ Broken or disconnected wiring or connections (Chapter 12)
☐ Blown fuse (Chapter 12)
☐ Faulty washer switch (Chapter 12)
☐ Faulty washer pump (Chapter 12)

Washer pump runs for some time before fluid is emitted from jets

☐ Faulty one-way valve in fluid supply hose (Chapter 12)

Electric windows inoperative, or unsatisfactory in operation

Window glass will only move in one direction

☐ Faulty switch (Chapter 12)

Window glass slow to move

☐ Battery discharged (Chapter 5A)
☐ Regulator seized or damaged, or in need of lubrication (Chapter 11)
☐ Door internal components or trim fouling regulator (Chapter 11)
☐ Faulty motor (Chapter 11)

Window glass fails to move

☐ Blown fuse (Chapter 12)
☐ Faulty relay (Chapter 12)
☐ Broken or disconnected wiring or connections (Chapter 12)
☐ Faulty motor (Chapter 11)

Central locking system inoperative, or unsatisfactory in operation

Complete system failure

☐ Remote handset battery discharged, where applicable (Chapter 1A or 1B)
☐ Blown fuse (Chapter 12)
☐ Faulty relay (Chapter 12)
☐ Broken or disconnected wiring or connections (Chapter 12)
☐ Faulty motor (Chapter 11)

Latch locks but will not unlock, or unlocks but will not lock

☐ Remote handset battery discharged, where applicable (Chapter 1A or 1B)
☐ Faulty master switch (Chapter 12)
☐ Broken or disconnected latch operating rods or levers (Chapter 11)
☐ Faulty relay (Chapter 12)
☐ Faulty motor (Chapter 11)

One solenoid/motor fails to operate

☐ Broken or disconnected wiring or connections (Chapter 12)
☐ Faulty operating assembly (Chapter 11)
☐ Broken, binding or disconnected latch operating rods or levers (Chapter 11)
☐ Fault in door latch (Chapter 11)

Notes

A

ABS (Anti-lock brake system) A system, usually electronically controlled, that senses incipient wheel lockup during braking and relieves hydraulic pressure at wheels that are about to skid.

Air bag An inflatable bag hidden in the steering wheel (driver's side) or the dash or glovebox (passenger side). In a head-on collision, the bags inflate, preventing the driver and front passenger from being thrown forward into the steering wheel or windscreen.

Air cleaner A metal or plastic housing, containing a filter element, which removes dust and dirt from the air being drawn into the engine.

Air filter element The actual filter in an air cleaner system, usually manufactured from pleated paper and requiring renewal at regular intervals.

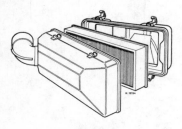

Air filter

Allen key A hexagonal wrench which fits into a recessed hexagonal hole.

Alligator clip A long-nosed spring-loaded metal clip with meshing teeth. Used to make temporary electrical connections.

Alternator A component in the electrical system which converts mechanical energy from a drivebelt into electrical energy to charge the battery and to operate the starting system, ignition system and electrical accessories.

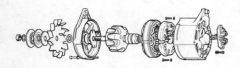

Alternator (exploded view)

Ampere (amp) A unit of measurement for the flow of electric current. One amp is the amount of current produced by one volt acting through a resistance of one ohm.

Anaerobic sealer A substance used to prevent bolts and screws from loosening. Anaerobic means that it does not require oxygen for activation. The Loctite brand is widely used.

Antifreeze A substance (usually ethylene glycol) mixed with water, and added to a vehicle's cooling system, to prevent freezing of the coolant in winter. Antifreeze also contains chemicals to inhibit corrosion and the formation of rust and other deposits that

would tend to clog the radiator and coolant passages and reduce cooling efficiency.

Anti-seize compound A coating that reduces the risk of seizing on fasteners that are subjected to high temperatures, such as exhaust manifold bolts and nuts.

Anti-seize compound

Asbestos A natural fibrous mineral with great heat resistance, commonly used in the composition of brake friction materials. Asbestos is a health hazard and the dust created by brake systems should never be inhaled or ingested.

Axle A shaft on which a wheel revolves, or which revolves with a wheel. Also, a solid beam that connects the two wheels at one end of the vehicle. An axle which also transmits power to the wheels is known as a live axle.

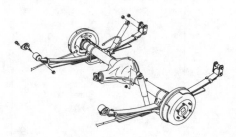

Axle assembly

Axleshaft A single rotating shaft, on either side of the differential, which delivers power from the final drive assembly to the drive wheels. Also called a driveshaft or a halfshaft.

B

Ball bearing An anti-friction bearing consisting of a hardened inner and outer race with hardened steel balls between two races.

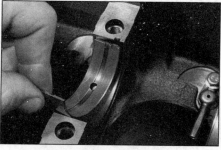

Bearing

Bearing The curved surface on a shaft or in a bore, or the part assembled into either, that permits relative motion between them with minimum wear and friction.

Big-end bearing The bearing in the end of the connecting rod that's attached to the crankshaft.

Bleed nipple A valve on a brake wheel cylinder, caliper or other hydraulic component that is opened to purge the hydraulic system of air. Also called a bleed screw.

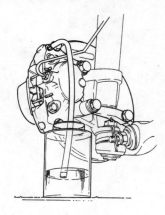

Brake bleeding

Brake bleeding Procedure for removing air from lines of a hydraulic brake system.

Brake disc The component of a disc brake that rotates with the wheels.

Brake drum The component of a drum brake that rotates with the wheels.

Brake linings The friction material which contacts the brake disc or drum to retard the vehicle's speed. The linings are bonded or riveted to the brake pads or shoes.

Brake pads The replaceable friction pads that pinch the brake disc when the brakes are applied. Brake pads consist of a friction material bonded or riveted to a rigid backing plate.

Brake shoe The crescent-shaped carrier to which the brake linings are mounted and which forces the lining against the rotating drum during braking.

Braking systems For more information on braking systems, consult the *Haynes Automotive Brake Manual*.

Breaker bar A long socket wrench handle providing greater leverage.

Bulkhead The insulated partition between the engine and the passenger compartment.

C

Caliper The non-rotating part of a disc-brake assembly that straddles the disc and carries the brake pads. The caliper also contains the hydraulic components that cause the pads to pinch the disc when the brakes are applied. A caliper is also a measuring tool that can be set to measure inside or outside dimensions of an object.

Camshaft A rotating shaft on which a series of cam lobes operate the valve mechanisms. The camshaft may be driven by gears, by sprockets and chain or by sprockets and a belt.

Canister A container in an evaporative emission control system; contains activated charcoal granules to trap vapours from the fuel system.

Canister

Carburettor A device which mixes fuel with air in the proper proportions to provide a desired power output from a spark ignition internal combustion engine.

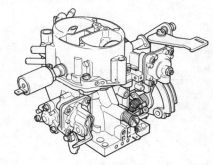

Carburettor

Castellated Resembling the parapets along the top of a castle wall. For example, a castellated balljoint stud nut.

Castellated nut

Castor In wheel alignment, the backward or forward tilt of the steering axis. Castor is positive when the steering axis is inclined rearward at the top.

Catalytic converter A silencer-like device in the exhaust system which converts certain pollutants in the exhaust gases into less harmful substances.

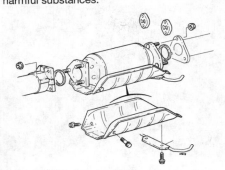

Catalytic converter

Circlip A ring-shaped clip used to prevent endwise movement of cylindrical parts and shafts. An internal circlip is installed in a groove in a housing; an external circlip fits into a groove on the outside of a cylindrical piece such as a shaft.

Clearance The amount of space between two parts. For example, between a piston and a cylinder, between a bearing and a journal, etc.

Coil spring A spiral of elastic steel found in various sizes throughout a vehicle, for example as a springing medium in the suspension and in the valve train.

Compression Reduction in volume, and increase in pressure and temperature, of a gas, caused by squeezing it into a smaller space.

Compression ratio The relationship between cylinder volume when the piston is at top dead centre and cylinder volume when the piston is at bottom dead centre.

Constant velocity (CV) joint A type of universal joint that cancels out vibrations caused by driving power being transmitted through an angle.

Core plug A disc or cup-shaped metal device inserted in a hole in a casting through which core was removed when the casting was formed. Also known as a freeze plug or expansion plug.

Crankcase The lower part of the engine block in which the crankshaft rotates.

Crankshaft The main rotating member, or shaft, running the length of the crankcase, with offset "throws" to which the connecting rods are attached.

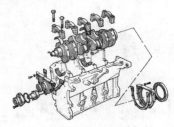

Crankshaft assembly

Crocodile clip See Alligator clip

D

Diagnostic code Code numbers obtained by accessing the diagnostic mode of an engine management computer. This code can be used to determine the area in the system where a malfunction may be located.

Disc brake A brake design incorporating a rotating disc onto which brake pads are squeezed. The resulting friction converts the energy of a moving vehicle into heat.

Double-overhead cam (DOHC) An engine that uses two overhead camshafts, usually one for the intake valves and one for the exhaust valves.

Drivebelt(s) The belt(s) used to drive accessories such as the alternator, water pump, power steering pump, air conditioning compressor, etc. off the crankshaft pulley.

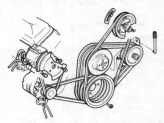

Accessory drivebelts

Driveshaft Any shaft used to transmit motion. Commonly used when referring to the axleshafts on a front wheel drive vehicle.

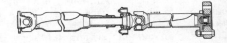

Driveshaft

Drum brake A type of brake using a drum-shaped metal cylinder attached to the inner surface of the wheel. When the brake pedal is pressed, curved brake shoes with friction linings press against the inside of the drum to slow or stop the vehicle.

Drum brake assembly

E

EGR valve A valve used to introduce exhaust gases into the intake air stream.

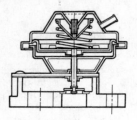

EGR valve

Electronic control unit (ECU) A computer which controls (for instance) ignition and fuel injection systems, or an anti-lock braking system. For more information refer to the *Haynes Automotive Electrical and Electronic Systems Manual*.

Electronic Fuel Injection (EFI) A computer controlled fuel system that distributes fuel through an injector located in each intake port of the engine.

Emergency brake A braking system, independent of the main hydraulic system, that can be used to slow or stop the vehicle if the primary brakes fail, or to hold the vehicle stationary even though the brake pedal isn't depressed. It usually consists of a hand lever that actuates either front or rear brakes mechanically through a series of cables and linkages. Also known as a handbrake or parking brake.

Endfloat The amount of lengthwise movement between two parts. As applied to a crankshaft, the distance that the crankshaft can move forward and back in the cylinder block.

Engine management system (EMS) A computer controlled system which manages the fuel injection and the ignition systems in an integrated fashion.

Exhaust manifold A part with several passages through which exhaust gases leave the engine combustion chambers and enter the exhaust pipe.

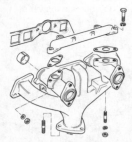

Exhaust manifold

F

Fan clutch A viscous (fluid) drive coupling device which permits variable engine fan speeds in relation to engine speeds.

Feeler blade A thin strip or blade of hardened steel, ground to an exact thickness, used to check or measure clearances between parts.

Feeler blade

Firing order The order in which the engine cylinders fire, or deliver their power strokes, beginning with the number one cylinder.

Flywheel A heavy spinning wheel in which energy is absorbed and stored by means of momentum. On cars, the flywheel is attached to the crankshaft to smooth out firing impulses.

Free play The amount of travel before any action takes place. The "looseness" in a linkage, or an assembly of parts, between the initial application of force and actual movement. For example, the distance the brake pedal moves before the pistons in the master cylinder are actuated.

Fuse An electrical device which protects a circuit against accidental overload. The typical fuse contains a soft piece of metal which is calibrated to melt at a predetermined current flow (expressed as amps) and break the circuit.

Fusible link A circuit protection device consisting of a conductor surrounded by heat-resistant insulation. The conductor is smaller than the wire it protects, so it acts as the weakest link in the circuit. Unlike a blown fuse, a failed fusible link must frequently be cut from the wire for replacement.

G

Gap The distance the spark must travel in jumping from the centre electrode to the side

Adjusting spark plug gap

electrode in a spark plug. Also refers to the spacing between the points in a contact breaker assembly in a conventional points-type ignition, or to the distance between the reluctor or rotor and the pickup coil in an electronic ignition.

Gasket Any thin, soft material - usually cork, cardboard, asbestos or soft metal - installed between two metal surfaces to ensure a good seal. For instance, the cylinder head gasket seals the joint between the block and the cylinder head.

Gasket

Gauge An instrument panel display used to monitor engine conditions. A gauge with a movable pointer on a dial or a fixed scale is an analogue gauge. A gauge with a numerical readout is called a digital gauge.

H

Halfshaft A rotating shaft that transmits power from the final drive unit to a drive wheel, usually when referring to a live rear axle.

Harmonic balancer A device designed to reduce torsion or twisting vibration in the crankshaft. May be incorporated in the crankshaft pulley. Also known as a vibration damper.

Hone An abrasive tool for correcting small irregularities or differences in diameter in an engine cylinder, brake cylinder, etc.

Hydraulic tappet A tappet that utilises hydraulic pressure from the engine's lubrication system to maintain zero clearance (constant contact with both camshaft and valve stem). Automatically adjusts to variation in valve stem length. Hydraulic tappets also reduce valve noise.

I

Ignition timing The moment at which the spark plug fires, usually expressed in the number of crankshaft degrees before the piston reaches the top of its stroke.

Inlet manifold A tube or housing with passages through which flows the air-fuel mixture (carburettor vehicles and vehicles with throttle body injection) or air only (port fuel-injected vehicles) to the port openings in the cylinder head.

J

Jump start Starting the engine of a vehicle with a discharged or weak battery by attaching jump leads from the weak battery to a charged or helper battery.

L

Load Sensing Proportioning Valve (LSPV) A brake hydraulic system control valve that works like a proportioning valve, but also takes into consideration the amount of weight carried by the rear axle.

Locknut A nut used to lock an adjustment nut, or other threaded component, in place. For example, a locknut is employed to keep the adjusting nut on the rocker arm in position.

Lockwasher A form of washer designed to prevent an attaching nut from working loose.

M

MacPherson strut A type of front suspension system devised by Earle MacPherson at Ford of England. In its original form, a simple lateral link with the anti-roll bar creates the lower control arm. A long strut - an integral coil spring and shock absorber - is mounted between the body and the steering knuckle. Many modern so-called MacPherson strut systems use a conventional lower A-arm and don't rely on the anti-roll bar for location.

Multimeter An electrical test instrument with the capability to measure voltage, current and resistance.

N

NOx Oxides of Nitrogen. A common toxic pollutant emitted by petrol and diesel engines at higher temperatures.

O

Ohm The unit of electrical resistance. One volt applied to a resistance of one ohm will produce a current of one amp.

Ohmmeter An instrument for measuring electrical resistance.

O-ring A type of sealing ring made of a special rubber-like material; in use, the O-ring is compressed into a groove to provide the sealing action.

O-ring

Overhead cam (ohc) engine An engine with the camshaft(s) located on top of the cylinder head(s).

Overhead valve (ohv) engine An engine with the valves located in the cylinder head, but with the camshaft located in the engine block.

Oxygen sensor A device installed in the engine exhaust manifold, which senses the oxygen content in the exhaust and converts this information into an electric current. Also called a Lambda sensor.

P

Phillips screw A type of screw head having a cross instead of a slot for a corresponding type of screwdriver.

Plastigage A thin strip of plastic thread, available in different sizes, used for measuring clearances. For example, a strip of Plastigage is laid across a bearing journal. The parts are assembled and dismantled; the width of the crushed strip indicates the clearance between journal and bearing.

Plastigage

Propeller shaft The long hollow tube with universal joints at both ends that carries power from the transmission to the differential on front-engined rear wheel drive vehicles.

Proportioning valve A hydraulic control valve which limits the amount of pressure to the rear brakes during panic stops to prevent wheel lock-up.

R

Rack-and-pinion steering A steering system with a pinion gear on the end of the steering shaft that mates with a rack (think of a geared wheel opened up and laid flat). When the steering wheel is turned, the pinion turns, moving the rack to the left or right. This movement is transmitted through the track rods to the steering arms at the wheels.

Radiator A liquid-to-air heat transfer device designed to reduce the temperature of the coolant in an internal combustion engine cooling system.

Refrigerant Any substance used as a heat transfer agent in an air-conditioning system. R-12 has been the principle refrigerant for many years; recently, however, manufacturers have begun using R-134a, a non-CFC substance that is considered less harmful to the ozone in the upper atmosphere.

Rocker arm A lever arm that rocks on a shaft or pivots on a stud. In an overhead valve engine, the rocker arm converts the upward movement of the pushrod into a downward movement to open a valve.

Rotor In a distributor, the rotating device inside the cap that connects the centre electrode and the outer terminals as it turns, distributing the high voltage from the coil secondary winding to the proper spark plug. Also, that part of an alternator which rotates inside the stator. Also, the rotating assembly of a turbocharger, including the compressor wheel, shaft and turbine wheel.

Runout The amount of wobble (in-and-out movement) of a gear or wheel as it's rotated. The amount a shaft rotates "out-of-true." The out-of-round condition of a rotating part.

S

Sealant A liquid or paste used to prevent leakage at a joint. Sometimes used in conjunction with a gasket.

Sealed beam lamp An older headlight design which integrates the reflector, lens and filaments into a hermetically-sealed one-piece unit. When a filament burns out or the lens cracks, the entire unit is simply replaced.

Serpentine drivebelt A single, long, wide accessory drivebelt that's used on some newer vehicles to drive all the accessories, instead of a series of smaller, shorter belts. Serpentine drivebelts are usually tensioned by an automatic tensioner.

Serpentine drivebelt

Shim Thin spacer, commonly used to adjust the clearance or relative positions between two parts. For example, shims inserted into or under bucket tappets control valve clearances. Clearance is adjusted by changing the thickness of the shim.

Slide hammer A special puller that screws into or hooks onto a component such as a shaft or bearing; a heavy sliding handle on the shaft bottoms against the end of the shaft to knock the component free.

Sprocket A tooth or projection on the periphery of a wheel, shaped to engage with a chain or drivebelt. Commonly used to refer to the sprocket wheel itself.

Starter inhibitor switch On vehicles with an automatic transmission, a switch that prevents starting if the vehicle is not in Neutral or Park.

Strut See MacPherson strut.

T

Tappet A cylindrical component which transmits motion from the cam to the valve stem, either directly or via a pushrod and rocker arm. Also called a cam follower.

Thermostat A heat-controlled valve that regulates the flow of coolant between the cylinder block and the radiator, so maintaining optimum engine operating temperature. A thermostat is also used in some air cleaners in which the temperature is regulated.

Thrust bearing The bearing in the clutch assembly that is moved in to the release levers by clutch pedal action to disengage the clutch. Also referred to as a release bearing.

Timing belt A toothed belt which drives the camshaft. Serious engine damage may result if it breaks in service.

Timing chain A chain which drives the camshaft.

Toe-in The amount the front wheels are closer together at the front than at the rear. On rear wheel drive vehicles, a slight amount of toe-in is usually specified to keep the front wheels running parallel on the road by offsetting other forces that tend to spread the wheels apart.

Toe-out The amount the front wheels are closer together at the rear than at the front. On front wheel drive vehicles, a slight amount of toe-out is usually specified.

Tools For full information on choosing and using tools, refer to the *Haynes Automotive Tools Manual*.

Tracer A stripe of a second colour applied to a wire insulator to distinguish that wire from another one with the same colour insulator.

Tune-up A process of accurate and careful adjustments and parts replacement to obtain the best possible engine performance.

Turbocharger A centrifugal device, driven by exhaust gases, that pressurises the intake air. Normally used to increase the power output from a given engine displacement, but can also be used primarily to reduce exhaust emissions (as on VW's "Umwelt" Diesel engine).

U

Universal joint or U-joint A double-pivoted connection for transmitting power from a driving to a driven shaft through an angle. A U-joint consists of two Y-shaped yokes and a cross-shaped member called the spider.

V

Valve A device through which the flow of liquid, gas, vacuum, or loose material in bulk may be started, stopped, or regulated by a movable part that opens, shuts, or partially obstructs one or more ports or passageways. A valve is also the movable part of such a device.

Valve clearance The clearance between the valve tip (the end of the valve stem) and the rocker arm or tappet. The valve clearance is measured when the valve is closed.

Vernier caliper A precision measuring instrument that measures inside and outside dimensions. Not quite as accurate as a micrometer, but more convenient.

Viscosity The thickness of a liquid or its resistance to flow.

Volt A unit for expressing electrical "pressure" in a circuit. One volt that will produce a current of one ampere through a resistance of one ohm.

W

Welding Various processes used to join metal items by heating the areas to be joined to a molten state and fusing them together. For more information refer to the *Haynes Automotive Welding Manual*.

Wiring diagram A drawing portraying the components and wires in a vehicle's electrical system, using standardised symbols. For more information refer to the *Haynes Automotive Electrical and Electronic Systems Manual*.

Note: *References throughout this index are in the form* **"Chapter number"** • **"Page number"**. *So, for example, 2C•15 refers to page 15 of Chapter 2C.*

Note: *References throughout this index are in the form* **"Chapter number"** • **"Page number"**. *So, for example, 2C•15 refers to page 15 of Chapter 2C.*

Note: *References throughout this index are in the form "**Chapter number**" • "**Page number**". So, for example, 2C•15 refers to page 15 of Chapter 2C.*

Haynes Manuals – The Complete UK Car List

Title	Book No.
ALFA ROMEO Alfasud/Sprint (74 - 88) up to F *	0292
Alfa Romeo Alfetta (73 - 87) up to E *	0531
AUDI 80, 90 & Coupe Petrol (79 - Nov 88) up to F	0605
Audi 80, 90 & Coupe Petrol (Oct 86 - 90) D to H	1491
Audi 100 & 200 Petrol (Oct 82 - 90) up to H	0907
Audi 100 & A6 Petrol & Diesel (May 91 - May 97) H to P	3504
Audi A3 Petrol & Diesel (96 - May 03) P to 03	4253
Audi A4 Petrol & Diesel (95 - 00) M to X	3575
Audi A4 Petrol & Diesel (01 - 04) X to 54	4609
AUSTIN A35 & A40 (56 - 67) up to F *	0118
Austin/MG/Rover Maestro 1.3 & 1.6 Petrol (83 - 95) up to M	0922
Austin/MG Metro (80 - May 90) up to G	0718
Austin/Rover Montego 1.3 & 1.6 Petrol (84 - 94) A to L	1066
Austin/MG/Rover Montego 2.0 Petrol (84 - 95) A to M	1067
Mini (59 - 69) up to H *	0527
Mini (69 - 01) up to X	0646
Austin/Rover 2.0 litre Diesel Engine (86 - 93) C to L	1857
Austin Healey 100/6 & 3000 (56 - 68) up to G *	0049
BEDFORD CF Petrol (69 - 87) up to E	0163
Bedford/Vauxhall Rascal & Suzuki Supercarry (86 - Oct 94) C to M	3015
BMW 316, 320 & 320i (4-cyl) (75 - Feb 83) up to Y *	0276
BMW 320, 320i, 323i & 325i (6-cyl) (Oct 77 - Sept 87) up to E	0815
BMW 3- & 5-Series Petrol (81 - 91) up to J	1948
BMW 3-Series Petrol (Apr 91 - 99) H to V	3210
BMW 3-Series Petrol (Sept 98 - 03) S to 53	4067
BMW 520i & 525e (Oct 81 - June 88) up to E	1560
BMW 525, 528 & 528i (73 - Sept 81) up to X *	0632
BMW 5-Series 6-cyl Petrol (April 96 - Aug 03) N to 03	4151
BMW 1500, 1502, 1600, 1602, 2000 & 2002 (59 - 77) up to S *	0240
CHRYSLER PT Cruiser Petrol (00 - 03) W to 53	4058
CITROËN 2CV, Ami & Dyane (67 - 90) up to H	0196
Citroën AX Petrol & Diesel (87 - 97) D to P	3014
Citroën Berlingo & Peugeot Partner Petrol & Diesel (96 - 05) P to 55	4281
Citroën BX Petrol (83 - 94) A to L	0908
Citroën C15 Van Petrol & Diesel (89 - Oct 98) F to S	3509
Citroën C3 Petrol & Diesel (02 - 05) 51 to 05	4197
Citroën C5 Petrol & Diesel (01-08) Y to 08	4745
Citroën CX Petrol (75 - 88) up to F	0528
Citroën Saxo Petrol & Diesel (96 - 04) N to 54	3506
Citroën Visa Petrol (79 - 88) up to F	0620
Citroën Xantia Petrol & Diesel (93 - 01) K to Y	3082
Citroën XM Petrol & Diesel (89 - 00) G to X	3451
Citroën Xsara Petrol & Diesel (97 - Sept 00) R to W	3751
Citroën Xsara Picasso Petrol & Diesel (00 - 02) W to 52	3944
Citroen Xsara Picasso (03-08)	4784
Citroën ZX Diesel (91 - 98) J to S	1922
Citroën ZX Petrol (91 - 98) H to S	1881
Citroën 1.7 & 1.9 litre Diesel Engine (84 - 96) A to N	1379
FIAT 126 (73 - 87) up to E *	0305
Fiat 500 (57 - 73) up to M *	0090
Fiat Bravo & Brava Petrol (95 - 00) N to W	3572
Fiat Cinquecento (93 - 98) K to R	3501
Fiat Panda (81 - 95) up to M	0793
Fiat Punto Petrol & Diesel (94 - Oct 99) L to V	3251
Fiat Punto Petrol (Oct 99 - July 03) V to 03	4066
Fiat Punto Petrol (03-07) 03 to 07	4746
Fiat Regata Petrol (84 - 88) A to F	1167
Fiat Tipo Petrol (88 - 91) E to J	1625
Fiat Uno Petrol (83 - 95) up to M	0923
Fiat X1/9 (74 - 89) up to G *	0273
FORD Anglia (59 - 68) up to G *	0001

Title	Book No.
Ford Capri II (& III) 1.6 & 2.0 (74 - 87) up to E *	0283
Ford Capri II (& III) 2.8 & 3.0 V6 (74 - 87) up to E	1309
Ford Cortina Mk I & Corsair 1500 ('62 - '66) up to D*	0214
Ford Cortina Mk III 1300 & 1600 (70 - 76) up to P *	0070
Ford Escort Mk I 1100 & 1300 (68 - 74) up to N *	0171
Ford Escort Mk I Mexico, RS 1600 & RS 2000 (70 - 74) up to N *	0139
Ford Escort Mk II Mexico, RS 1800 & RS 2000 (75 - 80) up to W *	0735
Ford Escort (75 - Aug 80) up to V *	0280
Ford Escort Petrol (Sept 80 - Sept 90) up to H	0686
Ford Escort & Orion Petrol (Sept 90 - 00) H to X	1737
Ford Escort & Orion Diesel (Sept 90 - 00) H to X	4081
Ford Fiesta (76 - Aug 83) up to Y	0334
Ford Fiesta Petrol (Aug 83 - Feb 89) A to F	1030
Ford Fiesta Petrol (Feb 89 - Oct 95) F to N	1595
Ford Fiesta Petrol & Diesel (Oct 95 - Mar 02) N to 02	3397
Ford Fiesta Petrol & Diesel (Apr 02 - 07) 02 to 57	4170
Ford Focus Petrol & Diesel (98 - 01) S to Y	3759
Ford Focus Petrol & Diesel (Oct 01 - 05) 51 to 05	4167
Ford Galaxy Petrol & Diesel (95 - Aug 00) M to W	3984
Ford Granada Petrol (Sept 77 - Feb 85) up to B *	0481
Ford Granada & Scorpio Petrol (Mar 85 - 94) B to M	1245
Ford Ka (96 - 02) P to 52	3570
Ford Mondeo Petrol (93 - Sept 00) K to X	1923
Ford Mondeo Petrol & Diesel (Oct 00 - Jul 03) X to 03	3990
Ford Mondeo Petrol & Diesel (July 03 - 07) 03 to 56	4619
Ford Mondeo Diesel (93 - 96) L to N	3465
Ford Orion Petrol (83 - Sept 90) up to H	1009
Ford Sierra 4-cyl Petrol (82 - 93) up to K	0903
Ford Sierra V6 Petrol (82 - 91) up to J	0904
Ford Transit Petrol (Mk 2) (78 - Jan 86) up to C	0719
Ford Transit Petrol (Mk 3) (Feb 86 - 89) C to G	1468
Ford Transit Diesel (Feb 86 - 99) C to T	3019
Ford Transit Diesel (00-06)	4775
Ford 1.6 & 1.8 litre Diesel Engine (84 - 96) A to N	1172
Ford 2.1, 2.3 & 2.5 litre Diesel Engine (77 - 90) up to H	1606
FREIGHT ROVER Sherpa Petrol (74 - 87) up to E	0463
HILLMAN Avenger (70 - 82) up to Y	0037
Hillman Imp (63 - 76) up to R *	0022
HONDA Civic (Feb 84 - Oct 87) A to E	1226
Honda Civic (Nov 91 - 96) J to N	3199
Honda Civic Petrol (Mar 95 - 00) M to X	4050
Honda Civic Petrol & Diesel (01 - 05) X to 55	4611
Honda CR-V Petrol & Diesel (01-06)	4747
Honda Jazz (01 - Feb 08) 51 - 57	4735
HYUNDAI Pony (85 - 94) C to M	3398
JAGUAR E Type (61 - 72) up to L *	0140
Jaguar MkI & II, 240 & 340 (55 - 69) up to H *	0098
Jaguar XJ6, XJ & Sovereign; Daimler Sovereign (68 - Oct 86) up to D	0242
Jaguar XJ6 & Sovereign (Oct 86 - Sept 94) D to M	3261
Jaguar XJ12, XJS & Sovereign; Daimler Double Six (72 - 88) up to F	0478
JEEP Cherokee Petrol (93 - 96) K to N	1943
LADA 1200, 1300, 1500 & 1600 (74 - 91) up to J	0413
Lada Samara (87 - 91) D to J	1610
LAND ROVER 90, 110 & Defender Diesel (83 - 07) up to 56	3017
Land Rover Discovery Petrol & Diesel (89 - 98) G to S	3016
Land Rover Discovery Diesel (Nov 98 - Jul 04) S to 04	4606
Land Rover Freelander Petrol & Diesel (97 - Sept 03) R to 53	3929
Land Rover Freelander Petrol & Diesel (Oct 03 - Oct 06) 53 to 56	4623

Title	Book No.
Land Rover Series IIA & III Diesel (58 - 85) up to C	0529
Land Rover Series II, IIA & III 4-cyl Petrol (58 - 85) up to C	0314
MAZDA 323 (Mar 81 - Oct 89) up to G	1608
Mazda 323 (Oct 89 - 98) G to R	3455
Mazda 626 (May 83 - Sept 87) up to E	0929
Mazda B1600, B1800 & B2000 Pick-up Petrol (72 - 88) up to F	0267
Mazda RX-7 (79 - 85) up to C *	0460
MERCEDES-BENZ 190, 190E & 190D Petrol & Diesel (83 - 93) A to L	3450
Mercedes-Benz 200D, 240D, 240TD, 300D & 300TD 123 Series Diesel (Oct 76 - 85)	1114
Mercedes-Benz 250 & 280 (68 - 72) up to L *	0346
Mercedes-Benz 250 & 280 123 Series Petrol (Oct 76 - 84) up to B *	0677
Mercedes-Benz 124 Series Petrol & Diesel (85 - Aug 93) C to K	3253
Mercedes-Benz A-Class Petrol & Diesel (98-04) S to 54	4748
Mercedes-Benz C-Class Petrol & Diesel (93 - Aug 00) L to W	3511
Mercedes-Benz C-Class (00-06)	4780
MGA (55 - 62) *	0475
MGB (62 - 80) up to W	0111
MG Midget & Austin-Healey Sprite (58 - 80) up to W *	0265
MINI Petrol (July 01 - 05) Y to 05	4273
MITSUBISHI Shogun & L200 Pick-Ups Petrol (83 - 94) up to M	1944
MORRIS Ital 1.3 (80 - 84) up to B	0705
Morris Minor 1000 (56 - 71) up to K	0024
NISSAN Almera Petrol (95 - Feb 00) N to V	4053
Nissan Almera & Tino Petrol (Feb 00 - 07) V to 56	4612
Nissan Bluebird (May 84 - Mar 86) A to C	1223
Nissan Bluebird Petrol (Mar 86 - 90) C to H	1473
Nissan Cherry (Sept 82 - 86) up to D	1031
Nissan Micra (83 - Jan 93) up to K	0931
Nissan Micra (93 - 02) K to 52	3254
Nissan Micra Petrol (03-07) 52 to 57	4734
Nissan Primera Petrol (90 - Aug 99) H to T	1851
Nissan Stanza (82 - 86) up to D	0824
Nissan Sunny Petrol (May 82 - Oct 86) up to D	0895
Nissan Sunny Petrol (Oct 86 - Mar 91) D to H	1378
Nissan Sunny Petrol (Apr 91 - 95) H to N	3219
OPEL Ascona & Manta (B Series) (Sept 75 - 88) up to F *	0316
Opel Ascona Petrol (81 - 88)	3215
Opel Astra Petrol (Oct 91 - Feb 98)	3156
Opel Corsa Petrol (83 - Mar 93)	3160
Opel Corsa Petrol (Mar 93 - 97)	3159
Opel Kadett Petrol (Nov 79 - Oct 84) up to B	0634
Opel Kadett Petrol (Oct 84 - Oct 91)	3196
Opel Omega & Senator Petrol (Nov 86 - 94)	3157
Opel Rekord Petrol (Feb 78 - Oct 86) up to D	0543
Opel Vectra Petrol (Oct 88 - Oct 95)	3158
PEUGEOT 106 Petrol & Diesel (91 - 04) J to 53	1882
Peugeot 205 Petrol (83 - 97) A to P	0932
Peugeot 206 Petrol & Diesel (98 - 01) S to X	3757
Peugeot 206 Petrol & Diesel (02 - 06) 51 to 06	4613
Peugeot 306 Petrol & Diesel (93 - 02) K to 02	3073
Peugeot 307 Petrol & Diesel (01 - 04) Y to 54	4147
Peugeot 309 Petrol (86 - 93) C to K	1266
Peugeot 405 Petrol (88 - 97) E to P	1559
Peugeot 405 Diesel (88 - 97) E to P	3198
Peugeot 406 Petrol & Diesel (96 - Mar 99) N to T	3394
Peugeot 406 Petrol & Diesel (Mar 99 - 02) T to 52	3982

* Classic reprint

Title	Book No.
Peugeot 505 Petrol (79 - 89) up to G	0762
Peugeot 1.7/1.8 & 1.9 litre Diesel Engine (82 - 96) up to N	0950
Peugeot 2.0, 2.1, 2.3 & 2.5 litre Diesel Engines (74 - 90) up to H	1607
PORSCHE 911 (65 - 85) up to C	0264
Porsche 924 & 924 Turbo (76 - 85) up to C	0397
PROTON (89 - 97) F to P	3255
RANGE ROVER V8 Petrol (70 - Oct 92) up to K	0606
RELIANT Robin & Kitten (73 - 83) up to A *	0436
RENAULT 4 (61 - 86) up to D *	0072
Renault 5 Petrol (Feb 85 - 96) B to N	1219
Renault 9 & 11 Petrol (82 - 89) up to F	0822
Renault 18 Petrol (79 - 86) up to D	0598
Renault 19 Petrol (89 - 96) F to N	1646
Renault 19 Diesel (89 - 96) F to N	1946
Renault 21 Petrol (86 - 94) C to L	1397
Renault 25 Petrol & Diesel (84 - 92) B to K	1228
Renault Clio Petrol (91 - May 98) H to R	1853
Renault Clio Diesel (91 - June 96) H to N	3031
Renault Clio Petrol & Diesel (May 98 - May 01) R to Y	3906
Renault Clio Petrol & Diesel (June '01 - '05) Y to 55	4168
Renault Espace Petrol & Diesel (85 - 96) C to N	3197
Renault Laguna Petrol & Diesel (94 - 00) L to W	3252
Renault Laguna Petrol & Diesel (Feb 01 - Feb 05) X to 54	4283
Renault Mégane & Scénic Petrol & Diesel (96 - 99) N to T	3395
Renault Mégane & Scénic Petrol & Diesel (Apr 99 - 02) T to 52	3916
Renault Megane Petrol & Diesel (Oct 02 - 05) 52 to 55	4284
Renault Scenic Petrol & Diesel (Sept 03 - 06) 53 to 06	4297
ROVER 213 & 216 (84 - 89) A to G	1116
Rover 214 & 414 Petrol (89 - 96) G to N	1689
Rover 216 & 416 Petrol (89 - 96) G to N	1830
Rover 211, 214, 216, 218 & 220 Petrol & Diesel (Dec 95 - 99) N to V	3399
Rover 25 & MG ZR Petrol & Diesel (Oct 99 - 04) V to 54	4145
Rover 414, 416 & 420 Petrol & Diesel (May 95 - 98) M to R	3453
Rover 45 / MG ZS Petrol & Diesel (99 - 05) V to 55	4384
Rover 618, 620 & 623 Petrol (93 - 97) K to P	3257
Rover 75 / MG ZT Petrol & Diesel (99 - 06) S to 06	4292
Rover 820, 825 & 827 Petrol (86 - 95) D to N	1380
Rover 3500 (76 - 87) up to E *	0365
Rover Metro, 111 & 114 Petrol (May 90 - 98) G to S	1711
SAAB 95 & 96 (66 - 76) up to R *	0198
Saab 90, 99 & 900 (79 - Oct 93) up to L	0765
Saab 900 (Oct 93 - 98) L to R	3512
Saab 9000 (4-cyl) (85 - 98) C to S	1686
Saab 9-3 Petrol & Diesel (98 - Aug 02) R to 02	4614
Saab 9-3 Petrol & Diesel (02-07) 52 to 57	4749
Saab 9-5 4-cyl Petrol (97 - 04) R to 54	4156
SEAT Ibiza & Cordoba Petrol & Diesel (Oct 93 - Oct 99) L to V	3571
Seat Ibiza & Malaga Petrol (85 - 92) B to K	1609
SKODA Estelle (77 - 89) up to G	0604
Skoda Fabia Petrol & Diesel (00 - 06) W to 06	4376
Skoda Favorit (89 - 96) F to N	1801
Skoda Felicia Petrol & Diesel (95 - 01) M to X	3505
Skoda Octavia Petrol & Diesel (98 - Apr 04) R to 04	4285
SUBARU 1600 & 1800 (Nov 79 - 90) up to H *	0995

Title	Book No.
SUNBEAM Alpine, Rapier & H120 (67 - 74) up to N *	0051
SUZUKI SJ Series, Samurai & Vitara (4-cyl) Petrol (82 - 97) up to P	1942
Suzuki Supercarry & Bedford/Vauxhall Rascal (86 - Oct 94) C to M	3015
TALBOT Alpine, Solara, Minx & Rapier (75 - 86) up to D	0337
Talbot Horizon Petrol (78 - 86) up to D	0473
Talbot Samba (82 - 86) up to D	0823
TOYOTA Avensis Petrol (98 - Jan 03) R to 52	4264
Toyota Carina E Petrol (May 92 - 97) J to P	3256
Toyota Corolla (80 - 85) up to C	0683
Toyota Corolla (Sept 83 - Sept 87) A to E	1024
Toyota Corolla (Sept 87 - Aug 92) E to K	1683
Toyota Corolla (Aug 92 - 97) K to P	3259
Toyota Corolla Petrol (July 97 - Feb 02) P to 51	4286
Toyota Hi-Ace & Hi-Lux Petrol (69 - Oct 83) up to A	0304
Toyota RAV4 Petrol & Diesel (94-06) L to 55	4750
Toyota Yaris Petrol (99 - 05) T to 05	4265
TRIUMPH GT6 & Vitesse (62 - 74) up to N *	0112
Triumph Herald (59 - 71) up to K *	0010
Triumph Spitfire (62 - 81) up to X	0113
Triumph Stag (70 - 78) up to T *	0441
Triumph TR2, TR3, TR3A, TR4 & TR4A (52 - 67) up to F *	0028
Triumph TR5 & 6 (67 - 75) up to P *	0031
Triumph TR7 (75 - 82) up to Y *	0322
VAUXHALL Astra Petrol (80 - Oct 84) up to B	0635
Vauxhall Astra & Belmont Petrol (Oct 84 - Oct 91) B to J	1136
Vauxhall Astra Petrol (Oct 91 - Feb 98) J to R	1832
Vauxhall/Opel Astra & Zafira Petrol (Feb 98 - Apr 04) R to 04	3758
Vauxhall/Opel Astra & Zafira Diesel (Feb 98 - Apr 04) R to 04	3797
Vauxhall/Opel Astra Petrol (04 - 08)	4732
Vauxhall/Opel Astra Diesel (04 - 08)	4733
Vauxhall/Opel Calibra (90 - 98) G to S	3502
Vauxhall Carlton Petrol (Oct 78 - Oct 86) up to D	0480
Vauxhall Carlton & Senator Petrol (Nov 86 - 94) D to L	1469
Vauxhall Cavalier Petrol (81 - Oct 88) up to F	0812
Vauxhall Cavalier Petrol (Oct 88 - 95) F to N	1570
Vauxhall Chevette (75 - 84) up to B	0285
Vauxhall/Opel Corsa Diesel (Mar 93 - Oct 00) K to X	4087
Vauxhall Corsa Petrol (Mar 93 - 97) K to R	1985
Vauxhall/Opel Corsa Petrol (Apr 97 - Oct 00) P to X	3921
Vauxhall/Opel Corsa Petrol & Diesel (Oct 00 - Sept 03) X to 53	4079
Vauxhall/Opel Corsa Petrol & Diesel (Oct 03 - Aug 06) 53 to 06	4617
Vauxhall/Opel Frontera Petrol & Diesel (91 - Sept 98) J to S	3454
Vauxhall Nova Petrol (83 - 93) up to K	0909
Vauxhall/Opel Omega Petrol (94 - 99) L to T	3510
Vauxhall/Opel Vectra Petrol & Diesel (95 - Feb 99) N to S	3396
Vauxhall/Opel Vectra Petrol & Diesel (Mar 99 - May 02) T to 02	3930
Vauxhall/Opel Vectra Petrol & Diesel (June 02 - Sept 05) 02 to 55	4618
Vauxhall/Opel 1.5, 1.6 & 1.7 litre Diesel Engine (82 - 96) up to N	1222
VW 411 & 412 (68 - 75) up to P *	0091
VW Beetle 1200 (54 - 77) up to S	0036
VW Beetle 1300 & 1500 (65 - 75) up to P	0039

Title	Book No.
VW 1302 & 1302S (70 - 72) up to L *	0110
VW Beetle 1303, 1303S & GT (72 - 75) up to P	0159
VW Beetle Petrol & Diesel (Apr 99 - 07) T to 57	3798
VW Golf & Jetta Mk 1 Petrol 1.1 & 1.3 (74 - 84) up to A	0716
VW Golf, Jetta & Scirocco Mk 1 Petrol 1.5, 1.6 & 1.8 (74 - 84) up to A	0726
VW Golf & Jetta Mk 1 Diesel (78 - 84) up to A	0451
VW Golf & Jetta Mk 2 Petrol (Mar 84 - Feb 92) A to J	1081
VW Golf & Vento Petrol & Diesel (Feb 92 - Mar 98) J to R	3097
VW Golf & Bora Petrol & Diesel (April 98 - 00) R to X	3727
VW Golf & Bora 4-cyl Petrol & Diesel (01 - 03) X to 53	4169
VW Golf & Jetta Petrol & Diesel (04 - 07) 53 to 07	4610
VW LT Petrol Vans & Light Trucks (76 - 87) up to E	0637
VW Passat & Santana Petrol (Sept 81 - May 88) up to E	0814
VW Passat 4-cyl Petrol & Diesel (May 88 - 96) E to P	3498
VW Passat 4-cyl Petrol & Diesel (Dec 96 - Nov 00) P to X	3917
VW Passat Petrol & Diesel (Dec 00 - May 05) X to 05	4279
VW Polo & Derby (76 - Jan 82) up to X	0335
VW Polo (82 - Oct 90) up to H	0813
VW Polo Petrol (Nov 90 - Aug 94) H to L	3245
VW Polo Hatchback Petrol & Diesel (94 - 99) M to S	3500
VW Polo Hatchback Petrol (00 - Jan 02) V to 51	4150
VW Polo Petrol & Diesel (02 - May 05) 51 to 05	4608
VW Scirocco (82 - 90) up to H *	1224
VW Transporter 1600 (68 - 79) up to V	0082
VW Transporter 1700, 1800 & 2000 (72 - 79) up to V *	0226
VW Transporter (air-cooled) Petrol (79 - 82) up to Y *	0638
VW Transporter (water-cooled) Petrol (82 - 90) up to H	3452
VW Type 3 (63 - 73) up to M *	0084
VOLVO 120 & 130 Series (& P1800) (61 - 73) up to M *	0203
Volvo 142, 144 & 145 (66 - 74) up to N *	0129
Volvo 240 Series Petrol (74 - 93) up to K	0270
Volvo 262, 264 & 260/265 (75 - 85) up to C *	0400
Volvo 340, 343, 345 & 360 (76 - 91) up to J	0715
Volvo 440, 460 & 480 Petrol (87 - 97) D to P	1691
Volvo 740 & 760 Petrol (82 - 91) up to J	1258
Volvo 850 Petrol (92 - 96) J to P	3260
Volvo 940 petrol (90 - 98) H to R	3249
Volvo S40 & V40 Petrol (96 - Mar 04) N to 04	3569
Volvo S40 & V50 Petrol & Diesel (Mar 04 - Jun 07) 04 to 07	4731
Volvo S60 Petrol & Diesel (01-08)	4793
Volvo S70, V70 & C70 Petrol (96 - 99) P to V	3573
Volvo V70 / S80 Petrol & Diesel (98 - 05) S to 55	4263

DIY MANUAL SERIES

Title	Book No.
The Haynes Air Conditioning Manual	4192
The Haynes Car Electrical Systems Manual	4251
The Haynes Manual on Bodywork	4198
The Haynes Manual on Brakes	4178
The Haynes Manual on Carburettors	4177
The Haynes Manual on Diesel Engines	4174
The Haynes Manual on Engine Management	4199
The Haynes Manual on Fault Codes	4175
The Haynes Manual on Practical Electrical Systems	4267
The Haynes Manual on Small Engines	4250
The Haynes Manual on Welding	4176

* Classic reprint

Preserving Our Motoring Heritage

< The Model J Duesenberg Derham Tourster. Only eight of these magnificent cars were ever built – this is the only example to be found outside the United States of America

Almost every car you've ever loved, loathed or desired is gathered under one roof at the Haynes Motor Museum. Over 300 immaculately presented cars and motorbikes represent every aspect of our motoring heritage, from elegant reminders of bygone days, such as the superb Model J Duesenberg to curiosities like the bug-eyed BMW Isetta. There are also many old friends and flames. Perhaps you remember the 1959 Ford Popular that you did your courting in? The magnificent 'Red Collection' is a spectacle of classic sports cars including AC, Alfa Romeo, Austin Healey, Ferrari, Lamborghini, Maserati, MG, Riley, Porsche and Triumph.

A Perfect Day Out

Each and every vehicle at the Haynes Motor Museum has played its part in the history and culture of Motoring. Today, they make a wonderful spectacle and a great day out for all the family. Bring the kids, bring Mum and Dad, but above all bring your camera to capture those golden memories for ever. You will also find an impressive array of motoring memorabilia, a comfortable 70 seat video cinema and one of the most extensive transport book shops in Britain. The Pit Stop Cafe serves everything from a cup of tea to wholesome, home-made meals or, if you prefer, you can enjoy the large picnic area nestled in the beautiful rural surroundings of Somerset.

> John Haynes O.B.E., Founder and Chairman of the museum at the wheel of a Haynes Light 12.

< Graham Hill's Lola Cosworth Formula 1 car next to a 1934 Riley Sports.

The Museum is situated on the A359 Yeovil to Frome road at Sparkford, just off the A303 in Somerset. It is about 40 miles south of Bristol, and 25 minutes drive from the M5 intersection at Taunton.
Open 9.30am - 5.30pm (10.00am - 4.00pm Winter) 7 days a week, *except Christmas Day, Boxing Day and New Years Day*
Special rates available for schools, coach parties and outings Charitable Trust No. 292048